The Civil Contract of Photography

Translated by Rela Mazali and Ruvik Danieli

The Civil Contract of Photography

Ariella Azoulay

ZONE BOOKS · NEW YORK

2008

ZONE BOOKS
633 Vanderbilt Street
Brooklyn, NY 11218

First Paperback Edition
Fourth Printing 2022

Printed in the United States of America.

Distributed by Princeton University Press,
Princeton, New Jersey, and Woodstock, United Kingdom

Library of Congress Cataloging-in-Publication Data

Azoulay, Ariella

    The civil contract of photography / Ariella Azoulay

      p.   cm.

    Includes bibliographical references (p.) and index.

    ISBN 978-1-890951-89-4 (pbk.)

    1. Photography — Social aspects. 2. Photography —
Philosophy. 3. Palestinian Arabs — Israel — Pictorial works.
4. Palestinian Arabs — Israel — Public opinion. 1. Title.

TR147.A96 2008

770 — dc22

                                 2007061955

Contents

Acknowledgments

Support for the translation of this book was made possible by the Center for Continental Philosophy at Bar Ilan University. Special thanks to Andrew Skmora, the thoughtful editor of the first drafts of several chapters of the English manuscript; to Bud Bynack whose excellent editorial work forced me to rethink some and rephrase many of my arguments; to Meighan Gale who vigilantly accompanied the manuscript through the production process; and to Julie Fry who gave the book its exact cover and proper design.

Introduction

I remember well the drone of the planes and the banister trembling as I tried to clutch it. My mother says I was shaking all over and that my teeth were rattling. When I shut my eyes, I feel as if I'm there, spreading the upper half of my body on the banister, arms wide open, and sliding down. The sliding never ends — a continuous snapshot with nothing before or after it. This is the only image I have of that day, mixed up with the rising-falling shriek of the siren, with strong pounding at the door and shouts of "Get up, get up" directed, I think, at my sister, who was sleeping through the whole thing. All the rest comes from stories. June 1967. I was five. The house we lived in on Weizmann Street in Netanya had no bomb shelter, and we ran to the next building. Two or three bombs fell on Netanya that day.

For years, this war was referred to with pride. My mother said I didn't cry at any point, and I knew this made me a part of the war's success. In time, I understood that this illustrious war, whose victory albums my father sold at his small, crowded shop, was none other than a conquest of people's lives, their ongoing dispossession of many things they had and many other things they would never have. The fact that I failed to understand this sooner, as it was actually taking place, has haunted me since.

I was twelve when I fainted for the first time. In Tul Karm, in the West Bank. My parents used to drive there every Saturday. My father would buy Uhm Kulthum cassettes at half price. I think that more than anything else, though, he loved going there so he could eat baklava. It was

9

the single foodstuff that disclosed his birth in an Arab country. When I came to my senses after fainting, I immediately was handed a slice of lemon and a glass of water. Someone on the street had taken over the situation and had rushed to provide me with a drink. I have no idea who. My mother was anxious to leave and said we wouldn't go "there" anymore. "The smells affect the child," she told my father. In hindsight, it turned out that I had fainted because I was menstruating, and my blood pressure had dropped. I have since fainted several times in Jewish towns. I knew my mother's decision not to go back "there" was not as well founded as it seemed, but I didn't know why. So I said nothing.

My mother wouldn't allow me to go to the beach on Fridays. That's the day the Arabs go. "They go in with their clothes on," she muttered. Ever since, I've carried around in my head an image of Arabs half-submerged in the middle of the sea, struggling to get up, with the weight of their wet clothes pulling them down. While I remember this image as if it were a photograph I actually saw, I know it was planted in my brain, courtesy of my mother's tongue as she tried to embody her warnings. When I was a bit older, in high school, and I went to the "territories" with Peace Now to demonstrate against the occupation, I saw only Jewish Israelis with crisp white shirts, equipped with a vision of how to wipe out the occupation. Even then, toward the end of the 1970s, the image from the sea remained the only image I had of Palestinians.

It took many years before this phantom picture was replaced by real photographs with Palestinian faces looking out at me. A girl with soldiers pulling her hair as they try to arrest her, a young boy tied up and lying on the ground with a group of soldiers and a rifle aimed at him, an elderly couple on the ruins of what was previously their home, shuttered store fronts with armed soldiers out in front, or an elegant woman of my age, standing tall, her arms hanging at her sides, on a background of magical wallpaper printed with a vista of lakes and palm trees. That was during the first intifada. At the time, I had just returned from a seven-year stay in France, and I avidly read the Hebrew daily *Hadashot*, where Palestinians' portraits and their names and stories were printed for the first time in Hebrew daily newspapers: black-and-white photographs in sharp contrast, the Palestinians in most of them taken from very close up, often in close physical proximity to Israeli soldiers. Every such photograph testified to the fact that the occupation should be ended and a Palestinian state established.

Around the same time, I began writing about art. But I was drawn to photography. There was very little writing on photography at the time within the discourse of art, and I was looking for a way to put photographs into words. I didn't know how to break the silence about it. I suppose the difficulty stemmed, for the most part, from the fact that photography wasn't considered an art form, that writing about it ran the risk of the directness necessitated by the writer's duty to look, first of all, at what is photographed, and only then to deal with issues of an artistic order. But the photographed persons went on looking out of the photographs and demanding something else, even when the gaze turned them into a sign to be drawn on in speaking out against the occupation.

Artistic discourse turned out to be an obstacle to seeing what was in the photograph, but it was not the only one. Postmodern theorists — such as Roland Barthes, Jean Baudrillard, and Susan Sontag — who bore witness to a glut of images were the first to fall prey to a kind of "image fatigue"; they simply stopped looking. The world filled up with images of horrors, and they loudly proclaimed that viewers' eyes had grown unseeing, proceeding to unburden themselves of the responsibility to hold onto the elementary gesture of looking at what is presented to one's gaze.

At the beginning of the 1990s, I began curating photography exhibitions. But I knew that my interest in photography didn't end with photographs taken by artists or professional photographers. In photography — and this is evident in every single photo — there is something that extends beyond the photographer's action, and no photographer, even the most gifted, can claim ownership of what appears in the photograph. Every photograph of others bears the traces of the meeting between the photographed persons and the photographer, neither of whom can, on their own, determine how this meeting will be inscribed in the resulting image. The photograph exceeds any presumption of

11

ownership or monopoly and any attempt at being exhaustive. Even when it seems possible to name correctly in the form of a statement what it shows — "This is X" — it will always turn out that something else can be read in it, some other event can be reconstructed from it, some other player's presence can be discerned through it, constructing the social relations that allowed its production.

My main interest was in photographs from the Occupied Territories, and the more I looked at them, the more I felt that they showed more than evidence of what was being done to the Palestinians. Over time, it became progressively clearer to me that not only is it impossible to reduce photography to its role as a producer of pictures, but that, in addition, its broad dissemination over the second half of the nineteenth century has created a space of political relations that are not mediated exclusively by the ruling power of the state and are not completely subject to the national logic that still overshadows the political arena. This civil political space, which I invent theoretically in the present book, is one that the people using photography — photographers, spectators, and photographed people — imagine every day.

By that time, at about thirty, I felt a strong desire to go back to the building on Weizmann Street. My photo album from that period of childhood was very slim. I had a feeling that simply going back there would nudge many things toward deciphering themselves. It was evening when I got there. Just entering the dark entrance hall felt oppressive. At the other end of it there was a large opening leading to the yard adjacent to the neighbors' yard that we ran to in order to reach the bomb shelter. If, in the course of my childhood at this address, I had entrusted anything there, I wasn't able to get it back on this visit. I don't know what I thought I would find there, but for days afterward, the picture of that stairwell stayed with me. Every time it began eluding me, I grasped at its edges as if it were a photograph, trying to keep it with me a moment longer. It dawned on me at the time that I could remember all the stairwells of all the buildings I'd lived in — eight in all. I have a fairly orderly archive in my mind. "It's the entrance hall that's the most dangerous"; "Don't open the door for strangers"; "Take a good look and make sure that no one comes into the entrance hall behind you." In the course of adolescence, these warnings were joined by a long series of prohibitions concerning me as a girl, as a woman. An entire world of moving freely through space and its related adventures had been gradually placed beyond my reach, because these had always involved walking at night, entrance halls, and public parks.

Each one of us carries with her an album of these planted pictures. In some cases, the violence needed for their insertion into the album is evident — as happens when the image is engraved through trauma. In other cases, the pictures have been planted while the "owner" of the album remains totally unaware of the violence involved, until the day she is able to see that this or that image that she had taken to be her own was in fact nothing of the kind. What distinguishes such pictures from regular photographs is the mode of their transmission. They are planted in the body, the consciousness, the memory, and their adoption is instantaneous, ruling out any opportunity for negotiations as regards what they show or their genealogy, their ownership or belonging. They lack the *objective* dimension possessed by an image imprinted in a photograph by virtue of its being, always, of necessity, the product of an encounter — even if a violent one — between a photographer, a photographed subject, and a camera, an encounter whose involuntary traces in the photograph transform the latter into a document that is not the creation of an individual and can never belong to any one person or narrative exclusively. The photograph is out there, an object in the world, and anyone, always (at least in principle), can pull at one of its threads and trace it in such a way as to reopen the image and renegotiate what it shows, possibly even completely overturning what was seen in it before. That evening at Weizmann Street made me understand the role of planted pictures in the restriction of my living space as a citizen and a woman, and the potential of photography for dissolving their power.

Photography has served me in ridding myself of these phantom pictures, or at least in reattributing them to their creators and detaching them from myself. Photographs, unlike phantom pictures, have no single, individual author, in principle, they allow civic negotiations about the subject they designate and about their sense. Advertising photography has come into the world with the wrong users' manual, photos tend to be confused with planted pictures and become phantom images. The existing common manual reduces photography to the photograph and to the gaze concentrated on it in an attempt to identify the subject. It takes part in the stabilization of what is seen, in making it distinct, accessible, readily available, easy to capture, and open to ownership and exchange. The wrong users' manual hinders the spectator's understanding that the photograph — every photograph — belongs to no one, that she can become not only its addressee but also its addresser, one who can produce a meaning for it and disseminate this meaning further.

Photography is much more than what is printed on photographic paper. The photograph bears the seal of the photographic event, and reconstructing this event requires more than just identifying what is shown in the photograph. One needs to stop looking at the photograph and instead start watching it. The verb "to watch" is usually used for regarding phenomena or moving pictures. It entails dimensions of time and movement that need to be reinscribed in the interpretation of the still photographic image. When and where the subject of the photograph is a person who has suffered some form of injury, a viewing of the photograph that reconstructs the photographic situation and allows a reading of the injury inflicted on others becomes a civic skill, not an exercise in aesthetic appreciation. This skill is activated the moment one grasps that citizenship is not merely a status, a good, or a piece of private property possessed by the citizen,[1] but rather a tool of a struggle or an obligation to others to struggle against injuries inflicted on those others, citizen and noncitizen alike — others who are governed along with the spectator.[2] The civil spectator has a duty to employ that skill the day she encounters photographs of those injuries — to employ it in order to negotiate the manner in which she and the photographed are ruled.

Events about which I wrote in that period, such as the gang rape in Kibbutz Shomrat or Carmela Boukhbout's killing of her violent husband, revealed to me the shape of women's narrowed living space, along with the fact that what has befallen them is a symptom of an *impaired civic* status that is characteristic of women in general.

The question of citizenship thus gradually became the prism through which I began observing things. At first, my writing progressed in several parallel channels: writing about photography, mainly photographs of Palestinians and the continuing injury caused them by the occupation, writing about women, mainly focusing on the violence directed against them and their abandonment, and writing about impaired citizenship as it concerned both Palestinians and women. It was the concept of citizenship that made it possible for me to conduct an extended discussion of seemingly distinct cases — the assassination of a prime minister, the killing of a husband by a wife whom he had abused and beaten for years, and the liquidation of a Palestinian individual identified as the planner of terrorist attacks. Unavoidably, this discussion led, in turn, to a reformulation of the concept of citizenship itself. When these incidents are discussed from the standpoint of citizenship, it is impossible to retain the label "domestic" with reference to the killing of a husband by his abused wife, just as the murder of a Palestinian can no longer be viewed as a "liquidation." The common framework of discussion proposed by this book for analyzing the susceptibility to disaster of distinct populations such as Palestinians or women thus resists some of the presuppositions of existing discourses on citizenship.

Because Palestinians are considered stateless persons, they are absent(ed) from the discourse on citizenship; because women are considered full citizens, their susceptibility to a particular type of disaster does not tend to generate an examination of their civic status. Circumscribing the discussion of Palestinians in advance through the scandalous category of "stateless persons" amounts to accepting a narrow reading of citizenship as a "natural" privilege possessed by the members of a certain class that administers the distribution of the good known as citizenship as if it were its own private property. Excluding the discussion of women's abandonment from the discourse of citizenship through the argument that it represents a factional issue overly narrowing the relevant "general" political perspective amounts to accepting the incidence of rape as a natural disaster or an ahistorical conflict between the sexes, rather than an alterable consequence of impaired citizenship.

In spite of my right-wing upbringing, I became convinced early on that injustice was being done to another people and that the solution lay in the establishment of a Palestinian state. This was what I believed for many years. When I started scrutinizing photographs in a serious, systematic way, I understood that terms such as "occupation," or "Green Line" or "Palestinian state" that I had been in the habit of using are part of the discursive structures of the regime and support it, even if one formulated her position toward them in just the opposite way than the one intended by the regime. These terms threaten to circumscribe one's field of vision and, perhaps worse, the boundaries of one's imagination, as well. They threaten to seal the photographs within a protective shield that will turn the photographed people into evidence that something "was there." However, in contradiction to the famous statement by Roland Barthes, which sought to capture the essence of photography as testimony to the fact that this something "was there," when these photographs are watched, not looked at, when they are read both out of and into the space of the political relations instated by photography, they seem — conversely — to testify to the fact that the photographed *people* were there. When the assumption is that not only were the photographed people there, but that, in addition, they are still present there at the time I'm watching them, my viewing of these photographs is less susceptible to becoming immoral. Addressing these photographs is a limited, partial, sometimes imagined attempt to respond to the photographed figure, an attempt to reconstruct the part it played, which is sometimes difficult to discern at first glance, and to realize, even if fleetingly, a space of political relations between those who are governed, a space in which the demand not to be ruled in this way becomes the basis for every civil negotiation.

I began working on this book at the beginning of the second intifada. In hindsight, I can say that observing the unbearable sights presented in photographs from the Occupied Territories, encountering them in the national context within which they were presented and enduring the difficulty of facing them day after day, formed the main motives for writing this book. *The Civil Contract of Photography* is an attempt to anchor spectatorship in civic duty toward the photographed persons who haven't stopped being "there," toward dispos-

16

sessed citizens who, in turn, enable the rethinking of the concept and practice of citizenship.

I employ the term "contract" in order to shed terms such as "empathy," "shame," "pity," or "compassion" as organizers of this gaze. In the political sphere that is reconstructed through the civil contract, photographed persons are participant citizens, just the same as I am. Within this space, the point of departure for our mutual relations cannot be empathy or mercy. It must be a covenant for the rehabilitation of their citizenship in the political sphere within which we are all ruled, that is, in the state of Israel. When the photographed persons address me, claiming their citizenship in photography, they cease to appear as stateless or as enemies, the manners in which the sovereign regime strives to construct them. They call on me to recognize and restore their citizenship through my viewing. At issue in this book is more than my insistence on using the term "citizenship" in analyzing the act of photography or in understanding the ways in which some populations are more exposed to catastrophe than others. At issue is an effort to disclose the inextricable relationship between the populations facing pending catastrophe and the citizens with whom they are governed, doing so by means of an examination of the civic space of the gaze, speech, and action that is shared by these governed populations.

The book seeks to arouse two dormant dimensions of thinking about citizenship and to recast them as points of departure for a new discussion of this concept. The first of these dimensions consists in the fact that citizens are, first and foremost, *governed*. The nation-state creates a bond of identification between citizens and the state through a variety of ideological mechanisms, causing this fact to be forgotten. This, then, allows the state to divide the governed — partitioning off noncitizens from citizens — and to mobilize the privileged citizens against other groups of ruled subjects. An emphasis on the dimension of being governed allows a rethinking of the political sphere as a space of relations between the governed, whose political duty is first and foremost a duty toward one another, rather than toward the ruling power.

Every day, as I leaf through the paper, looking out at me from its various pages are faces of Palestinians exposed to the rule of Israeli occupation.

17

Why are these men, women, children, and families looking at me? Why have they agreed to be photographed so as to look at me? At whom, precisely, did they seek to look — was it truly at me? And why? Does their use of photography express a civic skill that they possess? What am I supposed to do with their look? What is the foundation of the gaze I might turn back to toward them? Is it my gaze alone, or is their demand directed toward the civil position I occupy? What happens to my citizenship in its encounter with this look? What happens to it in this encounter with their catastrophe, knowing that they are more vulnerable than I to catastrophe?

The question "Why are they looking at me?" has enabled me to rethink the civic space of the gaze and our interrelations within it. Both the photographer's vantage point and the process of watching photographs have emerged as only one component within a whole, very complex fabric of relations. Within its weave, the photographed subjects' act of addressing the spectator bears decisive weight. For example, take the merchant from Hebron, one of many, many people from Hebron who staged protest strikes against the occupation in 1982 (figure I.1). On encountering the photographer, Anat Saragusti, the merchant faced the camera and demonstrated directly, for all to witness, evidence of the damage caused to him, the lock of his store forced open and destroyed by Israeli paratroopers sent in to break the strike. The photographed subjects of numerous photographs participate actively in the photographic act and view both this act and the photographer facing them as a framework that offers an alternative — weak though it may be — to the institutional structures that have abandoned and injured them, that continue to shirk responsibility toward these subjects and refuse to compensate them for damages. The consent of most photographed subjects to have their picture taken, or indeed their own initiation of a photographic act, even when suffering in extremely difficult circumstances, presumes the existence of a civil space in which photographers, photographed subjects, and spectators share a recognition that what they are witnessing is intolerable.

Vis-à-vis such photographed persons it becomes patently insufficient to account for photography through a focus on photographers or spectators, as occurs in any discussion suited to the title *Regarding the Pain of Others* with which Susan Sontag christened her last book.

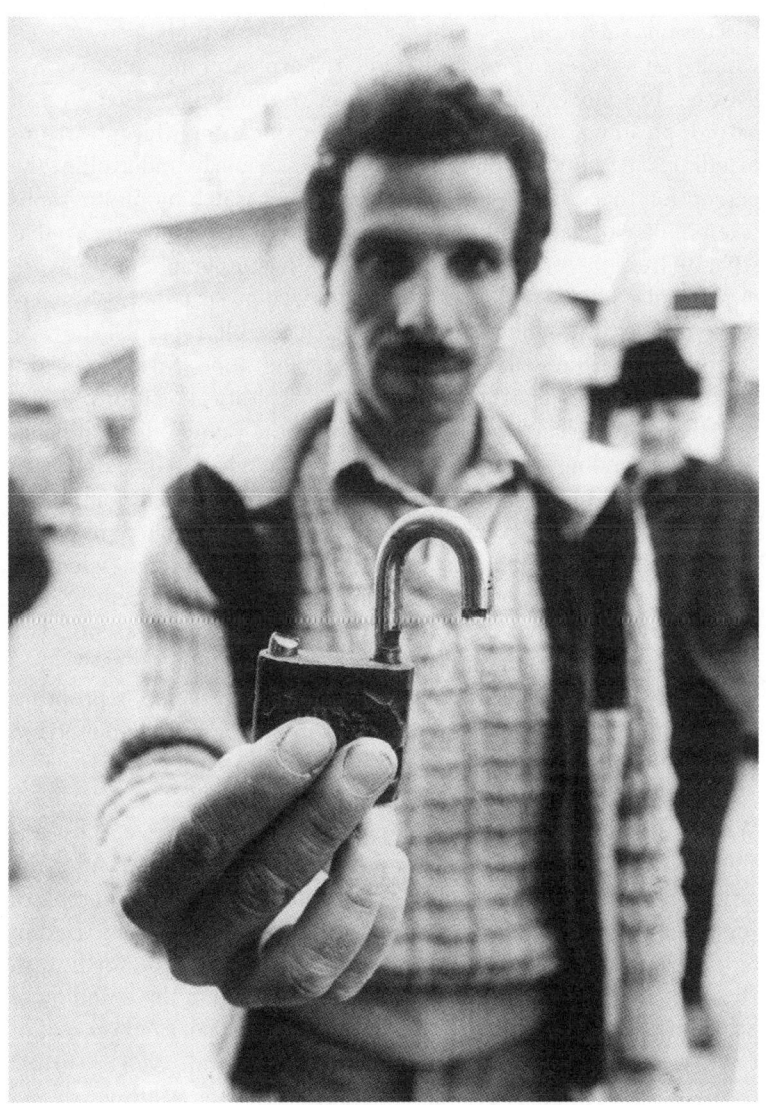

Figure I.1. Anat Saragusti, Hebron, 1982.

Discussions such as these elide the gaze of the photographed subject, which can vary enormously between sharp, probing, passive, exhausted, furious, introverted, defensive, warning, aggressive, full of hatred, pleading, unbalanced, skeptical, cynical, indifferent, or demanding. The photographed person's gaze seriously undermines the perception that practices of photography and watching photographs taken in disastrous conditions can be described and conceptualized as separate from the witnessed situation. When photographs or the work of particular photographers are characterized as "partisan," "subversive," or "critical," the assumption is that the photographs show or perform something that is already over and done, foreclosing the option of watching photographs as a space of political relations. When the Hebron merchant stands up in front of the camera, lock in hand, he isn't demanding remuneration for the broken lock. His stance is an insistent refusal to accept the noncitizen status assigned him by the governing power and a demand for participation in a sphere of political relations within which his claims can be heard and acknowledged. This book seeks to trace the blueprint of this political space through the construct of a civil contract whose main points it presents. The contract is one between the partner-participants in the act of photography and the various users of photography whom the book proposes to extract from the practices of both picture taking and the public use and display of photographs.[3]

What is the civil contract? I will present it through the earliest examples of the political use of photography. In 1845, six years after the official birth date of the technology of photography, a photograph of Jonathan Walker's palm was taken (figure I.2). Walker was tried in Florida for attempting to smuggle slaves out of the state northward. His sentence was imprisonment and a fine, as well as the branding of his hand with the letters "SS," denoting "slave stealer," the mark of Cain, as it were.[4] Following his release from prison, Walker turned to the Boston studio of photographers Albert Sands Southworth and Josiah Johnson Hawes to eternalize his branded palm in a photograph, which he proceeded to distribute as a protest against the court ruling. This resulted in a subsequent reinterpretation of the SS mark as denoting "slave savior."

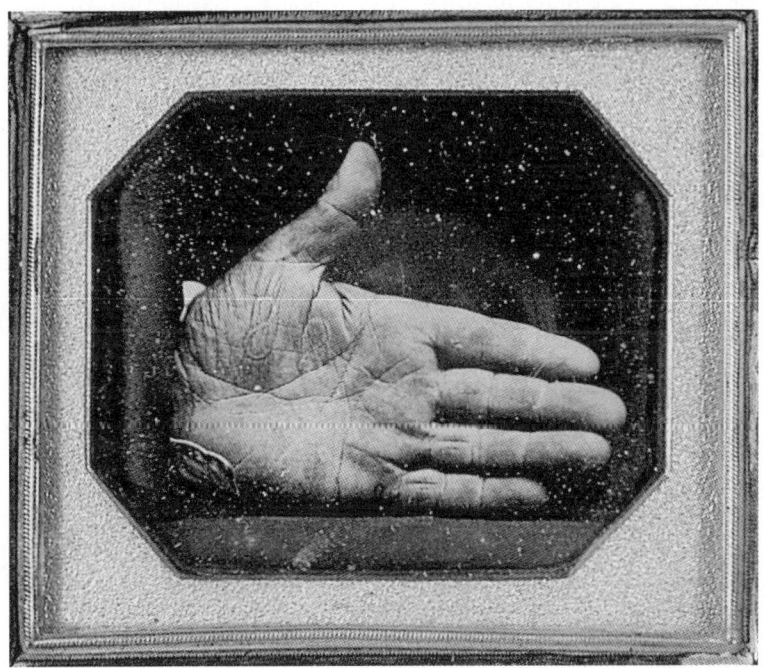

Figure I.2. Southworth and Hawes, *The Branded Hand of Captain Jonathan Walker*, daguerreotype, 1845 (reproduced courtesy of the Massachusetts Historical Society).

The photographic act initiated by Walker did not challenge the penalty that had already been seared into his flesh. The challenge was of another type, including three dimensions: to the *content* of the court ruling, according to which the assistance that Walker provided to seven human beings to escape slavery was a criminal act; to the stable *meaning* of the punishment, part of which was manifested through inscribing a mark of shame on the body; and to the boundaries defining the *community* authorized to reinterpret the court ruling.

What the encounter between Walker and the two photographers engendered was not the portrait of an abolitionist, but rather a direct and focused photograph of Walker's palm. The represented hand is reminiscent, in its directness, of a still life — a shell, a hat, a fossil. However, unlike the assorted articles usually photographed at the time in the genre of the still life, this hand was not meant to stay still and silent. Walker, Southworth, and Hawes sought to publicize and disseminate it and assigned it a place and a role in the sphere of speech and action. The daguerreotype had the power to publish the disgrace meant to exclude Walker from the public and, through this very act of publication, to overturn the disgrace.

In their act of photography, the photographers and the photographed person assumed the existence of a hypothetical spectator who would take an interest in the image and be aroused by it to show responsibility toward Walker and toward the ongoing injustice evidenced by the brand burned into his flesh. The spectators that Walker was assuming were not particular, familiar ones to whom he could have displayed his actual palm; he was assuming unfamiliar, anonymous spectators who — so he conjectured, presumed, or at least hoped — would form a community through the act of watching this photograph and others. Walker wasn't directing his attempt exclusively to the members of a particular community of abolitionists, but to possible, potential members of such a community. His photograph presupposes and is addressed to a virtual community, one that is not identical to the local community to which Walker belonged and from which he would supposedly be excluded by his mark of shame. The members of this presupposed community made use of the photograph as photographers, as photographed persons, as spectators.

These various and new uses of photography created a new community, in part actual and in part virtual. It was not a community of professionals or members of any particular church, party, or sect. It was a new political community of people between whom political relations were not mediated by a sovereign ruling power that governed a given territory. Neither were the people of this community subject to such a ruling power. The civil contract of photography that the emergence of this community exemplifies is the hypothetical, imagined arrangement regulating relations within this virtual political community. It is not dictated by the ruling power, even when this power attempts to rule and to control photography. When the ruling power interferes in this sphere, it amounts to no more than an additional player acting alongside the others. Even rude interference on the part of the ruling power in the encounter between the photographer and the photographed person or in a meeting between the spectator and the photographed person will fail to reach various other encounters between the same or other players committed to the civil contract of photography. Some of these will always elude intervention.

The political theory laid out below is founded on this new conceptualization of citizenship as a framework of partnership and solidarity among those who are governed, a framework that is neither constituted nor circumscribed by the sovereign. The theory of photography proposed in this book is founded on a new ontological-political understanding of photography. It takes into account all the participants in photographic acts — camera, photographer, photographed subject, and spectator — approaching the photograph (and its meaning) as an unintentional effect of the encounter between all of these. None of these have the capacity to seal off this effect and determine its sole meaning.

The civil contract of photography assumes that, at least in principle, the governed possess a certain power to suspend the gesture of the sovereign power seeking to totally dominate the relations between us, dividing us as governed into citizens and noncitizens thus making disappear the violation of *our* citizenship. Given the circumstances that Israel is an occupying and colonizing power, speaking of "our" citizenship — that is, of the citizenship of both Palestinians and Israelis — is based on the assumption that being governed along with and beside individuals who are not citizens also causes damage to the seemingly whole, unimpaired citizenship of the citizens who *are* recognized as such. No attempt is implied here to claim symmetry between populations of citizens and noncitizens or to lay a foundation for their comparison. Rather, this is an attempt to rethink the political space of governed populations and to reformulate the boundaries of citizenship as distinct from the nation and the market whose dual rationale constantly threatens to subjugate it.[5]

Although my claim is that the civil contract of photography is as old as photography itself (and although a lot has been written about citizens and citizenship), civil contracts and photography have been mostly kept apart in the theoretical discourses. Photography, its history, and its philosophy belong to the study of visual culture, media, or art history; contracts and citizens are the business of political theory or political science, sociology, or jurisprudence. *The Civil Contract of Photography* seeks to develop a concept of citizenship through the study of photographic practices and to analyze photography within the framework of citizenship as a status, an institution, and a set of practices.

The widespread use of cameras by people around the world has created more than a mass of images; it has created a new form of encounter, an encounter between people who take, watch, and show other people's photographs, with or without their consent, thus opening new possibilities of political action and forming new conditions for its visibility. The relations between the three parties involved in the photographic act — the photographed person, the photographer, and the spectator — are not mediated through a sovereign power and are not limited to the bounds of a nation-state or an economic contract. The users of photography thus reemerge as people who are not totally identified with the power that governs them and who have new means to look at and show *its* deeds, as well, and eventually to address this power and negotiate with it — citizen and noncitizen alike.

For the governing power, citizens can be equal among themselves, but not equal vis-à-vis others governed by that same power. Much of recent literature on citizenship ignores these two aspects of citizenship: citizens are governed together with noncitizens; citizens are governed differently from and therefore cannot be equal to others.

Citizens cannot be equally governed if they are governed with others who are not governed as equals. The proposed analysis of the photographic act and the space of photographic relations enables us to overcome the limit set on the concept of citizenship by the nation-state. The nation-state (re)territorializes citizenship. It provides a protective shield to those declared as citizens within a certain territory, and discriminates between them and others, noncitizens, who are governed with them, in the same territory, by the same power. Photography, on the other hand, deterritorializes citizenship, reaching beyond its conventional boundaries and plotting out a political space in which the plurality of speech and action (in Arendt's sense) is actualized permanently by the eventual participation of all the governed. These governed are *equally* not governed within this space of photography, where no sovereign power exists. Thus, citizenship can be restored at one and the same time as a relation to a state and a sovereign power and a relation between equals. These two aspects are constitutive of citizenship, and their logic will be retraced here from the French Revolution onward.

The conceptual valences between photography and citizenship are in fact twofold. Because, as we will see, photographs are constructed like statements (*énoncés*), the photographic image gains its meaning through mutual (mis)recognition, and this meaning (even if not the object itself) cannot be possessed by its addresser and/or addressee. Citizenship likewise is gained through recognition, and like photography is not something that can be simply possessed. Further, plurality is a prerequisite of both citizenship and photography. The principle of equality that citizenship upholds is supposed to preserve the conditions of plurality and to constrain the governing power. When citizenship is conceived and practiced as equality only between citizens, and not more broadly between the governed, it yields to the constraints of the governing power. Citizenship should be indifferent to the ties — from kinship through class or nation — that seek to link part of the governed to one another and exclude others. Free from the nationalist perspective, or any other essentialist conception of the collective of governed individuals, citizenship comes to resemble the photographic relation. Photographs bear traces of a plurality of political relations that might be actualized by the act of watching, transforming and disseminating what is seen into claims that demand action.

The civil contract of photography is a social fiction or hypostatized construct in the same sense that Rousseau's social contract was conceived of as something that has "perhaps never been formally set forth" previously, yet that is "everywhere the same and everywhere tacitly admitted and recognised."[6] Its theoretical recognition rests on the fact of its historical existence in every act of photography. It has been conceptualized here via its historical emergence as a convention that regulates the various uses of photography and its relations of exchange.

The book is organized as a progression of different, but related topics. The first chapter analyzes the Declaration of the Rights of Man and the Citizen, written at the time of the French Revolution (1789), and the Declaration of the Rights of Woman and the Female Citizen, formulated two years later (1791), from which it attempts to extract a blueprint of the figures of modern men and women as citizens and of the conditions either protecting them or exposing them to catastrophe.

The second chapter presents the civil contract of photography itself. It is, of course, not a document unearthed in some library or archive. I have encountered the traces this contract leaves at any and every site where there has been photography — that is, almost everywhere. This contract binds together photographers, photographed persons, and spectators. Each of them fulfills her role — persons are being taken in photos, photographers take pictures, spectators look, and all of them know what is expected of them and what to expect from the others. This shared set of expectations is a civil knowledge that amounts to more than just a technical skill. It is an assembly of civil skills that are not subject to nationality, but rather to borderless citizenship, to the modern citizenship of individuals who know, even when they are subject to boundless rule — and this is part of their civil skill — that the actual rule to which they are subject, in its concrete configuration, is always limited, always temporary, never final, even when there seems to be no exit from it. The photographs that they produce, that are made of them, that they look at, are traces of this civil skill, whose contract I have sought to make explicit, based on historical facts and a reliance on the experience of many people.

26

In the third chapter, I reconstruct the consent of the partners taking part in the act of photography to the binding contract between them, attempting to clarify the limits of this partnership. In order to outline the ethics of the spectator, I propose to understand the photograph's unique status as a product of the encounter between a photographer, a photographed person and a tool, in the course of which none of these three can treat the other as a sovereign such that even when one of them seems for a moment to possess the means of production, he or she is in fact no less operated than capable of operating. Introducing the dimensions of time and movement into the act of watching stills is the foundation for the ethics of the spectator. This ethics is based on a series of assumptions: Photographs do not speak for themselves. Alone, they do not decipher a thing. Identifying what is seen does not excuse the spectator from "watching" the photograph, rather than looking at it, and from caring for its sense. And the sense of the photograph is subject to negotiation that unfailingly takes place vis-à-vis a single, stable, permanent image whose presence persists and demands that the spectators cast anchor in it whenever they seek to sail toward an abstraction that is detached from the visible and that then becomes its cliché.

The fourth chapter describes the structural conditions of the field of vision in contemporary times, characterizing a certain type of photographic image — the image of horror — and examining the conditions for its transformation into what I will call an emergency claim. An emergency claim is an alert to a disastrous condition demanding urgent and immediate action. Through an analysis of various photographs from the second intifada, I cite the status of Palestinians as noncitizens as a central factor of the creation of conditions in which images of the horrors perpetrated against them were prevented from becoming emergency claims.

The fifth chapter discusses the ways in which injury to women appeared as a new object in discourse — since the 1970s, one distinguished from what had been perceived in the past as rape. This new object is characterized by a new understanding of what rape is, who a rape victim is, and who a rapist is, and also by new tools for dealing with rape that transform it into a phenomenon regarding which data and testimonies can be collected, in turn allowing its treatment and the implementation of means to prevent it. When the dimensions of rape relative to all women in the world emerge, rape appears as a catastrophe befalling a specific population, and its incidence — despite the change in its status in public discourse since the 1970s — indicates that the civil status of the population vulnerable to this type of injury is still impaired. The chapter points out that this is the only kind of catastrophe with no visibility in public discourse and attempts to understand the absence of pictures of rape as part of what leaves the dimensions of this catastrophe unchanged.

The sixth chapter presents the living conditions of the Palestinians as existence on the threshold of catastrophe and, through an analysis of photos and conversations with several photographers, addresses the question of how the threshold of catastrophe is photographed. The assumption is that the situation in Palestine is not on the verge of a catastrophe about to occur, but rather that it is a "threshold catastrophe" in the sense of a new configuration of catastrophe, a chronic and prolonged situation that doesn't interrupt routine.

The seventh chapter presents the figure of the universal spectator as an implied absentee presence in the act of photography and analyzes the relations conducted with her on the part of the photographer, the photographed person, and the actual spectator. The universal spectator, hovering, during the photographic act, above the encounter between the photographer and the photographed person, is an effect of the act of photography itself, necessary to the various protagonists taking part in this act so as to continue adhering to their mutual pact. Through observation mainly of portraits of Palestinians, the chapter attempts to reconstruct the face-to-face encounter between the photographer and the photographed person under conditions of threshold catastrophe.

The eighth chapter seeks to reject the prevalent perception of authentic or approved photography and to reconstruct the contours of the penal colony in Palestine (while discussing practices of detainment, imprisonment and torture) through a reading of existing and nonexistent photographs. The chapter points out the way in which the General Security Service (Shabak) employs photography as part of its methods of managing and oppressing the Palestinian population and, through a reading of missing photographs, proposes a rethinking of the category of collaboration.

The ninth and last chapter discusses the figure of the woman collaborator and the sexual violence employed by the Shabak against Palestinian women. Following the discussion of rape at the center of the fifth chapter, this chapter, too, deals with the manner in which the field of vision is sanitized of traces of this sexual violence, which is consequently compressed into an elusive rumor. Based on testimonies collected in the report by B'Tselem (The Israeli Information Center for Human Rights in the Occupied Territories) on collaboration in the course of the first intifada, the chapter tries to reconstruct how the modus operandi of the Shabak inscribes Palestinians with the sign of collaboration, whether or not they have consented to collaborate.

* * *

My work on this book began in parallel with the writing of *Once Upon a Time: Photography after Walter Benjamin*,[7] and for some time I believed that I was working on a single book or on twin books. While the two have since been separated and each has developed in a distinct direction of its own, there remains a strong link between them. The thinking of Walter Benjamin and the way in which photography percolates throughout his work are present in the background of this book. He wrote very little about photography relative to the whole corpus of his work, but the special way in which he read photographs and the place he allocated to the material aspect of photography — from the camera through the photographer's eye-hand relations — guided my first meeting with photography.

My reading of Benjamin was from the outset Deleuzian, and my debt to Benjamin is therefore also my debt to Gilles Deleuze. His discussion of caring for sense, along with the discourse of Jean-François Lyotard and his description of the duty to link phrases, has served me in discussing photography as a statement (*énoncé*) and in examining how and to whom it is being addressed as a civil act. I could not have developed my discussion of watching as a civil act and a rehabilitation of the political without Hannah Arendt's discussion of action and of the loss of common sense in modernity. The Declaration of the Rights of Woman and the Female Citizen, written by Olympe de Gouges (1791) and enunciating the way in which exclusion from the collective

29

has been inscribed on women's bodies, as well as Giorgio Agamben's *Homo Sacer* and its development of the concept of exception between the sacred and abandonment, helped me clarify the connection between abandonment and rape.

The discussions of rehabilitating citizenship under contemporary conditions are greatly indebted to the thinking of Étienne Balibar on citizenship and radical violence and to the thought of Azmi Bishara on citizenship in general and on the Israeli-Palestinian case in particular. Adi Ophir's work on the continuum between the particular injury and the condition of catastrophe contributed to my understanding of catastrophe as a preventable event. Joan Copjec's discussion of the condition of the gaze in modernity and her emphasis on its intransitive dimension enriched my formulation of the civil contract while posing an enduring challenge to it. Carole Pateman's discussion of the sexual contract as the repressed contract of the social contract and Juliet Flower MacCannell's work on the regime of the brother that has replaced patriarchy nurtured my thinking on women's impaired citizenship. This book also owes a great deal to my longstanding and unique ties with three artists, all of whom deal with photography and with theoretical thinking about photography: the project *Photographer Unknown* by Michal Heiman and her conception of photographs as subjects to be nursed and treated, Miki Kratsman's long-term work as a photojournalist in the occupied territories and his insights into what the act of photography is in the circumstances in which he practices it, and the tools that Aïm Deüelle Lüski constructs through which he dismantles the traditional rationale of the camera. To a large extent, their work has formed my understanding of photography and has allowed me to elaborate the civil contract of photography. The writings and photographs of many others likewise have made this book possible, and traces of their contributions are highly evident throughout.

CHAPTER ONE

Citizens of Disaster

Why try to think the categories of citizenship and disaster together? The answer is that the association of citizenship with disaster and the characterization of certain populations as being more susceptible to disaster than others show that citizenship is not a stable status that one simply struggles to achieve, but an arena of conflict and negotiation. The question of what constitutes the exception assumes a new meaning and helps distinguish two different political conditions: On the one hand, disaster is declared an exception because it is a situation in which citizens suffer immensely and need special protection from the state (or from their sovereign); on the other hand, certain people or populations governed by the state are declared an exception, and this makes them more vulnerable to disaster or abandons them in ways that turn their living environment into a disaster zone. In both cases, and from both perspectives, the political administration of disaster becomes a major scene for the claiming of citizenship or for its differential construction

Let us begin at the beginning. Common definitions of the term "citizen" can be divided into three main types. The first describes the citizen's status vis-à-vis the state: A citizen is a resident of permanent status in the state, with full legal rights and obligations. In the second type, the state is replaced by the body politic: Citizenship is membership in a political community (originally the polis, but now the nation-state), and it carries with it rights of political participation. A citizen is someone who is a member of such a community. The third type refers to the relationship between the citizen and the sovereign power that governs the state: A citizen is a person owing allegiance to and entitled to the protection of a sovereign state.[1] Permanent residence, membership in a political community, allegiance to a state: though not explicitly, these three definitions distinguish the citizen from the other — the noncitizen.

The ways in which the differences between these three definitions inflect this distinction play a crucial role in the conditions for exercising citizenship. The first type of definition is primarily concerned with the everyday, material experience of citizenship, while the second type is linked to more abstract dimensions, describing one particular moment in the life of the citizen — when he or she exercises the right to vote, a moment that occurs once every few years. In many cases, what legally distinguishes the citizen (who is described in the first type as having full rights and obligations) from the noncitizen (to whom only a limited number of rights and obligations apply) is what lies at the heart of the second type of definition: political participation.[2] In most cases, however, what separates the citizen from the noncitizen is what lies at the heart of the third type of definition: entitlement to protection.

None of these definitions, however, actually accounts for the other, from whom the citizen is to be distinguished, or for the reason the citizen should thus be distinguished at all.[3] Using the terms of the first definition of the citizen, we might define the noncitizen as someone who has no permanent status within the state where he or she resides and to whom only a limited number of legal rights and obligations — if any whatsoever — apply. According to the second type of definition, a noncitizen is someone who cannot participate in the political game, while for the third, the noncitizen is not entitled to the protection of the sovereign.

However they are distinguished, a recent UN report reveals another dimension at stake in the characterization of the noncitizen — he or she is someone who does not belong to the collective of citizens in a certain country and who is perceived as threatening to the security, purity of culture, economic welfare, and health of that country's inhabitants. The report cataloged 175 million noncitizens around the world, all of whom live alongside citizens who are distinguished from them: "In principle, noncitizens enjoy many of the same rights as citizens, with exceptions limited chiefly to political participation and freedom of movement. Nonetheless, states frequently subject migrants, refugees and other noncitizens to forms of discriminatory mistreatment which breach international norms, justifying this treatment with concerns of national security, cultural purity, economic welfare, and public health."[4] As revealed by the reasons used by states as justification for discriminating against and mistreating noncitizens, citizenship here is not concerned with all of those who are governed, but has been transformed into membership in a distinct collective.[5] To conceive of citizenship in this way is to elide power's basic relation to the governed *as* governed — citizens and noncitizens alike. Whether or not they are citizens, they are first and foremost *governed*,[6] a status that precedes any distinction between them.[7] Their status as citizens or noncitizens is what then characterizes the *form* of governance. The realm of politics exceeds the realm in which the politics of the nation-state is exercised by a sovereign power.[8]

Citizenship as a protection of all the governed, is a precondition for legitimate government in the modern era. Returning to the three general definitions, but now with the understanding that both the citizen and noncitizen are, first and foremost, fundamentally governed, what emerges is not simply the fragile status of the noncitizen, but the fragile status of the citizen as well. In the nation-state, the citizen's rights are granted insofar as he or she is a member of a distinct collective of citizens in which citizens represent themselves and also are represented. However, as one of the governed, the citizen remains exposed to the power of the state and unprotected from it by the allegiance owed to it, simultaneously being governed alongside other citizens as well as with noncitizens from whom the citizen has been distinguished.

The relationship between the citizen, as the governed, and the political power takes place under the aegis and in the name of what ostensibly unites them — the distinct collective of citizens and the need to protect it, which is allegedly common to the governed citizens and the governing power. The interests of the collective of citizens are supposedly served and protected by the political power. This misconception conceals the gap that separates the governed citizens from the political power, forging a false identification between the two that leaves the citizen exposed and unprotected vis-à-vis the power that enrolls her in its projects, from war and domination to exploitation and expulsion. The citizen's identification with this collective, which is designated either as the "nation," "state," "or body politic," obscures the core of his or her political existence as governed, obliterating the citizen's possible partnership with citizens of other nations or with noncitizens who, together, could stand up to the governmental power and confront it with the demand to be governed by the means, under the aegis, and solely in the name of their citizenship. Noncitizens are denied permanent status because they do not belong to the distinct collective of citizens in the state in which they are permanently governed. Treating them as the citizens of another hypothetical state, instead of the one in which they are actually governed, or, in the more severe case, defining them as stateless, are two ways of maintaining the temporary status of noncitizens in the state in which they reside and of continuing to govern them over time without the protection of citizenship.

In fact, if scrutinized, each of the three definitional types of citizens reveals the common submission to power of both citizens and noncitizens. The first type emphasizes that the citizen is a resident "of permanent status," while the status of noncitizen ascribed to another person who permanently resides alongside her and is governed by the same power in the same state is impermanent.[9] The second definition emphasizes political participation. Carole Pateman criticizes the conception of "the political" in the tradition of liberal theory because it "is identified with the 'state' and the latter is identified with a specific set of institutions."[10] Actual nongovernmental politics go beyond such a definition and limitations and enable citizens and noncitizens alike to initiate together other political relationships that are not totally identified with the interest of their government or even of their state (as conceived by that government) and that might challenge its sovereignty. In an open-ended political process, it is possible for the citizen and the noncitizen alike "to question" as Michel Feher writes, "the social norms that enable governing bodies to call upon unimpeachable principles in order to justify objectionable policies" and to "secure a social space" where they can "develop alternate ways of governing themselves and of relating to each other."[11] Finally, in the third type of definition, in which the citizen's entitlement to protection *by* the sov-

34

ereign is emphasized, what is in fact disclosed is the kind of protection that neither is entitled — protection *from* the sovereign. The lack of this type of protection is a blind spot in the existence of the modern citizen. The category of noncitizens, as the contrary of and in effect that against which citizens posit themselves alongside the sovereign prevents this blind spot from being revealed.

Now that we have juxtaposed the different types of governed that coexist within the same state, the difference in the types of disasters that affect the governed and the possibility of preventing or intervening in such disasters is more easily deciphered and acquires new meanings. Disasters "challenge the very principle of sovereignty," Adi Ophir has written, and reveal the broader, nongovernmental realm of open-ended political negotiations. "An emergency and a state of exception are created without being proclaimed by the sovereign, life is forsaken, and violent forces — natural as well as social — roam about, footloose, paying no heed to the sovereign's claim to have sole authority over life and death." And responses to disasters disclose "a new model of relations between politics, law, and morality in which a certain form of biopolitics turns into a mode of resistance to state power."[12] In the following, I'll show how disasters articulate a line that roughly distinguishes two types of population according to their relative exposure or protection. Tanks roll into city streets and trample everything they encounter; a pregnant woman is detained for hours at a checkpoint, resulting in the birth of a stillborn baby; vacationers die beneath the wreckage of a hotel, its façade torn apart by a car bomb; a woman is raped in the stairwell of her home. This is a random list of disasters that take place every day around the world. Although in many respects these disasters differ from one another, the ways in which individuals belong to the injured population and their civil status are significant for determining how vulnerable they are to the experience of disasters.

The first way in which individuals may belong to an injured population can be described as contingent, given the fact that the gathering together of this population in a given territory takes place for a predetermined length of time, before and after which the homogeneity of the population dissolves, and it breaks up into numerous subgroups. So-called terror attacks, which take place in the heart of powerful, wealthy countries, are one example of this type of contingent disaster. The contingent gathering of individuals at the site of a disaster gives the disaster that has struck them the status of an exception to the rule and introduces a factor of urgency to the efforts to address it. This shift in status entails that everything possible must be done to limit the scale of the disaster by contributing to its neutralization, preventing its recurrence, providing compensation to the victims, and rebuilding the ruins. The force of urgency affects all the individuals who happen to have been at the site of the disaster, regardless of their civil status. Various individuals who are outside of the zone that has been struck may suddenly find themselves sharing the common fate of victims, that is, with others who do not belong to the same economic, social, and political classes.

The second way in which individuals may belong to an injured population can be attributed to a differential system of citizenship that discriminates against certain sectors of the governed population on the basis of differences of religion, gender, race, class, ethnicity, or language. Such a system constitutes certain groups of citizens as "flawed citizens" and designates other governed subjects as noncitizens. Both noncitizens and flawed citizens are more exposed than "proper" citizens to hazards and risks, and their vulnerability is systemic. Although their status (as noncitizens or flawed citizens) is part of the rule, in times of disaster it is they, not the disastrous event itself, that seem an exception to the rule. The disaster that strikes such groups is conceived as part of the routine, not as an exceptional event, and the situation is emptied of any dimension of urgency. The stricken population may be at the disaster site over a prolonged period of time, such as the inhabitants of a chronically polluted area or of an occupied territory, but they may also be distributed over the face of the globe, as in the case of women. In any event, populations of flawed citizens and of noncitizens are constantly exposed to various kinds of injury.[13] These populations, for which disaster is chronic and does not constitute an exception, will be the focus of my discussion below.

The two injured groups I will consider at length in this book live alongside one another: female citizens in Israel and Palestinians living in the territories occupied by Israel since 1967. The first group may be conceived of as representative of a type: female citizens in more or less democratic regimes. The second group may be conceived of as representative of another type: people who have been abandoned by the powers that rule them. The former are citizens whose citizenship is impaired to a greater or lesser degree in different states and is certainly impaired in my own country, Israel. The latter are noncitizens who, for more than forty years now, have been ruled by Israeli authorities alongside Israeli citizens, but are deprived of basic rights that the latter enjoy and are totally excluded from the ruling power. The first group will be studied here with respect to the practices and situations that mark its past exclusion from and contemporary unequal access to the body politic and its inferior share in the advantages and protection of citizenship. The second group will be studied with respect to the practices and procedures used by the ruling apparatus that controls their lives through excessive use of violence, transforms them into nonpolitical subjects, and systematically undermines any effort to create a viable public sphere.

My assumption is that citizenship in any particular historical situation cannot be understood without taking into account the noncitizens who make up part of the governed population and constitute an excluded group *with and alongside which* the citizens are governed.[14] I myself am governed alongside Palestinians, but in a different way from them. This fact turns my investigation of the two groups, their political status, and their relative vulnerability in times and sites of disaster into an intimate matter. When I bring together these two groups and in my discussion move freely between them, I cannot forget the fact that I "naturally" belong to the former group and enjoy its relative privileges and against my will am taking part in dominating and oppressing the latter group. Because I belong to the one and take part in harming the other, I am responsible for responding to the injuries of the two groups in different ways, but these two ways are intimately related. It is my civic duty to address the plight of both groups, to understand the condition of their vulnerability to catastrophe, different from each other as they are, and to respond to the claims they are addressing to me. In the context of this work, I am interested in the claims they are addressing to me through photographs. I assume that photography — taking photos, being photographed, and disseminating and looking at photos — provides a privileged access to the problem of impaired citizenship, as well as a moral practice in face of the vulnerability this condition creates.

The analysis that follows deals with two matters: the role that citizenship plays in the modern era and the power it has to serve as protection, and the conditions under which this protection is itself left unprotected.

Unprotected Citizenship

One obvious text with which to begin a discussion of the concept of citizenship in the modern era, at least within the European political tradition, is the Declaration of the Rights of Man and the Citizen of 1789. It is a constitutive document in the history of modern citizenship as a certificate of political partnership. This partnership is based on the rights and obligations set out in the declaration's seventeen articles, which are preceded by a brief introduction describing the circumstances in which the document was written:

> The representatives of the French people, organized as a National Assembly, believing that the ignorance, neglect, or contempt of the rights of man are the sole cause of public calamities [*malheurs publics*] and of the corruption of governments, have determined to set forth in a solemn declaration the natural, unalienable, and sacred rights of man, in order that this declaration, being constantly before all the members of the Social body [*à tous les members de la société*], shall remind them continually of their rights and duties...and in order that the grievances of the citizens, based hereafter upon simple and incontestable principles, shall tend to the maintenance of the constitution and redound to the happiness of all.[15]

I will try to articulate the relationship between three concepts that appear independently in the declaration: citizenship, suffering, and presence. Although the declaration was formulated in France for the benefit of the French people, the rights and duties that appear in it are not derived from any specific French national characteristic or from any particular form of government, but from general principles regarding the relationship between sovereign power and its subjects/

citizens. The representatives of the French people were seeking to determine not only the political standing of the French people, but the abstract political standing of human beings and citizens, whoever they might be. The entire text, from the title to the last article, betrays the effort to avoid any local, historical, or contingent characteristics and to arrive at abstract formulations that would enable it to become an instrument of political protection with widespread distribution. The declaration was the outcome of the struggle of the French bourgeoisie against the nobility and ruling monarchy, but at the same time, it was the attempt of the male bourgeoisie to present itself as the entire French nation and to speak in its name, although in a language that refuses the particularities of the French context in order to espouse the universal claim of the nation as a body of citizens.

Hence the declaration reflects two different, but simultaneous struggles, a local one in which the bourgeoisie appears as one of the nation's three *estates* and a universal one in which it appears not only as the nation itself ("a complete nation" and "everything," in the words of a theorist of the Revolution, Abbé Emmanuel Joseph Sieyès in his 1789 manifesto *What Is the Third Estate?*), but as a model for citizens everywhere. The French revolutionaries saw themselves as having instituted the struggle of the modern man and the citizen against despotic rule as such, a struggle that could be conducted only by "citizens," whose very existence was supposed to be the harbinger of a new form of globalization.[16]

The political status of the man and the citizen, as constituted by the declaration, is not defined in terms of inhabiting a particular territory, but in relation to a power that governs a particular territory. Their rights are declared to be natural in order to ensure that no sovereign power, whatever it might be, will be able to abolish them. The declaration appoints new players in the political game and places itself at their service as a tool in their struggle. The declaration sought to guarantee political representation, which means participation in governmental power, while ensuring that this partnership, when resting on the principles of the declaration, can prevent the suffering that would be inflicted on individuals if they were not citizens. Citizenship guarantees not only that the subjects of sovereign power will enjoy equality before the law, but that the many laws, varying from one regime to the next, will have as their foundation a single, unchanging law, irrespective of place, one that would not require its reconstitution under each and every sovereign.

There are two aspects to the universality of the principle of citizenship. The first is formal and static, determining the principle's general sphere of applicability. The second is historical and dynamic, pointing to the changing gap, determined by historical and political conditions, between the fulfillment of the principle (in France, Europe, the West in general, and so on) and the entire range of its formal applicability (including all human beings and everyone who is governed). This second aspect presents an incongruity between the local and the global context as a structural principle of modern citizenship itself, an incongruity that the French declaration bequeathed to coming generations. As the declaration moves from the local context of the territory in which it was formulated to a nonterritorial principle of citizenship and then on to a universal principle, this shifting produces a residue, characterized by an invisibility, that includes all those whose status is located somewhere between territory and citizenship: individuals or populations who inhabit a given territory governed by the sovereign power, but are deprived of citizenship — which is to say, those who are missing from the political representation of the population in that territory. These individuals or populations are present in the territory, but their presence in the visual field created by the new political game is limited. As the declaration asserts, there is no guarantee that their suffering will be translated into "grievances based upon simple and incontestable principles," the voicing of which is a condition for the "maintenance of the constitution and the happiness of all."

The absence of citizenship places an obstacle in front of any attempt to turn the suffering of such noncitizens into a political object, which in turn effectively determines what matters can be spoken of in a political context, based on the specific political demands that can be made by the political partners responsible for this suffering or capable of preventing it or of mitigating its consequences. The flawed citizenship ascribed to these populations affects the responsibility that the government shows toward them, insofar as any dimension of urgency is removed from any calamity that threatens to affect them or any disaster that has already struck. The customary understanding of citizenship, which gives prominence to the formal aspect of the principle while veiling or suppressing its historical, dynamic aspect, is ultimately blind to this residue of noncitizenship produced by the declaration and thus contributes to the continual exposure of this residue of noncitizens to the same "public calamities" from which the declaration seeks to protect its addressees.

In other words, the text of the declaration presents citizenship as a way to prevent and protect against suffering. Not all suffering can be prevented, but there is suffering that citizenship, when it is inscribed in a declaration of an agreed-upon standing with manifest visibility, is indeed able to mitigate by granting basic rights to individuals. Because citizenship can prevent some suffering, however, from the moment citizenship is constituted as an instrument capable of doing so, all those who are not recognized as deserving to enjoy it — this residue of noncitizens, all those whose citizenship is flawed — are in effect the victims of unnecessary suffering, suffering that, according to the fundamental conception of citizenship itself, could have been prevented.[17]

The fact that suffering can be prevented is continually manifested in cases where different populations have demanded citizenship, with some coming gradually to acquire such status. In his essay on the declaration, Étienne Balibar ascribes great importance to the very act of enunciation of the declaration as what paved the way for the continual becoming citizen of those excluded from the original declaration, whereby populations are able gradually to extract their universal right to political existence from the same declaration that originally excluded them due to the indeterminacy that characterizes it, allowing them to return to its universality "without change, in order to reproduce the truth-effect without which there is no revolutionary politics."[18]

Given the declaration's indeterminacy, the commitment to repeat the act of enunciation "without change" prompts me to make the exact opposite of Balibar's assertion, although it remains along the same horizon: Not only are the man and the citizen separate, but the citizen is indeed threatened by the man, and the citizen's need to defend himself against the man is part of his citizenship. To demonstrate this proposition, I will look beyond the specific content expressed by each of the declaration's articles in order to point out the new conditions of visibility it has created for the appearance of the abstract figures of "man" and "citizen." The conditions that the declaration formulates are supposed to allow unnecessary suffering to be made visible, making it possible to translate this visibility into political action that could lead to the reduction or prevention of the suffering. The writers of the declaration use three terms to account for the possible causes of suffering when the individual is stripped of the protection of citizenship that the declaration manufactured and granted with its power. All three are related to a state of nonpresence or invisibility: disregard (or "ignorance"), forgetfulness (or "neglect"), and scorn (or "contempt").

Citizenship, as derived from the declaration, is not reducible to a matter of legislation or the formal recognition of legal status. Instead, it is the rendering of this status as present, explicit, and known to all — "in order that this declaration" shall be "constantly before all the members of the Social body." Giving the Tablets of the Law is not enough, insofar as a praxis of repeating the text must be instituted in order to transform the revolutionary act — citizenship for all — into an obligatory norm. Already in the eyes of the people of the eighteenth century, citizenship was a practice of repetition, citation, and performativity. The repetitiveness was intended to protect the recipients of citizenship from those who might threaten to rob them of it through the restoration of the old order.

The authors of the declaration sought to demarcate and restrict what was to be repeated to the single version of the text they had composed — "this declaration." But because the document is riddled from start to finish with obscurities and contradictions — discernible not only among its different versions,[19] but most explicitly the gap between the written text and the reality that it seeks to describe — it does not go without saying what this single version could possibly be or what this singular text is that should be repeated. The text is without concrete territorial demarcations, nor does it contain any other selective conditions or parameters that limit its pretension to generality. The foremost expression of this pretension is the declaration's addressee, who could ostensibly be anyone and everyone. It would not be presumptuous to recall that not only was citizenship not granted to any people other than the French, but it was also denied to entire segments of the French population: Women, blacks, the poor, children, and criminals were all refused citizenship.[20] This gap has not damaged the universal reputation that the declaration has enjoyed and continues to enjoy or the exemplary status that has contributed to making it a document to be reproduced and distributed. Nor has this gap defamed the declaration, which by means of a universalistic language conceals the concrete injuries it causes. Indeed, rereading the declaration today, the exclusion of these populations from citizenship is not evident within it, and the text appears amenable to citation by anyone demanding the very same thing denied to him/her by "this declaration."

"This declaration" — or the citizenship that it grants — is exactly what Olympe de Gouges had already repeated when the Declaration of the Rights of Man and the Citizen had been signed in 1789. When she published her own Declaration of the Rights of Woman and the Female Citizen in 1791, however, through her repetition, with the writer's gender affiliation was added to the introduction — "Mothers, daughters, sisters gathered here" — she exposed the particularistic dimension of the universalist declaration, turning it into a trump card in the political game.[21] She insisted on sharpening the rules of that game, emphasizing that it takes place in the gap between the *énoncé* (the assertion itself, what is said) and the enunciation (the act of saying). The universalist *énoncé* can be repeated in the enunciation, and through such repetition, the stated content can be given new meaning.[22] The Declaration of the Rights of Woman and the Female Citizen, which de Gouges proposed in the name of all women while repeating the original *énoncé* almost verbatim may be gendered, but it does not renounce the universalist pretension of the original. She turns inquisitively toward "man" — all men — who excluded her from the original declaration: "It is a woman asking the question — at least do not deny me this right." She thus posits, as a "natural and unalienable" right, a political right that is neither inscribed in the original declaration nor protected by it — the right to participate in the political game.

De Gouges in effect displaces the "man" of the declaration, but not the "citizen," from the position of the text's referent to the position of her own text's addressee, from Man (*Homme*) in the universal sense to the particular male individual (*homme*). In this position, she can appeal to "man" as the one who has excluded her, and thereby she implicitly creates a pact between herself as a noncitizen governed subject and the governed "citizen." This pact is based on a common attribute that allows de Gouges and the citizen of the declaration to take similar speaking positions: both are capable of issuing "grievances" in the public domain. According to de Gouges, this right — to ask, request, present grievances, or negotiate in the public domain — cannot be denied or violated, not because it is somehow natural, but because it is in the very nature of being governed in the framework of a modern body politic. Thus, de Gouges declares the right of *all* the governed — to talk back to the power that governs as a precondition for any further negotiation over the exclusion and abandonment of women.

In *Contingency, Hegemony, and Universality*, Judith Butler, repeatedly emphasizes that universalism is always tainted with particularism and therefore always includes an act of exclusion.[23] If we examine this assertion in reference to the declaration and the question of citizenship in general, the question arises: Does the universalist model of citizenship always have the intention of creating stateless individuals or, to be more precise, of creating noncitizens who are governed, even though they are denied citizen status?

Reconstructing the distinction made in the declaration between "man" and "citizen" is necessary in order to address this question. The distinction between them that appears explicitly in the title of the original document of 1789 is progressively blurred in the text, resulting in the terms being used interchangeably. Since this declaration has bequeathed to us the ambivalence between man and citizen, an ambivalence that persists to this day, I will dwell briefly on the relation between the two in the original text and apply my analysis to our contemporary discussion of citizenship.

Reconstituting the distinction is no simple matter, however, because it obscures the gap between the universality of the language employed by the declaration and the heterogeneous reality — including individuals who are not among the addressees of the declaration — that it seeks effectively to preserve. The declaration is under no obligation to identify its addressees; meanwhile, its direct addressees are known and acknowledge the declaration as knowing them in a manner that turns their standing as its addressees into something taken for granted. In other words, the declaration grants the rights of "liberty, property, security, and resistance to oppression" to all those who already enjoy such rights, even if only in a limited way, and for some less than others. In the same gesture, as something to be taken for granted, the declaration excludes all others, an exclusion that is conducted in a manner that is itself to be taken for granted. He who has "natural and unalienable" rights, the one who is the reason for writing the declaration, is "man." What man has is naturally his, and the declaration's task is to protect him. Neither property nor liberty are recognized by the declaration as political elements — it is only their protection that is grasped as a political matter.

Thus, the protection of the natural rights of man — the addressee of the declaration — is the crux of the document. "The aim of all political association," as stated in Article 2, "is the preservation of the natural and imprescriptible rights of man." The citizen, one might infer from the text, is the one who enters into political association and assumes this duty. Most evocations of the citizen in the declaration are of this kind. He shows up in a rather haphazard manner, primarily as a synonym for the new man born from the Revolution as a political entity. Man has the right to freedom of ideas and opinions, as Article 11 states, and in the same sentence — without a pause for breath — man is turned into the citizen who, by virtue of man's right, "may speak, write, and print with freedom."

The citizen portrayed by the declaration is a rather pale figure, working on behalf of man and his natural rights of "liberty, property, security, and resistance to oppression."[24] The declaration seeks to restrict the citizen's grievances so that they are "based hereafter upon simple and incontestable principles, shall tend to the maintenance of the constitution and redound to the happiness of all." A reading that seeks to rehabilitate the institution of citizenship that is latent in the declaration cannot be satisfied with the citizen that has been portrayed; it must recover the traces of the citizen to whom the declaration fails to address, but who nevertheless intrudes on the declaration, so as to make his appearance the political residue that has been left out and suppressed. If we momentarily put aside the citizen described by the declaration and look at the citizen who *arises* from the declarative act itself, we are faced with another citizen, different from his portrayed brother who is actually man's assistant. This is the citizen who is the *addresser* of the declaration. He is not the subject of the text, or one of its referents, but the author of this unusual speech act who uses it as a political act to affirm or create his association with his fellow citizens while at the same time negotiating with sovereign power or even putting in question the unitary and undivided sovereign.

This is precisely the citizen whose grievances the declaration seeks to contain. The citizen constituted as a political addresser is a persona that voices grievances — this is his essence, his function. In contrast to man, who is characterized by his "natural rights" and by what has always been his, even before becoming a player in the political game, the citizen is characterized as someone who seeks to negotiate with the governing power. The citizen, too, is characterized as being a new figure, but his subordination to man intends to obscure this and to lessen his power.

We thus have two citizens before us: one portrayed by the declaration as a pale figure who serves as man's bearer of arms and another who is unwilling to accept, a priori, his role as the protector of certain rights only because they are natural. He may be an addressee of the *Declaration*, and he may also be one of those that it excludes. The lack of congruence between him and man stems from the difference between all those who are actually governed and "all the members of the Social body" cited by the declaration. It is this gap that places the onus of voicing grievances on the citizen.

In the declaration, then, the discussion of man and citizen is split in order for man to be depicted as the one belonging to the order of *being*, while the citizen is placed in the order of *becoming*. As a figure motivated by grievance and demand and as a political addresser, the citizen is obliged to accept the protection ensured to man. In doing so, he is paradoxically left without protection against what may be done to him by the man who has set out to defend his natural and unalienable rights. If citizenship is understood not as "what man has," as a possession by natural right, but as a political stance from which grievances can be presented to power — to negotiate, for instance, over the form of governance — then the citizen is left without protection in the declaration. He is unprotected because presenting grievances is not

46

recognized as a right, and certainly not as one of the "unalienable" rights. In other words, when it is recognized that man and citizen are not synonymous, but rather two figures in tension and conflict with one another, it is necessary to reconsider what the declaration's legacy has actually been with regard to the governed, rather than just with regard to "man."

Who Speaks for the Governed?

Michel Foucault focused on the right of the governed in his essays on political issues of the day.[25] This right, while implicitly mocking the language of natural rights, is for Foucault "much more precise, much more defined historically than the rights of man."[26] The declaration of this right was intended to address the gap that often exists between all those who are governed and those who enjoy rights as citizens while at the same time explicitly making an effort to avoid any language that requires anchoring these rights in the sphere of the natural. Moreover, speaking about the governed and about an international community of the governed makes manifest what has been erased from the declaration in its portrayal of the citizen — the fact that the citizen is first and foremost governed.

Membership in an international community without borders carries both duties and rights, and the first of these, which is both a duty and right at the same time, is to take action, Foucault claims, against the "intolerable." Referring to the governed, which is to say to concrete political populations, Foucault universalizes them and attempts to formulate a program, as recently expressed by the editorial page of the periodical *Vacarme*, "in search after an international of the *governed*."[27] My attempt here is much more modest and limited. Here, there is no attempt to propose a document formulating what universal citizenship is or the minimum that needs to be protected, but rather an attempt to think about ways of rehabilitating the citizenship of a specific body of governed whose governance is an exception to the rule applied to the body of citizens in the territory in which they are governed together in given historical situations. What is attempted is the reformulation of the citizenship of the governed and of the citizens who coexist in the same territory in given historical situations with the hope of making them equal in standing.

What needs to be revealed is the continuity between the undermining of citizenship by the figure of "man," which was already contained in the declaration, and the existence of individuals and groups who have been excepted from the law. Modern citizenship is under threat from two directions: from the market and from the nation-state. These are two contrary forces with dissimilar interests, but both in effect serve as mechanisms for restricting the rights of citizenship, as well as access to citizenship itself. The state does so by governing what occurs in its territory, while the market controls the freedom of movement through its networks by means of its control over the cost of movement. One of man's natural rights is the right to property — which makes him, wittingly or unwittingly, an agent of the market and which threatens to limit the citizen's own citizenship.

The nation-state — although it is not mentioned in the declaration, it serves as its organizing matrix and presupposition — places limits on accessibility to citizenship. Rapidly, as Hannah Arendt wrote, the question of man's rights was conflated with "national liberation," and it came to seem that those rights can be guaranteed only by a "liberated sovereignty."[28] By means of ceremonies and rituals that have created a sort of civic religion,[29] the state enlists worthy citizens for the sake of causes that often have nothing to do with the citizens' association. Since its birth in the Declaration of the Rights of Man and the Citizen, citizenship has been sanctified by the state religion. While citizenship is enlisted for the sake of the nation and the state, citizens are commanded to defend the nation and the state instead of defending their citizenship. A split is thus created between the governed who become worthy citizens of the nation and noncitizens or subcitizens.

The civic religion displaces the relationship between citizens and their governance from the secular sphere of relations of control and the critique of government to relations whose organizing framework is transcendence.[30] The citizen is thus subordinated to "man," who has natural rights, while citizenship is subordinated to nationalism, which is anchored in the nation's natural rights.[31] This subordination acts as a mechanism of exclusion with a silencer. In its name, others who are governed in the territory are excluded from citizenship, and the silencer serves to make the citizens forget that they themselves are governed, preventing them from exercising their citizenship by preventing their participating in a common cause with the others who are governed, but who are not citizens. Thus, both the market and the nation-state have restricted access to citizenship, complicating it and making it dependent on a particularist affiliation. The combined action of these two mechanisms continues to pose as a daily threat to citizenship. Paradoxically, however, as long as these two mechanisms continue to manufacture citizenship as a status that is not easily accessible, citizenship will continue to retain its power as protection, and the need to defend it will continue to grow.

In 1948, the United Nations formulated a new universal declaration of the rights of man, the Universal Declaration of Human Rights, from which the term "citizen" was dropped. The deletion sharpened the distinction between man and citizen, positing man as prior to or independent of citizenship and turning man into a nonpolitical or pre-political entity, seeking to ensure that all men, whoever they might be and regardless of their civilian status, might enjoy a minimum of political protection. This abstract document is supposed to enable the various member states of the UN to be its spokespeople and is therefore devoid of any concrete reference to the situation of noncitizens or to flawed citizens and those in states of exception in their territories.

The citizen thus has indeed been omitted from the new declaration as its subject. But if we examine who the active *agent* of the declaration is, a more complicated picture emerges. The address of the declaration is a political act that gives voice to a political demand — even though its formulation strips the object of the demand of any political standing — in regard to the residue of the governed who exist while still remaining invisible in the territories they inhabit. Here the state paradoxically assumes a civil function in the framework of the international community. This is a task, however, that the nation-state is unable to perform unless it once again — to paraphrase Arendt — is transformed from an instrument of the nation to an instrument of law. But this declaration, like the declaration of 1789, is not controlled by its authors, who omitted the citizen; it has become a text in the hands of citizens and noncitizens alike, who may use it in the public arena in order to address power and who are capable of doing so independently of the logic of the market or the nation-state and its sovereign, speaking from the realm that exceeds the realm in which the politics of the nation-state is exercised by a sovereign power, speaking as and for the governed.

The addresser of the 1948 declaration is the governed citizen who understands that he or she is the inverted reflection of the noncitizen, of the residue left between citizenship and territory, to whose defense the citizen has come. This is the citizen who, since the mid-twentieth century, in the name of "the governed as such," has been establishing nongovernmental organizations that challenge the state's position as the restrictive spokesperson of the civilian *énoncé*.[32] "What distinguishes the various political involvements of the governed as such is that they are all predicated on an intolerance of the effects of a particular set of governmental practices — regardless of whether the governing agency responsible for these practices is a state, an international organization, a public institution, or a private corporation." Those who do so are "driven by a shared determination not to be governed thusly."[33]

> In other words. what specifically concerns nongovernmental activists is not *who* governs — who is in charge, for whose benefit, and to what alleged end — but how government is exercised. One can therefore speak of a dual relationship between nongovernmental politics and government according to what the latter term designates. Insofar it refers to the empowering mechanisms upon which governmental agencies rely, government is indeed that from which nongovernmental politics is severed. However, when it is understood as the normative procedures to which the governed are subjected, and especially when different groups of the governed are subjected to different normative procedures, government is the very object of nongovernmental politics.[34]

The citizen understands that global life in the company of noncitizens in effect deprives her of the universality of its basis — to be governed like anyone else or to participate in governmental power like anyone else. The organizations that this citizen has established, which are concerned with the rights of man and of the citizen, have extracted the expression "human rights" from the textual existence in which it appeared in this declaration and have made it a part of the negotiations over citizenship. These organizations are made part of the logic of globalization, providing assistance to those whose rights are being denied everywhere around the globe or administering global means of assistance to these populations in their own locales.

The presence of these humanitarian organizations typically indicates a crisis situation or evidence of the onset of a catastrophe.[35] In these situations, the presence of such organizations is fundamentally transient. They provide assistance chiefly in places where the urgency of the situation demands their presence, and they are supposed to depart when order is restored. Catastrophes that demand such an urgent response usually occur when sudden disaster strikes a population and destroys the material and organizational infrastructures that ordinarily sustain them. Although disasters that require an urgent response differ widely in cause, intensity, and effect (as in the case of the collapse of the Twin Towers or the tsunami in southeast Asia), they are similar insofar as each is a fully demarcated area that is turned into a disaster zone for a limited period of time, with various forces — local and global — mobilized to limit the damage and conduct recovery operations.

As I already noted, however, in what follows, I will not be dealing with this kind of disaster, but with conditions in which the injury that befalls populations does not create a dimension of urgency, a chronic disaster that goes on with no end in sight and in which there are no forthcoming plans for mitigating its effects. I will deal with two examples — women and the Palestinians.[36]

Vulnerable Citizens

Around the second half of the twentieth century, women's struggle for citizen rights and equal civil status was more or less completed in Western countries. This completion was marked by a new beginning — women's struggle to obtain right over their own bodies. The anti-rape and birth-control movements proclaimed women as sole owners of their bodies, subjects of their own sexuality, and authors of their own reproductive activity. However, the focus of women's struggles in various fields of knowledge and activity has gradually shifted from the realm of political rights to the realm of life. Whereas the first wave of their struggle was directed against their exclusion from the political sphere, the second may be defined as a struggle against their sexual abandonment.

The various rape-victim treatment centers that have been established throughout the world, the various focal points for dealing with violence against women, and the organizations concerned with domestic violence that have proliferated since the 1970s — all of these developments have a humanitarian dimension that obliges us to think about the civil or citizen status of the populations that they treat. Some act on behalf of women outside their own countries of origin, while most operate in their own countries in order to treat the domestic population. In contrast to civil-rights movements, which deal with various domestic infractions of the rights of the individual or the citizen, these organizations deal with the massive phenomenon of injury to women presently taking place, a constant threat hanging over this population. They provide assistance to victims of sexual assault of various kinds, committed in various contexts.[37] Over time, the extent of their assistance has expanded to include both emergency aid and support in working through medical, psychological, and legal processes.[38] In contrast to the way in which humanitarian organizations customarily work, these organizations negotiate with the sovereign over the limits of abandonment, even as they draw urgent attention to it and turn it into the topic of public and legal discourses.[39] Despite these activities and the significant changes in the field of lawmaking, women have not ceased to be abandoned to disaster. Even if they no longer live in a state of exception, they have not been fully integrated into the body politic bearing the marks of their previous exception. Hence their civic status remains deficient and the assistance they are offered in their distress is strictly on a humanitarian basis.

Although sexual injury to women is a phenomenon of global proportions, the fact that it is being dealt with locally by domestic organizations of a humanitarian nature makes manifest the deficiency of the civic status of women, and helps explain what makes this deficiency almost invisible, and certainly difficult to grasp and express in public discourse. If international humanitarian organizations were to provide urgent relief to victims of sexual assault, the label of humanitarianism would warn us of the existence of a disaster area and tell us that resources need be allocated to relieve it. If the domestic government were to address the phenomenon, it would constitute evidence that regular citizens were involved whom the sovereign is supposed to protect from injury and the threat of injury that so frequently hangs over them. The humanitarian activities conducted daily within each country's borders have lost any dimension of urgency, however, and thus constitute ongoing evidence of women's abandonment. Abandonment necessarily includes — for otherwise it would not be abandonment in the severe sense of the word — the sovereign's refusal to use all necessary means to prevent or to treat the disaster that befalls the abandoned and the concession of care in this arena to humanitarian organizations, even if a certain level of support for their activities is given.

The Declaration of the Rights of Man and the Citizen was a constituent document both for the political exclusion of women and for their abandonment in this strong sense. Returning to Olympe de Gouges' Declaration of the Rights of Woman and the Citizen and reading it alongside the more famous and certainly more influential declaration, I will expose the intimate relation, even the inseparability of this political exclusion and sexual abandonment, tracking its movement from its appearance in the first declaration to contemporary feminist struggles.

One instance in which we can see this exclusion and abandonment revealed is in Article 11 of the Declaration of the Rights of Woman and the Citizen, where de Gouges explicitly connects the protections of citizenship to the violation of the female body:

> The free communication of thoughts and opinions is one of the most precious rights of woman, since the liberty assures the recognition of children by their fathers.[40] Any female citizen thus may say freely, I am the mother of a child which belongs to you, without being forced by a barbarous prejudice to hide the truth; [an exception may be made] to respond to the abuse of this liberty in cases determined by the law.[41]

De Gouges reproduces the syntax and meaning of the corresponding, "original" article of the first declaration, but with crucial differences: "The free communication of ideas and opinions is one of the most precious of the rights of man. Every citizen may, accordingly, speak, write, and print with freedom, but shall be responsible for such abuses of this freedom as shall be defined by law."[42]

The situation de Gouges addresses is one in which illegitimate

53

children were a problem solely for their mothers and testified to their illegitimate deeds, and the generalized principle regarding the freedom to communicate ideas and opinions, in de Gouges' declaration, thus becomes a concrete instrument in the struggle against the forced silence inflicted on women who bear so-called "illegitimate offspring" and against the very notion of "illegitimate offspring" itself. Illegitimacy does not mean illegality. Whether or not sexual relations out of wedlock were considered illegal, they were regulated less by law than by religious values, social norms, and codes of honor. Illegitimate sexual relations existed in a twilight zone in which the law was actually suspended, neither punishing women nor protecting them, allowing unwritten codes to take their place. Women were forced into this indistinct zone and could not leave it through their own free will. Something went wrong with their sexuality, and the wrong done to them could not be perceived, seen, or heard. The civil liberty of free communication was interpreted by de Gouges as capable of pulling women out of this zone to enable them to negotiate their sexuality without falling into the trap of being either their husband's legal property or the illegitimate property of other men.

The exclusion of women from the protections of citizenship is manifestly their exclusion from the main arena of the political game. What de Gouges foregrounds in her declaration is the sexual background of this exclusion, which not only makes women illegitimate speakers in the political sphere, but renders their injuries inaudible as a result of this sexual exclusion. These injuries are manifested explicitly by rape and in more extreme fashion by the trade of women's bodies. Rape is the full realization of the injury, while the injury to women itself on the basis of their sexuality is still an integral part of women's lives.[43]

The declaration fails to mention these injuries, but nevertheless, they are legitimated by it through the very act of its enunciation. This act de facto excepts woman from the rule, abandoning them and making them susceptible to injuries that are left unpunished. Such injuries cannot be made public and cannot constitute a legal, moral, or political claim. The violation of women's bodies takes place in that twilight zone of illegitimacy, in the framework of which their injuries cannot be articulated as valid and negotiable claims and cannot become objects of emergency claims.

To understand how citizen status could enable women who bear illegitimate children to demand legal status for these children and the recognition of their fathers, one should take into account that the same women who were deprived of citizenship were party to a sexual contract whose rules they could neither establish nor change.[44] This contract determines the terms of their status as accessible sexual objects and holds their bodies in a sphere beyond the reach of law and sovereign power. Unwanted pregnancy, for which women were considered solely responsible, or the having of "illegitimate children" whose fathers could not be proclaimed in public, were not just the results of sexual relations outside marriage, but often — though how often we can only guess — of rape.[45] Both cases, however, reveal a situation in which women are deprived of rights over their bodies and cannot appeal to the law for protection. Thus, in the case of sex out of wedlock, women's bodies were violated symbolically; in the case of rape, they were violated both physically and symbolically.

As we have noted, the authors of the 1789 declaration state that "this declaration," should be "constantly before all the members of the Social body" in order to "remind them continually of their rights and duties." In order to be constantly present, to be memorized, the declaration itself had to be reiterated again and again. If we understand de Gouges' declaration to be responding to this demand, we may ask what "this declaration" is that is reiterated by her own declaration. De Gouges reiterates the style, the composition, the content, and the logic of the original declaration. But nothing in her text can stand for "this declaration" — except for the speech act itself, the very act of taking the addresser's position and becoming a political speaker who talks back to power in order to set its limits, negotiating different ways to be governed. Only this speech act reiterates the enunciation of "this declaration" as such. The declaration written by de Gouges thus is a cornerstone of women's struggles to acquire political standing and civil protection, the protection of which they were deprived in the Declaration of the Rights of Man and the Citizen. That declaration determined woman to be neither man nor citizen, and ever since, women's struggles should be seen as fought on both levels: to be equal to men, and to become citizens.

The first clause of the 1789 declaration states that all human beings are *born* equal. Giorgio Agamben has suggested that we regard this passage of the declaration, which emphasizes the moment of birth in relation to the rights of man and of the citizen, as a major turning point.[46] Henceforth, he contends, the law no longer was to rest on the traditional separation, originating in classical Greece, between political life (*bios*) and natural life (*zoē*), but made life itself the object of the law's interference and of government regulation. Instead of this distinction between political life and natural life, which disappeared, a new distinction arose between natural or real life, which the sovereign is supposed to defend as deserving of such protection, and what Agamben, following Walter Benjamin, calls "bare life," "the life that constitutes the first content of sovereign power," that is, "life's subjection to a power over death and life's irreparable exposure in relation of abandonment."[47]

Relying on the German philosopher Carl Schmitt, Agamben contends that by deciding on the exception the sovereign decides whose life is not deserving of protection and can therefore be abandoned, or forsaken — "sacred," in the sense meant under Roman law, in which the *homo sacer* was he who, living in a state of exception, was excluded "both from the sphere of the profane and from that of the religious, cannot be sacrificed, yet can be killed with impunity."[48] The rights defended by the 1789 declaration are said to be "natural and unalienable." But the sovereign, writes Agamben, can decide on their expiration or nonapplication.[49] From his discussion of the 1789 declaration, Agamben jumps to the authority of the sovereign, as if the declaration itself was not — even prior to the sovereign exercising the authority to except anyone from the rule — a document of exclusion.[50] Based on the distinction between man and citizen, women are doubly subject to exclusion — from the community of human beings and from the community of citizens: "Rights are attributed to man (or originate in him) solely to the extent that man is the immediately vanishing ground (who must never come to light as such) of the citizen."[51] Thus, the declaration, which asserts that natural rights are the basis for granting civil rights, grants civil rights only to those whose "natural rights" it seeks to protect and separates citizens from their fellows who are governed.

The declaration, which left women without any rights, effectively abandoned them: "He who has been banned is not, in fact, simply set outside the law and made indifferent to it but rather *abandoned* by it, that is, exposed and threatened on the threshold in which life and law, outside and inside, become indistinguishable."[52] In Articles 4 and 5 of the declaration, we see the civilian infrastructure for the harm and abandonment of women. Each of these articles places restrictions on the conditions in which citizenship can be exercised. These restrictions, which were intended to protect all citizens, ultimately determined the conditions for the abandonment of those who are not citizens, whose lives the declaration deemed unworthy of naturalization into the community that came into being under its aegis.[53] According to Article 4, "Liberty consists in the freedom to do everything which injures no one else; hence the exercise of the natural rights of each man has no limits except those which assure to the other members of the society the enjoyment of the same rights."

Recall that in Article 11 of de Gouges' declaration, she declares: "Any female citizen thus [assuming she is granted "the free communication of thoughts and opinions"] may say freely, I am the mother of a child which belongs to you."[54] Why is it necessary that the governed woman, whose right to question the power that governs her and negotiate with it is inalienable, according to de Gouges, is forced to claim the right to say freely to the man whose child she bears that she is the "mother of a child which belongs to you"? The answer lies in the special nature of this statement, which should be distinguished from the opening statement of de Gouges' declaration.

The statement declares who is responsible, or at least shares responsibility, for an "illegitimate" pregnancy. Uttering this statement constitutes harm to its addressee, the man; refraining from uttering it constitutes harm to its addresser, the woman.[55] The silencing of the woman involved is a precondition for the well-being of the man involved in an "illegitimate" pregnancy. The harm done to the man may easily be interpreted as an infringement on his right.

De Gouges' claim may therefore seem to contradict Article 5 of the 1789 declaration: "the exercise of the natural rights of each man has no limits except those which assure to the other members of the society the enjoyment of the same rights." But this seeming contradiction only exposes a basic relation between the two genders. Women are not discriminated against because they are deprived of citizenship in a de facto state of exception; they are deprived of citizenship and placed in a de facto state of exception because their citizenship may infringe on the rights and well-being of men, and they are abandoned by the law because allowing them to present their grievances in public, let alone to present these grievances as matters for political concern, would cause harm to the liberty of men. Lacking civil status, women are abandoned and subordinated to "barbarous prejudice" that forces them "to hide the truth" of their own bodies. It is out of this imposed concealment and suppression of their bodies and their sexuality that a halo of sanctity is born, together with the impunity of the men who transgress it. The woman's sexual body becomes a locus of secrets, kept outside the realm of public discourse, outside the reach of civil law.

The protection of the liberty of men and the institution of equality among them was accomplished on the basis of gender difference. Women, who were excluded from the Declaration of the Rights of Man and the Citizen both as authors and as objects of its wording, thus were left without civil protection and subject to the "sexual contract" that bound them to their fathers or husbands as sexual property.[56] Unable to enjoy their new citizen status, women are left unprotected. "The political discourse's separation of the social contract from the production economy of the home (*oikos*)," writes Susan Buck-Morss, has made it possible to establish the conception of liberty as the protection of private property, and the naturalization of the slave is emblematic of this type of property. In her version of the declaration, as well as in some of her other writings, de Gouges pointed to the analogy between the exclusion of women and the exclusion of slaves and claimed that these exclusions undermine the legitimacy of the universal declaration.[57]

The legal history of sexual violence toward women is riddled with wordings expressive of this state of affairs, whether through the lack of recognition of the possibility of rape between marital partners or the consideration of rape as an injury to the honor of father or husband.[58] The "sexual liberty" of the male citizen is not explicitly cited by the 1789 declaration, but the fact that the new citizen framework was constituted on the basis of gender difference, leaving the contract between the sexes unaltered, gave one side of the contract — men — a new status in regard to the other side, the status of a "citizen" with universal rights, a status that they previously had not enjoyed.[59] Sexual injury to women was not considered injury to *other* citizens, and the female noncitizen could not make a grievance of this injury. Thus the declaration of 1789 abandons women and fails to place any restrictions on the "sexual liberty" of men, because those for whom those restrictions might prove beneficial are granted no protection within its framework, remaining the property of the men who govern their lives.[60] The declaration's renunciation of women, by emphasizing that the acts or actions that it does not discuss are allowed, paved the way for doing injury to women and gave rise to the conditions for turning this injury into part of the social order.[61]

Since the 1970s, changes in lawmaking have reduced the range of women's abandonment by defining their injury as an object in the legal discourse that entails punishment. Hence, a new series of topoi and concepts have appeared in the discourse, including the rape of a woman by her husband and sexual harassment, along with the establishment of various centers and associations that have accorded these injuries discursive "visibility."[62] But not only has the injury to women not ceased, it has not even managed to create a clear field of visibility for itself. Being vulnerable to injury on a sexual basis is still an experience common to all women, and this is part of their status as flawed citizens, who have not yet achieved their full rights and the capacity to enjoy them. In some of these cases of injury, the perpetrators might possibly be prosecuted, but this merely testifies that without legal protection, women are still abandoned.

In the late eighteenth century, with the gradual acceptance of the principles outlined in the Declaration of the Rights of Man and the Citizen and the establishment of universal (male) suffrage[63] and the transformation of the body politic into a community of which all its citizens are members, women in effect were declared the exception.[64] Indeed, when "universal" suffrage was established in 1848, half a century after the French Revolution, it failed again to include women, despite the fact that they had already been participating in the political sphere through many different activities, including writing, teaching, hosting social and political meetings, health care, and photography.[65] Their exclusion from suffrage marginalized the modes of political participation that had already been accessible to women and actually expunged them from the representation of the political sphere, where the right to vote had become so predominant. At the moment when they were on their way to becoming equal members of the political body, they were declared an exception to the rule of citizenship and equal rights, even though they continued to participate in the political sphere through the avenues that remained open to them. Ever since, this ambiguity has characterized their political participation.[66] The human and civil rights of those born equal have been the rights of the male. Women remain abandoned by the law, which judges and punishes them without granting them many rights or protecting the rights they had.

Women's exception has rested on their sex, and nothing but their sex.[67]

The figure and image of Western woman was elevated and sanctified (in art, poetry, literature, public manners, and more) while at the same time as a person and a body she was excluded and abandoned. Women's sacredness was the condition of their desacralization and consequently their abandonment. The modern museum, whose rise is contemporary with that of modern citizenship, is a distinctive arena for identifying the traces of the interplay between women's sanctification and their abandonment. Within this framework, woman has been turned into a sublime and mysterious image that is beyond understanding and can at most be captured, but never deciphered by the great artistic master.[68] On the walls of the modern museum, nude women have been clustered, painted by men who began to exhibit to the public the bodies of women as if it were the men who owned them. Female nudity became a masculine game conducted in public — men showing naked women to other men. It took almost two hundred years until women began showing their own images publicly or those of other women, freeing these images from the mark of ownership of men, which permitted and enabled their abandonment.

In the heart of the equality to which all human beings supposedly are born, gender difference thus was inscribed as the constitutive element of the entire political order. But, as we also have seen in reading the 1789 declaration, man and citizen form a problematic duality. Though all human beings are born equal with respect to the same natural rights, only the civil rights that are granted to them can ratify these natural rights; although all citizens are made equal in the modern nation-state, they can be made equal only if they have natural rights.[69] This problematic duality between man and citizen — the simultaneous separation and creation of a circular dependency between them — is clarified by a reading of the preamble to the 1789 declaration, which sets forth the reasons for writing it. The new, modern political citizen appeared as a threat to the "old," natural man: "ignorance, neglect, or contempt of the rights of man is the sole cause of public calamities and of the corruption of governments." However, we must not forget that this "old" man is also a modern invention, which the declaration distinctively expresses.

Agamben notes that the basis of sovereignty, as formulated by the declaration, "is not man as a free and conscious political subject but, above all, man's bare life ... simple birth."[70] And as he notes, "the passage from divinely authorized royal sovereignty to national sovereignty" marked by the declaration "assures the *exceptio* of life in the new state order that will succeed the collapse of the *ancien régime*. The fact that in this process the 'subject' is ... transformed into a 'citizen' means that birth — which is to say, bare natural life as such — here for the first time becomes ... the immediate bearer of sovereignty."[71] As Agamben goes on to show, when "the fiction implicit here," that "birth immediately becomes nation such that there can be no level of separation ... between the two terms," eventuated in a "lasting crisis" in the twentieth century, this "natural life became the exemplary place of the sovereign exception."[72] However, Agamben's description tells only half of the story. Insisting on the ambiguity between man and citizen, he also confuses nation and citizenry. Agamben fails to consider citizenry and citizenship independently of sovereign power and as power's source of authority and legitimacy. When he identifies the man of the declaration as a trace of *homo sacer*, whose invention preceded that of political man, as the basis of political sovereignty, he misses the direct threat that man poses to the citizen, in the sense which I am trying to restore here.

The assembled representatives of the French nation were seeking to anchor "the natural, unalienable, and sacred rights of man" in their declaration, rights that were threatened by various political games. This is the reason for the invention of the abstract entity called the "citizen," who is not actually the governed, for in that case the dimension of exclusion that characterizes him would be dissolved. Only this entity can demand their protection. In other words, it is man's right that his natural life as someone born equal should receive protection: "Men are born and remain free and equal in rights" (Article 1). The purpose of this redundancy is nothing other than to maintain only those born equal in rights as such, and the citizen, subject to man, will be able to shape the law that preserves man as such: "Every citizen has a right to participate personally, or through his representative, in its [the law's] foundation" (Article 6).

In 1791, Olympe de Gouges exposed the absurdity of the exception of women from the rule: "Try — if you are only able to — to separate the sexes in the kingdom of Nature. Everywhere you will find them mixed together, everywhere they cooperate ... man alone has turned the exception to the rule into a principle."[73] Women's exception, in this sense, is not identical to the relegation of their activities to the domestic sphere nor to their exile to another demarcated social space. Following in the wake of the Industrial Revolution, accelerated urbanization, and the creation of modern markets, women began to play an active role in increasingly greater areas of modern human existence. Because of their very existence in the public space and due to the civil practices in which they began to take an increasingly active part — education, employment, care of others, exchange, and so on — women were at one and the same time a part of the political space while still lying outside of it.

Since the appearance of the Declaration of the Rights of Man and the Citizen, women have fought for civil equality and gradually, from the start of the twentieth century, began attaining the status of citizens.[74] As we have seen, in the declaration, civil rights are inseparable from human rights.[75] Citizenship was established on the basis of equality regarding the lives of "all human beings [who] are born equal." When women gained civil equality, however, this foundation and the relation it maintains with citizenship remained unchanged. The lives of women who have become regular citizens or those who participate in that abstract entity called the citizenry have remained in the state of exception in which they were placed by the originary and foundational declaration of the natural rights of the citizen on the basis of "equal" birth. "At the very moment at which native rights were declared to be inalienable" after the French Revolution, "the rights of man in general were divided into active and passive rights." Thus, as Agamben quotes Jean-Denis Lanjuinais addressing the Convention on the Nature of Citizenship, "children, the insane, minors, women, those condemned to a punishment either restricting personal freedom or bringing disgrace . . . will not be citizens."[76] As I said above, the stamp of women's exception from the body politic and from the abstract entity called "mankind" has been a stain on their belated political inclusion and impaired their status as citizens for a long time to come. Thus, even as citizens, women are still excepted, more easily abandoned than men, more often treated as bare life.

Since the 1970s, the focus of women's struggles in various fields of knowledge and activity has gradually shifted from the realm of rights and equality to the realm of bare life. It is not only a struggle for control over or possession of the body, but over women's position vis-à-vis the threshold between bare life and political life. Home, family, the street, and the workplace are reclaimed by women, not necessarily and not only as places in which their equal rights are to be protected by the state as sites of vulnerability, where the transition from a decent citizen to an abandoned body may take place rapidly, at any moment.

To understand the condition of possibility for women to be able to contest their vulnerability and the ease with which they are thrown into a state of exception, we must go back to the structural homology between the sovereign and the exception to the rule. The sovereign, Agamben contends, following Schmitt, is a type of exception to the rule — simultaneously within and outside the law — that determines the exception to the rule. The sovereign and the abandoned resemble one another as two poles of exceptions. Despite the resemblance, however, there remains a radical difference between them: while the sovereign abandons, the noncitizen or the flawed citizen is abandoned. The abandonment of women, which did not cease with their belated entry into the body politic, forced women to develop practices, norms, and skills of their own for governing their abandoned bodies, as happened, for example, in women's underground involvement in abortion. After women attained equal status as citizens, these skills proved useful in the negotiations they began to conduct with their fellow citizens and with the powers that be over what lay in its sphere of authority — the regulation of life and, most significantly, the determination of the boundary between life and death.[77] Such negotiations are the common denominator that in effect unites the three great arenas in which women have fought: over motherhood (birth control through contraceptives and the right to abortion),[78] over life (the management of birth), and over sexuality (the demand to recognize any kind of sexual assault as crime and any form of voluntary sexual relation as legitimate). All these struggles, far from acceding to a universalization of "the space that is opened when the state of exception becomes the rule,"[79] have offered a real challenge to the sovereign decision in establishing their status as exceptions.[80]

These struggles pose a demand that bare life be recognized as life worth living. The demand that bare life be protected poses a far-reaching challenge to the sovereign, because what it actually demands is an undermining of the biological boundary between life and death as the *decisive* boundary. In her essay on Antigone, Joan Copjec writes about the dead end to which Agamben's discussion leads, insofar as he continues to adhere to the same definitions that he critiques by accepting the biological as the decisive boundary between life and death. Near the conclusion of her essay, Copjec depicts the contrast between Antigone and Creon (or between her claims and Agamben's): "When she covers the exposed body of her brother, Antigone raises herself out of the conditions of naked existence to which Creon remains bound" by chasing after Polyneices "beyond death's border."[81] In the same spirit, it could be said that the various demands addressed to the sovereign by women have expressed a refusal to accept the reduction of the female body to bare life, to life itself. This refusal manifests itself, for example, in the redefinition of what constitutes a sexual injury and in women demanding that the legal discourse not limit sexual injury to "penetration" of the biological body. Moreover, this refusal manifests itself in the now common term invented by women themselves in order to describe a woman who was raped: a *survivor*.[82] This refusal is even further enhanced by the accumulating testimonies of women who have been raped, testifying to an experience of a kind of death that is not, of course, biological death.

Women challenge the sovereign by forcing him to renegotiate the line separating life from death, struggling to make their lives recognized as worthy of protection. But in defining themselves as survivors and the experience of rape as a form of nonbiological death, women transform the harm done to them into a nonpunishable crime whose perpetrators are impune, for no one can be accused of causing a metaphoric death. Paradoxically, by associating rape with death, women, who were formerly put in a state of exception by patriarchal rule are now voluntarily declaring their own exception to the rule. Violations of their sexual integrity are perceived as transgressions of their sacredness that have turned them into a new type of a living dead and not as injuries that should be addressed in political and legal terms. Stated differently, the secularization of the conditions for sexual violence against women has yet to be completed.

The abandonment of woman, which cuts across historical periods and political borders, is still in the nature of a nonevent. It becomes an event when a rape occurs, but even then, since what it involves is an event that lacks visibility and whose victims are not susceptible to exposure like the victims of other disasters, it remains in the nature of a nonevent.[83] Consequently, despite the fact that it is easier to bring rape to court today, the judicial system still finds it difficult to digest.[84] In other words, despite the fact that women have been able to acquire the status of citizens, their susceptibility to injury on the basis of their sex is still part of their daily routine, creating an extended link between them, as the governed and impaired citizen, and populations of noncitizens.

On the Verge of Catastrophe

The Palestinians in the Occupied Territories are not Israeli citizens whose citizenship is impaired or deficient, like that of women. Instead, they are actively denied citizenship by the power that has ruled them for more than forty years. They are thus Israel's noncitizens. In the last decade, they are constantly "on the verge of catastrophe."[85]

Being on the verge of catastrophe is a paradoxical situation in which the injury to the population of noncitizens is simultaneously visible and invisible.[86] The Israeli-Palestinian situation does not require an exceptional interpretative effort to expose the fact that the relation between citizens and noncitizens is the most general structural characteristic of the regime. Since 1967, Israel has governed millions of Palestinians who live beyond the Green Line, where the apparatus of rule that Israel maintains is responsible for the fabrication of Palestinians as noncitizens. The denial of their citizenship is not an accidental feature of their situation, but the form of the Palestinians belonging to the Israeli state: belonging through negation and exclusion.[87] The Israeli state does not contain them, but does not get rid of them, either. The state keeps them outside, although this outside is still under its sovereignty, given the fact that it is the occupying power in the territories and thus determines the limits of this outside.[88]

During several decades of rule, the state of Israel has prevented the creation and development of civilian and regional infrastructures in the Occupied Territories. In addition, since the outbreak of the al-Aqsa intifada, the Israeli Army has been destroying civilian infrastructure — which includes educational, medical, social, cultural, economic, and agricultural production and distribution — already existent in the territories. Various humanitarian organizations continually attempt to repair some of the damage in order to maintain a semblance of civilized life. As local and global citizens, the workers of these humanitarian organizations labor to try to maintain life at a minimally tolerable level. However, these organizations and individuals overlook the fact that the addressees of the assistance they offer still remain noncitizens.

The humanitarization of the occupation — evident first and foremost in the ongoing, permanent presence of humanitarian organizations and their assimilation into the apparatus of Israeli rule in the territories — is an integral part of what maintains the territories on the verge of catastrophe, postponing the occurrence of the catastrophe, making it invisible, even though it remains manifest to everyone. The daily presence of humanitarian activities of different international organizations, within the territories is usually perceived as a sign of a state of emergency. The activities of these organizations have become a part of the logic of military activity and part of the customs, conventions, and ongoing conduct of the occupation.[89] The mutual cooperation of the army and humanitarian organizations takes place to such a degree that the army invites organizations to intervene in the places where it operates. Moreover, the army has assimilated the humanitarian discourse, adopting its idioms and even institutionalizing the modes of humanitarian action by assigning special manpower to the topic and establishing humanitarian units. The humanitarization of the occupation, which occurs in conjunction with the growing harshness of the apparatus of rule over the Palestinian population, is emblematic of the current period of Israeli rule in the territories.

More broadly, however, being on the verge of catastrophe — postponed, invisible, yet also manifest to everyone — is the actual state of those who have been abandoned in the global era. This situation is a result of the new conditions of visibility that have signaled the collapse of the strict opposition between the visible and the invisible. Instead, it is the new model of catastrophic events in which the population of noncitizens becomes the very site of their occurrence. This population renders the presence of catastrophe in a new way within the field of vision of the citizens who live beside them. With their bodies, which are present in the territory but missing from its political representation, noncitizens manufacture new conditions of visibility for impending catastrophe to be witnessed.

Numerous visual and textual expressions can testify to the situation while still allowing the visible catastrophe to remain unseen.[90] The political transparency of the population of noncitizens is what renders the preventability of its situation — on the verge of catastrophe — invisible. On a daily basis, the communications media provide detailed information on what is happening in the Occupied Territories. The form of the reportage, however, prevents this information from being transformed into "emergency claims" due to the special structure of the *énoncé* of horror in the global era. The *énoncé* of horror is the textual or visual expression that describes the catastrophe as it occurs.

We must first distinguish between two types of *énoncé* of horror, which correspond to two types of victim. These two types are congruent with the two populations that I have described above that are currently scattered around the Earth. On the one hand, there are citizens, those who have permanent status as citizens, whose citizenship is taken for granted, people for whom citizenship is ensured, as it is for their children. Their citizenship protects them, offering them relative security from intentional or discriminatory injury, or at least the assistance needed to reduce the suffering such injuries may cause. Their citizenship does not protect them from accidental or unintentional injuries, such as environmental or mass disasters, which are indifferent to civilian distinctions. On the other hand, there are noncitizens, whose position is temporary and conditional. Even if they are woven into the fabric of life in the territory they inhabit, their status as noncitizens will preserve their temporariness at the mercy of the sovereign power.

The state may be interested in the specific goods this population can provide or obtain, but is definitely not interested in their permanent assimilation into the rolls of the citizenry, and thus their status remains transient. They themselves are not wanted. What the state wants is something that is in their possession—labor power, bodies, sex, knowledge, and skill in certain areas—but this interest is not enough to alter their transient status. Being temporary, noncitizens are eligible only for life-preserving treatment as bare life, life that ensures them the minimum for survival in each of these areas. But the bare minimum is never enough. Thus, they are placed on the verge of catastrophe. Noncitizens may be considered temporary, but their situation is permanent—a permanent state of being on the verge of catastrophe. Being temporary, they are unable to demand a change in their permanent situation. Those who attempt to aid them in any significant way, as well, are still unable to maintain them in any state except that of being on the verge of tolerable living.

When a disaster overtakes citizens, the *énoncé* of horror manufactured at the site of the disaster testifies to its urgency; it interrupts the routine of life. The depicted disaster is usually accorded a name or title of its own, which functions as a hook on which to hang additional *énoncés* describing, referring to, or interpreting the disaster, calling for intervention in it, limiting the suffering it causes, and ultimately making it possible to remember it and save it from oblivion. The *énoncé* of horror is thus linked to a series of *énoncés* that culminate when various systems restore order. This conclusion is accompanied by the annexation of the *énoncé* to apparatuses of memory, which ensures the commemoration of the *énoncés* of horror. But when a disaster overtakes noncitizens, an emergency claim is not necessarily produced, on account of the fact that before and after the disaster there will always be other similar *énoncés*. These *énoncés* will not necessarily be in reference to that particular disaster or attributable to that particular time and place, but may express similar disasters in other places and at other times that partake of the same general pattern of being on the verge of catastrophe. The use of photos of victims or disasters as illustrations for a newspaper article is a typical example of this. Regarding the population of transients, the *énoncé* of the horror of disaster has thus been confused with the *énoncé* of horror on the verge of catastrophe. In either case, they are most often retroactively made, without any dimension of urgency, and fail to demand the construction of a series of *énoncés* that would lead their spectator to the end of the story.

A short glance at a photo taken by Miki Kratsman during a visit of Physicians for Human Rights in the Occupied Territories may illustrate what being on the verge on catastrophe signifies (figure 1.1). This is not an image of an event that would make the news, but an image of the routine practice of a group of Israeli physicians (Physicians for Human Rights), who volunteer to periodically visit patients in Palestinian villages. What might look picturesque is in fact a document of unacceptable conditions of medical treatment: bare, dusty walls, a dirty space, the use of the natural light coming from the door due to the lack of electricity, the absence of proper equipment for examining X-rays, the conspicuously detached encounter between doctor and patient, the improvised clinic in which medical examinations are made amid people who are having a makeshift picnic after waiting for hours at the checkpoints. All these details are visual evidence of the invisible condition of being on the verge of catastrophe. The fact that nothing in the image is scandalous enough to be newsworthy or capable of interrupting the routine of well-protected citizens is the scandal of this image.

Although it is rare, from time to time, we can witness photographs that make it difficult to resist or avoid their urgency. One instance is Alex Levac's photo taken in Hebron in 2000 (figure 1.2). A Palestinian man is lying in the middle of the road with his face down. A puddle of blood spreads under his left knee. No one is allowed to approach him to give him medical care. The only one who can come close takes his time, holding his rifle — which might have served him a few minutes ago to shoot the Palestinian — commanding, threatening, abolishing the urgency with his display of naked power. The Palestinian lying on

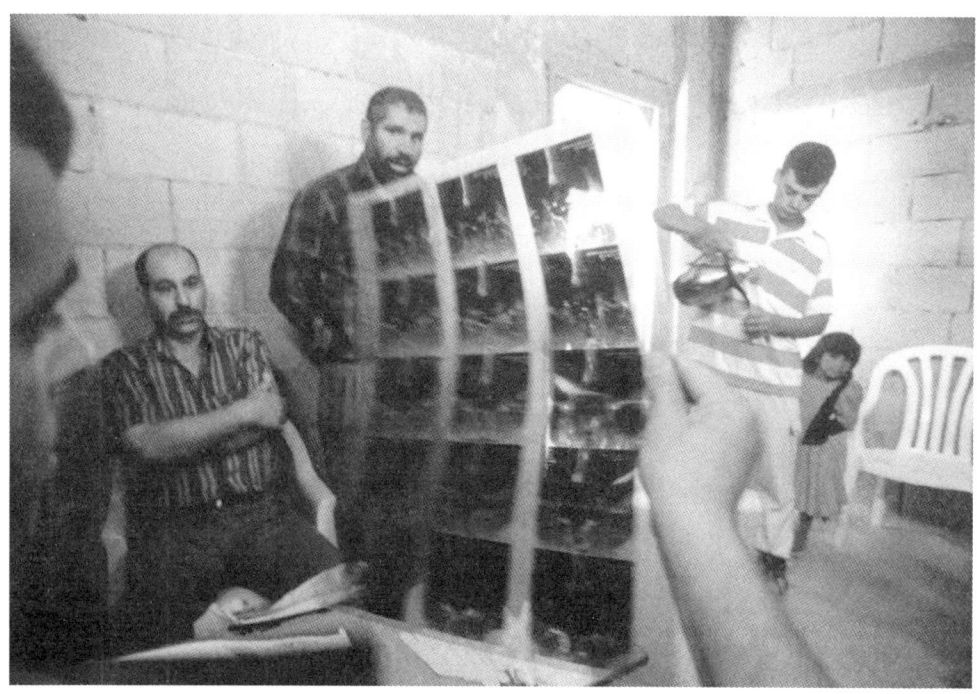

Figure 1.1. Miki Kratsman, visit by Physicians for Human Rights, Me'in village, 2000.

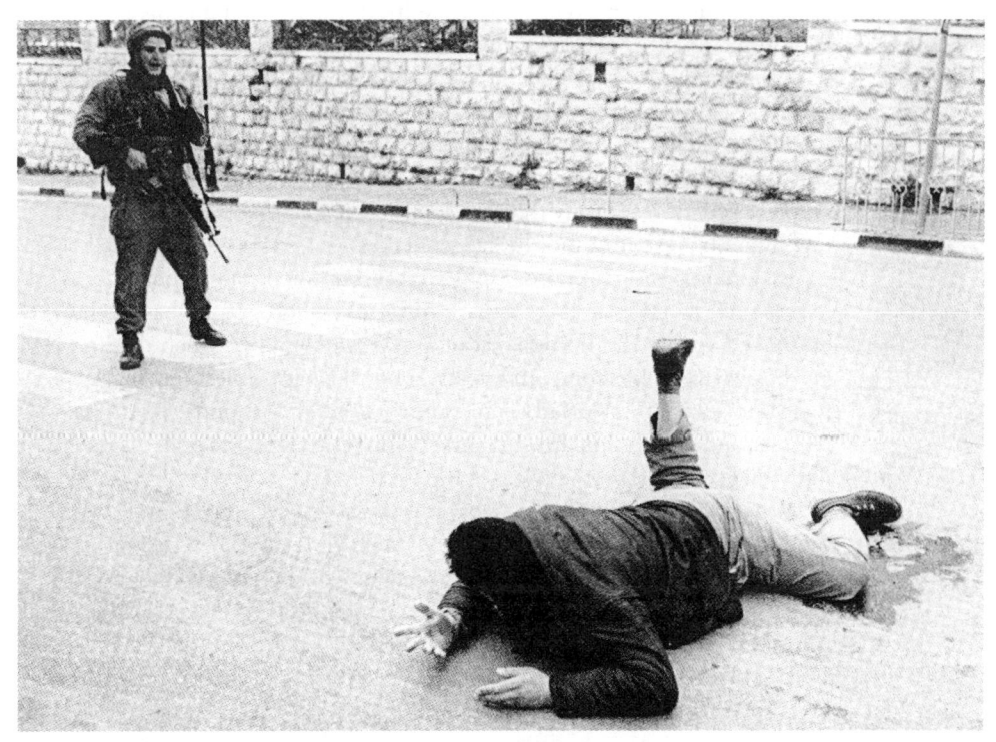

Figure 1.2. Alex Levac, Hebron, 2000. (Please see Color Plates.)

the road understands that no one can recognize his urgent condition — the critical wound in his leg, loss of blood, the ideal conditions for infection, evidenced by his hands, completely blackened from touching the road. All he can attempt is to overcome the urgency of his physical state and renew the civil skills and gestures he was forced to repress in order to protect himself. With difficulty, he pulls his head and shoulders off of the road to address the soldier, trying to negotiate with the soldier, to convince him with only his mouth and hands that he should stop hurting him, that he is not armed, that his body is wounded, that it was probably an error that he was shot, that he has been mistaken, that he ought to be treated as a citizen. The photograph is a silent testimony to the suspension of emergency, even when one might believe it cannot be suspended.

By looking at such photographs we can see traces of extreme violence, since what is at stake is bare life itself. Photography has been employed within the framework of a new topography, which distinguishes between life zones and death zones.[91] These zones may manifest themselves territorially — in suburban neighborhoods, frontier regions, and so on — but are currently being written on the body of the individual, as well, on the body of the excluded.

Wherever the excluded may be, it is there that we must search for the traces of this extreme violence. But such violence leaves its marks not on the extremities of the territory, but at its very heart, in the individual who has been excluded while remaining inside — disposed of as if he or she were an unessential excess of the system. The checkpoint system that has been planted within the territories by the Israeli state incarnates this new topography.[92]

In the absence of an official territorial divide between the state of Israel's citizens and its subjects (for the border already had been extended toward Jordan a few decades ago) and in a situation where the Palestinian has not been acknowledged as a citizen with equal rights, but only as an enemy of the state, the border shifts to the place where the Palestinian stands. Every time a Palestinian seeks to move, Israel takes advantage of the opportunity to reassert its sovereignty. It is wherever he would like to live his life that an ad hoc border marker is posited — not a border line. but a border point, a "spot."

This "spotted border" blocks the path of those who would pass through. The number of (potential or actual) border points is always equal to the number of subjects in the Palestinian-inhabited areas. According to a "military source" in the Israeli army, "the Palestinians don't know when we've received intelligence and think that yesterday there was just a spot check and rely on luck, and suddenly they arrive at a checkpoint with maximal inspection and then we catch who we're looking for."[93] Wherever there is a Palestinian who wants to go somewhere, that place becomes a point of transit, a border crossing, a checkpoint, an obstruction to movement. Whether he will pass the checkpoint or not will always depend on an arbitrary syntax consisting of successful negotiation, momentary generosity, a positive frame of mind, body chemistry, luck, a gamble, skill, cunning, artifice, or personal charm. Neither rules nor procedures, neither logic or plans of action — if any might be found — can explain or predict the behavior of the soldier at the checkpoint. By contrast, the fact that his behavior is unpredictable is part of a system that can be described. I will do so by analyzing the decision-making structure of the soldier at the checkpoint.

The Palestinian who takes his place before the soldier at the checkpoint, who shows her medical documents, and who tells the soldier his story and his woes recognizes the soldier as the sovereign, or at least as the sovereign's proxy. The soldier, who faces hundreds of Palestinian subjects every day, is required to make a new decision regarding each and every case that is presented to him. He is the law's representative. The law, however, has been suspended, and like the Palestinian standing before him, the proxy exists outside the law. In the absence of the law that he is supposed to represent, it seems that the soldier himself turns into the source of the law. The judgmental actions that he performs blur the line between the legislative and executive authorities, that is, the line between the legal and the political.[94] The soldier doesn't suspend the law; he is acting in a framework in which the law has already been suspended. It is the sovereign who has the authority to suspend the law, to decide on the exception to the rule. The soldier, however, functions — to borrow a phrase from Judith Butler — as a "petty sovereign," of which there is no short supply.[95]

In an article on the administrative detainees in Guantánamo Bay, Judith Butler revives Foucault's assertion regarding the relation between governmentality — the diffuse network of agents, practices, and institutions that employ political power to manage populations and goods — and sovereignty. She claims that the governmentality that characterizes our age has not replaced sovereignty, as Foucault is mistakenly understood to have claimed, but has created the conditions for the renewed appearance of sovereignty in another guise. To be more precise, another form of sovereignty has emerged: "precisely because our historical situation is marked by governmentality, and this implies, to a certain degree, a loss of sovereignty, that loss is compensated through the resurgence of sovereignty within the field of governmentality. Petty sovereigns abound, reigning in the midst of bureaucratic army institutions mobilized by aims and tactics of power they do not inaugurate or fully control." Whereas the suspension of the law, she writes, "can clearly be read as a tactic of governmentality, it has to be seen in this context as also making room for the resurgence of sovereignty." [96]

From Butler's description of the relationship between governmentality and sovereignty, however, we can neither draw a satisfactory explanation for the way in which sovereignty emerges as the field of governmentality nor an explanation of where governmentality draws the power reserved to the sovereign. If every agent of governmental power could suspend the law as he or she saw fit, not only would the political order turn chaotic, but these agents themselves would be consistently at risk of prosecution. Butler's description stops short of clarifying how the political order is maintained and how it is possible to orchestrate the activities of all the "petty sovereigns."

To address these questions, I will return to a distinct agent of governmentality — the soldier at the checkpoint. The range of options available to the soldier at the checkpoint, despite the visible arbitrariness that characterizes them, is limited and constrained. If he should decide to distribute flowers to the Palestinians, he will be detained and prosecuted — which indeed happened once to one soldier.[97] On the other hand, if a soldier examines a Palestinian's medical documents, thus impersonating a medical expert, or acts as one who has the authority to confiscate the keys to a Palestinian's car for not paying television license fees, he will not be prosecuted. These actions, occurring outside the law, do not suspend it. Rather, they take place within and are *inspired by* the framework that allows for the law's suspension. Otherwise, the soldier would be duly prosecuted.

I employ the rather vague term "inspiration" here, since in the absence of law, despite the fact that rules and regulations are issued daily to replace it, the soldier in the vast majority of cases must decide and attribute his decision to a source other than himself. His many decisions, taken in a variety of cases — whether he should allow a dialysis patient to get to the hospital, whether the woman before him is really pregnant, as she claims, whether labor contractions every two minutes justify calling an ambulance, whether he should let a second-degree relative visit grieving kinsmen, and so on — all must derive their inspiration from a source, or at least give the impression of having a source from which they receive inspiration. Although in all these cases the soldier is indeed a "petty sovereign," his sovereignty is nevertheless subject to — or inspired by — the sovereign power that appoints him as its proxy.[98]

We would be mistaken, however, to say that the sovereign's junior proxy draws his power from the sovereign alone, for in making his decision, he is creating the sovereign as the source from which he draws his power. Making his decision at the checkpoint, he feigns executing a decision of the sovereign power that was made before he was ordered to apply it. In other words, for his actions to be valid, the sovereign's junior proxy has to simulate a direct connection between himself and the sovereign. However, this is not a complete simulation. The sovereign indeed does not exist as the source of the soldier's decision — the soldier himself is the source of authority. But the sovereign is the one who created the space and time in which the law can be suspended in regard to the Palestinian as a governed individual. The decision to suspend the application of the law effectively selects persons as exceptions without renouncing control over them. On the contrary, control over them itself becomes exceptional. The sovereign's decision is manifested in relation to three dimensions: the time of control, the space of control, and the subject of control himself. There is a time of emergency, when routine has been disrupted, a space that is made exceptional, effectively suspending the Palestinians' ownership of it, and a subject, the Palestinian, who is abandoned to the whim of a junior representative of the sovereign.

Radical differences separate these three dimensions. Within the context of space and time, the sovereign's proxy submits himself to decisions that are issued from the chain of command that descends from the sovereign's decision. Yet the sovereign's decision abandons Palestinian subjects, leaving them at the mercy of junior representatives while concealing all traces of the chain of command that leads back to the sovereign. The abandonment of the noncitizen is the result of the sovereign's evasion of direct responsibility for its representatives' decisions and actions, but also the effect of its refusal to protect Palestinian subjects from these decisions and actions.

The repudiation of any responsibility does not consist of the sovereign's denial of any connection to its representatives.[99] On the contrary, the repudiation is specifically manifested by the sovereign's disruption of any attempt to reconstruct this connection, leaving the noncitizen with no possible way to move away from the sovereign's junior proxy and toward the sovereign itself. If he could manage to climb a little higher — as sometimes happens when an appeal is submitted to the High Court of Justice and the system comes to a decision — the noncitizen would almost certainly realize that this path does not necessarily lead to the sovereign.

The procedures for handling the people who pass through checkpoints every day are inaccessible. Even if they were accessible, they would still be worthless, because they offer nothing more than a general and abstract doctrinal framework that is consistently suspended in favor of local directives and commands that change several times a day:

> It's a very complex topic, the procedures ... since, for example, what I said regarding permits changes from checkpoint to checkpoint, and changes three times a day at the same checkpoint. Let's suppose some intelligence has come in, now they're working with a different directive at this checkpoint. It's not a written directive. It goes through channels from the district brigade command level to the checkpoint level. It's not a directive you'll find on some piece of paper. [It's a] directive that has come down following an operational directive based on intelligence.

The sovereign's junior proxy, then, is free to make his own decision, while the Palestinian subject lacks both the sovereign's protection and the political power to appeal the decision. He stands alone when facing the sovereign's junior proxy, or at most the checkpoint commander, who is merely another junior proxy of the sovereign.[100] The proxy, if he so wishes, will let the subject pass, and if he wishes otherwise, he will not. If he so wishes, he will exempt the person facing him from all the other exceptions to the rule, or if he wishes, he will acknowledge a particular urgency, a dire emergency that is different from the one declared by the sovereign, who has forsaken the subject, allowing those to pass who are in need of immediate treatment. If he wishes otherwise, he will deny the necessary assistance to the person with whom he is faced. Whatever the case may be, the Palestinian subject remains the exception — someone whose fate rests in the hands of a junior representative of the sovereign.

We Citizens

The reconstitution of Europe in the second half of the twentieth century was a historical moment at which the citizenship was redefined and redistributed all over the continent. Étienne Balibar has pointed to the fact that in the eyes of the citizens of the European Union, the non-European residents of Europe who form a large part of the European population have remained invisible.[101] Although Balibar has focused on Europe, this is certainly a global problem. Citizenship has not been granted to all, but only to those who can prove their entitlement to receive it. Entitlement is granted on the basis of national belonging. The citizenship that has been granted has been conditioned and limited by ethnic belonging, property ownership, or gender. Balibar calls this selective allocation of citizenship "European apartheid." These are not the inhabitants of the remote margins of Europe or those residing outside the European Union's borders who have yet to become part of it, but a population that occupies the very heart of Europe, serving the interests of "the system."

The existence of a European apartheid is a radical claim that few are willing to make and appears alien to the civilized continent, which claims to have overcome the ills of nationalism. However, the term "apartheid," which previously indicated discrimination between two groups of the governed population within the same determined territory, has today acquired global characteristics. Apartheid in the present global context is a general framework of what Balibar calls "extreme violence." There are many manifestations of this violence, both overt and covert. It exists both actively and latently: in border controls, in ethnic identification, in wars, in policies of cleansing and purging, in the perpetuation of backwardness, and more. "Extreme violence" does not refer to sporadic, localized forms of violence, but to a heterogeneous set of expressions of violence arising from a global order. This violence isn't necessarily planned in advance; only in retrospect do its various expressions come together as a single "system" whose modes of operation organize patterns of power and expansion and whose logic becomes clear through the distance of time and place. The radicalism of Balibar's claim lies in his understanding of extreme violence as a system bereft of agency in which what used to be scattered and scandalously exceptional events have become a series of banal daily occurrences. But, as I have shown, the necessary condition for this violence to become banal is the individual becoming an exception to the rule.

Under these conditions, there is still space for rethinking the mechanism that lies at the heart of the institution of citizenship that constantly produces a residue of noncitizens alongside the citizen population. This residue — which is huge and scattered across the face of the globe — taints all of the world's citizens with the epidemic of noncitizenship and threatens to undermine their own citizenship. A citizen is someone who is treated like anyone else, who is governed and participates in government like anyone else. As a matter of principle, and in the strictest sense of the term, under a regime in which hordes of noncitizens live beside citizens, there are no citizens at all.[102] This is as true of Europe as it is of Israel.[103] In this context, "rethinking the mechanism that lies at the heart of the institution of citizenship" entails one of two opposite and mutually exclusive strategies. We can, following Giorgio Agamben, renounce the concept of citizenship altogether as fatally compromised by the exception of the noncitizens that it always entails and therefore seek to replace it,[104] or, as I will argue, we can seek to rehabilitate the concept by overcoming the distinction between citizen and noncitizen and with it the state of exception that is its basis. To do so, as I already have begun to indicate, we also will need to rehabilitate the concept of a political community of the governed as the basis of politics in the coming age, not, as Agamben would have it, bare life.

At present, the political order grants "egalitarian" citizenship only to a part of the population, based on the existence of a residue of noncitizens who have been excluded from the political game.[105] It is of the nature of this residue that it is devoid of the right to rebel, or, to use Hannah Arendt's language, it is unable to demand "its right to have rights."[106] Insurrection is the requisite response to the perversion of the political order implicit in the concept of citizenship.[107] The ideal of being treated "exactly like anyone else," which has haunted modern citizenship since its inception, was the stimulus for rebellion and the gradual becoming citizen of the poor, Jews, women, and blacks. This ideal is a part of modern citizenship and its form of validation. Renouncing this ideal implies not only the preservation of the existence of the noncitizens and their becoming reconciled to their existence, but the acceptance of their existence as what one can only name the "pestilence"[108] of noncitizens within citizenship.[109]

How does the increasing presence of the noncitizen pose such a threat? By posing the possibility of transcending nationalism, the nationalism that threatens to conquer citizenship itself and turn citizenship into more or less than what nationalism itself actually is. Given the accelerated processes of globalization, the global space is characterized today by the growing gap between the number of inhabitants of a given territory and their representation in the census or voter registration rolls. These representations serve as a more or less stable point of reference (to which some citizens are added every so often, and others removed), in connection to which noncitizens are created each time anew as those devoid of political protection and rights. Citizenship, however, is an interface or point of contact between all of the governed and government. It is nothing more or less. Anything that increases its value and turns it into a form of national belonging, for example, or reduces its value and turns it into a form of behavior[110] is injurious to its sole function. In all of the countries in which there are noncitizens who are exceptions to the rule, there are also citizens who have an existing set of rights and duties from which the former have been excluded. Reinventing this set each time is unnecessary, as is the formulation of a document of universalist pretensions regarding what the minimum citizen is. The exceptions to the rule are governed together with others who enjoy citizen status. The only imperative is that the exceptions to the rule be made equal to the generality from which they have been excluded.

In a brief article, "We Refugees," Giorgio Agamben proposes the elimination of the naïve terms "people" and "citizen" in order to adopt "the refugee" in their stead as the central figure of our political history.[111] In designating the refugee as the only solution for untying the knot that links birth, nationality, and territory — all of which, since the French Revolution, have been responsible for the creation of noncitizens — Agamben includes the "stateless person" within the notion of refugee, claiming that any distinction between the two appears insubstantial. He cites Arendt's assertion that refugees "who have been expelled from one country to another are the avant-garde of their own people" in order to buttress the refugee's standing in the political game, which he subsequently outlines. Already in his reference to Arendt, however, Agamben commits himself to the strategy of reviving the transcendental figure of the people and its attendant notion of belonging that has formed the model for political relationships. The refugee remains tied to "his" people, and even if he should succeed in his mission — as the vanguard — he will at most lead his people after him, restricting himself once again to the nationalist game. Therefore, in order to overcome the mass production of noncitizens, Agamben turns to "the refugee," a term that itself is haunted by the specter of nationalism, as part of a project that seeks to get rid of "the citizen," which has its own ghost. But if we take into account that the citizen who was born from the Declaration of the Rights of Man and the Citizen is a twofold figure as I have shown, we can rid ourselves of the citizen of the nation-state, who is haunted by the ghost of nationalism, while rehabilitating the citizen of the state who still needs to be separated from the nation:[112] We should thus speak of "we citizens," not "we refugees."

In the same spirit, Agamben considers the issue of territory, proposing that we view the possibility of Jerusalem serving as the capital of two states as the desired political model:

> The paradoxical condition of reciprocal extraterritoriality (or, better, aterritoriality) that this would imply could be generalized as a model of new international relations. Instead of two national states separated by

uncertain and threatening boundaries, one could imagine two political communities dwelling in the same region and in exodus one into the other, divided from each other by a series of reciprocal extraterritorialities, in which the guiding concept would no longer be the *ius* of the citizen, but rather the *refugium* of the individual.

This ostensible solution for Jerusalem takes for granted that a nation — the Palestinian nation — would require a state for it to be fulfilled. In so doing, this solution suggests, another nation-state would have to be introduced into the region. What is neglected by Agamben's perspective, however, is the possibility of separating nationality from state, thus transforming the Israeli state (which actually governs these large populations of noncitizens) into a state of all its governed populations, a state of all its citizens.[113]

Two aspects of the global political reality further problematize Agamben's proposal. One concerns the power of citizenship, which, in contrast to that of the nation-state, is not in decline. This power is immediately manifest in the costs of access to citizenship, which are constantly on the rise. Citizenship, as an interface mediating the relation between the governed and government, remains the most stable protective armor in the face of existing forms and methods of control and certainly offers a more resistant interface than the status of the refugee. The second aspect relates to the processes of deterritorialization, which gradually is turning nationalist belonging into merely one out of many types of belonging, many of which do not necessarily require a territorial connection. These processes are currently preparing the ground for the separation of nationality from the state, a separation closely resembling the separation of religion from the state.

Under these conditions, we must find a way to do away with the conception that reduces citizenship to a certain status and identity granted by a state or its government to some, but not to all the governed populations. When citizenship is thus narrowed, citizens are expected to identify with the government that governs them and often are prompted to participate in the persecution of the noncitizens governed alongside them, while the basic solidarity of the governed, which is an essential aspect of citizenship, is prevented, ignored, or denied. In addition, we must find the means for rehabilitating citizenship as a negotiating position vis-à-vis the governmental power in which all of the governed participate.

The necessary condition for the restoration of citizenship in the global era is an agreement on the principle that everyone, everywhere, is entitled to citizenship in the state in which he or she lives. Within my local context, as in other countries around the globe, one additional condition is necessary: the separation of citizenship from nationality. Reorganizing the situation of noncitizens requires every state to extend citizenship, as a matter of routine, to everyone living in and governed by it. In this way, citizenship becomes a zero-sum game that is constantly distributed to the inhabitants of a given territory.[114] The electoral register, enclosed in restricted offices, could be replaced by a huge computerized screen placed in the city square, constantly updated in real time with data about the inhabitants of a given territory at a given moment. Everyone appearing on-screen would gain access to the rights granted by that territory.

Only such proposals as this — which contest the transcendental standing of entitlement to citizenship and in which it is merely a contingent matter that noncitizens have not become its citizens — can save the institution of citizenship in the present age. Once civilian representation is produced online from the registration of inhabitants in a given territory, it will be possible to overcome the flaws in the distribution of citizenship and to handle these virtual goods in a truly virtual manner.[115] Citizenship should become a matter of topographical location, a property allocated equally to everyone as each is entitled to it by virtue of their presence in the governed territory. Any stay within the territory beyond a given period of time should be the guarantee of citizenship, and citizenship should guarantee a political existence and the ability to demand protection from the governmental regime, most especially in cases concerned with existence on the verge of catastrophe. Moving away from a dividing line between citizens and noncitizens, what was on the verge of catastrophe will turn into the characterization of common living conditions of exceptional disasters whose delimitation, given the processes of globalization, will no longer reflect the territorial demarcations of nation-states.

At the present time, however, the same global system that renders the residents living within its jurisdiction noncitizens and strips them of their civic armor at the same time produces new conditions of visibility for the catastrophes to which it has exposed its noncitizens or has directly brought on them. The manufacture of this vulnerability is facilitated, first and foremost, by the structure of modern citizenship and its modes of distribution. These catastrophic events, whose site of occurrence is the population of noncitizens, are manifestly present in a new way in the field of vision of the citizens living beside them. With their bodies, noncitizens, present in the territory, but missing from its political representation, manufacture the new conditions of visibility of catastrophe. The threshold of catastrophe will then turn from a line separating citizens from noncitizens to a feature of shared conditions whose distribution according to the territorial boundaries of the nation-state is made impossible by the globalizing process.

CHAPTER TWO

The Civil Contract of Photography

We have seen that citizenship is a form of relations between the governed individual and the governing authority, relations ultimately based in a political equality between each and every governed individual. I will now explore the ways in which, when separated from nationality or any other essentialist conception of a group of governed individuals, citizenship comes to resemble the photographic relation. Exactly like citizenship, photography, is no one's property. It cannot be owned. Photography, at least the kind that I'm concerned with in this book in which photographs are taken on the verge of catastrophe, also is a form of relations of individuals to the power that governs them, a form of relations that is not fully mediated through such power, being a relation between formally equal individuals — individuals who are equal as the governed as such. It is a form of relation that exists and becomes valid only within and between the plurality of individuals who take part in it. Anyone who addresses others through photographs or takes the position of a photograph's addressee, even if she is a stateless person who has lost her "right to have rights," as in Arendt's formulation, is nevertheless a citizen — a member in the citizenry of photography. The civil space of photography is open to her, as well. That space is configured by what I call the civil contract of photography.

Photography is an apparatus of power that cannot be reduced to any of its components: a camera, a photographer, a photographed environment, object, person, or spectator. "Photography" is a term that designates an ensemble of diverse actions that contain the production, distribution, exchange, and consumption of the photographic image. Each of these actions involved in the photographic event makes use of a direct and an indirect force — taking someone's portrait, for example, or looking at someone's portrait. Much has been written about this violent dimension of photography — the potential for turning any concrete encounter into a violent clash. However, compared with the endless number of photographs taken, rare are those cases where eruptive violence replaces the relations between the protagonists. That is because a civil contract regulates these encounters, reducing and most of the time eliminating the possibility of direct violence. As long as photographs exist, I will contend, we can see in them and through them the way in which such a contract also enables the injured parties to present their grievances, in person or through others, now or in the future.

This turn to the rhetoric of the contractarian tradition in political theory may seem curious, and in need of explanation. After all, the contractarian tradition has left the moment of contract itself outside the political order and wasted no time on the relations between governed people that are not enabled, mediated, and constrained — let alone dictated — by the ruling power. In fact, many thinkers in that tradition have tacitly agreed with Carl Schmitt's reduction of the concept of the political to the space opened by and demarcated through the sovereign decision (or a series of sovereign decisions).[1] They were mostly interested in ways to justify and limit sovereign power, which many of them understood very differently from Schmitt, and this has been the main way in which the rights of individuals, the interests of the public, and the commotion of the multitudes have been taken into consideration. The individual, the public, and the multitude have always been considered with a view to the power that is at one and the same time the most dangerous for individuals and ultimately necessary for their protection, a condition for their coexistence in a group.

Thinking with Schmitt from the opposite direction, Agamben uses the image (or metaphor) of the contract to articulate the ways in which social and political relations manifest themselves in the realm determined by the sovereign decision. Concluding his discus-

86

sion of bare life as defined as "sacred life" under Roman law — the
life of *homo sacer*, he who "cannot be sacrificed and yet may be killed"
— he notes:

> It has been rightly observed that the state is founded not as the expres-
> sion of a social tie but as an untying (*déliason*) that prohibits (Badiou,
> *L'être*, p. 125). We may now give a further sense to this claim. *Déliason*
> is not to be understood as the untying of a preexisting tie (which would
> probably have the form of a pact or a contract). The tie itself originarily
> has the form of an untying or exception in which what is captured is
> at the same time excluded, and in which human life is politicized only
> through an abandonment to an unconditional power of death. The sov-
> ereign tie is more originary than the tie of the positive rule or the tie of
> the social pact, but the sovereign tie is in truth only an untying. And
> what this untying implies and produces — bare life, which dwells in the
> no-man's land between the home and the city — is, from the point of
> view of sovereignty, the originary political element.[2]

The incommensurability of contractarian political theories with
sovereignty which Agamben underlines is a superficial one, because,
as noted above, the original moment of the contract itself has been
left outside the political-historical domain, and concrete contracts
are always seen in terms of the authorities who can limit, impose,
induce, or invalidate contracts. The true opposition, I suggest, is not
between contractarian theories and theories of sovereignty, but between "sovereign violence," which "is in truth founded not on a pact
but on the exclusive inclusion of bare life in the state,"[3] and multiple
voluntary associations between many individuals, which reproduce
the original moment of contract without necessarily reproducing its
result, that is, the constitution of a sovereign authority.

And where Agamben insists (rightly) on the fact that "the state of
nature is, in truth, a state of exception, in which the city appears for
an instant" and "is thus not an event achieved once and for all but is
continually operative in the civil state in the form of the sovereign
decision,"[4] I would like to insist on the fact that "the state of contract," too, is continually operative in the civil state — in order to
reproduce not sovereign power, but rather a space relatively free

from its intervention, a space where "thinking a politics freed from the form of the State" becomes possible.[5]

"Thinking a politics freed from the form of the State" is Agamben's own project, described in *The Coming Community* (1993) as a politics founded on the "Whatever," on "singularity," "not in its indifference with respect to a common property (to a concept, for example: being red, being French, being Muslim), but only in its being *such as it is*."[6] But there is another way of thinking politics freed from the state, one that not only can receive a theoretical account, but that can do so because it is manifest, in the form of nongovernmental political activities of many forms and agendas, in empirical form throughout the world today. That is a politics founded not on singularity, but on the equality of the governed "as such" — as *they* are. It is based not on a community to come, but on a community, or rather several communities, both within and beyond the boundaries of the sovereign state, that already exist, communities that employ a variety of means — photography prominent among them — to edify an open political space where no one can decide on the exception, and a final decision cannot be made, a community in which a new beginning is a right preserved for each of its members and solidarity among its members precedes the submission and the identification with power. As Hannah Arendt has noted with regard to the power of the sovereign, "the moment the group, from which the power originated to begin with (*potestas in populo*, without a people or a group there is no power), disappears, 'his power' also vanishes." In a politics founded on the equality of the governed, power regains its meaning, not as a governmental tool, but as "a human ability not just to act but to act in concert"[7] and to negotiate, sometimes successfully, sometimes not — with sovereign power.[8]

The civil contract of photography, whose text I have drafted during the years of the second Palestinian intifada, bears witness to an attempt to find refuge amid the loneliness of being a spectator who has been addressed every day by photographs documenting the daily horrors of the Israeli occupation. Working out and making explicit the clauses of this tacit contract has been an effort to think my relation to and attitude toward these photographed individuals beyond guilt and compassion — outside of the merely psychological framework of empathy, of "regarding the pain of others" — on the basis of civic duty and the mutual trust of those who are governed. I will try to show that this mutual trust, mediated by photography, is a form of relations between individuals that was first established during the mid-nineteenth century and that has gradually developed ever since. The civil contract of photography can be extracted from existing photographic practices and uses, but is irreducible to any of them, nor can it be depicted as a product of their accumulation. Rather, positing this contract is a way to delineate part of the newly con-structed space of civil relations that has been opened — and even necessitated — by photography. In addition, developing the charac-teristics of this contract is my way of questioning photography's political configuration and reflecting on its effect on the modern form of sovereignty and its territorial articulation. Briefly put, the camera modified the way in which individuals are governed and the extent of their participation in the forms of governance. It is that change that I explore here.

The Invention of Photography

To this day, historians of photography persist in exploring the issue of the origin of photography's invention in a sustained attempt to determine its precise moment of birth. While the moment of birth is controversial, the consensus is that it exists — a single, magical moment reappearing as a constant anchor in all the narratives of photography's evolution, an axis relative to which the many alterna-tive chronologies are all presented, a time from which the age of photography is calculated and its centennials celebrated.[9] I'm refer-ring here to the summer of 1839, when the daguerreotype, named after one of its two inventors, was exhibited in the French Chamber of Deputies. This was the date that marked its transformation into an object of national legislation and a source of monthly payments to its inventors by the French state, entitling the state to render it a pub-licly visible invention, open and accessible to all, whose uses were not restricted by copyright. However, it is well known that before this official birth date, Henry Fox Talbot of Great Britain had already claimed the title of inventor of this new technology and had pro-vided evidence of his presentation of his invention to the British

Royal Society over a decade earlier. Another claimant to the title was Hippolyte Bayard, who went to dramatic lengths to make his claim. Nevertheless, the daguerreotype endured as the prototypical term for what soon became photography.

In 1931, about ninety years later, Walter Benjamin opened his essay "Little History of Photography" by noting "the fog that surrounds the beginnings of photography," obscuring the beginnings of this technology. And yet, he wrote, in contrast to the case of printing, the fog in this case is not all that thick, for "the time was ripe for the invention, and was sensed by more than one — by men who strove independently for the same objective: to capture the images in the camera obscura, which had been known at least since Leonardo's time."[10] Benjamin elaborated somewhat on each of those protagonists, in fact circumventing the question of the origin of photography whose answer converges into a single inventor's name. There was no single inventor. Instead, Benjamin proposed a new perspective of photography's beginnings. The origin, he suggested, was the appearance of a professional community.

In 1999, the American historian of photography Geoffrey Batchen published a book that he titled, with a quote from Daguerre, *Burning with Desire*. As I noted, Daguerre is conventionally considered the inventor of photography, despite repeated retractions of this title since the moment it was granted. In 1827, when Daguerre himself was still far from solving the question of how to fix and preserve the images created within the camera obscura, Joseph Nicéphore Niépce had already discovered the solution. At the time, however, it was considered unsatisfactory. Daguerre wrote Niépce: "I am burning with desire to see your experience from nature."[11] Batchen's thesis develops further Benjamin's intuitively written claim that photography was "sensed by more than one — by men who strove independently for the same objective." Traveling backward in time, Batchen's work periodizes the beginnings of photography at the end of the eighteenth century, joining together the findings of various scientists working in separate disciplines (optics, chemistry, and physics), all of whom were experimenting with means for producing images that would endure after the shutter of the black box had snapped shut over the aperture.

Batchen didn't do away with the question, but he can be said to have broadened the arena within which historians still attempt to pinpoint a moment of photography's birth. This, for instance, is the vein mined by the studies of the historians who contributed to the 2003 exhibition at the Musée d'Orsay and to the exhaustive accompanying catalogue, both centering on Daguerre and the daguerreotype. However, most of the historians who participated in the catalogue (including Quentin Bajac, Stephen Pinson, and Dominique Planchon-de Font-Reaulx) not only analyzed Daguerre's singular contribution, but also claimed primacy for it. The national dimension, intertwined from the outset in this debate and on which I will not elaborate here, thus surfaced, even in these recent studies.[12]

In his article in the catalogue, historian André Gunthert sought to offer an answer to a question that had already been posed by his predecessors: If the technical achievement of preserving an image was attained as early as 1825 by Talbot, and if Niépce and Daguerre had in fact possessed this knowledge while Niépce was still alive, why was it that they failed to publicize their discovery? In response, Gunthert has claimed that from 1835 to 1837, the scientists had invested their concentrated efforts in perfecting the invention, while from 1837 to 1839, they had focused on what he called the packaging of their invention and on the means of distribution, "What Daguerre wishes to present to the public is not a mere process or principle or recipe, but a finished product, containing both the necessary equipment, provided as a ready-to-use kit, as well as practical and symbolic instructions."[13] The development of photography after the daguerreotype, to which it put an end, Gunthert sees as a marginal phase in the history of photography, a phase that he described as "reprofessionalization by elitist photography militants." Their efforts toward liberation from the rigidity of the daguerreotype, toward opening up photography to individual creativeness as regards the photographic apparatus itself, were vanquished, he claims, by the photographic technology developed around 1880. This technology returned photography to the principle characteristic of the daguerreotype which, today, still remains a defining feature of photography — its condensation into a black box between whose walls all technical matters are obscured and buried, so that it works itself, so to speak, at the click of a button, making it accessible to all.

Gunthert accordingly ends his article with a call to view Daguerre "as a pioneer in the full sense of the term, not of the process of perfectly inscribing [an image] but, of photography as a practice."[14] Gunthert thus recognizes that Daguerre did not develop the process single-handedly and cannot, consequently, be considered its inventor. He does, however, seek to credit him with being the first to make this invention sufficiently simple and reliable for it to become accessible to the public at large. This achievement, though, in keeping with Gunthert's own claims, was attained only in 1907, about half a century after Daguerre's death.[15] While the accessibility and operational simplicity of cameras, according to Gunthert, was achieved only at the beginning of the twentieth century, he nevertheless views photography as a nineteenth-century invention.

None of the historians contributing to the Musée d'Orsay exhibition or catalogue perceived themselves as historians of the apparatus: the daguerreotype or camera. And yet, all of the histories they narrate are caught within a single narrative framework centered on the technological invention and on its inventor and distinctly converging toward this center. Contrary to these narratives, I'll contend that photography was invented at precisely the moment when the individual inventor lost the authority to determine the meaning of his invention. Thus the question "who invented photography?" is drained of its meaning. At that moment the use of a variety of technologies of creating images — daguerreotype, Calotype, Panotype, Talbotype, Crystallograph, or Ambrotype, to name just a few,[16] all placed at the public's disposal by their various inventors toward the end of the 1830s — exceeded the realm of control of this or that single inventor, this or that sponsoring state, and proceeded to create a new sphere of relations between people.

The invention of photography, then, is not the achievement of a single person who may have isolated several chemical elements and activated them by means of a certain mechanism. Instead, the invention of photography was the creation of a new situation in which different people, in different places, can simultaneously use a black box to manufacture an image of their encounters: not an image of *them*, but of the encounter itself.[17] Not only is the invention of photography the invention of a new encounter between people, but the invention of an encounter between people and the camera. Photography was invented at the moment when a space of plurality was initiated, at the moment when a large number of people — more than just a certain circle of acquaintances — took hold of a camera and began using it as a means of producing images.

Photography was invented at *that* moment, by *those* people. They cannot be identified; they do not belong to any milieu of professionals, but are ordinary people who, simply by using a camera, both promoted photography and initiated what I am calling the civil contract of photography. A description of them would be impossible to complete and could not provide a full account of the civil contract of photography's conditions of possibility if we failed to note explicitly that looking at photographs was an inseparable part of photography's institutionalization and that the validity of the contract is due, at least potentially, not simply to the new ability of photographers to take photographs, but to the oscillation between the photographer's and the spectator's position. This oscillation inherently undermines any legal or juridical claims that anyone does or can "own" a photograph. Not only can no single individual claim to have invented photography, but the properties of photography itself make it impossible for any single individual to claim exclusive property rights to a photograph.

The Space of Political Relations in Photography

The invention of photography offered the gaze an absolute plane of visual immobility, a plane on which all movement is frozen, transformed into a still picture that can be contemplated without disturbance. However, in this picture what has been established — what has been fixed and stabilized — what "was there," to employ the succinct phrase coined by Roland Barthes in *Camera Lucida* to characterize what every photograph says of its subject, that it "was there,"[18] is at most a testimony to the moment of the photograph's eventuation in which photographer, photographed, and camera encountered one another.[19] Even when this encounter occurs under the difficult conditions of distress or disaster, when a threat looms over or has already caused harm to the political space, as a space of plurality and

93

action, the act of photography and the photographs it produces might, at least potentially, restore it. In other words, although photography may appear to be a distinctive object of the contemplative life (*vita contemplativa*), a moment in which all movements have been eliminated, it is actually deeply embedded in the active life (*vita activa*); it attests to action and continues to take part in it, always engaged in an ongoing present that challenges the very distinction between contemplation and action.[20] The photograph always includes a supplement that makes it possible to show that what "was there" wasn't there *necessarily* in that way.

The disappearance of what "was there" from the first daguerreotype of 1837 and its transformation over time into an imageless monochromatic surface might serve as an allegory for this structure of relations. The daguerreotype shows "a section of wall and bench (or perhaps a window ledge) cluttered with various objects typically found in such places. These include the following: plaster casts of the heads of two putti or cupids, complete with small wings."[21] This description, which adheres to the plane of the visible as closely as possible, is revealed as an utter fabrication after inspecting the daguerreotype preserved in the vaults of the French Society of Photography (SFP) in Paris. The daguerreotype, which has (re)turned into a plane of silvery ash, is kept inside a safe-deposit box alongside a reproduction intended to attest to what *is* seen in it, despite it no longer being visible. The omission of this daguerreotype from the great Daguerre exhibition at the Musée d'Orsay in 2003 was based on the assumption that a yawning divide lies between what was seen in the first daguerreotype and what can actually be seen.[22] What lies in this in between, between what was seen in the first daguerreotype and what can actually be seen in it, is the very space of relations of photography.

This space is characterized by a particular relation to the visible. There has always been a regard for the visible. The world has a visible dimension; human beings are equipped with eyes and conduct themselves, to a large extent, in and through the world in keeping with the ways they observe it. The traditional distinction between the life of study and contemplation (*vita contemplativa*) and the life of action (*vita activa*), assigns contemplation a realm of its own that is essentially visual — reverie, wonderment, marveling, disinterested pausing vis-à-vis a landscape or a figure. Since the days of ancient Greece, the metaphor of this gaze has served to conceptualize abstract thought: theory, speculation, study, things that people imagine or understand through the use of their imagination, and so forth. However, attitudes toward the visible have always included two additional modes, as well, both of which are unrelated to the world of contemplation and, conversely, more closely approximate the world of action. The gaze, after all, is an inalienable part of action, of instrumental activities, of the effort to achieve goals and objectives, to grow more efficient and more sophisticated.

Hannah Arendt, who revisited the classical distinction between the realm of contemplation and the realm of action in *The Human Condition*, drew a distinction between three forms and three areas of action. The first form, which she defined as labor, consists in activity designed to provide for the basic needs of existence, allowing survival and the reproduction of life. The second form, which she defined as work, consists in activity creating products that do not serve immediate needs and that are not used up through direct consumption. Such products include instruments, tools, and tool parts that may be used in creating additional products and, finally, in creating an entire world, arranging the life of humans on the planet and allowing them to turn its space into their abode. The third form is action, which is unlike work in that it does not produce an end product or carry out a previously made plan. This form consists in individuals' venturing to generate something new through action or speech, doing so in public, among many other people, exposed to their gaze, in the recognition that the individual cannot fully predict the outcome of this venture or control the way in which it will evolve in the world.

I will draw on Arendt's distinction among three modes of *vita activa* to characterize various forms of active, noncontemplative gazes. The two most widespread ones are the identifying, orientative gaze, which, I propose, is analogous to labor, and the professional gaze, guiding and accompanied by certain types of action, which I'll present as analogous to work. Gazes of the first kind constitute part of the practice of orientation and survival based on the mechanism of identifying what is visible, which is a necessary condition for existence. The individual observes her surroundings in order to identify herself within them, to plan her movements, and to identify the objects, animals, and people that she encounters, discerning their intentions as well as the dangers and opportunities implicit in each encounter. Gazes of the second kind, which might be termed "directed" or "intended," are typical of professionals (doctors, artists, police, architects, educators, etc.) and allow the arrangement and control of what is visible through the use of a body of knowledge that is incremental, ongoing, and evolving. The professional gaze isn't necessary to basic survival, but, rather, to the ordering of certain types of activities, to the analysis of events and circumstances, to hand-eye coordination, and so forth, in situations where action is free of the need to satisfy immediate needs and is, instead, anchored to goals of a higher order.

The identifying gaze and the directed gaze have accompanied human existence from its very beginnings. Prior to the invention of photography, however, it was difficult to find a gaze of the type that was analogous to action in the sense defined by Arendt. Until then, the practical gaze was either an identifying, orientative one or a professional gaze directed toward a definitive activity. The gaze recognized as distinct from these two forms lay outside the realm of action altogether — the contemplative gaze that gives pause and wonders. Then, the invention of photography added a new way of regarding the visible, one that previously did not exist or that, at least, existed in a different manner. This gaze is based on a new attitude toward the visual. It constitutes in an approach toward items, situations, customs, images, or places that, before photography came into existence, were not held worthy of contemplation in and of themselves. This approach or attitude now exists in contexts of plurality, among people, in a public sphere, contexts within which every participant not only contemplates what can be seen but is also, herself, exposed and visible. Such regard for the visual departs from the disciplinarian gaze or the pattern of communicating prerecognized messages. It approximates at least the central distinguishing features of action: it includes the aspect of a new beginning, and its ends are unpredictable.

The members of the community of photography are, as stated above, anyone and everyone who bears any relationship whatsoever to photographs — as a photographer, a viewer of photographs, or a photographed person. While it is customary to draw distinctions between amateur and professional photographers and also, perhaps, between random or occasionally photographed persons and those for whom being photographed is a profession, the community of photography is not actually organized around these distinctions. It is a broad community, which I venture to call "the citizenry of photography," and it is borderless and open. The relations between its members cannot be defined in terms of a common professional interest in photography. Within the framework of this community, the third manner of gazing, the third form of regarding the visible, which I have related to Arendt's concept of action, appears from the outset with civil characteristics. Much like action, which always occurs within a political sphere of human plurality, the singular gaze enabled by photography, which I view as a civil gaze, also exists — always and only — within a plurality. The spectator activating this gaze views the photograph and recognizes instantly that what is inscribed in it and discernible in it are products of plurality — the plural participants in the act of photography (the photographer, the photographed person, and the spectator). Moreover, the spectator instantaneously recognizes them as products of the multiplicity of elements that enter into the frame, whether in keeping with the photographer's intentions, or despite these intentions, or unrelated to them. The civil gaze doesn't seek to control the visible, but neither can it bear another's control over the visible. In particular, it cannot consent to any attempt to rule the visible while seeking to abolish the space of plurality.

The Properties of Photographs and Photographs as Property

In *Techniques of the Observer*, Jonathan Crary postulates that the appearance of a new figure of the viewer was witnessed in a mixture of three positions: "An individual body that is at once a spectator, a subject of empirical research and observation, and an element of machine production."[23] The invention of photography, he claims, is secondary to the revolution brought about by the invention of various

97

seeing instruments during the first decades of the nineteenth century and to the new observer these apparatuses established. However, as Crary himself points out, photography also establishes "a new set of abstract relations between individuals and things" and imposes "those relations as the real."[24] Crary's understanding of that transition from the *camera obscura* to the seeing instruments of the nineteenth century, which created a new observer, will serve as a point of departure for my discussion of what the properties of photographs imply for the status of photographs as property.

Let us begin with the photographer. It is commonly accepted and legally established that the photographer owns the images that he or she makes — that the photographer's ownership of the image is his or her "right" under the doctrine of property rights. It is this putative "right" of ownership that, in the case of photographs, I want to contest here. My questioning of the concept of "right" in this instance is meant to challenge the assumption that the photographed individual has no right over the image made of him or her and that this right is "naturally" given to the person holding the photograph's means of production. Most importantly, I would like to challenge the transformation of the photograph into an object of private property. To do so, I will examine the distribution of those goods known as "images" within their social and political contexts silenced from the discussion over the regulation of photography's exchange relations through market forces and by the judicial system that legitimized this regulation.

Starting in the middle of the nineteenth century, when channels for the distribution of photography were established — the exchange of *cartes de visite*, shop display windows, exhibitions, newspapers, and so on — access has been provided to images of people, objects, and places that in the absence of photography would have remained outside the modern citizen's visual field. Here, I will dwell principally on the most obvious instance of this framework, the photographic situation under conditions in which at least two people gather around the camera and take part in the ritual of photography.

Men and women of the period celebrated this accessibility in a way that made them (and subsequent others) forget the fact that photography is the result of an encounter with an another and with an other, and, as such, does not have one obvious, constant owner. In that encounter, one is holding a camera, while the other, knowingly or not, becomes the photographed person. The encounter produces a photograph in which an image of the photographed person is inscribed. It is an encounter that always and inescapably involves a measure of violence, even when the situation is one of full and explicit consent between the participant parties. The violence is inherent in the instrumentalization of the photographed person in order to produce an image of him, within which context the photographed person can have as much of a vested interest as the photographer. Because ownership of the image has been assigned to the photographer, however, in only a few particular cases has a photograph been deemed to be in the public domain, and even then only after judicial intervention.[25] In rarer instances, typically involving well-known people, photographed individuals have been given certain rights in regard to *their* photographs taken in public, at least to the extent that they have been able to influence their mode of distribution.[26] At all other times, whether during moments of happiness or disaster, the photographed persons renounce in advance — or, more accurately, have been treated as if they have renounced in advance — any legal right to their own image, entrusting it to the hands of others.

The "right" to the ownership of a photographic image has been deployed retroactively in regard to the initial decades of photography. The question of who is the proper owner of a photograph did not emerge until the twentieth century.[27] The photographic situation, in which the photographer is whoever actually holds the means of production in his or her hands and controls its operation, effectively created the conditions for the photographer's designation as the "natural" owner of the photograph. When the photographer was working for someone else, the question of ownership went through an additional transformation, but the photograph in all cases was recognized as belonging to whomever possessed the instrument that created the photographic image and the support on which the original image was printed, rather than to the one who stood in front of the camera.

The precedence given to the ownership of the support (the artifact)

— a metal or glass plate in photography's infancy, photographic paper at a later stage — also made it possible for the opposite scenario to occur, in which photographs lacking the name of the photographer who made them wander throughout the world.[28] In those cases in which photographs are exhibited or printed without the photographer's name, the photographed individuals are presented as content, irrespective of its makers, content whose distribution is of prime importance for the public — an importance that usually suspends the question of legal ownership. In these cases, the photographed individual is usually not the owner of the photograph. Although the photograph is in the hands of someone who presents himself or herself as its owner, the only way of exercising this ownership is to share it with the public as a substitute for the photograph's owner. Thus, the individual or institution (newspaper, archive, etc.), having physical possession of the photograph, the material object itself, can act as if they were performing a "service" to the public, which is, in principle, the photograph's "true" owner.

When the question of ownership arises legally, before a court, it usually appears only indirectly and does not undermine what has come to be taken for granted — that the photographed individual is *not* the owner of his/her own image. The first instance of such a judicial case concerned a photograph of Napoleon III. The painter Adolphe Yvon had asked a photographer named Bisson to take a photograph of the emperor to assist Yvon while painting the emperor's picture. The painter posed the emperor in a certain attitude, under certain lighting, in a manner compatible with his own artistic conception. Later, the photographer made commercial use of the photograph, distributing numerous copies.[29] The painter, worried that the audience's appreciation of his painting would dwindle once it was recognized to be merely a reproduction of the photograph, pleaded with the court to prohibit the photograph's distribution. His legal argument, which persuaded the court to decide in his favor, was that he had composed the scene in the photograph and had paid the photographer for his work.[30] Over the course of the discussion of the photograph's ownership, the name and status of the photographed individual, the emperor himself, failed even to be mentioned as someone who might claim ownership.

Conversely, in the twentieth century, Dorothea Lange, who took one of the century's most renowned photographs, *Migrant Mother*, and lost her rights to it in favor of the institution for which she worked, attempted to challenge her loss of ownership by declaring that the true owner of the photograph was the woman who was photographed: "The negative now belongs to the Library of Congress which supervises it and prints it...until now it is her picture, not mine," she tried to argue (figure 2.1).[31] Lange's contention that the photographed woman owned the photograph, however, was largely a gesture of defiance and never prevailed. Had her proposal been accepted as law, the citizens of photography committed to the civil contract of photography would be just as inclined to contest her opinion in order to maintain citizens' ownership. Any final determination of the ownership of the photographed image, whether it is given to the photographer or the photographed person, negates the possibility that others can lay claim to it. It is not simply members of future generations who are entitled to reject these decisions. Not only are they entitled to reject them, as I will soon propose, but it is their moral duty to do so when the latter stand in contradiction to the civil contract of photography. When Florence Owens Thompson, the woman in the photograph, finally was identified and interviewed by the Associated Press in the 1970s in a story that appeared under the title "Woman Fighting Mad over Famous Depression Photo," she declared of Lange that "I wish she hadn't taken my picture" and complained that "I can't get a penny out of it. She didn't ask my name. She said she wouldn't sell the pictures. She said she'd send me a copy. She never did."[32] In effect, Florence Owens Thompson was complaining that her rights had been violated.

On occasions in which photographed individuals have brought a claim in regard to their photographs, it was not an issue of the ownership of the image that was at the center of the debate, but the right to protect the character of the image that was made of them. In addition to the right to ownership of the image, other juridical concepts, such as "the right to privacy," "defamation," or "malicious use" have thus been introduced into the discourse on photography. To this day, courts continue to ratify the absence of any rights of photographed individuals regarding the journalistic use of such photographs and tend

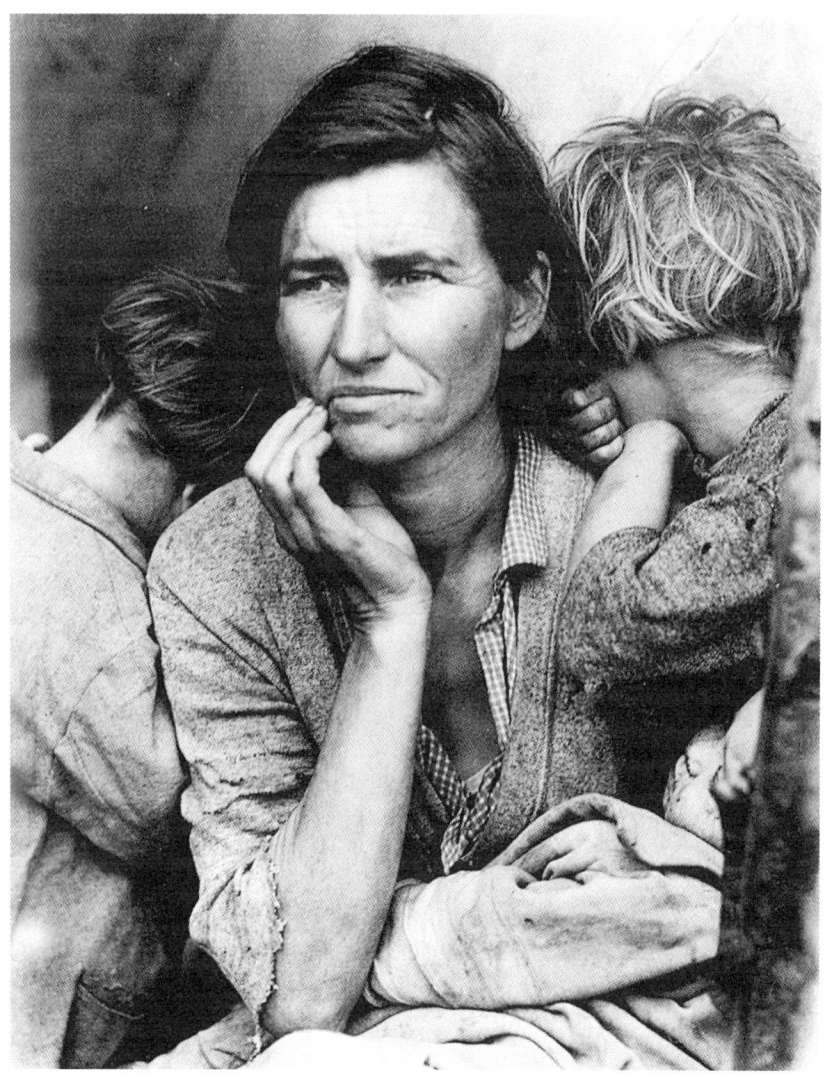

Figure 2.1. Dorothea Lange, *Migrant Mother* (Florence Owens Thompson), Nipomo, CA, 1936 (Prints and Photographs Division, Library of Congress, Washington, DC).

to impose restrictions only in cases of direct economic exploitation or violation of privacy at the moment of taking the photograph.[33]

However, the concepts of property and ownership are foreign to the logic of photography. What is seen in a photograph evades all criteria for ownership, and cannot be appropriated; from this it is impossible to establish a single, stable meaning of photography that would negate or supersede all others. A photograph is neither the product of a single person, despite the concept of "author" having been established in relation to photography, nor is it even solely a product of human hands. A photographic image, then, can at most be entrusted to someone for a certain time. It is a deposit, temporarily given over to whomever has it for safekeeping, but such persons are never its owner.

Not only is the deposit temporary, it is only ever partial, conditional, and with limited liability. All of these qualifications apply to the deposit because just as no one can claim ownership of a photographed image, no one can deem himself or herself to be the one who has renounced ownership and put it in someone else's hands. As stated above, the concepts of property and ownership are ontologically foreign to photography. At the same time that a photograph lies in someone's hands, someone else can always claim the deposited image for themselves, or at least demand to participate in its safekeeping. Since the safekeeping of the deposit ranges anywhere from burying it in the archives to giving it widespread circulation, from preservation "as is" to being exhibited in a different light, someone else may still wish to display it or cast it in a different light. The demand to participate in the deposit's safekeeping is not made in the name of a right to possess the deposited image, for this demand expresses a rejection of any right that might be given to someone in regard to a photograph. The demand to participate in the deposit's safekeeping stems from a duty toward the deposit as such, toward what has been deposited, toward whoever deposited it, and toward the archive itself. In what follows, I will try to show how this duty is produced.

It is here that the oscillation between the position of the photographer and the position of the spectator becomes most apparent and most definitively subverts the notion that photographs are the real property of those who take them. Ever since photography's emergence, there have been efforts to take photographs of areas in distress or those struck by disaster, to collect, distribute and interpret photographs from these places. The assumptions underlying these efforts have been, first of all, that what happens "there" is of interest not only to those concerned with it — those who've been struck by disaster — but to onlookers the world over, and, second, that photographs produced out of what happens "there" participate in constructing the event and the responses to it.[34] Since the second half of the twentieth century, this activity has been accompanied by the distribution of cameras within afflicted areas or areas prone to disaster in order to undermine any attempt to seal off such places to the photographic gaze.[35]

These uses of photography are part of the way in which citizens actualize their duty toward other citizens as photographed persons who have been struck by disaster. The exercise of photography in such situations is actually the exercise of citizenship — not citizenship imprinted with the seal of belonging to a sovereign, but citizenship as a partnership of governed persons taking up their duty as citizens and utilizing their position for one another, rather than for a sovereign. The camera in the hands of the citizen is indifferent to the question of whether or not the injured persons who are photographed are citizens "of" a state. The camera recognizes them as citizens of what I call the citizenry of photography. The civil contract of photography, the essentials of which can be derived from each of these uses, is its founding formulation. These uses are motivated by the duty actively to overturn any ownership that someone has obtained or that is being sought in regard to a photograph — regardless of whether it has already been taken or could in principle be taken — and with it the right to conceal the photographed persons from the eyes of other citizens bound together in the civil contract of photography. The duty derived from the civil contract of photography is simultaneously to reject one's claim to be the owner of a photograph that one possesses as well as anyone's attempt to appoint him or herself as a guardian of another in an attempt to prevent that other person from being photographed.

Photography's exchange relations were institutionalized in such a way that in addition to those recognized as the lawful owners of photographs, the public has been recognized as the virtual owner of all photographs. The familiar slogan regarding "the public's right to see" only partially expresses what is at stake and is thus a mistaken and misleading formulation. It is not simply the right to see, but the right to enact photography free of governmental power and even against it, if it inflicts injury on others who are governed. Photography provides modern citizens with an instrument enabling them to develop and sustain civilian skills that are not entirely subordinate to governmental power and allows them to exercise partnership with others not under the control of this power or acting as the extension of this power's operations and goals. In other words, photography is one of the distinctive practices by means of which individuals can establish a distance between themselves and power in order to observe its actions and to do so not as its subjects. Injury to this right, which is simultaneously injury to both the photographer and the photographed, as two citizens of photography — but fundamentally against all of the citizenry of photography — establishes a duty to protect it. If it is not protected, citizens will be deprived of the protection that can be granted by photography as an instrument that employs power that is in the hands of the governed and not only in the hands of the sovereign or those seeking to win sovereign power. Exercising this right — or discharging this duty — constantly undermines any attempt of founding an exclusive sovereign authority over the exercise of photography.

The Civil Contract of Photography: Terms and Conditions

As we have seen, in the classical photographic situation, the camera mediates an encounter between the photographer and the photographed, and an image is produced. In the legal institutionalization of this encounter, the photographed individual has not been recognized as its owner, whereas the photographer who produces the image has been given legal rights. However, this appropriation of the photographed person's rights, in which there is always a measure of violence, which was taken for granted by both sides from the start, and which has remained unaltered, cannot be understood without assuming that a certain pact or agreement lies at its foundation. Such an agreement is what makes the photographic encounter between the photographer and the photographed possible. It is important to emphasize, however, that this agreement does not mean there is willing consent, and in no way is it based on knowledge of the conditions of exchange or the possibility not to agree. What this agreement establishes is that the two sides reconfirm the balance of power that has been established between them, doing so without resorting to the use of overt force. When a camera initiates an encounter between the photographer and the photographed, each of the sides is generally responsible for its part and knows what is expected of it. Even the refusal to be photographed or the refusal to be photographed in a certain way is institutionalized — the photographed persons and the photographers act according to conventional expectations; everyone is supposed to know how to act and what to expect at the photographic encounter.[36] From the fact that in the photographic encounter itself there is no need for the formulation or signing of a concrete pact, we can assume there has been some kind of tacit prior pact or agreement between the sides that ensures the present encounter: not merely a contractual agreement or ad hoc understanding, but a civil contract.

If one reflects on the agreement between the parties to the civil contract of photography as it is usually enacted, it is clearly an unequal exchange. The photographer produces a picture of an event or place at which he or she is present, a picture that may include all others who are present at the same place. These people can either agree or refuse to be photographed by the photographer, or at least to have what is happening to them or the place they are occupying become the object of his or her photographs. If they grant the photographer the right to turn them into a photographic image, in most cases, they receive no material reward, except for being turned into an image. No photographer promises them anything regarding what the future of "their" photograph might be — whether it will be rejected during editing or widely distributed, whether it will be printed in whole or in part, with or without a name, and so on. They can only be sure of being turned into an image, which from the moment it is taken will be tucked away in a drawer or file in some archive, in some city, somewhere on the face of the Earth.

The photographer makes a living, and in some cases may even become wealthy; the photographer wins fame and prizes, is a member of organizations that defend his or her interests, is protected by publication contracts and agreements. The photographed individual, on the other hand, is abandoned. He or she has no control over the image; in most cases, the individual is unable to determine its composition and the modes of its distribution; like Florence Owens Thompson, he or she receives nothing in return except for being turned into a photograph — no monetary compensation or guarantee. The photographed individual remains entirely outside the economic transaction.

From an early stage of its history, the technology of photography offered itself as a convenient, inexpensive, and easily accessible and operable means of production that anyone could use. In principle, anyone could hold a camera in their hands, giving rise to a situation in which the importance of a photograph is never solely dependent on the specific means of production (high-quality camera versus instant camera), the photographer's professional skills, or his or her artistic talent. The importance of a photograph often transcends all of these qualities and quite possibly stems, in the first place, from the photographed object. In other words, the technology of photography created the relatively simple mobility between the positions of photographer and the photographed. This essential mobility finds no expression in the configuration of their established relationship, which has fixed the asymmetry I have described as the defining model of their relations.

The essential exploitation in the agreement between the photographer — or those for whom he is the agent — and the photographed is even more striking in light of this elimination of any possible reversal of roles. In the framework of this agreement, the photographed individual remains in an exploited position within the exchange — he or she is the one who relinquishes any rights in advance, subordinated to the photographer, who, simply by having the camera, is able to tell those who are photographed how to behave and appear, having the last word regarding the framing that will ultimately be shown to the public. But this description is only partial, at best, for its point of view restricts the contract to what is actually exchanged and recognized as having exchange value in the market.

To understand the nature of the agreement that lies in the background of any concrete photographic encounter, a roundabout path must be taken.

In *Leviathan*, Thomas Hobbes distinguishes between a contract and a compact or covenant in the transmission or exchange of property. In a contract, the right of ownership passes immediately between the signatories; in a compact, however, "one of the Contractors, may deliver the Thing contracted for on his part of the contract, and leave the other to perform his part at some determinate time after, and in the mean time be trusted."[37] A compact, then, is a contract based on mutual trust and an anticipated, future reward. The social contract, says Hobbes, enables human beings to renounce their natural right to defend themselves, meanwhile immediately awarding them security and the defense of their lives. Human beings in fact renounce their right to use force directly and in return enjoy the protection of a governmental power, which guarantees that this renunciation will not result in direct harm to them or to their property. The fear of being killed in the war of all against all and the insecurity that derives from the absence of any authority capable of ensuring that agreements and the fulfillment of promises are upheld lead humans to make the rational choice of constituting a community governed by a sovereign. In the course of constituting the community, each of its members renounces the use of force in favor of a collective power "as may be able to defend them from the invasion of Forraigners, and the injuries of one another, and thereby secure them in such sort, as that by their own industrie, and by the fruites of the Earth, they may nourish themselves and live contentedly." Individuals collectively agree to hand over their right to defend themselves to one person or a congress of persons known as the sovereign, "and every one besides, [is called] his Subject." [38]

According to the story told by Hobbes, along with others in the social-contract tradition, once it was "signed," human beings passed from natural state or patriarchal order to a social state within which a community was constituted on the basis of agreement.[39] The story is usually told and even more often interpreted as a thought experiment or a construct of reason, not as a "real" story about an actual agreement that marks the beginning of political states. It is usually assumed that the contract has such a binding force because human beings are rational creatures, and in the face of fear, they would no doubt have opted for a social contract that extends security to them and improves their condition.

In her critical reading of the various versions of the social contract, Carole Pateman points out that most, if not all presuppose that achieving security and improving the condition of individuals can be accomplished only through the means of sovereign government.[40] The social contract is nothing less than the text that justifies the form of sovereign rule. In Pateman's critique, she points to the way in which the first stage of the contract, which is described as the formation of a political community that establishes an obligation *between* the members of the community at the same time as it places authority in their hands, is rapidly pushed aside in favor of the second stage, which assumes that the members of the community will necessarily alienate their right to exercise political authority by granting it to their representatives, and in effect to sovereign government.

As mentioned before, the status of the civil contract of photography is likewise not that of an actual document, but a tacit agreement. It differs from the Hobbesian account of the contractarian origin of sovereignty, however, in that it echoes the first stage of the social contract, but seeks to differentiate itself by suspending the second stage. The intrinsic assumption behind this move is that photography is one of the only practices by means of which a political community has been formed that is based on a mutual obligation among its members, who hold the power to act in connection with this obligation.

To put it another way, the form that the civil contract of photography takes is the form of mutual obligation that precedes the constitution of political sovereignty. In the social contract as described by Hobbes, each individual renounces the power to defend himself or herself in favor of the sovereign, whether a single person or congress of people. In Rousseau's version of the social contract, the identity of the sovereign is altered, and the people as a whole come to substitute for it. In both cases, all individuals give the sovereign irrevocable power to govern them for the sake of the sovereign ensuring the protection of their lives. The sovereign exercises its governance by means of the monopoly it has on the use of violence to regulate social relations. If a subject should violate the contract and commit violence, the subject against whom this violence has been inflicted has the right to demand the protection of the sovereign and the restoration of order. In other words, the sovereign is the mediator among individuals in the framework of a closed and stable system of power relations arising from the fact that each individual is committed to the same contract vis-à-vis the sovereign.

By contrast, the civil contract of photography organizes political relations in the form of an open and dynamic framework among individuals, without regulation and mediation by a sovereign. Although individuals do indeed renounce their exclusive right to their own image and consent to becoming an image, such renunciation, as I will demonstrate, is not in favor of a sovereign that would have the exclusive power to produce an image out of them.

To illustrate the way in which photography's form of political relations are not organized around a sovereign power, I would like to return to the basic photographic situation. I will do so through a reading of an early photograph of Napoleon III's son taken by the firm of Mayer and Pierson in 1859 (figure 2.2). The photograph shows a boy three or four years old mounted on a pony and completely entranced by the camera. The child is posed in a chair strapped to the horse's saddle. Behind him is a monochromatic background typical of studio photographs of the period. Napoleon III, who recognized the importance and power of photography and had photographs of himself taken regularly, wanted to create a portrait of the imperial prince. In order to obtain it, his son had to go to the photographer's studio — a task he duly performed, accompanied by no less than the sovereign, who took the trouble to accompany him. It is almost certain that Napoleon III helped choose — from the repertoire offered to him by the photographer — the background and accessories used in the creation of his son's portrait. In his mind's eye, he may have pictured his mounted son in an oval or rectangular gold frame. Napoleon chose one of the most prestigious workshops of photographers of Paris and most likely relied on them to execute the portrait as he deemed appropriate. More than giving us a portrait of the imperial prince, the frame left from the ritual of photographing attests to the ritual itself.

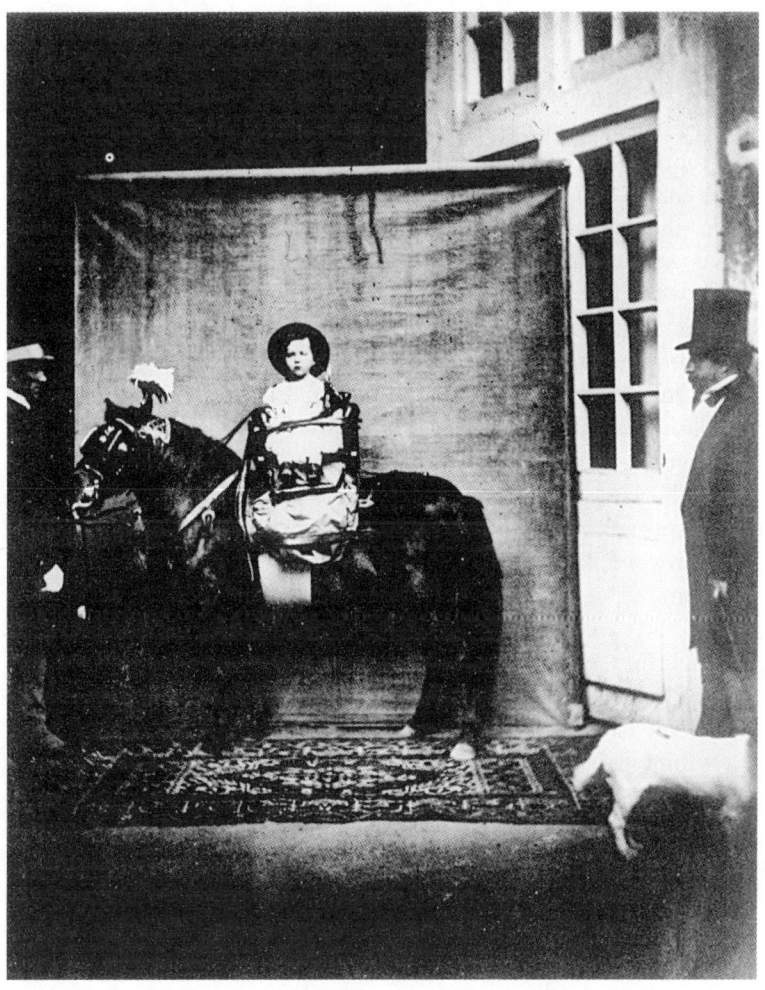

Figure 2.2. Mayer and Pierson, *The Imperial Prince*, circa 1859.

Jean Sagne, who discusses this photograph in "All Kinds of Portraits: The Photographer's Studio," describes the situation laconi-
cally: The emperor "commissioned a photograph of his son, the
imperial prince, on a pony. Quite by accident, the Emperor's profile
was captured on the right side of the negative."[41] Sagne sees nothing
more than a happenstance in the emperor's profile, and his reading
of the photograph thus eliminates, in an instant, the dynamic field of
power relations that the photographic situation portrays. On the one
hand, we have here a sovereign standing on guard, supervising his
son. He did not send one of the servants, but went to the trouble of
going in person to the photographer's studio to oversee the situation. On the other hand, we can discern a figure that is invisible in
the photograph, but that has nonetheless left its imprint; this is the
photographer, making sure that no detail of the photograph will
escape his control, who has been given a golden opportunity to defy
the sovereign, reorganize the frame, and steal Napoleon's image.
What we see, in short, is not Napoleon organizing himself before
the camera and seeking to control his portrait, but a pilfering of his
image.

Standing between the two men is the child. He is completely
subject to these two masters and to the power relations that are at
stake, yet he is the center of the event, the point around which
everything is built, and everyone is there to manufacture his photographic presence. The camera, as well, will get in on the action, participating in the erosion of sovereign authority at the moment of this
photographic encounter. In the margins of the frame, without con-
sulting anyone, the camera has captured the image of an assistant (To
the photographer? To the sovereign?), whose proximity to the boy
belies the fact that he is handling everything close at hand.

The photograph, then, does not exclusively represent the photographer's will and intention, those of Napoleon III, or those of the
photographed boy. In fact, the photograph escapes the authority of
anyone who might claim to be its author, refuting anyone's claim to
sovereignty. The photograph discloses the negotiations among the
parties to the contract — photographer, photographed, camera, and
spectator — as well as what the parties knowingly or unknowingly
achieve, through force, seduction, or even theft.

The meaning of the photographic situation thus cannot be under-stood without attempting to locate the general context of the praxis of photography and its modes of organization in political space. The photographic situation that I have described is one of many, one that exists simultaneously with many others. Photography, we should remember, is foremost a *mass* instrument for the *mass* production of images, which is not susceptible to monopolization.[42] The prolifera-tion of images that photography has facilitated is not simply a matter of quantity, but an essential vector of change in the perceptual matrix. The capacity to look can no longer be seen as a personal property, but is a complex field of relations that originally stem from the fact that photography made available to the individual possibili-ties of seeing more than his or her eye alone could see, in terms of scope, distance, time, speed, quantity, clarity, and so on.

To see more than they could alone, individuals had to align them-selves with other individuals who would agree to share their visual field with one another. Photography reorganized what was acces-sible to the gaze, in the course of which everyone gained the oppor-tunity to see through the gaze of another. In order to create this economy of gazes, each and every one had to renounce his or her right to preserve his or her own, autonomous visual field from exter-nal forces, but also acquired an obligation to defend the gaze in order to make it available for others to enter and intermingle. This was pri-marily the individual's renunciation of ownership of "his" or "her" image or point of view, just as he or she was prepared to give away that image or to become one. Photography, then, broadened the lim-its of the gaze to encompass a mixed economy of gazes that continu-ally flood the visual field with new data. This mass production of images offered to the gaze is not carried out from a centralized loca-tion. It is not synchronized or controlled by a sovereign power. It is performed in different places and by different people who are bound together in civil association on account of photography, but not nec-essarily with any explicit connection on the basis of a nation, race, or gender. With few exceptions, the mass production of images takes place unabated. Photographers turn into photographed individuals, and vice versa.

In exceptional cases, certain state apparatuses are able to suspend photography, typically in restricted areas and for limited periods of time. These are usually local prohibitions related to the declaration of a state of emergency — a state of exception. Such was the case during the early 1970s, when, following an order by Moshe Dayan, Ariel Sharon conducted an operation in the refugees camps in Gaza during which the army destroyed hundreds of houses to clear wide passageways in the densely populated camps, improve surveillance, and prevent clandestine movement of Palestinians through the narrow lanes. No photos from this operation are actually available.[43] Nevertheless, an innocent photograph that Moshe Milner took for the government press office in 1971, in which a young boy with lips tightly closed and a serious, inquisitive look is looking into the camera's lens, as if he wished that his portrait would seem like a portrait of a grown man to justify the issuing of an identity card, is troubling (figure 2.3). It is not troubling for what is seen in it, but rather for what is not seen and perhaps could have been seen in it: a testimony of the events that took place at that time in the refugee camps nearby. Was the photo supposed to show that life goes on as usual and that normal commerce continues, despite the violence and destruction in the camps? Or was it supposed to calm the Israeli public by showing the kind of cameras owned by Palestinians, for such a static, heavy camera would not be able to follow the army and document its action?

Even when such prohibitions pass into law, the ability to enforce them universally is difficult, due to the logic of the technology — its operational facility can be in anyone's hands — and the global travel networks that make it possible to smuggle the camera into areas that are off-limits.[44] There are rare instances that attest to this, when a set of photographs is disclosed from places and situations into which it is hard to imagine a camera could have penetrated. For instance, the four photographs recently discovered that were taken of the gas chambers at Auschwitz.[45]

It is the terms and conditions of the civil contract that explain people's compliance, again and again, in being made the objects of a violent act — photography — without necessarily receiving any immediate reward.[46] The photographer — who is usually on the edge of another, different institution — turns the photographed individual

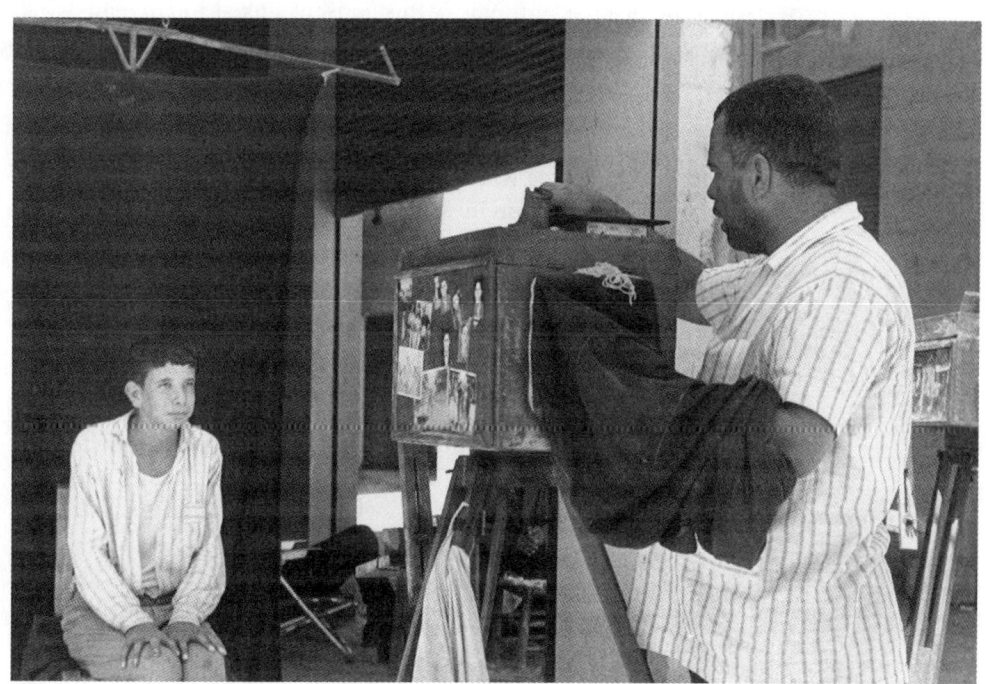

Figure 2.3. Moshe Milner, Government Press Office, Gaza, 1971.

into his or her object, shapes him or her without allowing the individual to have any direct control over the result. The photographer takes the photographed individual's image and appropriates it for himself. The photographed individual's consent has been given in advance — nobody, including the photographed individual himself, expects it to be given again. Nor is this consent linked to any concrete photographer standing and raising a camera in front of the photographed individual. This consent was given in the past, under specific historical conditions, and the continual disregard and forgetting of this consent perpetuates the problematic separation between the photograph as an image with exchange value and photography as the specific political condition in which this image is made.

I do not propose this contract as the outcome of a rational action that brought together people of different social, economic, cultural, and political classes who willingly have consented to an arrangement detrimental to their own interests. On the contrary, I contend that establishing a civil contract of photography was a mission imposed on the users of photography at the same time photography was imposed on them, perpetuating the inequitable division of goods, which blended nicely with the overall logic of the capitalist order. The civil contract of photography was "signed" when the invention spread, becoming readily available, sometime in the second half of the nineteenth century, between the time of the official declaration of the invention of photography (1839) and the invention of the portable and easily-operated camera (1877). Individuals were not asked for their opinions, quickly finding themselves living in a world in which photography began to mediate social relations, just as it was mediated, of course, by them. Despite the economic and class mobilization that photography afforded to some of its operators and users, photography, in most of its public appearances, nonetheless perpetuated the exploitative relations already existing in society.[47]

The initial deployment of photography on the part of the modern state contributed to the perpetuation of the social power relations of power, turning weak, disadvantaged, and marginal populations such as ethnic minorities, criminals, and the insane into utterly exposed objects of photography.[48] These groups served as guinea pigs for the mass utilization of photography by the modern state, which quickly turned the entire population into an object of photography, albeit in conformity with a predefined set of rules — various types of identification cards, personal documents, and so on.[49]

To this day, however, weak populations remain more exposed to photography, especially of the journalistic kind, which coerces and confines them to a passive, unprotected position. In most cases, they are deprived of the ownership of their own images.[50] In some cases, when one of these photographs breaks through the parade of images of its kind — photographs of horror — the symbolic or economic capital that accrues highlights the gap between their exploitation and the enrichment of others "at their expense." But this kind of critical stance still restricts our attitude toward photography to the question of ownership, positing the photographer and the photographed as opposing one another as the only possible owners of the photograph, leaving the citizens of photography in the background, preventing them from appearing as a crucial player in the practice of photography.

By contrast, becoming a citizen in the citizenry of photography entails seeking, by means of photography, to rehabilitate one's citizenship or that of someone else who has been stripped of it. She is someone who sees photography and its civil contract as something that can protect her from anyone who would violate another citizen, which amounts to violating her, insofar as citizenship itself is violated. The citizen — whether she is a photographer or spectator — can demand a role in the deposit, the photographed image, and is thereby a plaintiff, rather than an owner. She is someone who speaks on behalf of the photograph itself. Assuming that any harm to the principle of citizenship is a harm to her own citizenship, she is always already the spokesperson for her own claim as a citizen. As such, she is not reduced to her formal status as citizen. It is by actually practicing her citizenship that she becomes a citizen.[51]

To understand photography in the context of citizenship, and citizenship not merely as a status, but as a praxis of becoming threatened and restricted by the deeds of Man, a return to the 1798 Declaration of the Rights of Man and the Citizen is required. In the previous chapter, I discussed that distinction already made between "man" and "citizen" in its title. One might assume that this distinction was meant to ensure that all human beings would become citizens, but as is well known, not everyone became a citizen. The man of whom the declaration speaks is not the individual in a condition prior to becoming a citizen, but the precise opposite — he is supposed to restrict the dissemination of citizenship as a form of negotiation with power. Man seeks to reduce the citizen to a protector who will safeguard his "natural rights." In other words, man seeks to restrict citizenship to a status, either innate or acquired under stringent conditions, and to limit its content to the protection of his rights. The civil contract of photography, by contrast, affords enough distance to view a different type of relation between human beings, between the governed, in the framework of which the citizen aims to break away from his or her *status* as citizen and *exercise* citizenship — that is, to turn citizenship into the arena of a constant becoming, together with other (non)citizens.

Photography, which was given to the citizen half a century after the writing of the Declaration of the Rights of Man and the Citizen, is an instrument that thwarts the restriction of citizenship to a particular nation-state. Instead, it enables the citizen and the noncitizen (either directly or through the citizen's mediation), as those who are governed, to continue voicing civilian grievances despite the "natural and unalienable rights of man" continuing to be grasped as the reason and condition for citizenship. In other words, these civil grievances are distinct from the natural rights of man and are neither subordinate to these rights nor subordinate to the framework of the nation-state that legitimates them. Moreover, it is this citizenship, which is being trampled by "man" and the nation-state, that is being addressed by those actually practicing citizenship, who seek to rehabilitate and liberate citizenship from its subjection to "man" and his natural rights.

Here photography traps one in its paradox. To give expression to the fact that a photographed person's citizen status is flawed, or even nonexistent (as in the case of refugees, the poor, migrant workers, etc.), or temporarily suspended (citizens struck by disaster, exposed for a limited period of time), whoever seeks to use photography must exploit the photographed individual's vulnerability. In such situations, photography entails a particular kind of violence: The photograph is liable to exploit the photographed individual, aggravate his or her injury, publicly expose it, and rob the individual of intimacy. This threat of violation always hangs over the photographic act, and this is the precise moment in which the contract between photographer, photographed, and spectator is put to the test.

Is there any call to renew or reformulate it? Does the photographer not have a duty toward the photographic image — his or her deposit — even before it has been taken, before it has been deposited? Is the photograph, which now potentially lies in the photographer's camera, not the guarantee given to the photographed person that promises that the photographer will fulfill his or her commitment, even if the photographer might, in the last instance, at the moment of truth, seek to withdraw from it? To add a concrete example to this list of abstract questions, shouldn't the photographer who took the four frames inside the gas chamber at Auschwitz have had to click the camera out of respect for the photographed, who were naked in front of his camera? Should we leave it only to the photographer to confront the paradox of rehabilitation and violation, given the fact that he or she is the one who is "there" with a camera? Is this not a decision that the citizenry of photography agreed on when they acknowledged that they have no right to their own images — when they agreed to deposit the image as certainty of the fulfillment of their commitment, or the photographer's, or the spectators'? Did they not understand that their citizenship is stamped with the seal of photography, as distinctly made manifest by the identification cards we have been given?

Miki Kratsman's 1998 photograph, depicting a body lying exposed on the ground confronts us with these questions (figure 2.4). The body lying on the ground is silent; it is utterly exposed to the photographer who has arrived with his camera and calmly set himself in front of it, using the time at his disposal to compose a dramatic frame. Should the photographer not have taken this picture of the exposed body, abandoned without anyone bothering to cover it, or was it his duty to take the picture, to draw our attention to the length of time that elapsed between the disaster's occurrence and someone going to the trouble of honoring the dead by covering it, as is customary?[52] The laconic caption — *Migrant Worker* — that the

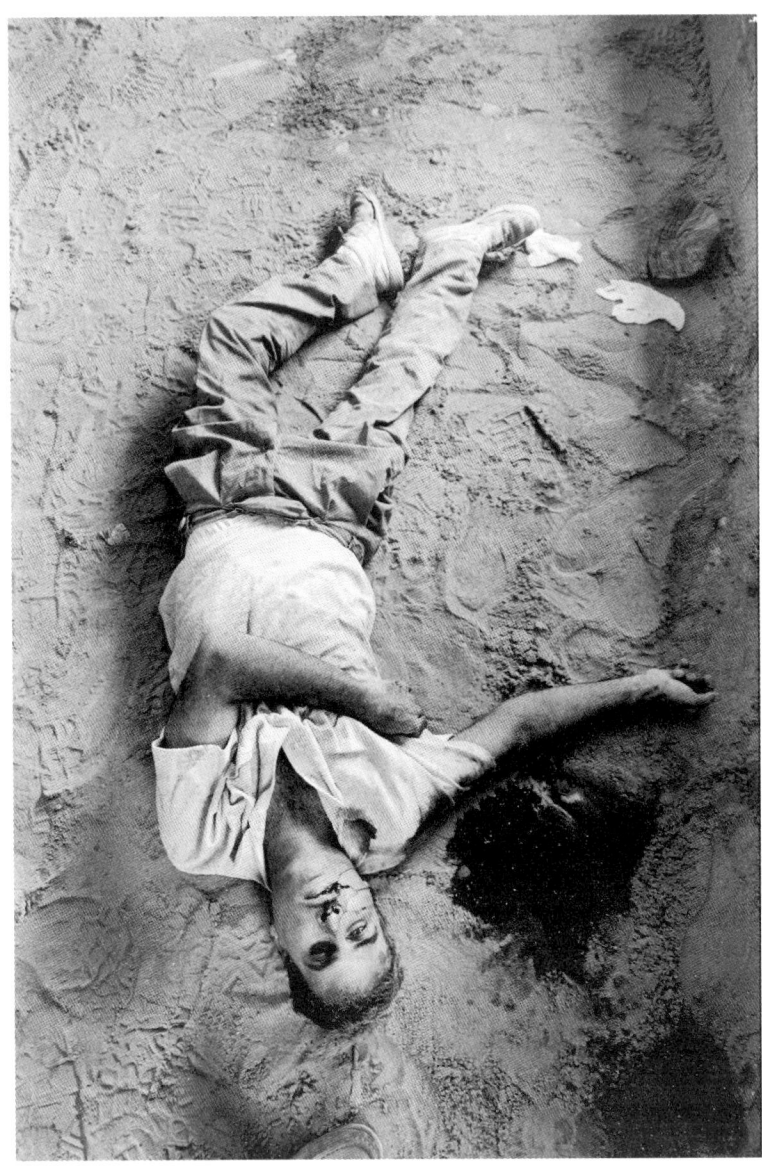

Figure 2.4. Miki Kratsman, *Migrant Worker*, Tel Aviv, 1998.

photographer appended to the photograph when he later exhibited it in a museum has turned the photographer into the bearer of the grievance. This grievance is not that of the photographed person, but of the photographed scene or event: the dispossession of citizenship, which the photographic act has posited itself against, in the manner of Antigone demanding that society allow the dead to be covered, and it has recognized as deserving such a minimum of respect.

Photography, at times, is the only civic refuge at the disposal of those robbed of citizenship. Thus, they incidentally benefit from the fact that citizens have accepted photography as a mediating agent in social relations. To trace how photography is tied to citizenship, we may return to France, in the year 1839. The same country that bestowed the Declaration of the Rights of Man and the Citizen, France, also nationalized the invention of photography in order to bequeath it, without delay, to all of humanity: "We believe we are acting in the spirit of the aspirations of this House [the Chamber of Representatives] in proposing to purchase, in the name of the State, the ownership of such a useful and inspiring invention, and that it seems to us in the interest of the sciences and the arts to bestow it upon the public in general."[53] A reading of the rhetorical gestures of the first proponents of photography demonstrates that they conceived of themselves as emissaries entrusted with the mission of bringing photography to all of humanity, as a gift of universal value with properties that no individual was entitled to hold: the reformative properties of rescue, preservation, and commemoration, as well as those of change and renewal.

Moreover, photography appeared as a new tribunal, a universal and impartial judge that could do justice to the past, present, and future. Its object has impressed an eternal seal — what is seen in it cannot be erased. Photography was depicted as history's representative on Earth, an instrument capable of perpetuating everything that was lost yesterday and of saving what may vanish tomorrow. In addition to being educated to look on photography as an event of importance to all of humanity, modern citizens experience it as events of which they are the direct addressees.[54] Photography has enabled them to participate in events beyond themselves, yet that have no existence without them. Photography has directly interpellated the citizen — he or she can become the bearer of history, both as photographer and as photographed. An unprecedented responsibility has been placed on the individual, who has the potential to preserve what takes place at the heart of the family for the sake of those closest to him or to her, as well as what takes place in public space, for the sake of people he or she doesn't even know. Thrown into the modern world, which took shape in the spirit of the civil revolution that came in the wake of the French Revolution and spread throughout the globe, and of the Industrial Revolution, which was already in full swing, the individual wordlessly consented. The individual simply became both the photographer and photographed.

The photograph, which preserved singular images on paper, was decisive proof for the individual that the proposed civil contract of photography was reliable. Mute at its inception, the photograph maintained its silence. Such silence, which can sometimes scream to the heavens, attests to the fact that it is our historic responsibility not only to produce photos, but to make them speak. Photography granted moderns the opportunity to be naturalized in their world — to know it, investigate it, contemplate it from various angles, bring it closer or distance themselves from it, critique it, and find answers. Since the eighteenth century, the public sphere has not been the sole origin for acquiring civil skills. The world of instruments opened new possibilities for looking and acting, as well for contributing to the shaping of the modern conditions for citizenship.[55] This mass naturalization refashioned the political game, reshuffling the cards in a profound way. The encounter between a public sphere and a new instrumental technology opened unprecedented opportunities both for change to take place within the political sphere and for new forms of exchange to occur within it. The camera opened the possibility of redefining the concept of citizenship and the conditions for its fulfillment.

People deprived of citizenship — women, first and foremost — began to take an active part in this formation of a new world.[56] As soon as the first daguerreotypes were distributed, hundreds of women began using the new technology to produce photographs of the same quality as those produced by men, although their careers did not enjoy the benefit of stability and protection that accompanied men's social and political status.[57] People began enjoying the right "to be included in the film," as Walter Benjamin phrased it.[58] From an opposite perspective, Susan Sontag has defined the introduction of the camera as "the right to something called news."[59] The camera embodied the possibilities available to the modern citizen to take part in the production, investigation, and distribution of what interests the public. These practices — in which the general public could in principle participate, either as active or passive agents (photographer or photographed) — constituted a significant stratum in the new exchange relations formed in the political sphere. In other words, the camera changed the way in which the individual is governed and the extent of his or her participation in the forms of this governance.

Photography, then, was the forerunner of a missed revolution. The body of citizens was given the means to instigate change, but the relations between these citizens were newly regulated through a unified sovereign power, most often on the basis of a national model, in conformity with coercive rules of exclusion, hierarchical order, discrimination, exploitation, and oppression. In the brief interval between the creation of the new political conditions and the exclusion of entire populations from equal partnership in the political game, the modern citizen signed a compact, the civil contract of photography, which the market and the nation-states shared an interest in weakening and even eliminating altogether.

The market and the nation-states had an interest in distributing photography without the contract that had been established with the invention of photography. The regulation of social relations with emphasis on ownership, on the one hand, and on national citizenship, on the other, in effect deprived modern citizens of what the contract had bequeathed to them. The political game in which the contract was involved — a game that cannot be predicated entirely on market logic, governmental power, and the nation-state is perhaps the only one of its kind in which citizens are able to fulfill their membership in a political community in a framework not dictated by a sovereign power, where they are able to act on their own behalf.

The civil contract of photography does not bind the photographed person to the photographer — or to those who might keep the photographer from standing opposite the person. It binds all individuals who take part in photography, both photographers and photographed alike. Every "signatory" to the civil contract has received, in return, the possibility of producing images of the other, that is, of supplementing the inventory of images that he or she can access. Every individual has been given the opportunity to see beyond his or her immediate surroundings and to use the gaze of others on people and places that the individual cannot access or photograph — including the individual himself or herself. The modern citizen has thus renounced the exclusive right to his or her image in favor of an economy of images that, in principle, includes the individual and all others. This consent is conditional on the consent of all others. Within a short time, the individual has been able to obtain photographic evidence of the consent of all these others, irrespective of their class, nationality, or whatever. Those who are enclosed solely in a private sphere are excluded from this game, but this limitation is temporary, for they might (re)appear in the public domain, (re)exposed to photography.[60]

The citizen's renunciation of the exclusive right to possess or distribute his or her photographic images does not mean that the citizen renounces the right to become a photographed image. It can be expected that the former renunciation would help produce one's images when one needs them, for example, when one considers what happens to a person as a matter of public concern. This is not simply a one-time agreement given to a particular photographer at the moment of an encounter, but is in principle a renunciation performed only once by each citizen, linking them all in the contract.

In *The Sexual Contract*, Pateman discusses contracts that concern not regular property but property in person — as in the cases of the marriage contract, employment contract, or prostitution contract. Irrespective of the eventual generosity of such contracts, in everything relating to the compensation given to the person whose body becomes property, they do not eliminate the fact that one side of the contract has the authority to dictate to the other side everything concerned with their bodies. Pateman contends that all of these contracts exist under the auspices of the "original" contract — the social contract — in the framework of which obedience is portrayed as free will. The act of photographing confronts us with the contract latent within it, an unusual type of contract in which what is at issue is also property in person. The act of photographing can take place within a broad spectrum of agreements, ranging from an absence of any explicit formulation of the principles of exchange (snapshot photography, for example), through hasty consent as to the nature of the engagement (a photographic studio), to a detailed contract in which the form and character of the exchange are described, including sanctions stipulated in the event of any noncompliance with the contract (fashion photography). Whatever the case, if there is a contract it refers only to the act of photographing. The civil contract of photography, however, which serves as a contractual framework for the regulation of photography's relations, refers to the different uses of photography, which includes spectatorship, and recontextualizes each of these concrete contracts, which could have threatened to impose on photography stable relations of exploitation and control.

Photography is one of the instruments which has enabled the modern citizen to establish her liberal rights, including freedom of movement and of information, as well as her right to take photographs and to be photographed, to see what others see and would like to show through photographs. Photography has become a means of viewing the world, and the citizen has become a well-trained spectator, capable of reading what is visible in photographs. With photography, the modern citizen found herself in a situation in which she was not previously familiar. On the one hand, she had been given strong and powerful tools — the production of images of herself and others, and the right to see and interpret what was disclosed in these photographs. On the other hand, as an individual the citizen felt cheated: "I'm tired of being a symbol of human misery, moreover my living conditions have improved," complained Florence Thompson, when *her* image as the *Migrant Mother* reappeared hundreds of times in the press decades after the photograph was taken.[61]

Despite the equality of means that are held in principle, "others" — institutional bodies, the rich and powerful, etc. — still have the ability to exercise these means in a discriminatory, and even oppressive manner. In other words, the gap between the power granted to the individual and the possibilities of personally exercising it has become even more glaring. She will be able to fully exercise her power — not merely symbolically, as one who is in principle the owner of the new technological instrument — only by means of a civil contract, which makes it possible to turn the mutual agreement to become an image into a way of securing a mutual guarantee. As stated above, this compliance to become an image was neither protected nor limited to the sovereign, but given to anyone and everyone. The mutual guarantee is supposed to ensure protection for the individual when her entitlement to become an image is threatened, or when her becoming an image is taken to an extreme that threatens to turn her into *only* an image. The mutual guarantee established amongst the citizens of the citizenry of photography is the basis for the formation of a political community that is not subjected or mediated by a sovereign.

This is not simply a mutual guarantee between individuals, but a mutual guarantee linked to the medium of photography and predicated on a mutual consent regarding the truth value of photography, the fact that what we find in it really "was there," in the words of Roland Barthes. In *Camera Lucida* and in his lectures, Barthes attempted to grasp the essence of photography, in its specificity as a medium. This formulation, which has since become classic, fails to exhaust the essence of photography, as Barthes wished, but undoubtedly offers a precise description of the social attitude toward photography. Barthes' expression, which he arrived at one hundred and fifty years after the invention of photography, succinctly captures the particular characteristic of the photographic medium, as it is grasped by the users of photography since its invention. Without understanding the civilian context of the medium, in addition to Barthes' definition, it is impossible to understand the institutionalization of photography as a medium of truth which attests to what "was there."

Critical discussions seeking to challenge the truth of photography, or argue that "photography lies," remain anecdotal and marginal to the institutionalized practices of exhibiting and publishing photographs. Only a glance at a newspaper kiosk is needed to realize the enduring power of the news photo. Photography's critics tend to forget that despite the fact that photography speaks falsely, it *also* speaks the truth. A photograph does in fact attest to what "was there," although its evidence is partial, and only in this sense is it false. What was there is *never* only what is visible in the photograph, but is also contained in the very photographic situation, in which photographer and photographed interact around a camera. That is, a photograph is evidence of the social relations which made it possible, and these cannot be removed from the visible "sense" that it discloses to spectators who can agree or disagree on its actual content. The social relation that "was there," to which a photograph attests, is an expression of a mutual guarantee, or its infringement. Either way, the realization of the contract is not something only subsisting in the photographic act, between photographer and photographed, but draws most of its strength and validity from the very fact that it is inexhaustible and does not flow merely in expected directions. Even if it appears, at a certain time and place, that an individual or group is capable of destroying the civil contract of photography, along with the citizens of the citizenry of photography, the contract itself surprisingly reclaims its place through the efforts of some of its numerous trustees. There is nothing inherent to the technology of photography that creates discriminatory or oppressive situations for different populations, and in the same way it cannot erect a barrier against movements between different positions in social reality. The most prestigious photographer, for example, might be caught in a disaster area, and turned into a passive photographed individual, whereas someone in the position of a photographed individual at the mercy of others can turn into an important photographer, having the power to provide visual evidence of events.[62] The mutual guarantee that is derived from the essential equality among the citizenry of photography — even if some are currently being recognized as full citizens of the states in which they live, and others are not — organizes social relations without the mediation of a sovereign, the place of the sovereign overtaken by the consensual social attitude toward the truth in photography.

Citizenship beyond Sovereignty: Toward an Ethics of the Spectator

The industrialization and dissemination of photography near the middle of the nineteenth century created a new citizenry — the citizenry of photography — whose citizens were equipped with the necessary tools for producing photographs, interpreting them, and acting on what they disclose. Although given to the modern citizen as another means of becoming a citizen in the nation-state, photography provided the possibility of becoming a citizen in this new citizenry of photography. Whereas the nation-state is based on the principles of sovereignty and territorialization, the citizenry of photography, of which the civil contract of photography is the constitutional foundation, is based on an ethical duty, and on patterns of deterritorialization. In principle, photography is an instrument given to everyone, making it possible to deterritorialize physical borders and redefine limits, communities, and places (processes of reterritorialization).[63] The citizenry of photography is a simulation of a collective to which all citizens belong. Neither taking precedence over citizenship or making it conditional, the citizenry of photography is fundamentally and solely defined by citizenship: Membership in the citizenry means citizenship, and citizenship means membership in the citizenry. The citizenry of photography has no sovereign and therefore no apparatus of exclusion. Each and every one is, in principle, a member of the collective. Membership in the collective is based on each one's renunciation of exclusive ownership of his or her image and on each one's willingness and right to be photographed and become a photograph.

The fact that the civil contract has only now been explicitly formulated does not contradict the fact that it exists and has existed as long as photography itself. That I am presently able to formulate its conditions rests on the abundant evidence we have of their existence. As early as the 1840s, the photographers David Octavius Hill and Richard Adamson, in tandem with their photographed subjects, saw photography as an instrument that establishes, on the ad hoc basis of each photograph, a universal tribunal that goes beyond local interests to see clearly what photography has to show.

These two men went to take photographs of the fishermen and fisherwomen of New Haven in an attempt to assist them at a time when their fisheries were failing. The gathering of photographers and the photographed around the camera was not contingent on a pragmatic answer to the question of whether photography could help them. Instead, it was motivated by the scopic regime that photography established — a photograph produced in the course of an encounter between photographer and photographed is created and inspired by a relation to an external eye, the eye of the spectator. It is not the same eye that is present in the situation, but one for the sake of which the photographed is willing to be photographed and the photographer is willing to take photographs: "She looked as if she knew my photographs might help her, so she helped me. There was a kind of equality between us," wrote Dorothea Lange in her diary about Florence Thompson.[64]

This spectator's eye deterritorializes photography, transforming it from a simple, convenient, efficient, (relatively) inexpensive and easily operable tool for the production of pictures into a social, cultural, and political instrument of immense power. The gap between these two dimensions of photography is newly expressed in each photographic act, summoning a supplementary eye, or at least alluding to the existence of an empty place, a potential place that enables the act of photography to occur while the participants acknowledge that they are not alone in front of the other. Photography thus enables its users to produce images that go beyond the simple technical actions required to produce them, attaining something that transcends the here and now. The reason they enjoy such a status is due to the fact that as soon as they have appeared in the world, it is impossible to dismiss them. Their presence cannot be subsumed under the reign of a higher authority. They are independent. The limits of their interpretation are not determined in advance and are always open to negotiation. They are not restricted to the intentions of those who would claim to be their authors or of those who participate in their production.

This particular characteristic of photographs tends to mislead the spectators who view them. A newspaper editor, for example, will add laconic captions to photographs, as if a denotative relation had been established between them. Such denotative relations assume that what is visible in the photograph exists there — somewhere —

awaiting the precise verbal formulation that would make it a proper object. However, contrary to what Susan Sontag has claimed in her own writings on photography, the transcendent status of photographs does not require what is visible in them to be given or assumed intrinsically to have a "grammar" of its own.[65] Although they write on the social context of photography, both Sontag and Barthes preserve the notion of a stable meaning for what is visible in the photograph and reduce the role of the spectator to the act of judgment, eliminating his or her responsibility for what is seen in the photograph. That judgment assumes a passive attitude toward the image and is primarily interested in questioning the extent to which the photograph succeeds in arousing a desired effect or experience. Sontag focuses on the photographer and sees him or her as responsible both for the photograph and for the fact that the photographed is represented one way and not another or conveys one experience rather than another. "Moralists who love photographs" writes Sontag not without a small measure of contempt, "always hope that words will save the picture."[66] According to Sontag, the picture's fate as good or bad is sealed as soon as it is printed on photographic paper. Any attempt to start speaking for the photo is akin to an effort to revive the dead. Her "ethics of seeing" is based on an aesthetic judgment and gives no attention to the civil contract of photography. It turns photographs into works of art that can be judged. Her ethics of seeing, in effect, reifies the new visual field created with the appearance of photography, leaving the photograph in possession of a special "grammar" that allows it to remain independent of its spectator.

The civil contract of photography shifts the focus away from the ethics of seeing or viewing to an ethics of the spectator, an ethics that begins to sketch the contours of the spectator's responsibility toward what is visible. The individual is not confined to being posited as the photograph's passive addressee, but has the possibility of *positing herself* as the photograph's addressee and by means of this address is capable of becoming a citizen in the citizenry of photography by making herself appear in public, coming before the public, and entering a dialogue with it by means of photographs, which, despite their power are often both silent and silenced.

Once photographs are spoken of, however, they are spoken of among many, in regard to many, and obtain the power to remind citizens that what brings them together, what motivates them to look at photographs, is the common interest, the *res publica*. In an era when speaking in terms of the *res publica* is becoming more and more rare,[67] photography is one remaining site, a place of refuge, from which the discourse on the *res publica* may be revived. Neither a local, sectarian, or national politics nor a politics of identity, photography remains part of the *res publica* of the citizenry and is or can become one of the last lines of defense in the battle over citizenship for those who still see citizenship as something worth fighting for.

This struggle links those who have citizenship and those who are threatened by the denial of citizenship or expropriation of the rights of others with those who have been robbed or denied citizenship, for whom photography and the citizenry of photography are often their first chance to become citizens despite being stateless.[68] In the Israeli context, for instance, the Palestinians became citizens of the citizenry of photography long before there was any possibility of their becoming citizens in the ordinary meaning of the word. The Palestinians are at one and the same time citizens of photography's global citizenry and noncitizens of the state that governs them. Photography enables them — along with many others — to make politically present the ways in which they have been dominated, making visible the more and less hidden modes in which they are exposed to Israeli power. Without the spectator participating in the reconstruction of the photographic *énoncé*, the harm to citizenship will not be perceived. Photography does not put an end to their position as noncitizen, but it does enable them and others who take part in the reconstruction of their civil grievances to exercise the legitimate violence of photography's citizens, regardless of their status as noncitizens deprived of rights who cannot use their citizenship to negotiate with the sovereign power.

Photography thus has formed a citizenry, a citizenry without sovereignty, without place or borders, without language or unity, having a heterogeneous history, a common praxis, inclusive citizenship, and a unified interest. The citizenry of photography is a global form of relation that is not subject to national regimes, despite existing within their borders, and that is not entirely obedient to global logic, even as it enjoys the channels of exchange and association the latter creates. Photography is a means of employing legitimate violence that is — or, in principle, that can be — in the hands of all of the members of the citizenry of photography, whether or not they are citizens of the space they inhabit. In the citizenry of photography, citizenship is rehabilitated and regains its essence. Not all of its citizens necessarily give active expression to their citizenship, and only a few have ever given their explicit consent to take part. However, even those who explicitly attempt to position themselves outside its bounds, or those who have never encountered a camera, are indeed a part of it.

In the ethics that photography requires of those who view photographs, it requests that its citizens — who are equally *not* governed in the citizenry of photography — not only try to avoid situations of degeneration into which the nation-state and the market often sink, but actively to resist them. For the citizen of photography, national citizenship is not the ultimate realization of citizenship and does not see property and ownership as the principle achievements of human existence.

Instead, photography, while personal, is a mobile and global recording kit for contesting injuries to citizenship. Official UN data estimates the existence of 175 million noncitizens worldwide. This figure does not take into account the millions who, despite being officially granted citizen rights, are far from able to assume their citizen status. Photography can be put forward and read as a nonmediated complaint attesting to situations in which citizenship has been violated. Simply flip through any history book from the last hundred years, any NGO pamphlet, any publication written by a human-rights or civil-rights group, or any humanitarian organization report, and you will see that photography marks the beginning of a demand to become citizens, even when that demand is hidden behind a demand for the protection of human rights. These collections of photograph-complaints would be worthless, however, if it were not for the citizenry of photography and its citizens who produce these photographs-complaints, as photographers or as spectators. When a photograph turns into a grievance, whoever articulates it becomes its civic subject.

Often, photography has been used, in one way or another, by the sovereign power. Photographers were rapidly integrated into routine tasks, ongoing documentation, the collection, classification, and storage of data, the use of data to enforce the law, and other governmental duties. Disciplinary and closed sites, in Foucault's terms, proved to be ideal places for the installation and regular employment of cameras.[69] Supervision and control, refinement and improvement, study and research — these have been the motivating goals behind camera operators and those who command them, even when they are themselves the ones exposed to the cameras.[70] Yet the formulation of these objectives, even in the form of written declarations, has not prevented the creation of a gap between the stated aims and what has actually taken place in the encounter between photographer, photographed and camera. Every photograph is a living testimony to this gap, even if some photographs may still lack an ethical spectator to notice them. In many instances, this gap is the place from which the spectator can become a citizen of photography, making it possible for the photographer or photographed to become a citizen, as well.

Photography plays a crucial role in the civilian status of its users, from their subordination to sovereign power to practices of civilianization that limit the control of this sovereign power.[71] Nonetheless, photography is rarely the object of legislation, nor does the state regulate its usage. The state's renunciation of any crucial governmental role regarding photography effectively abandoned photography to the logic of the market, and the governmental vacuum was filled with the technical jargon of capabilities and possibilities, and the language of neutrality and precision. Thus, the course of photography, which has been marked by different kinds of inventions, was confined to the framework of the market and determined according to public demand. Yet as in other fields, so, too, in photography, the course of development was dictated both by the resources of the state, which indirectly channeled photographic inventions into the fields of warfare, espionage, and supervision, as well as by the money of the masses, whose purchasing power led to the development of mobile, user-friendly cameras. Thus, for instance, the development of night-vision and aerial photography contributed to the process of restricting accessibility to photography almost to the point of monopolizing it (as in the case, for instance, of satellite photography), whereas the development of prepackaged film or the mobile automatic camera contributed to its popularization.

Even though photography was a French invention, it was anchored in a contract that was not limited to a particular nation.[72] Against the political order of the nation-state, photography — together with other media that created the conditions for globalization — paved the way for a universal citizenship: not a state, but a citizenry, a virtual citizenry, in potential, with the civil contract of photography as its organizing framework. Citizenship in the citizenry of photography asks not to be stopped at borders and plays a vital political role in making sure other cultures are accessible, in all of their prestige or misery, deeming local cultures to be worthy of documentation and public display. Photography, being in principle accessible to all, bestows universal citizenship on a new citizenry whose citizens produce, distribute, and look at images.

This citizenship, in principle, issues actual and virtual transit visas to all, allowing everyone to see, show, and be seen — though it is subject, of course, to supply and demand. The citizen of the citizenry of photography may move as she pleases in the visual field created by photography. It is part of the contract to which she's a signatory, a contract that, like any constitutive agreement, supposes a primal beginning and moment of creation, a moment of transition from a state of presence to a state of re-presence, re-presentation, a visual representation. This agreement — although it seems to produce a moment of unity, an unrealistic instant in which all citizens could be represented as if they were full partners in formulating the contract — collapses in the face of the structure of the camera, since its limitations are exposed. If this contract has any representation beyond the imaginary realm that this book seeks to give it, such a depiction exists in the entire body of photographs from which it was extracted.

From an instrument once recognized by the French state as having the power to fuel a revolution on the scale of the French Revolution, photography was reduced to merely its technical components. To this day, it has almost always been employed without any prior and systematic study of its legal, cultural, political, and moral ramifications or of the effects stemming from its omnipresence.[73] Photography has been naturalized as a disciplinary medium to such a degree that its very use appears to have been universally agreed on, avoiding not only any discussion of its procedures or mechanisms, but of the mode in which these have been adopted, as though they were common to all people who employ photography.[74]

Given this governmental vacuum, the civil contract of photography has a crucial role. It can serve as a regulative power, accounting for the different uses of photography, its modes of production and distribution, the exchange relations that are involved, its mechanisms of interpretation and authorization, its patterns of acceptance, as well as its public or juridical standing.

The exercise of that regulative power is the duty first and foremost of the spectator, and it is to the ethics of the spectator that I now turn.

CHAPTER THREE

The Spectator Is Called to Take Part

Photographs are present in our world as objects, products of work, even though photography ontologically resembles action more than work. That is because work, according to Hannah Arendt, is characterized by a clearly demarcated beginning and a predictable end. The products of work, although destructible, create the world within which we dwell. Some might say that the gesture of taking up a camera and pointing the lens toward someone or something may be described as the moment when photography begins and a photograph is produced, while the printed or computerized image may be perceived as the moment of completion of this work. But those who have engaged with photography know very well that this moment of the photographic act, which is said to reach its end when incarnated in a final product, a print or digital file, is in fact a new beginning that lacks any predictable end.

This is the precise definition of action that Arendt gives in order to distinguish it from work and labor. Even when a spectator merely glances at a photograph without paying special attention to what appears in it, the photo rarely appears to the gaze as a mere object.[1] The photo acts, thus making others act. The ways in which its action yields others' action, however, is unpredictable. In addition to noting this indeterminacy, which is oriented toward the future, Arendt describes action in terms of overdetermination when she contends that action is irreversible. The deed cannot be undone. Photography is bound to this description: The image inscribed within it cannot be undone. But as Arendt further argues, the action depends on others' actions, and as a result of this plurality, it will never reach its goal. On account of this plurality, the overdetermination of action should be reconsidered.

Photography as Civil Action

A diagram of a photograph might be of help here. Two armed soldiers stand behind the dead body of a Palestinian (figure 3.1).[2] They are posing for a photo being taken by another soldier, preparing a souvenir to take back home. Their action is irreversible — it is inscribed in the photograph forever. Only a few yards from where they stand, however, outside their visual field, is another photographer. Although they probably could not glimpse his presence, their action is entangled in this photographer's action and is thus prevented from attaining its end. Even if the three soldiers travel home with their desired photo still hidden in their camera, the action of the other photographer, who shot the photograph we are now viewing, will have caused their action to deviate from its path.

If the action's sense is articulated only through a subsequent action in which it comes about and is potentially completed by others, we should ask what is irreversible in the action.[3] The action's sense is never in the action itself. It can take many different, even contradictory paths, depending on the next *énoncé*, which will determine how the action will be articulated through the determination of one out of many senses and directions. What is irreversible in the action is this node or conjunction of potential plural senses.[4] As Arendt claims, no one can destroy or undo her own action, even if one does not like the action or its possible results. This is why, for Arendt, forgiveness is the only action that can relieve a person from the irreversibility of her action. If we focus only on this node as the kernel of irreversibility, what is revealed is the fact that the entanglement of actions in others' actions constantly pulls the initial actions away from what might be perceived as their irreversible results.

Let's return to the photograph. Shuttered shops can be seen in the background. The soldiers are wearing uniforms and helmets, armed with submachine guns in the manner of soldiers on a combat mission. But in the photograph, they look relaxed, as if they have completed most of their work and can now unwind to pose for a pic-

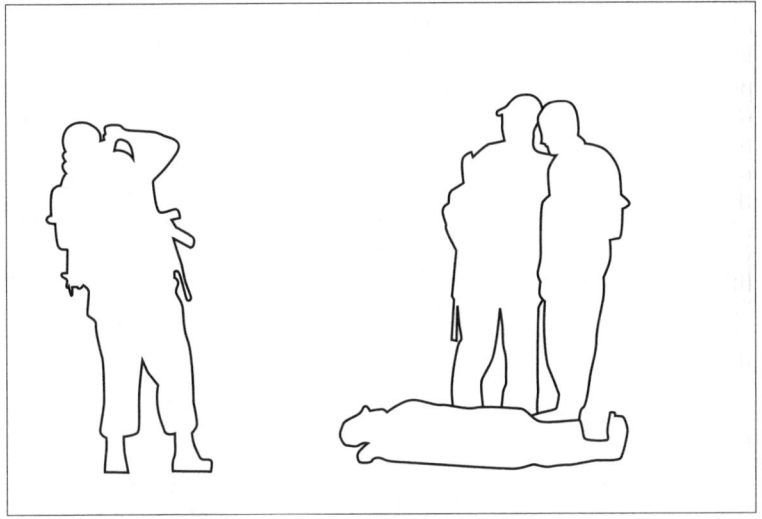

Figure 3.1. Based on a photo by Yariv Katz which was taken at Baqa Al Sharquia in 2002 and is now shown on the Web site: http://commondreams.org/headlines02/0224-04.htm (last accessed on March 20, 2008).

ture to commemorate the day's victory. Each soldier brandishes his rifle with one arm, pointing it at the corpse of the Palestinian lying on the ground. One of the soldiers appears unable to tear his eyes away from the body lying at his feet; the other gazes directly at the camera. Both soldiers are laughing. One laughs as he looks at the body, as if to say, "Look at that!" The other soldier is smiling, as if preparing himself to be photographed, and trying to look his best. He may be recalling that years ago, he was taught to smile when having his picture taken, otherwise the photo might look stiff or frozen. From his perspective, the situation seems appropriate for picture taking and an occasion to smile. The soldiers' laughter would presumably have been erased from the photograph if the presence of a "foreign" photographer — foreign, that is, to the masters of the land — had penetrated the purified space in which they were freely and happily posing for pictures. This laughter, even if involuntarily uttered, is addressed to the soldier who is taking their picture, a photographer of whose presence they are fully aware. It is laughter that

139

assumes a partnership, displaying a total insensitivity toward anyone who is not part of that partnership. The camera that the soldier levels his gaze on is not that of the photographer from whose position we now view the photograph. It is rather the camera held by the third soldier within the photograph, the one who is taking his friends' picture, whom we, as spectators, see from behind. This photographer, the soldier with his back turned toward us, is unaware of the presence of those watching him — first and foremost that of the other photographer, Yariv Katz, taking his picture. The soldier-photographer himself does not focus on the other two soldiers, because his camera is aimed beyond them, as though he were saying to them "Be patient with me; the dead man isn't going anywhere" while he chooses to take pictures first of some Arabic inscription or graffiti on the wall.

The soldier who is staring at him appears insistent. He is determined to have his picture taken with the body of the Palestinian, having assumed that his comrade, the photographer — the soldier taking the picture — wouldn't want to miss this opportunity to take such a picture. Most likely, he is not mistaken, and it is highly probable that their picture with the body was in fact taken. There is no need to see the picture they have taken in order to discern the tacit agreement between the three soldiers that there is no dimension of urgency in regard to the dead person beside them. The dead body lying at their feet can be seen as a silent testimony to this fact. It is covered with a military blanket, its bare feet protruding from one end of the blanket and the head protruding from the other. If it were completely covered, the soldiers themselves, or perhaps some of the viewers they imagined when they gathered around the body, might not have been convinced that they actually took a picture with a dead body. This attention to detail is also visible in the positioning of the shoes that have been taken off the body. Even if, for some reason, their friend actually had failed to press the camera button and had failed to produce the picture they had hoped for, this wouldn't in any way cancel out what is visible in the photograph before us — that is, the soldiers' preparation to secure a souvenir or trophy photo with a dead body. It seems more likely to assume, though, that a few moments later, their soldier-photographer friend finished the aimless photos he was busy with and turned his attention to his two friends. It is evident that in his view, too, nothing seemed urgent except the collection of trophies of the kind that enable soldiers to run their gaze over the governed person's full submissiveness and to mark, like a chasm separating them, that this dead person is of no importance — he is not "one of them." And yet, staking their claim through the act of photography, this dead person is "theirs," and they are entitled to decorate themselves with his death.

The Palestinian in the photograph is dead. He can no longer act. It is impossible to comprehend what it is that that allows the display of this indifference in broad daylight unless one studies the background of the photo. Just a few meters away from the dead Palestinian, hundreds of thousands of Palestinians are imprisoned in their homes under orders that prohibit them from approaching the dead person, from covering him properly, from paying their last respects and burying him in the ground. We do not know whether it is a curfew order, full or partial, that prevents them from approaching the dead, or if there are other orders from the penal colony. One way or another, they are the present absentees of this photograph. They are not imprisoned in jails — they are sitting behind shuttered shops a few yards away, hidden on the roofs of surrounding buildings, locked in rooms, confined to their homes, or simply expelled from the arena, fully aware that no one will take care of their dead. Their space of living is strictly controlled by the Israeli Army.

The space of plurality, which is the necessary condition for any action in Arendt's sense, is forbidden to the noncitizens. Once excluded from citizenship, their access to the space of action has been restricted. Many channels for negotiation have been blocked from them, and only occasionally can their action take place in a space of plurality, or in what Arendt has called "the space of appearance." When the three soldiers transformed the dead Palestinian into a mere decoration in the background of their photograph, they intensified the Palestinians' condition as noncitizens.

In so doing, the soldiers unintentionally expressed a flaw in their own citizenship whereby their action lost the space of plurality and became a uniform action. The photographer who found a gap in the curfew and pointed his camera toward the soldiers, deviating the sense and direction of their action, thus restored the conditions of plurality to the space of action. Although plurality cannot erase structural inequalities and discrepancies between the different protagonists, the space of plurality undermines the apparently stable conditions of domination.

In the situation exemplified by this photograph, the game of negotiation over the distinction between what is just and what is unjust, what is correct and what is incorrect, thus has, once again, begun. The game has only partially opened up, as stated above, since the Palestinians are noncitizens, and, as such, they are excluded from taking part in the political game in which this negotiation takes place. Palestinians participate only at the margins of this game, through alternative channels where they can impose themselves as players.

Although Jean-François Lyotard names this game where the just and unjust are objects for negotiation the "pragmatics of obligation," the civil dimension of photography challenges Lyotard's claims about the nature and structure of this negotiation. According to Lyotard, in this game of prescriptions, orders, and obligations, the addresser's position remains hidden: "One does not know who is speaking, and one does not know why what is said is said." Consequently, he argues, "to understand what a prescription or an obligation, the pole [instance] of the sender [addresser] must be neutralized. Only if it is neutralized, will one become sensitive, not to what it is, not to the reason why it says what it says, not even to what it says, but to the fact that it prescribes or obligates."[5] The addresser of the prescription, the commanding other, has a transcendent character, though only if "the transcendence is empty."[6] Obligation cannot originate in someone's address, and, whatever the case may be, no one has the authority to address an obligation.[7] The addressee has a considerable responsibility: "for us, a language is first and foremost someone talking. But there are language games in which the important thing is to listen, in which the rule deals with audition. Such a game is the game of the just. And in this game, one speaks as one listens."[8]

However, when cameras are in the hands of so many, new modes of questioning and arguing over how citizens coexist and how they are governed are available. From the moment when photography became a tool available to the masses, a new form of civil relations was enacted that was not mediated by sovereign power. Whether one occupies the position of the addresser of a photograph or its addressee, one is always, at the same time, a citizen. Even if one is a noncitizen in the state where one is governed, in the citizenry of photography, one is a citizen. Under these conditions, by neutralizing the pole of the addresser and preserving the "transcendent character of the other," one actually intensifies the harm done to the addresser.

By contrast, when an injured person tries to address others through a photograph, she is becoming a citizen in the citizenry of photography. We can illustrate this by looking at a few photographs from the Occupied Territories. These photographs show Palestinians receiving medical care under unbearable conditions (see figure 1.1), a crowd of workers waiting at the checkpoint for hours (see figures 4.2 and 4.3) or the photo of the two women whose babies died at the checkpoints (the photo of Chaira Abu-Hassen and Amia Zakin, see figure 7.1). In each of these photographs, I can read the consent of those who are photographed. They are ready to take the first step of making a civil address: the presentation of a grievance. *Over there, within the photo, someone addresses me; she claims my civil gaze, struggles for her citizenship in the world of photography, and puts my own citizenship in the state into question.* A photograph is an *énoncé* within the pragmatics of obligation. It commands the restoration of the addresser's position — as the governed and as a citizen under the civil contract of photography — whenever this position is endangered or harmed.

No special talent is required in order to listen to an injury claim. The traces of the injury are imprinted on the surface of the photographic image, awaiting a spectator to assist them. An addresser initiated the restoration of the conditions of visibility through the reconstruction of the four elements of the photographic *énoncé*: addresser, addressee, referent, and meaning. The spectator is called to take part in this restoration. She is not expected to complete the job. The photograph she faces testifies that *an* addressee has already taken part in the restoration of civil conditions. Since photography is always an action taken in the plural, no one can be the author of the photograph: "as nobody does [the action], it is not done."[9] In order to participate, to take part, the spectator, too, should become a citizen of photography.

The photograph is sealed by the injury, which it frames as an object of intervention. Within a new framework of time and space, the photograph creates new conditions for moral action.[10] These conditions differ from their predecessors in that the "here and now" no longer serves as the sole organizing framework of moral action, which thus allows for new objects to appear.[11] Photography is one means for the deterritorialization of national boundaries: in the modern era, the spectator can be anywhere at any time. At the time and place of the photographic act, a spectator has the power to translate her gaze into action — whether as a photographer, as one of the various agents who have commissioned the photograph, as a member of the public who demands to see by sending the photographer as proxy, and even after the fact, in some other place. The citizen of photography enjoys the right to see because she has a responsibility toward what she sees. Never before has there been such a responsibility of such a dimension, directed toward all of the potential citizens of the citizenry of photography. Once the modern citizen had in her possession the modern technology capable of documenting the horrors perpetrated throughout the world, she found herself sharing with others the responsibility toward the photographed.[12]

In *The Imperative of Responsibility*, Hans Jonas asserts that the concept of responsibility emerged with modern technology. The latter gave rise to the conditions for turning the Kantian imperative from "you can because you must" into "you must because you can."[13] Every citizen in the citizenry of photography has equal rights, but photography continues to testify to the enormous inequality that reigns outside. This inequality among equals imposes a common, though not equal, burden of responsibility on the shoulders of all citizens of photography.

Observing, once again, the scene depicted within the photograph of the soldiers posing over the body of the dead Palestinian, one may track down the soldiers' behavior. Excluding the Palestinian from having citizenship in the state where he was governed is perceived by the soldiers as all-out permission to exclude him from the sphere of civil action altogether — which means exclusion from citizenship in the citizenry of photography. In the citizenry of photography, despite behaving as if they were masters of the Earth, these soldiers are not given preferential treatment, and the very photograph in which they manifestly have assumed the dead Palestinian to have been excluded from the sphere of civil action is their writ of indictment. Their photograph of themselves with the body was presumably distributed among friends, for whom the dead Palestinian was merely a laughing matter. Among the soldiers' audience, no one was called by the photograph to testify to the civil status of the photographed.

A citizen of photography, however, would take part in the restoration of the photographic *énoncé* and its transformation into an emergency claim. The photo taken by the soldier — from which we can view, through another photograph, only the action of its being taken — was never distributed. Its end is unknown, but only several yards away from the soldiers stood another photographer who watched what was happening and thought it was proper to record it: not a photograph of soldiers next to a body, but of soldiers having their picture taken with a body. This is the photograph we are looking at now. It is a photograph whose addresser, the other photographer, used the civil contract of photography in order to protect the photographed dead Palestinian from the omnipotence of the soldiers, who thought they could do as they pleased within the citizenry of photography.

The Conquest of the World as Picture

Shortly after photography's appearance, the process of what Martin Heidegger called "conquering the world as picture"[14] commenced. In the modern technological era, "We are in the picture," Heidegger wrote:

> "Picture" here does not mean some imitation, but rather what sounds forth in the colloquial expression "We get the picture" [literally, we are in the picture] concerning something. . . . "To get into the picture" [literally, to put oneself into the picture] with respect to something means to set whatever it is, itself, in place before oneself just in the way that it stands with it, and so to have it fixedly before oneself as set up in this way.

Thus, "'to get the picture' throbs with being acquainted with something, with being equipped and prepared for it.... Hence, world picture, when understood essentially, does not mean a picture of the world but the world conceived and grasped as picture."[15]

In this era, photography became a prime mediator in the social and political relations between citizens, as well as the relations between citizens and the powers that be.[16] We thus live in an era in which it's difficult to conceive of one single human activity that does not use photography or at least provide an opportunity for it to be deployed in the past, present, or future.[17] Newspaper reportage, jurisprudence, medicine, education, politics, family, entertainment, and recreation — everything is mediated by photography.[18] There are virtually no restrictions on the use of photography in public space.[19] Everyone and everything is liable to become a photograph. However, there are exceptions — military zones, for instance, and other enclosed spaces where rules concerning the use of photography are fabricated by those in charge.[20] In certain domains, the use of photography is a duty (identity photos for official documents) or normative (class photographs for official ceremonies). Most often, though, the encounter with photography does not require an explicit consent from its users, whether they are photographers or spectators.

What has yet to be conquered, however, is always susceptible to being conquered. The conquest of the world as picture was not hastily undertaken, nor did it emerge out of oppression. This process was not directed from on high, by means of a central body that administered the use of photography, nor did it regulate the infinite output that was produced. Photography functions on a horizontal plane. It is present everywhere — actually or potentially.[21] The conquest of the world as picture is enacted simultaneously by everyone who holds a camera, serves as the object of a photograph, or looks at photographs.

The conquest of the world as picture was photography's vision from the very beginning and is newly performed at each and every moment. The dynamic partnership of "everyone" in the fulfillment of this vision, their participation in the conquered world (as picture) and in the powers that conquer (the photographer and spectators), however, actually prevents the completion of the process of turning the world into a mere picture. This partnership makes the conquest of the world through the accumulation of more and more pictures an ongoing and unfinished project. Within a social context, the logic of photography exceeds the singular act of photography and is woven into the net of a plurality of people where all are photographing at the same time, lending their human gaze and their mechanized gaze to others in a way that essentially escapes their control. This is the origin of the ontological difference that marks the status of the image in an era that began with the invention of photography. This is what allows the logic of photography to overpower social relations while at the same time providing a point of resistance against photography's total domination, initiating the responsibility to prevent the overdetermination of this domination.[22]

Here is a photograph which exemplifies the civil contract of photography. In 1988, the newspaper *Hadashot* sent reporter Zvi Gilat, translator Amira Hassan, and photographer Miki Kratsman on assignment to report on a soldiers' post built on the roof of the Abu-Zohir family's house. Mrs. Abu-Zohir demanded that the photographer take a picture of her legs, which had been shot with rubber bullets by soldiers from the Israeli Defense Forces. The photographer — who regularly took pictures of the marks of the occupation left on the Palestinian body, who had seen rubber bullet injuries before, and who was familiar with the *habitus* of his editors and their expectations in regard to photography — dismissed her request, claiming that rubber bullets do not make good pictures. He still had not seen her wound. His knowledge, however, was based on past experience, which was abundant. But the woman was insistent. She knew that her wound was singular, that her right to be photographed does not oblige anyone to see the photo, and certainly that she could not demand that an editor publish it. But she acted, nonetheless, as if it was her right to demand her photo be taken and that it is everyone's duty to witness it, a duty that does not stem from the law, the state, or the sovereign, but from the civil contract of photography. She is seeking to be recognized as one of the governed by means of, through, and with photography.

She has come face to face with a citizen: the photographer. He asks to see the wound before he fulfills her request. She refuses. She will not expose her legs in public — her body is her own. Her partic-ipation in the civil contract of photography in this case is an agree-ment to be photographed — but not to be seen — by a photographer (figure 3.2).

> *Photographer:* Show me your legs.
> *Mrs. Abu-Zohir:* I won't show you my legs. You're not going to see my legs.
> *Photographer to translator:* Explain to her that this photo is going to appear in the newspapers, and the entire world is going to see her legs.
> *Mrs. Abu-Zohir:* A photo's a photo. I don't care if the photo is seen, but you're not going to be in the room with me when I ex-pose my legs.

An agreement on being photographed? "Yes," says Mrs. Abu-Zohir, but there will be no wholesale agreement on photographer-photographed relations as the press dictates them. Instead, when Mrs. Abu-Zohir demands that the picture of her wound be taken, the photographer prepares the camera, directs its gaze, determines the exposure length, focuses the lens, deposits the camera in the female translator's hands, and leaves the room. The translator shoots an entire roll of film in order to obtain a single image, the one in front of which you and I now are placed as spectators. Mrs. Abu-Zohir's bare feet are planted on the ground, pressed to the floor, supporting the entire weight of her body as she stands staunch and upright. She levels her gaze at the camera — not at the photographer — he is clearly of no concern to her. She rolls up her pant legs, pulls up her skirt, and frames the injury. It's as if she were saying: "I, Mrs. Abu-Zohir, am showing you, the spectator, my wound. I am holding my skirt like a folded screen so that you will see my wound."

Alongside her stands a little girl, perhaps her daughter, who feels comfortable enough to walk barefoot. She is allowed to look. Perhaps she's even required to look, unlike you and me — the spectators of the photo. The girl signifies the distance between whoever looks at her and whoever looks at the photo. Mrs. Abu-Zohir has placed the girl beside her as a reminder, so that no one can mistake the photo for

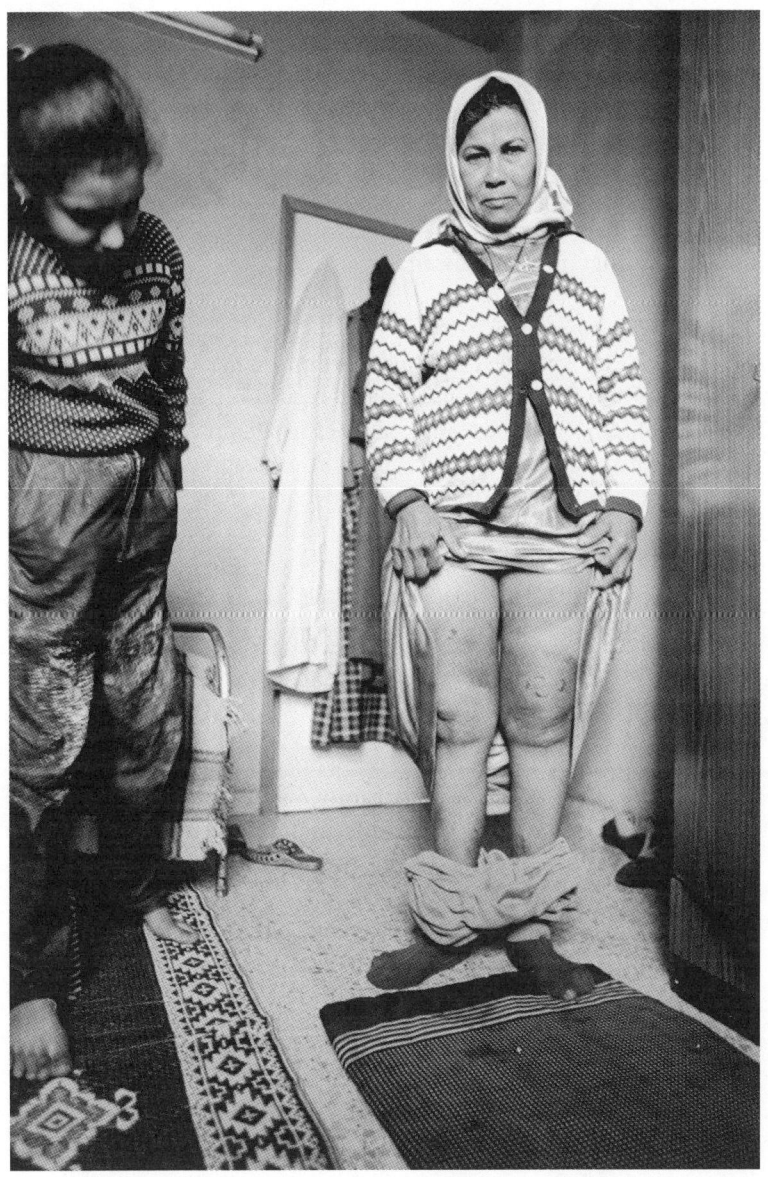

Figure 3.2. Miki Kratsman, Mrs. Abu-Zohir, Balata Refugee Camp, 1988.

what is photographed in it, but also to ensure that no one will forget the continuity between the photo and what has been photographed.

Mrs. Abu-Zohir, when she lets her skirt fall back down, seeks to put an end to the photographic act. But the photo, existing in the public space, will not allow photography to end, nor will she alone dictate its course. This photo, from which her silent gaze looks out at you and me, will not let go. Nothing has concluded, though the hour of photography has passed.

Trust in Photography

Mrs. Abu-Zohir's request for a photograph of her injury is based on the assumption that the camera makes it possible to obtain as sharp, clear, and lifelike an image as possible of what appears in front of the lens. This is more than an assumption, it is an agreement among the citizens of the citizenry of photography concerning the status of the photographed and the possibility of a transition from the photograph to the photographed — that is, concerning access to what is imprinted on the photograph. This agreement is the *convention* of photography, which can be exemplified by two anecdotes that are well known to those who have studied or worked in the fields of cinema and photography.

The first concerns responses that the pioneering Russian documentary filmmaker Dziga Vertov received after he presented his films to peasants who had never seen a movie. Surprised and embarrassed by the close-ups, they adamantly objected to the cynicism of decapitating people for the sake of cinema. The second anecdote concerns an anthropologist who showed a Bushman woman a snapshot of her own son. The woman could not recognize her son's face until those around her pointed to every detail in the photograph, saying "here is the nose" or "here are the eyes." These two anecdotes describe people's first encounter with the medium of the image, whether it is cinema or photography. In the first anecdote, identification is extreme — to the point of total identification — between the filmed image and its reference, to such an extent that what appears on the screen seems to the peasants to be an actual person who has just been decapitated. For the woman in the second anecdote, the identification is so unfeasible that she does not recognize her son in the reference. The gesture of identification, expressed in pointing out "This is X," thus characterizes the viewing of a photograph by the spectator. The absence of this gesture, which reaches the extreme among inexperienced spectators such as those described in these anecdotes, indicates that the experience of the narrators of the anecdotes, their confident assumption of the referential character of photographs, was in fact gathered through practice and socialization.

When various teachers and writers use these anecdotes, they wish to expose the fact that photography and cinema are practices of representation that are culturally dependent and that a particular mode of representation is not to be taken for granted. So far, so good. But these narratives obscure as much as they reveal about this convention that is the photographic image. The narrators distinguish themselves from other spectators by the mere act of revealing that the image is constructed as a convention. The ritualistic dimension of repeatedly revealing the existence of convention transforms the act of storytelling into an instrument of the socialization of the spectator — socialization into an allegedly "critical position" of suspicion of any photographic image because its conventional mode has been revealed.

Attention paid to the socialization of the spectator leaves out a crucial element of the civil contract of photography. Although restricted to a general claim about the cultural conditioning of photographic representation, such narrations allow the one who relays them to believe that a deep truth has been exposed, all the while ignoring the obligation she has toward the social agreement of the *photographed*, which lies at the heart of the civil contract of photography. The narrator considers photography's cultural dependence to be a negative feature, the secret of photography that must be exposed, rather than what characterizes the conditions of the visible in this era. In other words, transmitting such anecdotes often absolves the transmitter from actually grappling with their content. As soon as they are spoken, everyone knows that the storyteller is aware of photography being a convention, and critical analysis of the further elements of the convention stops. However, the fact that these anecdotes can be told again and again (and by a vast number of people) and that the narrator or her listeners can reveal the secret every time without ever exhausting the secret should necessitate a new inquiry into the convention of photography and its status as a secret.

Even in a society accustomed to photography, one in which disputes occur over what is represented, carried on by various experts who linger over the image in order to make it speak, the fact that photography is a convention is simultaneously visible and concealed. The secret that unveils photography as a convention is usually related to the level of representation — what is seen in the picture can be identified by people belonging to the same culture in which they have been trained to see photographs and to identify similarities between such photographs and the photographed object. Graphics (arrows indicating who or what is shown in the picture) or linguistic signs (words or concepts that organize the seen so that it will not escape the eye of the spectator) assist in the construction of meaning out of the various marks printed on the surface of a photo. These signs facilitate the gesture of identification — "This is X." The signs themselves, as well as the disputes over their reference, attest to the fact that the photograph does not speak for itself, that what is seen in the photograph is not immediately given, and that — yet again — its meaning must be constructed and agreed on.[23]

As demonstrated by the above anecdotes, however, the inquiry into the convention of photography focuses on the plane of the visible while leaving in shadow, and perhaps even in secret, the convention of photography as it exists on the plane of political relations. Speaking of the convention as "the thing agreed on" — that is, the object of agreement — undermines the fact that a convention is first and foremost a gathering, as indicated by the Latin root of "convening," *con-venir*, meaning coming together, coming to an agreement.

Most histories of photography ignore this element of the agreement that is involved in photography,[24] along with the social relations shaped by this agreement. These histories are written from a hegemonic viewpoint that accepts the institutionalization of photography as a movement toward progress in the finalized determination of knowledge. Accepting the motif of progress as the self-evident, central axis for the unfolding of events, these histories overlook the fact that from its very beginning, photography has been a mass medium that violently and rudely fixes anyone and anything as an image in ways that resist finalized determinations and that invite the participation of others in the negotiations of what and how that images signifies. Despite this, for almost two centuries, photography has still attempted the realization of the moment of convening that has existed within it from the very beginning.

In order to understand this agreement, it is necessary to question the conditions that brought about its achievement among people who were unfamiliar to one other. The origin of this agreement can be located at the point when a *certain type of photography* became established and acquired a monopoly within a very short span of time.[25] It is the conquest of the world as picture: photography as a representation of what "was there" and therefore as a basis for a decision concerning what is — what is true — based on limited episte-mological criteria of identification. The various practices in which photographs are used tend to relate the photograph less and less to a framework of political relations in which one becomes a citizen and more often to a distributive system of finished products. Photogra-phy is presented as a dispenser of photos that requires nothing more than sorting, grading, presenting, rejecting, or framing. In discursive fields that regularly use photography — journalism, law, politics, social struggles, and humanitarian activities — this photography is thus reduced to the function of pointing at a reference.

The famous enthusiastic speech of the French physicist François Arago, delivered before the French Chamber of Deputies in 1839, allows us to isolate one constituent moment in this establishment. In his speech, Arago hoped to convince his colleagues of the impor-tance of the invention and the necessity of the state to take steps to protect and promote it.[26] Arago pointed to the great potential of photography to assist in various fields of human endeavor, as well as in many different fields of knowledge, including philology, astron-omy, archaeology, and art. However, the benefit of photography seems of secondary importance when compared to the truly great project that he implies in his remarks — and it is indeed the conquest of the world as a picture.

He saw that everything could be turned into an object of photog-raphy, more or less the entire world, while emphasizing the fact that anyone could participate in realizing the capabilities of the inven-tion. According to Arago, the invention does indeed yield "experi-mental results among the curiosities of physics," but if this was the only benefit of the invention, as he clearly states in his speech, "it would never have become a subject for the consideration of this chamber."[27] It is under discussion not only because a much larger community than scientists could handle it, but also because it has created a shift in the possibilities of conquering the world. Much more than single visual representations resulting from a large investment of practice, time, and resources, photography is an endless multiplicity of images of which anyone can become the producer and agent, simply by following a short set of instructions. "When, step by step, a few simple prescribed rules are followed, there is no one who cannot succeed as certainly and as well as can M. Daguerre himself."[28]

When reading Arago's vision it is difficult to miss the prophetic announcement of the imperialistic power of photography. Arago's enthusiastic arguments were intended to weaken or perhaps even to silence the voices of those opposed to photography and its institutionalization. Traces of those voices have barely survived in the discourse on photography, and the few times they are mentioned they are generally presented as reactionary and primitive for having ascribed magical properties to photography. Even when Walter Benjamin, who dreamed of writing alternative histories, and an alternative history of photography in particular, presented such voices through the dichotomy of conservatism and progress, he scornfully described such voices as opponents of the "Black Art from France."[29] Ever since photography's appearance on the stage of history, any possibility of repudiating what has turned into the self-evidence of photography, or photography as self-evident, has been drastically curtailed.[30] If, in photography, there was any measure of otherness — as its opponents at the outset insisted — it has been effectively denied and domesticated while photography has rapidly spread into every field of life and been assimilated into the modern landscape.[31]

Arago concluded his speech to the chamber on a patriotic note, depicting France as the bearer of glad tidings: "France has adopted this invention and from the first has been proud to be able to generously present it to the entire world."[32] The state responded to Arago's panegyric to photography and his demand that its inventors be rewarded by purchasing the patent rights and transforming the invention into common property.[33] The object of these glad tidings was no longer a mere technological invention, but a political revolution — a second French Revolution. Like the first, which formulated the "rights of man and citizen," this revolution reshaped the status of both man and citizen.[34]

The French state purchased the patent rights of the camera as fabricator of images, but it couldn't make the action of photography its own, because, as we have seen, photography, as such, can not be appropriated. Selecting the daguerreotype, Daguerre's invention, over the competing inventions of, for example, Talbot or Bayard, whose photos appeared less accurate and more pictorial, was a decision in favor of photography as a scientific tool for producing representations of nature with high "exactitude," to be used as an instrument of truth and transmitter of information on what "was there." This visual information could be used not just for scientific inquiry, but for legal, historical, or cultural purposes.[35] Distinguishing photography from painting (which does not hold an indexical relation with its object) separated photography from the logic of collections and exhibitions that were merely presented to the eyes of curious individuals. In the type of photography that was thus established, epistemological criteria set the standard for the relation between the photographic result and its object, so that photography is supposed to enable the identification and recognition of the photographed.

In addition to a few specific operating instructions for each chosen model, the instruction manuals supplied with every camera have given expression to these epistemological criteria: "the instrument you have in your hands is intended to help you obtain an image of reality that is as clear, sharp, exact and reliable as can be, under all visibility conditions, from any distance or angle." These criteria guide any use of photography, including the purchasing of photographic equipment, the ordering of a photo, looking at a photo in a newspaper, noticing an event by means of a photo, photographing a certain person or situation, or being photographed in order to provide identity for an official document. Photos have a contractual standing that is presumed to ensure a clear, sharp, legible, decipherable, and true image, such that what "was there" in front of the camera lens, was also really "there." The subject engaged in photography

155

expects it to serve as a means for that end. The purpose of photography reproduced in most instruction manuals echoes an "original" purpose, which results, each time, in the renewal of its sanction. The technical language and the phrasing of the instructions refer directly to the instrument and its operation, but the principles of the presupposed agreement among the users can be derived from both the technical language and the various uses of photography that they attempt to support. Those principles are generality, accessibility, publicity, transparency, neutrality, and impartiality. Although these principles are often violated under varying circumstances and are typically subject to constraints and restrictions of different kinds, they nevertheless serve as the rules of the game that have been agreed on by all. But the camera itself does not fulfill these principles. A photographer is required if these principles are to be applied.

Let's look at the work of a photojournalist. When she comes to the arena of a certain event, she can search for many various subjects and try to capture them through her own unique viewpoint or that of the newspaper she represents. Whatever the scope of her work and its specific motives (economic, professional, moral, cultural, or others), in one way or another, she will act according to principles that are supposed to be respected no matter what specific circumstances in which she finds herself. The photographer's duty is to supply an accessible image, sharp, clear, readable, and impartial. It is very rare to come across a photographer who has intentionally created the situation that she has photographed, and the public scandal erupting around a few such events is a testimony to their occurrence being rare and exceptional. The rule is that the introduction of a camera into any place participates in the creation of the event. Taking part in the situation doesn't mean that the photographer has created the situation she was about to take in photo. The photographer is motivated by an unwritten contract with the public, and she is supposed to bring her gaze to rest on what is considered of public interest.

It is for this reason that the public — including those who may someday be photographed, or those who, like Mrs. Abu-Zohir, hope to be photographed — trusts the photojournalist to perform her work faithfully and to negotiate consistently with the institutions responsible for regulating access routes to potential photographic objects. At times, this contract is updated to conform to the demands of a newspaper or the consequences of a particular event, but its essence is stable. Even if a critical study were undertaken of a set of photographs taken by a certain photojournalist and the pattern of their appearance in a newspaper were to be scrutinized, particular interests might be revealed, but this would not weaken the photographer's belief in universal principles that guide her work. Without this belief, she and the society that, in principal, defends her freedom of action would have difficulty granting her the professional title of "press photographer."[36] She acts in accordance with the political motto of "the public's right to know" and the moral "duty to report" as that duty has been carried out in the international arena. Astonishingly, even when visual matters are at stake, demands for the transparency of information do not use terms from the visual field, such as "the right to see" or "the right to take photos." The conversion of the visual into the conceptual, into knowledge, exposes the instrumental approach to photography that characterizes various fields of legal, political, or moral discourse that constantly make use of photography. Photography is thus perceived as a transparent means of achieving the same general, universal goals.

However, the public assumes that photography is an instrument that can be controlled, one that is capable of supplying its demand. But the public cannot trust the photographer unconditionally, since she may be biased by some particular interests. The civil contract of photography is not a specific contract made with a specific photographer, but the expression of an agreement over certain rules among users of photography and the relation of those users and the camera. Yet conversely, if and when the photographer betrays her mission and wishes to distort the visible, the camera — as the impartial emissary of the public — will ensure the immortalization of reality as it stands, so that this reality will one day reveal itself. If the camera goes out of control, the photographer (as the public's emissary) will know how to regain control over the instrument and continue to produce what is demanded. Similar to the Lacanian "subject supposed to know," the subject "supposed to know that from which no one can escape,"[37] the contract at hand allows the public to see the camera as what is supposed to show. The camera, however, is not a subject and is usually dependent on whoever operates it. But from the moment this operator takes hold of it, she, too, is no longer sovereign.[38]

Establishing the hegemony of photography as a representation of what "was there" was part of a double effort: to purge photography of the religious or magical dimensions that opponents ascribed to it and to structure it as a secular invention that could be integrated into the liberal ethos of equality and progress. The depiction of photography as a medium under the control of the photographer was intended as a counterproof to the claims of those who equated photography to black magic, while presenting it as a technique that requires very few skills was intended to establish photography as a medium of equality. However, a contradiction arose between the concerted effort to remove the religious dimension of photography and the effort to secularize it.

The medium is not under the control of the photographer, any more than what "was there" is. The image that appears on photographic paper is never simply reducible to a man-made image, but is an irreversible recording of what "was there" before the camera, what is nonnegotiable, what in itself and by itself has impressed its stamp on the emulsion. The object of photography, present in the world of experience, imprints an image on the emulsion that — although the hand of the photographer certainly interferes by adjusting the lens, opening/closing the shutter, setting the frame, and so on — always contains an element that exceeds the world of experience, thus exceeding any interference. What we see in the photo was made by someone from a particular viewpoint. It is the outcome of focus, excision, and framing. Yet the image maintains a direct connection with the depicted object, because it was written by the object's own reflected light, by its aura. The secularization of photography, therefore, was accompanied by the creation of its transcendent standing.[39]

Among the users of photography, there is a silent agreement over the double way in which the medium of photography links the photographer and her object. The photographer and the photographed each act on the medium and, intentionally and/or unintentionally, each undermines the other's exclusive control over it. This agreement concerning the act of photography both assumes that the photographic product — the photograph — testifies to what "was there" while nonetheless claiming that its framing is culturally dependent. Indeed, this agreement is only ever a partial version of what appears to the eye of the spectator. What "was there" certainly existed, but not necessarily in any finally determined way, and no determination of it significance has exhausted the possibility of other such determinations. Instead, the spectator must reconstruct what was there from both what is visible and what is not immediately manifest, but what can — in principle — *become* visible in the exact same photograph. A person's responsibility to the historical agreement over the status of the visible in photography requires this reconstruction, and to do this, she should become a spectator.

Barthes Watching Photographs of Horror

While in many public-policy fields the hegemonic conception of photography has been as a referential representation of what "was there," for quite some time, the discourse of art has subordinated photographs to the very different logic of the artistic object.[40] Looking at a photograph, within this discourse, is characterized by a suspension of direct access to the photograph's reference and a declaration of the primary interest in photography as a visual surface that stands in relation to a canonical repertory of images.

Within the discourse of art, the regime of the art museum is based on a subject who is constituted in front of the field of the visible — a photograph, for instance — as the one supposed to make an aesthetic judgment. Visiting the museum, contemplating visual items, and passing an aesthetic judgment are all necessary actions performed by the modern citizen. Confronting a work of art in the museum space or through its mediation, the citizen gains the recognition of her citizenship at the same time as the image becomes the object of an aesthetic judgment. These mutual relations of recognition are expressed when the modern citizen encounters a picture in a museum.[41]

The effect of this regime has been and continues to be powerful enough to make a philosopher such as Roland Barthes, writing on photography in the 1960s, completely subject to it. As such, he can serve admirably as an example of the way in which in the discourse of art, as in other areas in which the hegemony of photography conceived as representations of what "was there," has foreclosed recognition of the role of the spectator as a citizen participating in the civil contract of photography. Barthes' work is canonical in the history of photography that addresses horror photos, especially since it appeared at a time when they were rarely exhibited in museums. I will not read his work as a theoretical text and address its claims, however, but rather attempt to extract traces of his gaze in front of particular photographs.

In the essay "Photos-Choc" ("Shock-Photos") in the original French edition of *Mythologies*,[42] Barthes briefly discusses an exhibition of the same name held at the Galerie d'Orsay in Paris. Barthes' report of his impressions of the exhibition displays a certain discomfort with certain feelings that were aroused in him — or to be more precise, *not* aroused — at the sight of the photos:

> Most of the photographs exhibited to shock us have no effect at all, precisely because the photographer has too generously substituted himself for us in the formation of his subject: he has always *overconstructed* the horror he is proposing, adding to the *fact*, by contrasts or parallels, the intentional *language* of horror: one of them, for instance, places side by side a crowd and a field of skulls; another shows us a young soldier looking at a skeleton; another catches a column of prisoners passing a flock of sheep.[43]

The photos that Barthes describes — of skulls, skeletons, and prisoners — indeed sound disturbing. Barthes notices them, describes them in detail, identifies them within the composition, and in the course of his description testifies to his aesthetic reaction: The photos prove unsuccessful in moving him. Skulls are too stylized, and the skeletons are too organized, the prisoners too poetic. In other words, not only is the photo entirely legible as it appears before Barthes' eyes, it seems as if anyone can read it in exactly the same way. In other words, the photo doesn't challenge Barthes, it doesn't posit him as the singular addressee who must revive the photo by extricating it from its anonymous, silent thrownness into the world.

Barthes' critique is centered on the photographs' "over-construction." He feels that they deviate from the appropriate measure of legibility that the photographer should have maintained, so that the photos would not be accessible to everyone in advance. Thus, Barthes feels that he's been denied his place, and he describes the feeling of having his position expropriated:

> Now, none of these photographs, all too skillful, touches us. This is because, as we look at them, we are in each case dispossessed of our judgment; someone has shuddered for us, reflected for us, judged for us; the photographer has left us nothing — except a simple right of intellectual acquiescence.... We can no longer *invent* our own reception of this synthetic nourishment, already perfectly assimilated by its creator.[44]

Barthes complains that the photos have robbed him of his faculty of judgment and feels he's been cheated, stripped of his possessions, and denied his position. After all, he's the one who was supposed to have shuddered before the photo, to have been provoked to think before it, and most of all, to have passed his own judgment, but someone else has already done this before him.

Barthes makes no attempt to question why he is unable to shudder, think, or judge if someone else has already done this before him. Nor does he question why, if someone else does it simultaneously with him, shuddering at the horror would require seclusion or privacy.

The answer to these questions is connected to the way in which Barthes understands photography. Barthes looks at a photo as the product of an author who has signed his name to the way in which what is seen within the photo has been organized. In *Camera Lucida*, published two decades later, but still echoing the logic hidden in this early text on photography, Barthes designates the "studium" as the organization of what is seen in the photo, at the same discussing what evades this organization, which he designates as the "punctum." The "punctum" of the photo, Barthes claims, cannot be predicated on what the author wanted to include in the photo. Instead, it is a residue that has been caught in the photo and that wounds and undermines the spectator. As something elusive, the definition of which fixes it as something undefined, lacking a precise name, it is not planned by anyone. However, instead of contending that what this involves is two basic elements, with the identification and distinction between them, with respect to the photo, depending on the spectator, Barthes falls into an essentialist trap. By assessing the quality of the photo according to the presence or absence of the punctum, Barthes actually deprives the punctum of its potential status as the reversible element of photography, as what remains open and makes an ethics of the spectator possible. Seen instead in this way, the punctum has the capacity to transform the photo and the power to extend outward to the social relations in the framework of which it was made. In other words, rather than preserve the punctum as something that makes possible the transition from the photograph to the moment of photography and thus to the photographed, Barthes inscribes himself in the finest aesthetic tradition, turning the punctum into a stable characteristic of the photograph.

Even in "Shock-Photos," the residue that Barthes discusses turns into a category for classifying photos, only in this instance, what are being classified are photos of horror. In the absence of a punctum, or whatever we may choose to call this "something," and even in the face of horrific photos, Barthes as spectator will remain indifferent and impassive. For the singular encounter between the photo and the addresser Barthes substitutes aesthetic intention, which comes to shape his viewing experience. This residue is not of the order of the singular — what Barthes called what "was there" — that is burned into the photo and displayed for the spectator. The residue that Barthes is looking for is the aesthetic experience. His remarks indicate that the photo's purpose is to make this experience possible. In this aesthetic experience the photo is expected to make the spectator feel both in control and undermined at the same time. The photo must respect the spectator's physical and spiritual autonomy, and enable him to feel that he's the master of his own judgment of the photo. The photo serves as an opportunity for him to acknowledge himself again as an independent spectator or connoisseur, who may be distinguished by his ability to judge independently and to voice such judgments publicly. In other words, the spectator assumes the aesthetic position that posits the object before his eyes as an aesthetic object, in such a way that allows him and the image to acknowledge one another.

Standing in front of the photos, Barthes' initial action is to bracket what "was there." Thus, he precludes the possibility of any encounter between himself and the singularity of what "was there." In advance, the aesthetic position includes predispositions that neutralize any possibility of shocking the spectator. Instead of the photo positing the spectator as its addressee, Barthes as spectator posits the photo as the object of aesthetic study, effectively turning his viewing of the photo into the same "acquiescence" that he feared. But instead of "intellectual acquiescence," to use Barthes' own term, what we encounter is an aesthetic acquiescence in the framework of which the spectator determines whether the photo makes him shudder or not. Barthes displaces the sentence "it makes me shudder" from the ethical field, where it refers to the object of moral concern, to the aesthetic field, where it refers to the experience of the subject. In regard to the photo, instead of judging whether "it's beautiful" he judges whether "it makes me shudder."

Barthes confines the photo to a vicious aesthetic circle that works in the following way: a good horror photo is supposed to make the spectator shudder. The spectator is both active and passive. He is passive insofar as he must be made to shudder by the photo. He is active insofar as he is the one who determines or judges whether he has effectively been made to shudder. To make a statement of taste, the spectator must place the photo within the aesthetic order — here, the order that determines what a photograph of horror is supposed to do: make a spectator shudder. We thus return to the original aesthetic judgment concerning the photo, regardless of whether it has succeeded in arousing the desired experience — here, to be made to shudder. The vicious aesthetic circle, then, has three effects: it places what is seen in brackets and puts the spectator in a position of expectation ("It does [or does not] work for me") that, although passively waiting, has a strong component of demand; it restricts the viewing to the framework of a search for the punctum, an otherness or mark of artistry that is supposed to be in the photo and make it do what it is supposed to do; and it transfers the weight from the visible event that makes one shudder to merely the possibility that one might shudder.

The marks of the aesthetic order here place not only the singularity of a photo in brackets, but the singularity of the ethical position that it requires. The leap that Barthes makes from facing a horror photo to judging an aesthetic image is easily performed, given the current conditions of visibility in which the circulation of horror photos is conducted according to a logic similar to — and possibly even more intense than — what applies to works of art. The modern work of art, whose nature was shaped in the mid-nineteenth century, exists within an endless movement of searching for the new, rare, and different. This movement imposes a logic of negation on the work of art in order for it to prove its difference from what came before it or what lies ahead. The logic of this movement is to negate and challenge what exists and is motivated by an insatiable hunger for the new. The discerning spectator of art is the one who seeks the new and is proud to make it his — not the work of art itself, but his identification and determination of its innovation. Thus, he acknowledges the work of art as new, and the work in its turn — with the mediation of the entire art world — acknowledges this spectator as someone who has acknowledged the new that it represents. The assumption that underlies this mutual acknowledgment is that there is a direct relation between the development of the work of art and the development of the gaze. The work of art, then, is pumped into a movement that exists prior to its construction, a movement that is managed and regulated by social structures, political mechanisms, and cultural positions.

Within the hegemonic channels for disseminating information in the present era, the horror photo's existence follows a pattern similar to that of the work of art described above. An entire institutional complex — structures, mechanisms, and positions — is prepared to manage the horror photo. From the front page of the newspaper to the museum wall, this kind of photo is supposed to present a different image, one never seen before, that challenges the gaze and exposes it to something unfamiliar. The horror photo is not only supposed to be shocking, but it is supposed to be either more shocking or shocking in a novel way each time it appears.

Horror was not already omnipresent by the 1950s, when Barthes was writing "Shock-Photos," in the newspapers, in entertainment, and on talk shows. Regarding what he saw in the Galerie d'Orsay, Barthes formulated the early position of a critic who warns others of insensitivity in the face of horror. One can easily be led astray by Barthes' formulations and fail to notice the way in which it produces the exact same insensitivity that is the object of his critique.

The concept of "insensitivity," which a number of critics employ today, participates in the acceleration of the horror. If we are not to be reconciled with death, so as not to be insensitive to it, the photo must be more and more shocking each time. As if horror itself were not enough, it is called on to assume a new form each time. The concept of "insensitivity" obscures the fact that this doesn't concern the sense faculties of one group or another, but the conditions of the discourse that enlists its best critics in order to render the visible horror unseen. They consistently declare that the omnipresent horror – the photos of which are distributed everywhere – is unseen.

In the era of the conquest of the world as picture, such an oxymoron is not only made possible, but is prevalent; it is the catalyst of the desire to see more and more of the visible horror. Such a discourse conditions spectators to look on the horror and, given its invisibility, demand more and more of it in order to see it. This field of vision is common both to those who assume an impartial aesthetic position and those who assume an "entertainment position" that, in being subject to the logic of ratings, cannot claim impartiality. These two positions serve as mirror images of one another. They are supposedly contrary positions – the first is reserved for the discerning spectator, while the second is open to everyone. In actual fact, they share the same three elements of waiting, passivity, and demand that place the photo's reference – horror – in brackets and facilitate the passing of judgments that grade or classify it into irrelevant categories.

In other words, both positions accept the citizenship offered by photography in a passive way and impose their own logic, from a position of expectant demand: It must touch me, it must arouse or shock me. Thus, the desire for more effective horror – when trapped inside the vicious aesthetic circle – can never be satisfied and is doomed to further intensification: "Most of the photographs exhibited to shock us have no effect at all, precisely because... none of these photographs, all too skillful, touches us."[45] I've deliberately broken off this passage at the point where he attempts to explain the reason for his indifference: "This is because...." Whatever reason he may supply, it does not alter the pattern of relations I've described, in the framework of which the horror right in front of Barthes' eyes cannot satisfy this hunger. It is placed in brackets and made invisible.

Barthes comes to the conclusion that the horror photo has failed its task — to shock. He has reversed the relation between spectator and object in such a way that the horror itself is not worth looking at unless it manages to intensify the excitement of the spectator who stands in relation to it. Thus, the focus of his discussion is not on what appears to the gaze, but on whoever is doing the gazing — the spectator. The concrete event, the event that has already ended, is forced to give up its place for an event of a different order — a "pure" event, something that has already happened but hasn't happened yet.[46] It is the desire for an event in the raw, an event stripped of its mundane significations, that finally appears in a refined form. This desire, which in principle can never be satisfied, functions as a mechanism of aesthetic distinction, and as such, it manages to capture important theoreticians such as Barthes and turn them into its agents. The agents of this desire enjoy citizenship in the citizenry of photography, but are limited to the possession of an entry permit, or passport. It makes the citizen forget his responsibility always to become a citizen, that is, to experience his citizenship as an unfinished task that will remain unfinished and to experience photography as an unfinished event that will remain unfinished. To become a citizen of the citizenry of photography means giving renewed sanction to the agreement on photography, to come together (con-venir) for photography, remembering that the photographic image is unlike any other image — it is the product of being together through photography.

Becoming a citizen of the citizenry of photography means rehabilitating the relation between the photo and photography, between the printed image and the photographic event — that is, the event that took place in front of the camera, constituted by the meeting of photographer and photographed object that leaves traces on a visual support. There is a gap between the photo and the photographic event that both those who take an aesthetic position as well as those who take an entertainment position seek to eliminate. Becoming a citizen means replacing these impartial positions with a position that is partial to the civil contract of photography, a contract without which modern citizenship is invalid, insofar as it is the contract that made the conquest of the world as picture possible.

Citizens have been bound together in an agreement on photography, through the convention of photography, according to which what appears in the photo "was there." But the conquest of the world as picture means that what appears in the photo is *not* all that was there — this has been agreed on by the civil contract of photography — but was, however, photographed from out of what "was there" — and this, as well, has been agreed on through the same civil contract. In an era that witnesses the conquest of the world as picture, an era in which social relations are mediated through photography, to be satisfied with citizenship as merely a legal status implies an agreement to close the gap between the photo and photography, agreeing to the absolute conquest of the world as picture while eliminating the social relations that, merely by existing, possess the power to prevent this absolute conquest. Becoming a citizen in the citizenry of photography means giving renewed sanction to the gap between the world and the picture. Becoming a citizen is in opposition to the absolute conquest of the world picture, on account of the same civil contract in which the conquest of the world as picture was agreed on when political relations had been the guarantee against its absolute conquest.

Becoming a Spectator, Becoming a Citizen

Since the 1990s, the conditions of visibility for photography have altered within the museum space. A new spectatorial position has emerged within the museum, a position from which a responsibility to the sense of the image has coalesced with the responsibility toward the photographed. As a result, an influx of images of horror has transformed the museum into an alternative site vis-à-vis the media and its particular logic. Not only have present images of horror been gazed on in this space, but a widespread review of photographs from the past has been initiated in which early moments of the civil contract of photography have been restored. The contemplative act, which previously characterized the museum subject, has thus been replaced by the subject as civil spectator who watches the image in order to view its conditions of fabrication and the new possibilities for intervening in what it frames.

The term "spectator," much like the verbs "to observe"[47] or "to watch," is not typically employed with reference to still photography. It is customary to use such terms with reference to natural phenomena and, within the sphere of art, to movie screenings or other modes of entertainment. With the photograph, the tendency is to "look at" or "contemplate," and what is photographed is customarily "seen." The distinction refers to the object — the stationary object accessible to immediate and exhaustive viewing (that is, seen in its entirety), which gives rise to such clichés as "a picture is worth a thousand words." A moving image, however, eludes the stable gaze, but only through its constant replacement by successive images: "It" must be watched continuously, as long as there is something to see before one's eyes. A photograph, being a fragment taken from a flow or a sequence, is supposedly a stationary object. What is seen in the photograph is not given, and the gaze on it can never immediately exhaust it. The gesture of identification — "This is X" — frequently used in reference to photographs, homogenizes the plurality from which a photograph is made and unifies it in a stable image, creating the illusion that we are facing a closed unit of visual information. This gesture, frequent in so many domains, is part of an ongoing effort to suspend the civil power of being a spectator and to neutralize the power of the civil contract of photography. To combat that effort, it is necessary to rethink what it means to be a spectator.

The dictionary defines "spectator" as a "one who looks on or watches,"[48] that is, a person who takes no part in an event that takes place before her eyes. But this language refers not only to the placement of the spectator in regard to the event, but also to the way in which the action unfolds in time. The spectator's work also is one of *prolonged* observation, performed on the margins of a particular activity or event. The spectator observes a certain space and has the capacity to report on what she observes. From her position, the spectator can occasionally foresee or predict the future. Thus she is able, through skilled observation, to identify and forewarn others of dangers that lie ahead. The secrets of the future can be revealed to her, in photographs of horror, as well as the atrocities of the present.

The act of prolonged observation by the observer as spectator has the power to turn a still photograph into a theater stage on which what has been frozen in the photograph comes to life. The spectator is called to take part, to move from the addressee's position to the addresser's position to take responsibility for the sense of such photographs by addressing them even further, turning them into signals of an emergency, signals of danger or warning—transforming them into emergency claims.

As an example of the spectatorial act, let us take the example of the artist Michal Heiman as she looks at a book by the photographer Eadweard Muybridge, who was active toward the end of the nineteenth century. In Plate 171 of his book appears a series of eighteen consecutive photographs of a woman spanking a child (figure 3.3). Both the child and the woman are stark naked. The woman, with her arm raised, is kneeling on one leg as she holds the boy down on her other knee, propped against her stomach. On the surface of a reproduction of the two-page spread in Muybridge's book, Heiman has embedded her own two imprints: "Raped into Being a Photograph" ("Anusim lee-Hyot Zilum" in Hebrew) and "Photo Rape" in English.[49] The use of the plural form (*Anusim*) in the Hebrew indicates that it is not only the child being spanked who has been "raped" into becoming a photograph, but both the woman (mother? model?) and child. Both are naked and have been given over to the gaze of the photographer, who has attempted—as Muybridge explicitly stated—to record scientifically, one fraction of a second after another, the precise progression of movement. Heiman's imprint points to the perverse choice of his example—the spanking as a demonstration of discrete physical motion—and the violence of the camera that has "raped" both of them, woman and child, into forever enacting the spanking scene and serving, with their naked bodies, as the object of the insatiable gaze of the photographer. Along with many others, Heiman implies, Muybridge was involved in the flourishing late nineteenth-century business of traffic in photographed images of naked women and children.[50] Heiman draws the spectator's attention to the fact that hiding behind the veil of a scientific investigation of motion lies the violence that the photographer has exercised on his photographed subjects, who unwittingly became the victims of a

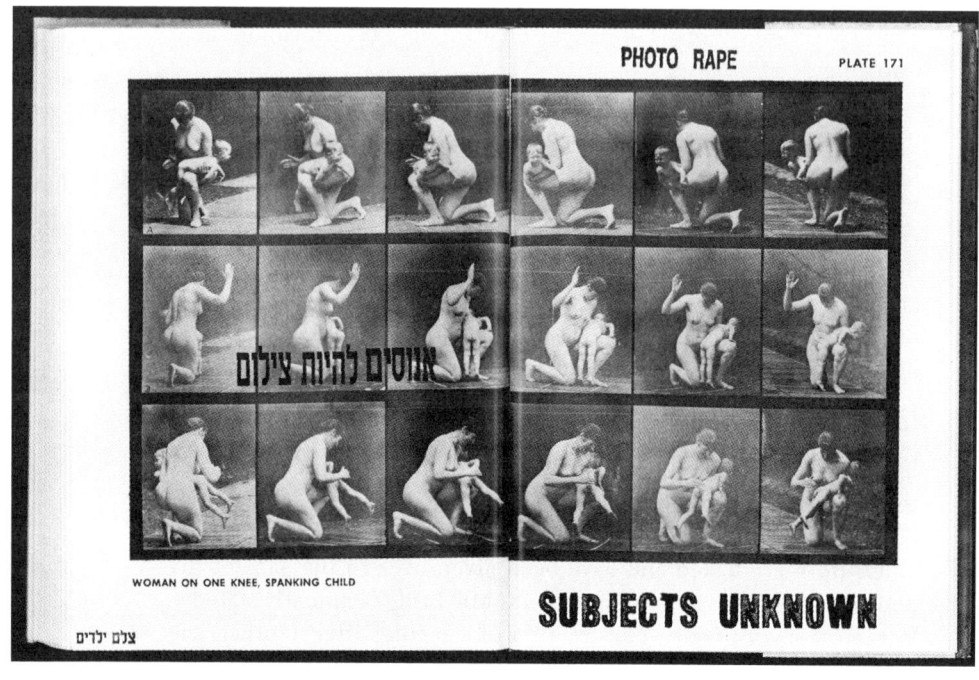

Figure 3.3. Michal Heiman, *Subjects Unknown #1, Woman on one knee, spanking child (Photo: Eadweard Muybridge, plate 171, 1884)*, chromogenic print, 78.0 x 114.0 cm, 2002.

game of desire and truth, oppression and sexuality. A Foucauldian reading might even tempt us to claim that this series of eighteen frames captures the logic of the entire Victorian regime.[51] Under the cover of scientific investigation, this same regime, which ostensibly suppressed sexuality and prohibited any public display of nudity, encouraged and supported the production of photographs that provided a detailed, intrusive, and multidirectional gaze on the naked body and in the context of these specific photographs exposed the relationships between education, sexuality, and violence.

In the encounter she produces between Muybridge's series of photographs and her own imprints, Heiman attempts to shift the balance between the photographed subjects as the object of the scientific demonstration of a photographic principle and their existence as concrete individuals who, for the purpose of a demonstration, have been stripped of their clothes and forced to perform, for the benefit of the photographer's gaze, a scene lying somewhere on the borders between sexuality, parenthood, and violence. With her imprint, Heiman loudly protests for all to hear — "Raped into Being a Photograph" — making a demand on the spectator to look squarely at the photograph, at the photographed individuals, rather than take refuge behind the knowledge that they may have of the undertaking as a study of human movement or an important station in the development of photography and cinema. Heiman's demand is an act of becoming a citizen of photography and a declaration that in principle, the work of watching is not hers to complete — that this work can never be finished.

Because in principle, photographs evade an ultimate reading, a last judgment, Heiman's reading of Muybridge's photographs, in opening up a perspective previously obscured, constitutes an invitation to further reading. Otherwise, photographs of this kind would appear only as instruments of oppression that rape women and juveniles, and the photographer is confined to the position of an executor of a certain social order, the spectator merely someone who takes part in preserving this order. The power of the gaze, which Heiman exemplifies, is witnessed in the demand of the spectator to linger over the photograph and to reconstruct the photographic situation, the encounter that took place "there." This twofold demand makes it impossible to see photography simply as an instrument of brute force that ruthlessly operates on its victims. Instead, we must assume that the photographed subjects also have the ability to use force at the moment of photography and can undermine, though paradoxically in cooperation with the photographer and with the mediating assistance of spectators — the explicit aims of the photographer and those who sent him.

Behind the fences and locked doors of the University of Pennsylvania, Muybridge staged his photographed subjects within small dramatic scenes that typically consisted of a single movement captured in a loop. From a scientific perspective, the intention was to use photography to break down human motion by fractions of a second so as to capture what the human eye cannot see. This was the explicit intention of a research program that was certified and supported by the university and authorized for publication in the form of an elegant book. But when we look at the series of Muybridge's photographs that Heiman has chosen to isolate, the motivation to show the human eye what it cannot see is revealed to in fact be of secondary interest. The photograph confronts the gaze with the fact that the gaze tends primarily to see what it is told to see. As the caption states, "WOMAN ON ONE KNEE, SPANKING CHILD." But is this really the case? A methodical appraisal of the eighteen frames will immediately show that the woman is not really spanking the boy, that she is in fact maintaining a clear distance from his exposed buttocks lying on her knee. Another glance at the photographs invites the spectator to trace the logic of the movement dissected in them: An arm that is raised supposedly falls on the buttocks, repetitively. This loop, however, is fictional, too, and fails to describe what is visible in the photographs. The series consists of three rows of six photographs, and in each set of six photographs, the woman is in exactly the same position. Thus we do not have eighteen photographs, each still a different instant of motion, but three sequences in which a single motion is repeated in six different frames. When we look at the entire series, the whole does not appear to consist of only three photographs that repeat themselves, but gives the impression of a dissected, continuous movement spread over eighteen different frames. The riddle is solved when we realize that the illusion of

motion is not produced by any movement by the photographed subject, but by the camera's movement. In each set of six photographs,
the woman never moves. It is the photographer who moves around
her in a semicircle and who shows her from different angles.

We thus do not have an attempt by the photographer to record
the woman's motion, but a testimony to the movement of the photographer around the woman. A prolonged examination of this
series of photographs discloses to the spectator how badly she has
been tricked by the name of Muybridge's project — "the investigation of motion." The photographer may hide behind the scientific
title he has given his project, but what he seeks to observe is the
woman and child stark naked — and to observe himself observing
them. It is not just their naked bodies that he wants to observe, but a
sort of beating, in the course of which the photographer places himself in the position of an angel who might be telling the woman,
"Lay not thine hand upon the lad." Yet it is quite apparent to everyone that it is not the woman who has wished to lay her hand on the
lad, but the photographer who asked her to do so, just as it is he who
wants, despite the title, to halt the action, to suspend and prevent it
from going further.

In the central row of photographs, the woman is shown with her
arm suspended in the air, like Abraham's raised arm; in the upper
and lower rows, the woman is shown in exactly the same position. In
the first case, the photographer circles her to the right so that the
spectator's eye can follow the movement from her back to her face
and glimpse her subtle smile. In the second, the photographer circles
her to the left so that the eye can catch the boy's enraptured expression. "Despite all the photographer's artistic talents and systematic
staging of his model," writes Walter Benjamin in his brief history of
photography, "the beholder feels an irresistible urge to search such a
picture for the tiny spark of contingency, of the here and now, with
which reality has (so to speak) seared the subject."[52] As the spectator
continues looking at the action, now following the photographer
through the eyes of his photographed subjects, she sees the way in
which the photographer, who has positioned himself in the heroic
role of someone with the power to beat the boy or stop the beating,
has himself been turned into an object of the mocking gaze of the

woman. She, on the other hand, is trying to hide her smile as she and the boy, who is half giggling and half frightened, mischievously play at spanking and thus fail to follow the details of the director's instructions. Although the woman and boy may have been forced into becoming a photograph, forced into being the objects of a voyeuristic or pornographic gaze, they are also acting as agents who leave vibrant traces in the photograph that attest to the photographer's having become the object of others' gazes — the gazes of the photographed subjects at the time the photograph was taken and the gazes of the spectators afterward.

This series of photographs by Muybridge stands apart from the rest of his work. They do not record the movement of the photographed subject, but the movement of the photographer himself and his attitude toward the object of his photograph. The photographer, with his camera dizzyingly encircling the raised arm and the possibilities it holds of beating the boy's naked body, of beating the naked body of the woman herself, ultimately chooses another option — not to allow the beating to occur. He could have made it happen, yet frame after frame, at the time the photographs were taken and in the process of editing, he chose to prevent it. Muybridge, who is no less present in the photographs than his photographed subjects, is training himself through the photographic situation to subdue and suspend violent action.

Once the photographer has turned into an object of the gaze, the code of scientific discourse that leaves his biography out of the photographs no longer applies. It proves difficult to resist allowing a significant event in his biography help us understand both the photographs and the era in which they were made. A few years before he began working on the dissection of human motion, Muybridge married Flora Shallcross Stone. Two years later, in 1874, she bore him a son. When the boy was six months old, Muybridge came to suspect that he was not his, but the progeny of his wife's lover. Seeing the boy as the product of this sinful union, he would not so much as touch him, and as for the boy's father — his wife's lover — he murdered him, leaving the boy an orphan. Muybridge was ultimately acquitted of the murder charge on the grounds that it had been "justifiable homicide" and "a crime of passion." Thus, Heiman's imprint,

"Raped into Being a Photograph," imprinted in the plural, allows us to reorganize the power relation with the protagonist who participated in the act of photography. Although forced by the photographer into a passive position, the photographed subjects are looking at the photographer's gestures with an ironic distance, actually watching the impossibility of forcing one to become a photograph without being trapped in the same fate. No less than a woman spanking a child, this photo is of Muybridge photographing a woman spanking a child, as well as of a woman and a child looking at the photographer photographing a woman spanking a child.

Of course, on its own, a reading such as this will not suffice without the reconstruction of the photographed subjects' civic status and without recalling that their ability to participate actively in the game of power relations between themselves and the photographer was not supported by any political recognition. Both the woman and the boy were among those excluded from the rights of citizenship enjoyed by men. The photographed individual, then, can become a citizen of photography and yet remain a noncitizen in such a way that this conflict between being and not being a citizen turns the photograph into a complaint that attests to the fact that the photographed figure is fundamentally a political entity, an entity that is governed, and that this political being was robbed of its citizenship.

Against this background we should revisit the universal claim of photography that was advanced by the French state, which presented itself as the state that had given the invention of photography to all of humanity: "anyone can in principle operate a camera." When there is someone who falls outside of this principle, such deprivation exposes the shadow that this universal "anyone" casts on the citizen of the state. Attributing the threshold of opportunity for using photography to the technology itself — it is easy to operate, widely available, inexpensive, and so on — masks the fact that not everyone is truly equal before the photographic technology. Despite the steady lowering of photographic costs, poor populations were nevertheless unable to enjoy the same possibilities that this technology opened for the realization of citizenship.[53] Cultural conditioning and economic limitations have posed, and continue to pose, obstacles to certain populations in their ability to employ this technology beyond it becoming a means for taking an identity picture, that is, for the purposes of power, not of the citizen.[54] This "anyone in principle can" should not be understood as technological accessibility, but as a civilian partnership: From the point of view of the citizenry of photography, anyone can become a citizen.

Large parts of disenfranchised populations are prone to turn into photographs taken by others, more than they tend to become photographers themselves or self-photographed subjects. However, even as merely photographed persons, they take part in the power play on which they leave their photographed mark, even as they remain excluded from the hegemonic political game. This is true of the contemporary photograph of the Afghan girl that I will address later on, and it was also true in 1850, as photography was just coming into being, of Drana, Delia, Jacques, and Renty, Afro-American slaves whose pictures were taken by Joseph T. Zealy for Dr. Louis Agassiz, the noted Harvard naturalist.

Their daguerreotypes are part of a series of fifteen images of seven slaves whom Agassiz selected out of a large number of slaves presented to him on the Taylor plantation in Columbia, North Carolina. Agassiz arrived at the plantation through the mediation of his friend Dr. Robert Gibbes, a North Carolina paleontologist who was friendly with the local slave owners.[55] According to the entries in Agassiz's journal, he was interested in finding slaves who were born in Africa and their offspring who were born in the United States.[56] After choosing the ones who suited his study and with the consent of the slave owner, they were sent to the studio of the photographer in charge of producing a scientific documentation, of which they were the raw material — a full frontal view and a profile (figures 3.4, 3.5, 3.6, 3.7).[57] Very little is known of these pictures, and even less is known of what preceded their creation — of the meeting between the slaves and Agassiz, or the manner in which he examined them in order to select those suited to become his research samples, or the way in which they were told that they would be required to pose for photographs, or just how they arrived at the photographer's studio.[58] The details that are known — Agassiz's hope to enlist the aid of photography so as to prove his claims that not all humans are of the same species and that the black race is inferior to the white one, alongside

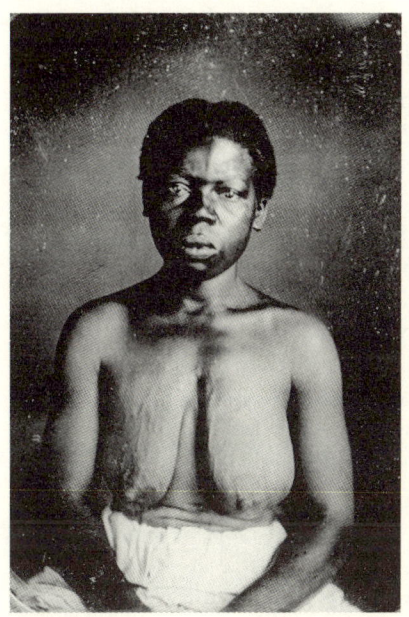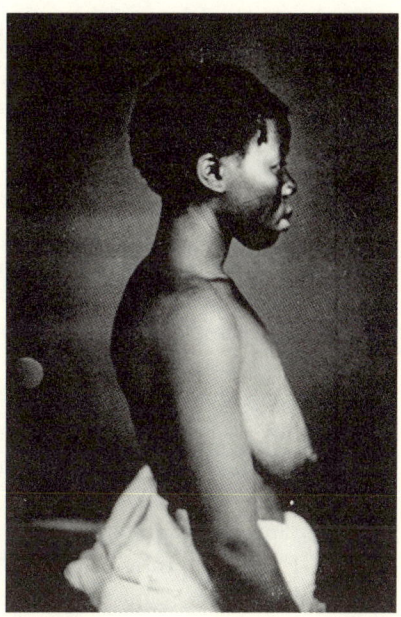

Figures 3.4 and 3.5. Joseph T. Zealy, Drana, country born, daughter of Jack, Guinea, Plantation of B.F. Taylor, Esq. Columbia, S.C., 1850 (Peabody Museum, Harvard University).

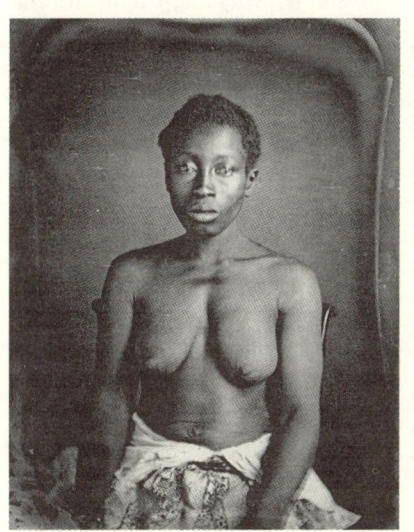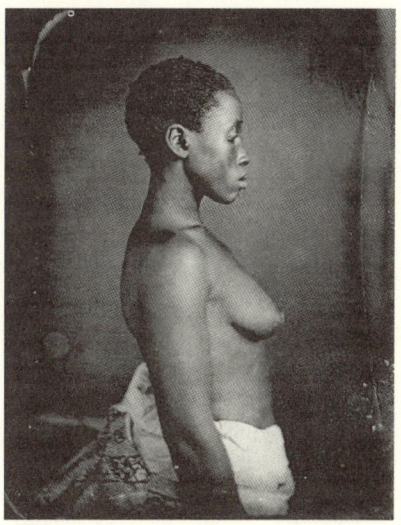

Figures 3.6 and 3.7. Joseph T. Zealy, Delia, country born, daughter of Renty, Congo, Plantation of B.F. Taylor, Esq. Columbia, S.C., 1850 (Peabody Museum, Harvard University).

the transformation of these photographed people into illustrations for a scientific claim — tend to obscure the little that can be salvaged from the photographs about the photographed people and their point of view.[59]

The daguerreotypes are preserved at the Peabody Museum at Harvard, along with identifying labels that were carefully prepared by Gibbes to assist Agassiz in his study.[60] The photographed people are identified by their first names and their owner (B. F. Taylor); the photographed women are also identified by their kinship — daughter of "Jack" and daughter of "Renty." The portraits of the two women, who were actually very young, almost girls, are taken in a similar manner: dress undone down to the waist, its upper edges visible within the frame, body upright, head turned almost imperceptibly to the right, gaze directed straight ahead — almost certainly toward the site from which they received instructions in the course of the photography session.

For a long time now, I've been placed at the site toward which each of them is directing her piercing gaze, trying to understand what it is that makes these harsh portraits so stately and glowing, so permeated with the powerful presence of the photographed women, attempting to revive the mark they left on the photograph through a reconstruction of their point of view and its placement opposite the viewpoint responsible for their oppression. I'll begin by asking who they were posing for and what precisely was the photographic situation to which they were subjected.

From the sparse details that are identifiable from Gibbes's notes and Agassiz's letters, it emerges clearly that negotiations between four white men — Gibbes, the scientist colleague and liaison; Agassiz, the scientist who initiated the photographic project; Zealy, the photographer; and Taylor, the slave owner — formed the basis of the agreement regarding the photographs we see before us. No mention whatsoever is made of the role of the photographed men and women, but they were clearly not parties to this agreement. If their photographs had not been before us, they could have been said to have been completely invisible to all the parties involved. However, not only do we have before us photographs in which they are present, but all that is left of the agreement between the four men are these photographs taken in the photographer's studio. Even if the four men were not present together in the studio along with the photographed women, it would be a mistake to analyze what our eyes behold as an encounter between the women and the photographer alone, just as it is a mistake to analyze the photographic situation only in terms of an oppression whose forms and modes are realized, completely, through the threatening whip of the master. The relations of exchange between the four men in question preceding the photographic event form an inseparable part of this event, while the sexualized and racialized violence reflected in it cannot be deciphered without taking these relations into account. However, it would also be unduly limiting to discuss the photographs as if they were only and completely expressions of the deal forced on the photographed people, as if these people were absent and as if the act of photography were only and completely an execution of a scientific claim that bears no testimony to the encounter — violent though it may be — between the photographed people and the ones commanding them to pose.

The violence of the daguerreotypes before us doesn't stem exclusively from the encounter between the photographer and the photographed women. It is no less a result of the multipartite encounter between the latter and those who agreed on the photograph in their stead. The photographer alone lacked the power to force the slaves to stand half-naked before the apparatus that he was operating. Moreover, we have no information at all about what the photographed people knew of the ritual they were forced to take part in, beyond the general fact that slaves did not participate in the flurry of activity surrounding the invention of photography, which enabled people to create images of themselves: "Few slaves, however, had the luxury of projecting any look at all. That slaves were denied individual identity in the antebellum South, is merely underscored by the near-total absence of photographs depicting them."[61] We can, however, assume that even if they didn't know exactly what this technology was, and even if none of the people present showed them the results — that is, their own image — they were well aware that as the event took place, they were serving as the objects of a gaze that transcended the here and now. During the taking of the photograph, the gaze of the photographed women is directed toward the photographer, but it also reaches beyond him, in the knowledge that there is the photographer and there is the person who selected them as objects of a gaze, and the person who permitted their transformation into objects of this gaze, and the person who is now in fact gazing at them. In other words, their gaze, even if it doesn't fully comprehend what photography is, understands that the situation in which they are gazed at is one that departs from the direct meeting of gazes between those present opposite each other.

The symbolic violence employed by the photographer in his exacting instructions was an extension of the violence with which they were already familiar, but it is also distinct from the familiar violence in that it is a subdued, symbolic form that does not directly touch the body. Gibbes, who was present during the photography sessions, ensuring through his gaze that they were following the instructions in a manner that would achieve successful results, most probably took an active role in bringing them to the studio. He served as a kind of liaison for their master, who authorized their transportation to the studio and their supervision, for Agassiz, whom he served faithfully throughout the photography project, and for the photographer, who presented certain conditions in order that his work might achieve success, with the photographed women, whose full cooperation was a condition for the fulfillment of his task. Taylor, who was not present in person at the studio, was present through the other men, whom he had empowered to use the photographed women in order to produce the daguerreotypes. These men, even if they were not all supporters of slavery, recognized the slave owner's ownership of these slaves by virtue of their common agreement on the act of photography.

Agassiz, initiator of the photography project, who was already back home at the time the photographs were taken, was present in the arena as a specter through his representatives, but also through his particular choice of the slaves to be photographed, which brought together fathers and daughters. The choice of fathers was explained by his wish to study "pure" Africans, born in Africa, of the kind that by this time could be found on U.S. soil mainly in the person of slaves. Although Agassiz also sought to study the U.S.-born progeny of African-born slaves, there is no explanation in his notes as to why these progeny ended up being daughters. Even if Agassiz's journals or letters had elaborated in detail on this issue, the information, at the very most, would have illuminated the way in which he viewed and justified his selection, rather than explaining the meaning of this selection in the context within which it was realized and carried out.

In his essay on these photographs, Brian Wallis writes, "Agassiz was doubtful about finding 'pure' examples of the race in America."[62] It is seriously doubtful whether the specimens Agassiz found on the plantations around Columbia were indeed "pure," for the importing of slaves from Africa was banned in 1808, and most, if not all of the photographed men do not look as if, by 1808, they had already attained an age and a capacity that would have made them profitable imports for a white master. Be this as it may, the photographed men disrupted the pure or purifying categories. It is highly likely that some of the photographed people were not "pure" Africans in the sense intended by Agassiz, because they had been born in the United States or smuggled into the country after the legislation that cleansed the language of the Constitution of the stain of slavery, but that authorized the local trade and ownership of slaves.

However, the emphasis on place of birth deflects the discussion from what was actually bothering Agassiz as regards the purity of the photographed men. His skepticism about the possibility of finding pure specimens stemmed from the widespread phenomenon of racial interference due to the ongoing mixing of black and white blood. At issue, of course, in his worries was not what is known as "mixed marriages," but rather the rape of black girls by their white masters and the birth of "hybrid" offspring.[63] The rape victims, often very young girls, were totally without protection, either legal, because the law didn't recognize black women as subjects whose violation could at all be addressed, or social, because the men to whom they were married were powerless to fulfill the role preserved for members of their sex in the white society they served — that is, as protectors of their wives.[64] The sexual violation of black women is represented in the literature on slavery in the United States in the nineteenth century as a widespread and common phenomenon with numerous implications for the structure and form of kinship relations among blacks.

181

The main characteristic of these relations that is relevant to a discussion of the photographs in question involves the attribution of offspring to mothers, rather than to fathers. This attribution was not a feature of the social relations prevalent among the blacks before reaching the United States. It emerged as an effect of their way of life among the whites, who operated on many levels and in many ways to disrupt family structure in the slave society.[65] Children's attribution to their mothers served their masters, first and foremost, because the latter were consequently freed of any responsibility toward their offspring, meanwhile positioning the mother as the sole anchor of certainty as to children's lineage.

Within this context, Agassiz chose to ignore the prevalent kinship relations that had developed in the United States among slaves, instead displaying a paternal model of family relations in which the fathers served as the source. However, given the circumstances described above, even if the identity of the specific fathers selected could indeed be determined as that of the biological fathers of their offspring, the photographic event, in the frame of which their daughters were forced — before their fathers' eyes — to strip in front of strange men, undermined their symbolic status as fathers who protect their daughters. The fact that the photographed people — both men and women — were stripped half-naked in the photographic situation both enhanced and illustrated the fact that these were people stripped of power.

Thus, the act of photography through which Agassiz sought to attain the hard facts supporting the inferiority of the black race turned into a performative event occasioning an acting out of the white man's supremacy over the black man and the black man's subjection and subaltern status. The two women selected for the photography project — the daughters of Renty and Jack — served as currency through which the four white men once again demonstrated to the black men just who it was who possessed the power and authority to issue commands to the women while commanding them to witness their daughters' subjection to these commands.[66] The photographs thus indeed "proved" what Agassiz sought to prove, but they did so not as the result of a scientific inquiry, but as a result of the power structures that they reveal.

In the daguerreotypes, the photographed people, both men and women, stand motionless, like statues — upright and balanced, mouths shut, eyes staring ahead, heads held high on tall necks, arms symmetrically dropped at their sides, palms placed on their thighs pointing toward each other at an angle to the arms and wrists. It is a stance requiring concentration and effort. The time required for taking such pictures was fairly long. These subjects were required to display their bodies to a gaze, to spread them like anatomical maps, and they appear to have done so solemnly, with total obedience. Their pose conformed so precisely to the instructions that the similarity between the contours of their perfect silhouettes within the frame becomes troubling.

However, the similarity forcefully imposed on the photographed people by the director arranging them in the photographic situation is disrupted by the different looks in the eyes of each subject. It can be determined with near certainty that all of the people photographed were required to look straight ahead.[67] In the full-frontal photograph, all of them indeed comply with this instruction. In the profile, the gazes of Delia and Jack (Drana's father) are slightly lowered. Their bodies remain upright, as if they could feel the gaze fixed on them, expecting them to stand firm, but the dissolved eye contact seems to have reconnected them to themselves, to have allowed them to curl up into their pose and retreat momentarily into a private reverie. Delia's gaze in the frontal photograph looks frightened. Her shoulders are pulled very slightly forward in a gesture expressing discomfort, as well as a groping attempt to understand who stands before her and what is to be expected from him. The possibility of (re)gaining protection or help does not seem to be dismissed outright.[68] In contrast, Drana's gaze is tougher, more seasoned, grudging and scornful toward those seeking to photograph her look at this given moment. Similarly, the gaze of Renty (Delia's father) is full of anger and resentment, even discernibly hateful toward those who have placed him in this position. Jack's eyes are slightly squinted, as if they sought to turn the tables, scrutinizing those looking at him, transforming them into objects whose despicableness makes him wonder just how far they can go with their crudity.

The different gaze of each of the photographed people, expressing their attitudes toward those who have cast them into the photographic situation, distinguishes them from each other within the overall framework, which sought to turn them into perfect illustrations. However, the uprightness, the broadened chests, and the bodies spread on display cannot be attributed exclusively to the violent game of the instructions and their fulfillment. It is difficult not to see the way in which they take this pose as both a challenge and an expression of pride, as if they fully understood the situation created by the act of photography, the opportunity being offered them to present scientific proof of their noninferiority.[69] As I've noted above, something in the situation allowed them to understand that the gaze resting on them at the moment didn't exhaust the gaze to be directed at them. And the gaze that they returned was not addressed exclusively to those who were there in the room with them. The scorn, the contempt, the anger, the call for help, the indifference, the wonder are all expressions of an address extending beyond total subjection and suspending it in order to utter and express. These photographed people address someone who is not present, an addressee who opens up the space in which they are placed, who undoes — albeit very slightly — its oppressive limits. Though they know nothing of the category of a universal addressee, their gaze is addressed to someone like her whose existence they assume when they address their gaze to her, revealing something of their feelings toward their enslavers.

Using photography, Agassiz sought to produce scientific proof of the inferiority of the people photographed. However, photography exposed the performative content of his claim and documented the cyclic manner in which it produced the required results. Photography subverted Agassiz's presumption to use it for showing the blacks in their purity. It not only documented the objects that he sought to photograph, it also recorded the manner in which these were designed for gazing at, in the spirit of the slave auctions at which they were displayed on podiums and required to exhibit their bodies, enabling examinations of the merchandise. After enactment of the law prohibiting the importing of slaves from Africa, the bodies of women turned into a precious resource for the reproduction of slavery. Deborah Gray White describes how, frequently, women's display at auctions involved feeling up their bodies, both by sellers, who wished to convince potential buyers of the quality, and by buyers, who wished to verify and examine the merchandise themselves.[70] The main areas handled were the belly and the breasts, as if these could teach the handlers how many children the women could bear and suckle.

The photograph forced on the people enslaved at the Taylor plantation served them as an opportunity not only to subvert the claim that they were inferior, but also to provide a rare replacement for the never-taken snapshots of life in slavery — an exposure of the black woman's body to the gaze and arm of the white man and its transformation into a battleground.[71] Drana's breasts are furrowed with vertical scars left by beatings or by their damaging overuse for nursing or sex. The exhausted breasts, which look like those of an old woman, whose history is inscribed on her body, are all the more striking on the background of her young body, leaving a silent testimony to her abuse in the photograph.

The same year that these daguerreotypes were taken, Sojourner Truth, lecturing in Ohio, asked accusingly, "Ain't I a woman?" Her rhetorical question was a response to a comment from the audience by "Dat man ober dar say dat woman needs...to have de best place every whar." Truth, never treated in the manner the man had claimed was preserved exclusively for women, called on the audience to take a good look at her and her body — "Look at me! Look at my arm!" — and to judge for themselves whether she, too, was not a woman. Eight years later, in 1858, during a lecture at Silver Lake, Indiana, a man stood up and voiced a rumor that had been making the rounds through the audience — that Truth was in fact a man disguised as a woman. He demanded that she consent to an examination of her breasts by a number of women who would verify her sex. In an unprecedented act, facing an audience that had reacted with great enthusiasm to the idea that Truth consent to an examination behind closed doors in a seeming gesture of respect for her privacy, Truth bared her breasts publicly for all to see. In her choice of the anonymous public gaze over the supposedly intimate framework she was offered, Truth challenged the distinction between private and public that relegated slavery and its injustices to the private sphere in an attempt to retain them beyond the public gaze and the political arena, the latter being the only sphere in which a new beginning would occur. Drana, unlike Truth, didn't choose to display and turn her breasts into a living proof. But when forced into a situation where her body was examined behind the closed doors of the photographer's studio, she didn't miss the opportunity of staring at the spectator and causing her to connect her disgusted look with her scarred body.

Chapter Four

Emergency Claims

American attacks on Iraq in 1991, conducted under the framework of what was called the "Gulf War," marked the beginning of a new era in the imagery of war.[1] This epoch has subsequently and repeatedly been described as one of sterilized or sanitized news coverage.[2] Such formulations indicate the emergence of the ruling power's ability, during times of war, to manipulate the production and distribution of images. Coalescing around such figures of speech as "smart bomb" and "precision target," this discourse has, in effect, allied itself with expressions coined by the ruling power. Rather than look at the images themselves and the ways in which they expose the evils of war, news editors, journalists, and critics focused at length on the nature of the new imagery of war, of which the general conditions of appearance had been formed through the cooperation of the media with the military and other branches of government. Susan Sontag has described this situation as "techno-war": "the sky above the dying, filled with light-traces of missiles and shells — images that illustrated America's absolute military superiority over its enemy."[3] The flickering, green nocturnal photographs of Baghdad have become icons of an era of warfare conducted and photographed remotely at a distance.

The preponderance of such icons has made the gaze forget the fact that photographs were taken in this war, just as in all other wars perpetrated since the invention of photography. Slightly more than a decade later, daily bombings of Afghanistan and Iraq continue to be depicted as if such assaults occur under the same visual regime, one overseen by a distant gaze. As Sontag contends, "Television, whose access to the scene is limited by government controls and by self-censorship, serves up the war as images. The war itself is waged as much as possible at a distance, through bombing, whose targets can be chosen, on the basis of instantly relayed information and visualizing technology, from continents away."[4]

The prevailing critical description of the new age that emerged with the American attack on Iraq in 1991 characterizes it as one exclusively made of sanitized images or, even further, as one wholly sanitized of images. Such a description adopts a remote stance toward its object, a position from which one cannot even take images into account or what is evident within them. Instead one can only derive an image from them — an image of the end of the image. This position, voiced by critics of the government, uncannily resonates with the government's own position, complementing the latter's effort to homogenize the field of vision, creating the conditions for its own images to be viewed in such a way that all others images will hardly be seen.[5] If the Gulf War represents a significant turning point in the annals of the photographed image, it is not by virtue of having emptied the field of vision of images, but on account of it signaling a new stage in the government's efforts to monopolize control over the visual image and to impose its self-produced images on the media.

This attempted takeover was conducted along two parallel and complementary channels. One was made of the autonomous, real-time production of images via the weapons of war, distributed to the media as the most accurate and reliable record of military operations.[6] The other involved the assignment of press photographers to specific fighting units, fully integrating them in the array of forces as "embedded" reporters. The first channel transformed the military into a major player within the visual field, allowing greater participation in a competitive domain where images are produced and distributed by a multitude of different agents vying with one another. The second channel effectively held the media hostage to the government's command.

In light of these developments, it is important to recall that cameras did not cease taking pictures once the age of sanitized "techno-war" was declared. Photographic production has found its way into the media, with some photos appearing within mainstream outlets, others on the fringes, and, as always, with some remaining temporarily buried in archives. Without a doubt, the registry of images from the war in Iraq includes a wide variety of photographs. Among the more horrifying of shots one can find the charred corpses of Iraqi soldiers frozen in position or burned vehicles with dead occupants caught inside. Other photographs depict the experiences of American soldiers in action, as well as the sights that inevitably follow the horrors of war: the ruins of buildings, refugees and camps — all part of the consequences of war.[7]

Either viewed individually or taken in their cumulative abundance, these photographs refute the widespread assumption that postmodern war has made it impossible to see war and its horrors. These photographs are indubitably part of the repertoire of postmodern warfare, and they are constantly seeking spectators.[8] The press photographer has not vanished from the arena of war and continues to take pictures. However, she now finds herself surrounded by other photographers who either work on behalf of various interest groups or others who come to be designated as "amateurs." All these photographers share her labors, competing over access to the various media outlets. Thus, for example, when the U.S. Army at the start of the attacks in 1991 successfully blinded spectators' eyes, making them believe there were no more images to view, press photographer Peter Turnley refused to join the pool of photographers assigned to various military units and roamed Iraq on his own, taking photos without the supervision of the military. The images he captured were distributed through various channels. On the eve of the Second Gulf War, the photographs he was able to capture were redistributed over the Internet in the form of a digital book entitled *The Unseen Gulf War*.[9]

The many photographs taken during the Gulf Wars and other horrifying occasions are not necessarily broadcast on the prime-time news or printed on the front pages of major newspapers. But these photographs do indeed circulate, and with a few simple steps, anyone can locate them through various information networks.[10] Texts written *about* these images, despite the images themselves having found distribution through diverse communication channels, still are not sufficiently exhibited — not on prime-time television, or on the front pages, or in color, or with such immediacy. Such texts, however, are testimony to the *existence*, rather than the *absence* of images. With each photograph — whether taken by a professional press photographer, an amateur photographer, or one working for a cause — there always remains the possibility of reading traces of an event (as well as its "counterevent"), or at least the ability to bring such an event into view through the photograph. Thus, for example, in the Web site album of Tim the Soldier,[11] pastoral views of American soldiers stationed in the desert appear alongside photographs showing Iraqi prisoners being forced to pile up the bodies of dead Iraqi soldiers. Without having been given the proper tools to perform the job, some Iraqis can be seen dragging a corpse unsteadily on a blanket in one photograph. Another shows six American soldiers carrying the corpse of a single Iraqi soldier on a stretcher. Looking comparatively at these two photographs, it is difficult not to observe the humiliation imposed on the Iraqi prisoners and the disrespectful treatment of the enemy dead. Even further, one cannot fail to see these photographs as a portent of the infamous torture photographs, also taken by American soldiers, a decade later in Iraq's Abu Ghraib prison. Efforts to monopolize control over photography thus will only partially succeed, and for only a limited period of time. As long as there are cameras in this world, photographs will continue to be made simultaneously by different people, and heterogeneous realities will be presented that will eat away at any supposed monopoly.

"Everything Could Be Seen"

The assertion that a sterile field of vision is operative is generally accompanied by an additional insults and accusations aimed at spectators, claiming that they turn away from images of horror and prefer to watch other things instead.[12] Critics claim that the vision of spectators has been blinded. The spectators are oblivious; their attention has waned; they prefer entertainment; they would rather avoid looking; they are weary of horrific images; they need more stimulating sights and more powerful images to move them. When spectators are conceived in this way, the question of how to stimulate them continually arises for professionals in many fields. But when the assertion that war has been sanitized of images is coupled with the assertion that spectators are blind, it remains unclear why spectators would actively avoid images that simply are not supposed to exist. These two contradictory assertions — one claiming that there are no images, while the other claiming that there are too many — are generally voiced in succession by the same speakers. According to the first claim, there are too few images, thus there is nothing to look at. According to the second claim, there are too many, and therefore it has become impossible to look. Both claims leap over what is visible to the gaze — fragmentary images of moments within the whole of what is called war — subsequently rejecting what has been rendered visible on account of not conforming to a phantasmatic model of the object of vision, the existence of which has been assumed by the critics. With this phantasmatic model, the much sought-after object of vision is a sort of pure object that makes it possible to see war with utter clarity. It is an ideal object of vision, which is why all the available images are either more or less than what is supposed to be offered.

The other side of this passion for a pure object of vision, which no existing image can equal, is the passion for a pure spectator who will encounter the image, be appalled by what is revealed, and successfully change the world through her active response to it. Such a hope inevitably results in disappointment through the repeated confrontation with the absence of such a spectator. There is no field of vision in which such an image may be found and no such image in existence. It is vain to wait. In its very essence, the image is partial, obscured, fissured, and questionable. Though mendacious, it nonetheless discloses something truthful, yet is nebulous at the same time. Handicapped, the image is not sufficient in itself and requires visual and verbal support — a spokesperson to bring it forth and to have it speak. A solitary image cannot testify to what is revealed through it, but must be attached to another image, another piece of information, another assertion or description, another grievance or piece of evidence, another broadcast, another transmitter. An image is only ever another statement in a regime of statements.

Photography's inclusion within a discourse reasserts the civil contract of photography, enabling the promise to continue to protect the last means of employing legitimate violence that is left in the hands of the modern citizen — photography. The civil contract of photography enables citizens and noncitizens alike to produce grievances and claims that otherwise can't be seen and to impose them by means of, through, and on the citizenry of photography. The civil contract of photography protects the citizen vis-à-vis power, endowing her political existence with a dimension beyond the bounds of being subject to power. The civil contract of photography is frequently threatened by the ruling power. When the citizen's gaze is diverted from photographs, and directed toward the field of vision created by the ruling power, where, in fact, there are no images, individuals abandon their commitment to the contract and effectively collaborate with the ruling power even when they may be explicitly opposed to its actions.

In order to protest against power, critics continue to monitor the field of vision it created — where, at most, only ideas can be "seen" — and relinquish the civil field of vision, where concrete objects await their gazes. To steady one's gaze on the photographs, to direct one's look at what is revealed by each and every one and to assume responsibility for how what is visible is articulated into discourse — this is sometimes all that a citizen can do. Indeed, in various places throughout the world, citizens are acting exactly in this way. They *themselves* are looking at what is presented to their gaze and are in no hurry to describe what the "spectator" may have seen or felt in relation to what is visible. Instead, they assume their own singular vantage point. Looking at what is visible as it is revealed from their own point of view, they attempt to extend the limits of this angle of vision, rather than renounce it so as to adopt the viewpoint of power, which ostensibly enjoys a birds-eye view of things. From their own localized perspectives, as citizens with multiple positions of speech and action, they take responsibility for what is visible and the way in which it unfolds in the discourse. As activists participating in various public associations, as parents, teachers, lecturers, artists, workers, and merchants, citizens of the citizenry of photography assume local responsibility toward what is visible, although the visible cannot be separated from its global conditions. In the following, I will linger over the responsibility demonstrated by several photographers and artists toward what is visible in the reality of the Israeli occupation of the Palestinian Territories.

The existence of images within a discourse that does not cease to describe their absence is part of the current general conditions of the image. In other words, the visible threatens to turn invisible, and the invisible threatens to manifest itself as visible. Local conditions affect the generalized form of relations between the visible and the invisible. With the rising homogenization that characterizes the global age, local conditions perform a process of heterogenization within the field of vision. Based on an exhibition I curated in the summer of 2004 at the Um El Fahem Art Gallery in Israel, entitled Everything Could Be Seen, I will examine the viewing conditions specific to Israeli rule over the Palestinians.[13]

What could be seen? Where? In real time or in pictures? From nearby or from afar? When could it be seen? When it happened? After the fact? Under what conditions? Who said there was anything to see at all? What does seeing "everything" mean? And what does "could be" mean? If it "could be seen," who prevented it from being seen? And if it could be seen, why is no one seeing it? Is it all over? Is there, perhaps, nothing to see? What does "seeing" mean? Is seeing possible? Does the fact that pictures exist imply that seeing is possible? Can one see at all without speaking about what one sees? And besides, who is saying that nobody saw? No one knew? Who's asking all these questions, and why? What are the conditions of possibility for the question "Could everything be seen?" Was the title of the exhibition an answer to a question? To a contention? To an accusation? To a court order? Who is posing the question? And why doesn't she address the question to herself?

The sentence "Everything could be seen," which served as the name of the exhibition, is not a reply to any message arriving from the outside in the form of a question, a contention, or a court order. On its own, the sentence seeks to establish an urgency, to allow the images to give a warning, and to declare a state of emergency. The exhibition presented a series of images that had been conceived, collected, classified, created, or processed out of the continuing everyday reality of the state of Israel's "temporary" dominion over three and a half million Palestinians. On display were visual traces of a people on whom a framework of control has been imposed, one that does not cease controlling their lives, denying them — usually in violent fashion — any political status. In collapsing the distance between the machinery of control and the body of the subjected, the denial of political status facilitates direct intervention in their lives. Whoever is placed in this position is a *noncitizen* of the state of Israel. A multi-layered relationship between a noncitizen and a citizen of the state subsists on several levels. Here I will dwell on one constitutive aspect of this relationship.

Urgency with respect to the citizens' situation (usually in defense of their security) requires and provides the justification for the state's direct intervention in the lives and bodies of the noncitizens. The transformation of one population (noncitizens) into a "human shield" for another population (the corpus of citizens) over a period of several decades makes it impossible to discuss the one isolated from the other. Despite gestures of separation and withdrawal, as the structure of relations between the two populations based on the hostility of mutually exclusive sides, the prolonged dominion of one over the other has tied them to a common destiny. In this framework, the noncitizens — Palestinians living in the West Bank and the Gaza Strip — are paying the greatest and gravest cost. With growing frequency, they are completely abandoned, subjected to the damage of their property, and exposed to mental suffering and physical injury. However, within this situation, the ruling power's privileged citizens (Jews), its second-class citizens (Palestinians with Israeli citizenship), and the Palestinian refugees living outside the borders of the state of Israel (whose fate is still dictated by the state on account of their perpetual designation as refugees) — all pay a price. Citizens, on the whole, try to avoid paying and are repeatedly surprised when the bill arrives at their table. They take offense when the price to be paid is exacted from others, and not only from those who "should" pay it by virtue of their status as noncitizens. The chronicle of events — the daily news and the agenda it determines — coalesces around the price citizens are paying, depicting the transaction as something that could be or at least should be prevented. One sees on the margins of the daily publication and dissemination of this reportage, without even a hint of emergency, traces of the ravages being inflicted on the population of noncitizens. Such traces appear divested of the function of civility that, to a greater or lesser extent, holds the power of turning the harm that has been inflicted into something that is not to be taken for granted.

In reading several images, I will focus on the price that is paid by noncitizens, which is supposedly extracted only temporarily, although such transience has in fact become the permanent and daily reality of their lives. I'll attempt to point out the structural gap that prevents the horror depicted in each of these images from turning into a state of emergency or an audible cry for help. Curating an exhibition made of these images was guided by the intention of turning a flash of time from the future — some distant day when one will be able to claim that "everything could be seen" — into the present, to contend that this day has already arrived.

As I write this text, and while you spectators are reading the text and contemplating the images, "everything" can already be seen. And this is not because the omnivoyant gaze has suddenly been revitalized or because messianic conditions have arisen that would allow a glimpse of the end. "Everything" can be seen because what one can see, even within the frames of the few images I will address, is enough for one to see "everything" and to understand its outline. What I'll consider is sufficient cause for the establishment of an indictment against injury done to citizenship. What I will show is *not* seen in the existent tribunals, nor is it translated into an emergency summons, given the current conditions of the gaze we are faced with and the particularity of the statement of horror that I will analyze below.

In the early 1930s, Walter Benjamin wrote that "photographic records begin to be evidence in the historical trial. This constitutes their hidden political significance."[14] The images under discussion are evidence, incontrovertible evidence, of destruction, humiliation, injury, manslaughter, abuse, suffocation, suffering, misery, and injustice. They are the basis for seeing everything, despite the case that not everything could be seen. There is a decisive rift, however, between the substratum of visual facts that have been compiled and the gaze that will rest on them. This gap prevents the gaze from seeing the visual fact that is disclosed. The fact that visual materials remain from one event or another or from a certain situation doesn't necessarily insure their visibility. Not everyone who looks effectively sees. Seeing requires a special intention, which is manifested by a certain responsibility on the part of an addressee toward what is in fact seen. The collected pieces of evidence I gathered here for the exhibition Everything Could Be Seen will perhaps serve, at some point in the future, as exhibits to be admitted at the "historical trial." In the meantime, it seeks the responsibility of citizens for what has been shown. It does not suffice that the evidence is merely put on display. If the spectator fails to demonstrate responsibility toward it and to give it a place in current discourses, it is liable to be dismissed from the historical trial, like dust blowing in the wind.

Jean-François Lyotard's theory of discourse, developed in *The Differend*, provides means for conceptualizing an ethics of the spectator, in order to discuss her civic responsibility.[15] The statement, which is the smallest element of discourse, cannot be reduced to merely linguistic content or an expression; it is a structure of relations made among an addresser, an addressee, a referent, and a meaning. One cannot discuss the statement in isolation from these four elements (*instances* in French), although it is not necessary for all of them to be active. To discuss the damage that discourse cannot express, Lyotard develops a theory of discourse that is organized around the pole of the injured. To harm one of the elements of the statement, he writes, makes it impossible to express the damage, turning it into injustice and transforming whoever complains about the damage done to him into a victim. Harm inflicted on the element of the addresser can occur when the addresser is physically silenced, or when the authority of the addresser is undermined, or when the right of the addresser to maintain his or her ground and political status is subverted. Harm can also occur if the addresser is deemed to be insane or if what he or she says is labeled incoherent.

Harm to the element of the addressee occurs when the addressee is simultaneously the one who has inflicted the damage and the tribunal that decides on the damage, but also when the addressee is simply not present, does not understand his or her role, rejects that role, is negligent in carrying it out, or neglects it deliberately or out of indifference. Harm to the referent is caused when its existence cannot be established, or when the procedures allowing it to exist are not recognized as valid, or when they are not available to the addresser, or because the evidence that would help establish its existence has been erased. Despite the fact that the referent can be established, harm to meaning is caused when the conditions of discourse distort the meaning of the statement.

My discussion will divert from the path that runs, according to Lyotard, from damage to injured person to victim, opting for a particular kind of *énoncé*: statements produced from and in the face of horror. *Zva'a*, the Hebrew word for horror, describes mists rising from the earth toward the clouds, ascending above a place where disaster has struck. But horror is not simply the view afforded to the gaze — "a horrific sight" — it also functions as a description of the state of the spectator of horror. Horror is the emotion that is aroused in the spectator by what she sees: the feeling of shock or alarm, a trembling, dismay, or fear. In the Hebrew Bible, the word "horror" appears only in Isaiah 28:19, although the Revised Standard English translation uses a different equivalent: "as often as it [judgment] passeth through, it shall take you; for morning by morning shall it pass through, by day and by night: and it shall be nought but terror [*zva'a*], to understand the message." Within a context that undermines the power of the visible in order to shock on its own, horror appears to demand that an emphasis be placed on the part of hearing for any understanding of horror as horror: "That he should give his heart to understand the rumor of calamities, his heart shall not be quieted, only shall be full of trembling and trepidation."[16] In other words, horror already enfolds within itself the flawed nature of the statement in which it will be transmitted.

Such a flaw is due to the absence of the conditions required for a statement of horror to turn into what I call an emergency claim. An emergency is a situation involving calamity or mortal peril that demands immediate treatment. It is produced from a situation entangled in disaster, war, terrorist attacks, massacres, catastrophes, or accidents, but it also emerges from ongoing situations of poverty, misery, abuse, or humiliation. "Emergency," as a term, encompasses both the description of the calamitous or perilous situation and the prescription of how it ought to be handled. A horror that takes place in conditions that turn it into a situation is thus designated as an emergency, the termination of which requires action to be taken.

But not every statement of horror turns automatically into an emergency claim. In the modern era, when the relationship between the ruling power and its subjects is mediated through citizenship, the ruling power is committed to alleviating situations that arise for citizens in conditions of disaster and holds the authority to declare a state of emergency. In Israel, a permanent state of emergency was declared in 1948 and has never been abolished since then. The alleged presupposition and justification for this unusually prolonged state of emergency is that the Jewish state and the Jewish citizens are under constant existential threat. Under the aegis of the state of emergency, Israel has ruled for more than forty years the Palestinians in the Occupied Territories as noncitizens and in the last decade has turned the territories themselves into a zone of emergency, without this other emergency ever constituting an object of legal or political concern.

Emergency claims are not necessarily articulated with the ex-plicit hope for a declaration of a state of emergency. Rather, emer-gency claims are produced on a daily basis in the face of disasters of varying degree. These claims exist within a discursive framework in which the ruling power is indeed a powerful player, but has not com-pletely monopolized the means of turning statements of horror into emergency claims.[17] The modern citizen is capable of standing up to power and can negotiate and even contest the limits whereby her — or her neighbor's — statement of horror is turned into an emergency claim.

The meaning of a statement of horror as an emergency claim — even when the horror is clearly visible — thus is not something given or taken for granted. The emergency claim is open for negotiation. In principle, the civil contract of photography enables anyone to negotiate or to contest the transformation of a statement of horror into an emergency claim, even if under certain conditions (as a citi-zen or noncitizen of her country) this right has been taken from her. An emergency claim testifies to three facts: that a disaster exists; that it is an exception to the rule, one that necessitates immediate action in order to terminate it; and that there is someone who wants to assume the position that allows immediate action to be taken in order to terminate it.

The statement is embedded in a discourse, and the related elements of addresser and addressee are not predetermined, fixed, and linear. The actualization of these elements (which involves the question of who is acting as addresser or addressee) and their restoration take place within a dynamic and decentered space dependent on negotiation between various factors. No one, including the addresser, has sole possession of the statement. Under occupation, war, or other situations of extreme violence, statements of horror are susceptible to harm at each of their four levels — that of the addresser, the addressee, the referent, and the meaning.

Let us examine these injuries in turn, beginning with their effect on the position of the addresser. In the photographic statement of horror, the position of addresser is in principle divided among at least three possible addressers who often act simultaneously and out of conflicting relations among themselves. This divided position can be detected as shared among the photographed person, photographer, and the photograph's editor, as I'll demonstrate in what follows in an analysis of three newspaper photographs. Even if we were to focus on the photographer as the addresser of the photographic statement, his address cannot annul the addressing of the photographed person, who may be looking for a different addressee than that of the photographer and the editor in an effort to allow a different meaning to appear. The heterogeneity of the addressing position, coupled with the fact that the photographic énoncé will always include more than what any addresser who has been party to its creation has hoped to include within it, turns the photographic sign into an active statement that can never be completely and ultimately sealed. This instability enables the spectator of the photographic statement to take responsibility for its meaning.

When Palestinians are depicted in newspaper photographs, for example, their address tends to be pushed aside by the addressing of others. In most cases, the statement is transmitted from the viewpoint of the state, the Israeli-Jewish perspective that looks on the Palestinian mainly as an enemy, rather than as a governed population on whom injury has been inflicted — viewing her as an exception, rather than as a fellow man. Even when the reporter or photographer responsible for creating such statements makes the effort to deviate from this pattern, their statements are reconfigured by the routine framework of editing by the newspaper, television program, or news report.

Removing the Palestinian from the position of addresser, or at least casting a shadow on him by the introduction of another addresser, constitutes a disservice to the possibility of his addressing. In the conditions of constant disservice, which disrupt the possibility that the statement of horror will appear, insisting on having the picture speak by way of a text, as well as on the sectioning of the text through the resuscitation of traces of addressing that have been stamped on the picture, makes it possible to restore the flawed statement of horror.[18] In most cases, the Palestinian is denied a direct addressing position, being instead effectively interwoven into the body of the dominant narrative that attempts to justify the occupation or into the terms of the leftist Zionist narrative that is opposed to the occupation, but views it merely as a temporary aberration that Israel has to eliminate. Despite the differences between these narratives, both positions, insofar as the Palestinian is designated a noncitizen, integrate his grievance into a general narrative, thus putting in brackets the fact the he has been harmed by the ruling power. "The occupation" is a framework that does not expose urgency, yet statements of horror circulate. The actual state of emergency in which the noncitizen is captured is prevented from being seen when it is addressed under the terms of "the occupation." This very term, "the occupation," limits what should be negotiated to negotiations between two national entities, and thus any injury inflicted on the noncitizen is supposed to be part of these eventual ulterior negotiations. Under the present conditions, however, "the occupation" functions as a mechanism of neutralization that prevents statements of horror from emerging as emergency claims.

With regard to the position of the addressee in the conditions of occupation, the danger of turning into the secret ally of the ruling addresser hovers over the spectator or watcher of the statements produced from the places that are on the verge of catastrophe. The addresser often behaves as someone who can foretell the addressee's level of openness to the horrifying information to be presented, what dosage she'll be able to bear, and the vantage point from which she'll be able to digest it. Many of these addressers are likely ("in private conversation") to declare themselves opposed to the occupation, but that their responsibility toward the profession and the tasks it entails obliges them to be "attentive" to the addressee, whose atrophied position they themselves have created. This covert cooperation between this addresser and the addressee thus addressed, whereby everything is apparently already known in advance, limits the statement's capacity to appear as an emergency claim that would place the spectator in a position of responsibility toward its meaning.

However, under the conditions of occupation, as we just noted, even the "interested" addressee may miss this position of being addressed that the statement has assigned her and simply regard the statement to be confirmation of what she already knows. In the conditions of occupation, failing to be addressed is always already structured into the manner in which the statement of horror is presented. The spectator must have a special interest and already be prepared to turn herself into the civil addressee of a singular statement — a position that requires a deviation from the side to which she belongs. Even the addressee who may in principle empathize with the Palestinians adopts a similar position that enables — without it being her explicit aim — the statements of horror to pass by without generating a dimension of emergency. This addressee looks at emergency claims and witnesses only as generalized statements of horror — "the Palestinian misery" — which are topics for negotiation only within an eventual political dispute between two national sides (the Israeli state and the Palestinian Authority). By transforming the emergency claim into a generalized statement, the addressee relinquishes her civil point of view and adopts one that has been created by the ruling power, the point of view from which this emergency claim has been contextualized.

The ruling power seeks to homogenize the heterogeneous scopic regime through the active reduction of objects seen within it to the logic of a national struggle. Under this scopic regime, which always seeks a monopoly, the possibility of statements becoming emergency claims is limited, if not fully erased. The generalized statement is always assimilated into the ruling national discourse, even when it apparently claims that the ruling class is responsible for the injury inflicted on the noncitizen. This discourse amplifies the existing division between citizens and noncitizens in such a way that they are placed against one another, with the citizens on the side of the ruling power. The citizen as addressee acts like someone whose knowledge and position exempt her from being singularly addressed, since she has in fact become the addressee of the *generalized* statement. In this way, she can regularly speak out against the occupation. Such people — specifically, those who are the natural target audience for arguments about the status of the Palestinians on the verge of catastrophe — are the ones who repeatedly say, in an apparently experienced and "critical" manner, that there is no need for them to peruse such articles or look at such photos, because they claim already to know what they contain. Perhaps, due to the proliferation of pictures of horror, they have been left numb, which is a retroactive justification of the newspaper editor's position.

In such conditions, where addresser and addressee have been made to agree in advance on the meaning of the statement — which in effect amounts to injury to each of the elements — the referent is usually assimilated to the meaning. The meaning of the statement is usually located within predetermined brackets, restricting the referent of the horror to an already constructed container of meaning. This prepackaging enables the addressee to participate in a community of citizens capable of recognizing a disaster through a commonly accepted framework while ignoring the particular details of the new situation surrounding the disaster site. On the one hand, the addressee acknowledges the statement's existence, but on the other, she presents herself as sufficiently experienced in statements of its kind to allow her to skip lightly over it to pass on to the next item on the agenda. She thus confirms the structure of the statement, which has been classified in advance, and feels exempted from having to contemplate its particular referent. Not only can the addressee separate herself from those who unrelentingly deny the existence of the disaster and run the risk of looking at the situation in an unrealistic manner, she also can separate herself at the same time from those who demand to learn something from this specific case or who seek to do something about it now.

Statements of Horror

Although in some cases, statements of horror narrate the horror directly, requiring relatively no effort from the viewer to establish its presence in the context of emergency (one need only think of images in which we see wounded people, people already marked by the ravages of starvation, or mutilated bodies or demolished homes), under the conditions that we have just examined, other photos require a special discursive effort for the production of their visibility as emergency claims (one need only think of images in which we see families who have lost their loved ones, or views of desolate streets, ongoing dereliction, or diseases caused by inhuman living conditions). Despite the fact that horror is present in these photographs on one level of visibility or another and that most of them have been produced out of the horror itself, through the taking of stills or motion pictures, these statements are inherently flawed on account of the injuries we have just examined. These injuries are closely tied to the civil status of the photographed subjects. Such statements are flawed when they do not successfully generate an emergency, when the horror transmitted by these statements fails to appear as something that needs to be stopped immediately, or when they fail to depict something that requires preventative actions to be taken to ensure it from continuing through either direct rehabilitation or remuneration being offered to the victims.

In both flawed and the unflawed visual statements, the horror does not belong to the victim who is depicted, and it is not merely among those who are directly identified with the victim or who share the same territory with her that interest is aroused. Interest in the statement of horror and responsibility toward it constitutes one of the characteristics, abilities, and skills of the modern citizen of photography, part of what makes her what she is in a world stretched between domestic and global spaces. Despite the singularity of each and every statement and the incontestable particularity of the historical, political, and cultural circumstances from which it is manufactured, each has global characteristics that derive from the means of

203

its production, distribution, and the systems of exchange in which it circulates. The modern era has shown that anyone is liable to be the object of a statement of horror — perhaps not every kind of horror, and not in the same way, but in the modern era, equality before horror can unite populations whose differences are generally thought to be unbridgeable. Thus, for example, a disastrous train wreck or an earthquake can bring together rich and poor, the rulers and the powerless. The presence of citizens amid such disasters often contributes to the production of a proper statement of horror. The citizenship of photography may not be able to protect people from disaster, but can at least serve as a means for spectators to structure within the framework of a discourse the way in which the disaster has struck them and can enable them to limit the suffering that such calamities generate while accelerating the processes of recovery.

The statements of horror that will be discussed here are those in which noncitizens appear. The Palestinians are the noncitizens of the state of Israel. Ruled by the state of Israel, but as the exception to the rule of Israeli law, they have been effectively abandoned by the sovereign, and in most cases injury inflicted on them not only escapes penalty, but is rarely considered to be something that deserves notice. If injury to the Palestinians is sanctioned, any statement in which an attempt to report this injury fails to appear as an emergency claim in the framework of the existing discourse. Such a situation, then, creates particularly difficult conditions for the appearance of emergency claims as such. For instance, a photograph showing Palestinian detainees whose eyes have been blindfolded appears as a routine arrest procedure, rather than as a statement of horror, because the practice of blindfolding has become a commonplace procedure (figure 4.1). Such images are frequently printed in the media without any sense of urgency, which, if aroused, could expose this practice as a blatant violation of proper arrest procedures. In order to endow such images with urgency, the responsibility of a spectator is required to overcome the banality of their presentation.

Blindfolding is a characteristic treatment of prisoners of war, whose captors seek to prevent them from identifying the areas from which and to which they are being transported. Instead of the

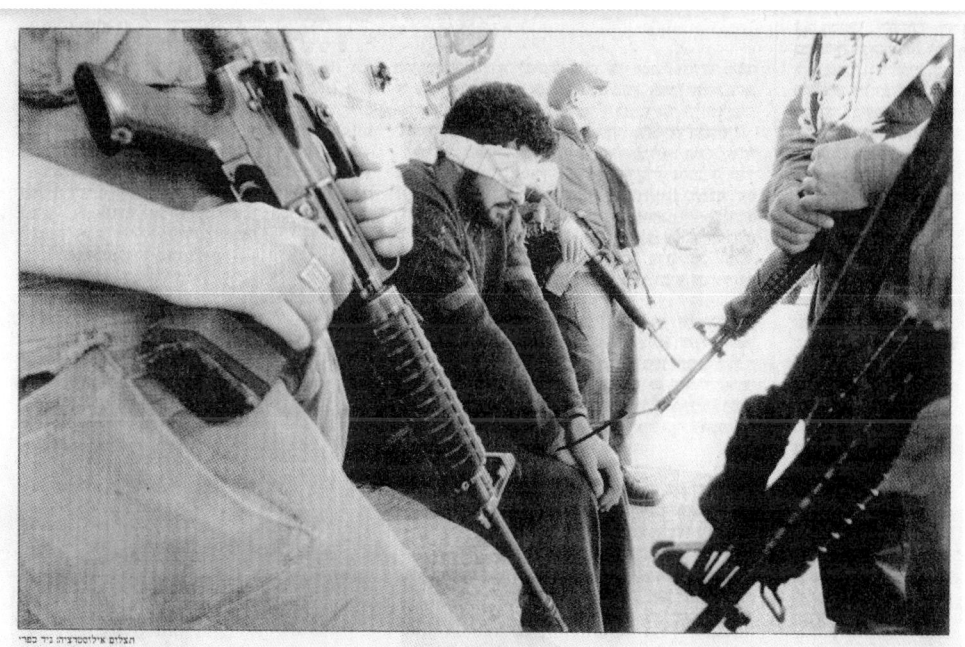

תצלום אילוסטרציה: ניר כפרי

מעצר חשוד, נובמבר 2002. למצולמים אין קשר לכתבה

Figure 4.1. Nir Kafri (published in *Ha'aretz* with caption: "Suspect arrest, November 2002, no connection between the photographed person and the article"), *Ha'aretz*, 2002.

blindfold appearing as evidence of the constant conversion of an arrest procedure into the procedure for taking war prisoners, the distorted iconography constructed by the occupation presents it as an attribute of the Palestinian — of every Palestinian — as the mark of a dangerous enemy. The fact that the Palestinians lack political protection allows the occupation regime systematically to take actions that ensure that the existence of Palestinians in their own homes will remain temporary, making conditions such that the injury inflicted on them will be taken to be part of that liminal state.[19] Not only does every movement by Palestinians require authorization, currently for tens, if not hundreds of thousands of them, even permanent residency in their homes requires a "permanent resident" permit, which has to be renewed every three months. Even at the time when the state was interested in commodities that could be obtained from Palestinians — for example, cheap labor — it was not interested in allowing their assimilation into the permanent register of citizens. Since the beginning of the occupation, transience thus has become a permanent feature of the Palestinians' condition.[20] The state of Israel finds them, as transients, to be eligible only for life-preserving treatment, thus providing them only with the bare minimum that would be required to fulfill the necessities of life.

Not only is this population excluded from participating in the ruling power to which it is subjected, but its very existence has been reduced by the authorities to the existence of mere life. By employing the services of more than thirty dedicated humanitarian organizations, the state of Israel attempts to ensure the Palestinians the bare minimum necessary for their survival. Certainly, the bare minimum will not suffice for those receiving it, especially when this has been their condition for such a long time. It does seem to be sufficient, however, for those responsible for a situation in which so many have consistently been deprived, leaving this population on the verge of suffering a humanitarian disaster, and in fact, many organizations warn that the situation in the Occupied Territories is closer than ever to this catastrophe. Those who survive for extended period of time on this bare minimum exist in a perpetual state on the verge of catastrophe.

Existence on the verge of catastrophe is not the kind of situation that can be sustained before the actual outbreak of catastrophe.

Rather, it is a new form of catastrophe itself, a prolonged situation lacking any spectacular means of interrupting its routinization. On the contrary, this formation is a catastrophe that can be sustained for a long time without necessarily producing any warning signs, except for those stamped on the bodies of its victims. Existence on the verge of catastrophe is the formation of catastrophe that currently assails populations of citizens around the world, populations whose existence is transient, but whose condition — on the verge of catastrophe — is permanent. Forced into being transient, such populations are denied any way to demand a change in their situation, and under such conditions, whoever is still able to come to their aid can do no more than preserve their existence at the very edge of what is bearable — on the verge of catastrophe.

When citizens are struck by disaster, the statement of horror produced from the site of disaster area attests to an emergency and interrupts routine. The depicted disaster is generally accorded a name of its own, which serves as the support for additional statements that describe, refer to, and interpret it. Designated with a title, the disaster calls for an intervention, for a limit to be placed on the suffering it causes, and, finally, the title allows it to be remembered, saving it from sinking into the depths of oblivion.

Although the statement of horror is chain linked to a series of statements, such a connection ends once various systems manage to restore order. When this happens, the statement of horror is usually annexed to the mechanisms of remembrance, which ensure the commemoration of the disaster. When noncitizens are struck by disaster, however, a statement is not always produced, or the statement produced is not always a statement of horror. Even when such a statement is produced from a disaster, it is doubtful there will be any mechanisms of remembrance to preserve it. The incidence of disasters among the population of noncitizens and the fact that such disasters are not recognized as intolerable situations often turn their statements of horror into generalities. Such generalized statements are kept in storage, not necessarily referring to the particular disaster that has been reported, nor are they remembered as having been photographed at a given time and place. Instead, they come to express similar disasters in other places at other times. Captions such as the "illustrative photo" or the "people depicted have no relation to the actual events" are conventional types of such generalized statements. When photographs are being used to illustrate a type of situation, rather than to testify to a singular event, it is a sure sign that a disaster has become chronic, that the worst is yet to come. The statement of the state of plight of noncitizens always arrives belatedly. But nothing is more urgent.

The conversion of statements of horror into generalized statements teaches us something about the status of the disaster and the blurred boundary between it and the routine existence of the population that exists on the verge of catastrophe. Statements produced from the disaster and from the routine of existing on the verge of catastrophe are usually produced retrospectively. They lack any real dimension of emergency. The personal and private disaster is assimilated into the population's collective situation and in so doing staves off the necessity for an active linking of statements that would put an end to the disaster. To demonstrate this further, I will present two examples of two different statements of horror: one produced from the situation of being permanently on the verge of catastrophe and the other produced from a concrete and singular disaster.

The front page of the *Ha'aretz* newspaper on January 19, 2004, featured a photograph in which a crowd of hundreds of Palestinians could be seen crushing each other while trying to exit the Erez crossing (figure 4.2). The photograph, having made it to the front page, apparently suggests an interruption of routine. But when one reads the caption beneath the picture, one understands that what is actually presented is merely stale news that has been retrospectively produced. The caption states: "Erez crossing, yesterday. The crossing was closed after the [suicide bomber] attack on Wednesday; with its reopening yesterday, long queues formed — at the end of which only a tenth the usual number of workers entered."[21] It should be noted that it is not clear who was damaged by the situation that the caption reports, the Palestinian workers who remained unemployed, or the Israeli employers who were left without their workforce. However, if the reader turns to the next page of the newspaper, as directed by the caption, she will encounter another photograph taken at the same location, while the article beneath it reports on the wounding

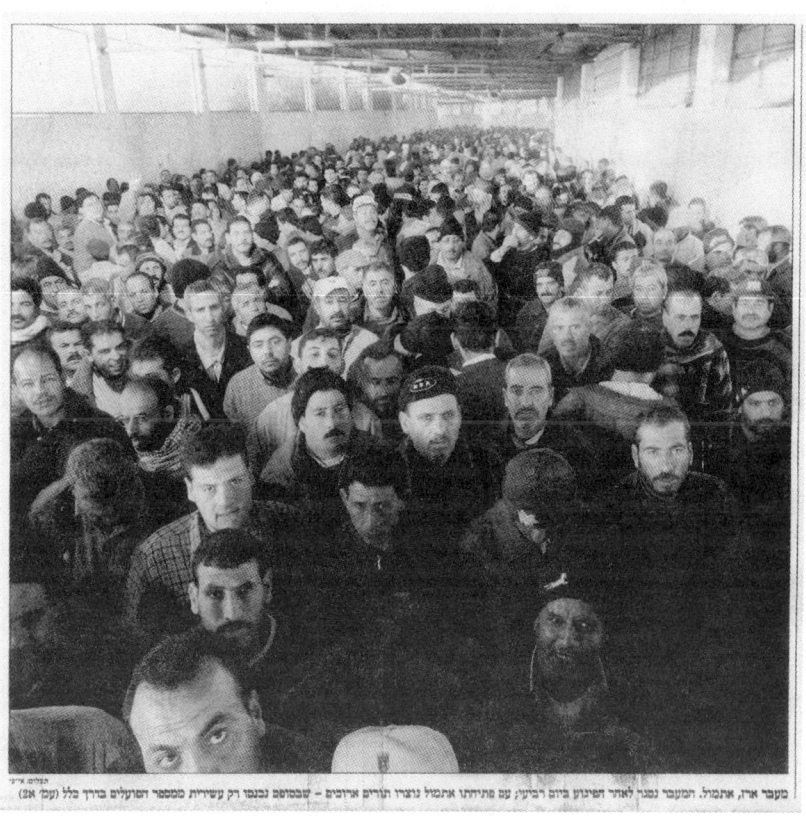

צילום: א״פ

מעבר ארז, אתמול. הממשבר נסגר לאחר הפיגוע בדום רביעי; עם פתיחתו אתמול נוצרו תורים ארוכים - שבמהלך נבנו רק עשיריית ממספר הפועלים והרעלום בדרך כלל (עמ׳ 8א)

Figure 4.2. Erez crossing, *Ha'aretz*, January 19, 2004 (AP/Wide World Photos).

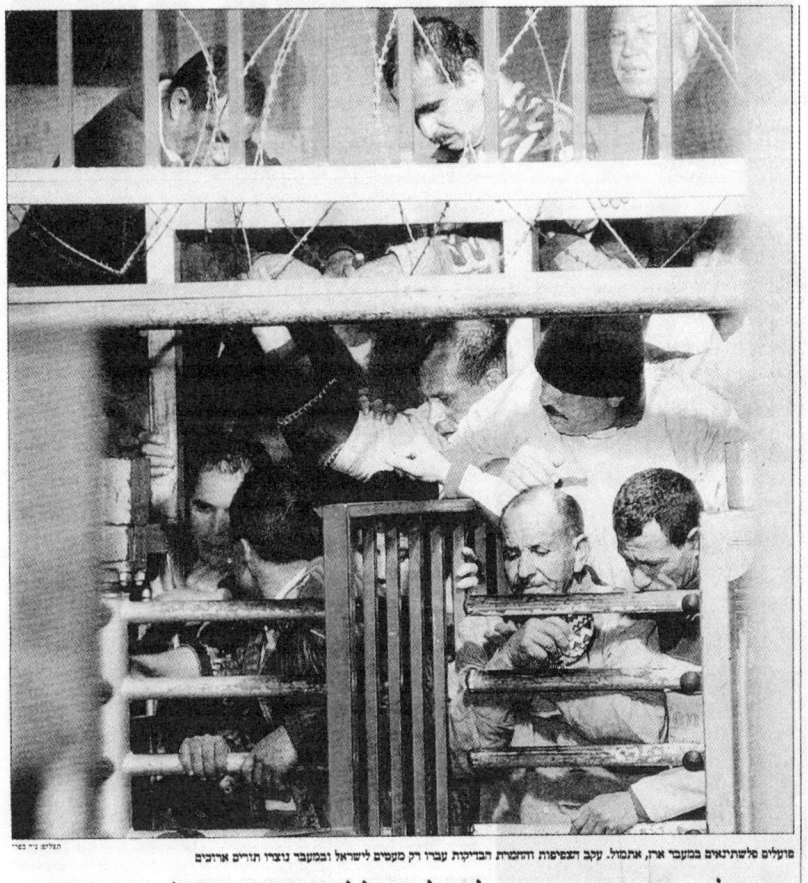

פועלים פלשתינאים במעבר ארז, אתמול. עקב הצפיפות והחומרת הבדוקות עברו רק מעטים לישראל ובמעבר נוצרו תורים ארוכים

מופז הוציא צו לפינוי 3 מאחזים
נוספים; עדיין לא פונה אף מאחז

ישראלי נפצע בינוני מירי ליד לרמאללה

מאת עמוס הראל

בדרכה הדרומה. תושב ההתנחלות מחות והביטחון ניסיון של בסיסי
נהליאל כבו 40. שישב ליד הנהג. לשגר במכריל שתי יתרארדיות

Figure 4.3. Nir Kafri, Erez crossing, *Ha'aretz*, January 19, 2004.

of an Israeli by gunfire near Ramallah (figure 4.3). This juxtaposition of these two modes of presentation is a regular and effective mechanism of justification that does not require too many words, arguing, in effect, that the citizen's injury serves as justification for the ill-treatment of an entire population of noncitizens. The statement of horror that describes the plight of the noncitizen is reinscribed as a necessary link in the attempt to address the emergency that is produced by the citizen's statement of horror.

Although the injury to the Palestinian has been erased, visible traces are left in the form of a mute emergency claim. Within the narrative framework that attempts to justify their injuries, effort is made to deny the misery and rage staring out from the eyes of thousands of Palestinians crammed inside a space too small to contain them — an attempt to deny the plight of people whose existence has been reduced to their desire to move from one place to another. In being part of commonplace and self-evident measures taken in the wake of terror attacks, the closing of the Erez crossing that took place four days earlier did not turn into an event from which a statement of horror was produced. The event might be reported, but implicitly or explicitly as an aside, only ever in the form of a dry report intended to deliver information about the implementation of a common, routine procedure. Reducing the existence of the procedure to a picture caption — "The crossing was closed after the attack on Wednesday" — turns the event into something taken for granted, as though it were a customary practice of the policy, so that the effects of this policy are simply unable to appear as emergency claims.

Any emergency regarding the situation of the citizen population thus requires and justifies direct intervention in (that is, injury to) the population of noncitizens. Law and justice are absent, and implemented in their place is a policy that functions as a system of reward and punishment against which those who are hurt because of it are unable to defend themselves. Punishment of tens, if not hundreds of thousands of Palestinians without due process — who lost their livelihoods during those four days; the absence of a compensation mechanism for the lost workdays; the lack of any arrangement to pay for the cancellation of work or for the disruption of their employment on account their having been herded for hours inside transit halls in intolerably crowded and suffocating conditions — none of this appears to be news worth reporting. Evidence of the Palestinians' situation is constantly present in the media, but rarely as the enunciation of emergency claims. Their misery is either presented as justified or personalized. The neutralization of their emergency effectively substitutes compassion for responsibility. If only one of the thousands of people in the photograph were a citizen, an injury to his livelihood would be enough of a reason to demand an accounting, if not the immediate return of his means of supporting himself. Repeated injuries to his livelihood, the restriction of his freedom of movement, and the continual endangerment of his health would be sufficient cause to launch a series of statements demanding that the situation be immediately rectified.

Figure 4.4 is the second example of a statement of horror produced by a disaster. Every few days after the outbreak of the al-Aqsa intifada, many such statements appeared in the newspapers. On the front page of *Ha'aretz* on April, 25, 2004, a small, solitary headline appeared without the supportive body of an article: "8 Killed in the [West] Bank: A University Lecturer and 6 Activists." On page four, alongside a photograph of an armed soldier pulling the arm of a Palestinian youth, a report appeared that was intended to be the follow-up story to the small headline on the front page. However, its subject was "IDF Operations in the Territories." The report was an assemblage of information gathered from "military sources," within the Israeli Defense Forces, most of which provided apparently incriminating details regarding each of the men who were killed — data that was supposed to justify their killing ("recently accumulated intelligence about his links with two wanted men from Hamas"). It also cited information from "Palestinian sources," most of which refuted the selfsame "incriminating details" (for instance, "he was beside his sister on their way home"). The collation of information in this way functions as a kangaroo court, announcing a verdict that has already been passed by the army. Of the disaster that has struck those killed and their relatives as a result of the miscarriage of justice and its swift execution there is no mention in the report.

Since the meaning of this series of statements of horror is not given the status of an emergency claim, such statements — which

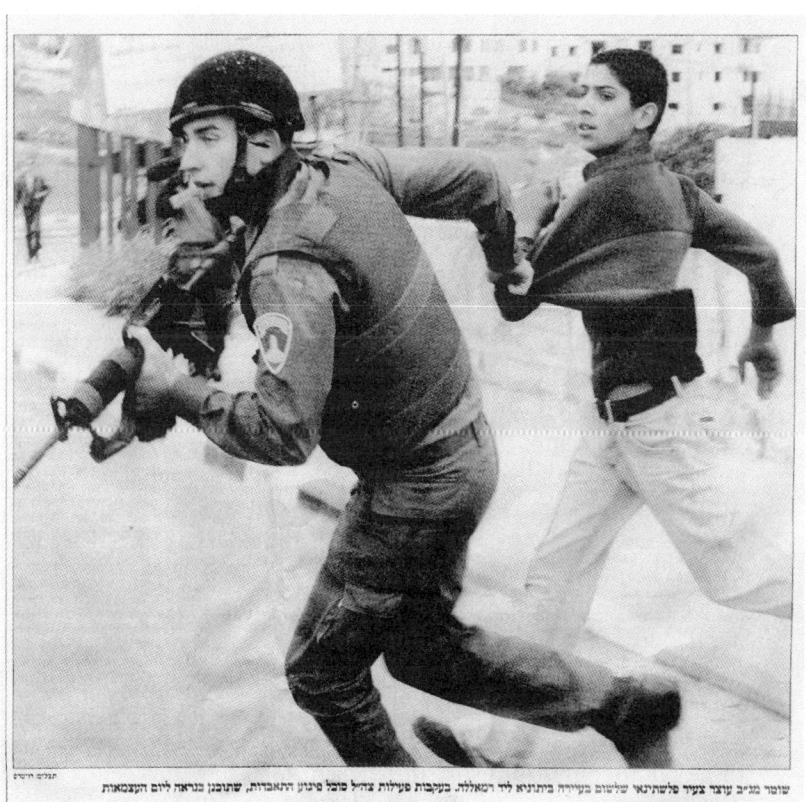

צלם: יוטרם

שומר מג"ב עוצר צעיר פלשתינאי שלשום בעייירה ביתתניא ליד רמאללה. בעקבות פעילות צה"ל סוכל פיגוע התאבדות, שתוכנן בגראה ליום העצמאות

Figure 4.4. Bitounia, *Ha'aretz*, 2004.

nevertheless bear the traces of the disaster — lack any dimension of urgency. Instead, the emergency that arises from the statements (especially from the photograph), is the urgency to deal with a threat — depicted in the form of a Palestinian youth — that hovers over the citizen. The soldier is seen rushing ahead, with his left hand holding a cocked rifle that is pointing forward, while his right hand grips the arm of an unarmed Palestinian youth whom he is dragging away in order to detain. The photograph's caption provides an explanation for the erasure of the emergency of the noncitizen's situation in favor of the emergency of the citizen's situation: "Border Patrol policeman arrests a Palestinian youth in the town of Bitounia near Ramallah. IDF activity forestalled a suicide attack that was planned apparently for Independence Day." Random arrest and mistaken identification ("An attack dog was sent to chase after the wanted men. The dog assaulted Abu-Limon, rather than the armed wanted man, Imad Janajara, who was running beside him, and then the soldiers shot and killed him from a distance, thinking he was the suspect"); unjustified suspicions ("Border Patrol men shot at the two who were unarmed. According to the IDF, they were trying to escape. One was killed and the other mortally wounded. No belt of explosives was found in their possession"); mortal wounding; killing — all of this awaits the Palestinian over the course of his daily routine. When such events occur, they are depicted as part of a larger plan of action or part of a policy that is logical and justified — obscuring the disaster that strikes the individuals who have been harmed so that the policy may be implemented and subsequently represented as a necessary price that has to be paid.

These two examples illustrate the gap between the use of these three photographs to justify these events and the emergency claims that could have been produced from them, as well as the production and distribution of statements in the media outside of any emergency context. The gap between the visible and the invisible places great responsibility onto the spectator and an even greater demand on the spectator-citizen, whose protection and well-being as citizen has been the source for legitimating injury to the noncitizen. The visibility of the horror is not an objective matter, because it has been entrusted to those who are its addresser. The structure of the statement enables the citizen to participate actively in establishing the reference and in creating the meaning of the statement through a process of addressing and being addressed. As mentioned above, the four elements of the statement — addresser, addressee, reference, and meaning — are not stable. Every statement can be retransmitted, dictated by a different addresser and to a different addressee, while insisting on establishing the reference and extracting its meaning. Such a process is not subject to an economy of justifications, but rather is part of a civilian discourse that is faithful to the elementary principle of equality among those who are ruled.

In the exhibition Everything Could Be Seen, I tried to show the civil attitude taken by several artists, Israelis and Palestinians, toward emergency claims. Demonstrated in their work are multiple articulations that attempt to establish a set of necessary, but not completely sufficient conditions for the rehabilitation of the photographs' referents: attempts simultaneously to expand the site of their meaning while aiming to get rid of the generalized meaning of "the occupation," which presently contributes to the perpetuation, rather than the changing, of the existing situation. "The occupation" is a countereffective term for two principal reasons. First, it is related to the extended period of time that has elapsed since Israel occupied the territories, which has turned Israeli rule of the territories into a permanent arrangement, rather than a temporary matter. The second reason relates to the fact that the term "occupation" regularly diverts attention away from the control of humans toward the control of territory. While the framework is territorial, all discussion on "ending the occupation" focuses on territorial solutions, most of which aim for a separation and redivision of the physical space. The emergency claims gathered together in the exhibition space tried to bypass the dominant dispute over the land of Israel/Palestine and its territorial partition to open a debate on citizenship and to emphasize its distribution. Statements of horror are obscured by the term "occupation." What can be seen in these statements of horror is an ongoing situation in which territorial control is only one element in the large-scale subjugation of the Palestinian population taking place through a discriminatory distinction between citizens and noncitizens under a single governmental framework.[22]

CHAPTER FIVE

Has Anyone Ever Seen
a Photograph of a Rape?

During the years that I have worked on this book, I looked at thousands of images of horror of different kinds from all over the world: famine, disease, epidemics, terror attacks, houses torn down, butchered bodies, bombings, torture, mass death, and poverty.[1] Time went by, and numerous images were registered in my memory, until I noticed that one image was absent from the various sites — newspapers, photo albums, television programs — in which images of horror are shown: the image of rape.[2]

This surprised me, because it stood in stark contradiction to the activist discursive and legislative effort to turn rape into an object of discourse.[3] As we will see, from the 1970s on, an entire discourse had been constructed around rape that turned it into an object that is present in various fields of knowledge and action.[4] The passing of laws,[5] rape victims' becoming frequent talk-show guests,[6] rape's becoming an object of research in diverse fields of knowledge,[7] the establishment of support groups and the publication of pamphlets to raise awareness of its existence, the establishment of rape-victim treatment centers, the collection of data on rape, and the publication of ads in the newspapers — these are just some of the practices that indicate a fundamental shift in attitudes toward rape in modern Western culture that have given rise to the conditions for talking about it as a frequent phenomenon whose existence cannot be denied and whose presence cannot be camouflaged behind existing norms. In what follows, I will be examining the changing codes of knowledge that have constituted what has been meant by "rape," and I will confront the astonishing fact that rape isn't accessible to the gaze in any of the discursive frameworks in which it is posited.

The New Discourse on Rape

In May 1970, Paul Tabori concluded his introduction to *The Social History of Rape* with the following remarks: "This is not a bid for sensationalism or for the exploitation of prurient interest but a straightforward and modest examination of a segment of human urges and actions that has received comparatively little attention."[8] His book surveys the representation of rape in the anthropological, legal, and biological discourses, as well as in humor and in history books. Tabori analyzes rape as the expression of a human drive that has been known since the earliest times, and his book is an attempt to write the social history of the phenomenon. A year later, the radical feminist movement published a manifesto that begins with the following statement: "When more than two people have suffered the same oppression, it is no longer personal but political — and rape is a political matter."[9] The authors of this text also identify rape as being omnipresent; from their standpoint, however, its omnipresence is expressive not of a universal human drive, but of particular arrays of political relations.

Tabori's text unknowingly summarized an epoch, while the feminist manifesto consciously and deliberately ushered in a new one.[10] Three years after the manifesto was written and presented to the conference of the radical feminist movement, it was published as part of a book written by the women of the movement, the subtitle of which was *The First Sourcebook for Women* (figure 5.1). The book's characterization as being "first" referred not only to its content — everything published previously, which had not included the voice of women, could not be considered a reliable and significant source for the understanding of rape — but to its target audience as well: everything published about rape prior to this book hadn't been addressed to women and hadn't allowed them to make use of it. However, the use of the term "first" should also be understood as a speech act — this was the first sourcebook that women could use in a new way, politically, socially, and culturally. It appeared to say: "Take me and use me for political action."

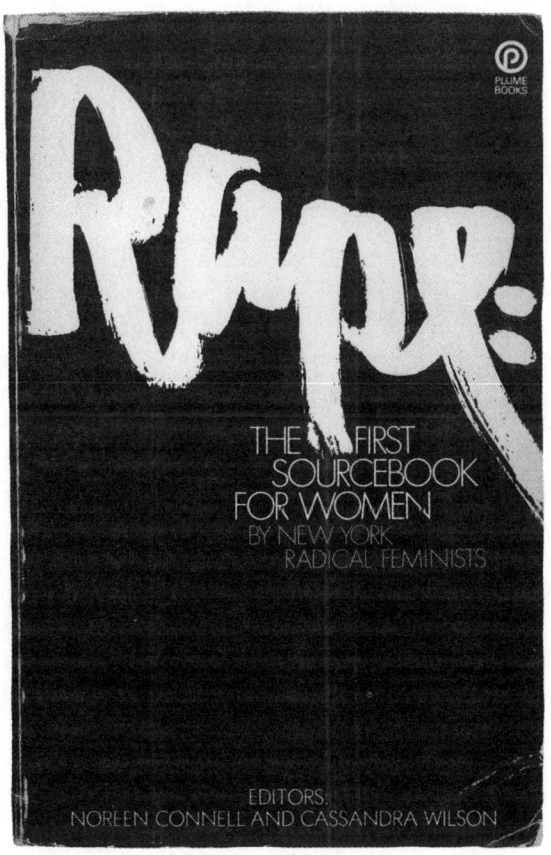

Figure 5.1. Front cover, *Rape:The First Sourcebook for Women*,
New American Library, 1974.

In this period, the early 1970s, rape appeared as a new object in the legal/scientific/political discourse, a discourse held to be rational and deliberative. One mysterious aspect of it, however, remained beyond any controversy: this new object of the discourse of rape was not to be shown or seen. At the center of this chapter lies an attempt to show that the 1970s not only heralded the new discourse of rape but also constituted rape as a new object; subsequently I will critically analyze this new object's extraordinary conditions of visibility.

A New Object of Discourse

With the 1971 antirape declaration and the publication of *Rape: The First Sourcebook for Women* in 1974, when opposition to rape matured into a social movement, its focus was on refuting three prevalent assumptions regarding women and sexuality: that women are not raped against their will, that women want to be raped, and that women make false accusations.[11] These assumptions, which locate rape in the context of the woman's sexual behavior, imply that women are interested in sex that is forced on them and contest the reliability of the woman's contentions regarding herself both at the time of the rape, when she attempts to resist it, and afterward, when she claims to have been raped. These three assumptions place the emphasis on the woman's stance in regard to rape and on her contribution to its happening, but remain indifferent to the issue of rape itself — its consequences and frequency, its image and "standing" as a type of crime, its definition and the possibilities of intervening in it. As opposed to these assumptions, the feminist movement's purpose in the struggle against rape was twofold: on the one hand, to remove rape from its sexual context and restructure it as an act of violence, and on the other, to constitute the rape victim's position as one of legitimate grievance. However, what was at stake here wasn't just establishing a social movement and obtaining broad support on the issue of rape, but the constitution of rape as a new object in culture and the law so that its very existence would no longer be dependent on the subjective experience of one woman or another.[12]

Rape does not belong to the class of objects that are present in the discourse, but whose presence is not an object of the gaze (such as God or the idea of the good, for example). Neither does it belong to the class of objects that cannot be seen themselves, but that can be seen only by means of objects that represent them or in which they are manifested (such as the state, the Renaissance, or the process of secularization). Rape is an event, like a murder, a traffic accident, or an avalanche, to which there may not be any witnesses, but that can in principle be seen and shown. This is exactly how it's spoken of — as a visible object. In fact, however, due to the special rules of the new discourse on rape, and due to the prohibition on showing rape, in particular, rape's visibility is nearer to that of an idea that cannot be grasped by means of the senses.[13]

"Rape" is not a new term, but the use of it to describe such widely divergent cases as the rape of Susannah by the elders as described in the Book of Daniel, the rape of the Sabines, the rape of Artemisia Gentileschi, and the gang rape of a girl from Kibbutz Shomrat[14] raises the question of what we are dealing with when we are dealing with rape. In much of the literature on rape, it is treated as something that is always already the same. In fact, however, it is something whose contours, significance, and implications have changed over time.

In *Rape: A Philosophical Investigation*, Keith Burgess-Jackson asserts that rape is an obscure term: "There is, I believe, good reason for the vagueness of the term 'rape.' We need/want a category in our thinking for morally problematic sex."[15] Due to the obscurity of the term, he contends, it has been surrounded by debate from which several parallel theories of rape have emerged: conservative (which views rape as damage to property, assuming that men — or a particular man in regard to a particular woman — have rights of ownership over women), liberal (which views rape as an offense against the woman's right to her body and as the imposition of nonconsensual sexual contact), and radical (which places emphasis on rape as an instrument of social oppression whereby women are kept in an inferior position).[16] However, Burgess-Jackson's discussion never rises above the textual level — even when discussing the law, his analysis focuses on the language of the law — and reducing rape as an object in a discourse to a concept it assumes the stability of this concept itself as described in the language of the law throughout history, a concept, moreover, that he characterizes as "morally problematic sex." The theories in regard to rape may be different from each other, but what Burgess-Jackson in effect claims is that rape is rape and has been so from the time of the Code of Hammurabi to the present day.[17]

In opposition to his claim, I will attempt to show that the revolution stirred up by the feminist movement in regard to rape did not produce new theories for an existing and obscure term, but produced first and foremost a new object, which cannot be predicated only on its new linguistic meaning. As I will show in what follows, this object does not conform to the description of "morally problematic sex." It has a cultural, economic, political, and legal existence separate from the terminology of "rape" that preceded it. In it, rape is present and unfolds itself differently in space and is accessible to the gaze in other ways. It generates new forms of speech and invites new forms of intervention.

Likewise, George Vigarello's book, *A History of Rape* (2001) which offers one of the most comprehensive histories of rape during modern times, from the sixteenth century to the present day, also assumes rape to have stable historical significance, the course of which the author seeks to describe.[18] "It requires that the citizen be seen on the basis of his or her own self and not on the basis of some presumed 'owner,'" writes Vigarello in regard to amendments made to French law in 1791.[19] However, from this change in legislation, he contends, one cannot infer an immediate change in the autonomy of women. In support of this view, he cites the case of Laurent Geeraert's wife (the woman's name herself is unknown), who lodged a complaint against her husband for his brutal treatment of her. The government representative's summation for the defense, which Vigarello quotes, summarizes the rapist's standing in the late eighteenth century: "If a public action was admitted for abuse and cruelty between husband and wife, there are persons who would spend a large part of their life in prison."[20] Women's exclusion from citizenship denied them all the rights attributed to the citizen, first and foremost the right to be treated on the basis of one's own selfhood and not as the actual or potential property of a particular male.

It is because Vigarello's discussion is indifferent to the issue of citizenship and women's exclusion from it that he is consequently able to preserve rape as consistent throughout history, although he does point to significant changes that have occurred in it. The French law of 1791, which ostensibly changed the standing of rape in those days, was written exactly at the time that Olympe de Gouges was writing her Declaration of the Rights of Woman and the Female Citizen, in which, as I attempted to show in Chapter One, she pointed out the necessary connection between the rehabilitation of women's status as citizens and their ability to negotiate with the sovereign over the extent and manner of intervention in what is called "bare life."

The introduction to the manifesto of the radical feminist movement of New York, which was written 180 years after the amendment to the French law, states: "Rape became an issue when women began to compare their experiences as children, teenagers, students, workers and wives, and to realize that sexual assault, in one form or another, was common. Conditioned to believe that the rapist was sick and a social aberration, while at the same time held accountable for attracting and precipitating the sexual violence we often experienced, many women repressed their memories of rape."[21]

Not just the content of these remarks, but the very fact that women began to hold such discussions attests to the appearance of a new discourse on rape, distinct from what had previously been called "rape." In the past, the category of rape had referred to cases in which a woman was attacked by a man and forced to engage in sexual relations with him. But this description of the act didn't suffice in its application to the woman who'd been raped. It was not every woman who could occupy the rape victim's place in this description of the act, and it was not every woman who could be raped. For example, a wife could not be raped by her husband, regardless of the degree of violence inflicted on her, nor could a prostitute be raped by a client or any other man, and it made no difference if the act itself conformed 100 percent to the description of rape. Rape presumed damage to the value or physical integrity of the woman, and toward this end the woman had to be considered property of value, and somebody, usually a man, had to show interest in that property and demand restitution for the damage to it.[22] The rape of a maidservant or orphan carried much less risk than the rape of a married woman or a woman of standing, and according to Vigarello, such cases were quite rare.

223

In most of the reported cases — not necessarily those that came to court — the rape victim came from the lower social and economic classes or was either mentally or developmentally retarded, and some male relative was interested in pursuing the case of injury for her and conducting negotiations properly.[23] This, however, wasn't enough. A few additional conditions were required for such cases to come under the category of rape. The violence or brutality toward the woman had to be exceptionally severe, so that the public could be shocked and horrified, and the rapist had to be a stranger or someone with whom the woman had no relation whatsoever. The rapist's behavior was seen as reprehensible because he refused to wipe the rape victim clean of the stain on her and would not take her for his wife; or he may not have paid the damages due her family; or the rape may have involved some conspicuous affront to customary moral values, for example, taking the virginity of too young a girl.

The radical feminist's manifesto challenged the clear-cut boundaries of rape in its traditional conception by alternately employing two terms: "rape" and "sexual assault." In speaking of rape as sexual assault, and of sexual assault as rape, they were referring to a new object. The limiting conditions that previously had defined rape underwent a severe makeover. From now on, the victim of rape or sexual assault could in principle be any woman (or, in effect, any person), and there were no longer any prior conditions to prevent what had been done to her from being recognized as rape. The rapist, too, had changed and was no longer a freak, deviant, or stranger who came from outside the rape victim's social circle or a man of higher social standing than the rape victim, allowing him to subdue her to his will and get away with it unpunished.[24] The woman could be any woman, of any age, and the rapist could be any man and did not necessarily have to harbor any criminal intent (*mens rea*).

In other words, the term "rape" was rendered banal — not in the sense of the feeling it should arouse, but from the aspect of the act's characterization and possible participants. Rape now did not necessarily entail physical assault. It could take place without any violence having been inflicted on the woman and without including an element of surprise. The rapist could be someone near and dear, and the rape victim could be of any age and stand in close familial or social relationship to him. She could be a daughter, wife, sister, friend, or acquaintance, and the rapist may have exploited this to rape her. Furthermore, the rape victim might not have understood what happened to her at the time, but only in hindsight, because what happened to her at the time hadn't yet entered into her language, or into that of society, as rape. In other words, as I will show in greater detail below, an event could be defined as rape in hindsight, even years later.

The determinant factor now was the woman's rebellion against what has been forced on her, which may emerge only after the fact. A woman might submit to a man because she is paralyzed with fear when he attacks her, she may cover up the act because she is paralyzed with shame, or she may repress it because she is unable to deal with the trauma. And during all that time, the event will not have been a rape to anybody — man or woman. However, it will be constituted as a rape the moment the woman voices her rebellion, when her apparent giving of herself is exposed as coercion and her prolonged silence is understood as part of the ongoing scandal of rape, which in effect has continued to act on the woman's mind and body during all those days — or years — of denial.

In the text I have quoted from the introduction to the feminists' manifesto, women describe a different experience from what had characterized rape in the past; they share it with other women and understand that their common experience, which they've now exchanged with each other, has created a new object that didn't exist before, and that it is their task to make that object manifest in the discourse. At a particular historic junction — the early 1970s — these women understood that what lay at stake was no less than *sexual accessibility to their bodies* and that this had to be posited at the heart of their struggle.

Until the end of the nineteenth century (and sometimes well into the twentieth), women were still excluded from the body of the citizenry and left in a subordinate position. Their exclusion and subordination were amplified by their special status as objects in a system of sexual exchange. A women's subordination to her husband, father, or brother was a specific expression of her subordination to that system. Claude Gauvard describes rape as being "by preference a crime committed against defamed women who must be clearly distinguished from married women."[25] In other words, a woman's value as a sexual object was determined by her sexual accessibility or inaccessibility to men. Raping a "defamed woman" was nothing, compared with the relatively rare case of raping a married women.

Marriage was a normative way to protect women from being abandoned after losing their value as sexual object or as a secure procedure to prevent this loss. Once outside the institution of marriage, a woman who remained sexually inaccessible would be acclaimed as pure, perfect, and elevated to sanctity. But a woman who'd already become accessible to men out of wedlock — whether willingly or through rape — was abandoned. In accordance with the prevailing mores in society, she'd be considered unfit and consequently be targeted, defamed, ostracized, or left for dead. Hence, in the case of women before the twentieth century, the sacredness of *famina sacra* was split into two, a quasi-religious purification and sanctification of the unmarried virgin, on the one hand, and a quasi-political abandonment of the defamed, permissive, unmarried women, on the other hand.[26] These were two opposite exceptions to the rule of marriage; whether they played it by the rule or chose — or were driven into — a state of exception, they were treated as sexual objects, and not as political subjects.

This duality of sanctity and abandonment created the "female body," with which women were required to conform and to which they were subordinated, no less than to the men who exchanged that body among themselves — from father to brother or husband, and from husband to husband. While man's "bare life" had been suppressed and clothed in the garb of citizenship, the "bare life" of the female body was given prominence, made manifest in the public space, openly displayed and sanctified — or abandoned — to a point where no citizen's garb could conceal it. As Jean-Paul Sartre remarked of the naked body: "The body . . . symbolizes our defenseless object-ness. Getting dressed means to camouflage its object-ness, it is to claim the right to see without being seen, or in other words to be pure subject."[27]

The visual field is filled to overflowing with testimonies to this process. Gender inequality was lauded and glorified. The female body can be understood as a medium on which different social and economic forces have impressed their designs by various means — such as clothing, jewelry, cosmetics, and plastic surgery — and through the mediation of diverse practices of representation, from paintings to photos, films, and advertisements.[28]

In the 1960s, however, shortly after women achieved equal citizenship status and shortly before they began their struggle against rape, the female body itself became an object of struggle. In the course of this struggle it underwent a transformation from a body accessible only to whomever had legal title to it to a body whose accessibility would from now on be determined by woman herself. This woman was a new actor on history's stage — a female citizen with equal rights who sought to manage her body, its ends, and accessibility to it as she saw fit. The sexual revolution, in the framework of which this transformation took place, was conducted cooperatively by men and women together, in intergenerational conflict with the generation that symbolized the transfer of possession of the female body among men. As it turned out, within a short period of time, however, the sexual revolution failed to extricate women entirely from the logic of this system, in the framework of which they were exchanged among men.

Although the sexual revolution is a defining moment in the modern history of woman's abandonment, there is a puzzling tendency to disregard or to overlook it in the discussion of rape. It is the moment at which the rules of the game concerning sexual relations were redefined on both the symbolic and the practical level. The invention and marketing of the birth control pill played a crucial role in transforming women into active agents in negotiating their bodies and accessibility to them. For the first time in history, women experienced the possibility of owning their own bodies and making their own decisions in regard to them. But this was only a possibility, and its realization was limited within the framework of the unequal power relations between men and women as shaped and institutionalized over thousands of years.

The antirape movement, however, which came into being a few years after the sexual revolution, attests to the change in the way women now experienced their bodies. About a decade after they began to recognize the legitimacy of a certain separation between the institution of marriage and the conduct of sexual relations, as more and more women began to have sex before marriage, with different partners and in deliberate contravention on their part of the institution of virginity, the sanctity of which symbolized their subordination to men — they felt threatened, assaulted, accessible, and available against their will. The spoken and written texts that women began to produce in regard to their bodies attest to the harsh experience of prejudice against their sovereignty over their bodies, which had just been achieved in the framework of the sexual revolution, and the possibilities of which they had only just begun to understand.[29]

The answer to the question regarding to whom the female body belongs, the body that recently had been "liberated" from the bonds of sanctity and from the patriarchal regime that managed it, was not at all self-evident. Women conceived of it as belonging to them and of having sovereignty to make decisions in regard to it. Men conceived of it as being more available and of having contributed to the struggle for liberation and as partners in this accomplishment. Paradoxically, this mutual struggle, which women had conducted alongside men, reinforced their status as men's hostages. They had deliberately sought to mar the image of the female body and had rebelled against the imperative to conform with it, but without its protection in the framework of the former system of exchange and absent a radical change in gender power relations, they found themselves abandoned and again subordinated to fortuitous males, who were now supposed to protect them from other fortuitous males.

The female body was stripped of all the traits and symbols that had curtailed its availability in the past and had turned it into a unique object intended in principle for one man only, and it had become available, more accessible to many more men — a seductive body that could be seduced, a body that takes an active part in various sexual games, on frequent occasions and in various venues, not necessarily restricted to the bedroom. This body came into the world without any of the normative defenses of citizenship to regulate its standing and the relations that could be conducted with it. The body itself underwent a process of secularization, but this didn't encompass the value system in which the body appeared and was conceived, managed, and desired. Since the sexual revolution, every situation involving an encounter between a man and a woman had become a possible arena for conducting sexual relations. However, as became increasingly clear from the 1970s onward, every situation involving sexual relations had become a possible arena for rape. But the same process also turned the arena of rape itself into an arena of conflict, since the relative availability of sexual relations to men and women alike, as well as a woman's relative liberation from the ownership of a particular man, also made it possible to turn sexual relations into an arena of negotiation, which could at any moment turn into an arena of conflict. In other words, a new abandonment of the female body took place, even under conditions in which women could refuse sexual relations that are offered to them and could rebel against any attempt to impose sexual relations on them.

The latent potential for rape in an intimate situation draws a sharp line between two types of rape: rape by a stranger and rape by someone with whom the victim is familiar.[30] The analysis that I will undertake below refers only to the second type. Rape can no longer be taken to refer only to the behavior of a man who imposes sexual relations on a woman — rape is a moment of the woman's rebellion against this coercion. Into the situation in which a man and a woman have physical relations, a new element has been introduced, which has the potential to turn the situation all at once into rape.[31] This element consists of the woman's willingness or unwillingness to continue these relations, or, in other words, the woman's unilateral withdrawal from a situation in which the man had the impression that the woman he was in company with would agree to have sexual relations with him.

Such a withdrawal was and continues to be experienced by men — and by women, too — as not at all self-evident, but as a step that is often accompanied by anger, humiliation, and a feeling of guilt. The famous title of Robin Warshaw's book *I Never Called It Rape*[32] repeats itself in different variations in the testimonies of many women who have been raped and in the reactions of both men and women to the rape of women by familiar partners.[33] Warshaw relates that it took three years until she was able to call what happened to her rape.

Even if more women today are able to comprehend that they are being raped at the time of the act itself, "belated rape consciousness" is still a very common phenomenon that might not arrive for hours or years, until it is attained either alone or through the agency of others.

The woman's withdrawal from the situation, which is seen not only as a rejection of the physical contact (sometimes even after such contact has already taken place), but as a unilateral withdrawal from something else that doesn't belong to the concrete moment of rape, exacerbates the difficulty of calling what happened "rape": "It was very clear that I wanted to go back home and he didn't respect that, he was very embarrassed that he was unable to control himself. I always have this gesture, even now when I talk about things of this kind. I don't know why that is — I right away defend the boys."[34] From the testimonies of many men and women, what emerges is that both sides experience the withdrawal as treachery of a sort, as a breach of a contract or promise that was ostensibly latent in the developing relations between the two. It is as if by merely agreeing to be in the man's company, the woman had agreed to have sexual relations, and so her withdrawal constitutes a unilateral breach of faith. Since in effect nothing had been agreed on by the man and woman, we must go on examining what this ostensible treachery is — this agreement that the woman ostensibly violated when she voiced her desire to stop the physical contact or leave the man's company, a desire that from this point on transforms the behavior of the man, who won't let her leave and imposes continued physical contact on her, into an act of rape.

A study of the circumstantial conditions points to part of the answer, but this still doesn't suffice. Here are some familiar situations: She went out with a partner and went up to his apartment; she was living with her husband; she invited a man into her home; she stayed at work until a late hour with a colleague; she bathed naked in a pool with a friend. The intimacy, or ostensible intimacy, fortuitous or institutionalized, arising between a man and woman in a demarcated private space is taken for the woman's consent to the development of sexual relations from which she is not at liberty to withdraw: "Where do you think you're going? . . . I thought I was to blame."[35] Although in none of these situations did the woman promise that it would turn into a sexual encounter, she is trapped in a promise not of her own making. Above this model of relations, in which a man and woman are together in a relatively secluded space, still hover the historic conditions that predicated women as being *for* men, whether in the form of the patriarchal sanctification or in the modern form of the objectification of the female body and its being made available. In these conditions, the withdrawal of a woman from the physical space where she's in company with a man is tantamount to a breach of promise. The source of the guilt, which so many women talk about in their rape testimonies, lies in that ungiven promise.

The feelings of betrayal or guilt aren't confined only to the event itself, however. They recur, sometimes even with greater intensity, when the event is identified as a rape and the assaulting male is labeled a rapist. The woman, who only a moment ago was the man's wife, girlfriend, acquaintance, or date, unilaterally declares that a rape has occurred here and that the man in whose company she has been, a man who put his faith in her (believing at least that she would respond to his advances), has raped her. He is usually a respectable man of some standing, known to be law-abiding, and here she must shatter his dignified image, betray his familiar figure, stand facing him alone, point to him, and say: "He raped me; he's a rapist." In other words, what turns rape into rape in its modern sense is the woman's retreat from a promise she never made to be available to the man whom she's with.

At the time of the rape or afterward, when she's again by herself, at home, at the police station, in court, or in public, what happened between her and the man will still be sexual relations, and sexual relations only. Her retreat from a promise she never made is a necessary condition for rape in its modern sense to take place. It follows that rape in its modern sense is based on the woman's objection not only to the rapist who demands the fulfillment of a promise she never made, but also to the promissory structure imposed on her. Even if at the time of the rape the woman is unable to resist or rebel, merely proclaiming what happened to her to have been rape and demanding public acknowledgement of that fact are in themselves an act of rebellion.

231

The legislation against rape and the new discourse on rape have placed women's consent to have sexual relations with men at the center of the debate on the assumption that women are ordinary citizens and that rape is expressive of a violation of one of their rights. This has aroused widespread criticism from many feminists, who have shown that consent doesn't necessarily stem from volition and that coercion doesn't necessarily entail violence and who have demanded that lack of consent be recognized even when coercion is perpetrated by symbolic means. Radical feminists have even demanded that the category of consent be stricken from the law.

The category of consent, which refers to circumstantial consent — whether the woman agreed to be with the man in the pool, in his room, or in her home — makes it impossible to see rape as an arena in which women rebel against their continued oppression in spaces that have remained in the grip of the ghosts of their sexual domination. The rape of women continues to occur, in tremendous numbers, and it remains a matter of individual combat, of one-on-one warfare. The feminist campaign hasn't succeeded in placing this struggle at the focal point of the effort to change the sovereign's attitude toward women, who are abandoned under its aegis and exposed as existing in a state of exception each time anew.

The imposition of sexual relations on a woman, the fact that the discourse on rape appeared only ten years after the sexual revolution and that the rape situation didn't appear as self-evident from the start — all these things point to the obscurity surrounding the meaning of the availability of the female body that was ushered in by the sexual revolution of the 1960s. In this obscurity, women remain haunted by the ghost of previous attitudes toward women, attitudes that perpetuate their subjection to men and their existence in a state of exception. Women understood the female body as belonging to them and themselves as responsible for its availability and for deciding on accessibility to it, while the male assailant to whom they have denied this body behaves, once they are together, as if this body still were his by right. He knows or supposes that this body is available to others; he knows or supposes that until a moment ago it could have been available to him and he doesn't understand why it has been taken away from him at a given moment. Furthermore, he doesn't understand why the woman is the one who determines the rules of the game in regard to this body, which was never supposed to have been hers.

The female body was indeed stripped, made available, accessible, and more readily obtainable, but in the concrete encounter with the bodies of concrete women, the availability of the female body, which the sexual revolution lauded and acclaimed, quickly revealed itself as a new type of abandonment. The rise in the number of opportunities for sexual encounters between men and women (and between members of the same sex, as well), much more than prior to the sexual revolution, gave rise to a new situation in which women are constantly viewed as sex objects while their opposition to this exposes them to rape. The new incarnation in which the female body appeared thus was not much different from the former one. Its omnipresence — exposed, sexual, seductive, and seducible — threatened to trap concrete women in its image and to identify their availability.

Whereas in the 1960s women had had to fight against the image of the female body to deliver themselves from it, now they braced themselves to fight over the character of this new female body, which threatened to become their own. At one and the same time, the sexual revolution created both the omnipresence of the female body as a sex object and the availability of women's bodies. The "female body" had been over-secularized, turning it from a sanctified object into a sex object that different agents have sought to claim possession of and manage accessibility to through open display, trade, and rape. As women began to conduct campaigns on all fronts against the sexual representation of the female body, they also stood up as owners of their own bodies and as possessing their own criteria for the ways they could be used and made accessible. But even though the body had lost its transcendent status, the woman's "No" was not just a concrete statement that meant "I don't want to, because I don't want to now and in this way," but also the manifestation of a new general rule: "I don't want to and I am the owner of this body, and that is why I'll decide, and it's not a matter for negotiation." Their claim on their body is a political claim, insisting that it will be respected not because of its sanctity, but because of its new

233

political status. The fact that women must make this general rule manifest time after time attests to the fact that their integration within the political community of citizen was not yet completed.

And so, even after achieving citizen status and equal rights in everything relating to sexual accessibility to their bodies, women were left exposed to the strength and power of men and unprotected by law. It wasn't only their own bodies that were abandoned in this way, but also the image of the female body itself, which had become a part of them. They had to conduct the struggle over it while continuing to struggle in the first person, each over her own private body. The sexual attack of which they were the object didn't come about because one of them had seduced a man who happened to be in her vicinity, or because another had dressed provocatively, or because yet a third had drunk one glass of wine too many. None of them bears the blame or the responsibility for the abandonment of the image of the female body made manifest in her own.

This fluctuation between the image of the female body and the body of each and every woman is a crucial piece in the emergence of a sharp divide between what had been called rape in the past and the new understanding of rape that came into being from the 1970s onward. The sharp divide these new objects created brought about a transformation of the field of vision, of the capacity to speak about what appears in it, and of the possibilities of intervention in what occurs in it. The new field made it possible to see the abandonment of women, all women, by the law: not necessarily the actual injury to each and every one, but the abandonment of each and every one as a result of the abandonment of the female body. Therefore, the fact that one woman or another hadn't been sexually assaulted could no longer refute the new claim, which became widespread from the 1970s onward, showing that the female body itself was abandoned, accessible, and exposed to sexual use by men and that as long as it was abandoned, all women would be abandoned as well.

The revolution wrought by women in regard to their bodies makes it possible to reconstruct three central arenas in which the female body was sanctified and abandoned: civilian, legal, and visual.[36] The civilian arena was the first into which women carried their struggle at the time of the French Revolution, fighting to gain equal rights and political representation. But the struggle against rape revealed how partial and unsatisfactory the political representation they had achieved was and it hadn't taken their abandonment off the agenda. The political status they had achieved didn't make it possible for the conditions of female existence to become part of what is contested in the framework of civilian struggles. They and their concerns were left unrepresented allowing the sovereign to remain indifferent toward injury inflicted on them.[37]

The legal arena was distinctly understood as where injury of a sexual nature to women could not receive satisfactory expression and where whoever harmed them need not fear retribution because of impunity. In their struggles, women pointed out that the law and the legal system generally tend to protect the sexual assailant more than the victim and that the various changes in legislation introduced since the French Revolution were unsatisfactory. In effect, most rape cases were never brought to court, and when they were, existing laws were only rarely enforced.[38] The feminist struggle exposed the structuring of rape as a crime involving injured dignity, the injured parties being first and foremost the men with ties of ownership to the woman, rather than as sexual violence in which the woman herself was the injured party. It pointed to the perversion of law that enabled the courts to demand that the woman prove that the rapist had forced her to have sexual relations without her consent, that violence was employed against her, and that she had resisted forcefully.

The visual arena shows how the female body is produced and exhibited in the tension between sanctification and abandonment. In this context, the female body appeared as a sex object, an object of lust, exposed to abandonment. The processes that had contributed to this since the French Revolution reached a peak with the sexual revolution in the 1960s. Among them were the proliferation of female nudity in museums beside a noticeable decline in the display of male nudity; the institutionalization of pornographic visual culture;[39] the institutionalization of various art and fashion practices that transformed the female body into a walking fetish in the public space,[40] the object of desirous gazes and a sex symbol; and the use of new technologies since 1840 as channels for distributing images of

235

the female body (photography, *cartes de visite*, advertising, and film) that exhibit it as both a desired commodity in diverse exchange relations and a sanctified object.

Until the 1970s, the abandonment of the female body enjoyed cultural, social, and legal legitimacy in certain defined sites of the public space. In parallel and as part of the same process, the institutionalization of the universal, impartial male gaze took place, which drew its legitimacy from the separation between "bare life" and "political life." Thus, on entering various sites of the public sphere — courts, museums, parliaments, and so on — man, protected by his uniform dress, could experience himself as an abstract, incorporeal citizen. In parallel, the nude female body turned into a desirable and accepted object in various exhibition spaces, while woman herself was refused admittance to these sites and institutions as an active player.[41] It was there that the modern spectator practiced observing the exposed and abandoned presence of the female body.[42] Sexual assault of women was institutionalized as an inseparable and inevitable part of the residue of violence that constitutes the body politic and accompanies it as a constant potential, the occasional realization of which is necessary to its existence.

Since the 1970s, coincident with the consolidation of the anti-rape movement, feminist discourse developed a lively critical discussion of these various representations of the female body scattered about the public space — in its hallowed sanctuaries, such as museums and churches, or in various mass media, such as advertisements and magazines — and problematized all such representation. The female body was posited as an object of negotiation in various frameworks (the public discourse, legislation, theoretical research, etc.) and by various means (demonstrations, the production of counter-images, etc.). What lay in the balance in these negotiations wasn't only the question of ownership of the female body, but also the ways of, use of, and right to exhibiting it and its representations. These issues may have been similarly problematized in action or speech prior to this historical moment, but a new object in discourse is never the outcome of such isolated instances. When Mary Richardson stepped into the National Gallery in 1914 in order to deface Velasquez's *Venus*, she sought to challenge the self-evident manner in which women were exhibited inside the museum as belonging to other men — or at least this is one way her action could be interpreted. It was immediately cast, however, as a felony that fell within the criminal sphere, and so it remained episodic and made no ripples. Since the 1970s, however, acts of this kind are also registered as attempts to problematize the representation of the female body, and the questions in this regard have spread to every field of thought and action and have been assimilated into various fields of discourse. Both men and women have dealt with these issues, honing concepts, debating, censoring, proposing alternatives, creating new contexts, joining battle — all to turn the display of the female body as sex object into a matter that demands attention.

Women have fought — and some continue to fight — over the manner in which the female body is represented as if it were their own.[43] They have fought against its unitary image and sought to make it banal and commonplace, to allow it to appear as multifaceted, to diverge into countless manifestations, and to enable every woman to enrich its repertoire of representations in her way. As a result of these battles, what had been considered *the* female body in the past and had turned into an object of exchange value in negotiations among men lost its distinctive outline and with that also its monopolistic power in various cultural arenas. The female body underwent a transformation, in the wake of which its various appearances could no longer be subsumed as the manifestation and representation of "woman as sex object," not in the sense of this expression prior to the sexual revolution and not in the later sense, when women became more available than ever for casual sexual relations. There is one arena, however, in which the abandoned female body that women have fought to get rid of in every other arena comes back to life each time anew, where its ghost haunts the feminist struggle itself and frequently threatens the citizen status of woman as having the right to protection by the sovereign. This is the arena of rape.

Rape usually occurs in a private space. Private space in this context doesn't correspond with the domestic space or an individual's private space. It is a space whose privacy is constituted by dint of the intimate relations forged in it or the violence employed in it — and sometimes the intimacy turned violent. The violence creates a closed space here. It isolates or seeks to isolate the woman from anything or anyone who might come to her assistance and leaves her stripped of her strength, facing her assailant.[44] In the public space, the rules are more or less clear — few incidents of rape take place in public, and when rape does occur in the public space, it is usually during wartime or in the course of ethnic cleansing, when all systems collapse. The private space in which rape is perpetrated is a new space of relations, rich in contradictions arising out of the concrete encounter between woman and man, but always also out of the traditional models of relations between men and women to which both unwittingly cling. Here the norms customary in the public space, where the woman is already an ordinary citizen and has the ability to negotiate over the way in which she is ruled and, in the wake of the sexual revolution, over the way in which she manages her sexual availability, intersect with the norms of the private space, in which woman is still seen as a sex object, permitted to the man in whose company she shares this space. In this intimate space, she is seen as available and accessible, but she is no longer anyone's property. She has perhaps been (or is thought to have been) with other men, but she continues to preserve her sexuality as something that isn't entirely under the thumb of the open sexual game that may be conducted between them. The woman posits herself as having the freedom to decide if and when to have sexual relations in a manner that is necessarily independent, directly or indirectly, of the behavior or charm of the man whom she's with. Rape begins the moment the man is unable to reconcile himself to the fact that he has no proprietorship over this decision, that its source is completely alien to him, and that he can in no way appropriate it. Despite all the changes in the status of rape, this space has been and remains abandoned and outside legal language, a twilight zone in which woman's abandonment continues.

This is the background against which rape has gained new prominence since the 1970s. Various spokespersons of both sexes have continued to use the term "rape," but have had to recourse to additional terms all the time in order to describe accurately the gamut of experiences for which the term "rape" alone, in its new legal sense that was taking shape, was inadequate. The change didn't take place only with the appearance of new definitions of rape and a new glossary of terms to describe the event. It took place as a result of the fact that women began to talk about rape by themselves, in the first person, to attest to the experience of rape from the primary source, and they began to do so both among themselves and generally in the public sphere. The new definitions were a response to the new confessional discourse, and the latter on its part made use of the new terms in ways that didn't always accord with "legislative intent." The women who spoke thus in the first person changed the meaning of rape; they fought against it in the arena in which it took place, but also in other arenas that gave rise to conditions allowing rape to continue and even proliferate. They linked the incidence of rape to a complex world of experiences in the framework of which they felt abandoned, exploited, available, and coerced. They began to turn to the courts, muster support, apply pressure, demonstrate, collect data, cross-reference testimonies and documents, prevail on women to confess, promote awareness, write by themselves, formulate rules, establish treatment centers for victims, instruct various agents active in the field, write and distribute the history of their activities, invent new genres of writing and art on the topic of rape, teach women's self-defense, and more. They created a place in the new discourse for the conditions of female existence and exposed the boundaries responsible for their structured absence from previous discourses.

The new conditions of female existence in space, plus the fact that some of these conditions had become visible and amenable to being spoken of and changed through intervention, turned "rape," "sexual assault," and "sexual injury" into new objects of discourse. Data regarding them was collected using various sections and categories, which made it possible to expose their frequency and probability, their physical, emotional, and social damages and consequences, their patterns of incidence, and their modes of eventuation. That data made it possible both to distinguish among the abundant types and forms of woman's abandonment and to subsume them all under a single general concept.[45] In these conditions, it became possible at last to dispel the fog that had shrouded coercive sexual relations for centuries in the framework of various cultures.

239

That process extended also to women who had become accustomed in such cases to choose silence, when possible, as the wiser course.[46]

For the first time, rape turned into a distinct and independent category of knowledge and action in a way that made it possible to think about it in political terms, create conditions that would lead to its reduction and prevention among susceptible populations and at susceptible sites, and provide treatment to victimized women. In the framework of the new discourse, rape is no longer an event that disrupts a system of exchange relations in which the woman is an object (as when rape is "solved" by forcing marriage on the rapist or a rape victim is "redeemed" through marriage to a man of inferior position who agrees to disregard this "stain" on her past),[47] but something that is simultaneously specific and general. As a specific term, it is one of a cluster of available terms that may be chosen to describe a specific case in the most accurate and appropriate way. As a general term, it is used in regard to various types of sexual injury to women — their common denominator being the coercion of women to make themselves sexually available to other men — in order to declare the nature of the injury to the woman and to generate urgency in her regard. The latter use of the term refers to the conditions of women's abandonment, while the former describes a specific case of abandonment.

The polemical debates regarding the definition of rape, which continue to this day, have led to the creation of a differential network of signifiers that point to rape even in the framework of relations and types of assault that formerly hadn't been understood as such, including rape within the family, attempted rape, gang rape, sexual extortion, incest, date rape, and sexual harassment.[48] These new signifiers gave rise to new conditions for the appearance of women's abandonment and exposed the fact that it has extended into various arenas of the entire social space, including those that formerly hadn't seemed relevant to the debate on rape: the home, workplace, sites familiar to the victim, and so on.

Both the rapist's identity and that of the victim of sexual assault underwent a transformation. He turned from an unknown pervert into a completely ordinary man who might be known to the woman and even close to her. The victim herself appeared, for the first time in history, as someone who'd found herself, against her will, in a situation in which any woman could find herself. When this was done and the data on sexual assault was examined, the figures that emerged were horrifying. Rape had become omnipresent.

The feminist activists who collected and analyzed these data sought to use them in order to create a dimension of urgency. They warned that one out of every three women is likely to become a victim of sexual assault in her lifetime, and one out of four women is likely to become a victim of rape.[49] Seven out of ten victims, the data revealed, were raped or assaulted by someone they knew, that is, in the ordinary frameworks of their lives.[50] The collected data attest that women's bodies continue to be abandoned, but rape as a category is less and less neglected. It has turned into an object of research in various disciplines — history, philosophy, critical theory, statistics, sociology, psychology, and so on. It has become the target of governmental and public intervention and an object of management, treatment, examination, attestation, police investigation, rehabilitation, categorization, and financing. The women and men who began to deal with it are waging a daily battle to keep rape at the center of attention and not let it slip off the public agenda.

The Presence of Rape to the Gaze

How, then, are we to account for the astonishing fact of the effacement of rape from photographic representation under existing conditions of visibility? In *The Birth of the Clinic*, Foucault emphasizes three dimensions by means of which the appearance of something new may be discerned: a change in its presence before the gaze, in what can be said about it, and in the means of intervening in it.[51] These are three separate dimensions, each of which represents a different type of accessibility to the object in question. They are interdependent, yet facilitate each other: Presence before the gaze generates new conditions of speech and makes intervention possible, while at the same time accessibility to the gaze is mediated and restricted by the possibilities of speech and intervention, just as intervention is possible due to presence or speech, while at the same time it changes their conditions. An object's accessibility to the gaze in discourse, as Foucault describes it, is a necessary dimension of

241

existence in discourse — all the more so in reference to the emergence of something new. However, accessibility to the gaze doesn't mean that the object is necessarily visible. Thus, for example, God, the rule of contradiction, and the fall of the Roman Empire are not objects of the gaze, at least not directly. Their presence in discourse is manifested by means of intermediaries that represent them — miracles, the created world, archaeological remains, and so on. Rape could have been shown and seen, just as murder and traffic accidents are shown and seen, but it has become an object of the same order as God and the rule of contradiction.

Surprisingly enough, however, rape shows up in discourse without the mediation of visual images, either direct or indirect. Rape is the object of neither the gaze nor visual representation.[52] Its appearance in the new discourse is that of an invisible object. Everybody's talking about it, talking about its images as if they were here in front of us — present before the gaze — but the images are absent. When I set out to look at them, I found to my surprise that they were missing. From here on, I will attempt to reconstruct this absence and to ascertain what role it plays in organizing the discourse in which the object "rape" appeared. At this stage of the discussion, I will postpone the inevitable normative question — whether and in what conditions it may be desirable or permitted to show images of rape — and return to it later.

Rape's integration into daily language came about through the creation of ready-made catch phrases, such as "men can stop rape," "no sex without consent," "rape is evil," "rape or sex: the difference is consent," "kill the rapist in you," "men get raped, too," and so on.[53] These phrases describe rape from the combined heterogeneous viewpoints of the assailant and victim. A randomly chosen, but illuminating example of this is a full-page ad that appears from time to time in the U.S. press (figure 5.2). I happened on it in a local Boston newspaper. The ad begins with the following three lines:

It was 2 A.M.
She was in my room.
We were drunk.[54]

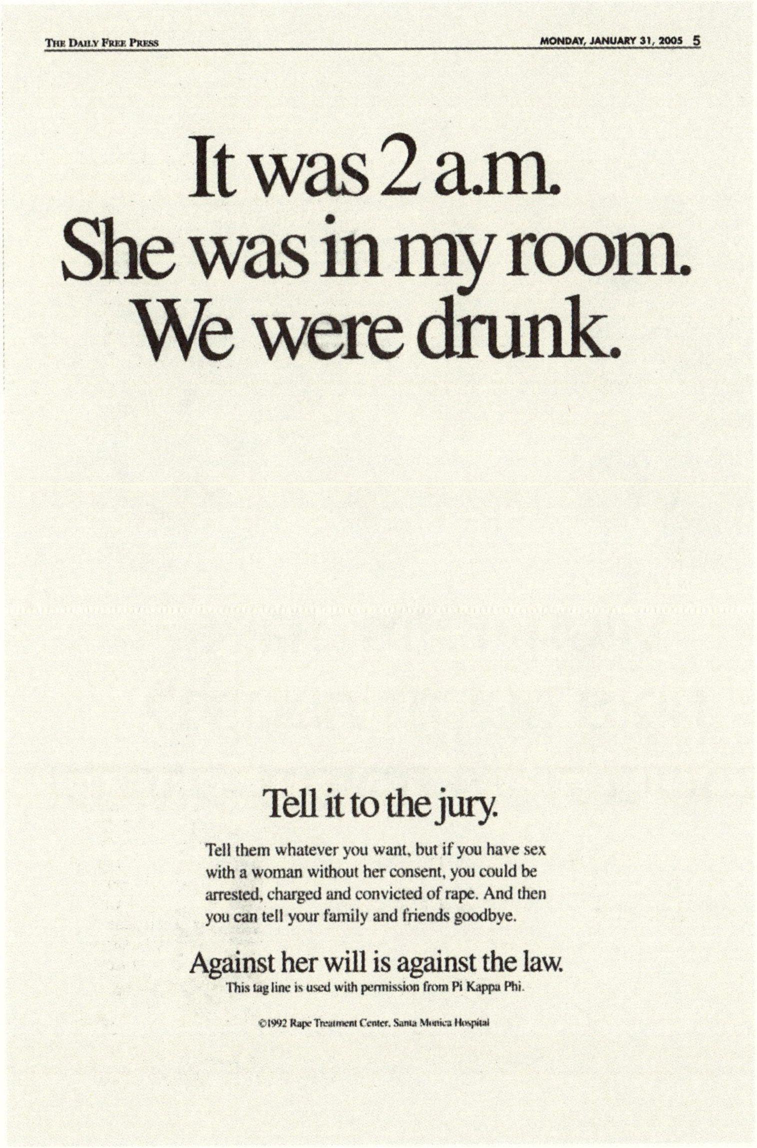

It was 2 a.m.
She was in my room.
We were drunk.

Tell it to the jury.

Tell them whatever you want, but if you have sex
with a woman without her consent, you could be
arrested, charged and convicted of rape. And then
you can tell your family and friends goodbye.

Against her will is against the law.

This tag line is used with permission from Pi Kappa Phi.

©1992 Rape Treatment Center, Santa Monica Hospital

Figure 5.2. Advertisement, *Daily Free Press*, Boston University, January 31, 2005.

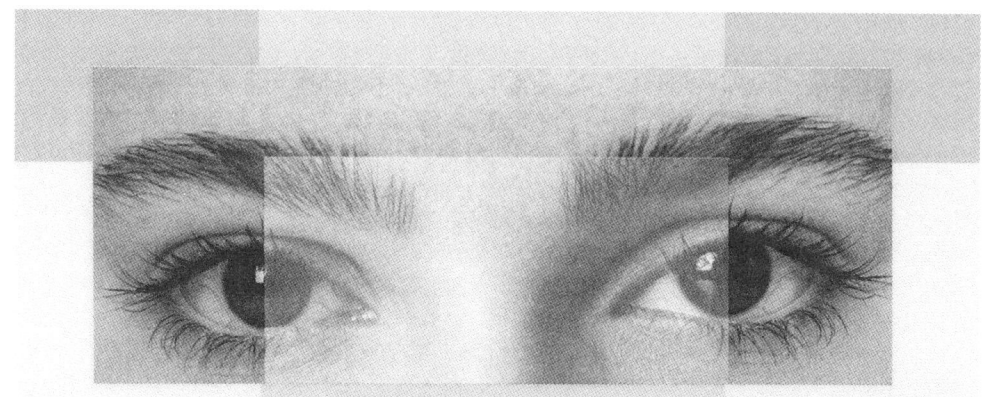

איגוד מרכזי הסיוע
לנפגעות תקיפה מינית
ולנפגעי תקיפה מינית בישראל

Figure 5.3. Cover of Report on Sexual Violence in Israel, 2003–2004.

At the bottom of the ad, in small, but still very legible lettering, the assailant's voice is answered by another voice, reminding him that it's no longer possible to talk like this: "Tell it to the jury." In even smaller lettering, for the benefit of anyone who still hasn't understood what should be self-evident, a final caption reads: "Tell them whatever you want, but if you have sex with a woman without her consent, you could be arrested and convicted of rape. And then you can tell your family and friends goodbye." The ad supplies a code of behavior. It indicates to its readers what's allowed and what's not, what was formerly customary and what is now no longer legal, and what the social and legal consequences are of behaving according to a repudiated norm. It also provides them with ready-made catch phrases for use in critical situations in which someone might yet enjoy the benefit of the doubt: "Against her will is against the law."

This ad — just like all the books that deal with the topic and the various publications produced by rape-victim centers, such as reports, manuals, fundraising pamphlets, and so on — is devoid of images of rape or of any other situation involving sexual assault.[55] This systematic absence is indicative of a policy that can best be characterized by the dictum "Do not show." Before trying to ascertain exactly what the origin of this dictum is and what conception it represents, I will linger over what *can* be seen in such published material besides the written text.

There may be abstract images of tables of data, graphs and pie charts, or official photographs of functions and fund-raising events. In some publications, use is made of a visual motif with an overtly expressive, yet somehow vague charge that can take on various meanings. A distinctive example of this is the pair of eyes that have appeared in recent years as a recurrent motif in the various publications of the Association of Rape Centers for (Female and Male) Victims of Sexual Assault in Israel (figure 5.3). The eyes appear on their own in a narrow, horizontal strip, detached from any concrete or identifiable figure. They are there to level a gaze at the spectator. In another version of the same image, the eyes appear together with a nose, a face-to-face encounter, albeit with a dissected face that lacks concreteness. The face lacks identifying features. Like the eyes, the partial face, too, is leveling a gaze at the spectator. The choice of this

245

image would appear to be a counterproposal to what has been described in feminist visual research as the hegemonic representation
of women: a passive figure with no gaze of her own who serves as
the object of the masculine gaze.[56] The woman gazing out of these
ads appears to be a subject with a penetrating gaze who literally
won't take her eyes off anyone looking at her. The woman as subject
of the gaze here is a manifestation of the new female figure that
these publications wish to promote: a woman whose consent must
be sought. This figure is meant to replace that of woman as the
object of the gaze that posits her as an object of sexual conquest.

The use of the strip with the eyes is distinctly expressive of a
prevalent conception in the treatment of victims of sexual assault
that has taken form around the concept of "empowerment." Paradoxically, however, the strip with the eyes (even including the nose)
is reminiscent of Identi-Kit pictures that are used by police to construct profiles of suspects — including, of course, profiles of rapists.
With all the effort to remove any identifying feature from the face
and not reveal any concrete figure, the outcome is a facial section
that can in principle be adapted to any woman — or in which any
woman can be identified. It functions in the same way as the profile
of a rape victim that is generated by the media when it covers her
face with a mask of pixilation. The resulting image posits the "unidentified" rape victim in the sphere of identification and verification and leaves her in the custody of the police discourse, alongside
suspects, criminals, and their weak, vulnerable, and exposed victims.
It is most unlikely that this is the result that the "authors" of this icon
intended. It appears to be the exact opposite of everything they represent. Nevertheless, it is no marketing error, but as an effect of the
new discourse on rape that I have tried to describe here and as a
symptom of the conditions that make it possible.

The rape victim's uncovered face — the only visual image that has
escaped the taboo against the display of images of rape — attests in
fact to the obscure face of rape itself. This single norm that "everyone" seems to have tacitly agreed on is something that gives one
pause to wonder: What are these images that the codes of knowledge who treat rape as unrepresentable have effaced, and what is the
meaning of this effacement?

In a heavy (720-page) volume published in 2004 entitled *The Face of Human Rights*, there is only one image of a woman that does refer to rape, which itself remains unseen, and the caption reads: "Sierra Leone, 2001. A survivor of sexual violence."[57] The photograph is in black and white, and in it, we see a woman sitting on a bed in an empty room — the emptiness might be taken to indicate that it's a temporary place of abode, a transit. Her elbows rest on her knees, and she's holding her head in her hands, thus hiding her face. This photograph joins the paltry collection I've managed to put together over the years.

The collection contains very few items that are explicitly connected to rape. It consists almost entirely of photographs showing items of testimonies of rape incidents that took place against a background of ethnic or national conflict.[58] Four images are from the rape in Nanking (of Chinese women by Japanese soldiers during the city's occupation in 1937), showing clear and explicit traces of the sexual violence against the photographed women (figures 5.4 through 5.7).[59] The rest of the (few) photographs that I've managed to collect show women whose demeanor or face bear the traces of grave injury. Without the benefit of captions referring to the context, however, it would be impossible to tell whether these were specifically women who had been raped.

In one photograph taken in Sudan, for example, about twenty women can be seen walking through a desert landscape, some of them pregnant, others carrying infants in slings.[60] The story that accompanies the photograph hints at the possibility that the children being carried by the women are the outcome of rape. In another photograph, a woman can be seen leaning against a fence, her face hidden behind the palms of her hands, which attest to her advanced age. The caption refers to a rape camp in Bosnia.[61] In addition, there are a few recent photographs taken in Abu Ghraib that were later declared forged by the American administration. It is unclear whether these photographs, which depict violent scenes of rape of Iraqi women by American soldiers, are part of an existing hoard of rape scenes or testimony to the way in which people fantasize about rape. I'll come back to them later.

It is indeed a very meager collection. Some readers may perhaps

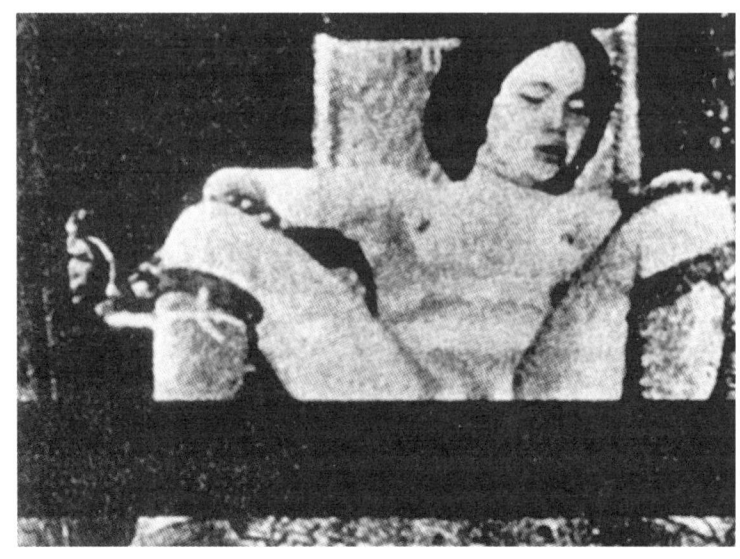

Figures 5.4 and 5.5. Rape in Nanking, 1937.

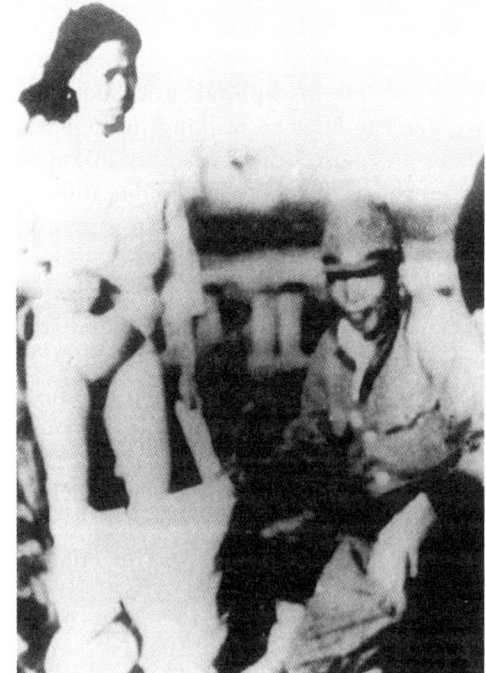

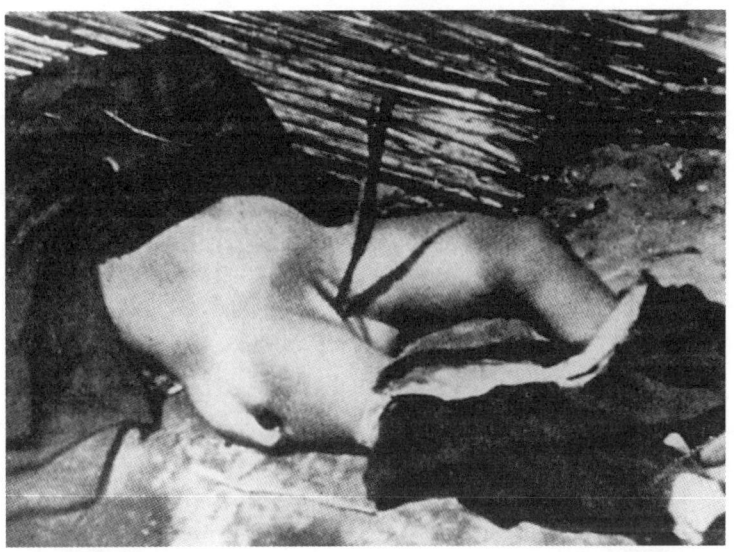

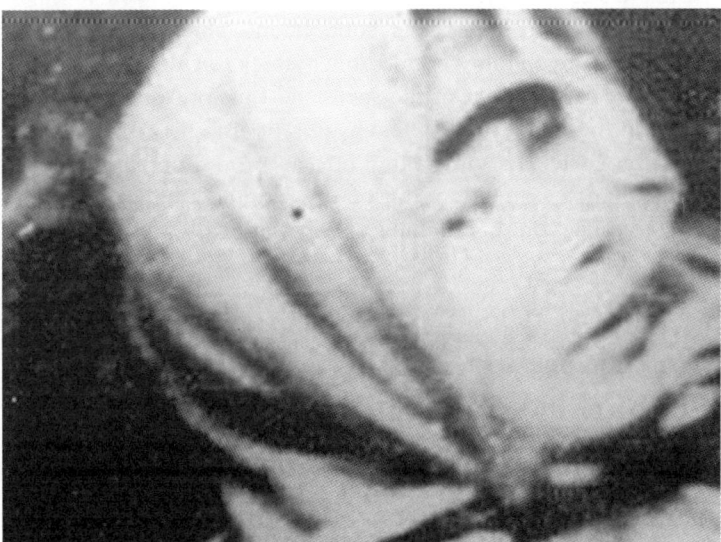

Figures 5.6 and 5.7. Rape in Nanking, 1937.

recall some other photograph they've encountered in a newspaper, book, or catalogue. These are merely the exceptions that attest to the rule: In the public space, one that is not closed, but that is well defined, there are very few photographs of rape, just about all of them from war zones or regions of ethnic conflict. Few people are familiar with them, and their accessibility to the public is restricted.[62]

This contention regarding the absence of rape images does not refer to any essential nature or principle. It is a historical contention regarding the current, transient state of the rape image in the public space. In order to understand the historicity of this state of things, we must go back to the moment of rape's appearance as a new object in discourse. As mentioned above, the explicit purpose of the feminist activists who fought to make rape manifest in public discourse was to detach rape from its sexual context and fix it in consciousness as an act of violence. The objective had been to refute the assumptions that the assailant was motivated by uncontrollable passion, that rape was a form of sexual relations, and that the victim was in fact interested in sexual relations of this kind. This stance — which sought to distinguish rape from its sexual context, and which set the general tone in the debate on rape — came under attack for preserving sexual relations as a battle between the sexes and thus preventing women from seeing the men around them as potential rapists, or for being too comprehensive and not taking into account a possible mistake in the assailant's understanding of the woman's behavior.[63] The controversy raged on the sidelines of what gradually turned into the dominant chorus, voiced by treatment centers for victims of sexual assault. In effect, rape became established as a violent crime, with the term "consent" at the heart of the issue.[64] It was no longer a matter of uncontrollable passion on the part of the assailant or unwitting seduction on the part of the victim, but a game with established rules that if broken meant violence.

This outline of rape's representation repeats itself in the legal discourse, in the public discourse via the media, and in the therapeutic discourse. There remains only one field — the visual — in which the debate remains rooted in the soil of sexuality in a way that reveals how unrealistic it was to detach rape from its sexual context. The enormous abundance of images of violence that have flooded the public space in recent decades includes documentation of many and sundry kinds of violence. The fact that photographs of rape are missing from these repositories can possibly be explained by the fact that rape usually occurs in a space without witnesses. This, however, is not a satisfactory answer. Many cases of violence generally occur in a space without witnesses, but this hasn't prevented the buildup of a large body of photographs documenting such cases over the years.[65] Photographic evidence exists in rape cases, too, as attested by occasional reports in the newspapers of film rolls or videotapes having been found in a rapist's home. These photographs are never published, but they exist and are accessible to the gaze of those allowed or authorized to see them.[66] In truth, such photographs represent only a tiny proportion of all rape cases, but even so, they teach us that rape is not in principle devoid of an image — the public gaze on images of rape is what's missing.

I therefore assume that there are photographs of rape that have been taken at the scene of the crime, from close quarters, uninterruptedly, by a camera in the hands of an authorized spectator or by a camera mounted on a tripod and tripped automatically. Like any other still photograph — here I'm not dealing with videotapes — these photographs cannot speak by themselves, but bear traces that need to be coaxed into speaking. Likely enough, these photographs, some of which are probably stored in police archives, show either sexual contact from which traces of violence or coercion can be extracted and reconstructed or scenes of violence from which traces of sexual contact can be drawn. It may be supposed that some of them are stomach-turning, others ambivalent and even seemingly innocent. In some of them, by their very nature, people will be seen having sexual relations without any traces of violence. Others will resemble pornographic photographs involving some degree of violence. Still others will show violent scenes without any traces of a sexual connection. In any event, they are all partial, insufficient to tell the entire story, and certainly not sufficient to show what rape looks like at a glance. Rape "itself" cannot be photographed except in part, and in such a way that an active gaze is required to reconstruct the event and acknowledge it as rape.

I would like to linger here over the published images from the scene of the rape in Nanking.[67] Viewed superficially, one of them —

in which a woman is seen seated on a chair, her legs spread apart and tied to its arms — might appear to be a pornographic photograph (figure 5.4). This reading of it changes, however, the moment it is printed in a book that deals with the mass rape committed in Nanking. The context makes it difficult to continue interpreting the female figure's slightly open mouth and pouting lips as an expression of sexual desire, inviting one to see them instead as part of a face convulsed with pain and swollen from weeping. But even if her pouting lips do attest to sexual pleasure, the context doesn't negate the fact that the body may have enjoyed pleasure, but makes it possible to understand that this pleasure, to which the photograph may perhaps attest, was violently forced on her. In any event, the meaning of the photograph doesn't reveal itself at once. Constructing its meaning is no less important than the very testimony it bears.

A second photograph shows a woman with her clothes torn away, the hem of her garment in the hands of a Japanese soldier (figure 5.5). Already at first glance, this photo appears less ambivalent — sexual and ethnic violence is right in the forefront. This image could have been photographed before or after the rape, but itself doesn't show rape. In a third photograph, we see the lower half of a female body — most likely a corpse — lying on its back, a branch protruding from her genitals (figure 5.6). Here there is clear evidence of sexual brutality toward the woman, which also apparently led to her death. Signs of abuse of the body are certainly evident in the photograph. Not one of them on its own (or any other photograph of rape) can turn into an index of rape images — a finger that can point and say "Here, this is what rape looks like."

The last photograph is apparently a photograph from the moment of rape itself: a naked man is seen penetrating the body of a woman whose blouse is ripped way; both are visible only from the waist up (figure 5.7). This photograph too, however, is unable to speak for itself. The woman appears frightened, and her gaze is turned away from the situation, seeking help, assistance, perhaps the cooperation of witnesses present at the site, or perhaps compassion or mechanized attestation from the photographer. Her left hand, however, resting gently on her left breast, is a disturbing element, making it difficult to fix the unequivocal content of the picture.

Even in the case of photographs produced in laboratory conditions by the rapist, the information conveyed will always remain no less partial than the information conveyed by photographs that attest to rape by means of allusion. In other words, photographs of "rape itself" will not necessarily illuminate rape better than peripheral photographs. Corresponding repertoires of *énoncés* of horror that attest to other atrocities that have been committed over the course of the twentieth century weren't necessarily produced out of actual proximity to the disaster, either. A familiar repertoire of images on themes such as execution, famine, the demolition of houses, or poverty will include photographs of objects, places, dominant figures, key moments in the annals of the "field," demonstrations, posters, and the front pages of newspapers, all of which exhibit various aspects of the theme. No special conditions are required in order to produce similar *énoncés* in instances of rape, and the fact that rape itself may have occurred in the dark makes no difference. So how could it be possible, for example, that Inez Garcia, who stood at the center of the first "rape trial" that was accompanied by massive support from the feminist movement and that stirred up a storm in the United States, never became a familiar, iconic figure?[68] How could it be possible that the rape camps in Bosnia, which everyone knows about, have left us no images, not even such as might have been taken from afar or after the fact? How is one to explain the fact that the underground tunnel beneath Arlozorov Street and the Ayalon Highway, which cast its pall of terror over the women of Tel Aviv in the late 1970s because it had become the site of repeated rapes, never became a familiar icon? Why haven't images from the rape parties that are occasionally held under the auspices of fraternities in college campuses across the United States ever leaked into the public space in an age when so many of the participants have digital cameras? Discussing the absence of such images leads directly to the question in regard to the restrictions imposed on their accessibility.

If rape were indeed only an act of violence, as the feminist movement has tried to depict it since the movement's inception, it is difficult to understand why it is thus set apart from other images of violence and why there is such a comprehensive abstention from distributing images of rape or any other iconography connected with it.

In this case, it is also impossible to understand why there has been no open, public debate over the question whether such images should be shown and in what way, just as similar debates have been and still are conducted over other issues, for example, showing victims of terror attacks or the bodies of soldiers killed in combat.[69]

Two reasons are usually given for this comprehensive abstention from exhibiting images of rape: out of consideration for the victim, to spare her further humiliation, and for fear of accentuating the sexual connotations of the images or fear of the pornographic use that might be made of them.[70] Although each of these two reasons ostensibly refers to a different pole of the rape act — the former to the viewpoint and experience of the victim and the latter to the viewpoint and experience of the assailant — they share a common assumption. Both assume that it is not just a matter of violence employed against an ordinary citizen, causing her injury. Both thus make manifest the sexual aspect of rape and the normative system involved in it. Both reasons imply that it is impossible to rid rape of its sexual aspect, and both assume that exhibiting the image intensifies this aspect as well as the injury to the victim — to the entire public, in fact — and increases the likelihood that others might derive (sexual) pleasure from this injury.

This sexual aspect of rape, however, is what Catherine MacKinnon, in her analyses of the obscenity law, presents as a moral — or, more precisely, moralistic — context. The injury, which by dint of these reasons would be spared the victim, is the stain that accompanies her identification in public with the act of rape, that is, disclosure of the fact that she has been a victim of coerced sexual contact. Whether one shows sympathy toward the victim's milieu, which grasps her as desecrated, or toward her own emotional plight, the assumption is that the victim's body is a sacred object which has been desecrated by impure, coerced sexual contact. To overcome the desecration of her body, the victim must distance herself as far as possible from the act in public and take refuge in a therapeutic private space, which will allow her to deal with the stain on her from an emotional aspect.

The debate since the 1970s over whether or not to reveal a rape victim's face emphasizes the shattering of the stereotypical view according to which rape happens only to other women who belong to another class, but it has been also part of the discourse of empowerment, which has called on women not to be ashamed of what happens to them. From time to time, the media will showcase a woman who is prepared to do what most rape victims avoid: reveal herself in public and say in the first person: "I was raped." Every such confession reawakens wonder at the courage required of and the support for the rape victim who will have dared to identify herself, and this fact shows how widely prevalent the conception remains that rape stains its victim and that talking about rape in the first person still should be an exceptional act.[71]

Although over thirty years have passed since the beginnings of public speech about rape in the first person, it thus remains trapped in the problematic framework of the confessional. Speech as confession assumes secrecy, prohibition, desecration, trespass, transgression, besmirchment, and sin. It places the confessor in the nonpolitical position of a woman who must confess to her actions, even if she isn't to blame for them. The confessional position and the authentic speech produced therein are supposed to enable her to be purified of the actions that she describes. The confession functions as a test of truth. It has validity only if the woman delivers detailed testimony about everything that has happened to her — otherwise she has no right to speak. Despite all the time that has elapsed since women began to confess publicly: "I was raped," confession still remains the only speech position offered to women to talk about rape. This position also forces the rape victim to associate herself once again with the cultural image of the female body and, by means of its mediation, to recognize the fact that rape has diminished this body's value and killed it: "Something very important was killed in them, perhaps the feeling of their personal value, of their identity, of being a woman."[72] When the confessional position is the only one offered to the rape victim, she is forced to choose between rejecting the invitation to confess, reconciling herself to the stain on the female body, which she manifests by her silence, or confessing in public, which brings in its wake understanding and sympathy that reassure her that "rape bears no stain," a statement that needs be repeated each time anew exactly because rape is indeed seen as besmirching.

The understanding and sympathy that confession is expected to elicit are themselves highly compromised and problematic. In "Survivor Discourse: Transgression or Recuperation?" Linda Alcoff and Laura Gray-Rosendale analyze the potential dangers in the sensational dimension of survivors' appearances on television programs and their susceptibility to becoming victims again — this time of the discourse of experts, which tends to challenge their legitimacy and thus enables program editors to confine their presence to the status of spectacle. The essay describes the incriminating series of questions to which a survivor named "Tracy," who appeared on one of the talk shows, was subjected. Alcoff and Gray-Rosendale reject the validity of judgmental questions that attempt to examine the rape victim's behavior at the time of the rape and even the very right of the studio audience to judge her behavior. They advise survivors not to give interviews if they are to appear on a program beside experts who may turn them into therapeutic or diagnostic objects and deny them their status as authors of their own stories: "We need to transform arrangements of speaking to create spaces where survivors are authorized to be both witnesses *and* experts, reporters of experience *and* theorists of experience."[73] The authors seek to create a new form for the production of knowledge wherein there is a breakdown of the boundary between the witness and the person who collects, classifies, and analyzes her testimony to produce new knowledge.

While the effort to efface this boundary is in itself laudatory, the alternative form that the authors propose for organizing knowledge about the act of rape — based on distancing other speakers, who "weren't there," from speech positions on the topic of rape — echoes a familiar form of previous modes of organizing knowledge characteristic of the masculine, militaristic discourse on "security." This discourse until not long ago posited men as the sole legitimate speakers concerning the act of warfare, because having been fighters, only they "were there." Alcoff and Gray-Rosendale take no account of the inherent problematics of placing the survivor and her "authentic" portrait at the forefront of the struggle against the patriarchy, and they do not contend with the question regarding what Tracy — or other survivors — appear as on the talk shows.

When Alcoff and Gray-Rosendale propose to get rid of the

experts and turn the rape victim into an expert on her own behalf, the only one able to relate and analyze an event and an experience that have become utterly private, they contrive for the rape victim a speech position outside the hegemonic discourse, a nonnegotiable position that is unwilling to come into contact with any other discourse. She bears the stamp of someone who has been there in the authentic "here and now," in the name of which speech is given her and with which there can be no discussion.

The women "to whom it happened" thus are demanded to put their singular testimony to the test, and it is this singular testimony that grants them the right to speak. In order to exercise the new public position offered to them, however, they are required to forget the general context in the framework of which what happened to them occurred — they are there for their story — and to answer sincerely, without omitting any detail, any question asked regarding the sexuality forced on them. They are thus placed anew in a state of exception, excepted from women in general as exceptions to the rule among those who have been raped. Even when the statistics are one in four, they are still the exceptions to the rule. In this fashion, the overall conditions of women's exception to the rule and abandonment are reproduced.

Talking about rape in the first person, which in the 1970s was supposed to spark a revolution as a certain type of speech act, has turned into a repetitive ritual, and as ritual it preserves elements of sanctity, which its initial speakers specifically sought to take leave of. They aspired to talk in the first person about their own bodies and in this fashion to concretize and secularize the female body, while incidentally combating its customary images. The rape victim with her authentic speech, however, who is required to confess in detail and with precision to what has happened to her, and who is invited to speak as someone that can speak only from this position and only on this topic, turns into a spokesperson of the female body, rather than someone who seeks to challenge its monolithic unity, as she has tried in the past.[74] Paradoxically, while women have struggled over the appearance and image of the female body for decades, each time it threatens to emerge anew, intact and undivided, and to trap women in its web. It is their body — the body that was theirs, but also the body of which they wish to take their leave, at least in its familiar form, that they are fighting to change. The struggle hasn't been decided yet, and it is this that has left women's citizenship flawed and has sustained their injury or at least hasn't made it possible to prohibit it entirely. It is not just the injury that desecrates the female body and drives the victim to the confessional position, but the everyday injury that lurks in ambush everywhere and threatens to reconfine them within the boundaries of the female body and to suspend their concrete existence to enable its appearance. In the arena of rape, they appear as an obstacle in the path of a man bent on gaining hold of this body.

Alcoff and Gray-Rosendale's contention that only female survivors can be experts on the event they have survived is based on the demand for an authentic speech position. Dropping this demand, however, is the only thing that will enable every citizen, female *or* male, to describe the abandonment of female citizens on the basis of their sex, talk about its conditions, and fight against it. Women could be excellent candidates for becoming experts on the quotidian conditions of their abandonment and for talking about these conditions with other experts, without having been raped and without attaining a position of authentic speech.[75] Authentic speech in the first person, which seeks to point the finger of blame and musters all the details of the case toward this end, belongs in the courthouse. There, authenticity is required to ascertain the legal truth, which will afford the female citizen legal protection. In the public space, women need another kind of protection — political protection that will make injury to them of a sexual nature, including injury that doesn't end in rape and is not cause for legal complaint, a nonnormative matter and unacceptable situation. The process of politicizing the speech position, which will enable women to appear as experts on the conditions of female existence, need not stem from their having been raped, but from the very fact that they experience their everyday abandonment in their daily lives (as I will attempt to show below), and this position need not be reserved only to them. Men, too, can attest to the everyday abandonment of woman.

Rape victims' status as exceptions to the rule is even more prominent if we take into account the fact that their portraits as rape victims, disclosed in the public space and exhibited as those "to whom it happened," follow one after another as in a police lineup — and these are the only sketchy pictures in our storehouse of rape images. But if these are almost the only pictures of rape, how, then, do women nonetheless know to recognize rape? What tells a woman facing a situation or image that is susceptible to being called "rape" that something in the situation isn't quite right? What teaches her to sense the threat, to suspect that there has been a sexual injury here, that someone is trying to hide something in regard to such an injury? Moreover, in the absence of a public space wherein images of rape can be observed and talked about, any premonition or intuitive knowledge a woman may have is susceptible to being undermined, denied, and eliminated.

A short passage from Sylvia Plath's diaries allows us to follow the gazes of two women who meet around a situation-image, and the lack of a common public space in which this image might exist doesn't enable them to make the situation-image manifest there, either for themselves or for others. The image continues to exist for each of them separately, apart from the other, and thus it shatters into fragments of images that don't coalesce into a clear picture. The image remains in their private consciousnesses; they stand facing each other, lacking the tools to exchange with each other the fragments that have been violently seared into them:

> So I called, "Have you finished John's picture? "Oh, *ja, ja.*" He smiled. "Come and see. Your last chance." He had promised to show it to me when it was done, so I ran out and got in step with him on his way to the barn. That's where he lives.
>
> On the way, we passed Mary Coffee. I felt her looking at me rather strangely. Somehow I couldn't meet her eyes. "Hullo, Mary," Ilo said. "Hello, Ilo," Mary said in an oddly colorless voice.
>
> ...He kept walking up, so I followed him hesitating at the top. "Come in, come in," he said, opening a door. The picture was there, in his room. I walked over the threshold. It was a narrow place with two windows, a table full of drawing things, and a cot, covered with a dark blanket. Oranges and milk were set out on a table with a radio. "Here." He held out the picture. It was a fine pencil sketch of John's head. "Why, how do you do it? With the side of the pencil?"

It seemed of no significance then, but now I remember how Ilo had shut the door, had turned on the radio so that music came out. He walked very fast, showing me a pencil. "See, here the lead comes out, any size." I was very conscious of his nearness. His blue eyes were startlingly close, looking at me boldly, with flecks of laughter in them. "I really have to go. They will be waiting. The picture was lovely."

Smiling, he was between me and the door. A motion. His hand closed around my arm.[76]

In the lines preceding this description, Plath shares with her readers the silence that has been imposed on her, a silence that, being described as an emotional event — as "being struck mute," just as trauma victims are customarily described — has erased the social and political conditions of this muteness. Plath knew that it was best not to share what happened to her with other people — with her mother, in particular: "I have just got to put down what happened to me this afternoon. I can't tell Mother, not yet, anyway."[77] This is not the only silence revealed by the tale. Plath's encounter with Mary Coffee just moments before Ilo attacks her is also characterized by silence. In retrospect, Plath understands that Mary knew what was in store for her, yet nevertheless maintained her silence. Perhaps this was because it is impossible to prevent a man from realizing the potential abandonment of women, or perhaps it is because Mary herself had been a victim of his sexual violence and, had she warned Plath of what was about to take place, would have had to admit this to her, and perhaps she, like Plath herself, did not want everyone to know *about her*, that this had happened *to her*, as if being the victim of sexual assault meant that, one way or another, she bore a certain measure of guilt. And perhaps she simply didn't know what to tell her, for what could she say? That there was danger lurking? That to go behind closed doors with a man could mean being trapped in a promise she never made? And how would she be able to back up her words, to support her case? All she had was a fragment of an image, a thought, a glimmer. It had to be eliminated; it wasn't real; it was saturated with the fears she wanted to get rid of; it was only her. She had best keep her silence. But it is not just Mary Coffee who knows what is in store for Plath. Even Plath herself knows it. She, too, clings only to fragments of knowledge, to glimmers. She, too, throws them aside. It's impossible to live like this. Not everyone is a rapist. But in retrospect, as she describes it, all the details were there: "At the moment I didn't notice, but now I remember exactly how...."

Sylvia Plath, Mary Coffee, or any woman who has just begun reading Plath's description will know more or less what is about to happen, even if she won't be immediately able to state it as such. She will know it simply because this will not have been the first time she has experienced her body as abandoned. Like the women close to her, she will not have succeeded in putting together the fragments of feelings and images in time and in forging a clear picture out of them, one that would have made it possible to give warning out loud, that would have given her the strength to protest in the knowledge that others, too, will immediately identify the action she has identified and take action against it. The internal images do not suffice. They have left her on her own, replete with words, but devoid of images, lacking the resources to make others see what she has seen, to signal to others, to be assisted by them in taking action without delay to prevent the occurrence of what is happening, because what is happening should be prevented.[78]

The ability to create a common community around shared images isn't required to create the ultimate repository of rape images or only distinctive images of rape. Neither are these shared images meant only as an injunction to remember and not to forget, as the cultural function of photographs is sometimes understood.[79] The photographs are part of the tools that enable us to rehabilitate the sensus communis and construct around it a common community of negotiation, in the framework of which we are able to agree on the boundaries of disagreement. When rape images lie outside the sphere of discussion, are removed from it suddenly or in incisive fashion, we are completely unable to manufacture the boundaries of our agreement or disagreement in regard to them, and we are prevented from negotiating over turning at least some of them into emergency claims.

Photographs of the rape of women in the public sphere pose a threat to the public order not because of what is seen in them, but specifically because of what is not seen in them. If they were to be shown, they would not look like the absolute opposite of everything we're familiar with; they would look a little like familiar images of violence, a little like familiar images of sexual relations — and there are, of course, plenty that are an admixture of both. If they were to be shown, it would be possible to read them in continuity with both and in this way to secularize the images of rape, manufacture differences among them. By means of talking about the visible rape, which emerges from the photographs and returns to them, it would be possible not only to show the differences, big and small, but also to structure them within the framework of a civilian discourse and allow them to become negotiated. Above all, when talking about rape will not be accompanied by the omission of images of the rape of women, all women may be able to know more easily, at the time of the act, that it is indeed happening to them and that what is happening to them is not their private hallucination or a fantasy of the man who is raping them.

Rape in Visual Culture

Even in the field of contemporary art, however, there are few visual representations of rape.[80] In the absence of an identifiable body of images, the few allusive images that do exist haven't coalesced into a distinct iconography.[81] An installation by Karen Russo, which was shown at the Israel Museum in 2000, is still one of the first attempts to deal with this topic in art (figure 5.8). In the center of the installation, a young woman can be seen lying on a bed inside a wooden house.[82] Beside her stands a wheelchair. Her dress is disheveled, her legs exposed and taut. She lies unmoving, eyes riveted on the ceiling, arms folded over her breasts, lips pursed. She appears frightened as she lifts her gaze toward the woman standing over her, as if she were awaiting her judgment or perhaps some intervention on her own behalf. In any event, she isn't protected. Another male figure can be seen slipping outside through the window. The man and woman standing over her are talking about her between themselves, but she has no part in the conversation. There is a forced smile on the woman's lips. Although she stands leaning slightly toward the girl, her gaze is directed away from her, toward the man standing on the

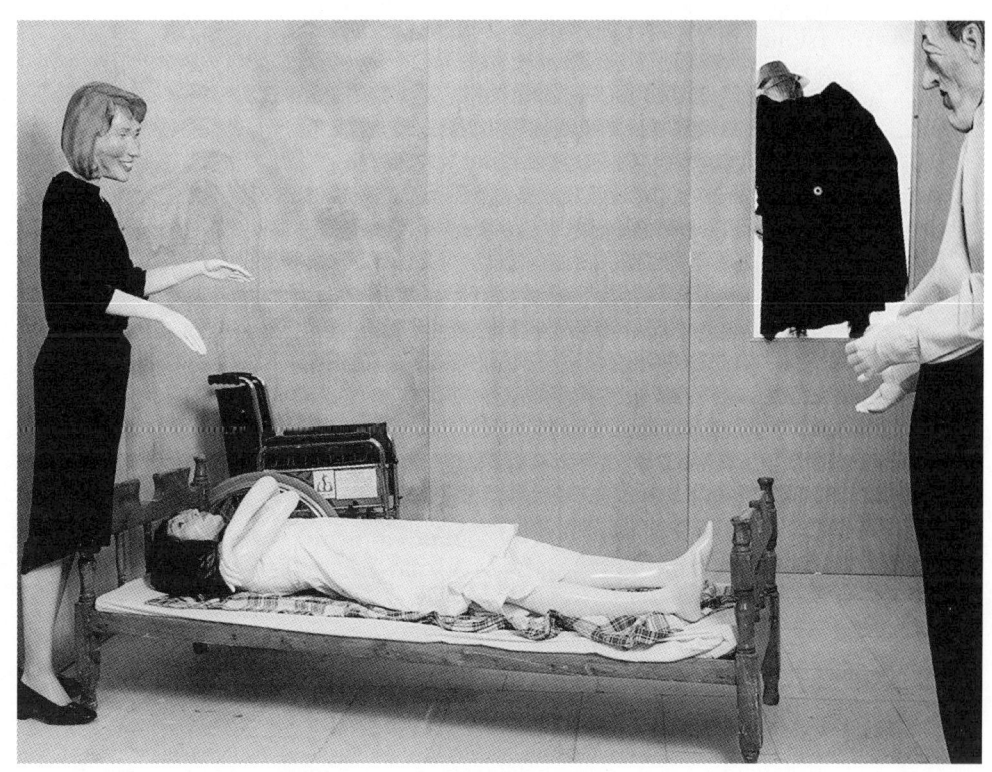

Figure 5.8. Karen Russo, *The Mute*, installation view, Israel Museum, 2000.

other side of the bed — seeking to soothe him, appease him, or obtain his consent. He, for his part, is staring back at her with a resolute and menacing gaze. The girl looks like a hostage of the situation she's in. The wheelchair tucked away in the corner strengthens the impression that she can't get away from there. But even without it, the initial circumstances don't seem to be in her favor. She is trapped inside a domestic space that betrays itself as open to trespass inside and out. "It's impossible to know what there is inside, it's impossible to know what there is outside."[83]

What we have before us is not an image of rape. We don't actually see rape. But the spectator "sees" that the girl has suffered sexual injury — it's difficult to ignore all the hints scattered about. The spectator cannot know exactly what happened, how, or when. However, she can't but begin to speculate. A notice hanging on the wall beside the girl's bed tells the story of the two rapes she underwent, one by her father, the other by an unknown assailant.[84] The story relates that the second incident restored her capacity for speech. But the raw voice restored to her didn't suffice. Now she is again silent, if she ever talked at all, lying again on her bed, petrified, wound up, and threatened.

Despite the fact that the story employs the past tense, it's hard to dismiss the feeling of a threat looming over the present. The spectator knows this is a case of rape or sexual assault and that a threat now looms over the girl, even without recourse to the text that tells about the rape. This knowledge cannot rest on prior familiarity with pictures of rape, for these don't exist, but only on something else.[85] The spectators, both women and men, are familiar with the situation. Perhaps not in just this way, not in this setting, not with these protagonists — but nevertheless familiar with the feeling that the girl is abandoned and threatened. She is familiar to us "from life," and she also has a visual presence. This visual presence is the other side of the missing images of rape. It is the omnipresence of images in which the abandonment of the female body is exhibited in visual culture. You don't see rape, you don't see any woman being raped; what you do see are lots of abandoned female bodies, susceptible to rape.

What do we see in these images? Feminist visual studies have ramified and grown since the 1970s.[86] They have adopted various

264

theoretical approaches and deal with a broad range of issues. But despite the differences among the researchers and their objects of study, it is possible to identify one common understanding, which may be expressed and formulated in different ways, but which recurs in almost all of these studies: In her various representations, woman is always structured *for* a man.

Agnès Varda, a film director who is also a researcher in visual culture, summarizes the situation with accuracy: "In films made by men, female nudity is the climax of a process of a woman's being stripped of her clothes, or of voyeurism, or of exposure which organizes the female nudity in the framework of the overall purpose of a love scene. *Immediate use* is made of this body."[87] It doesn't matter what she does, what work she's employed in, where she lives, where she goes, what she wears, or what she says — ultimately, her presence there is *for* a man. Being for a man attests to woman's status despite her having become a citizen.

When woman was left out of the entire body of citizens, she was left belonging to man, subordinate to him under "the sexual contract."[88] Once she achieved citizenship and ceased "belonging" to a particular man, she was left *for man*. Since the French Revolution, women's struggles have played an active part in removing veils of sanctity that might attest to any claims of essential, rather than socially structured difference between women and men. One after the other, the various levels of difference were historicized while the formal equalization of rights became ever broader and spread to many fields, until it appeared that no field was nonnegotiable. From an object and a possession, woman turned into a subject who owned property.[89] Representation of woman as existing for a man, however, repeatedly strips her of everything she has managed to acquire in the public sphere. Thus, the visual culture perpetually reconstitutes the difference between women and men as ineradicable and nonnegotiable, as a difference that lies outside or beyond the political game and the civilian space where women and men mingle together.

To sustain this difference, photographs of rape must remain outside the public space, as well. Disclosure of rape images to the gaze would reveal that there is nothing in them more terrible than in other images of women, which exhibit their sexual accessibility and make manifest their abandonment. The terrible thing in rape images — access to a woman's body and sexuality without her having the real opportunity to choose it — is not vouchsafed to the unmediated gaze anyway.[90] In order to see it, one must reconstruct the context of the image and coax it into speaking, as I have tried to show in regard to the few rape images that have been distributed, such as those of the rape in Nanking.

The fact that rape images have been left "outside" has another function, this one related to the constitution of rape as an object of discourse. The absence of these images makes it impossible to produce a common fund of images, the negotiations over whose boundaries are exactly what gives concrete existence to it in the public space. What happens "there," in that place where rape occurs, remains wrapped in mystery, difficult to identify and decipher, something that only the rape victim herself can recognize. All of the images that she has previously encountered at the visual level are supposed to be distinct from it. They are permitted to be seen; therefore, what is seen in them is permitted, whereas these others are forbidden to be seen; therefore, what is seen in them is forbidden.

What happens "there" appears in its absence as something that cannot be shown, something that is so very different, terrible, threatening, and injurious. But is what happens "there" really always so different from what happens "here," with which she's familiar as the customary norm, as what is permitted and sanctioned, such as, for example, sexual relations that she herself didn't initiate or really want? In effect, within this continuity between what she's familiar with and has seen around her and the situation in which she finds herself at the moment of rape, the likes of which she has never seen, there is only the smallest of differences. The overall matrix is much the same, and it is just this difference that makes all the difference.

Does this difference really justify her making an issue out of it? "Leave it alone, nothing really happened."[91] The demarcation of a clear boundary between permitted and forbidden images also threatens the *meaning* of what happens to a rape victim and prevents her from properly understanding — before, during, or after the rape — the situation she's in: "Don't make an issue out of it," as if everything that happens to her at the time of the rape is unlike what happens to her all the time, in everyday life, the apprehension of which is forbidden to the gaze and remains abstract.[92] Challenging the trustworthiness of the rape victim and her story, which frequently accompanies her attempt to turn her private story into a complaint, relies exactly on this absence, strengthening the rape victim's uncertainty in regard to the meaning of what has happened to her: Was she raped, and will this be interpreted by others, as well, as an act of rape?[93]

Female existence as being for a man thus is what makes it possible to continue woman's abandonment. The state of abandonment continues to loom over her as a threat that might be fulfilled anew at any moment. Each of these researchers describes women in different ways and by means of various categories: "fetish," "object," "receptacle of desire," "object of conquest," "subordinate," "subservient," "belonging," "property," "exploited," "abandoned," or "debauched." The heterogeneity inherently structured into female existence withdraws or disappears the moment a concrete woman is modeled and represented as someone who exists for a man and is exchanged as concrete currency that expresses the general cultural value of what I have termed the image of the female body. It is not the fact that the female body is omnipresent in its nudity, sexual and provocative, that makes it abandoned. It is the fact that it is omnipresent while marked with the seal of the female body, that is, marked as a body that is susceptible at each and every moment to becoming a *body for a man.*

Out of the various images analyzed in these studies, the abandonment of woman can be reconstructed, but these are not images of rape. There is, however, a continuity extending from these images to the missing images of rape. This is so because rape is the ultimate fulfillment of woman's being for a man. In the absence of images of rape, the existing images of abandonment have turned into the flip, manifest side of the missing images of rape. The fact that the latter are missing while the former are present is a symptom of the conditions for acts of rape to occur and for producing the *énoncés* of rape. By dint of the separation between the invisible images of rape and the images of abandonment visible everywhere, it is possible to make rape images the exception to the rule and to formalize images of abandonment as the rule in regard to the representation of women.

267

With the advantage of hindsight, we can discern that some of the scholars who dealt with visual aspects of modern female reality unwittingly structured the object of research in a way that preserved this homogeneity in the representation of women, missing dimensions of their existence that extend beyond it, while others managed to avoid this trap and proposed subversive readings of texts that appear hegemonic and conservative at first sight.[94] In any event, these studies created the conditions for problematizing the representation of woman, a process that became ever more complex over the years due to critical analysis of oppressive images and the production of alternative images in more complex contexts. Also contributing to this process were insights that came to the field of visual research from the queer and postcolonial discourses in a way that made it possible to loosen the Gordian knot between the female body and the masculine gaze and to open a new field of possibilities for understanding gender relations. Despite all these changes in the status of women, the representation of their bodies, and the critical understanding of these representations, however, the statistical data continue to point to a level at which all differences among women collapse and are assimilated into the cultural image of the female body. Those are the statistics that indicate that one in every four women is compelled to make this general body manifest in her own personal one and becomes the victim of sexual assault.

The removal of rape images from the cycle of images in the public sphere makes it possible to maintain this consistent, unifying minimum in representations of women in visual culture. Rape images are taboo. As I have tried to show, the taboo applies not only to direct images of rape, but to an entire gamut of images stained by the term "rape." They are all contaminated, and showing them is prohibited. "The passion for the real," writes Joan Copjec, that is "the frenzied desire to cast aside every veil, penetrate every surface, and transgress every barrier in order to reach the real that lies behind it" is touched with obscenity, is part of the "implicit conviction that there is ultimately no ob-scene, no off-screen, that cannot be exposed to a persistent, prying look. Obscene is the belief that a subject is reducible to what can be seen or captured in a photograph, or more generally, in what can be known about her."[95] The systematic concealment of images of rape manufactures rape — which can be seen and shown — as an object prohibited to the gaze. So if we ask once again why, in the obscenity of this "frenzied desire" for the real, which has been translated into the right to see and to know, rape is the last object left outside the field of view and produced as its beyondness.[96] Two possible answers present themselves: one, that there is nobody interested in images of the object called rape and there is nobody who wants to attain them; and two, that the obscenity of the passion to expose the object and to do so completely betrays itself in rape, as the application of direct violence to remove every barrier in the way of attaining the object.

Yet nobody seeks to expose rape as an object. Rape is an event that has been left in the dark, a consecrated residue that attests to a flaw in the citizen status of rape victims. The various institutions that produce and distribute images avoid any dealing with it. Above images of rape looms a taboo that prevents turning the horror of rape into a common reference, which is a condition for mustering agreement on the need to prevent and stop it. This state of affairs attests to the fact that casualties of rape are not really full citizens — the imprint of their being excepted to the rule continues to shape the way in which sexual injury to them is treated and managed.

The sexual violence that strikes woman is thus not an exception to the rule. As I showed in Chapter One, in conditions wherein the disaster that strikes a particular population is not an exception to the rule, the stricken population itself is the exception to the rule. The frequency of rape, as demonstrated by the staggering numbers issued by rape-victim treatment centers around the world and the fact that these figures haven't dropped during the years since the data were first brought to public attention indicate that rape has turned into a mass disaster that strikes its victims one by one and it has not succeeded in becoming an exceptional event, an exception to the rule, against which all the resources of government and civilian society are mustered to prevent its occurrence or at least make it rare.

In a culture of images, where everything is susceptible to being made into an image and when the economy of catastrophes and intervention in them relies massively on images and is conducted by their means, the absence of images relating to rape prevents its prevalence from being recognized as a state of emergency, a mass disaster on a worldwide scale that urgently needs to be dealt with.[97] Even as rape was reconstituted in post–1970s discourse, it failed to figure in political discourse, in the arena in which the sovereign has an obligation to exert its full power and authority to protect the female citizens whose welfare is supposed to be its concern.[98] Instead, in these conditions, in which woman is an exception to the rule, every act or statement that recreates the exception to the rule — and this is exactly the effect of the implicit prohibition on showing any images of rape — preserves this residue and contributes to its perpetuation.

Images of Rape

When the grisly photographs from Abu Ghraib prison came out, in the initial days of publication, they included a few pictures of the rape of women. These first appeared in the *Boston Globe*.[99] A short while later, these photographs vanished from the media and slipped entirely off the agenda. An authoritative source, it was said, had examined the photographs and found them to be faked. The source had also located their origin on a pornographic Internet site and asserted that the American soldier's uniform in the photographs was clearly bogus, at which the debate came to an end.[100] Everyone accepted the determination of the photographs' status, and none of the people who continued to deal with the images from Abu Ghraib asked why the women's rape photographs had disappeared without a trace. These photographs were not included in an exhibition devoted to the photographs from Abu Ghraib at the International Center of Photography (ICP) in New York, nor were they mentioned in the text written to accompany the exhibition. They were also not mentioned in most of the essays written about the Abu Ghraib photographs,[101] or in those by feminist writers and scholars of photography. The traces of these photographs can now be found almost exclusively on the Internet alongside other pornographic images in which rape appears.

Even Susan Sontag, who published an essay on the photographs from Abu Ghraib in the *New York Times*, ignored the women's photographs and unquestioningly accepted the distinction between documentary and staged photographs, between true and false photographs. Sontag opens her own discussion of the well-known Abu Ghraib photographs, which had been confirmed to be authentic and not staged, with a critique of remarks made by Secretary of Defense Donald Rumsfeld: "There was also the avoidance of the word 'torture.' The prisoners had possibly been the objects of 'abuse,' eventually of 'humiliation' — that was the most to be admitted. 'My impression is that what has been charged thus far is abuse, which I believe technically is different from torture,'" Donald Rumsfeld said.[102] To support her contention, Sontag cites the definition of torture from the 1984 convention against torture, to which the United States is a signatory: "any act by which severe pain or suffering, whether physical or mental, is intentionally inflicted on a person for such purposes as obtaining from him or a third person information or a confession."[103] But what we see in the photographs is not the infliction of pain and suffering in order to obtain information. The acts to which the photographs attest don't appear to be inspired by any "higher" purpose, as is usually the case with torture, for which an entire array of reasons is invoked in its justification, and therefore Rumsfeld seems to be in the right, at least on this matter: These acts do not constitute torture, and the definition cited by Sontag merely supports his position.

However, despite the difference of opinion between Sontag and Rumsfeld to which Sontag points, Rumsfeld's remarks reveal a common denominator he shares with Sontag: the assumption that torture is more serious than what is clearly sexual abuse. Rumsfeld refuses to see the photographs as torture and asserts that it is only "abuse." If the photographs had been photographs of torture, as Rumsfeld believes, or if they had not been acknowledged as photographs of torture, as Sontag believes, the difference would have been not only in the meaning of what is seen in the photographs, but in the nature of the interventions they would have required. In effect, both Rumsfeld and Sontag see sexual injury as less serious and are accustomed to its not generating any real urgency and not necessarily turning into an emergency summons. The rape of women was immediately eliminated from the discussion without generating even the beginnings of an *énoncé* of horror over which negotiations could afterward be conducted on turning it into an emergency claim, and what was left was only the injury — including the sexual humiliation — inflicted on the men.[104]

It is possible, of course, to contend that the photographs of the rape of women are fake and therefore don't deserve mention in this context. However, I would like to reexamine this contention. First, why should we accept as definitive the determination by interested parties in the American administration that the photographs are fake? Second, even if they were fake, the question yet remains: Why must the discussion of their status begin and end with an authoritative determination beyond any doubt that was made by an interested party and why has hardly anyone among those who have discussed the photographs from Abu Ghraib demanded additional information, beyond the general statement that something about the American soldier's uniform in the photographs is amiss? Isn't the sudden disappearance of the photographs from the agenda without leaving almost any trace yet another an orchestrated repetition of the same explicit injunction "do not show" that is generally applied to photographs of the rape of women?

The photographs of the sexual injury to Iraqi detainees that remained on the agenda are repulsive, horrifying, no more and no less so than other photographs of sexual injury, but they were nevertheless distributed numerous times through various channels. Any fear of pornographic use being made of them was eliminated — in contradistinction to these others, they were judged not to be pornographic. Some of them have achieved an iconic status that casts a shadow over what is seen in them and makes it possible to look at them casually, with perhaps only a bare acknowledgment of identification, such as "Oh, that's a photograph from Abu Ghraib."

As opposed to these photographs, the photographs of women being raped, which are suspected to be fake, have been suppressed, as are people who supposedly pose a threat to government. Immediately after they were suppressed, the site that had been disclosed as the ostensible source of the pictures, www.iraqbabes.com, was also suppressed (figure 5.9). When one tries to log onto the site now, one finds only the home page, a collage consisting of some of the photographs. Additional photographs that were not defined as fake in

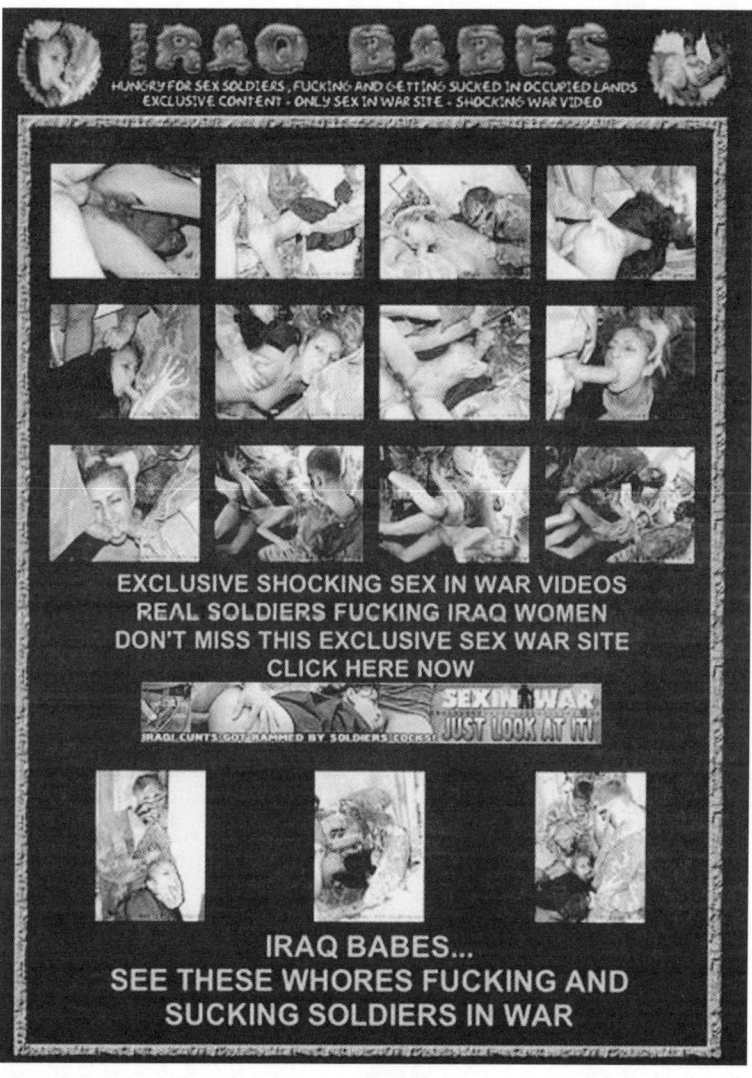

Figure 5.9. Home page of www.iraqbabes.com (site does not exist anymore).

which sexual injury to women is seen and that Army Major General Antonio Taguba has confirmed as being part of a cache of eighteen hundred photographs from Abu Ghraib, have also been obliterated from public view.

Despite the disappearance of these photographs, on the margins of various media reports and in the heart of humanitarian organizations that collect information, verbal and numerical data are accumulating in regard to the sexual injury, abuse, and rape of Iraqi women. These data reveal the severe and ongoing injury to Iraqi women since American soldiers entered Iraq. They are based on first-person accounts by the victims themselves, which tell about rape, abuse, and sexual injury. A report on the topic was submitted to the UN in March 2005 by Kristen McNutt, a researcher for a humanitarian organization of lawyers, and figures from a report in preparation for Amnesty International, which is based on data collected by Professor Hoda Shaker, are quoted extensively in an article by Luke Harding in the *Guardian*. From the testimonies gathered by Professor Shaker, it is clear that "sudden suppression" extends beyond photographs as the treatment of choice for the rape of women. The report tells of at least one Iraqi woman, among those who have been raped and made pregnant by American soldiers, who was abducted from Baghdad, together with her family.[105]

Just as in the case of women in the Western world, the sexual injury to Iraqi women is being reported, but the photographs that attest to their being raped are defined as pornography. So let us try to deal at face value with the contention that the photographs of Iraqi women being raped were indeed staged, that is, that they are a product of an American pornography site in which photographs were staged and distributed. I propose to reflect for a moment on the circumstances of their manufacture as staged images and on their status. We are talking about a huge number of photographs — as I noted, close to two thousand are known at the present time, but clearly, the actual number is much larger — produced by a relatively small number of soldiers. Unlike the photographs of the rape of women, which were defined as real pornographic photographs, the photographs of sexual injury to Iraqi detainees can be defined as real photographs that mimic real pornographic photographs. Indeed, a great many of the photographs shown to the public imitate scenes that are commonplace in hard-core and soft-core pornography: masturbation, forced masturbation with the aid of accessories, sexual contacts in view of spectators that are present in the picture, group nudity before the camera lens, and nude bodies intermingling.

The vast extent of the photographs and their deliberate resemblance to pornographic photographs make it possible to gaze anew on what happened in Abu Ghraib Prison and conclude that the injury and humiliation inflicted on detainees also included the administration of a porn industry in miniature. This tiny production plant for pornographic material, which operated in wartime and as part of the routine of military life "with real American servicemen and women" and "real Iraqi detainees," operated at the margins of a much more sophisticated and resourceful porn industry, which also operates in wartime and continues to operate as part of civilian life. This industry, which operates by means of the Internet and distributes standard pornographic photographs in which women are raped, in time of war and in its spirit also dealt in the rape of "real Iraqi women" by "real American soldiers," as declared on the home page of the iraqbabes.com site.

Iraqi Web sites used the pictures that were shown on the American site, in which the brutal rape of Iraqi women could be seen, to support their reports of sexual injury to Iraqi citizens. Two women, one with black hair, the other a brunette, are in the hands of several soldiers who grip them firmly, pull their hair, overcome their resistance by tugging at their arms and legs, and penetrate their vagina or their mouth. On some of the sites that have reported on the photographs, the American soldiers' sex organs were pixilated, perhaps for reasons of modesty or in an attempt to stay in good taste.

On all of the Internet rape sites, the signified "rape" is linked with the signifier "rape" and the sign that they create stands alone as if untouched by time, as if rape weren't part of the chains of signifiers that take part in undermining its stable meaning, as if the status of women hadn't changed since the term "rape" was coined thousands of years ago, as if rape hadn't become an arena of women's struggles.[106] The site on which the photographs of the rape of Iraqi women were distributed, like other rape sites of which the Internet is full, wasn't shut down by the government until the "Iraqi enemy" made use of it and presented the photographs as evidence of the American army's injury to Iraqi women. The humiliation of the Iraqi women, their being made the object of a group rape on a porno-graphic site, turned into dangerous material and demanded government intervention only after the Iraqi enemy treated these photographs as real and thus revealed the continuity extending from the signifier "rape of women" to the signified "rape of women," or from the image of rape to rape.

In her essay on the Iranian film director Abbas Kiarostami, Joan Copjec discusses the obscenity of the photographs from Abu Ghraib of injury to men, the very photographing of which was inspired by the belief that everything can be shown, including intimacy. The ostensible protection of the intimacy of women, injury to whom is not shown in photographs, rests on exactly the same mistaken under-standing that Copjec criticizes, according to which the intimate can be captured in a picture. Photographs in which sexual injury to women will be shown as such pose a threat to the public order, but not because of the detriment to moral values attributed to them, or because there is in them something contagious and infectious, which must be avoided like the plague. When they are removed from the public space, photographs of the rape of women make it possible to continue to preserve the unstable meaning of rape, to put off per-petually the meeting between signifier and signified and to leave it somewhere out there between sexual fantasy and emotional halluci-nation. The implicit prohibition on the distribution of rape images postpones the constitution of a common community of men and women who could demonstrate mutual responsibility toward the meaning of rape and regarding its reference, over the meaning of which they could negotiate.

When there is an unwritten prohibition on showing "real" images of rape, "staged" rape images are freely shown on porn sites.[107] Rape there is an uncamouflaged headline act. Access to such sites is easier and simpler than might be supposed. All one need do is to type the four letters of the word "rape" into a search engine. Hundreds of sites offer a wide-ranging, shivering repertoire that is organized according to categories that classify rape by its degree of severity or the responses of those involved in it. The brief tour I conducted of porn sites that specialize in rape was a difficult thing, like going into an unprotected urban zone where violence lurks at every corner, there is no law, and attacking women is permitted and invited, even in the public space.[108] The images emerge from every part of the screen. They flicker and strike the gaze with violence, and many of the sites even obstruct attempts to leave them, so that one must turn off the computer itself to do so. The massive presence of rape photographs on pornographic sites, as opposed to their almost complete absence in other areas of culture, demands study.[109]

In the 1960s, Robin Morgan coined the slogan "Pornography is the theory, rape the practice." To this day, one tradition of antipornographic writing views pornography as the theory that legitimizes rape as a practice. This causal linkage is problematic, not only because the writers do not present proof of the influence of "theory" on "practice," but because of the conception of translation that underlies it. Opposite this bent, a new tradition of pornography studies is becoming established that contends that opponents of pornography talk about an entire field with which they are unfamiliar and reject it without looking at its products.[110] These studies, however, provide only a very limited account of the presentation of rape on porn sites and do not contend with the rape fantasy that these sites distribute.[111]

In *Hard Core*, Linda Williams describes the pornography known by that term as an attempt to achieve certainty that what is being seen is "not the voluntary performance of feminine pleasure, but its involuntary confession." Woman's ability to fake orgasm lies at the basis of this search for certainty, in which a man attempts to extract from a woman's body something whose reliability cannot in fact be assured: uncontrolled verification of pleasure. Rape, she writes, is one of the ways of obtaining the "proof of a sincerity that under other conditions might seem less sure."[112] However, this formulation, which criticizes prevalent conceptions of pornography, treats rape in a nonproblematic manner and views it as merely a means to an end. Williams pays no regard to the way in which rape is classified and structured on these sites: wild rape, bestial rape, a woman raped before her husband's eyes as he's tied to a chair and cannot rescue

277

her, rape of brides on their wedding day, brutal rape, or rape based on the ethnic origin of the victim (Asian or Russian girls). When one examines this wealth of topics, despite the variety they seem to offer, they all turn out to revitalize a single common fantasy: the lust to achieve absolute possession of a woman, the most consummate expression of which, even more than possession of a woman who is another man's property, is the willing delivery of a woman in the possession of one man to another.

The value of women in this exchange does not derive from any essential quality of theirs, but from their manner of belonging to other men: women who are about to become the property of a single man (brides on their wedding day), women of other men who can be obtained only by means of rape (the enemy's women, for example), women who are inaccessible due to ethnic or cultural differences ("exotic" women), or women who are the property of a man where he must watch her being expropriated (rape before a husband's eyes). In all of her appearances on these sites, women are seen as actually or in principle the property of another man or intended to become such. In order to view "the involuntary confession of pleasure," as Williams defines it, there is no reason for the raped women to be Iraqi, Asian, or brides on their wedding day. Their being raped is not a means of achieving possession of them, but an effort to strike at someone else's ownership and its foundation — their value as property. So that her value can be damaged, the site grants the raped woman special value that marks her as deserving to be raped. Paradoxically, the rape of a woman of value who has been found deserving to be raped recalls her status as a woman like any other, living testimony that in fact, the value of all women is the same — all of them can be raped. The narrative in those sites is consistent — every woman deserves to be raped and cannot escape it, and no man is able to protect her. The pictures of rape on these internet sites are an attempt to stake out a reservation in which rape has a single, stable meaning — injury to their men. As such, rape regains its old meaning here, and it is presented as not only inevitable, but unchangeable. Despite the appallingly large figures regarding the incidence of rape, it is not yet the field of a lost battle for women, because men are invited to fantasize on these sites, as if they were trying to rescue a

278

lost and vanishing world, one in which men could go on exchanging women among themselves.

The visual status of rape makes it possible to illuminate the connection between rape and pornography from another angle. Pornography is considered a marginal area, a gray, borderline, dubious, and dirty zone, a sordid occupation that is always in friction with the law. All the same, when viewed from an economic standpoint, the income from it in the U.S. market exceeds the income produced by professional football, basketball, and baseball combined, which shows that it is a culture and product consumed by the masses.[113] Rape isn't just invisible in the public space, it is not associated with the behavior of respectable people. Not only are very few images of it, if any, accessible to the public, but when they do exist, they are considered damaging to the reputations of the victims. Nonetheless, when one examines the statistical data, it becomes clear that rape occurs everywhere, that it is spread across the entire social space, regardless of status, age, or nationality.

The pornography sites offer pictures and videos that are tagged by their makers as "high quality" or "real," and some of them are said to be taking place "online," that is, in real time, not recorded. It isn't entirely clear whether this is a marketing ploy meant to give the spectator the feeling that he is looking at real "material" or whether these sites are simply a bastion of criminality bluntly and unveiledly directed at women, existing in a sort of twilight zone immune from the guardians of the law. The latter option would not be entirely implausible, for after all, there is even a trade in women that is openly conducted in many Western nations in which legislation regarding women is considered advanced.[114] Under current conditions, when the biblical injunction that "thou shalt not make any graven image" applies to rape, the images posted on these sites function like the golden calf: They permit the transgression of all prohibitions. Women are brutally raped while the spectator is afforded a semipublic gaze on the event, and with it the structural possibility of claiming that no rape ever really took place — it is all only the product of a porn site in which everything is fantasy, and make-believe substitutes for reality, and the visual posture toward the rape that is experienced in this private-public space is one of only voyeuristic stimulation and sexual arousal.

279

Rape cannot remain in the dark. Darkness lurks in wait for it anyway, providing it with ideal conditions for development. The new discourse on rape established in the past few decades made it possible to see that rape is omnipresent, but also that it is an injury amenable to intervention, prevention, or reduction. To consent tacitly to the suppression of the object's visual dimension is to consent to the relegation of images of rape — their collection, design, distribution, meaning and action — into the hands of sites in which rape is presented anew as an ahistorical and apolitical fantasy. The public display of photographs of rape is not something to be taken for granted, not something that can be performed in a bureaucratic and automatic fashion or by predesigned rules. On each occasion, it again and again demands cautious, reasoned, flexible, and critical thinking. Such thinking cannot rest on a universal rule or a universal consensus, but requires all decision makers to take a risk, consult, and make a civil judgment that can — and should — stand up to critique.[115]

The film *Antonia's Line*, by the Dutch director Marleen Gorris, which won the 1996 Oscar for best foreign language film, might serve here as an example. Toward the middle of the film, the narrator's voice interrupts the cinematic narrative and informs us in a matter-of-fact tone that the child Theresa has been raped. From this, the film goes on to the next scene, where we see her lying in her bed, supported and consoled by her mother and grandmother. It was only after I'd watched the movie several times that I noticed the precisely reasoned manner in which the director punched this visual hole in her film. Gorris rejected depicting the rape of a girl, which would have required staging the rape of a girl on the movie set, without a blink of her cinematic eyelashes.[116] The film goes on, the narrative is comprehensible, and the spectator is confronted with a reasoned position in regard to the presentation of rape in cinema.

A few minutes earlier in the film (several years earlier, in terms of the narrative), the young man who raped the girl had assaulted and raped his sister, too, a woman named Didi. That rape came to an end when the young man is attacked by Theresa's mother, who wounded him in the arms and groin, causing him to leave town. Gorris chose to show Didi's rape, the first presented by the film, from when it began until the intervention by Danielle, Theresa's mother, who stabbed the rapist with a pitchfork. Gorris presents the rape in continuity with the previous sexual harassment of Didi by her brother and father in full view of everyone. During the rape, Didi won't let go of her eyeglasses, which she holds in her left hand, crushing and breaking them, the splinters embedding themselves in her flesh. Spectators experience the rape from the perspective of Didi's pain, horror, and nightmarish ordeal. This rape is presented as the product of tacit consent on the part of the community in which the rape victim lives and thus as not an intractable decree of fate.

Showing or not showing images of rape in this way and reintroducing them to circulation won't eradicate rape, but it may pry rape free from its last grip on worlds in which women are yet subject to the norms of the frater-patriarchy. Breaking the taboo on showing images of rape will challenge the clear demarcation between images that are allowed to be shown and those that are not — the line of demarcation that distinguishes rape from the other horrors that afflict humanity and preserves women as the exception to the rule — and it will also challenge the division between the arenas in which they are allowed or forbidden to be shown, which leaves the visual treatment of rape, with the dramatic decisions that involves, to porn sites.

Fighting in the visual arena today is thus an inseparable part of any struggle in the political arena, for it is in the visual arena, through and by means of images, that women and men train themselves to feel, see, think, judge, and act. It is not possible to refer to the publication of direct or indirect photographs of sexual injury and rape only in instrumental terms of warning or commemoration. The movement of images in the public space doesn't consist only of cause and effect. Their movement — including the argument over what to show and what not to show, how to interpret such images and others, the various meanings attributed to them, the ways in which they posit addressees and solicit addressers — this is all part of what creates a community to negotiate over the boundaries of the prohibitions and sanctions it sets for itself, fashioning norms of behavior, action, speech, and viewpoints.

Epilogue

"I was there" writes Michal Heiman on a photograph in which a female figure lies sprawled on her back among some thorn bushes (figure 5.10). The figure appears to be lifeless; her legs are spread, her pubis shaven. The place where she lies might be the interior of an unidentified building or a space outside it. The wall intervening between the spectator and the body is what generates the confusion, as if beyond the wall lies an internal, delineated, private space. This wall, which separates the spectator from the figure and the event that took place where she lies, has been penetrated. There is a gaping hole in the middle of it, and it seems as if somebody has broken inside through it. The trespasser has disappeared, apparently having concluded his business and departed. The body lies there unmoving, all but for the left arm, which is upraised and holding a burning candle. The upraised arm looks like the flag planted by a foreign army on soil that doesn't belong to it, to mark its conquest.

"I was there" is a sort of declaration, confession, or comment regarding a particular site that people speak of, a phrase typically uttered after something — an event — has taken place. This phrase is part of a conversation. What is now on the agenda is the specific "there" in question, and the phrase is addressed to anyone who knows something about it, even if only where it is or what has happened there. This phrase may guide the conversation in a particular direction, but neither initiates nor brings it to a conclusion. It is possible to deduce from this phrase that the speaker — "I" — is not alone. The "I" exists only in relation to a certain "you" or "them." This phrase expresses the speaker's interest in a site or an event. This is not an abstract interest, but an indication of the first-hand involvement of someone who happened to be at the site or within the situation that now preoccupies her interlocutor. Although this phrase stamps the site or event with the speaker's presence, what she has attempted to say, in fact, is that the site or event has indelibly stamped her.

This is how Michal Heiman uses the phrase, literally turning it into a stamp that appears on the surface of the photographic image. The stamp is not, however, the result of an external mark, but is actually embedded within the image itself, becoming an indistinct

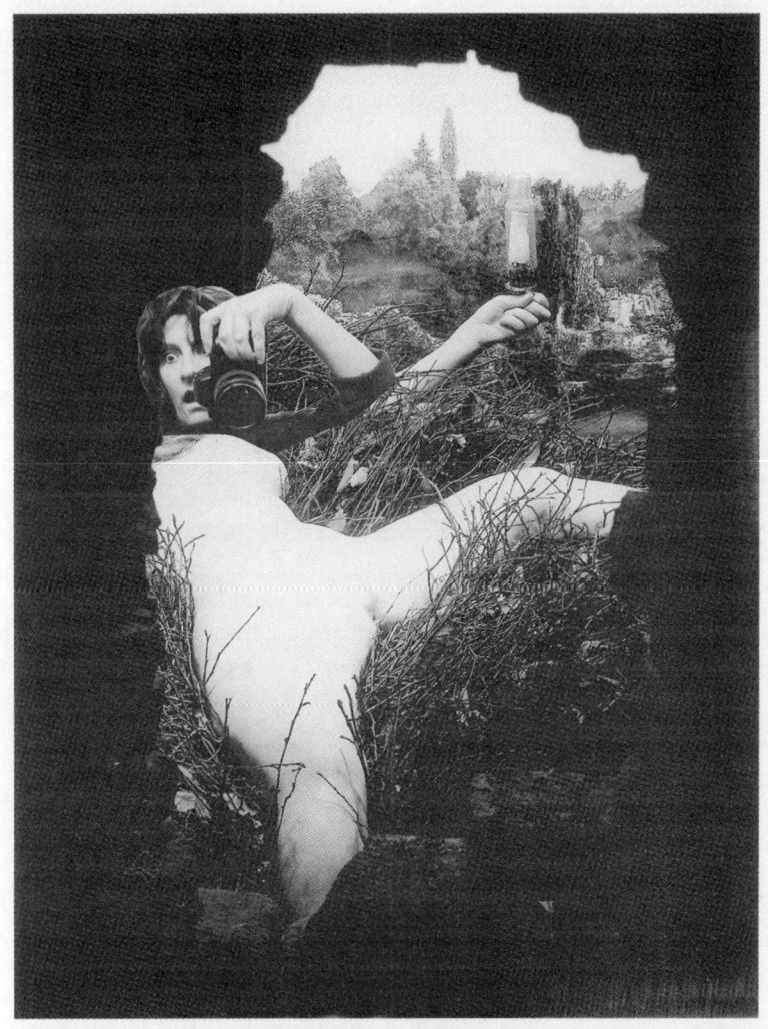

I WAS THERE

Figure 5.10. Michal Heiman, *I Was There #6, Etant Donnés (Marcel Duchamp, view through the door of the installation, collection the Philadelphia Museum of Art, 1946–1966)*, color print, 121 x 88 cm, 2004.

and indispensable part of it. When embedded in the photograph of Marcel Duchamp's *Étant donnés* that I have described above, this phrase suddenly turns the photograph — of a situation, an installation, or reproduction of a painting — into the record of a particular event to which "I," the speaker ("I was there"), refers, aiming to suspend, with her words, any other explicit content of the photographic image. She draws the spectator's attention to the existence of this event in the expectation that their mutual gaze on it will render it present and visible. This imprint shatters the illusion that an image can immediately be seen or read, disrupting any possibility of reconstructing the event that "was there" through a single voice. Instead, there is an imposition of several voices: the photographer's voice; the voice of someone who was (or was not) there versus the "I" ("I was there") who defiantly attests to the fact that she herself *was* there, denoting herself as someone from whose mouth more has yet to be extracted about that "there"; and the voice of the spectator, who is invited to determine where exactly she or he had been when "I was there."

The statement "I was there" is a primary, basic verbal confirmation that the "I" is a black box in which "there" is inscribed. This "there" is not simply a place or event, but a place where something happened that brought the "I" into confrontation with an unbearable sight or unspeakable information. *I* was there, but never really alone; you, too, who know what I mean when I say "there," have already been there — or know at least where you were when you were not there — and are now suddenly forced to reconsider your own existence in relation to "there"; I, who *was* there, cannot remain exactly as I was before I was *there*. In other words, being there means that the "there," the site that has become meaningful enough to note that "I was there," has left traces that from now on must be interpreted or made to speak, and whoever bears these traces is sentenced to do something with them, or, alternatively, to share them with someone else, to replace or get rid of them. "There" is a place between the "I" who was there and the person to whom this phrase is addressed, the one who serves at this moment as a witness or party to the fact that the "I" had been there.

There is no need to mention its name. Saying "there" already presumes a certain knowledge, even if vague, that in this place, something happened that cannot be erased, even if it seeks to elude memory or perception and leave anyone whom was there in a fog of uncertainty as to what exactly happened there. When the imprint of "I was there" is embedded, the photographic image turns into a clue, and looking at it becomes watching it — a moment in an encounter or a conversation.

Most of the writings on this artwork by Duchamp deal with its spatial organization, Christian symbolism, the life cycle, or voyeurism. Heiman, who in the words of her signatory "was there," points to what was previously unseen in the photograph, though it lay openly on the surface: the woman lying sprawled is the victim of sexual assault. When Heiman's stunned gaze looking out from the photograph, the recording camera that she holds in her hand, and the news reportage element of the imprint "I was there" are all produced from the vantage of a woman, the place is interpreted as the arena of a sexual crime.[117] The spectator won't know whether the woman lying there was beaten, if she was abused or raped. The details are lacking. As always, the photograph is only partial. The viewpoint that has been introduced into the plane of the photograph, however, no longer permits a simple retreat to the previous thematics that preoccupied modern research into art history.[118] "I was there," says the language of the imprint. But Heiman is not there. She is outside, or, more precisely, on the threshold, between the space in which the woman lies and the space in which the spectator stands. This location of hers — neither inside nor out — makes it necessary to rethink this notation of place, "there," and its connotation. "I was there," the statement itself, is a paraphrase of the famous statement by Roland Barthes about the essential claim made by photography: it deals with what "was there."

The indexical nature of photography enables us to come face to face with what was there, in front of the camera, from the light rays out of which an image has been produced, an image of that fraction of a second of an event. Heiman's paraphrase reminds us that this description is neutral and that somebody had to have been there with a camera in order for a spectator to be able to look at the photograph later and say "It was there." The statement "I was there" makes manifest the fact that someone actually was there, and when it is linked to Heiman as a woman photographer, the gender uncertainty is removed. It is clear that a *woman* was there. That "there" in which she was could perhaps be the specific site recorded in the photograph, but it could also be the situation in general. It is as if the fact that she, too, "was there," in a place similar to that of the injured woman, enables her to tell the spectators "Don't be mistaken, what you see here is not the artistic examination of a figure in perspective — I was there and I know what it's like to be there."

The camera in her hand — not in both hands, as is customary — expresses the fact that "here," neither the quality of the photography nor the framing, focus, or length of exposure are important. Here, in this situation, what matters is simply to press the camera shutter and not relent, to take as many photographs as possible, to record, and to not allow this picture to be erased. Standing there on the threshold, neither inside nor out, Heiman's horrified gaze doesn't rest, however, on the figure sprawled there, apparently the victim of a lethal injury. The photographer's gaze is directed beyond it, as if seeking to signal that the wounded figure is not the end of the matter, that the danger hasn't passed yet. At this very moment, in that place called "there," another event similar to its predecessors is taking place, and her gaze, accompanied by the camera, is looking for it.

Even if Heiman is seeking explicitly not to function and not to be identified as a photographer, when her own image holding a camera has been embedded in the site of Duchamp's *Étant donnés*, one can hardly avoid thinking that a film is hidden in her camera. It is not her private film — neither what is in it nor the gaze to which it attests. What is branded on the film is branded on the gaze of many who were there, in or beside these scenes, who saw, but did not see, didn't know what to do with what they saw, didn't know that their standing referred to what has been branded on their consciousness, didn't understand how only they could have noticed what everyone else can see. In order to develop the film that lies hidden in Heiman's camera, a citizen spectator is required — a spectator for whom the visible is never the last word, a spectator dedicated to the necessity of deciding what must be done with these images and which of them must be shown in public. This film requires someone who understands that it is her duty to distinguish between a photograph openly depicting violence and one that appears banal, from which the protagonists may have even been removed, only the arena itself remaining exposed. Returning to these open cases, such as those which have been documented by press photographers or sketched by painters in the annals of art, Heiman's camera in such scenes might be an exemplar of such a citizen gaze. It should be a gaze that holds itself humble before the image, recognizes the fact that not everything can be seen and shown, knows that removing the social prohibition of the visible will not lead to full visibility, and understands that not only is such visibility impossible, but that the passion for such visibility is precisely what thwarts the eye from seeing what is visible on the surface.

CHAPTER SIX

Photographing the Verge of

Catastrophe

To photograph what exists on the verge of catastrophe entails one's presence at the onset of a catastrophe, looking for its eventuation, that is, being able to see it as an event that is about to occur. As I have described in Chapter Four, however, since the beginning of the second intifada, the verge of catastrophe is the actual, ongoing condition of Palestinian existence. Catastrophe has altered its form, turning from a sudden event that affects someone into a perpetually impending state. The new conditions of catastrophe still include elements of the old form of catastrophes with which we are familiar, elements that have the potential to disrupt routine. An entire village street is wiped off the face of the Earth; a building is destroyed by bombs; or an entire area is subjected to heavy artillery fire for several days, with inhabitants suffering severe physical and emotional injuries and unable to treat their casualties. The fact that such events are so numerous and frequent is what transforms them into a routine aspect of daily life. In Chapter Four, I discussed the flawed conditions of visibility related to being on the verge of catastrophe as conditions preventing or disrupting the transformation of an *énoncé* of horror into an emergency claim. In this chapter, through a close reading of a few photographs, I will attempt to understand the stakes for photography in confronting this new face of catastrophe.

Photography as Resistance
My readings of such photographs are limited, demarcated, marred by the territorial and civilian separations created by the occupation,

289

which prevent me from having the same access to Palestinian photographs that I have to those by Israelis. Since these separations are
not a momentary obstacle but what shape the visual field of the
occupation in the eyes of an Israeli Jew, I prefer to consider these
demarcations also as objects within this field. Israeli citizenship — my
own, that of most of the photographers whose photographs I shall be
looking at, or of anyone else stamped with the seal of this citizenship
— is the dominant condition for the noncitizenship of the Palestinians, the general measure of the depth of their oppression and the
extent of their exclusion, in the same way that Palestinian noncitizenship defines and conditions the essence of Israelis' citizenship and
the boundaries of the democracy that they ascribe to their regime.

Beside the direct and eruptive violence that occurs in being on
the verge of catastrophe, another kind of violence is widespread, one
that is withheld, suspended, while still clearly intensifying its effects
on the lives of the people against whom it is directed. Power is
deployed over the entire territory as though in a state of war, but
there is no war — mainly only targeted assassinations, the destruction of infrastructure, violent arrests, restrictions on travel, roadblocks, bombings from the air, eradications on the ground, raids on
residential neighborhoods, the expropriation of rooftops for military
purposes, the prohibition of demonstrations, and other aggressions.
Most soldiers in the Occupied Territories do not actually occupy
anything, and the safeties on their rifles are on most of the time.

The threat of violence, most often suspended, is still signaled
with the presences of clubs, rifles, patrol cars, the voice announcing
a curfew, the gate of a roadblock, or the building that serves as an
inspection facility. Imposing constraints on the movement and behavior of those who are ruled, violence is always present, and every
place is a potential site for it to arise. This is well known — it is liable
to arise anywhere, at any moment. The suppressed violence takes a
toll without necessarily having to erupt, having no direct connection
to the measure of obedience of those who are ruled, as it prevents,
delays, complicates, disrupts priorities, upsets plans, hurts the sick,
hampers students, destroys livelihoods, intensifies hunger, creates
malnutrition, harms family relations, inhibits growth, fosters diseases, and drives people out of their minds. Its results can be no less

and sometimes even more catastrophic than those stemming from the application of direct and eruptive violence. Existing on the verge of catastrophe means being exposed at all times, with no relief, to injuries of all kinds.[1]

Catastrophe, as it is usually understood emerges, erupting as an event, sharply drawing the line between before and after, manufacturing its emergence as a riddle: How and why is this happening? Why now? Why in this manner? What to do about the catastrophe requires exhaustive research that could bring to the surface more and more facts to explain its eventuation. But the verge of catastrophe, does not emerge, is not exactly an event, and has no power to create a difference. It exists on the surface, completely open to the gaze and yet evading it, because there is nothing to distinguish it from the surroundings in which it exists. Its contours are indistinct; one could easily fail to notice it, passing in front of it without stopping. It meets all the conditions necessary to escape most existing systems of representation. It is a nonevent or an event that never was and never will be. Its being depends on the ability we have of producing *énoncés* from it, on there being someone to address and someone to serve as the *énoncé*'s addressee, someone capable of establishing a reference and of discussing its meaning.

To photograph or to look at what exists on the verge of catastrophe is to assume or to manufacture the position of enunciating, the position from which it is possible to look at this surface and produce *énoncés*. For this to happen, the photographer must first assume she has a reason to be in the place of the nonevent or event that never was, which no one has designated as the arena of an event in any meaningful way. She, or those who dispatch her, must suspend the concerns of the leading and dominant figures of the mass media regarding the ratings of the finished product and with her camera begin to sketch a new outline capable of framing the nonevent.

Photographing what exists on the verge of catastrophe thus is an act that suspends the logic of newsworthiness, a logic that is manifested today by what we can call "the hit parade of *énoncés* of horror." The standard that is applied here does not examine the images in relation to what appears to be photographed within them, the singularity of what has been photographed, but judges them in connection to similar images of the same kind. It is a measure that values the images and determines their distribution according to a principle reminiscent of the radio hit parade — the ten best, the most powerful, the most surprising. These, however, must retain some similarity with "successful" images, those that maintain some point of reference to a previous, familiar image.

In her series entitled *Holding*, for example, Michal Heiman collected and arranged a number of photographs taken by various photojournalists printed throughout the press over the course of the second intifada. Out of her classificatory criteria, the image of rescue — a figure holding another — emerges as the iconic image that is promoted by the press. Without even speaking of a guiding hand, she points to a regularity in the photographer's or editor's decision to emphasize images in which the vulnerability of the victims and the harm inflicted on them gives way to the assistance and protection granted to them. This image's referent stems from a long tradition of fables in which a valiant hero emerges to rescue the damsel in distress.[2]

This hit parade is one aspect of the larger conditions of postmodernity that are often described by a number of thinkers from many different angles.[3] The victim is the vanishing point of this hit parade, the medium on which this logic is impressed and illuminated. The typical depiction of the victim makes it possible to observe — as if under a microscope — the elements that maintain the distance between being and nothingness. Being and nothingness are the two ends of the spectrum, limits in which the hit parade takes no interest. Between them extends an entire world of nuances capable of infinitely diversifying the register. When the victim is posited as a vanishing point, the media at times are able to act independently of the political-military perspective that seeks to deprive the Palestinian of the victim's position permanently in order to portray him as the aggressor.

Alongside the media's interest in circumstantial victims, the Israelis also evince interest, to a certain degree, in these permanent victims, the Palestinians. When deprived of the political context in which the harm done to him is inscribed and the shield of citizenship necessary to protect him, the Palestinian appears to lack the means of providing for his own basic needs — housing, food or medicine — and his injured body turns into a site where this truth is revealed.[4] While liberation from needs was a condition for the appearance of the beautiful body in the classical time of Greece, in modernity, the appearance of needs evokes the image of the injured body, [5] which has functioned as a sort of signal to the various mechanisms that govern the regulation of needs to swing into operation. Photography serves as a vital link, feeding the humanitarian chain, when supplying needs becomes the primary object of concern.

As opposed to the attack on the Palestinian, the attack on the Israeli is almost always represented as carried out against his civil status and is therefore an attack on the sovereignty of the state. His injury is an opportunity to restore and reveal sovereignty's presence in the space. The photograph *Time Capsule No. 1 (3 minutes)*, made of twelve intersecting photographic reproductions, depicts the scene of a Palestinian bomber attack in Jerusalem three minutes after the event (figure 6.1). The photograph discloses — albeit through a deliberate intensification the already large number of security, rescue, and medical forces at the scene — the way in which these agents, who are called on to restore order, brush the site clear of the attack and of anything that might be construed as damaging to sovereignty.

When one looks at the photographs of Israelis rescuing and being rescued in Heiman's *Holding* series, the scenes are fraught with tension, with signs of the state of emergency declared at the time of the attack plainly visible from everything and everyone who is present in the arena (figures 6.2–6.5). The scene is characterized by frantic movement, an atmosphere of panic and alarm that the power of the rescue forces is supposed to subdue. The wounded are laid out on stretchers and evacuated in ambulances. Emergency lights place the area under full surveillance, and the catastrophe is immediately contained within the model according to which everything is under control and order is soon to be fully restored, but structured so that "we" are used to the routine and know what's expected of "us" — casualties and rescuers alike, citizens and sovereign.[6] The rescue operations are conducted in an exemplary fashion, despite the commotion and difficult conditions that erupt when any catastrophe causes a large number of deaths and injuries. The work is efficiently

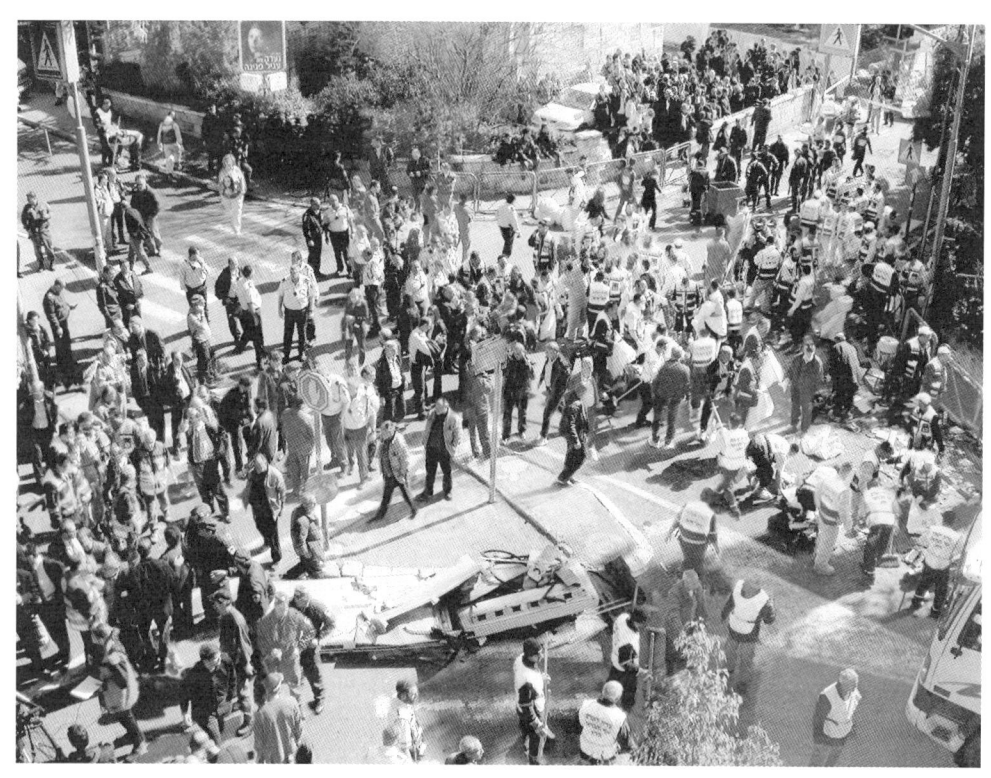

Figure 6.1. Boaz Aharonovitch, *Time Capsule No. 1 (3 minutes): Girl with a Pearl Earring*, digital image, 160 x 120 cm, 2004. (Please see Color Plates.)

divided among the different elements. The area is quickly covered with all of the signs of authority, prepared in advance to participate in the state ritual surrounding the attack, introduced in order to confirm what the sovereign already knows about the circumstances of its occurrence.

In these photographs, an eternal couple, a man rescuing an un-protected woman in his arms, usually appears in the foreground of the frame, as Heiman has pointed out.[7] The casualties have been made the victims of a crime in which they had no part. Alongside the randomness hovering over their injuries — for they could have been elsewhere — is the looming shadow of the sovereign, who promises that it is within his power and authority to prevent further injuries and is capable of frustrating evil intentions, securing the borders, expanding security checks, and purging the territory that is under his jurisdiction. Each such photograph in which citizens are rescued by proxies of the sovereign seeks to reaffirm the power of the sover-eign within a framework that defends citizens by abandoning the Palestinians to a state of exception.

This ritual, while creating a point of identification between the citizen and the sovereign against the Palestinians responsible for the attack, also serves as another opportunity to shield the citizen's eyes, not only from the sovereign's responsibility for abandoning the Palestinians, but from the citizen's own ongoing abandonment per-petuated by the security turnstile that permits the uninterrupted use of violence: The figure of the security guard standing at the door of almost every location within Israeli public space — restaurants, cof-fee bars, public buildings, shops, schools, and elsewhere — is a kind of Israeli oxymoron in which his hand, resting on his gun, is inter-preted as protective, rather than threatening. For Heiman, the res-cuers running with the injured in their arms — Israelis and Palestinians alike — are part of the mechanism that enables the attack, actually facilitating and being responsible for its outbreak prior to occupying their position as rescuers: "This is the great deception on the part of the rescue. The rescuer is part of and party to the creation of the vio-lent option, and his part in it remains invisible. He reappears in the photograph only as a rescuer."[8]

Five years after the outbreak of the al-Aqsa intifada, an article

295

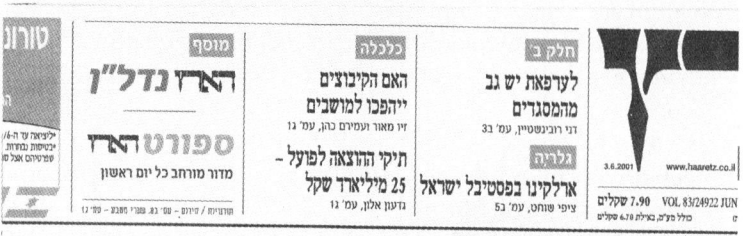

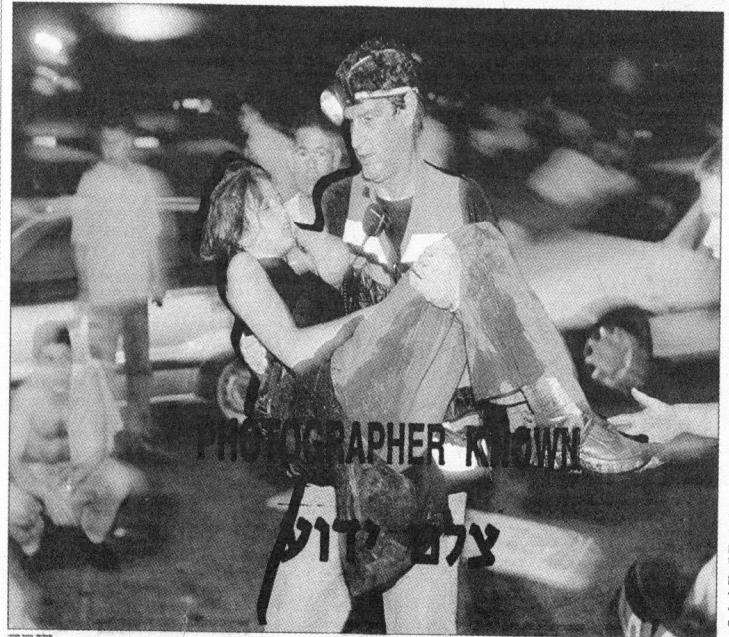

Figure 6.2. Michal Heiman, *Holding # 3 (Photographer Known, Photo: Moti Kimchi, Ha'aretz, 3.6.2001, Tel Aviv)*, color print, 160 x 120 cm, 2004.

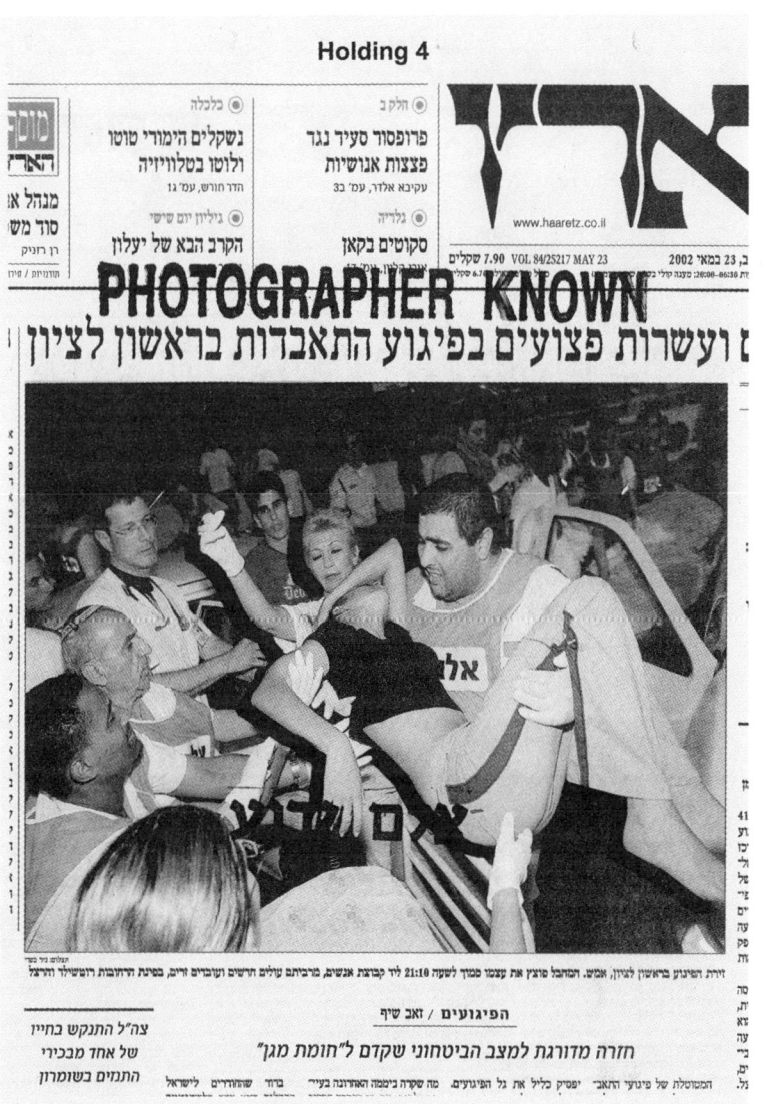

Figure 6.3. Michal Heiman, *Holding # 4 (Photographer Known, Photo: Nir Kafri, Ha'aretz , 23.5.2002, Rishon Leziyon)*, color print, 160 x 120 cm, 2004.

Holding 7

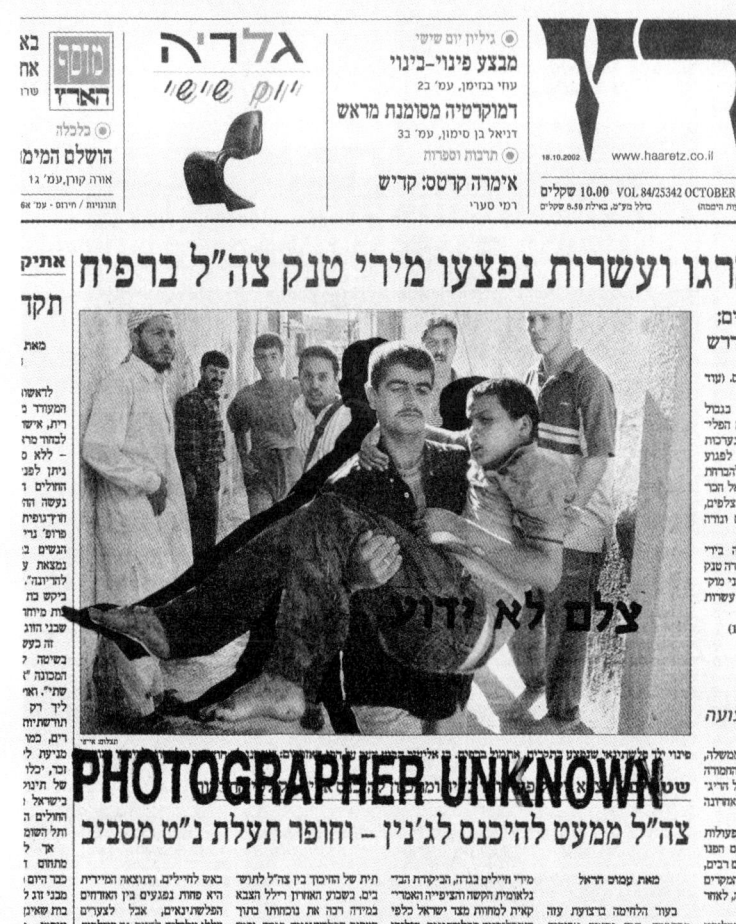

Figure 6.4. Michal Heiman, *Holding # 7, (AP, Photographer Unknown, Ha'aretz, 18.10.2002, Rafah)*, color print, 160 x 120 cm, 2004.

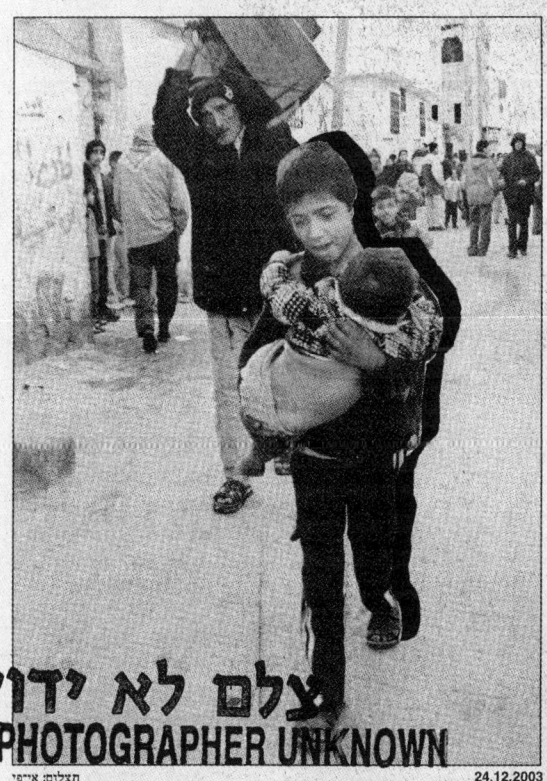

Figure 6.5. Michal Heiman, *Holding # 12 (AP, Photographer Unknown, Ha'aretz, 24.12.2003, Rafah)*, color print, 160 x 120 cm, 2004.

that had appeared first on the Web site of *Ha'aretz* under the head-line "47% of Wife Killers — Security Guards or Agents," appeared in the newspaper the next day under the headline "They're Expected to Contain the Horrors of the Intifada and Keep Silent." This article clearly diverts the focus away from the troubling data on the do-mestic violence committed by security guards to the emotional state of women and their vulnerability in the face of the intifada. (The subtitle read: "Women Are More Vulnerable in the Face of Terror Because They Are Supposed to Take Care of the Men and Chil-dren."[9]) The article presents the details of a study in which three female researchers cross-referenced the data related to injuries to women by men with the al-Aqsa intifada and its victims. The study reveals that in half of the cases, the murder of women is a direct result not only of easy access to weapons, but of the skills and tactics acquired in the name of the law in order to defend it as security guards, soldiers, or policemen — those "who carried a licensed fire-arm."[10] Likewise, the study points out that in the course of the inti-fada, the number of women murdered rose by over 150 percent (38, as opposed to the 14 in the four years prior to the intifada).

The article was accompanied by a photograph by Uriel Sinai, together with a disclaimer from the newspaper that "the photograph serves as an illustration of the article." The photograph shows a woman being led away by a man and woman from the "security forces" (figure 6.6).[11] Contrary to the nature of the gestures of res-cue and containment in Heiman's *Holding* series, this scene plays on the common trope of the bride being led off to her wedding. We see the two people in uniform — field uniforms — each clutching a hand and shoulder, and it is difficult to tell whether they are supporting the woman or making sure she doesn't slip from their grasp as they resiliently carry her away to a place the spectator is not shown. From her look, however, coupled with the fixed stares of her rescuers, the scene does not at all seem comforting or protective.

Although the article focuses on women murdered by men be-longing to the security forces, it is thus accompanied by a picture that portrays the survivor of a terrorist attack, over whom the secu-rity forces have spread their blanket of protection, as if the photo-graph were intended to exonerate the Israeli security agents of the

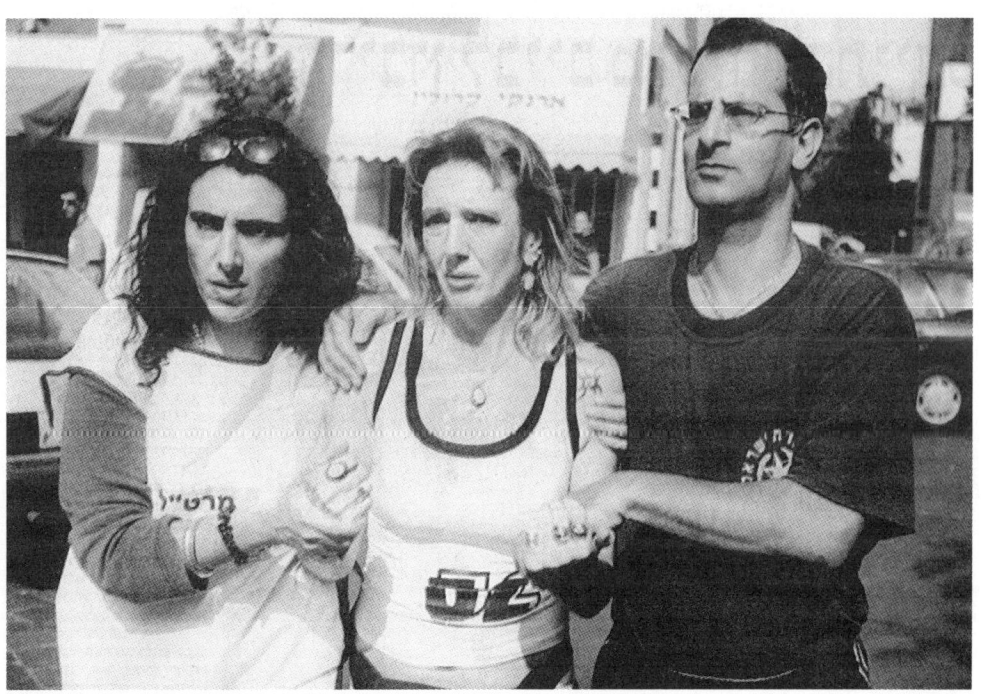

Figure 6.6.   Uriel Sinai, *Ha'aretz*, November 28, 2005.

crimes they are accused of in the article. Despite the fact that the study is concerned with injuries to women committed by Jewish Israeli men belonging to the security forces, the photograph chosen to illustrate the report nevertheless shows a female survivor of an attack that has been carried out by a Palestinian. The camera angle, however, positioning the figures against an urban background devoid of the typical signs of a Palestinian attack, suspends the immediate context of the attack that only the caption for the photo prevents one from forgetting.

The woman, more than anything else, appears almost entirely exposed to the force of law, thus becoming a thin surface that allows national and gendered violence to come together. Her abandonment as a woman, left on the margins of the great national story, is presented as no more than a side effect, as an unquestionable necessity. So, too, her abandonment as a citizen, together with male citizens also abandoned by the sovereign, is a sort of necessary side effect of the sovereign's duty to protect and defend its citizens. The ongoing injury to the Palestinian, his abandonment to the unrestrained power of the sovereign, is the great blind spot of the picture presented in this newspaper article, which, despite the radical cross-referencing of data presented in the article, sustains the ethnic separation that divides the Jewish and Arab subjects of the sovereign.

Heiman's *Holding* series enables an examination of how the Palestinian, as the regular victim of the occupation, appears as a survivor. The scene is characterized by a type of chaos from which all the typical marks of sovereignty and hierarchical organization that assign each figure a given task are missing. The injured Palestinian is generally in the custody of others in the vicinity; they are trying to pull him from the disaster area, the disaster to which they've all been subjected. The relations between the casualties at the site and the rescuers are not the typical relations of contingent casualties and recognized rescuers deployed by a sovereign power. The disaster is without limits, it is spreading, and the inability to delineate it can be read in almost every photograph: from the rescuing gestures shown when treating and evacuating the wounded, activities not carried out by trained professionals experienced in limiting the extent of injury while taking the wounded to a safe location, of which the child as rescuer is the epitome, to the inhabitants of the streets in the background of these gestures, who lack the authority to declare a state of emergency.

This is similar to Heiman's series of large photos of demolished houses in the *Photo Rape* series,[12] which is based on the classification of photographs primarily taken from the local press, where the absence of any state of emergency regarding the Palestinian's ongoing catastrophe is manifested at the level of both the provision of assistance and of the photographing of the event (figure 6.7). Even when her home is being destroyed, the Palestinian is usually portrayed as idle, sitting and wondering, contemplating, or haphazardly collecting something from the ruins, exposing what has happened to her by the look of her gaze. Traces of shock can sometimes be read on her face, or mute dread. Generally, however, the photograph appears in an Israeli newspaper a bit later, by the time the emergency has faded, returning it to the routine, as if there were nothing new about the fact that the Palestinian's body has once again been abandoned to the violence of the occupation. The Palestinian has become accustomed to it; the photographer is accustomed to it; the hit parade is accustomed to it.

Distinguishing the two types of victims teaches us that the difference in photographing them is initially derived from the gap in time between the moment of the violent event and the photograph. From the moment she is injured, the Israeli victim is surrounded by photographers. The occasion of her injury disrupts the flow of routine, causing media networks to interrupt their schedules. Bodies are removed from the site to permit the entry of photographers. Hereafter, until the site is cleared and purified of all traces of the event, it occupies center stage. The photographs show the victim bleeding, his body torn apart — gruesome, living testimony to what the Palestinian has done to him.

In the series of panels entitled *Blood Test*, Heiman sampled bloodstains shown in photographs printed in the newspaper (figure 6.8). The details of bloodstains are isolated from the photographs of the attack or of the arena from which they were taken and have been inserted into a consistent format according to size and shape. Heiman uses bloodstains appearing in the newspaper without making

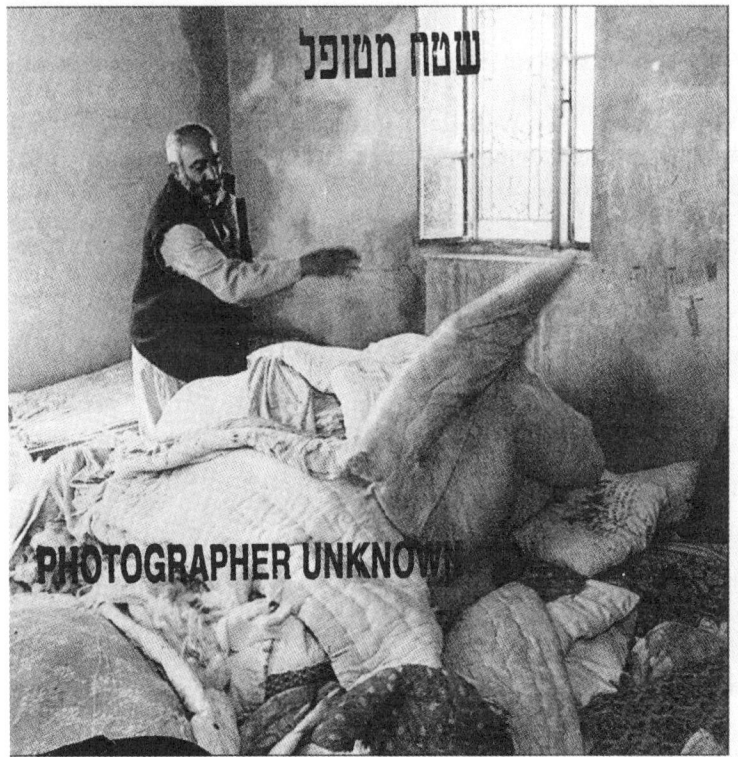

Figure 6.7. Michal Heiman, *Attacks on Linking #1– Photo Rape – Rearranging His Room (Photographer Unknown, Ha'aretz, 16.11.2001, Taleb Darawi, Shawarwa village)* (from her solo exhibition, "I Was There," Andrea Meislin Gallery, New York, 2005), color print mounted on canvas, 480 x 270 cm, 2001.

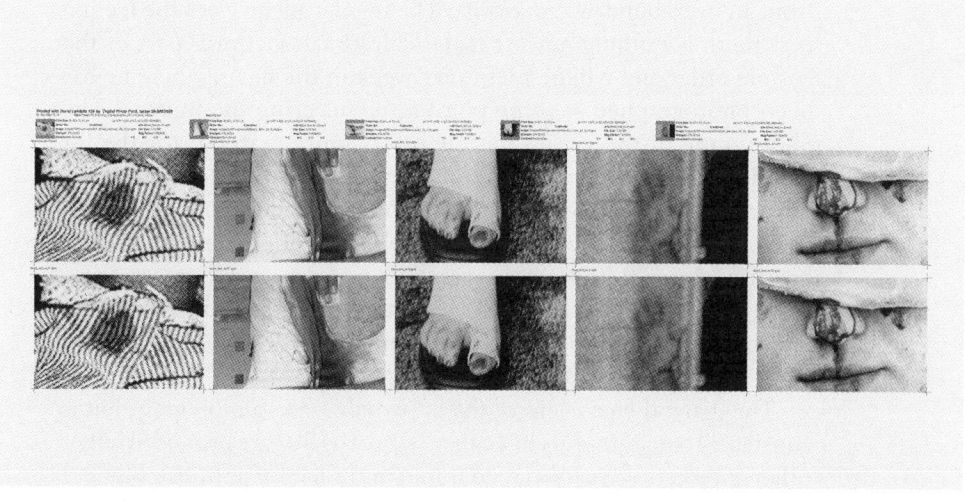

Figure 6.8. Michal Heiman, *Blood Test #4 (Series A)*, color print, 52 x 101 cm, 2002. (Please see Color Plates.)

any distinction between "Jewish blood," "Arab blood," or "migrant worker's blood." Despite her indifference to the ethnic identity of the person whose blood has been spilled, the conditions of the images of horror of the Palestinian are such that, in the Israeli press, Palestinian blood usually fails to generate any sense of urgency and therefore in most cases has dried long before the cameras arrive at the scene. Even though in the series of twelve samples Heiman has managed to cull at least half of them from Palestinian blood that was shed in the recent intifada, this symmetry with samples of Jewish blood merely emphasizes the fact that in proportion to the number killed (thousands on the Palestinian side, hundreds on the Israeli), only Jewish casualties generate a true state of emergency in the local media.

On the Palestinian side, there may be an exceptional case, a particularly spectacular bloody incident, such as the hundreds of bloodstains on the steps to the Temple Mount. Although the Palestinian victims do not manage to disrupt routine, a small number reach the regular niche reserved for them in which only one item is extracted from an overabundance in reality. The regular niche gives the feeling that there is nothing new, that the Palestinian victim is part of the cosmic order and will be met every week in the news, where he has been photographed at some point after suffering the injury.[13] The photograph of the victim merely offers more material for the hit parade of images of horror, temporarily employed, destined to be discarded and replaced by the next photograph. But to take the place of its predecessor, the next photograph must offer something more horrific, closer to those photographed, or a new angle, more gruesome or more intense. The logic of the hit parade functions on a principle of repetition and escalation and in the process detracts from the singular value of each photograph.

The general equivalent of the hit parade seeks a monopoly, but is constantly competing against other standards that are produced out of other interests — national, economic, military, or political. Since it frequently shares the same interests as these standards, they do not actually threaten to undermine its logic.[14] In addition, it can also live peacefully alongside moral or humanitarian interests, as long as they serve its purposes and provide new merchandise. Under the conditions of prolonged occupation, of existence on the verge of catastrophe, sensational news appears routine. To observe and to photograph it, the photographer must suspend the hit-parade logic of images of horror, deterritorialize the field of vision, punch holes in it, and create lines of escape within it or out of it, thwarting the constant attempts to regulate what is seen. To photograph the verge of catastrophe, then, is an act of resistance. Each of the four vectors of an *énoncé* is a point of resistance: addresser, addressee, referent, and meaning.

How the Visible Becomes Invisible

Under the conditions that subsist on the verge of catastrophe, however, the hit parade of horrors threatens the visibility of any referent. Even under other conditions, however, the referent of photography is not given or self-evident. Photography's appearance on the stage of history, which facilitated the conquest of the world as spectacle, created new conditions for the gaze. Looking at photographs gave rise to the "identificatory gaze" based on the discriminating gesture that determines that "this is X" or "this is Y." The identificatory gaze performs a twofold reification — for what is seen in the photograph and for its meaning. This identificatory gesture toward the photograph is demanded by the gaze, but nonetheless threatens to restrict the gaze solely to this gesture.

This reification is not an essential element of the medium, but a specific dimension of the gaze that came to be dominant with the advent of photography. To observe this gesture more closely, I will look at the traces it has left in a text referring to a specific photograph:

> One day, quite some time ago, I happened on a photograph of Napoléon's youngest brother, Jérôme, taken in 1852. And I realized then, with an amazement I haven't been able to lessen since: "I am looking at eyes that looked at the emperor." Sometimes I would mention this amazement, but since no one seemed to share it, nor even to understand it (life consists of these little touches of solitude), I forgot about it.... I was overcome by an "ontological" desire: I wanted to learn at all costs what photography was "in itself," by what essential feature it was to be distinguished from the community of images.[15]

This is how Roland Barthes begins his book on photography, a canonical text in the discourse surrounding the medium. A phenomenological reading of Barthes's description will allow us to extract a mode of looking at a photograph. In other words, this written document, which details the observation of a photograph, allows us to trace obliquely the author's act of viewing and to outline its character to the degree that we can point to what has escaped his eyes in the course of its observation.

Barthes doesn't show this photograph to his readers. The absence of this image, an absence that is not even mentioned, is curious, because he claims that all other photos he refers to in this book are printed except the one he omitted purposely. That is the photograph of his mother, which he deliberately and explicitly veils from his readers, turning this avoidance into the point of departure for most of his assertions in the book. Instead, the photograph of Jérôme is described for the fact that it evoked excitement. However, the excitement is not derived from what is seen in the photograph, but from what the photograph's object — the person who is photographed — is likely to have seen. Barthes is not excited by Napoléon, whom he cannot see, but by the fact that the eyes he's looking at have looked on Napoléon. Had this been a photograph of Napoléon himself, Barthes may not have been moved at all. It is the possibility of proximity that moves him — proximity, through someone else's gaze, to a mythic and inaccessible figure outside the economy of photography who in principle cannot have been photographed: Napoléon died in 1821, eighteen years before the invention of photography. Barthes is not moved by Jérôme's gaze, but by what these eyes have apparently seen. In other words, he's moved neither by what is seen in the photograph — the eyes — nor by what was seen by the eyes of the person in the photograph — Napoléon. Barthes takes no special interest in either Jérôme or Napoléon, but rather is excited by the closeness between the two, a closeness to which the photograph bears witness. We should even restrict this supposition, however, and emphasize that the photograph does not attest in itself to any such relation and at most has allowed Barthes to imagine it.

Barthes does not interrogate this proximity; he later abandons it, going on to address something else. The fact that Jérôme saw Napoléon has nothing to do with the specific photograph in front of Barthes' eyes. Barthes sees neither Jérôme nor Napoléon, but only *a photograph of Jérôme*. The knowledge that the photograph before him is a portrait of Jérôme allows Barthes to project a field of vision onto the photograph in which Jérôme and Napoléon can encounter one another, identifying this field of vision as "Jérôme's." Barthes does not argue — nor could he have argued — that the gaze revealed to his eyes, Jérôme's gaze, could have seen Napoléon at the precise moment when Jérôme was photographed, for Napoléon died before the photograph was taken. He knows only that at some moment in time, Jérôme saw Napoléon, and in Barthes' eyes this gaze, which had rested on Napoléon, bears the touch of this light.

Such an encounter, had it occurred, would have had to take place at least eighteen years before Jérôme's photograph was taken, as Jérôme could only have seen Napoléon in his youth. Barthes may indeed be looking at a photograph, but what he sees is "Jérôme" — not the portrait, but the name. Thus Barthes' looking on the photograph is accompanied by an erasure of the visible, which is overshadowed and rendered superfluous by the knowledge that the identificatory gaze determines to be revealed. In other words, the discriminating gesture of the identificatory gaze is accompanied by another distinctive gesture of the gaze on photographs, the gesture of the projective gaze.[16] Everything Barthes attributes to what is seen in the photograph emerges from this projection.

In using the notion of a projective reading based on the gesture of the projective gaze, I am not proposing that we see a flaw in Barthes' form of reading, but only acknowledging an inevitable dimension of any reading of a photograph. The psychoanalytic concept of projection includes two dimensions: the displacement of certain affects from one site to another and the disavowal or refusal of these feelings or passions, which the subject rejects by placing them on the other. Barthes looks at the photograph and sees nothing other than what he attributes to it. He doesn't see Jérôme, the brother of Napoléon. He most likely was alerted to the image being of Jérôme from a caption appearing beside or above the photograph. He does not focus on Jérôme's figure as reflected in the specific photograph he was looking at, nor does he see Jérôme seeing his brother Napoléon. Extrapolating from the family connection, Barthes assumes that Jérôme had seen Napoléon and projects this supposition onto Jérôme's eyes. The photograph doesn't disclose itself to the gaze "of Barthes," it is Barthes who projects onto the photograph what *he* sees and what is visible to *his* eyes.

The reported excitement does not belong, then, to what is seen in the photograph. In other words, Barthes' observation of this photograph, as well as of others, confronted him with a rupture in his field of vision, the instability of the visible, the possibility of seeing through the medium of someone else and, even more, the possibility that someone else might see through him as a medium. In general, he encounters the fact that "his" gaze is not his. Looking obliquely, we witness Barthes overlooking this rupture with which he is faced.

Barthes' text is inexplicit testimony, insofar as he remains unaware of it, to the modern citizen's dramatic encounter with photography: What appears to the eyes of the spectator is not what she sees in the photograph, and what he sees in the photograph does not appear in it. The "ontological desire" Barthes speaks of is symptomatic of this encounter. What he attempts to grasp is the nature of this medium, which is believed to reify the visible completely, framing it within the boundaries of the paper, fixing it so that it can be looked at again and again. Nevertheless, this visibility, apparently imprisoned within the confines of photography, shows itself to elude every gaze. Barthes does not allow these dimensions, which undermine the stability of the singular gaze and the homogeneity of the field of vision, to appear. Instead he proposes a "new science for each object," "a *mathesis singularis* and no longer *universalis*," at the heart of which is an attempt to reconstitute the individual as the prop of the gaze.[17] Barthes unwittingly denies the fact that his gaze is not his own, that it is stolen, borrowed, expropriated, undermined, and not fully visible, that the visible does not appear before him "like an image in a photograph." Instead, he projects a stability and sovereignty that are not in it, seeing it as "the absolute Particular, the sovereign Contingency, matte and somehow stupid, the *This* (this photograph and not Photography)."[18]

Barthes' main contention, according to which the essence of photography is manifested by the claim that something "was there," remains in solidarity with what is written in every instruction manual of photography, and in the process, it overlooks the civil contract of photography, of which any collection of instructions is but a technical echo. Barthes writes: "What the photograph reproduces to infinity has occurred only once: the photograph mechanically repeats what could never be repeated existentially. In the photograph, the event is never transcended for the sake of something else; the photograph always leads the corpus I need back to the body I see."[19] Barthes explicitly rejects various discussions of photography — sociological, formalistic, and others — on the grounds that they miss the essence of photography that he sought. While identifying photography's problematic — the elusiveness of the visible in the medium that is assumed to reify the visible — he still confines the problematic to a relatively secure area, missing the fact that it is the precise characteristic of photography in all of its dimensions: "Whatever it grants to vision and whatever its manner, a photograph is always invisible: it is not it that we see. In short, the referent adheres."[20] Barthes thus considers photography to be invisible, given that the viewer passes too quickly on to what is signified within it. Presenting what is signified in it in a simplistic manner, as though it were a given, easily accessible piece of visual data that can be determined without any negotiation, Barthes fails to account for the fact that the referent of a photograph — and not only the photograph as signifier — is given for negotiation. In addition, he overlooks the fact that the adhesion of the referent to the photograph is not to be taken for granted, that the photograph does not exist in its own right, but always in connection to an external text (such as the knowledge that "this is Jérôme"), that the spectator does not only see what he claims to see in the photograph, that the gaze "of" the spectator is not his, and that photography is a projective surface that never discloses anything in itself. Disregarding all of these points, Barthes eliminates the fact that photography is a social practice that mediates social relations by being anchored in a civil contract of photography.

The Shadow of the Rifle

As I've shown in Chapter Two, the civil contract of photography was part of the institutionalization of photography in the first half of the nineteenth century. This contract lies at the foundation of the practice of photography, even when remaining unspoken or when photography is employed without being aware of its existence. The civil contract of photography is a part of modern citizenship, and anyone in contact with photography, from the amateur to the professional, is implicated in it. The contract is interwoven with photography as technology, preventing technology from remaining only technology. Commitment to the contract exists in different realms and with various degrees of intensity. There are those who accept their citizenship in the citizenry of photography as simply given, and there are others who constantly seek to negotiate over the implications of this citizenship, seeing in every act of photography — its production or viewing — an opportunity for renewing discussions over their citizenship and that of others. Given these aspects, both the reification and the elusiveness of photography characterize the gaze in relation to photography, and not the photograph itself. The spectator has a responsibility toward photography that obliges her to recognize that what is in the photograph actually "was there" and that what is in the photograph is only part of what "was there," or sometimes is only a point of departure to arriving at what "was there."

The situation from which the photograph was taken should always be reconstructed, and the photograph itself attests to the limits of what could be photographed.

> Q: Do you have photographs of those retracing their paths after being detained at the checkpoint without being permitted to enter Israel?
> *Miki Kratsman*: No. Because it doesn't photograph well. It could be a video shot, not stills. The only thing I can express in stills is when you see lots of people with small children standing in front of the barrier, waiting.[21]

Every day till the second intifada, thousands of Palestinians used to pass the Erez checkpoint between Gaza and Israel on their way to work and back.[22] Miki Kratsman and Boaz Arad placed a video camera on a tripod at the checkpoint, letting it run for the entire forty minutes of the tape (figures 6.9 through 6.11).

> Q: Where was the video shot from?
> *Kratsman:* I stood with my back to the barrier and looked in the direction of the buses. When they step down from the rides to return to Gaza, they run in the direction of the barrier to get through as quickly as possible. More and more people arrive all the time. It doesn't stop.
> Q: Was there any reaction from the people you photographed?
> *Kratsman:* People came up to me and said I should take pictures in the morning. It's harder in the morning, harder to get through. In the morning, they're coming into Israel. The inspections are more stringent. I asked them what time I should come in the morning, and they told me twelve o'clock at night.

The Palestinians' movements, regardless of where they travel, are systematically restricted. Every checkpoint is a temporary suspension of motion, and every movement is only temporary, until the next checkpoint appears. The checkpoints, supposedly meant for

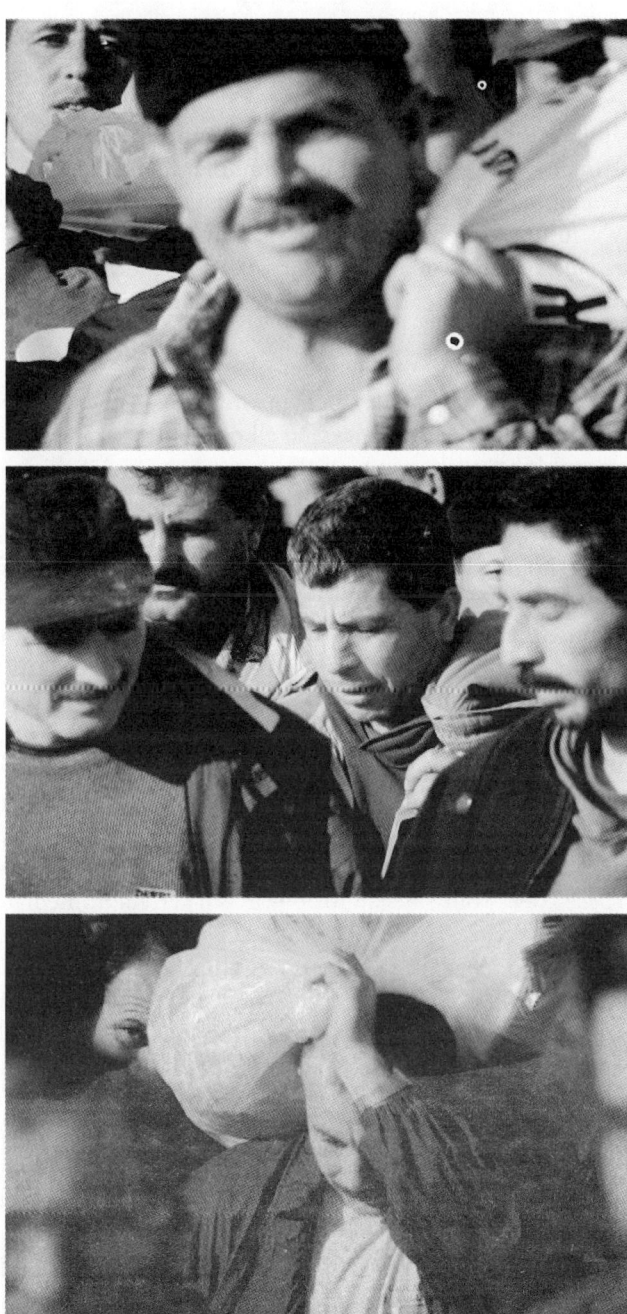

Figures 6.9–6.11. Boaz Arad and Miki Kratsman, *Untitled* (a sequence from video), 2003.

inspecting and supervising, are above all instruments of detention. Through segregations, lock-ins, checkpoints, and roadblocks, the Palestinians' space is divided into innumerable isolated units. Any movement between these units is conducted — if at all — through the army's authorization. Under the shadow of the rifle, hundreds of thousands of Palestinians are cut off from their workplaces and homes, their relatives and families, and from health care, education, and other basic services.

It is not only the exact number of Palestinians that should be of interest, but the fact that it can happen to any of them on any given day — and even, on certain days, to all of them several times a day. It is impossible to photograph all the cases, but even if this were possible, there would be no one to look at all of them. But this technical impossibility to photograph, show, or view does not mean photographs should not be taken, that it is pointless to take photographs, or that the difficulty of the situation absolves us of the responsibility to document and collect every detail, gather testimonies, and amass proof of each and every case — to expose, beyond all events, the permanent confiscation of time as fragments of life. Even further, we are still obliged to give an account of the situation in its entirety and to develop implementable methods for what fails to be photographed when no cameras are present or are contingently or systematically forbidden or when a camera is present, but there is nothing to see or to show.

These checkpoints began to appear as a system immediately after the Oslo Accords.[23] In recent years, their presence has multiplied, spreading from very few on the roads out of the major towns into a dense network of hundreds of checkpoints and roadblocks scattered in a grid over the length and width of the West Bank. In addition to causing innumerable injuries, this policy has resulted in many Palestinian women bearing stillborn babies at the checkpoints. It's difficult to obtain the exact numbers, but estimates are in upward of several dozen. There have been no photographs taken of a woman in childbirth at a checkpoint. Sometimes, when cameras prove inadequate when faced with the verge of catastrophe, painting offers its services in order to recreate the photograph that was never taken of what threatens to be forgotten, what has been erased, or simply ren-

dered nonexistent.[24] Such is a painting by Faten Nastas: "The painting is based on a true story I read in the paper," she said, "about a
woman who gave birth to twins at the checkpoint, and they died
because they didn't get medical treatment on time.... If there had
been a photograph of the event, I might have not painted it."[25]

Nastas's painting is in the form of a snapshot (figure 6.12). The
baby is about to emerge from the woman's womb as she lies on the
back seat of a car that has been detained at the checkpoint. The door
is wide open, and her legs are sticking out of the car. She's gripping
the front seat with her right hand, taking her pain out on it, holding
her head in her left hand, trying to dull the pain. Around her are
three Israeli soldiers who are looking away, behaving as if a birth
is not taking place, as if a new life were not trying to emerge into
the world, as if they were not presently taking the life of someone
yet to be born. The soldier sitting inside the guard post is completely
lethargic, distracted, exhausted by the situation, perhaps even miserable about it, but his passivity does not absolve him of his complicity
in the murder. A second soldier is talking to the woman's husband,
lecturing him on the checkpoint policy, scolding him with a finger,
informing him that these are the rules he must obey. If he wishes, he
can respect them; if not, he can go somewhere else. As for the third
soldier, who is just as apathetic toward the woman's cries of pain and
distress, he might be staring at the insolent husband, who has the
audacity to argue with the "masters of the land,"[26] but out of the
corner of his eye, he cannot help but see what is happening inside
the car. Only obstinacy, insensitivity, recklessness, or malice — or
perhaps all four — allow him to continue to look ahead stubbornly,
remaining motionless in the face of what he has certainly witnessed.

The civil contract of photography binds us in a commitment to
the referent of photography. Concern for the referent or its meaning, however, does not allow us to forget the prejudice of photography — the fact that it borders on the deceptive. This is not because
anyone has manipulated it or allowed the conditions of its production to be sabotaged, but because, despite the fact that it is an *énoncé*
within a discourse, it is only a single component in a sentence — the
trial of history — that tends to conduct itself in the world on its own,
independently, as though it carried its truth on its back.

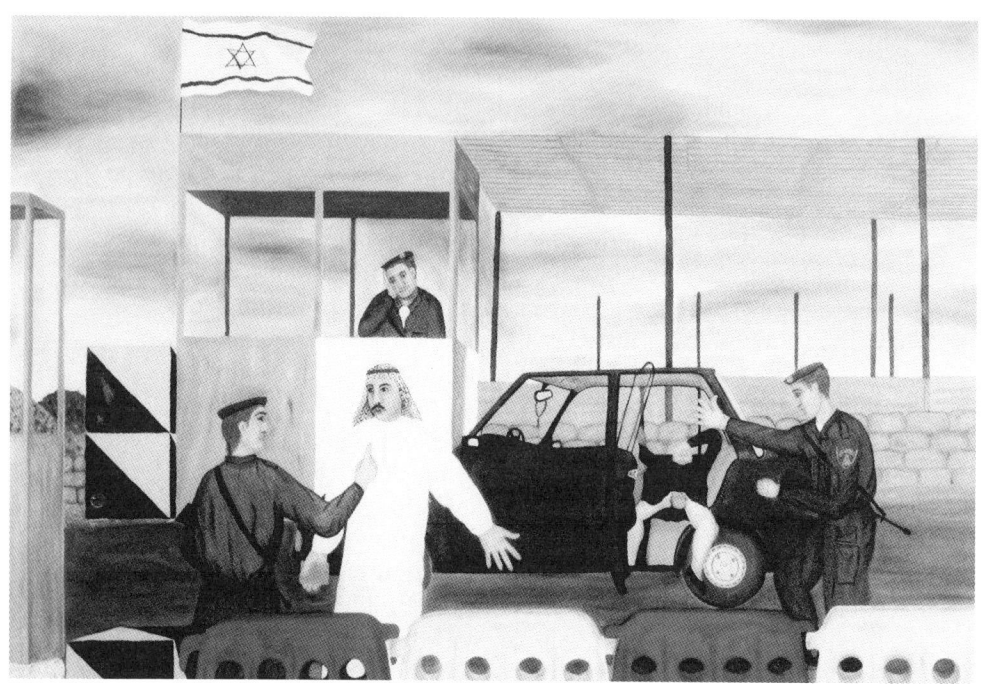

Figure 6.12. Faten Nastas, *Birth and Death at the Checkpoint*, 1996. (Please see Color Plates.)

Consider, for example, these photographs of the way in which food is transferred from trucks outside the Occupied Territories to trucks that are supposed to supply the Palestinians within them. It is done via the "back-to-back" method (figures 6.13 and 6.14).

Officer at back-to-back device: Back-to-back is simple, level areas about the size of a football field, maybe more, at which a Palestinian truck and an Israeli truck arrive. Merchandise is loaded, merchandise is unloaded. Merchandise is exchanged, and each one departs on his way. Back to back. One vehicle opposite another vehicle. Back to back.

Head of Economic Branch, Office of Coordination of Government Activities in the Territories: It's not some kind of gizmo, yeah. It's a solution. It's new to the events, more than a year and a half.[27]

An open sand lot. A thick row of huge boulders, each as tall as a sturdy adolescent, divides the lot in half. Scattered among the boulders are heavy concrete cubes. A scorching sun shines from above, and there is nowhere to hide from it. Long cargo trucks arrive at the site, some are full, others empty. Within a few hours, they will exchange roles. The ones that are full will be emptied, and the empty ones will be filled. Everything will be carried out under the supervision of armed soldiers, who will hurry back and forth between the two sides, climbing into the trucks, opening some of the sealed crates to check whether they contain only what they're supposed to, inspecting the declarations of goods, invoices, and transit permits. If feeling agreeable, they may allow the bartering to be completed and show humaneness toward people who have been prevented from trading their own produce, growing it, marketing and distributing it, and taking an active part in a free market. Sometimes they may even exhibit excessive humaneness, sending the driver off with a good word, a word that might occasionally cut the taste of the hands that have gone through the food the driver brings home to his village. But on other days, this same armed soldier might be inconsiderate, without understanding or benevolence. He might monkey wrench the process, be obstinate about the stamps, stubbornly asserting — especially when a weapon is hanging from his shoulder — that only

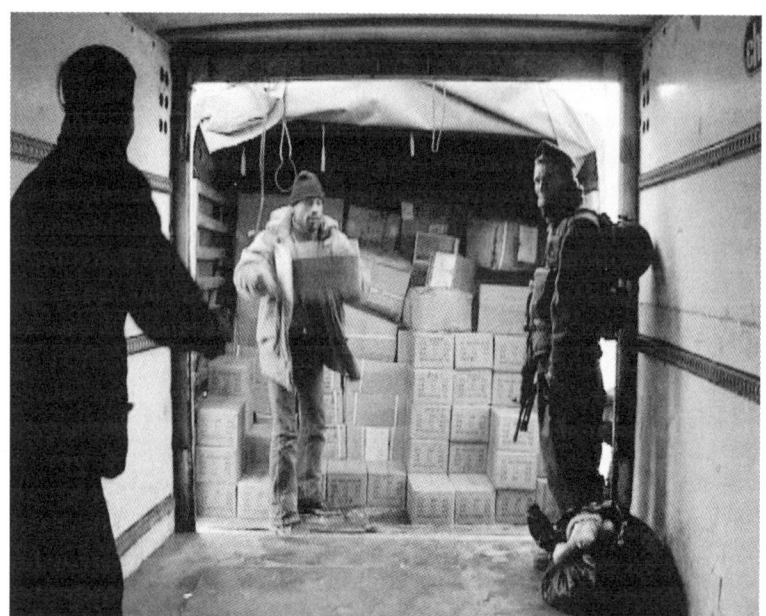

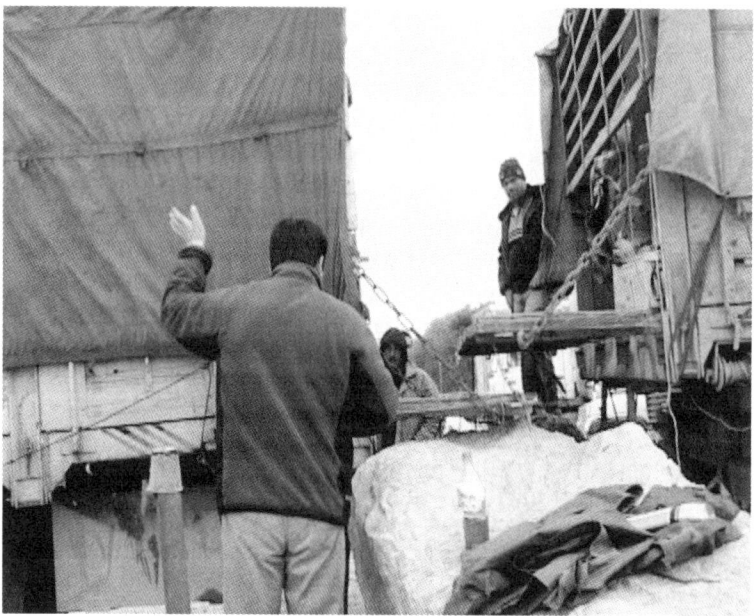

Figures 6.13 and 6.14. Miki Kratsman, *Back-to-Back*, Bitounia, still from *The Food Chain* (a film by Ariella Azoulay), 2003.

stamps from the Haifa and Ashdod ports will be honored. Those who've come to load goods are sent away empty-handed, and those who have come to unload will return with their trucks still full.

Head of Economic Branch, Office of Coordination of Government Activities in the Territories: There is no shortage of food, it's flowing. A Palestinian can pick up the phone to the Coordination and Liaison Administration in Hebron and say to them: "Listen, there are hungry people here or there aren't any hungry people here."

There is no shortage of food, it's flowing. And to help the river of goods to flow, the army has opened back-to-back lots. No, it's not some kind of tricky scheme, I was told when I asked — "It's a solution." The problem was that food had not been circulating, but now, thanks to the back-to-back lots, it is flowing. Wholesale. But there are retail currents, as well. A Palestinian can call the same office making his life miserable and ask for food, call the same officer who prevented him from collecting his crop a couple of hours earlier or caused the fruit that had ripened in his orchards to fall from the trees and rot. That same officer, or a soldier under his command, will pick up the telephone and call one of the thirty humanitarian organizations that will make sure he is provided with sacks of rice. There is no shortage of food — it's flowing. *Its flow is being photographed.* There it is, passing from hand to hand, from truck to truck, and though the shadow of a rifle may slightly impinge on the proceedings, what does that matter if food gets to the mouths?

The Shadow of the Camera

And the shadow of the camera? Where does this fall when photographing what occurs on the verge of catastrophe? To answer that question, I will make use of the instruments that Aïm Deüelle Lüski has constructed beginning in the 1970s. I deliberately employ the term "instrument," rather than "camera," in order to suspend the common meaning of the Hebrew translation of the act of drawing (*graphia*) with light (*photo*). Hebrew subsumes photography (*zilum*) into the craft of portrait making, the creation of an image, *zelem*. In this same respect, we may speak about photographing inanimate objects or open landscapes, but this, too, implies the creation of an image from them — that is, an image in their form. This type of image is the product of a single-focus camera. Deüelle Lüski's instruments offer an alternative logic.

In order to understand this logic, it is necessary to return to the moment of photography's invention and the institutionalization of the format we are familiar with today. In the invention that became dominant, the camera bisects the photographic space, creating a sharp division between what is in front of it and what is behind it. In other words, the camera viewfinder becomes the primary axis of photographic space, moving from the photographer toward the photographed and thus producing a coherent picture that fixes the visible to a single, consistent viewpoint. It is troubling, however, that this complex structure of relations finds no explicit expression in the space of the photograph, which reveals to those who look at it something that "was there," facing the camera. It is this logic of traditional photography that Deüelle Lüski exposes and reflects on, questioning the necessity of positioning the photographer along a "vertical" plane, parallel to the photographed.[28] The various cameralike instruments he has constructed are aimed at deconstructing this vertical structure and propose different ways of thinking the photographic encounter. Each of the horizontal, multisided, or multifocused cameras that he has created address one of the components of the traditional camera, revealing its problematics: lens, camera obscura, viewfinder, photographic film, and so on.

What is common to all of these camera constructions is the fact that the image obtained is nothing like the image offered by all the cameras manufactured since the invention of photography. The difference, first of all, is that the image from his cameras is unreadable, or at least cannot be read all at once. More precisely, the image that he captures is not really that type of image, *zelem*. This immediate unreadability of the image suspends the common gesture when facing with a photograph, that of pointing directly to the photographed and exclaiming, "That is X" or "That is Y." This typical gesture disregards the problematic status of what is signified in the photograph, denying the threat it poses to the stability of the spectator's gaze, taking it for granted. Deüelle Lüski's cameras (and, even more, the images they produce) defy the self-evidence of the photographic blot, which under the dictates of technological development and the market — constantly improved on in terms of the quality of the image, the sharpness, clarity, realism, and so on — is presented as if it were incontestable.[29]

In the act of photographing, Deüelle Lüski's instruments have an enigmatic presence (figures 6.15 and 6.16). Generally, they look like dark boxes of varying design, devoid of a "front" side in which the lens is situated. They cannot be operated like ordinary cameras. They are heavy and cumbersome. Using them requires an anchor of some kind, on a tripod or some other support. They do not have a single mechanism, a viewfinder or, in recent years, a small digital screen, that allows the operator to believe he is in control of the frame of the "picture" prior to its capture. The instrument is sealed off from its surroundings, except for a number of perforations that cannot be seen by the naked eye. It starts to run without prior knowledge of the results — not only as to what will be seen in the photograph, but even the kind of image the camera will produce.

Designed each time in order to deal with the logic of one of the components of the traditional camera, the constraints built into the instrument deal with the question of what type of instrument should be applied to a particular event or situation. These questions do not revolve around the end product — the photograph. The photograph is produced as a hieroglyph, and the code to decipher it needs to be studied, not on its own, but in connection with the mechanism responsible for its production. The instruments constructed by Deüelle Lüski are, in the true sense of the word, iconoclastic. They shatter belief in the photographic image as the sacred product of the act of photographing. Deüelle Lüski's instruments wage a guerrilla campaign against the single-focus gaze that looks from above, dominating, observing, watching, standing guard, the gaze that seeks to normalize and police the disrupted flow of life and to disguise the traces of the civil contract left in the photograph.

Photography, as I said before, borders on the deceptive. A photograph can never serve as the final, unquestionable and irrefutable proof. Given the tendency for photography to be looked at and read as though it attests to what "was there," rather than only exposing

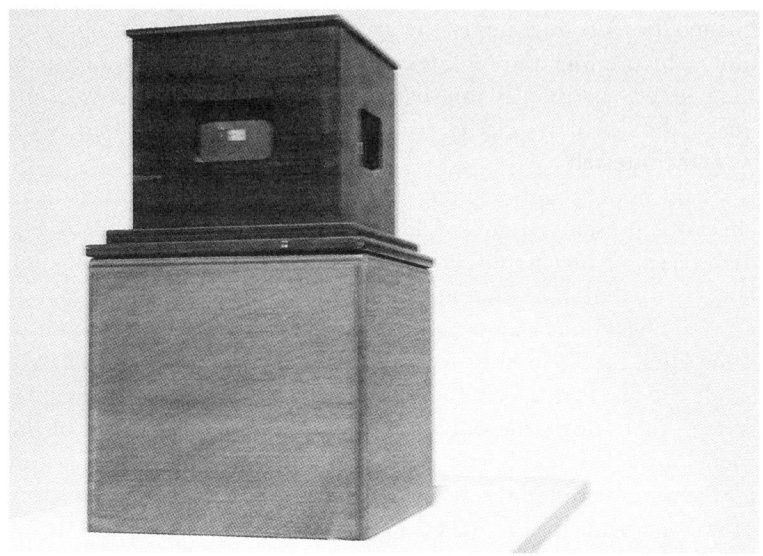

Figure 6.15. Aïm Deüelle Lüski (collaboration with "Doing Photography") (Camera N.E.S.W., 20 x 20 x 20 cm, razor lens, negative in 45 degrees), 1991.

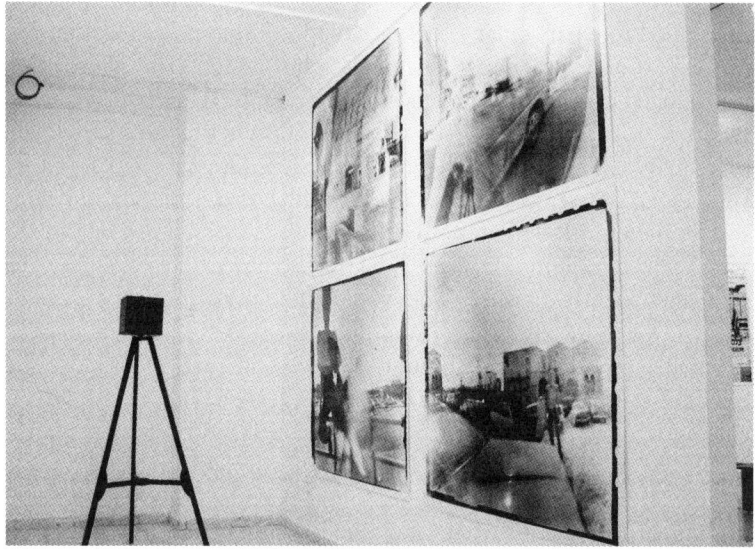

Figure 6.16. Aïm Deüelle Lüski (collaboration with "Doing Photography"), *Seam Line, Jerusalem* (photos taken with Camera N.E.S.W., black and white negative, 4 x 5 inches), 1991.

what was there as seen by a single-focus camera from a particular angle, it would be more accurate to compare it to a statistical datum. A statistical datum attests to its object, but does so only from the position of the statistical instrument that is used to generate the object. Whenever the question arises of whether or not there is malnutrition in the Occupied Territories, only its superficial symptoms are treated, for example, by adding iron to flour.[30] One statistical datum — there is malnutrition in the territories — is replaced by another: there is no malnutrition in the territories. But the reduction of the Palestinians to biological beings whose needs must be provided for has not altered as a result of this substitution. Nor can this situation of theirs be captured in a single photograph.

Head of Economic Branch, Office of Coordination of Government Activities in the Territories: [Hunger is] when people are hungry for food. In Biafra, for instance. When children are wandering around with swollen bellies and have no food.[31]

The head of the economic branch, who views the photograph as bearer of the truth — a swollen belly equals hunger — exposes the deception of photography. It's not because the child in Biafra doesn't suffer from hunger, but because photography as an instrument is incapable of photographing ideas. Photography is a modest instrument that lacks the Kantian categories of understanding, having only a single sense, and its forms of intuition (time and space) are limited and determined by a single program: only drawing with light what is visible to the single eye located in its foreground. Its modesty is not a disadvantage, but an important quality as an *énoncé* whose meaning can be stated only by being linked to a chain of other *énoncés*.[32]

The instruments constructed by Deüelle Lüski put obstacles in the path of constraining the meaning of the photograph to simply what lies in the photograph itself. Each instrument does this in a specific way, although each suspends the instrumentalist attitude toward the camera that views it as a means of producing an image as close as possible to reality. In ordinary cameras, this connection is formulated in terms of pursuing an objective, which is almost always the same — to obtain an image as close to reality as possible in such a way that the instrument succeeds in overcoming every obstacle of light, distance, sharpness, and so on that reality places before it. In other words, every ordinary camera is a partial realization of the ideal camera that will be capable of eliminating the discrepancy between what is visible on the photographic paper and what appears in "reality."

Deüelle Lüski's cameras play in a new space, where there is no place for an ideal camera and its objectives, whereby the common ground of all ordinary cameras is elided. Deüelle Lüski's cameras thus are research tools, mobile experimental laboratories, and the images they produce are the records of laboratory experiments. The connection between camera and image undergoes a reformulation through the use of these cameras. The image is not a universal sign, but depends on a specific camera. To read these photographs, it is necessary to reconstruct the specific conditions of the act of photography and to confront them with the specific conditions of what was photographed. The often misrecognized distinction between photography as mechanism, instrument, or act and the photograph as the image or paper is reconfirmed.

The photograph did not come into the world by chance; it is the product of a camera that expresses a particular scopic regime, and Deüelle Lüski's instruments reveal the shadow of the camera and its place in that regime. All single-focus cameras are part of the same scopic regime, and for this reason, its hegemony appears to receive no discussion. Deüelle Lüski's cameras oblige us to think about the limits of this scopic regime and the possibilities of escaping from its total grasp — of getting out from under the camera's shadow. Underlying this move are some novel ways of thinking about the position of the photographer and even fundamental transformations of her function, or at least for altering the familiar single-focus viewing regime within which the photographer is embedded.

Let's return to the back-to-back platforms, specifically the one at Bitounia. Deüelle Lüski went there with a black, flat, circular instrument with a segment cut out of it, like a piece of pita bread ready to be filled with falafel balls (figures 6.17 and 6.18). For the instrument, which he calls a "pita camera" on account of its shape, this was a premiere performance without prior rehearsals. He had no idea what sort of image the camera would produce or any idea where to place

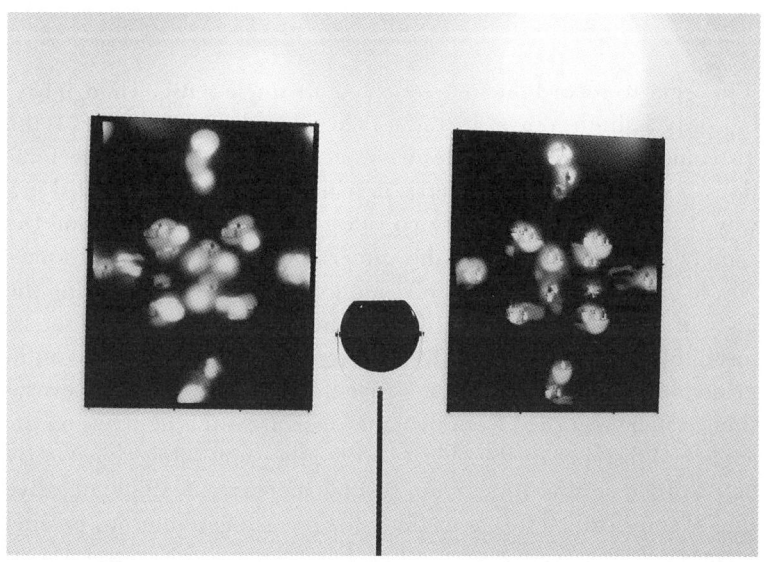

Figure 6.17. Aïm Deüelle Lüski, *Pita Camera*, diameter 20 cm, 2.5 cm thick, black perspex, miniature holes, minimum focus, variable length, 2003.

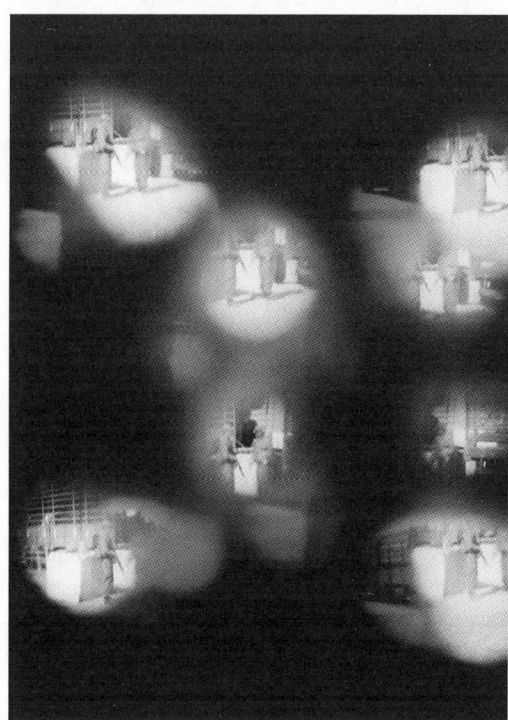

Figure 6.18. Aïm Deüelle Lüski, *Back-to-Back*, Bitounia, photo taken with Pita camera, color negative, 4 x 5 inches, 2003. (Please see Color Plates.)

it in order to record the impressions of its single sense. Though having only a single sense, it was served by multiple apertures — the instrument's two convex sides were pierced with dozens of perforations. As with his other cameras, in which the image is recorded in a way that erases the logic of two sides — in front of and behind the camera — it made sense that this camera should be positioned somewhere in a space where this division exists. While destabilizing the logic of such a dividing line, this camera makes it possible to see its instability in space, as well. Everything surrounding the pita can in principle be recorded on the negative that fills its pocket. Not everything will be recorded from the same aperture — this depends on the angle and distance of the object to the pita — and some objects may be recorded several times from several apertures. A single negative thus is transformed into a medium for recording numerous parallel images rubbing against each other, lying beside and on top of one another. The printed negative displays the pita's internalization of light infiltrating the volatile space.

Clusters of images clearly stand out against a black background. Some are bright, appearing as if photographed in daylight — overexposed by the harsh local sun burning the outlines and eliminating any subtlety of shading. Others look as if they were photographed at night without a flash, saturated in dense shades of red and orange. The seemingly unbroken, coherent space of the back-to-back platform loses its logic and is broken down into what appear to be grapelike images, with each capturing a moment of what is happening. Two soldiers are lazily conversing. A Palestinian is waiting, idly sitting on a concrete cube — what else can he do in the suffocating heat, while the soldiers are chatting? He simply accepts the conditions, since this is not the first time (or apparently the last) that performing a simple action requires an exorbitant amount of time. In one grape-image, the soldiers appear full size, tall and resolute, with their hands taking pleasure in gripping their weapons. In the next, the camera has produced a close-up that seems completely intentional, framing their hands gripping the rifles as though the camera was directed at capturing their essence — their weapons.

These grape-images are like raw data that an artist's hand had no time to trim, mold, form, or polish with the regular touches customary for it to appear as an autographed image. The gaze attempts to pull the life out of the image that has been trapped inside the grape. The ring of footsteps crunching gravel and the drone of a truck moving in reverse disturb the silence. The spectator holds her breath; the color rises in her cheeks. These are sour grapes. This is a keyhole, peering into a restricted military zone. Who gave you authorization to peek? I wasn't peeking — I was looking, watching — and given permission by the civil contract of photography. The pita steals images without anyone noticing the presence of a camera. Its eye is hidden inside its body, seeing without causing commotion. It's just a sample. A food sample.

Deüelle Lüski constructs cameras, and the cameras produce images. He himself is not a photographer in any normative sense. The images produced by the camera are not "his," but more accurately the products of the singular camera responsible for their production.[33] Deüelle Lüski did not perform the elementary series of actions that turn the person holding the camera into a photographer. He didn't peer through a viewfinder, compose the frame, or delimit what he saw.[34] What he has done is create a destabilizing instrument that displaces the entire burden and responsibility away from the photograph to the scopic regime and from the photographer to the circumstances of photographing. These photographs show, in the most raw and clear manner, that photographs escape the bounds of ownership. The impression of what was there is not Deüelle Lüski's. The intention to record a certain place, however, and under certain circumstances, extracting evidence of the verge of catastrophe from the plane of immanence — this is something that can be attributed to Deüelle Lüski. But once the negative inside the pita is exposed on both sides and the image is produced, the work is not complete. The photograph is still in need of an addressee who will attempt to give it meaning, linking it to the next *énoncé*, until someone else links it to another.

Photographer Unknown
We encounter photographs every day, floating in the world, unmoored from the original context of their production. Many years of training and practice have turned us into knowledgeable spectators

who evidently go to the heart of the matter — focusing in on the photograph, identifying what it makes visible.[35] On billboards, ID cards, and passports, in newspapers and books, "orphan" images lacking an author flood the world. Generally, not knowing the name of the photographer does not mean she is absented from the photographic act — at least not in the familiar case of single-focus cameras — but this effacement of the photographer is actually a common practice, insofar as so little importance is given to the photographer that it is uncommon even to mention her name.

Omitting the photographer's name, like glorifying it in other instances, is part of the same scopic regime that reifies the visible while absolving the spectator of responsibility for the visible and for commitment to the civil contract of photography. The reification of the visible is carried out either as a result of reliance on the photographer as someone with the authority to manage the photographic act or as the result of the instrument's apparent neutrality, which assumes an absence of human involvement. In both instances, there is a rejection of the complexity of the photographic act, which cannot be predicated on any of the principles it involves, just as the information evidently given by the product, the photograph, does not suffice.

For over two decades, Michal Heiman has been collecting photographs. This collection constitutes another point of departure for continuing to inquire into photography's procedures and rituals. What is common to all of these photographs is, first of all, that the photographer's name is missing. Heiman has gathered them together under the general heading "Photographer Unknown," emphasizing the omission of the name with an imprint that establishes their common name — "Photographer Unknown" — as a substitute for the personal name that has been erased.[36] This black imprint gives each the appearance of a tomb, reminiscent of tombs for the unknown, grouped together by someone courteous enough to give them a textual existence. This textual existence allows them to be found within the sea of names, enabling the dead to reside among the living so their souls will never be erased from the scroll of life. The photographic remains are thus not left among the living in themselves, but are accompanied by the shadows of those who participated in their making.

There is a gesture of generosity toward these photographers in

Heiman's act, which is displayed in the exhibitions she has curated and the actions initiated regarding past photographers who have been forgotten or who have not received their rightful place in the pages of history.[37] This artistic and curatorial work illuminates the effacement of the photographer not only in the general context of photography, but in particular in the context of photography that deals with the verge of catastrophe. Reintroducing the photographer's presence is a method that brings social and political relations to the surface, without which the photographic act fails to take place. Mutual mediation – social relations mediated by photography and photography mediated by social relations – prevents the final conquest of the world as picture, making it impossible to close the gap between world and picture.[38]

When Heiman stamps the statement "Photographer Unknown" onto the photographic surface or when she embeds it in the photograph as part of a digital intervention into the image, she effectively perforates the smooth surface of the photograph, making a photographer suddenly emerge, bringing forth testimony to the fact that he or she was there at the spot in which the photograph was taken. The stamp is thus a declaration that what appears on the photographic paper was seen not only by the lens, but at the same time by a person. This reminder of the photographer's presence at the site of the event dispossesses the photograph of its reification as an event that took place, reinscribing it in the network of exchange relations in which a photographer and photographed take part.

The return of the photographer to the instant of the photographic act allows Heiman to revitalize and begin reading the scene in which the photographer encountered the photographed, raising questions and analyzing the photograph as evidence of the scene – to begin watching the photograph. Some questions are liable to evade a gaze carved out by the boundaries of the frame that accepts what is visible while omitting the actual encounter. The spectator, or the position from which a spectator's reconstruction is possible, is not wholly alienated from the photographer's position. The conditions of the modern gaze, which are mediated through photography, no longer permit a clear-cut separation between the position of the photographer and that of a spectator.[39] The photographer who raises a camera toward what will become *his* or *her* photograph does so from the position of a trained spectator of photographs. The prominence of the screen in digital cameras is simply one literal manifestation of this latent gesture of spectatorship in the photographer's position. In the position of spectatorship mediated by photographs, it is possible to witness the modern configuration of common sense, the loss of which Hannah Arendt has described as a result of the gaze's withdrawal from the world, which is a process that began with Descartes and became widespread with the onset of the instrumental gaze.[40] The movement between these two positions — photographer and spectator — neutralizes the specific gravity of each, which could have allowed one to judge the other as though it were completely foreign, and thus exposes them as interdependent, conditioning and conditioned by one another as either allies or adversaries.

Heiman's work is exemplary for the way in which it presents the mutual dependence existing between the photographer's position and that of the spectator. Perhaps this could be accounted for in her transition from the position of someone who used a camera within the framework of newspaper journalism during the 1980s to the position of someone who stopped taking photos for the press and started to question critically the relationships between the photographer and photographed person. The mere gesture of pointing a camera toward the photographed is at the center of her inquiry, as can be seen by the way she introduces her own image holding a camera into a number of arenas where a photographer had already been — and from which a photographer is absent (see figure 5.10).

This shift, however, is already visible in her early work, where the photographs bear traces of the very act of looking — including imprints, enlargements of newspaper pages, and typographical editing and display. In the early 1990s, after stopping her work as a photographer, Heiman drew a clear line of separation between her work *with* photography and the traditional work *of* a photographer. Not only did she cease taking the act of photography for granted, but she began to question the possibilities and the modes of displaying photographs in public — particularly photographs of people who have encountered catastrophe, which became one of the most crucial questions in her work.

Each time she has exhibited her work, Heiman has returned to these questions, examining them through the framework of the archive that she began to assemble in the 1980s. This is an active archive, and she continues to collect images and photographs from various sources: photographs from family albums, reproductions of canonical works of art (Goya, Degas, or Duchamp), canonical works of photography (Muybridge, Claude Cahun, Nan Goldin, and Cindy Sherman), and those of unknown photographers (sorted and labeled "PHOTOGRAPHER UNKNOWN"), in addition to photographs that she herself has taken from the time she used to work for the press (such as the series *What's On Your Mind?* from 1984–85). The archive provides the framework in which Heiman handles her photographs — or more precisely, as Heiman defined it in an interview, where she "nurses" them.[41] She not only performs technical manipulations, such as trimming, rephotographing, restoring, and retouching, but she borrows the techniques of therapeutic and psychoanalytic discourse in order to address spectators, along with photographed persons and the photographers.

The archive turns every image into part of a series, undermining its potentially iconic status by inserting it into a mental and political discourse, transforming it into a visual document that the spectator is called on to read, or rather, to watch. Sorting through and cataloging the archive's photographs under several categories — such as "Photographer Unknown," "Photo Rape," or "Holding" — is part of the therapeutic activity through which she extracts what "was there" from the silence imposed on it, through a direct appeal to the photographer, spectator, or photographed person. Through her inscription on a photo of a drawing by Goya, for instance, in which a man is seen spanking a woman's exposed buttocks, Heiman repeats Goya's type of questions addressed to the spectator, "See?" With this question, she echoes the spanker's own rhetorical question to his victim as he's spanking her and the conventions of the historical period that gave him the authority to spank her in public as punishment for adultery — "See?" — as if he were seeking to teach her that witnessing is part of the punishment.[42]

Twenty years after the fact, Heiman "asks" women whom she had confronted with her camera *What's On Your Mind?* (figure 6.19).

331

Though belated, her goal is to start a conversation that failed to take place when the camera originally stood between them. The power of this query, however, lies in the fact that once she has addressed it to the photographed woman and placed the question on the surface in which the woman is embedded, it acquires an independent existence. With only a slight change of intonation, this shift emphasizes that the reflexive appeal in the second person can be directed at Heiman herself, as if she might be asked, "And you, what was on *your* mind?" What was she thinking when she photographed them as she did — from afar, and in most cases without eye contact, so as to ensure that they wouldn't notice her or so they wouldn't wrap themselves around anything other than what she identified in them — something that appears with the passing of time as a kind of shared destiny written in the faces of these women.

These photographs were taken at different times, under disparate circumstances, and it is only Heiman's belated act of viewing that groups them together in a series that enables the spectator to reconstruct the stance Heiman took when confronting the photographed women. It is only from this new series that the spectator sees those points when she observed the women in their isolation, when their thoughts were wandering far from where they were. No one, it seems, shows a bit of interest in knowing what's on their minds. Their moment in front of the camera is the moment in which their exhaustion at the end of the day is exposed, peeking out from under the aura of the evening's glamour they were forced to wear. Heiman's photographed women, under harsh lighting, are exposed to gazes, near and far, surrounding them, giving themselves over to the roles constructed for them while simultaneously remaining detached from such positions, caught by the screen that they have erected between themselves and those who surround them. Heiman's return to arenas where she had previously worked as a photographer and her interventions into arenas photographed by others — allowing her to look in a way that suspends the photographer from his or her job, effectively rearranging the visible and underscoring what could not be seen — enables her to invite the characters who were there, at the front of the stage or behind it, to participate in reconfiguring the field of vision that has been woven around them.

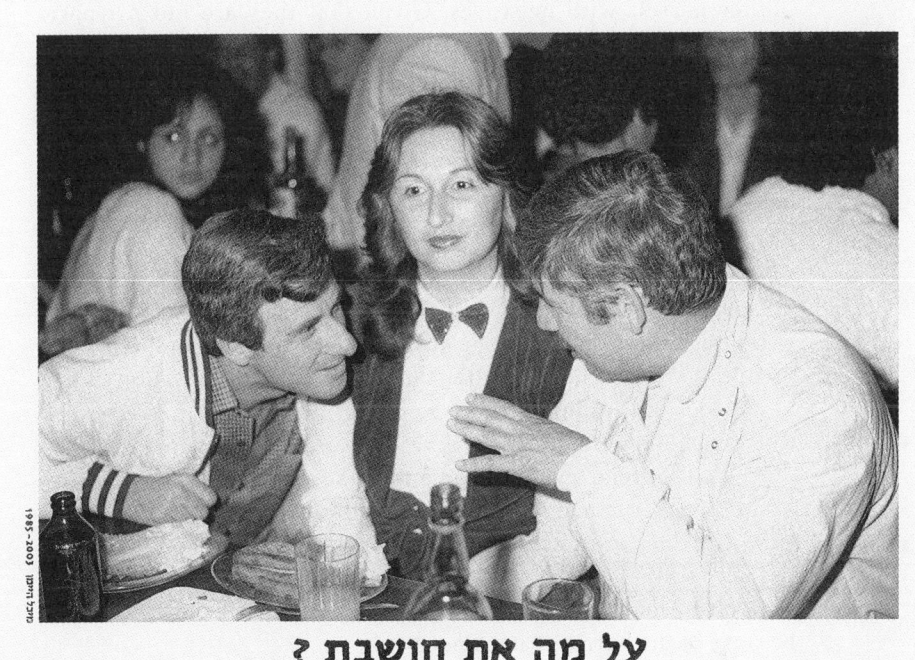

על מה את חושבת ?

Figure 6.19. Michal Heiman, *What's on Your Mind? #4*, chromogenic print, 65 x 90 cm, 1985–2003.

The series of works that she produced in the course of the second intifada is based entirely on looking at press photographs as they appear in the newspaper.[43] *Her* viewing of a disaster is always mediated by photographs. The photographs, appropriated and made her own, are scanned from prints. She takes only photos that have been already printed on photographic paper or newsprint. She doesn't bother herself with negatives. Given that they are not *her* photographs, she has no access to the negatives. When Heiman works with photographs that have already had an existence in the world — in a newspaper, family album, or archive — she uses them in relation to such contexts and in relation to the gazes and interpretations that have already encountered them. By turning the photographs of other photographers, which appeared under their own names in the press, into *her* photographs, Heiman shows that the work of editing is an essential part of photography, as well as the way in which the spectator encounters it. The scanning of photographs from the newspaper raises questions concerning the demarcation and framing that would seem to have lost meaning after the photograph's publication in the newspaper. By scanning the photograph, removing it from its surroundings, and reframing what is visible in it, Heiman employs procedures that suspend any hope of a direct gaze. Serving as an apparatus of mediation, Heiman's work protects the — her — gaze at the same time as it does so to what is included and not included in the image. In the conditions of the verge of catastrophe, many of the images are difficult to look at, not necessarily because of what they show, but because of the horror that cannot be shown.

As mentioned above, Heiman's series *Blood Test* is composed of blood samples from photographs of the wounded that appeared in the press. These are troubling photographs, showing the bodies of people with torn limbs, bleeding profusely. Heiman gathered the photographs of the wounded into a series, looking at them through the mechanical gaze of a computer, reframing the blood, the source of the blood, and the body with its gaping wounds until it disappears behind the bloodstain that now fills the entire frame. The slow zoom into the bleeding body demonstrates the impossibility of seeing the horror. The deeper the gaze seeks to penetrate, the more blotted and distorted it becomes — the poetics of the blood stain. Heiman's series demonstrates that the obligation to look at the wound does not necessarily mean one must penetrate deep into the heart of the horror, as if this could be revealed to the gaze, but means one must become its addressee, restoring it as a referent of the gaze, producing its meaning as injury and opening the possibility of its continual address.

A voice rings out from the ambush, sounding the order: "Raise your shirts!" (See figures 6.20 through 6.23.) Cocked rifles emerge from the bushes, steadied by determined hands, bodies dressed in uniforms with metal accessories, all of which join together to form an operational force. This force confronts ten youths, giving them the order to disrobe. Before the youths encountered this military voice, which barks commands in broken Arabic, they had been traveling home after a day of peddling small goods, a day that began with the salvaging of items from the garbage dump to sell on the main street of Um al Fahem, which borders on their village. Early in the morning, they snuck across the border, and now, just as they are about to repeat the offense in order to return home, their secret is exposed. The voice doesn't scare them, but this does not mean they can disobey the command. In resignation they stop, dropping plastic bags full of the day's pickings, and in accordance with the belligerent voice that calls them, they organize themselves into an attentive bloc. "It's routine, because everyone immediately understood the procedure," says the photographer Miki Kratsman. "They all lifted up their shirts as one. And then there's the children's smile, which I can't know if it's the outcome of embarrassment, nerves, or who knows what."[44]

The photograph is silent. Not only here, not only this time. It is always silent, unable to share with the spectator the voice commanding the children. The traces of the voice can be recreated only from the posture of their bodies. Kratsman, the photographer, has removed the source of the voice from view, leaving the soldiers outside the frame. We can than ask, "Where are the soldiers?" as David Reeb has, which serves as the title of a series of paintings he rendered from Kratsman's photographs. "I wanted to remove it from the context of an event and put it in the context of routine," Kratsman says. "When there's a soldier and rifle it's already an event. The

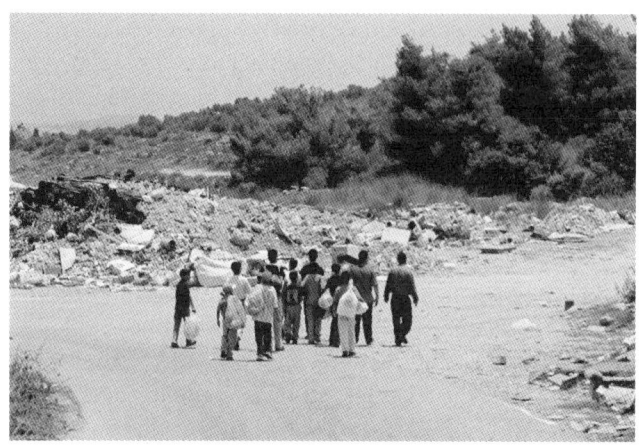

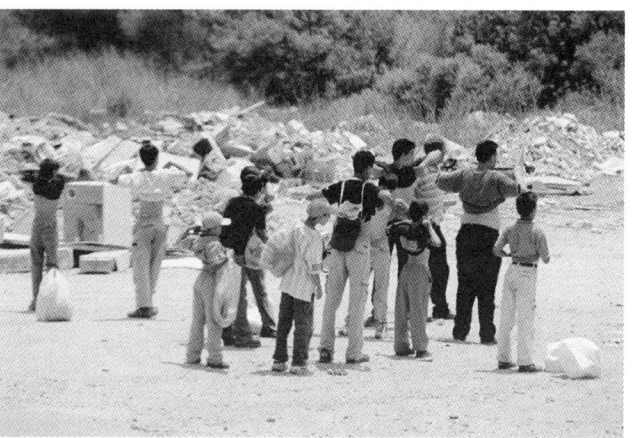

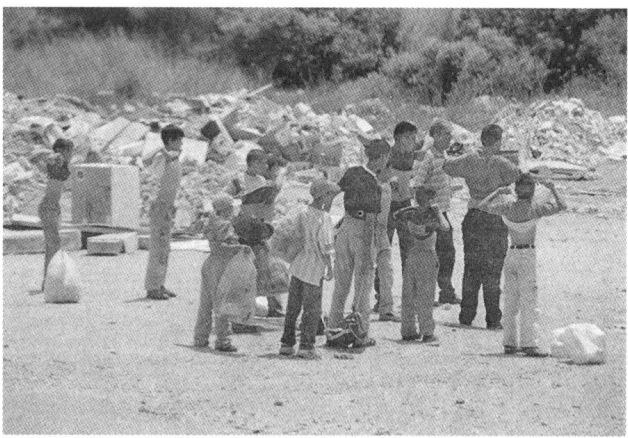

Figures 6.20–6.22. Miki Kratsman, *Rubbish Dump*, Um El Fahem, 2003.

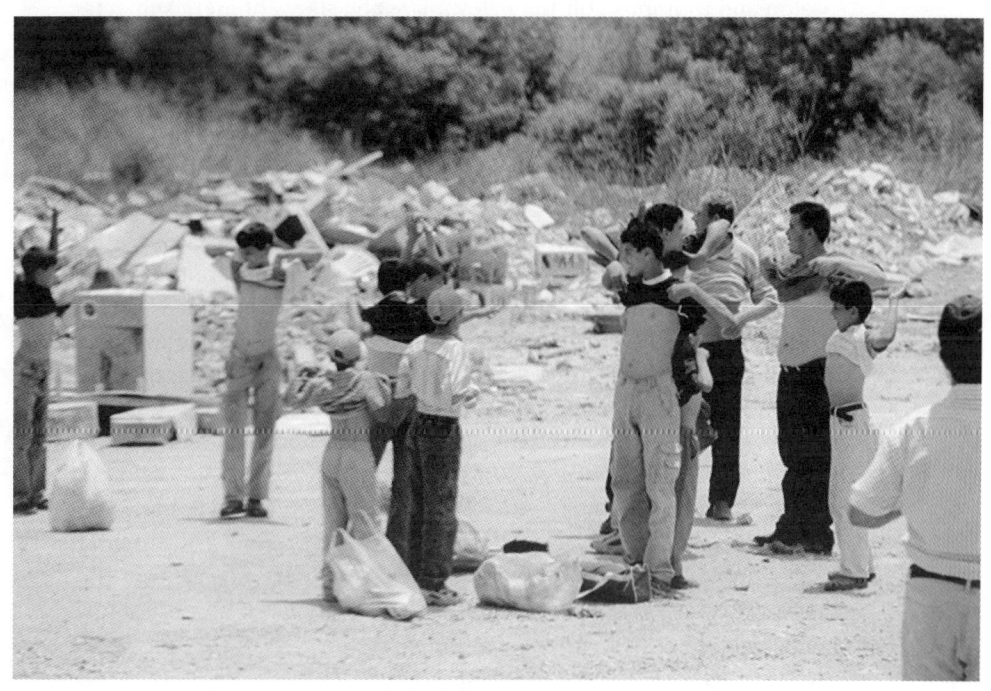

Figure 6.23. Miki Kratsman, *Rubbish Dump*, Um El Fahem, 2003.

moment he's gone, a suspension arises until you realize what the game is here."[45]

The soldiers are absent, yet they nevertheless establish the tone of the photograph. They're trying to take charge of the boys; they're losing their breath; their presence threatens to suffocate the field of vision and to impose on the Palestinians the status of mere subjects. All of this occurs despite the lack of an exceptional event. It's all purely routine, an event made into routine. The photographer shot a roll and a half of film, nearly fifty pictures, that attempt to grasp this nonevent: a thin cloud of dust rising from the encounter between soldiers in uniform and boys in gaudy shirts, on the fringes of the garbage dump, near the remains of an old washing machine and other random parts of derelict objects. In one frame, however, the photographer left the soldiers outside the frame. This photograph is not silent. It utters a laugh, capturing the mischievous voices of the youths who, having no choice, obey the orders while maintaining a distance between themselves and the authorities, a distance that the soldiers are trying to eliminate.

Wordlessly, punctuated by giggles, in their bodies' imperceptible movements, the youths' upright posture directed at the soldiers begins to break down, eventually breaking down the marching formation they were ordered to assume. In gazing back and forth at three photographs — the first, in which the youths alertly face the soldiers; the second, where the formation falls apart; and the third, in which they fool around among themselves — it is possible to reconstruct this process of disintegration. We can assume it began with the boy in the dark blue shirt on the extreme left. He managed to roll up his shirt over his chest, keeping it there even after letting it go. As he was apparently discovering the marvel of his shirt resisting gravity, raising his arms in the air and calling out, imitating the soldiers' tone, "Raise your arms!" The youth in front of him turned to look, instantly forgetting the soldiers' command, pulled away by his friend's instruction, resting his gaze on his friend's body and being seized by laughter, fascinated by the trick. His friend's docile shirt entices him to try his own luck, and in the meantime, the boy who's dropped the blue pouch from his shoulder joins the game of looks and gestures. The three of them have become engrossed in their own affairs. They practice pulling in their bellies and sticking them out, raising their arms and stooping their shoulders, gazing at their friend's bodily control. The laughter overtakes them, making them forget the original reason for raising their shirts, going on to imitate the soldiers and each other, tossing commands into the air. These commands are suspended, defused of their malice, falling back down — as in a children's game — on the youths' exposed bodies, who are now enjoying the warm caress of the spring sun.

The Hague Convention (1907) and the Fourth Geneva Convention (1949), which address the notion of occupation, unequivocally state that occupation refers to territory and by extension to the territory's inhabitants: "a territory is considered occupied when it is de facto under the authority of the hostile army" (paragraph 42). The occupation of inhabited territory, then, is always temporary, not only because regulations point to the horizon of its conclusion — "when peace shall be made" — but on account of the existence of a population in such a territory, on account of which it cannot be occupied not only legally, but also ontologically. "It is forbidden," says paragraph 45, "to force the inhabitants of the occupied territory to swear allegiance to the hostile ruling power." A state of occupation, then, is a situation in which the rule of a territory is imposed on the inhabitants by means of military force, turning the occupants into subjects, but not citizens.

The Israeli regime has not only failed to acknowledge the Palestinians as its citizens and thus has turned them into subjects, but has branded and continues to try to brand this status into their consciousness in every possible way. The Palestinians' ever-present refusal to adopt this imposed consciousness, as a subject of occupation, is at the same time their refusal to recognize Israel as a legitimate sovereign. With the few resources at their disposal — the unceasing vitality with which they deal with the occupier — the photographed Palestinians expose this ongoing refutation of the fanatical military effort to achieve what is actually impossible, the forceful occupation of their consciousnesses. The photographer, who has left the soldiers out of the frame, joins in the Palestinians' efforts, allowing them to resist by means of photography.

However, there is a gap between the supply of images and the

339

singular gaze motivated by the obligation to look. Michal Heiman told me in a conversation:

> I receive the *Ha'aretz* newspaper every day and, on my initial perusal, extract what interests me and put it aside. I don't always necessarily know why I keep this or that page. There are periods in which I don't even leaf through the newspaper, I just keep it complete. In the short periods when I'm away from Israel, I ask others to buy me a newspaper. On days after dramatic events, I make sure to have other daily newspapers besides *Ha'aretz*. Very often, the pages I've kept drown in the chaos of the studio. Very often, I understand in hindsight why I've kept something. [There are] newspapers that I didn't classify immediately and kept in large boxes. I usually do the classifying myself. There was a time when someone else used to help me. I would give them exact instructions what to look for: images where one can see shut eyes, smoke, ropes cordoning off arenas, a presence of a photographer taking pictures in the arena of disaster, bloodstains, baby carriages, someone running and carrying someone else in his arms, cars that have been damaged, an outline map of a certain area alongside a photograph of a damaged car, wounded animals, search dogs participating in the scenes, people with yellow boots (sterilization of the scene), fences, demolished houses, sofas, photographs in which there is entry into the house itself, rooms that look like a psychoanalyst's clinic, places that have interesting pictures on the walls, buildings with holes in the walls.[46]

The newspaper contains more than the eye is capable of seeing. This is true not only of the random eye of a spectator, but of the eye that has taken up the task of looking in a systematic manner — of watching photographs.[47] Heiman organizes this task by breaking it up into distinct actions that are not necessarily performed in an unbroken sequence. For her, the newspaper is not a mere vehicle of information, but a precious object, a valuation to which she intimately testifies. It arrives on the door every day, bringing material she feels it is her duty to address, even if she is unable to do so at the moment it appears. Thus, the images are neutralized, detached from the immediate context of the news, becoming visual testimony to psychic and political mechanisms relating to photographed persons:

"A good part of the classifying categories is set from the beginning, with some of them following my feeling that there is something obsessive about their appearance in the newspaper. Afterward, I go over the materials again and keep only a small part of it."[48] What became clear from Heiman's description is the need to spatialize the gaze through the dividing up of the mass of images and distributing it in portions among different viewpoints and moments of the gaze.

The Decentralization of the Gaze: Watching

However, spatializing the gaze, making it more efficient under the conditions that pertain on the verge of catastrophe, conditions that produce images of horror every day, is not sufficient explanation for understanding this mode of spectatorship. The element common to the various procedures employed by Heiman in preparation for seeing what is in the newspaper is suspension. Purchasing the newspaper doesn't necessarily lead to contemplation; flipping through it doesn't ensure there will be any insight; turning to an item in the archive doesn't immediately rationalize what is seen. The classification is not final, and the gaze is not necessarily hers. The procedures of collecting, classifying, cataloguing, numbering, archiving, filing and removing from the file, scanning, and stamping — these are activities that generally proceed directly from gazing at the photograph or from the moment when what is visible in the photograph becomes clear.

Watching photographs taken on the verge of catastrophe is a gesture that should take place in public. It transcends the private acknowledgment of horror. Whenever it is witnessed, horror is never fully visible to the eye. A citizen can only hope to produce public emergency claims from what is visible. In her *Tests*, Heiman already was making use of assistants and museum spectators in order to look at the photograph and speak what it reveals (see figure 7.9). The camera, followed by the computer, has participated in the de-centralization of the gaze, as well as in its spatialization, effectively suspending the conditions for a direct encounter by distancing and alienating the image. Looking at photographs, Heiman simultaneously seeks to observe the photographer's instrumental gaze while breaking free from it by applying editing techniques to digital reproductions. Enlarging and reframing the visible in an image already distanced from the event makes it possible to challenge the assumption of a stable, two-dimensional image's unified field of vision, opening up new perspectives. Her reorganization of the visible plane enables her to suspend the act of looking, putting distance between herself and the photographer's viewpoint, which is frequently imposed on the spectator.

Whether instinctive or intentional, this twofold suspension is a reaction to conditions in which there is a real threat to the civilian gaze. This intervention, as in slow motion, makes it possible to see the way in which the citizen, without this suspension, is close to losing her civilian skills, threatened to be captured by the logic of the occupation, coerced into the field of vision it organizes, without being able to see reflexively other possibilities. Heiman's move to decentralize the gaze marks a return to the photograph as a singular point from which all possibilities are opened, possibilities that are generally suspended or quickly hidden from view by the "correct" meaning of the photograph, which tempts one into choosing a single, stabile significance, typically the least controversial. In this sense, the suspension of the act of looking doesn't remove the photograph from the gaze, but suspends the gaze's hold, demanding that the fleeting gesture of seeing, which disappears as soon as the object is identified, be replaced by the gesture of watching, which occurs over an extended duration.

Watching something as a spectator means fixing the gaze for a period of time in order to allow the visible to unfold, like a picture in motion. Watching as a spectator means thoroughly investigating the visible phenomenon: watching it like a movie, where picture after picture disappears while the eye stays focused on the fixed frame and follows the show. In the case of stills, the gesture of spectatorship requires a special intention from the spectator who seeks to reconstruct the situation of the act of photography from the surface of the photograph. This motion does not belong to what is seen, as in a movie, but to the spectator. On the one hand, it occurs in the same fashion, frame after frame, before her eyes. But on the other hand, watching still frames is quite different, more passive. It has duration, even though the photograph remains motionless.

"The public has the right to know," as is often demanded, is a mistaken and misleading formulation of the civilian stakes of the gaze. It predicates the civilian stakes on the right to see, that is, to exhaust the object with the gaze. On its own, however, the right to see currently lacks any civilian logic. Demanding that the right to see be respected assumes that someone — an individual or organization, private or governmental — is hiding images whose disclosure will expose the truth that is being concealed from the public. But with the contemporary conditions being such that injury to others is largely visible, the problem is not so often the concealment of objects from the gaze, but the constant threat to the public's civilian capacity to see as spectators.[49]

For example, in the wake of the publication of several dozen photographs from the Abu Ghraib prison, pressure mounted against the American administration to release all eighteen hundred photographs in its possession. Releasing the photographs from the control of the American administration is important, but the fundamental issue is not the call to release another several hundred photographs, but in what we can see as spectators not looking at, but watching the several dozen already published, in addition to the hundreds of images of the American occupation of Iraq and Afghanistan, and the public has yet to carry out this civilian duty. In most cases, the struggle over the right to see disavows the duty to behave as spectators and by this spectatorship to criticize governmental power, reflect on its actions, and impose constraints. The duty to watch as spectators is at the same time both the duty to resist injury to others who are governed and the duty to restore the civilian skill of spectatorship: to be an addressee of this injury, to produce its meaning as injury, and to continue to address it.

Since the beginning of the second intifada, Heiman has looked at thousands of photographs appearing in the newspaper, torn from their printed existence, turning dozens of them into digital files, and recreating their status through computer alterations, as images in her archive. One from her series is based on photographs of demolished Palestinian houses throughout the West Bank. These are rather chilling photographs that show the gutted remains of houses with utterly destroyed walls, reduced to ruins. The occupants remain, wandering around inside the remnants in a daze. The intifada has made newspaper readers penetrate, with their gazes, into exposed houses that peer out at them from underneath newspaper headlines. The spectator finds herself in the position of an uninvited guest looking into the home of a stranger. In this clumsy manner, to a spectator looking on the loss and damage suffered by the person who owned the home, which was suddenly and violently destroyed, she and the remains of her home are now exposed to all eyes. The house is subsequently violated by the gazes of diverse groups of spectators, more or less distanced from the actual invaders — acquaintances from the adjacent neighborhood, photographers, reporters, and newspaper readers. The photographs depict multiple situations, from those taken at the time of the military operation, when the presence of the invading military force appears in the frame, to those after the fact, which establishes the photographic record of the military operation's effects, when the gutted house and broken walls allow the gaze to penetrate inside, recording the private space and the evicted occupants through the use of force, that is, without knocking on the door.

In some cases, the photographer's identity is unknown, whereas in others, at least the identity of the agency for which he worked can be determined. In the first type of photograph, his specific identity is secondary to the essential position he has assumed — that of a photographer penetrating into a space that is not his, thus becoming part of the military force that violates a private border. Regarding these photographs, the force's proximity to the lens allows us to assume they were not taken by one of the casualties, whose minimal rights, including the right to photograph and record the damage that has been done to them, have all suddenly been abolished.

Over the course of the intifada, several photographs have appeared in the newspapers from which cooperation between the army and the photographers can be inferred. This is not simply one or two isolated incidents (see figure 9.1). The series of images that Heiman has created out of photographs of destroyed houses under the title *Photo Rape* is, in a certain sense, indifferent to this distinction. Regardless of the specific identity of the photographer or the specific circumstances of the scene, the photo rape of domestic space, its forced exposure to an external eye, is the moment to which Heiman seeks to direct the spectator's gaze. Even if motivated by a desire to unrelentingly question the photographer about his presence at the scene, by enlarging these images to gigantic proportions (the standard size of a professional photographer's back drop) and hanging them from the ceiling to the floor in a series, as a kind of updated catalog of the occupation's injustices, Heiman aims at the spectator, refusing to free her of bearing witness to the act of photographing.

Photo Rape

And that act is a violent one. As we have already seen, the civil contract of photography was established on the basis of an agreement to conquer the world through pictures. This agreement implies that everyone participates in conquering the world through pictures, at the same time being conquered by them. Nobody is left outside the frame. These are not symmetrical relations, but dynamic relations in which there is no stable, external point of view. Both the spectator and the photographed person can limit their interactions with photography. They can even make themselves believe that they are not participants in the game. But this delusion has no basis in reality. The world cannot be wiped clean of photography, nor can social relations evade it. This delusion is unsustainable for the press photographer, who in the framework of his job must regularly produce more and more photographs, and photographs that are images of interest to the public.

> Raising the camera is a very violent action. When the camera is hanging from your neck or shoulder, it's like in a Hitchcock movie — soon we'll be using the gun. That is how you obtain wordless assent from whomever you're photographing. The act of raising the camera is very violent, and every time, I want to skip over it again. It's of great importance. Here I am exposing you; here I am looking at you. When you ride a bus, you catch the gaze of someone looking at you. There are few who have the courage to look anyway. Here I'm like someone inside a bus, and I'm telling the people I won't lower my gaze. And it's through the camera as well, so it's much easier.[50]

345

The wordless consent that Kratsman speaks of cannot be understood as merely the photographer imposing what he wishes onto the photographed person, but as the reinscription of the consent already given to the framework of the civil contract of photography. In facing the camera, there is someone who wants to be photographed, who wishes to speak, but there may also be someone who wants to hide, though she also has something to state for the public record, but she wishes to do so under her own control, rather than through the eye of the photographer. The arena of photographing is actually an arena of disclosed and undisclosed power relations that do not always act in anticipated directions or necessarily as a function of the "real" power relations among the protagonists. Despite the fact that the photographer is the one holding the camera or the soldier is the one supervising the situation with his rifle, neither are necessarily able to conquer the situation or fully control it from their single viewpoint.

In a photograph that appeared in a weekend edition of *Ha'aretz* (April 19, 2002), two Palestinian women and a little girl are seen sitting in what had been the living room of their home. The picture was accompanied by the caption: "A.P. photograph." Michal Heiman scanned the photograph as it appeared in the context of the newspaper (above the title of an article by Amira Hess, "War over the Home") and imprinted three different stamps on its surface (figures 6.24 and 6.25). The stamp "PHOTOGRAPHER UNKNOWN" (which she has used for over a decade), positioned at the bottom of the photograph, leaves one ill at ease. In this specific use, it cannot be interpreted as a reference to the omission of the photographer's name from the printed photograph or seen as a monument to the unknown photographer. The photographer was in fact there — I am facing the photograph he made. Standing opposite such a shimmering, chilling photograph, is there any significance to the fact that he is unknown, that his name has not been recorded? The fact that he's a photographer working for a foreign news agency may already be more significant than his specific identity. The newspaper's decision to publish an Associated Press photograph already indicates the absence of another photographer in the field — the Israeli photographer, or more accurately, the photographer who is occupying the position of an Israeli photographer sent by Israeli newspapers.[51] The presence of the latter photographer is felt less and less in the areas of conflict between Israel and Palestine, and his place is being taken over by the photographers of foreign agencies. He is no longer allowed to roam freely through the territories as he once did. Now he is permitted access only to specific destinations that have been coordinated in advance.[52]

A glance at the front pages of *Ha'aretz* from 2002, the same year in which this photograph was taken, reveals that photographs such as those of Hamas cofounder Ahmed Yassin's attempted assassination in an Israeli Air Force bombing in Gaza or those of demonstrations against the Israeli occupation in Ramallah all bear the signature of Reuters or the Associated Press, whereas "official" photographs — such as the finance minister writing "improved standard of living" on a blackboard, the judges of Israel's Supreme Court studying the Or Commission report on the killings by Israeli police during the intifada in 2000, or policemen practicing the dispersal of unruly demonstrations "by nonlethal means" — bear the signature of Israeli photographers. Without attempting to reconstruct all the conditions that are responsible for the production of these photographs, this systematically repeated division shows us that the Israeli photographer and the "foreign photographer" (who may also be an Israeli citizen) are not given the same degree of freedom of movement.

The general category — "A.P." — already sheds some light on the photographer's unknown identity. The newspaper reader will know that he is foreign, working for a global photo agency that supplies images from around the world. The reader may even pay attention to the fact that this photographer can move around the Occupied Territories with greater ease than his Israeli counterpart. Hidden behind what can be interpreted as his freedom of movement, however, is often a sad reality. A large number of these photographers are local Palestinians whose presence in the field may only slightly help them find employment, which has become progressively more difficult to obtain over the course of the second intifada, given the obstacles that the occupation authorities ceaselessly put in their way: delays in granting travel permits and in renewing their press credentials, as well as direct injury to them and their equipment.[53] The army

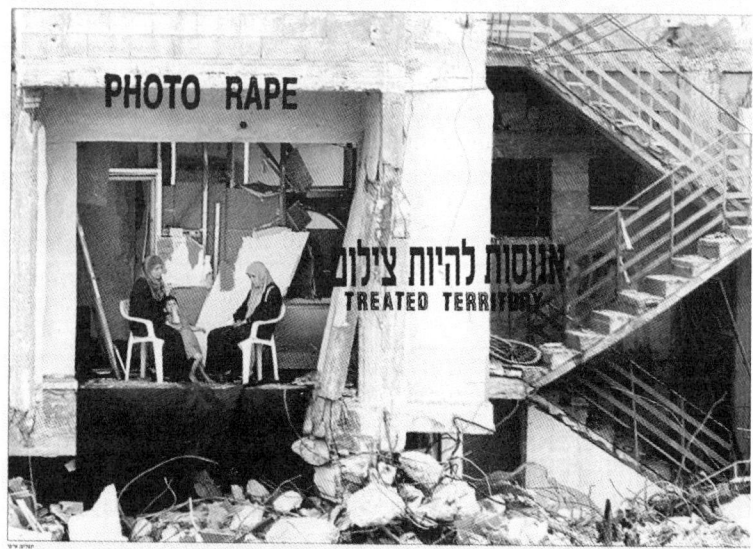

Figure 6.24. Michal Heiman, *Attacks on Linking #3 – Photo Rape – War over the House (AP, Photographer Unknown, Ha'aretz, April 4, 2001, Jenin refugee camp)*, color print mounted on canvas, 480 x 270 cm, 2001.

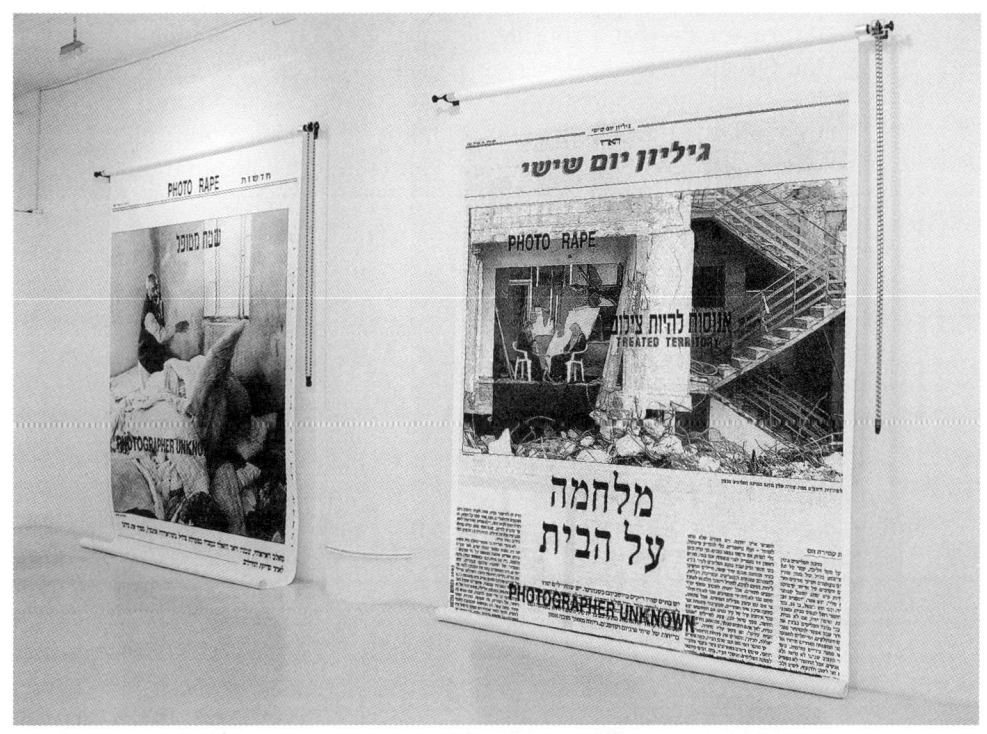

Figure 6.25. Michal Heiman, *Attacks on Linking #1 & #3 – Photo Rape*, 2001, installation view, 2 color prints mounted on canvas, 480 x 272 cm each, Artists House, Tel-Aviv, 2003.

accuses them of biased reporting and therefore feels free to sabotage their work. The newspaper editors need their daily merchandise, and covering up the photographer's identity, turning the Palestinian into a "foreign agency photographer," helps them obtain and supply it to the market. Thus they are able to avoid explicitly admitting, in print — in what would get them condemned as providing biased information — that a considerable part of their photographs from the Occupied Territories were actually taken by Palestinians. This known-unknown identity of the Associated Press or Reuters photographer is thus a local-global identity on which a multitude of seemingly opposed interests and contradictory collaborations are inscribed.

But if we pass from the question of the photographer's official identity to the photographic situation and the traces of identity remaining in the photograph, we will again see that the photographer is indeed unknown, at least to the photographed women. Sitting slumped in their chairs, the women look sullen and withdrawn. Their gazes are lowered, and the photographer — no matter where we imagine he stood — was not visible to their eyes, remaining unknown. Except for the little girl, who may have encountered the photographer with her eyes looking off into the distance, the women and the photographer are placed in two separate spaces. In this photograph, as in many others of its kind, "PHOTOGRAPHER UNKNOWN" does not denote someone whose identity is unknown, but someone whose presence is unknown, someone invisible to the eyes of the objects he is photographing. He has not been revealed to them, just as he has not shown himself to them.

The pile of ruins in front of the house indicates that the photographer was standing relatively far away from where the women were sitting. It is difficult to find traces of agreement or cooperation between the photographer and the photographed women in the photograph. Rather, what is presented in the photograph is the unbridgeable gap between the photographer's remoteness, his retreat into the background, and the magnified presence of the photographed women, prominent in the foreground of the photograph, framed within the façade of their demolished home. Above the stamp "PHOTOGRAPHER UNKNOWN," Heiman has imprinted another two stamps on the photograph — "FORCED-RAPED INTO BEING PHOTO-GRAPHED" in Hebrew, and "PHOTO RAPE" in English.[54] The Hebrew refers to the photographed women in that they have been forced to submit to being photographed, and the English refers to the element of rape in the act of photographing. Either way, Heiman depicts the photograph as an invasion, as a photograph illicitly captured by use of force, given that even if the photographed women found themselves consenting, the conditions in which this consent was obtained are such that their civilian autonomy has been breeched, and even consent is a form of coercion. An act of rape has been committed "here." But, unequivocally, this "here" is not a single, distinct place. The "here" of the photograph is always many, a simultaneous multiplication of several spaces, each of which is organized differently. At the very least, we can identify four spaces that are heterogeneous to one another: the space of the photographed, the space of photographing (constituted at the moment the photographer enters the scene), the space of the photograph itself (represented on the photographic paper), and the space of spectatorship (constituted at the moment the spectator enters the scene). Seeking to examine the invasion, one cannot ignore this multiplicity of spaces.

The agreement in principle between the photographer and photographed person that I have discussed as being anchored in the civil contract of photography takes on different qualities, depending on the different spaces and relations that are presented, giving rise to rules and norms that are constantly updated as a result of the diverse uses of photography and the local negotiations between public and private groups and institutions.[55] These changes are only occasionally given a legal or political ground, but usually become established norms. The contract connects citizens who are willing to be made into a photograph and those who are capable of turning someone else into a photograph. In the case of citizens, this agreement is part of their citizenship and is thus protected — its existence is not an object of debate or discussion. It needs to be opened up to discussion only when the photographic situation occurs in a disaster area, where the photographed are not citizens or have suffered the loss of their citizen status as a result of the catastrophe that struck them.[56] In this kind of situation, it is no longer possible to speak in the same

way about a civil contract that links the photographer and photographed. Citizenship is typically a shield that protects on the basis
of consent and the possibility of exercising it. The photographed in a
disaster area is missing this shield, along with the ability to revive the
hypothetical agreement between her or him and the photographer.

The tradition of photographs from disaster areas, beginning from
the time photography appeared, regularly supplies photographs of
victims. These have been captured by a photographer who has exercised his citizenship and his duty toward the civil contract of photography by photographing the noncitizen, determined to bring this
photograph to the attention of the world.[57] In most cases, the photographed is no more than a ghost in whose name photographs are
taken, on whose behalf photographs are looked at, and for whose
sake they are distributed. Consciously or unconsciously, the photographer turns himself into a part of the forces that make the photographed person a ghost. From the advent of photography up to the
present, the photographer's ethics in facing the victim have remained
virtually unchanged — the duty is to photograph above all else.[58]

The A.P. photographer's penetration into the private space of the
photographed in the photograph of the women in their demolished
home multiplies the violence that destroyed their house, tearing
away its front wall and exposing them to the gazes of pedestrians. It
is important to remember, however, that the women's rape into
being photographed occurred prior to the photographer arriving at
the scene of crime. The photographer exacerbates the effects of the
exposure, fixing it to paper, but his act is simply one more gaze
showing others who are not there at the site of the event what his
eyes have seen. To us, the spectators, he makes the chilling sight of
penetration into the private space available, providing access to the
invasion and violation of intimacy that is perpetrated by the occupation. He offers us this scene from the position of a spectator, outside
the frame — a privileged spectator with a camera in his hand — behaving as if he were fulfilling his duty, giving the public what it is supposed to take an interest in seeing.

The photograph can serve as a critical *énoncé*, equal to stating
"Look what they did to the Palestinians," just as it can serve as an
énoncé justifying government policy, as in, "See? They got what they

deserved" — that is, punishment for their actions or those of their countrymen. The photographer may momentarily be closer to one of these positions and even attempt its expression in the photograph, but his mission will always include — if not from the very beginning — the professional injunction formulated in universal terms as the duty to show.[59] The photograph that he has issued, on account of one motive or another, is generally channeled into the economy of the hit parade of images of horror. In this framework, the photographer's position serves only a small and even at times a marginal role.

On December 6, 2001, on the front page of *Ha'aretz*, a photograph appeared of a half-naked Palestinian walking with his arms raised toward an Israeli armored personnel carrier (figure 6.26). Policemen of "the special antiterror unit" are seen sitting behind sandbags with helmets on their heads and rifles pointing at the Palestinian. Although the Reuters photographer captured only one Palestinian with his camera, there had been six Palestinians who underwent the humiliating ritual, according to the report by journalists Amira Hess and Amos Harel, a procedure that, according to the Israel Defense Forces (IDF), was carried out in order to allow the policemen to check whether the Palestinians had any explosives strapped to their bodies.

A photograph printed on the newspaper's front page generally signals its importance in relation to the day's news. At least two opposing possibilities are offered to the newspaper reader's gaze: either viewing the scene as the demonstration of the harsh and humiliating procedures to which the IDF subjects the Palestinians, making them walk naked in front of soldiers, or, alternatively, thinking that in these days of terrible attacks and with the growing sense of insecurity among the country's citizens, we can now witness how hard the army is trying to serve the land, penetrating to the Palestinians' very bodies in order to insure the citizens' safety and protect them from suicide bombers. In either case, the Palestinian in the photograph, who has been photographed such that he can easily be recognized by his own people, at the same time has turned into a ghost for the newspaper's Israeli-Jewish readers, coming to represent the abstract figure of "the Palestinian." The Palestinian is abandoned, with his body being imprinted with the lesson: "See, such and such is being done to a Palestinian who. . . ."

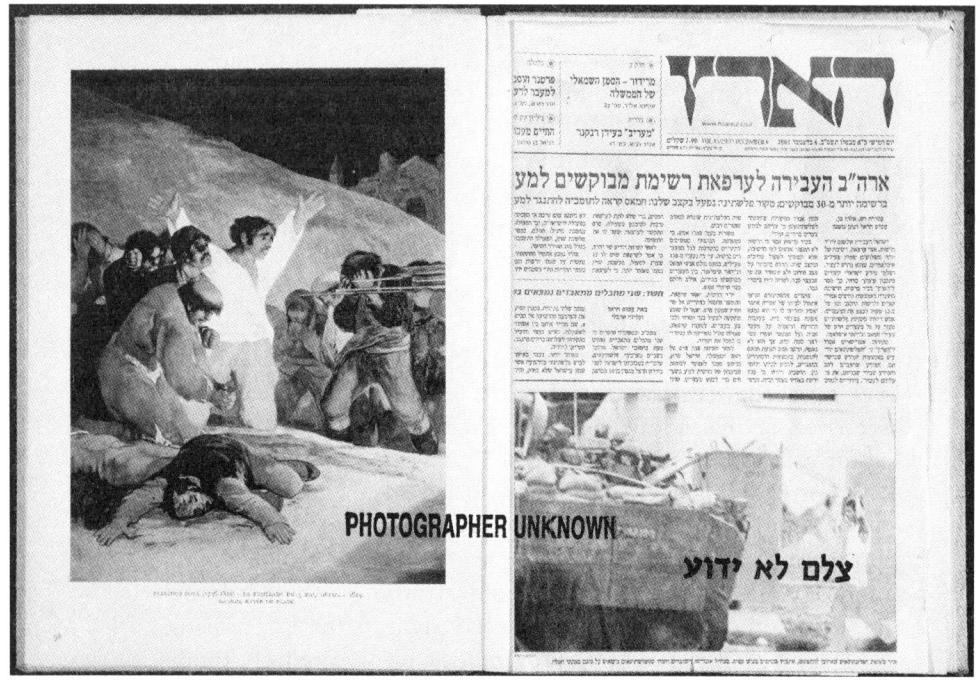

Figure 6.26. Michal Heiman, *May 3, 1814 – December 6, 2001 (Francisco Goya –1814, Photographer Unknown – 2001)*, color print, 120 x 176 cm, 2002. (Please see Color Plates.)

If we look a little while longer at the photograph, not as an icon with a decipherable message, but as something to be watched, we see a concrete Palestinian, easily identifiable even if his name is unknown. Before our gaze stands a noncitizen who can be arrested at any time. With a megaphone and the barrel of a rifle, it is possible to force him to undress and expose himself to the whims of those who have detained him. When presented as an icon, without his own story, he is raped into being only a photograph. He is raped into being someone who can continually be humiliated by the gaze, his naked body captured by the photograph, fixing him as someone who strips on command. Seen from this angle, the publication of this photograph on the newspaper's front page magnifies the ritual of humiliation he undergoes at the checkpoint. The position of spectatorship offered to the one looking at the photograph, suspended on the front page without the voice of the photographed, is that of the soldier in the armored personnel carrier. This provocation compels the gaze to act violently, be invasive, humiliating, and degrading toward the helplessness of the photographed.

He is a Reuters photographer. Nothing in the photograph makes it certain whether he has been given authorization by the army to see and to show or is someone from the outside casting a voyeuristic gaze on the scene. Something exceptional was occurring in front of his eyes, and he felt that it was his professional duty to photograph it. A photographer is unable *not* to record such an event. Gathering testimonies is his obligation, even if they strike him as disturbing or meaningless. Completing the work is not his duty.

This is the ontology of photography — it always includes more than what one wants it to contain. The photographer is responsible for photography, and his act is a necessary, though small link in the chain of acts responsible for fulfilling the injunction "to watch" or "to show." The chain is constituted by several people, performing different functions, and their concerns cannot be predicated on one another. Not every photograph that has to be taken has to be shown. Not every photograph can be separated from its context, without explanation or any public disclosure of the photographed person's "side of the story." That is, not every photograph can be transformed into an illustration used by the editors to maintain or to build interest

355

in their newspaper. The duty to photograph derives from the nature of the event revealed to the photographer's eyes. The perpetration of violence, which is the perpetration of injury, is an event that places an obligation on the photographer. Even if at the time of the event she does not have all the tools at her disposal to judge the event, the fact of the injury alone obligates her to create testimony. This is an immediate duty, which typically leaves no room for personal considerations. It derives from the congruence between the nature of photography as a medium that captures a moment and the transitory nature of the event.

Everything That Happens in the Occupied Territories Should Be Headline News

The photograph of the Palestinian being humiliated by the soldiers in the armored personnel carrier is one example of the duty to photograph, but it is at the same time an excellent example of the distance between this duty and the duty to show — two distinct duties that are often mistakenly conflated. The editing process, which occurs through a series of stages, does not have the same quality of immediacy as the photographic act, nor can it be reduced to only the publication of the photograph. Performing a few technical manipulations allows the editor not only to show the photograph, but to show responsibility toward the photographed: highlighting, disguising, framing, sectioning, obscuring, or exposing the identity of the photographed, captioning and clarifying, recreating the details of the event, turning it into an object of research, and other tasks to continue to reflect on what is seen. On its own, the photograph is incapable of conveying the event to which it attests. The photograph is thus only a point of departure for the reading carried out by whoever stands before it, for who decides to look and to watch. It is the spectator who transforms what is photographed, what happens, into an event.

Michal Heiman shows us one way of looking at this photograph (figure 6.26). As a condition for an extended gaze, she proposes first to clothe the Palestinian, transforming his naked body from an object of the direct gaze into a sign that scars the surface of the photograph. The apparel she has chosen for him — yellow trousers — instantly turns him into a figure resembling the condemned man of

Goya's painting. Heiman places the newspaper page on top of an open book of Goya's work, lying to the right of the page showing the central section of his *The Third of May 1808: The Execution of the Defenders of Madrid*, which Goya completed in 1814. Thus, when the Israeli occupation of Palestine and the French occupation of Spain are posited alongside each other, the Palestinian subject turns from an object of humiliation — whose humiliation has been recorded for posterity — into a condemned man voicing his grievance a moment before it's too late. From a photograph of ongoing humiliation, which the spectator perpetuates, this juxtaposition turns the photograph into a warning, one that exposes the occupation as being a kangaroo court in which unharnessed power is employed, leaving the subject exposed and unprotected. At every moment, he is liable to be condemned, on the spot, to execution, without a trial.

In the context of this photograph, however, with the stamp "PHOTOGRAPHER UNKNOWN," this situation receives another meaning, a statement of protest against the photographer who hides his identity or who has his identity hidden by others. Who is this photographer whose identity is concealed? Never mind his name — why is his identity concealed? Did the ruling apparatus go out of control that day, so that he must hide himself when using his camera? Why does the newspaper not report on the new conditions of photography? And if the photographer was welcomed by the army, providing him with services, why does the newspaper not report on their relations — with him or with the agency he works for — and the agreements signed with the army to have access to his data. The photograph was not created by itself. Paraphrasing the famous invocation by the poet Chaim Nachman Bialik, "If there is justice out there, let it appear at once!" We can claim: "If there is a photographer out there, let him appear at once!"

The caption appended to the photograph by the editorial staff gives us the army's position: "The IDF says: The policemen suspected the Palestinians of carrying IEDs [improvised explosive devices] on their bodies." This statement is supposed to turn the fact that the Palestinian was ordered to parade naked before the eyes of the stubborn soldiers into something reasonable and even necessary. Within Israel, in public places where security checks are conducted every day, citizens may be required to submit to inspection, due to the fear that one of them may be a Palestinian in disguise, but are not required to undress and certainly not forced to parade around naked until someone decides that their inspection is over. The physical inspection, which itself strikes the citizen as invasive, is conducted quickly by means of a metal detector. The nature of the inspection, which is an examination of the body, hides the existence of the body from the gaze by displacing the field of vision to the field of hearing. If the detector encounters a suspicious object or material, it will begin to beep. The inspection is routine, and most people go through it, given that it is widespread in many parts of the world, conveying to those who are examined that the system knows how uncomfortable these procedures may be, but these are the rules that apply to all. However, this is not what is conveyed by the photograph of the Palestinian who was asked to undress. The removal of the Palestinian's clothes in broad daylight, exposed to the gaze, vulnerable, and at gunpoint, is not necessary. A superfluous dimension exists within the orders that force him to undress and parade naked. Every Palestinian required to undress is not only a suspect, but an imposter, disguised as someone who is not carrying an IED.[60] As I will elaborate in Chapter Eight, the checkpoints enable the army to expose the Palestinians, one after another, until the real Palestinian body is discovered — the one that threatens to shatter the authoritarian power of the Israeli gaze by striking at its body.

Over the course of the Camp David talks and afterward, the figure of the Palestinian was reconstructed. Ehud Barak, than Israeli prime minister, forged the model, and Israel's political and military leadership has been searching for someone to fit it ever since: This Palestinian has no interest in peace, speaks only lies, and conceals his corporeal truth. Thus, the Palestinian's corporeal truth must be neutralized in the same way that his speech was neutralized at Camp David. The truth of his body must be shown to the entire world. If the army had sufficient means at its disposal, no doubt each Palestinian would be stripped of his disguise, culminating in the discovery of the real body, the one with the belt of explosives strapped to its waist. In the meantime, the army must busy itself with arbitrary inspections and representative samples.[61]

If I were to let through everyone who said they weren't feeling well, then all the Palestinians would come and say they were ill. Not long ago, someone at a checkpoint was found to have a packet of medical permits with a doctor's signature. By chance that day we spotted many people arriving with the same permit, the same signature.... [The soldier at the checkpoint] doesn't treat every Palestinian as an enemy or a suspect, but to our regret just a month ago a woman, a mother of children, was [caught] smuggling explosives in her handbag. Apparently that shows us that we even have to check people like her.[62]

Around twenty Palestinians are sitting on the ground in a close circle (figure 6.27). It is dawn, with the first light appearing. The two soldiers guarding them are wrapped in heavy coats, standing stiff and on guard, with rifles hanging from their necks. A roll of barbed wire passively assists them in their mission. The Palestinians appear to be in their thirties and forties. They are manual laborers who were simply on their way to work, but today it is their turn to be suspects. Tomorrow there will be others. They are sitting on and wrapped with the same gray woolen military blankets, and their eyes are covered with strips of flannel, their hands tied with bright plastic handcuffs. Their guilt hovers over them, but it is likely they will not be informed about what they actually did wrong. Meanwhile, until something happens, the army feels justified in leaving them as utterly defenseless prisoners of war. They are prevented from moving, seeing, or talking. At first sight, one might think that the soldiers have crowded them together in order to make it easier to control them. But on looking at the photograph, the organizing principle of their seating emerges — each of them is facing a different direction, with no one facing his neighbor. The flannel and handcuffs are not enough — they are even denied the possibility of speaking with one another. They sit there completely submissive.

A Palestinian who wants to pass through a checkpoint has to have a reason. He can't simply arrive at the Coordination and Liaison Administration office and tell the clerk sitting there, "I simply feel like going out for some fresh air."[63] The Palestinian must provide an acceptable explanation for why she wants to move from place to place. She must give precise reasons in order to procure the necessary

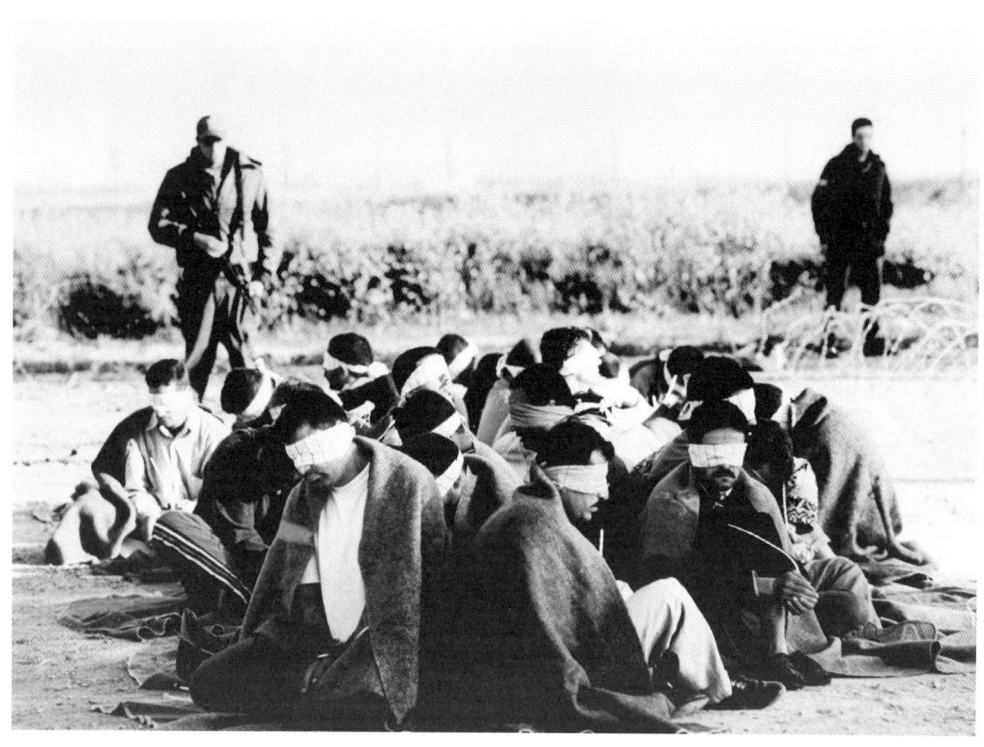

Figure 6.27. Orel Cohen, refugee camp, Tul Karem, March 8, 2002.

authorizations. If it's a matter of consoling the bereaved, she must prove the closeness of this relation to the deceased. If it's a hospital matter, she must prove that she's already ill, and not with some sort of psychosomatic sickness. If it's a matter of employment, she must prove that she actually has work and that someone is waiting for her on the other side. Needs, needs, and more needs. Anything else is a luxury that doesn't even bear the slightest discussion. This is what the army wants to hear, every day, from the mouths of hundreds of thousands of Palestinians: only the pure voicing of needs, the murmur of urges whose satisfaction cannot be prevented, but this, too, should not be overdone. Every day, all the time, the soldier wants to hear the chorus of broken chatter, raw bodily noises, the language of medical permits and death certificates, the testimony of the next of kin. Only then can he be certain that the situation is under control, feeling comfortable that the vast majority are trapped in a tangled web of needs, seeking satisfaction.

From the army's standpoint, demonstrations by Palestinians in Palestinian territory are a luxury. I will not discuss all of the reasons why this is the case, but will only concern myself with the major cause. The checkpoint is a tool for fracturing Palestinian society into individual bodies. Everybody has his or her own authorization. There is no collective at the checkpoints. No organized groups are permitted. The checkpoint strips the individual down until she's finally separated from her companions and can care solely for her own personal needs. When the individual gets into any sort of dispute with a soldier, all others must silently remain in line, standing in single file. There are no groups at the checkpoint, because a group begets a public, and a public begets discussion, argument, action, the forging of plans, dreams, visions, and delusions. In the line, revolutionary dreams are cut up into a few meaningless words that can be dropped from the corner of one's lips directly into your neighbor's ear, words that never go beyond the bodies, the general mood, and the progress of the line.

"In this photograph, which was taken at a checkpoint," Miki Kratsman says, "they are being told 'Stand in a row,' and 'Don't pass the line'" (figure 6.28). "Usually, a stone serves to mark the terminus, and they line up in a row behind it and wait. At the checkpoints,

I've often seen Palestinians being told 'not to pass the yellow strip,' and then the driver who mistakenly crosses the yellow strip has his car keys confiscated."[64]

Ever since the idea of "the Wall" separating the West Bank and Israel began to materialize, Palestinians, in cooperation with a few Israeli and international anarchists, have regularly attempted to demonstrate along its perimeter. The army tries to distance these demonstrations from the Wall and break up the enthusiasm surrounding them, to prevent them from becoming an event, from entering into the public space of civil discourse. Occasionally the army will grant permits for specific periods of time — a half-hour's demonstration, for example — in remote locations, difficult to access. In this way, the Wall, which is detrimental to the lives of hundreds of thousands of Palestinians, spreads fear and panic even without being seen — a concrete tyrant that is remotely controlled. The soldiers, it seems, are required for defending the Wall from nonviolent Palestinian demonstrators — perhaps it is suspected that through their megaphones they will huff and puff and blow the Wall down.

Most attempts to turn the Wall into a public square as a site for demonstrations fail before they even get off the ground. In his diary, Oded Yedaya, an Israeli demonstrator and photographer, writes of attending demonstrations "walking inside the village, since the army will not allow us to walk along the Wall, which actually borders the village," or "walking in a demonstration, also for fear that the army would obstruct the buses' departure and the arrival at the checkpoint."[65] Some of the demonstrations do in fact take place in the Wall's shadow, or at least in the shadow of the bulldozer that is busy leveling the foundation for the Wall's continual construction. Most of the time, the demonstrators are forced to hold the demonstrations — even if only for short periods of time, until the army comes to break them up — inside the villages. The dozens of photographs taken over the past two years by Yedaya have made it possible to identify several models of relations between the soldiers and demonstrators — who, in most cases, are Palestinians — at the opposite end of the spectrum, away from the relations at the checkpoint.

In almost every sphere of life, the Palestinian has been forced to depend on the goodwill of the soldier, the sovereign's junior proxy,

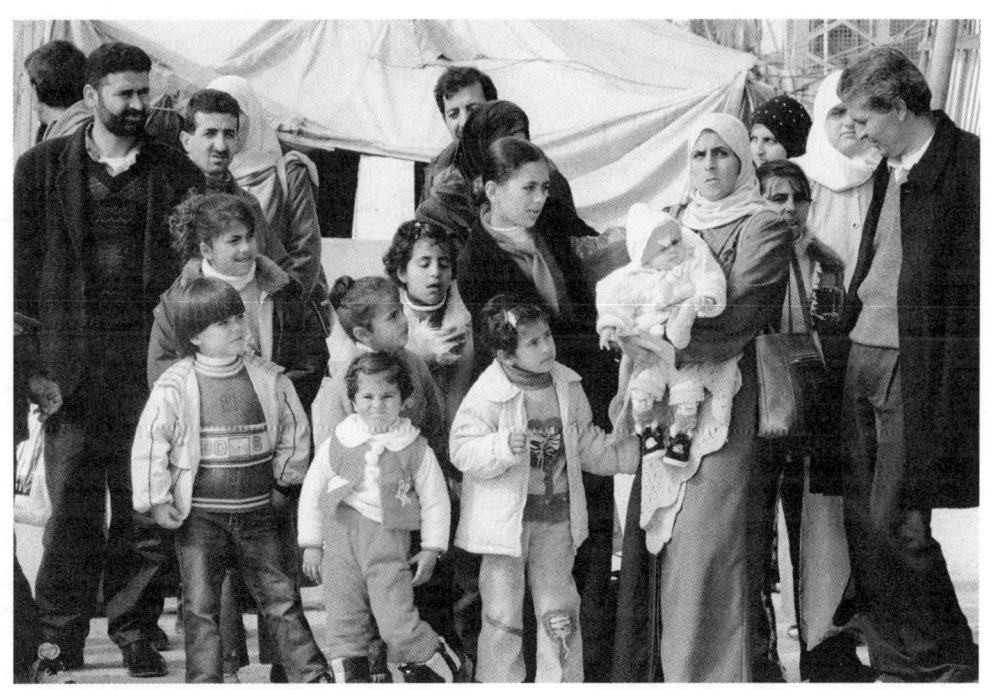

Figure 6.28. Miki Kratsman, Beit Ibba checkpoint, 2004. (Please see Color Plates.)

who is supposed to decide his fate — allowed to pass through, or
made to wait.[66] The demonstration is currently the only public
medium in which the Palestinian's movement is not dependent on
the Israeli soldier. Even when the latter asks demonstrators to dis-
band, the Palestinians simply move on to the next spot. Demonstrations momentarily challenge the army's preference to meet the
Palestinian at the various types of checkpoints. Demonstrations create a moment of unity that has the potential of developing into the
creation of a mob scene or the production of a public. Either way,
the army prefers to handle the Palestinians in individual units, one at
a time. Even further, it prefers the Palestinians to be separated from
the Israelis, for then it can treat them like a mob, with no obligation
to make distinctions between the individuals who compose it. The
Israelis become a nuisance when they join the Palestinians' demonstration, and they cause a disturbance when they sticks their noses in
at the checkpoint.[67] The Israeli is embarrassing to the soldier, given
his familiarity not only with the procedures employed by the soldier,
but with the fact that they can be reversed. He can even resort to
threatening to appeal to a higher authority: As Oded Yedaya reconstructs a conversation between him and a soldier at a checkpoint, the
soldier says: "Don't interfere in my work." Yedaya replies, "I'm entitled to state my opinion." "Don't stand here hassling me, go back to
the taxi," the soldier retorts. "I have a right to stand where I want to;
it's not a closed military zone here," Yedaya declares. "I'll arrest
you," the soldier threatens. "You can't. I'll call the police," Yedaya
threatens in return.

The soldiers at the checkpoints expect the Palestinians to have
been trapped in a tangled web of needs, isolated as individuals and
deprived of the citizen's ability to say "You can't," but the Palestinian
demonstrator does not express an urgent need, one that would position the soldier in a demiurgic position as the one who can rescue
him from the burden of his needs. The demonstrator is exercising a
civilian right — in the case of the noncitizen, a demand for the recognition of the inalienable and irrefutable right to demonstrate. The
nonviolent Palestinian demonstrator deviates from the course that
the army has prepared for her and from the framework in which its
soldiers have been trained to deal with her.

The soldier at the checkpoint expects the Palestinian to express his needs and to present the reasons and evidence that her needs are justified, because from the soldier's standpoint, these needs are often a disguise for something else. In other words, these needs have become the Palestinian's truth, but this truth is illusory and can be unmasked as false. At the demonstrations, however, the Palestinian arrives empty-handed, his arms limp at his sides, free to perform light, energetic motions. In the demonstrations held with Israeli and international activists, the Palestinians can be distinguished from the others by their empty hands and light strides. The Israelis and foreigners are always clumsier, walking around with bottles of mineral water or a backpack, or sometimes with a camera. The difference between these groups doesn't stem simply from the fact that the former have just walked from their nearby homes, whereas the latter have come from afar and therefore carry things as if they were going on a trip. The Palestinians' empty hands express the fact that they are not carrying anything superfluous, suspicious, or questionable. It is as though they want, in advance, not to appear to be suspects in the soldier's eyes — as they typically are viewed when passing through a checkpoint. Along similar lines, they don't carry information that the authorities would need to validate and authenticate. They intentionally break from the mold in which the Israeli soldier habitually places them.

Photographs from the demonstrations against the Wall, which take place inside Palestinian space, attest to their participants' motivation to create a distance between themselves and the army, sustaining a public space that is unscathed by its control. Usually there are several dozen demonstrators, often demonstrating by walking and sometimes by sitting. When women demonstrate on their own, they typically choose to sing (figure 6.29). In all instances, the demonstrations are unambiguously nonviolent. They also lack any mob mentality, which has been known to gain momentum on the way to a funeral.[68] However, at times, the demonstrators exploit the physical strength of the gathering in order to remove the obstacles that the army has placed within the public space or to use its own methods to thwart it in its pursuit of them. With a few shovels, a relatively modest group of participants can use the occasion of the demonstration to remove a sand pile that has plagued a village for

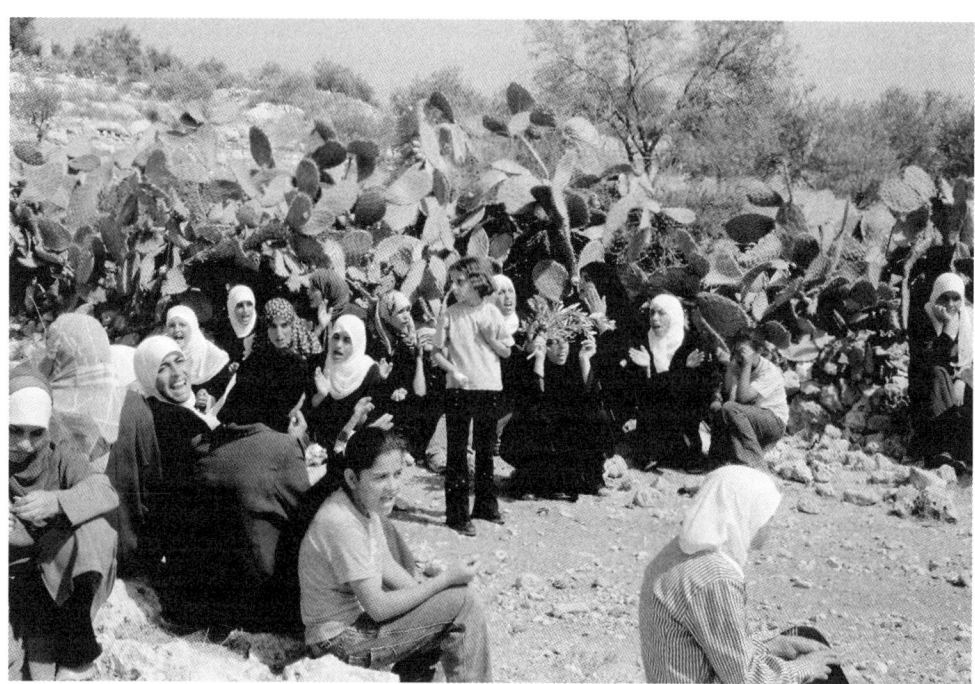

Figure 6.29. Oded Yedaya, demonstration of women, Boudrus, 2004.

days or in other instances to scatter heavy rocks across the road in order to slow down the pursuing army's entry into the village, enabling the public space created by the demonstration to continue (see figures 6.30–6.33).

In a photograph from the demonstration at Zawiya in September 2004, more than a hundred demonstrators are seen walking along an exposed ridge beside a row of olive trees (figure 6.34). They are marching under the blistering sun. Some are carrying flags. Alongside them, only yards away, armed soldiers are walking, looking like security guards on an excursion organized by some government agency. A few randomly scattered Palestinian flags are the only reminder that the soldiers are not working on behalf of the demonstrators, but are actually their explicit enemy, not only those who continually prevent them from moving from place to place and stop them from fulfilling their needs, but those who want to prevent them from demonstrating and to deny them the possibilities at their disposal, wishing to neutralize the power that the demonstration has by restricting the location in which the organizers choose to hold it, nullifying it as an event. On this particular occasion, too, the army, in a gesture of "goodwill," allows the demonstrators to hold a "half-hour's demonstration."

Most of the demonstrations, as mentioned above, stop at the outskirts of the village. So it was at Hrebata in May 2004. Oded Yedaya describes what happened, writing about himself in the third person:

> The procession passed in front of him, and he jumped from the fence and continued at a run beside the road to overtake the head of it again, to catch the moment of encounter and confrontation with the army. But the army's megaphones stopped the procession at a range of a hundred meters from them, without any confrontation. Meanwhile, and all the photographers immediately scattered, looking for a camera angle and cover.

With a photographer's instinct, Yedaya ran ahead, seeking to position himself at the forefront, where events were apparently going to unfold (figure 6.35). But as the army attempted to suspend the event, the camera lens revealed different events, less perceptible, presumably not even intended for photography. From the photograph,

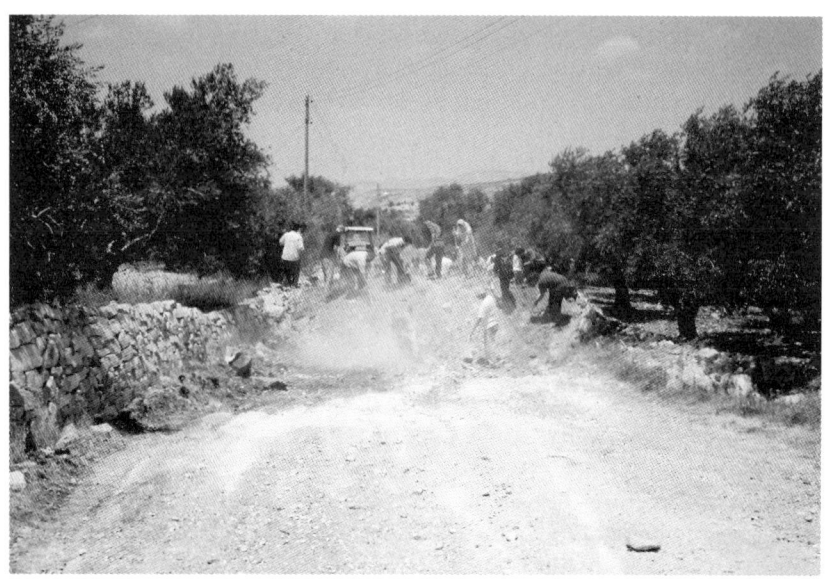

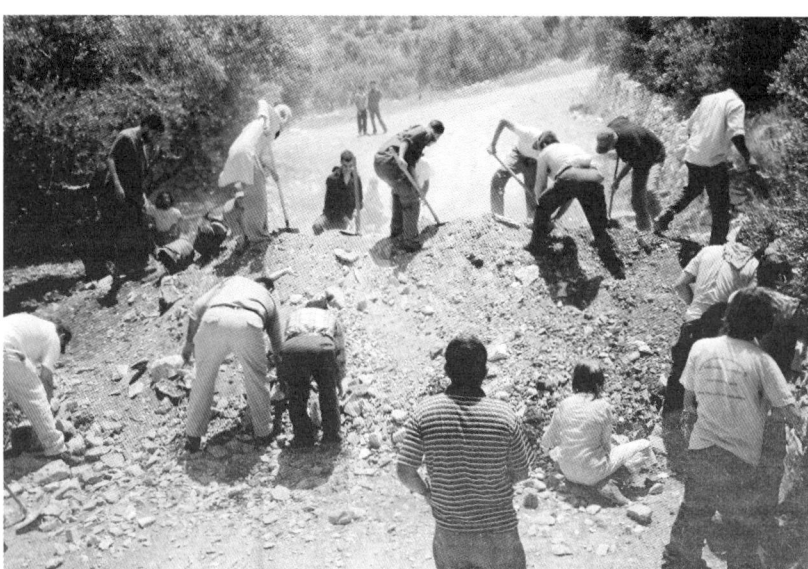

Figures 6.30 and 6.31. Oded Yedaya, dismantling soil barrier, Asira A-Shimalya, 2005.

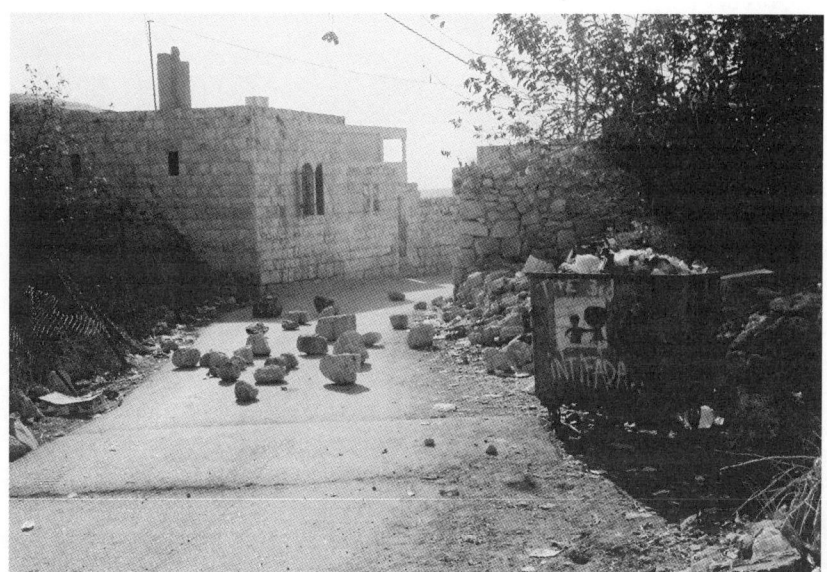

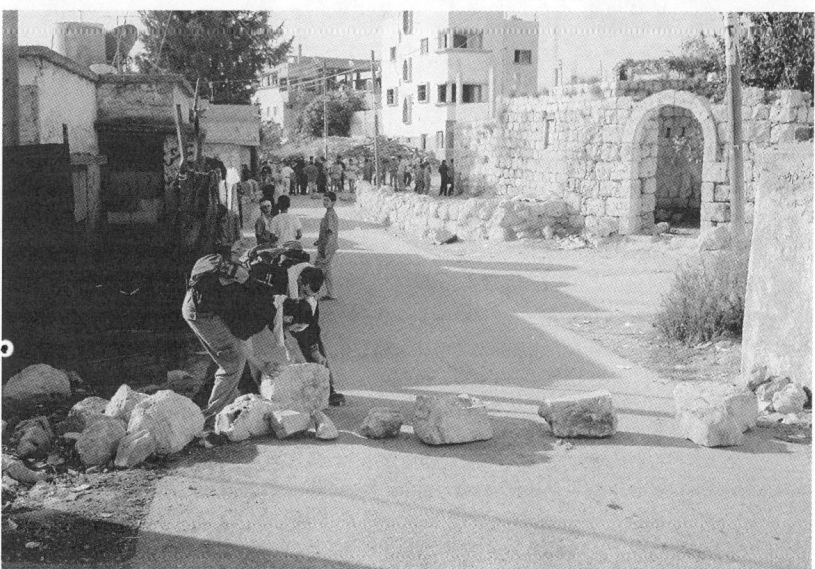

Figures 6.32 and 6.33. Oded Yedaya, stone barrier, Bil'in, 2005.

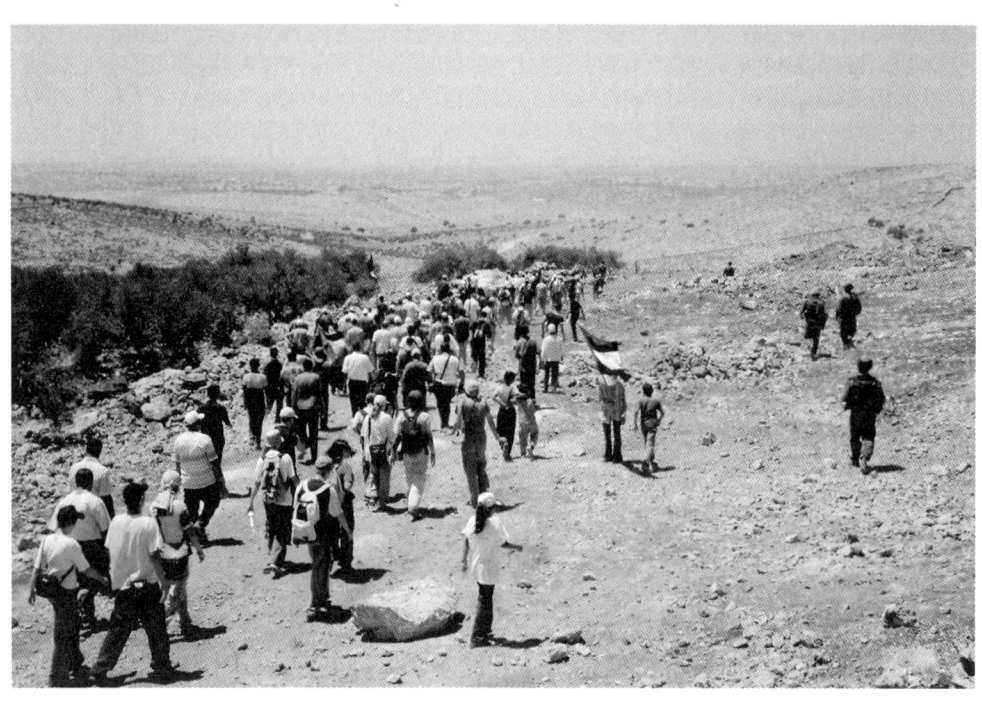

Figure 6.34. Oded Yedaya, march along the line of the Wall, 2005.

however, the event suddenly appears as an epic image, releasing the familiar protagonists from the face-to-face encounter to which they are accustomed, positing them as two antagonistic sides (figure 6.36). Toward the demonstrators — Israeli citizens and Palestinian noncitizens alike — the megaphones in the soldiers' hands demand an end to the proceedings. Not seeking a violent encounter, but merely demonstrating against new decrees, the demonstrators come to a standstill, crowding together to create a human wall. Acting as though they were familiar with the Palestinians, knowing how they cannot be trusted, the army sends a few soldiers out of the camp to stand atop a hill with cocked rifles to remind the subjects — even if there are a few Israelis traitors in their midst — that there are not and never will be two sides. There is a sovereign power and there are subjects, with junior proxies who occasionally decide what the rules are for all the subjects. The Palestinians do not constitute a side, and certainly not a public, so they are advised to disperse. The sovereign power has denied them citizenship, and now it attempts to deter them from shaping their own modes of becoming a citizen. Their demonstration, exuding a youthful spirit and civilian vitality, is the exact opposite of the might and tyranny of a military group that rules another group by force. If any violence should erupt, it will only be on account of one side — the group of soldiers — knowing only how to use force.

The Palestinians will wait a little longer, slowly withdrawing from the spot, entering the village and looking for a quieter street where it is less likely that the army will come to disrupt them. In choosing the location of their demonstration, there is no need to head to the town square or to some other central site under the authority's surveillance. In any event, if someone is to be a spectator of their demonstrations, it will be through the mediation of photography. Meanwhile, these demonstrations are a training ground for becoming citizens under conditions in which the army, for several years, has decimated all outlets for becoming citizens, systematically destroying any potential for a public space.

Under these conditions, a narrow path will suffice. With resilient strides, the demonstrators will soon leave, entering the village, drag some rocks to block the route to their gathering place, and hope that

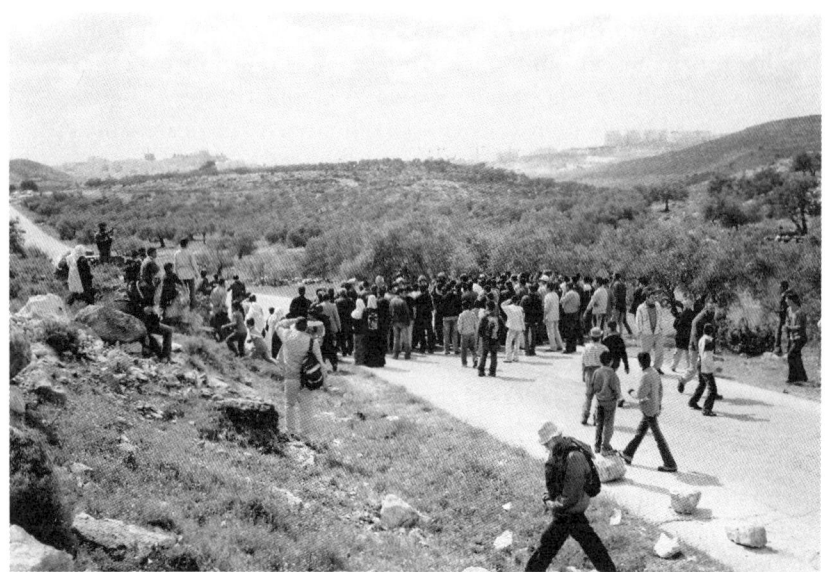

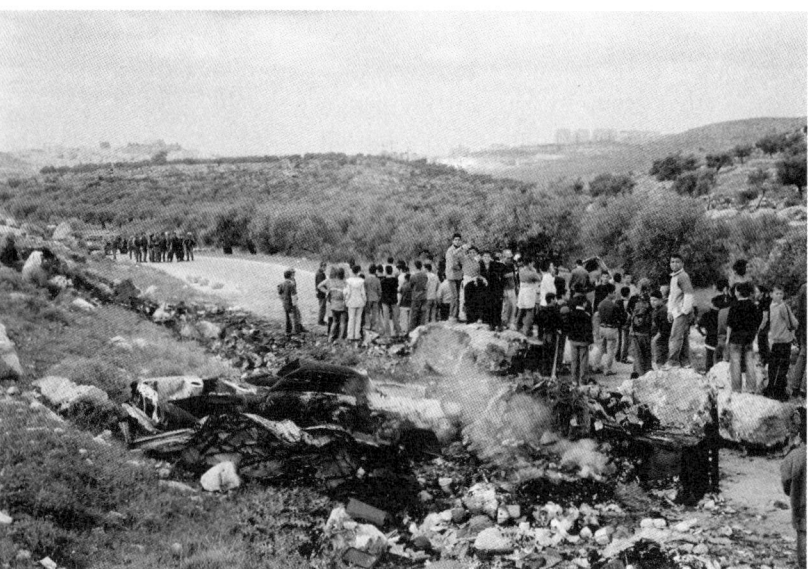

Figures 6.35 and 6.36. Oded Yedaya, diversion demonstration, Hrebata, 2004.
(Please see Color Plates.)

this time, too — not from "goodwill," but by virtue of the rocks — they will gain another half-hour of training in nonviolent demonstration. In their minor spatial language — which they have developed using the occupier's language, assimilating and altering it for their civilian needs — they will block roads here and there and remove the mounds of dirt that the army has placed at all the exits of the village.

> They raised the rifle and said it's forbidden to pass here. Why? Because. Who says it's forbidden — why? This is inside the village, a public space; people are allowed to move around inside the village. It's not beside the bulldozers of the barrier. "What are you doing here anyway?" the soldiers remembered to ask. "I'm a photographer." "And have you got a press card?" "No." "So get the hell out of here before we arrest you. This is a closed military area."[69]

On the verge of disaster, the citizen's gaze might sometimes be more threatening to the ruling power than that of the press photographer, who has been given permission to see and has been sent by the newspaper to photograph events. For the citizen — if her gaze is not damaged — everything that happens in the Occupied Territories is an event: headline news.

CHAPTER SEVEN

Whose Gaze?

The person in the photograph wants something from me. She's staring at me. Her stare doesn't falter. The first photographs ever made already bore the mark of a human presence reaching beyond a mere image.[1] The denotation of the photograph appears in them, but exceeds the boundaries of the material presence of an image printed on a sheet of paper. The photograph frames a new space of observation and action for the person who is shown in it. The spectator employs the gestures of identification to banish the ghost of the photographed person, which threatens to use and to act from the space that the photograph has opened up for it. The spectator attempts to circumscribe this presence, to identify it, determining "This is X." But this gesture never exhausts what or who it is that is shown in the photograph. At best, it allows the spectator to suspend her encounter with the person in the photograph, to imagine that this person isn't present, to act as if what she's looking at is no more than a photograph. However, the person in the photograph comes to life out of the picture, makes demands, activates, tries to pull strings, hovers in the air, commands, seduces, repels, troubles, and irritates. But she always also remains opaque, dumb, distant, locked in a space separate from the surroundings of the spectator. In order to remove her presence, the spectator can file away the photograph in a family album; she can bury it in a drawer or turn to the next page of the newspaper. Then, the photographed people will go away for at least a while. When the gesture of identification is suspended and the photographed people are allowed to come back out of the photos, to become present, however, the distress may become overwhelming.

The photograph emerges, then, as a field of evasive presences, loaded with details that escape consciousness and knowledge while awakening the anxiety that I may be missing what I'm called on to do in front of it, alongside the phantasm — that if I just fix my gaze for a few more minutes, more hours, the photograph may divulge its secret. In the meantime, all that's possible is to assist this process with varied uses of the photograph: a long unbroken gaze, intermittent recurring looks, blowing it up, shrinking it, embedding it, framing it, cropping it, hanging or printing it. These actions are confessions, as it were, of the impossibility of maintaining a direct gaze between the spectator and the photograph and between the photographer and the photographed person, or — alternately — confessions of the fundamental incapacity of the photograph to show and the spectator to see: "Imagining that the blowup — like a magnifying glass — would explain the photo to me."[2]

Under these conditions, when the photograph is at one and the same time no more than a piece of paper and a space of relations between spectators and photographed people, the civil contract of photography allows photographs to call up a complex system of relations between photographed persons and spectators.

For example, a photograph of Amia Zakin and Chaira Abu-Hassen was printed in *Ha'aretz* at the beginning of 2002. Taken by Miki Kratsman, it accompanied an article by Gideon Levy in their joint weekly column "The Twilight Zone." The column centered on an encounter with two Palestinian women with similar stories. Levy and Kratsman used this similarity in order to point out a recurring practice in the checkpoints. Amia Zakin and Chaira Abu-Hassen hadn't known each other before the article was written. Their analogous stories converged on a single common denominator: their victimization by soldiers at checkpoints, which prevented them from reaching the hospital in time while in labor, resulting, in both cases, in the death of their newborn babies.

For fifteen hours the two women in labor — each separately — had to travel roundabout paths, looking for a passageway at one of the many checkpoints that separated each from the respective hospitals that they were trying, desperately, to reach. Their persistent movement among checkpoints for such extended periods in their condition testifies to the fact that the soldier standing guard at the checkpoint repeatedly either presented himself to them or was positioned by them as someone who might be the addressee of their plea. To no avail. Not one of the soldiers helped them, and they each reached the hospital too late. The infants they bore died soon after birth. Fifteen hours, phone calls to commanding officers, quite a few soldiers with various ranks and authority who were called on to decide on the case before them, to make and implement decisions: The death of the two babies wasn't caused by the "mistaken" decision of one individual soldier at this or that checkpoint, but rather by the very system that turned the women's trip from their homes to the hospital into a route strewn with decision makers bearing directly on their lives.

An encounter with a photograph in a newspaper always occurs after the fact. Most, if not all of the channels of assistance that were open during the fifteen hours of these women's tortuous trips among checkpoints are already closed. And yet the photograph is nevertheless branded with a seal of actuality — the actuality that attributes the photograph to a concrete event, that gives the photographed people names, that frames their story in time and place. This actuality, Walter Benjamin wrote, is compellingly visible in the portraits from the age of the daguerreotype, in which "there remains something that goes beyond testimony to the photographer's art, something that cannot be silenced, that fills you with an unruly desire to know" — in the case of a portrait of a fishwife, for example — "what her name was, the woman who was alive there, who even now is still real."

No matter how artful the photographer, no matter how carefully posed his subject, the beholder feels an irresistible urge to search such a picture for the tiny spark of contingency, of the here and now, with which reality has (so to speak) seared the subject, to find the inconspicuous spot where in the immediacy of that long-forgotten moment the future nests so eloquently that we, looking back, may rediscover it.[3]

The photograph's presentation as evidence and as a remnant of what "was there," of a "here and now," realizes one of the possibilities embedded in portrait photography. Benjamin, however, hints at more than that. Actuality lends the picture an unequivocal title, permanently stabilizing and finalizing the meaning of the photograph, nailing it to that "here and now" and accordingly robbing it of all the other possibilities and meanings that have so far not been realized or manifested. "The human countenance" in these daguerreotypes, Benjamin wrote, "had a silence about it in which the gaze rested."

In contrast to Benjamin's claim, I will argue that even if actuality does hover, like a constant threat, over photographs, it will never succeed in locking a given photograph completely or in totally cutting off its transmissibility, its potential for conveying an experience that is not merely information. At most, actuality can seal the photograph for a while, until the storm passes, can block the civil horizon of the person looking at it, can damage her capacity to see, but it cannot totally remove the unease, the uncertainty, the ground-level observation point that will affect the next spectator, will unnerve and compel her to rethink what appears before her, including the boundaries of her own gaze.

Chaira Abu-Hassen's Laugh

If, for a moment, we suspend the actual information and detach the photograph from the concrete event that it is purported to document, we will be able to see how alongside the topical content, a chasm opens up in the same picture between the photographed figure and the photographer, between the woman in the photograph and anyone who seeks to situate herself in front of her. Something in the photograph of this double portrait by Kratsman, something that at first I couldn't decipher, indicated this abyss and led me to ask Kratsman to show me the rest of the photos he took during his encounter with these two women. From "the human countenance" of Amia Zakin and of Chaira Abu-Hassen there indeed radiates silence, ease, containment, and all these seemed in a stereotypical gaze as alien to the picture's actuality. A woman who just days ago had lost her newborn after carrying it in her womb for nine months, — how can this woman emanate a silence "in which the gaze rested"?

I studied the whole series of photographs that Kratsman took. In almost all of them, the face of Chaira Abu-Hassen bore an insuppressible laugh (figure 7.1). This laugh increased my sense of disconnection between the tragic incident and the photographed portrait. This time, suspending the actual meant responding to the undeciphered strangeness conveyed by the photograph, to the inscrutability arising from it, and to the way in which the situation it depicts defies exhaustive explanation. Watching the photograph, I envisioned the moment when the camera in Kratsman's hands stripped its protagonists — both the photographer and the photographed women — of their "here and now," hurling them into a situation that was impossible for both. She, whose words — quoted in the article by Gideon Levy — were razor sharp, was overcome by an insuppressible smile-laugh. He found himself embarrassed by this laugh, mechanically clicking the camera again and again as if willing the camera to capture randomly what the encounter between him and the Palestinian woman did not allow — a serious face, reserve, poignancy, a face from which laughter had receded. And indeed, among the series of almost unbearably repeated images, the photographer found a single frame that he sent to print, a single frame that he felt he could own up to as a photographer assigned to convey the photographed woman's story. This frame, too, however, was not devoid of the troubling traces of Chaira Abu-Hassen's laugh.

It is possible, of course, to ask why Chaira Abu-Hassen laughed. And it's possible to attempt an answer as follows: In front of the camera, she was revisited by the ghost of the photographer's traditional instructions to "smile" when taking a portrait photo. The classic demand of the studio photographer is designed to cause his subjects, without letting them sense it, to put "all else" aside and allow a smile to spread across their faces. And the smile does indeed spread, perhaps more a response to the demand's absurdity than to the demand itself. The smile is an effect of the photographed person's posture in front of something — the camera — before which she is supposed to simulate standing in front of someone and therefore is supposed to smile in response to the person acting as proxy for that something or someone. The gradual erosion of the status of the studio photographer's demand that his subjects smile, hasn't weakened the troubling structure of the relations embodied in the circumstances of portrait photography. Therefore, it might be assumed that this is none other than the trace of the laughter or the embarrassment overcoming the photographed person — a person for whom the camera has not become a daily routine — before a camera that is raised toward her.

The camera, in this case — and this should not be forgotten — is raised in the hands of an Israeli photographer, who vis-à-vis Chaira Abu-Hassen will always also personify the position of occupier. Confronting him, Chaira Abu-Hassen laughed, as if saying without addressing him: "Oh no, not again." It might, perhaps, be assumed that this is the forced laughter of a woman whose moment of encounter with another woman who experienced a trauma similar to hers — a woman she hadn't met until the moment of the photograph — and with an Israeli man from the other, occupying side divested her of the ability to contain her condition. In this case, the laugh on her face will amount to a testimony of sorts to her effort to rid herself of a foreign body lodged in her throat and seeking a nonverbal outlet.

However, all these explanations, however accurate or misled, seek to give the laughter reasons and justification; they seek to erase the laugh of Chaira Abu-Hassen as an inscrutable, undecipherable, and troubling presence. This presence, in the mere fact that it is not open to exchange or communication, protects the Palestinian woman from the Israeli before her who stands for those responsible for the loss inflicted on her. This is not the reason for her laughter. This is its effect. The laughter makes present the open abyss between occupiers and occupied, the observer's inability to understand, as well as the uselessness of any empathy or sorrow after the fact, which will never amount to much more than self-righteous gestures. This abyss, embodied in the photograph, is much closer to what "was there," what happened there when the photograph was taken, than any factual report conveyed by the photographed details.

There is something in the presence of the camera that reaches beyond its technical attributes. It is a relatively small, usually black box with a seeing apparatus sticking out in front — an adjustable lens. The lens embodies a gaze, which can best be described with reference to Lacan's use of the term, following Sartre.

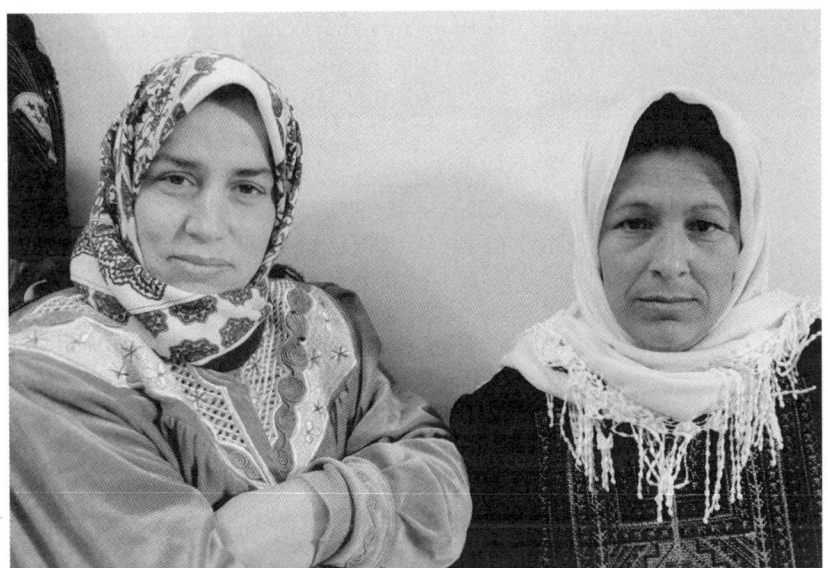

Figure 7.1. Miki Kratsman, Chaira Abu-Hassen and Amia Zakin, Yamoun village, 2001.

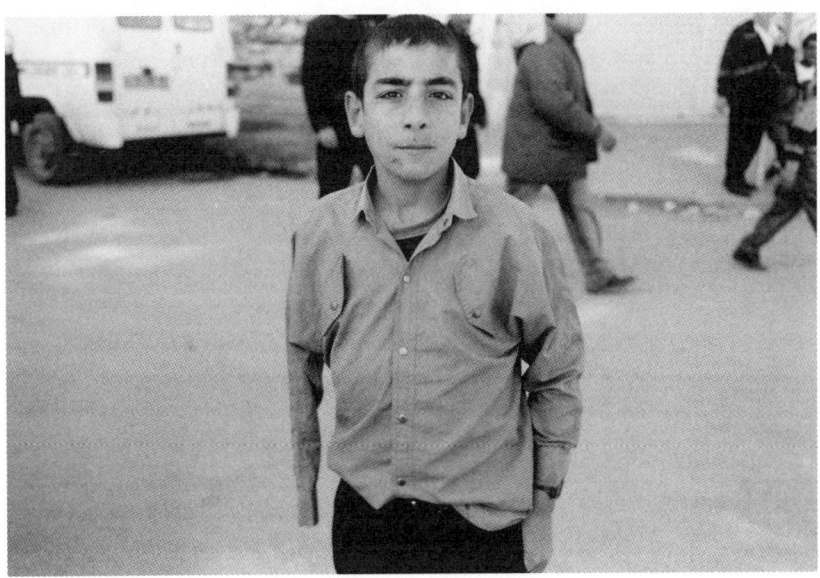

Figure 7.2. Miki Kratsman, Ramallah, 1995.

Sartre ... brings it [the gaze] into function in the dimension of the existence of others. Others would remain suspended in the same, partially de-realizing conditions that are in Sartre's definition, those of objectivity, were it not for the gaze. The gaze, as conceived by Sartre, is the gaze by which I am surprised — surprised in so far as it changes all the perspectives, the lines of force, of my world, orders it, from the point of nothingness where I am, in a sort of radiated reticulation of the organisms.... In so far as I am under the gaze, Sartre writes, I no longer see the eye that looks at me and, if I see the eye, the gaze disappears.[4]

As long as the lens, along with the gaze embedded in it, hasn't been directed at someone or something, the gaze remains a secret. Even when it is directed, the secret is not totally revealed. At most, it may be possible to follow its axis, its direction. The black body of the camera with the lens fixed in front threatens with its gaze. But it also seduces: "Sawarani, Sawarani! ('Take my picture, take my picture!'), the children of the [occupied] territories shout when they spy a camera, as if conditioned," Kratsman wrote during the years of the Oslo Accords (figure 7.2).[5] At times, the camera's gaze also arouses violence of the type that is exhibited to it, for it, or that is directed at it. Either way, although the camera has become a routine part of modern life, its presence always arouses some degree of discomfort or at least disrupts the situation that preceded its entry. The knowledge that there is a gaze in this black box makes it an object unlike other objects. The threat embedded in this gaze can take on many forms. Common to all of them is the fact that the gaze inside the camera is not the gaze of another looking at me, but rather, the gaze of the camera.

The Gaze of the Camera

The gaze of the camera is not the gaze of the photographer, because the viewpoint of the camera is not the same as the viewpoint of the photographer. The photographer points the lens and adjusts the shutter (or skips the latter when the camera is automatic) and positions the camera at a specific point relative to what she wishes to turn into the object of her photograph, after which she sets the frame and presses the button that activates the camera. The photographer repeats this action several times with slight shifts in lighting, angle, distance from the object, all in order that the variety of pictures will allow her to choose the one that meets her expectations from the photographic situation.

Skilled photographers usually know — or at least pretend to know — how to decrease the gap between the photographed result and the way in which they imagine it while taking the photograph.[6] In some cases, they use Polaroid cameras to teach themselves, in real time, how to decrease that distance, and those working with digital cameras use the screen that actually displays the picture before it is taken. Sometimes, the photographer is positioned opposite a ready-made frame predetermined by a public-relations person, an impresario, the security forces, or other agents in whose power it is to employ legal or illegal violence. Even then, the photographer's point of view is not totally erased.

For instance, in a photograph taken by Kratsman in 1989, during a funeral in Nablus, he was pushed by the Palestinians walking behind the coffin to a standpoint right in front of the coffin, a standpoint from which he couldn't move: "It's one of those photographs where the frame is set for you; you don't need to plan much. You take the picture from where you're standing; you're not free to move. It's like a political event where there are cordons, and you're told up to what point you can proceed. That's your spot, and this is our spot"[7] (figure 7.3). The viewpoint of the photographer extends beyond the skills she may display during the photographic situation or beyond her freedom to craft the frame. Her position is distinctive both culturally and in relation to other positions, before she has even raised the camera to point it at some object.

But just as the photographer's position cannot be removed from the photograph, neither can the photographer totally remove another viewpoint. Photographers, despite their skill and professionalism and despite technical aids such as Polaroid cameras or digital screens, are unable to lock the frame around their viewpoint alone. The photograph will always include something else that is not reducible to the photographer's viewpoint. It is a viewpoint, or perhaps it should be termed a viewing position, that is not attributable to anyone but the camera.[8] This viewing position is not reducible to a single point distinct from the other points, but it is a focal point, as it were, connecting all the other viewpoints. The viewing position of the camera is not equivalent to a human viewpoint and cannot be replaced by it. During photography, the camera does not respond totally either to the photographer or to the photographed person. The photograph is a result of the encounter between the two, with the camera in between. Each vantage point is imprinted in the photograph, and none of these vantage points can be reduced to the others.

The single photograph itself is, accordingly, a montage of the heterogeneous viewpoints of those who participated in the act of photography. This heterogeneity doesn't result from a montage of different shots, but exists simultaneously within the single frame (or within the single shot in a video recording or a film camera). The various and conflictual viewpoints that leave their mark within the frame split the frame itself. The frame offers the human gaze a rectangular, steady, frozen field of vision in which, by moving the gaze, every millimeter of its length and breadth can be studied without losing what was seen before. Because it freezes the gaze, everything seen in a photograph is retained in a manner distinguishing it from what can be seen from a human viewpoint.

I'll return to the photograph of the funeral taken by Kratsman in Nablus in 1989 (figure 7.3) to exemplify the way in which the single photograph connects a heterogeneous multiplicity of viewpoints. A multitude fills most of the photo frame; the people in it are seen to be crowded together. They are pushing ahead and forming a circle of sorts around an open casket displayed at the center. The white cloth wound around the face of the dead man lends him a peaceful and restful look, in contrast to the furious hubbub and the violence surrounding him.[9] The bodies of those present slant markedly toward the dead person. Each of them is pushing his way through in order to be as close to him as he can. Many hands are stretched forward in a V-for-victory sign, and together they assemble over the head of the dead man like a crown rising upward. The crowd's looks are also focused on the dead man, directed at his visible face, mouths open in a shout of outrage or loss and revenge. The dead man is the visible

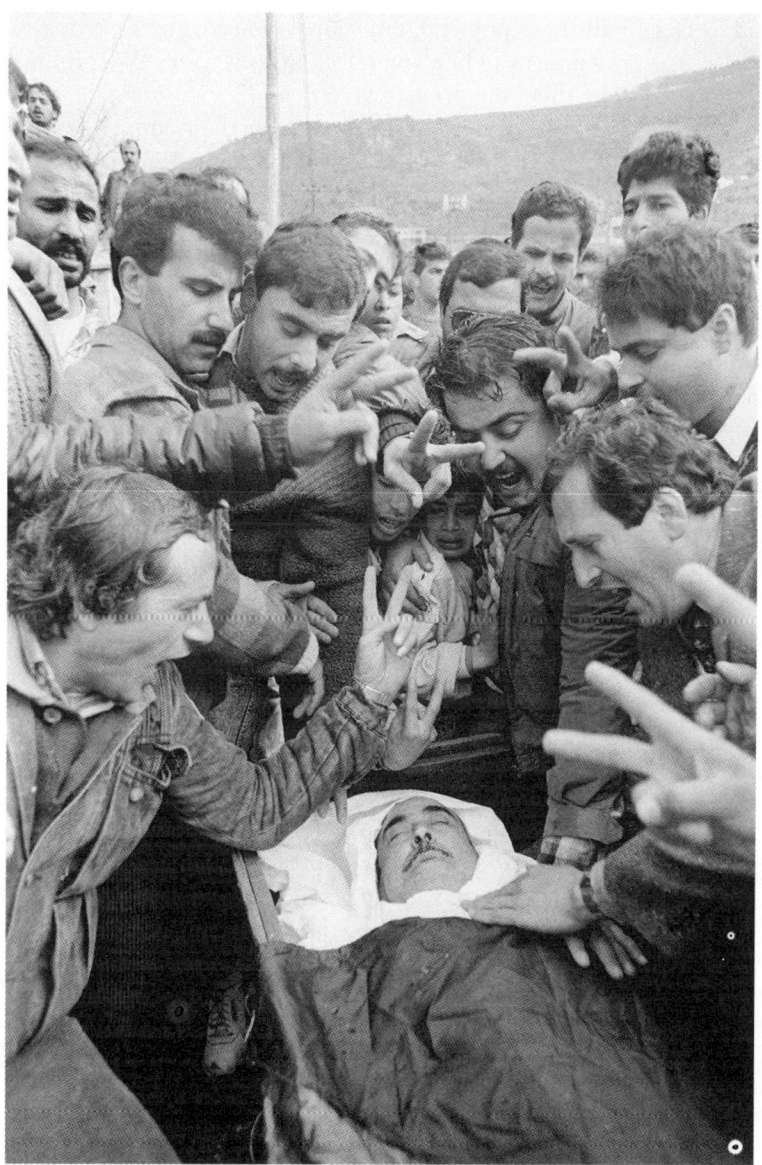

Figure 7.3. Miki Kratsman, Nablus, 1989.

addressee of all these physical, emotional, voiced, and optical gestures. The crowd turns to him and tells him, as it were, "We promise 'you' we'll show them the price of your death."

But the addressee is dead and cannot hear their address, yet he continues to exist. The crowd converging on the coffin deepens its message to the dead man with movements and gestures. This address, however, is actually directed at someone else who is present opposite the coffin at the time. It is the photographer invited to the site of the event to witness this address to the dead. The address, whose traces we can see in the photograph, is thus carried out while doubly inverting the addressee of the crowd's physical signs and actions. The crowd turns to the dead man so as to turn to the photographer, but the message to the photographer is merely intended to show him to whom the address is truly directed. The address directed toward the photographer doesn't confirm the photographer as their addressee. On the contrary, it denies his stand as addressee by displaying before him the true addressee and exhibiting the crowd's commitment to him. The true addressee is dead, and yet he continues to exist.

One of the early photographs in Michal Heiman's *Photographer Unknown* series shows the body of a person who has just been beheaded (figure 7.4). The head is lying beside the body, turned toward the camera, like a flower arrangement at the center of a still life. Autographing the picture with the "PHOTOGRAPHER UNKNOWN" signature allows Heiman to direct attention to the fact that someone "was there" and went to the trouble of creating this composition.

The composition, she says, is the result of an attempt to bear witness, through the photograph, to two things: first, to the fact that an execution was indeed carried out; second, to the fact that the executed person was indeed the one who had been sentenced to death. The photographer may have been compelled by his superiors to organize the scene in this specific way, or this may have been the way in which he understood his role, but it is also not unlikely that he simply wished to demonstrate an aesthetic sensibility or to lessen the horror destined to be revealed to the sensitive eyes of future spectators. Be this as it may, he was there, and he negotiated the character of the image for whose creation he was responsible. In the

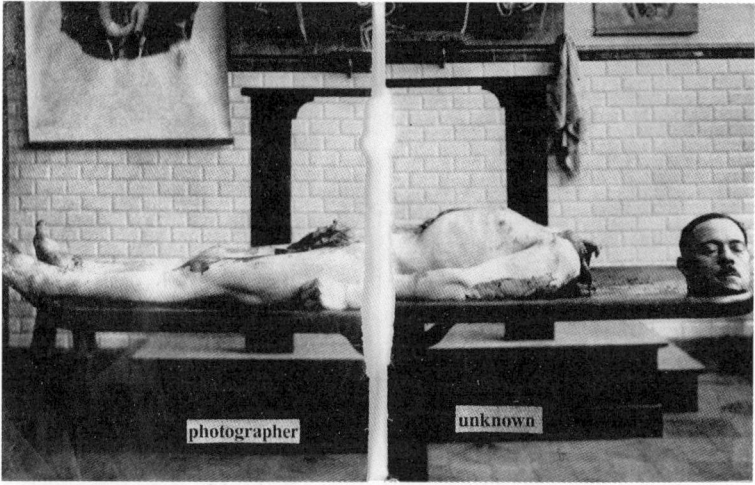

Figure 7.4. Michal Heiman, *Photographer Unknown, Photo magazine, 1978,* (*Les Archives des exécutions – La section des corps,* head and body of Fournie, Tour, France, 1920*)*, duratrans, light box, 120 x 160 x 10 cm, Ian Potter Museum of Art, University of Melbourne, 1994.

case of this particular photograph, he was there "alone," or in other words, the photographed person was a corpse that was totally at his mercy, his to arrange as he willed. And yet, even in such circumstances, the world seen in the picture is not totally vanquished by his point of view. What is imprinted on the paper of the photograph is never completely circumscribed by what the photographer meant, and it always includes something else requiring clarification.

The future spectator of the photograph may identify that "something else," but even if she ignores it, the photograph, the hard copy of a given event, will never turn into words graven in stone. Another spectator, at another time, may return it — this "something else" — to the complex of relations of exchange that are always part of a photograph. Heiman tore this particular photograph out of the French magazine *Photo*.[10] Because it was published by the magazine without a photographer's name, it became a natural item for her archive of photographs by unknown photographers. Her gaze at the photograph opposes the erasure of the photographer and draws attention not only to his presence in the arena of the photograph, but also to the extra effort he invested in designing the appearance of death.

Let's watch the photograph briefly. Before us is a carefully crafted museum look — pictures hang on a wall, a podium hosts the full weight of a naked body. The white-tiled walls are sparkling clean. The head is detached from the body, aligned with it precisely, turned toward the spectator, indifferent to the cold metal of the bed on which it rests. This arrangement looks like a shop window, carefully designed, well lighted, drawing the eye. A perfect phantasmagoria. Traces of protocol are clearly discernible in the frame. It must include the main exhibit; the exhibit must be clearly identified so as to serve as an archival record; the frame must be cleaned so that nothing will interfere with the visibility of the centerpiece. However, in the background, as a silent testimony to the entire event, a rag remains hanging on a hook. This must be the rag that allowed the photographer to position the dead man so that his head would look like a flower arrangement, an artifact of the effort that must have been invested in cleaning the arena of everything that a gaping body could leave in it. The arena looks both perfect and chilling — an icon of covered tracks, removed spots, wiped-up fluids and secretions — a purified space. The rag, which could have uncovered the conditions of the production of the phantasmagoria, serves as part of it in its spotless cleanliness.

This is a cyclical phantasmagoria internalizing into its logic what threatens for a moment to reveal something of its conditions of production. The rag may have simply been forgotten there, but it might be conjectured that at the last minute, with the next body already knocking at the door, so to speak, the photographer had to accelerate his craft and, not knowing where to dispose of it after cleaning the area, decided to make it part of the whole. Perhaps it was out of respect for the deceased that shame overcame him when he was about to hide the dirty rag, as if he were caught in the act of someone who saw fit to conceal a dirty rag while remaining indifferent to the display of a naked body. If the photographer experienced such deliberations, the dead person remained unmoved by them, totally indifferent. But it is not as easy to take for granted the indifference of the living man toward the dead. Even if the photographer treats him as

388

dead, the dead man goes on staring at him. A very short time has passed since his death. His face still bears the imprint of an expression. Repulsion? Skepticism? Scorn? His beheaded head rests silently on the podium, his eyes closed, but signaling tension under their lids. It seems as if "he" is waiting in ambush for the photographer, for anyone who seeks to look at the naked body, telling him yes "I'm" dead, yes "I'm" bodiless, but "I'm" still a presence that returns a gaze, that stands guard and won't let the spectator look placidly at the uncovered private parts of the dead.

The "PHOTOGRAPHER UNKNOWN" stamp displayed in the middle of the photograph reintroduces the presence of a photographer into the arena while returning the photograph into the context of the act of photography, thus allowing the extrication of a complex theater of relations from the photograph — power relations, only some of which are manifested in the single photo, just as only in some can the protagonists retain control, determining, as a result, how they will leave their mark in the picture. The photograph always includes more as well as less than what they may seek to include in it. What links them — photographer or photographed person — with a future spectator cannot be reduced to what they seek to deposit in the photograph, or, conversely, to what they take pains not to deposit in it. The civil contract of photography removes in advance any possibility that one of the protagonists may be subjugated to someone else. This is a contract according to which all are in principle equal before photography. Every reading of a photograph that is carried out in the service of the photographer or the photographed person and in deference to a message that one of them has sought to place in the picture is prone to be overturned. The photograph will equip the next spectator with the tools allowing her to yank the carpet out from under what others before her have tried to determine.

The Universal Addressee of Photography

The description "the addressee is dead ... yet he continues to exist" characterizes the type of address performed by photography in general. Photography is an encounter of a very special kind between a photographer who is holding a camera, and a person who knowingly or not, becomes the photographed person. The violence inherent in their encounter is due to the instrumentalization of the photo-graphed person in order to produce an image. This violence is there even if the photographed person is interested by the photograph no less than the photographer. In most of its occurrences, the encounter between the photographer and the person photographed is not intended to bring them together. Each takes part in the encounter or happens into it in order to actually address someone else who is not present at the encounter. This someone changes according to the specific circumstances or the genre of the photograph (photojour-nalism, family snapshots, or a passport photo), but in every case, whoever may have been the addressee of the gestures and move-ments of those who were photographed, the photographer is not the final addressee of the photograph itself or its "true" addressee. She is, rather, the addressee's proxy.[11] The photographed person's con-sent to become an image is always given not with regard to this proxy, who is an actual and concrete realization of the vantage point of the picture's "true" addressee, but, rather, with regard to another or end addressee.

This end addressee is purported to see clearly, to be free of prej-udices, so that nothing will mar her gaze. To paraphrase Lacan, she is cast as the "subject supposed to see."[12] She is supposed to see what appears in front of her eyes beyond the narrow considerations of time and place or local interests. Such a subject is an ideal concept, a necessary logical postulate, of which actual addressees, defined by precisely those considerations, are at best imperfect copies or repre-sentatives, but — at best, as well — an ideal which they can at least aspire, a limit concept embodying the ethics of the spectator. With-out positing her existence, it is difficult to envision such a sweeping consent to become a photograph: "A family in distress may think mistakenly that the press will help it," Miki Kratsman once told me. "This is where you feel a bit dishonest. Sometimes you make a point of saying that we'll merely print it in the paper."[13] The photographer is perceived here as a proxy, a service provider who can bring to the eyes of the true spectator what his eyes see.

The sight of the true spectator is supposed to be free of any personal interest save the common interest in the civil contract of photography. She is a universal spectator, a moral addressee — an addressee who is situated outside of the time and place of the photograph and to whom the photograph can be addressed as the "subject who is supposed to see." In this book, I deal exclusively with photographs in which the photographer or the photographed person addresses this spectator. (See, for instance, the case of Abu-Zuhir.) This universal spectator, hovering above the encounter between the photographer and the photographed person at the time the photograph is taken, is an effect of the act of photography. The photographer or the photographed person each needs her in order to continue entering into this covenant with each other. The fact that she is dead — "the fact that the other is dead is beyond dispute"[14] — and that she doesn't respond to requests, hasn't destroyed the need for her existence or the reality of the gaze of the other she continues to return to us after her death.

Without assuming the existence of such a universal spectator — whether alive or dead — there is no explanation for the willingness of individuals to conquer the world as photographs and to submit to the violence this involves. The place of the universal spectator is kept after his death as a vacant space, allowing individuals to continue to be looted in the act of photography and moreover to participate in this willingly and consentingly. In a conversation with him, Kratsman described the violence embedded in the act of photography as the aspect of this act which is taken for granted: "My part in the contract is that I apply violence. Okay. That's a given. You want to have your picture taken, you want to prevent a photograph, I want to photograph. From here on, how do we keep the contract?"[15] Kratsman speaks of keeping the contract, not of signing it. The fact of the contract's existence isn't a subject of doubt, either for him or for his colleagues.[16] What is repeatedly at issue is how the contract will be adhered to.

Relatively rarely, the person photographed seeks to challenge the power relations between him and the photographer while employing a directly resistant force. When he does so, he is usually doing this out of a commitment to the same universal spectator. Thus, for instance, in the photograph of the funeral in Nablus (see figure 7.3), the photographer was forced by the Palestinians following the coffin to be present at the funeral and to fulfill his role as photographer:

"We saw a funeral procession and we were surprised that there were no photographers there. When we started taking pictures, still from a distance, a few youths who had been leading the procession came up to us and pushed us in a very violent way into the cemetery. There, they started shouting 'Take this, take this.'"[17] The Palestinians knew what Kratsman and another photographer who was with him didn't know when they arrived on the spot. Only later did they understand, from an officer who ambushed them as they were leaving the cemetery: "He explained that there had been a deal between the army and the photographers that the funeral wouldn't be covered so there wouldn't be a mess. That was a time when there were a lot of claims that when there were cameras, the Palestinians made more trouble and that it heated things up."[18]

The Palestinians demanded their right — the possibility of showing the universal spectator what they considered to be worth her gaze, or, alternately, what only she would be able to see. Moreover, they preferred the civil contract of photography, in the framework of which they could both address and not just "willingly accept" the situation forced on them by the army. Kratsman himself, despite the violence used against him, took the photographs out of his commitment to the same universal spectator. Retaining the empty space of the [dead] universal spectator was what enabled him to maintain his contract with the photographed on another level as well: "I had my eye glued to the viewfinder the whole time, I understood that this was what was protecting me there, being a photographer, I didn't press the camera button all the time. With all the noise, they had no way of knowing when I was taking pictures."[19] As long as his eye was glued to the camera, Kratsman knew that he was relatively safe in the violent situation into which he had been physically pushed, shouted, and threatened. As long as his eye was applied to the camera viewfinder, the Palestinians' violence could ignore his concrete existence as an Israeli and see him as a photographer who is equally committed to the universal spectator. This was why Kratsman tried to extend the situation of photography for as long as possible. It allowed their tense relationships to take place under the aegis of the civil contract of photography.

392

Codes and Signals of the Civil Contract of Photography

Kratsman's reliance on the gesture that signified he was in the act of taking photographs helps illuminate the way in which the civil contract of photography simultaneously signals its presence and signals the ways in which its presence entails the concrete interests of those being photographed, even if — or especially when — those interests may be in conflict with the interests of others, without the contract being reduced simply to the partisan service of any particular interest. For example, since the end of the 1980s, Kratsman has been photographing in the Occupied Territories.[20] During the initial period, the daily press in Israel usually dealt with "events" in the territories from an abstract perspective or from one totally subservient to the Jewish-Israeli perspective. The Palestinian was faceless, nameless, one of a crowd — a rampaging, riot-spreading, injurious crowd that needed to be contained and taught a lesson in order to restore the peace.[21] The daily *Hadashot* took a revolutionary step when it turned the spotlight on the individual Palestinian, her life story, the injustice caused her, her daily tribulations, her biography, her worldview, her struggle against the occupation, her national aspirations, and the way in which she viewed the reality of occupation. During those years, the struggle was over the very act of making the Palestinian's photograph present and introducing his point of view.[22] In practice, the struggle was over making the victim present and drawing attention to her very existence as a victim.

The uniqueness of Kratsman's photographs from this period lies in the fact that they also simultaneously proposed the marginalization of the soldier, pushing him to the edge of the frame and even out of it. In other words, alongside the growing specificity of the Palestinian, they stripped the soldier of concrete facial features and transformed him into a generalized soldier figure. This was how Kratsman succeeded in carving out a space for the Palestinian in the discourse that tried to suppress him while relieving the specific soldier of direct and exclusive responsibility for his actions and addressing the question of responsibility to "the Israeli" in general.

In a collection of photographs from the first intifada that only in hindsight can be defined as a series, this double approach is manifest within the single frame. These are photographs of encounters —

393

usually extremely violent ones — in which there is physical contact between Israelis and Palestinians, physical contact leaving no space for doubt as to just who the ruled subject is. The subject appears in these photographs in his nakedness, as one who is at the mercy of someone else, for instance, in a photograph of a youth whose hair a soldier is clutching from behind, in a photograph of the Palestinian lying bound on the ground and doubled over in a futile attempt to protect himself, in a photograph of a girl whose hair is being pulled by a soldier, or in a photograph showing a terrified, running boy with a soldier's hand raised toward him.

Simultaneously making one group present and another abstract cannot follow from a grounded position of a single protagonist — Kratsman, in this case — but rather provides a striking example of the way in which the civil contract of photography links individuals with differing interests. In the abovementioned pictures of the first intifada, one could say that Kratsman's photography responded to both the Palestinian and the Israeli. In the context of the occupation, the Palestinian is the party with a damage claim, but his damage claim can be heard only before a nongovernmental court.[23] Regularly and for several decades, harm has been caused to the Palestinian. The harm done to her, accompanied by the lack of any institutional means for demanding that it be recognized and compensated, means she is forced to ignore the local judiciary and employ other channels offered by the local and global public sphere. In many cases, photography may serve as the sole solution at her disposal.

The Palestinian might thus be described as a party interested in photography and the photographer as a party who responds to this interest on reaching the arena of the Palestinian's injury. In contrast, the Israeli soldier, who is directly responsible for the damage and the injustice being caused to the Palestinian, is less interested in the photograph.[24] Kratsman indeed reaches him to photograph him as he retreats from the picture, that is, as one who is not too keen on being photographed. Accordingly, the contract of the photographer — Kratsman in this particular case — is not just with the future spectator of the photograph or universal addressee. It is always also a contract here and now with one or several concrete photographed persons who he encounters through the mediation of the camera.

394

His not necessarily intentional response to their demands — that of both the Palestinian and the Israeli — to transmit or not to transmit the content of the photograph occurs out of a clear stance that acknowledges the fact that the photograph never merely transmits content, but always also transmits the given stance vis-à-vis this content. In other words, Kratsman understands that the photograph will *always* reveal something about the act of photography, about the attitudes of the photographed people toward this act. Therefore, Kratsman's consent to photograph does not constitute an action serving this or the other party. Even if he had wished to, he could not satisfy both these adversaries. It is, rather, an act of implicit responsibility to the civil contract of photography and toward his professional position in this context.

The encounter of photography usually takes place within the framework of a clear protocol that, in most cases, need not be reiterated, because it is thought to be taken for granted. A camera raised in the hands of the photographer is thought to signal the beginning of the act of photography, and a flash or a click are conventional signals for the end of the action. In between, for as long as the photographer's eye is pressed to the viewfinder, everything may be photographed. The click or the flash of light are agreed-on signals, like the change of lights at a stop light, turning people's behavior in the presence of these signals into a conditioned reflex. Photographing in Nablus, Kratsman used this code in order to maintain his status as photographer, a status that in this specific case served him as a personal bodyguard.

The raised camera, like the clicking sound or the light flash it emits, allows the ritual to take place around mechanical signals that, at least on the face of it, neutralize the sense that it's the photographer who is controlling and manipulating the photographed people. Thus, when the click is heard, the photographed person can free himself of the pose he has taken without the photographer having to tell him explicitly to be "at ease."

These signals are characteristic of still photography. In a series of family portraits that Kratsman took in collaboration with Boas Arad in the Bedouin village Kasser El Sir, they used a small home camcorder similar in size to a still camera. The portraits were intended

395

as part of a public-relations film that they were preparing for the NGO BIMKOM (see figures 7.5–7.7). They asked the family to assemble for a family portrait in a single space. The family came together and formed a line in front of the photographer. Due to his habits as a still photographer, Kratsman raised the camera and put his eye to the viewfinder, rather than using the video screen of the camcorder. Time passed, and the family members stayed in place. None of the expected signals appeared, and the photographed people turned into captives of the act of photography. After about two minutes, as recorded on the camcorder, a small boy who had had enough started walking off and, following him, the rest of the family members scattered.

The absence of a signal that the photograph was done created a moment of embarrassment for both sides. The reactions of each side to this situation intensified the power relations between them. The photographer, who didn't lower the camera, maintained his position as photographer, although the act of photography was supposed to have been over quite a while before. The people being photographed stayed in place, didn't dare negotiate their status, accepted their subjection to the authority of an other without challenge, although the act of photography was supposed to have been over quite a while before.

The intensified power relations were not just those that brought these parties together as photographer and photographed people, but also those that form their civil world — the photographer as a first-class citizen and the people being photographed as citizens, true, but second-class ones whose abode and everything involved in that term are not recognized by state authorities. The people in question lack minimal services such as electricity, education, garbage removal, housing, and so on whose infrastructures the state is supposed to provide for all its citizens. The photographed people who remained hostage to the act of the photographer, who awaited the signal as an external, nonnegotiable force, in fact assigned to the photographer the authority to release them. The photographer appeared before them as the representative of two machines — the camera and the state. Their powerlessness vis-à-vis both, making them subjects of the sentence that each mechanism metes out, is

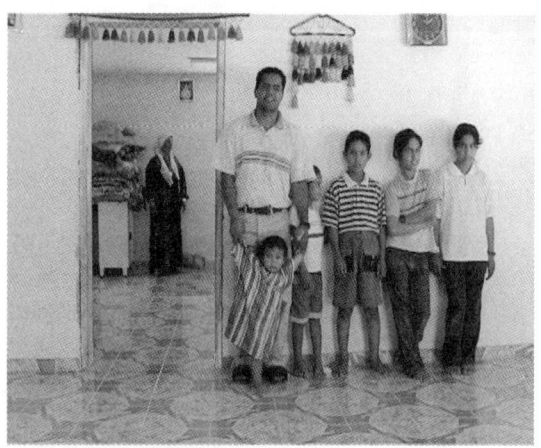

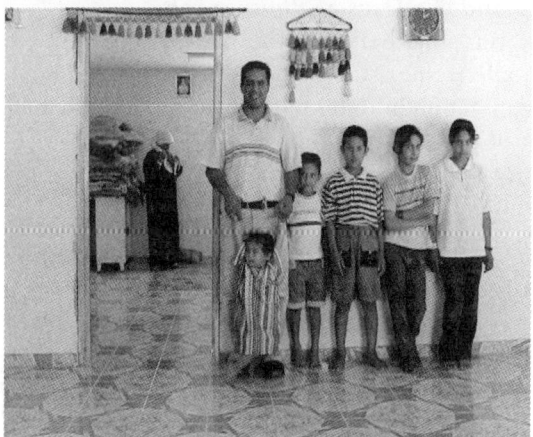

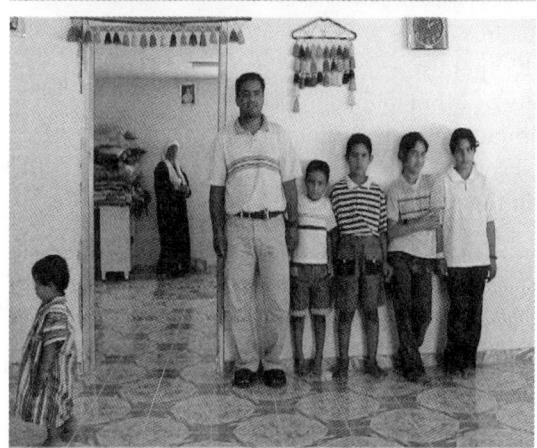

Figures 7.5–7.7. Miki Kratsman and Boas Arad, Kasser El Sir,
2003.

manifest in the "photograph." The spectator is invited to stand in front of the "photograph," projected in the space of the museum on a thin plasma screen, allowing the temporary illusion that this is a still photograph. Despite the illusion of stills, the picture isn't totally steady, and the spectator can slowly notice signs of discomfort on the faces of the photographed people and watch the way in which it is only the small boy who has the strength to "call out," in his act of desertion, that the king has nothing on, while he demonstrates by walking off that neither the photographer nor anyone else is possessed of the reasonable authority to hold them all hostage.

Ownership and the Uses of Photography
The power relations between the photographer and the photographed people are not stable. Neither do they unfailingly intensify in only one direction in times of confusion. They are malleable during the act of photography, but in cases where they're distinctly unequal, any temporary and symbolic changes are incapable of totally erasing the actual power relations between the photographer and the photographed person. The angry crowd at the funeral treated Kratsman violently in order to force him to photograph, but even in the context of this temporary inversion placing Kratsman in the hands of the Palestinians, he was the one whose gaze was perceived as the gaze toward which it is worthwhile orienting, the gaze that it is worth attracting, along with the series of future gazes that it generates.

Both this instability and malleability and the underlying power relations that persist are visible in Michal Heiman's work on the photographs of other photographers. Scanning their photographs into the computer unravels their boundaries and establishes them as potentials. From then on, they can be stabilized in different ways, emphasizing the photographer's point of view, making its existence present or, alternately, dropping it altogether, moving away from it and looking at the photographed people from another angle. Heiman takes (the) pictures that other photographers took (of/from others).[25] Even if in the act of taking the photographs the photographer has provided a direct or indirect service, the image is nevertheless one he has *taken*. Heiman doesn't play impostor or claim that *these* are her photographs. Within *her* frame she includes the credit in which newspaper acknowledged the photographer, as printed underneath the photograph, and she also includes additional fragments of the newspaper, enabling a reconstruction of the scene of the photograph's viewing. Her gesture to the unknown photographer, which contains an element of generosity, also contains a blunt, violent, and challenging gesture that forces a reopening of the issue of the ownership of a photograph of another as victim. "Her" collection grows incessantly and includes thousands of photographs taken by others. Some of them are probably seen by their authors as achievements, perhaps even the best of their work, and the agencies to which they are credited consider them their exclusive property.

The instability and malleability of photographs, as exemplified in Heiman's work, thus returns us once again to the problematic of ownership with regard to photographic images, this time to the related issue of the appropriation of images for uses other than those for which they were created. Bernard Edelman, in a Marxist reading of the history of photography, describes the ways in which the relations of production created the need to stabilize the issue of ownership, with the judiciary preferring to employ old and accepted categories that transformed the photographer, described just a short time before as an apprentice to the machine, into an independent creator leaving his mark on the photograph. [26]

In the rare instances where the photographed people themselves have been party to lawsuits, they have been highly skilled citizens possessed of the means and tools enabling them to manage their image in the world and to hone it as they wish. A famous case of this type was that of Jacqueline Kennedy-Onassis, who sued the fashion house of Dior for publishing "her" picture in an advertisement. Kennedy-Onassis demanded that the photograph be suppressed, claiming that she had never given consent to the use of her image for purposes of advertising consumer goods. Dior claimed, in its defense, that the image was not that of Kennedy-Onassis, but rather that of a model by the name of Barbara Reynolds, employed by an agency for celebrity look-alikes. The court ruled in favor of Kennedy-Onassis and in fact undermined the indexical relation between the photograph and the person standing in front of the camera. It established this relation as secondary to the relation between the photograph and what it looks like.

Jane Gaines, who analyses this case, compares the claims of Dior, (the photograph "is what it is") and of Kennedy-Onassis (the photograph "is what it *says*").[27] She claims that the precedent set by this case is one that views the photograph as what it says. Her claim and the precedent set by the lawsuit are part of the same ongoing attempt to formulate an understanding of the medium of photography and determine its status as an independent image-producing technology.[28] If this ruling is not turned into a claim about the essence of photography, however, a very different claim about the relation between the image and the individual's civil status may be extricated from it. The court totally ignored the question of the photographer's and Dior's ownership of the picture, therefore evading any challenge to the normative attribution of a photograph to its author. And yet it reinforced Kennedy-Onassis's civil status and determined that a person is entitled to decide what uses are to be made of her image.

The court thus distinguished between ownership of the photograph and the social uses to which it may be put. In so doing, it activated the civil contract of photography, which is supposed to protect the citizen not from the act of photography itself, for he or she has given hypothetical consent to conquering the world as a picture, but from improper uses of the photograph. Improper uses of photography, along with the injustices they generate, tend to disappear from sight when legal discourse or its interpretation reduces photography to a unified procedure derived from its "essence" and isolates its characteristics from the civil relations of photography.

I won't elaborate here on the entire range of unworthy uses of photography but, rather, on a particular strain, the type that derives from a breach of the civil contract of photography, either in advance or during the act of photography — in other words, from the abuse of the civil status of the photographed person. To illustrate, I'll address the case of the Afghan girl whose picture was taken in a refugee camp in the mid–1980s by the photographer Steve McCurry for *National Geographic*.[29] Her picture was published on the cover of the magazine, printed in ads publicizing the monthly, reprinted in the organization's fiftieth anniversary book, and became the subject of

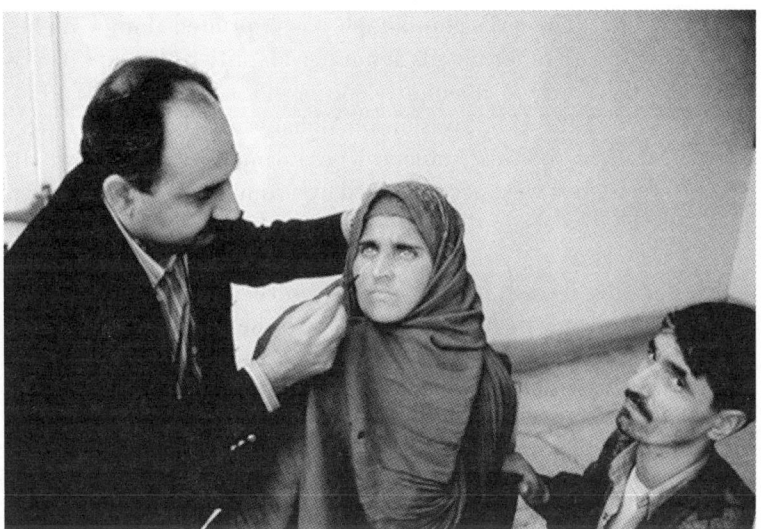

Figure 7.8. Steve McCurry, Sharbat Gula, still from documentary film by *National Geographic* on the search of Gula, 2003.

follow-up articles that brought the magazine millions of readers. Before she met Steve McCurry, Sharbat Gula had never had her picture taken (figure 7.8). The technology of photography had not reached her or her environs so the civil contract was not familiar to her. This in and of itself doesn't make her out of bounds for photography, but neither does it exempt anyone wishing to photograph her from an extra degree of responsibility for dispossessing her of her civil status under that contract. Since that single photograph, Sharbat Gula had no other pictures taken of her until Steve McCurry went back to search for her with the intention of telling millions of people the world over, all of whom had made her acquaintance through the first photograph, what had happened to her since — not what fate had befallen the Sharbat Gula who lived in a refugee camp, but rather what fate had befallen "the Afghan girl who was on the cover of *National Geographic.*"

When first printed, in 1985, the photograph illustrated an article on a refugee camp of Afghans who had fled their country due to the

Soviet invasion. The girl's photograph wasn't printed along with her name or with any other details about her identity or her life. It was present in the article as an empty signifier of the exotic and of afflic-tion. Following the U.S. invasion of Afghanistan, the photographer went on a search for "his" subject, whose name he didn't know. His efforts to trace her were accompanied by a simulation of legal proce-dures intended to verify that the woman in the new photograph was indeed the same girl who had appeared in the old photographs, which not only framed her story between two *National Geographic* covers but, indeed, turned the covers into the real story. The pho-tographer had to screen various candidates attempting to claim the coveted title of "the Afghan girl who was on the cover of *National Geographic*" so as to reject impostors, and he employed a series of humiliating examinations — of the pupils of their eyes, of their cheek bones, of their skull structure, and so forth. The testing process was documented, displayed to readers, and recorded in a film on the whole affair. Experts in various fields carried out the process of ver-ifying the photographed woman's identity, not in order to substanti-ate her ownership of her image, but, on the contrary, in order to substantiate the photographer's and the magazine's ownership of her image. Her consent to have her picture taken and her renewal of this consent, when it was proven to all that the person reaffirming the consent was the same photographed subject, made the photographer and the magazine the eternal owners of the image, relieving them of the need to share with her their ownership of the image or, needless to say, the profits they made from it.

When the first photograph was taken, Sharbat Gula was indiffer-ent to the medium of photography. She didn't ask to voice her com-plaint through it. Most likely, she didn't know that a photograph could be used for such purposes, and she therefore didn't expect it to free her from her predicament. The first photograph printed on the cover of *National Geographic* didn't express the civil contract be-tween her and the photographer or the readers of the magazine. It was more like a business contract that one side manages without the knowledge of the other side. Her breathtaking beauty and her exotic dress, coupled with her dissociation from any concrete reality and the concurrent preservation of the abstract "otherness" of the landscape and surroundings, helped turn her into an icon, a logo selling itself. Her beauty — her green eyes and her dark skin, her look, her otherness — all these turned into signifiers of affliction of the kind that remains unseen, unknown, and that therefore is mainly moving.[30]

Fifteen years later, the magazine, through the photographer, could not but offer the anonymous and nevertheless universally known figure a new contract. Between the first and the second photograph, between the first random encounter with the camera and the second intended one in whose realization large amounts of money and effort were invested, Gula became part of the civil contract of photography. She gave her consent to a series of photographs, the common element of which was the attempt to stress their linkage to the anonymous icon of the past. In return, she was promised that no identifying details would be disclosed regarding her whereabouts. The contract between her and the photographer (and the magazine) included a commitment on the part of *National Geographic* to construct a school for the education of young Afghan girls, and she, in return, enumerated in front of the cameras — this time the ones recording the *National Geographic* film about the search for her — the many advantages that the U.S. liberation of Afghanistan represented for her and for her people.

It is difficult to overlook the propaganda interests present in this search or its role in the American effort to build up a lobby supporting the invasion of Afghanistan. However, it is also difficult not to see that this time, the camera could not kidnap Gula's image as it had in the past. Whether it was she herself who demanded that a school be built in return for the photograph or the magazine that proposed the barter, the second photograph could no longer be hijacked like the first one.[31] Neither she nor the readers could remain indifferent to the act of photography. Readers who had for years been interested in her fate prepared the ground for a fairer barter, one from which Gula herself could benefit and whose conditions she would take an active role in formulating.[32]

Let us return now to the image of the two Palestinian women in their destroyed home and to the stamp "PHOTO RAPE" imprinted on it by Heiman (see figure 6.24),[33] for there is another dimension to the appropriation of images for uses other than those for which they were created, a dimension exemplified by what Heiman has, in turn, done to the image. It is an appropriation not for unworthy ends, but for worthy ones.

In the photograph, we can see the traces of the decisive moment that was hijacked from the photographed women, as if the women had been violently forced by the photographer and his camera to turn into a photograph. These women are refugees whose home in the Jenin refugee camp has been destroyed. They are sitting in its ruins. The content of the house has been pulverized, and blobs of color at the front of the frame, between the fragments of wall, are visible remnants of belongings that have lost their identity. Nothing is left whole under the rain of bombs and the force of the bulldozers. The walls are broken apart, and the home is transformed into a past home. Its inhabitants have nowhere to go. Where they sit is neither a private nor a public space. They are there, exposed to the gaze of passers-by. Day and a night, they are there. Sitting on borrowed chairs in the place that was their home — "in" it. There are no rescue forces, no emergency aid agencies, no rehabilitation plans. The photograph in front of us does not capture a single decisive moment. It is static — a "report from a disaster zone," as Amira Hess called it in the article that this photograph accompanied. In Heiman's series of photographs of destroyed homes (*Attacks on Linking*), the stamp "PHOTO RAPE" can't refer to the moment of the photograph. The "Photo Rape" in the Jenin refugee camp depicts a permanent condition. These are people who are totally exposed to others' gaze, dispossessed of their citizenship and, in this series of photographs, of their homes, as well, people who are unable to obstruct the act of photography. Whether physically or contractually, these are people who are utterly exposed.

In using the stamps, Heiman forces herself on the photographs. She positions herself as a party in the image and in the relations between the photographer and the women, as if she herself wished to bear witness. The women in the picture were raped, she tells us. Don't be misled by their heavy clothing, their bodies wrapped from head to foot, the silence surrounding them. There was an act of rape here. It's just that their bodies survived and are now forced to become a photo. It is not a photo of rape but a "Photo Rape." The photograph realizes the rape of these women, the act that potentially turned them into a picture. They are forced to become a picture from the moment they have lost their capacity to refuse to do so. Their right not to become a picture has been denied without their having had any means of resisting or anyone to protect their right. The stamp embedded in the photograph addresses the spectator, admits to the incapacity of the photograph alone to address the spectator assertively, to demand her attention, to demand her recognition of the injustice.

When the name of the photographer who took a photograph such as this one is known, Heiman seeks his permission to use the page of the newspaper on which the photo appeared. However, when the photographer is inaccessible, she uses the photo anyway and justifies her decision with the claim that the photographed women did not give the photographer their permission to print it either. In the spirit of the civil contract of photography, one might offer an alternative formulation to the effect that their consent to be photographed can be assumed, while this by no means includes consent to anyone's ownership or exclusive claim to their image and certainly not to its concealment from the public eye.

Through a series of intervening actions — sorting, cutting, re-photographing, emphasizing details, naming, stamping, enlarging, embedding, and others, Heiman "activates" the photographs. Their "activation" causes them to lose what might have been thought to be their stable content — the content answering to the gestures of identification that is thought to be owned by the photographer or the agency that employs him. As a result, the pictures invite reexamination. These are never photographs that have made the top of the hit list of horror images. They are pictures representing a banal, mundane, nonspectacular evil of a type that some of the spectators consider a legitimate act of punishment. The victims photographed in them are "routine victims." The Palestinians whose home has been destroyed around them do not stand at the center of a mass relief effort to assist them and to reconstruct their ruins. These static photographs include no dimension of urgency, either on the part of official bodies or on the part of the people photographed, and the spectator, following them, leafs calmly through her newspaper. This is the fate of the routine victim in the procession of horror images.

When the spectator enters the museum space in which this photograph is re-presented, however, she knows she is not alone. The doctored ("nursed") photograph clarifies what she missed about the photographed women earlier, in the picture's former incarnation as a newspaper item. She is not alone vis-à-vis the photograph. Neither is she alone in her shortsightedness. She is invited to reexamine both. Now, when the photograph has been blown up to giant dimensions, it would be difficult to miss either the photograph or what she previously had not seen. This series was displayed in the form of backdrops hanging from the ceiling like the ones displayed in photographers' studios. The photograph as backdrop constitutes an invitation to the spectator to stand in front of it and take a picture. The spectator is invited to use the photograph as a backdrop and take a snapshot. A souvenir. A monument to horror.

This invitation causes a form of discomfort that can be described in the following paraphrase: "Their catastrophe, my souvenir." It forces the spectator to decide, in full view of additional spectators, whether or not to take a picture. In using the invitation, the photographed women become a backdrop allowing the spectator to take a picture with her back to them and then to go home, taking their image along with her as booty. In declining the invitation, the spectator expresses her unwillingness to turn them into booty and her criticism of or reservations about those who do so.

Spectator A: Whatever they're handing out, I'm taking.

Spectator B: These are human beings. They've just been through a disaster. How can you loot them?

Spectator A: I'm not looting, and I'm not stealing, I'm shouting out my protest.

Spectator B: You don't care about anything at all. It's all the same to you as long as you've got something to take home with you.

Spectator A: That's so self-righteous — as if you didn't take home your morality?!

Spectator B: It's not the same thing.

Spectator A: Right. I take the photo home and give it life, show it to others — "and you shall tell to your sons. . . ."

Spectator B: Stepping on corpses, huh?

Spectator A: The scandal isn't here, where you're looking for it. The scandal is in what you see, and not in the fact that it's seen or that you take a picture.
And so forth.

Spectator A and Spectator B are formulating their stands. The photograph is silent. The fact that it is a backdrop invites them to act. The scene in the photograph is painful. If they look at the photo and see in it the suffering and affliction, their helplessness in the face of it simply increases. What could they even presume to do about it? The first proposes using the picture; the second proposes refraining from using it. The first suggests seeing and showing, distributing widely, prodding, transmitting, activating, deforming; the other suggests viewing it herself and abstaining from showing it. She calls for compartmentalization, sanctification, ritualization. Every day, as they leaf through the papers, they see photographs like it. They have already adopted a particular viewing practice.

Most likely, the predominant viewing practice is a quick glance at the photo while reading the caption and a hop skip and a jump to the next page. This practice was instituted after they had already seen painful pictures. It's the practice of one who has been there, not that of one who first encounters a photograph of suffering, horror, or affliction. At some point, they don't remember when it happened. Usually, when they flip through the paper, no one is watching them. It's just them and the photograph. It's hard for them to stay with it, to watch it; they're more comfortable when it passes. The space of the museum and the implicit invitation to take a picture causes them to stop for a moment and examine other options, to offer themselves an account of their attitude toward photographs in general and to horror photographs in particular.

The first spectator can't bear the loneliness she feels in the face of the picture and proposes getting herself out of it. She doesn't know what worthy viewing is, she just knows that it's hard for her there alone. Maybe if she shares the photograph with someone, shares her presence vis-à-vis the photograph, something will become clearer — the photo, her attitude toward it, or maybe her attitude toward the world. The second spectator may or may not feel lonely, but she prefers to stay that way, to immerse herself in her singularity opposite the picture and, through this, to determine what improper viewing is. Not only doesn't she want to peep at the photographed women in their misery, she would also like the newspaper editor to think similarly, and perhaps also the photographer. But the horror goes on, and it generates more and more photographs; what is left is examining the various uses and politely rejecting those that propose making no use of photography.

Heiman is a spectator of the first type. For years now, her work has expressed a refusal to remain alone in front of the photographs. Testers, spectators, photographers — everyone is invited to help her look at the photographs, whether in private or in public. In 1997, she created her first "test" of the spectator — *Michal Heiman Test No. 1* — in the framework of which spectators entering the museum were invited to talk about photographs that were shown to them by an "examiner" (figure 7.9).[34] The discussions of the photographs that this generated publicly transgressed the photograph's dumbness and the museum's silence.[35] The tests created by Heiman, like her transformation of destroyed homes into backdrops offering the conditions for re-creating the photographic situation within the museum, express the anxiety/phantasm invested in the act of viewing horror: "Don't leave me alone in face of these photographed people. Talk about the photographs to me." At the same time they are an attempt to replace the anxiety/phantasm with a civil collaboration that will place it between brackets. "What is in the photograph?" "What is seen in it?" "Who is seen in it?" "Why are they looking at me like that?" "What is she doing?" "What is he up to?" "Why is she silent?" "What is that blob?" "Where is she looking from?" "What does he see?" — myriad questions, all of which are troubling and all of which will remain, in the final analysis, without conclusive answers.

The anxiety in the face of the photograph's silence is transposed onto a double phantasm: that it will stay silent and its truth will be buried beneath it forever, that it will speak loudly, directly or via mediators, and will betray what ought to be silence. These anxieties/phantasms derive from the double status of the photograph as transcendent and as the handiwork of a person. Thus, the procedures employed with relation to the photograph ask it to speak, to explain

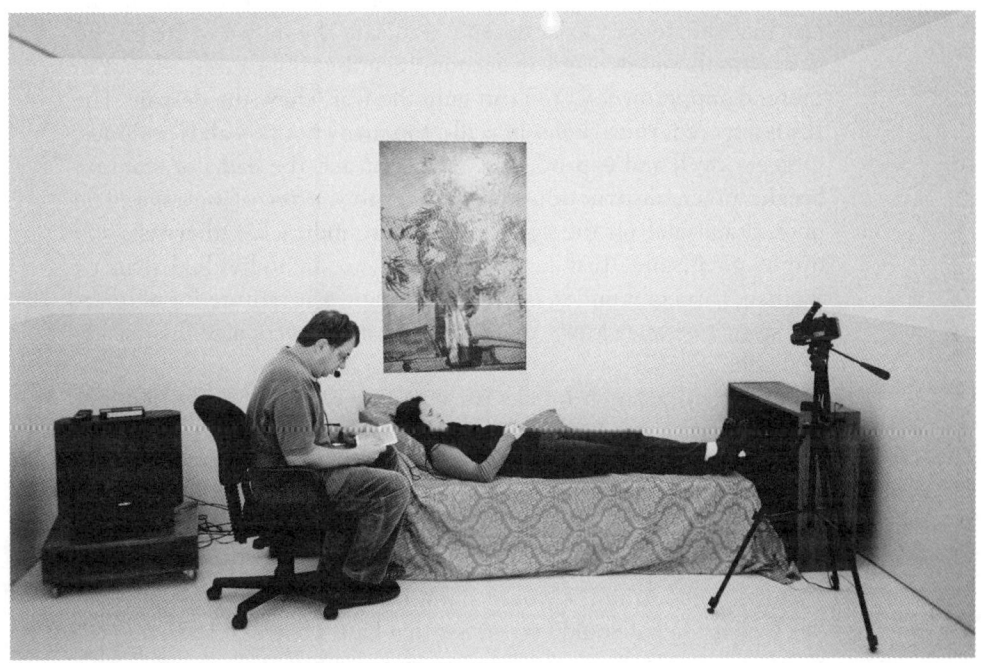

Figure 7.9. Michal Heiman, *Enactment, Michal Heiman Test (M.H.T.) No. 1 – My Mother-in-Law*, 1998 (Le Quartier, Centre d'art contemporain, Quimper), installation, projection test, green box, 4.5 x 17.5 x 24.5 cm, Herzliya Museum of Art, 2000.

itself, and see it as "supposed to know," while the procedures creating the network of speakers ask them to speak, to explain the photograph, and with their assistance — examiner, assistant, museum
spectator, and so on — to recognize that the one who is "supposed to
know" does not exist.

The one who is supposed to know has long ago evaporated. The
fact that she doesn't exist doesn't eradicate the desire to latch onto
her coattails and demand an account. See the suffocation? It's hot in
there, damp, crowded. You can gulp the fear, chew the despair. The
sky is angered, ruins, holes in walls, too many hours — all is ominous.
Objects swell and expand, the walls contract, the dams of emotion
break: anger, destruction and devastation, cries of outrage. The
photographs deliver the sights without a soundtrack. Otherwise, you
might go insane. Just faces, portraits, of an individual man or
woman, parts of families, emblems of death, a substitute for obituar-
ies, so that we may know the face of the dead, recognize the malady
of death.

And then a laugh breaks in, bursting out of the photograph,
taunting, grating, relentless. This time the photographer didn't erase
it. And again the routine silence, measured movements up and
down, endless skill, you could go crazy every day, every day, the
clenched lips, the razor-sharp direct gaze. The photographer is long
gone, will be back tomorrow; the soldier, still there, stays within the
frame — without him, I would stand face to face with the lady and
her baskets. What could I say to her that hasn't been said to her yet —
what? You could go insane, but I go insane when she's absent, when
the pictures disappear, when all goes on as usual, but the photographs refuse to appear, turned down, politely rejected, the editor
making time for another type of color, better suited to the season,
lighter and more transparent, a pastel-tinted chiffon skirt, and again
on the next page, you can go crazy, rummage through boxes, use old
newspapers, eat breakfast with them — if they hadn't turned yellow,
one would never know that what's printed in them isn't new, as
fresh as if they were this morning's paper — five killed, four portraits,
one missing, the family refused to cooperate, soldiers in night lighting, ready to counter the fall of Qassam rockets. "Like in a David
Lynch movie," the editor thought and stretched the photograph

across a double spread: The plaintiff will be charged, her face blurred, intentionally, perhaps *sub judice* or maybe not. The question whether it's a paper from this morning or a year ago is important only this morning — by noon it evaporates, the pages jumbled on the desk, piles of yellowing newsprint, a paper dam.

But whether there are or aren't any photographs, the pictures are present all the time. When the photographs are absent, only words are left; when the words are on their own, language is foreign, threatening, unreliable, abstract, used, sometimes overused, homogenized, without cracks, without blemishes, without a stranger who held it and staked a claim to it, the same stranger who always arises out of the photograph, who has acted on the photograph, acted on the photographer's action, collaborated with him, no, not consentingly — it can happen without consent, as well. The photographer didn't even know, and here she is, the stranger — there in the picture, no, not the photographed person, another stranger, strangeness that has turned the action into a joint one through acting on it, deflecting it from its course, robbing its meaning, returning it to its owner, who no longer recognizes it, who thought it was his, promised better times, as if he were the giver.

Without photographs, one can go insane. The photographs testify that those photographed are still there: Look — they participated in the act of photography, always a joint action, a multiparticipant action, and the photograph is a dam holding back someone's words, a living contradiction. There was someone else there, and sometimes it takes weeks to see the part of it that is the foreign presence, sometimes days, never immediately, at least an hour. Sometimes the photographed man or woman has no part in it — the photograph may have no people in it, nothing in it but landscape, the landscape that all have abandoned. Then, too, you need hours of looking, possibly days, weeks, or years, but in the end, the silver iodide will burst into dance and disrupt the limits of the photograph.

The photograph is the site where the collaboration coughs up its secret. There is no noncollaborative action except when life ends. When life ends on one side, the air thickens on the other. The sky is open and clouds float, laughing above at the border traced on maps in a sure hand and transcribed onto the stony fields.

CHAPTER EIGHT

The Public Edge of Photography

Lying folded on my desk for over a year in a transparent plastic folder is the front page of the October 14, 2004, Hebrew daily *Ha'aretz*. The photograph it features, which is the reason I saved this page, shows a Palestinian man, his upper body naked, in the custody of armed soldiers (figure 8.1). The caption accompanying the photograph describes the "event" that it apparently documents, but retains total indifference to the photo itself and to what it shows: "Quasma's arrest yesterday in Hebron. His interrogation to examine the role of Hamas's Damascus branch in directing terrorist attacks in the territories."[1] Imad Quasma, commander of Hamas's military wing in Hebron, is standing at the center of the photograph, his hands pulled back, most probably handcuffed. The strip of flannel cloth around his forehead is slightly confusing. It adorns his forehead as if he were an athlete taking part in some kind of game, but a look at the photograph on the next page of the paper will verify that moments earlier, this flannel strip served as a blindfold, "as is customary in these parts." The strip of flannel cloth usually allows soldiers to hold Palestinians they happen to encounter, marking them as unauthorized to resume whatever journey they were on for the duration of the time when the soldiers, who are overburdened with surveillance and control tasks, are unable to tend to them. Using minimal means, the multipurpose strips of cloth facilitate this violent detainment while removing the Palestinian as someone they must engage in their own field of vision by shutting off the gaze with which he, in turn, could engage them. In the photograph in question, the traces of this use of

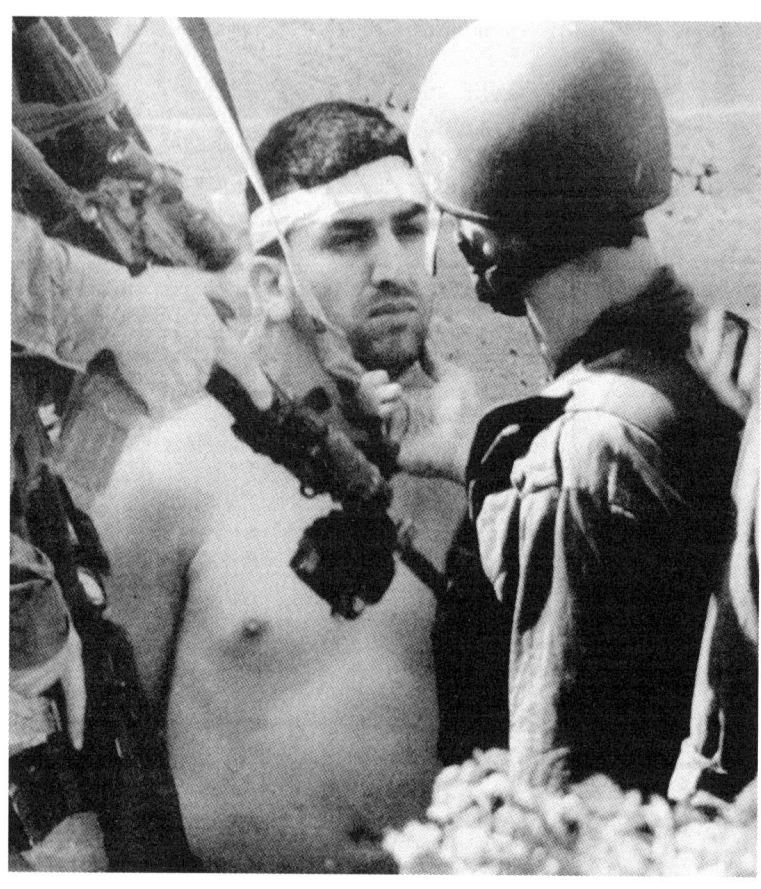

Figure 8.1. Imad Quasma Arrest, Hebron, *Ha'aretz*, October 14, 2004 (Reuters).

flannel strips are visible, but at this point, the cloth strip has been slid up onto the forehead, above Quasma's eyes, which are now free to stay wide open. There's no ignoring the fact that the flannel strip has not been removed altogether. It remains tied around his head, threatening to lower the curtain once again, a reminder for Quasma, and possibly for others, that it is the soldier who determines the visible limits of the field of vision as he covers and uncovers the eyes of detainees at will.

It is precisely the front-page photograph in which the eyes of the Palestinian are uncovered just after being blindfolded that not only enables a view of the extensive force at the disposal of this junior representative of the sovereign, who is authorized to play with the flannel strip as he sees fit, backed by at least three other armed soldiers (not by one, as the spectator might think at first glance), which reveals the insane logic of Israel's rule in the Occupied Territories, seeking total occupation of the Palestinian's gaze, its neutralization, and its subjection to manipulation at will. "Following soldiers' orders," reads the news item coupled with the photograph, "Quasma stripped down to his underwear to verify the absence of an explosive belt."[2] On the face of it, this is a common scene, one in which soldiers are seen seeking a deepened gaze at the Palestinian, a gaze aimed at deciphering his intentions and desires, his worldview and his plans. The gaze of the soldier serving in the Occupied Palestinian Territories is *authorized* to scrutinize the Palestinian. The dubious skill of serving as a human x-ray machine has been constituted by the no less dubious authority to render the Palestinian accessible to the gaze of a conquering power.

The soldiers' gaze at the Palestinian plays a crucial role in the soldiers' daily routine. As we have noted before, every single one of their encounters with Palestinians turns into a localized checkpoint: an observation point at which the Palestinian's movement is intercepted and blocked so that the soldier can examine him. The gaze in question is a violent one, invasive, investigative; through it, the soldier presumes to learn the truth hidden in the given body. In the wake of this gaze, the soldier creates a signal marking the Palestinian as either "authorized" to or "prohibited" from proceeding. In a conversation I had with a "military party" to whom I was referred by the

Israel Defense Forces spokesperson, I enquired about the skills possessed by the soldier stationed at a checkpoint, equipping him to look and determine people's fates based on this look. The party in question responded in amazement, "What do you mean? He isn't blind." The soldier not only sees, he also understands fully what it is that he sees, and anyone else who "isn't blind" would see just what the soldier sees. In other words, looking at the Palestinian as a suspect requires no particular skills, nor does it result from a gaze that is in any way exceptional. On the contrary, this is the normal gaze of any Israeli citizen, the common gaze characteristic of any who aren't "blind." This gaze is shared by both the citizen and the ruling power — the citizen who recognizes the Palestinian as a threat and supports the power's authority to look directly at the Palestinian without the mediation of citizenship or of any particular field of knowledge, which it does on behalf of citizens to achieve their protection.

The soldier, who is at one and the same time both a citizen and an authorized representative of the sovereign, demonstrates this point of view. However, the photograph allows an encounter with this point of view not as it is described by the soldier, but as it leaves its traces in the frame testifying to it. The soldier claims to verify that Quasma has not concealed a belt of explosives on his body. A look at the photograph, though, distinctly clarifies the extremely slight connection, if any exists at all, between this task and what it shows. In most of the photos showing Palestinians in the process of raising their shirts before soldiers' eyes, it is usually obvious that several meters separate the two parties, ensuring — to the soldiers — that they will not be injured if the Palestinian is indeed wearing an explosive belt that he proceeds to detonate. In the second photograph accompanying the news item, Quasma's arm is being gripped by an armed soldier who is leading him. The physical proximity between the two indicates that the actors have already completed the stage in which Quasma was made to bear testimony through his body. His nearly naked body has already finished providing the answer. Nevertheless, the soldiers have left him in his underpants, without his clothes. They are not satisfied with an instrumental, examining look at him, and they do not opt for employing the strip of flannel cloth as a blindfold to free themselves of the Palestinian's gaze, thus removing any engagement with his own gaze. The photograph indicates that in this particular encounter, they are seeking something else. This thing, which is nameless and pointless, has for several decades now entrapped them within its web, forcing them again and again to intercept the Palestinian and, with his participation, to stage the same piece of theater over and over. Difference and repetition. Here it is before us.

True. You don't have an explosive belt strapped to your body, but that doesn't mean you don't intend to put one on or to dispatch someone else with such a belt strapped to his body. Let's look you in the eye, let's see what you have to say for yourself. You think I don't know you people. So what if you're the head of the military branch. You will let me look at you as much as I like. I'm the one making the rules here.

The soldier persists in the erratic presumption that Quasma will be revealed to him in his nakedness. He tries to make the gaze go deeper, to look inside and uncover the truth that Quasma is trying to hide. He knows Palestinians like him; "he's not blind." He is not alone in his presumption of knowing the naked Palestinian or in the persistence he discloses in his endless attempts to realize it: "The fact that Quasma chose to turn himself in to IDF forces is somewhat surprising. Other activists, serving as the heads of the military branches of the Hamas in Hebron and Nablus, such as Ahmed Bader and Mohammad al Hanbali, opted for a fight to the death when soldiers arrived to arrest them — and sometimes even succeeded in killing IDF soldiers." These are the words of Amos Harel and Arnon Regular in the article accompanying these photographs. True, they are citizens, but they represent the national gaze of the regime. They're not blind. They, too, know the Palestinian, foresee his actions, surprised at his surrender, but in fact not really so surprised, for their surprise is merely temporary, since it is obvious that there's no relying on what seems visible at the surface. If Quasma has turned himself in, he must have ulterior motives that will surely be revealed in the future, affirming this suspicion.

The journalists don't pause to wonder about the disproportionate force amassed by the military in order to remove Quasma from his home or about the damage inflicted on his neighborhood and its residents. In the manner of reportage on military actions, they report

417

dryly that on the morning when Quasma came out of his house carrying a white flag to turn himself in, "The Egoz unit of the Golani Brigade" assisted by "forces from the Nachal Brigade" surrounded the group of homes around Quasma's house, fired in the direction of his house, and let loose a bulldozer that commenced destroying the building. Even the fact that the fire power directed at such "heads of the military branches of the Hamas" turns the phrase "a fight to the death" into a euphemism raises no questions for these journalists.

The soldier in the photograph is forcefully gripping Quasma's chin. He has locked it between his index finger and thumb, preventing the face from moving, as if he is seeking to fix Quasma's gaze onto him alone, to force the Palestinian to look at him as he — the soldier — speaks to him. This is a pattern of the use of force that is familiar to many from recent personal history, mainly as a gesture of parents' or teachers' education of a child. It seems rather out of place here on the background of the explicit, armed violence that serves as an organizing principle central to the entire scene.

Don't you dare move while I'm looking at you. Sure, I took off the flannel blindfold, but that doesn't mean that you can look wherever you please now. I'm looking you in the eye. You've gotta look back at me. Look back at me right now and go on looking until I tell you that you can stop. Look me straight in the eye while I'm talking to you.

Quasma unlike other "wanted men" as they are described in the article, didn't "fight to the death." Quasma laid down his arms, and now he stands naked before a proxy soldier. Quite soon, the soldier will pass him on to his "superiors." He knows that the head of the Hamas military branch in Hebron is "in his hands" for just a short time. He will soon have to part with him, pass him up along the chain of command into the appropriate hands. But he wants something for himself, too. A look. Recognition: "I caught you. I'm a low-ranking soldier, yet I'm the master." But the master cannot be awarded the recognition of one who is not a master. So the soldier will have to grip Quasma's chin for a long time to come. He won't be able to achieve the recognition he seeks. Quasma will not grant it. In the face of the empty gestures of the soldier who acts as if Quasma, who is in his custody, is listening to what he says, Quasma stands determined, staring, not lowering his gaze, not delivering the desired gaze of recognition, but rather one implying *I do not recognize you as someone deserving my recognition.*

Reorganizing the Plane of the Visible

The horrors generated by the ruling apparatus over the occupied Palestinian territories have generated numerous images, especially during the second intifada. The dissemination of this particular image, like that of other images, through various channels does not by any means ensure that they will turn into objects of the civil gaze. The instrumental point of view that is embodied by the soldier in the photograph, while also serving as the vantage point from which he directs his gaze, is a point of view that permanently endangers the civil gaze. The instrumental gaze is powerful, widespread, threatening, prevalent, simple, easily skimmed through, and well fit to the conventional conformist narrative. It is commonly served up along with justifications and proof of its necessity. As the photograph of Quasma shows, his detainment is not prohibited as a subject of photography. Photographs like this one are readily accessible, and they are often printed without batting an eye. It might even be said that the power of the regime, through its myriad representatives (those fulfilling appointed positions and those volunteering to represent it) makes use of such photographs, turning them into yet another apparatus of rule.

A Reuters photojournalist documented Quasma's detainment. He was there, photographing the military success. The photograph is unequivocal evidence of this success. But also evidence of the interest shared by the army and the photographer in showing Quasma's face. The strip of flannel over his eyes would have left his identity uncertain. This way, with the flannel pushed up around his forehead, it's possible to see that he has been detained and that the detained person is indeed him. Photojournalist Ronnie Schitzer documented the detainment of Azam Nabil Diab — or, in the words of the headline and caption printed in *Maariv* on August 19, 2001: "The facilitator, the man who guided the suicide bomber." Here too, the photographer followed the capture at very close quarters. Here, too, the nearly total nakedness of the Palestinian demonstrates that as he was being handled by the military, the photographer was walking around nearby in order to document the event and doing so with the encouragement, the permission, and the inspiration of the army. The army's penetration into more and more areas of Palestinians' lives and the permeation of its presence throughout the entire space extend the level of publicness at which its actions are carried out while slating them for more frequent exposure to the presence of a photographing eye.

However, an understanding of the extension of the visible surface of military actions is impossible without an account of the way in which the security forces produce and maintain areas that are insulated from public view. The connection between both these simultaneous motions — opening up and shutting out — is characteristic of the ruling apparatus in the Occupied Territories in general, extending beyond the issue of gaze. When one closely scrutinizes the field of vision that they produce, it is clear that what is at issue is not two contradictory motions that allow a reading of what appears in the field of vision and what is excluded from it as manifestations of the ruling apparatus's efforts to hide what it is perpetrating from the public. Such an attempt to understand the difference between what can and cannot be displayed in the field of vision as an expression of moral or legal boundaries is outdated for purposes of understanding the mode of action of the ruling apparatus, and it may create the false illusion that the disclosure of more and more images of the horror it is perpetrating might bring about its end.

A discussion of the field of vision of the occupation in simple, binary terms such as "open"/"closed," "hidden"/"explicit," or "legal"/"illegal" further blurs the ability to understand that what is at issue is a mechanism of action that incessantly produces differences that operate in a manner that is independent of the nature and essence of the differences produced: differences between a full citizen and a partial citizen, between a citizen and a subject, between an illegal sojourner and a foreign worker, between a prison and an incarceration facility, between a detention center and a curfew, between closure and siege, between administrative detention and detention under Military Summons 1500, which allows the army to detain Palestinians incommunicado for up to eighteen days with no access to judges or lawyers and then to renew authorization for detainment under similar conditions for an overall period of up to ninety days — and on and on, amplifying the direct damage inflicted by the ruling apparatus on those it rules through the extension of its options and range of action. When these series of differences are subjected in the final analysis to a binary logic, they succeed in creating a semblance of law and order and of logic and method. Thus, this incessantly reproduced binary logic allows the state of Israel within the "Green Line," the 1949 Armistice Line separating Israel from Egypt, Jordan, and Lebanon after the 1948 Arab-Israeli War, to continue operating as a democratic regime while another distinct regime — which is nevertheless an inseparable part of the state — is in place outside the sovereign territory.[3] What is in question here is not just what the ruling apparatus allows to be viewed or prevents from being viewed, as if an agreement could be constituted between the ruling power and the civil gaze as to what the objects of this gaze can be. The central question can no longer be how to make visible what the ruling apparatus seeks to keep invisible, but rather how to reorganize the plane of the visible.

This can be achieved by employing two procedures. One of these is extricating from existing photographs what is inscribed in them, but remains in the margins, pushed aside by familiar figures, easily readable, that appear at its center and overshadow the rest of what is visible — a bracketing of figures that will help me to emphasize and construct a visual object that, at first glance, seems not to exist in the photographs. The second procedure involves reconstructing and fabricating images from verbal testimonies in order to achieve this reorganization of the plane of the visible through a refusal to recognize the category of "authentic documentation" as the sole criterion for determining the borders of the visual reservoir and through an acknowledgment of the role of textual elements in organizing the plane of the visible.

The Penal Colony

"Prison photos?!" was the rhetorically incredulous answer I got from photojournalists and activists working with various human-rights groups. There's no such thing, all of them claimed, explaining that, most of the time, taking photographs in prisons is forbidden.[4] And indeed, equating the space of imprisonment with the official space of the prison may well entrap one in the illusion of a visual vacuum and an interdiction on photography. However, deflecting the discussion from the official boundaries of the prison space to the practices of detainment and imprisonment and gathering together photographs testifying to these practices allows the emergence of the incarcerating logic in the enormity of its pervasiveness, in the fact that it has become the daily routine of all the Palestinians who inhabit the Occupied Territories, their penal colony. Moreover, such a shift not only enables one to face a huge repertory of photographs, but also to take into consideration the numerous photographs that are *absent*, inaccessible at present, but at least known to exist, for there is evidence that they have been taken. I'm referring to photographs taken by the army and the General Security Service (the "Shabak") that are used to facilitate their management of the penal colony. The existence of these photographs and their inaccessibility necessitate a careful reconstruction, not only of what is visible in them, but also of the photographic utterance in general in circumstances of repression. The reconstruction of this imagery is necessary in order to make present what is visible in the photographs, as well as the conditions in which they were created.

There are dozens of amateur photographers serving in the ranks of the Shabak. They release the shutters on their cameras as a matter of routine, as part of the regular series of actions they perform vis-à-vis Palestinian detainees. I am not referring to the widespread procedure of taking mug shots of each and every detainee, but rather to the photographs produced in the course of an interrogation for future use. This is a unique type of photo that might be termed a "torture photograph." These photographs do not show torture, but serve, themselves, as a mode of torture. Partial and limited information on the use of photography in the course of interrogations appears in the margins of the testimonies of detainees that are regularly collected by the Public Committee Against Torture in Israel and by the B'Tselem human-rights information center. This information has never been collected or researched as a separate category, nor has this form of torture been recognized as a singular phenomenon or as an item on the list of methods of torture produced and periodically updated by these organizations.

The testimonies indicate two types of photographs. In the first, relatives or someone who is dear to a detainee under interrogation are photographed in harsh conditions of detention or of severe abuse, and these photographs are placed in front of the detainee during his interrogation. In the second use of photography in the service of torture, the detainee himself is either photographed or threatened that he will be photographed in such a way as to be potentially incriminated within and by his social environment, based on his appearance in the photo. In both cases, the photograph is presented as a bearer of truth related to the figure photographed in it, and the very display of this truth is designed to lead the person under interrogation to disclose the secret he is assumed to be attempting to hide. In this process, the photograph is not the object of a gaze inviting its spectator to pause over what it shows so as to discern, through what is inscribed in it, the traces of an encounter surrounding the camera and of the power relations that allowed the photograph. Rather, it is reduced to its denotative existence and pared down to an object possessed of a distinct and stable identification and designation of the type "This is your mother in solitary confinement" or "This is a collaborator."

Had these photographs been accessible for public viewing, they could have been liberated from the instrumental meaning that the Shabak interrogator sought to impose on them. What is visible in them could have been prodded to speak. After being briefly displayed to the people under interrogation, from who we learn of their existence, and after serving the interrogators as a means of acting on these people, they are either destroyed or archived in inaccessible basements. As part of the ongoing injury inflicted on the Palestinian person and his capacity for employing civic skills and abilities, of which looking at photographs is one, the interrogator circumscribes the photo to its value as a vehicle of unequivocal truth — "a mother in solitary" or "someone collaborating" — imposing this truth on the person under interrogation.

The inaccessibility of these photographs threatens to turn us, those who are viewing the occupation, into collaborators with the interrogator if we accept without question that what the photograph indeed shows is the bit of information that the interrogator seeks to elicit from it: "a mother in solitary" or "someone collaborating." In order to see in the photo what it is that the interrogator wishes to show the detainee under interrogation, we are called on to perform a violent and intentional erasure of what we know or what we are capable of knowing about the circumstances of this act of photography. In fact, that is quite a bit. After all, the testimonies of the people who have undergone interrogation provide us not only with the identified content of the photograph, but also with the circumstances of its production.

Here is an example of such a testimony. "From time to time, Benny would catch hold of my shirt collar and bang my back against the wall," 'Abed A-Nasser 'Ubeid testified.[5]

> In the course of the interrogation, Captain Benny brought out a piece of white surgical tape, stuck it on my chest, and wrote the word "collaborator" (*amil*) on it in Arabic, as well as the number 745421088. He started teaching me the number. It took me about 3 hours to learn it. Afterward, he took my photograph and told me: "I'll spread your pictures all over the detainment center and all over your village, and masked men will throw Molotov cocktails at your house and burn your three little daughters, and at the detainment center they'll interrogate you and torture you."[6]

In many cases, the Shabak interrogator doesn't need to disseminate the photo beyond the limits of the prison. The "birds' cell," as detainees call the collaborators' cell, has been used to fulfill the required role "in house."[7]

"Captain Benny" created an entire sight-and-sound spectacle in order for 'Ubeid to be revealed in the photograph in the identity of a "collaborator." Using this identity, eternalized in a photograph, he threatened the man under interrogation, attempting to reveal his true identity as a member of the Hamas movement. Captain Benny was obliged to create a complex spectacle because a photograph alone, always and in principle, cannot convey truth and definitely cannot convey the whole truth. A photograph is a fragment that can be prodded in to speech only if it is woven into a discourse. The interrogator sought, by means of torture, to drive into 'Ubeid's consciousness the identity number that the Shabak assigns to someone whom it has forcefully drafted into its service. 'Ubeid was forced to say the number aloud and in a manner seeming to indicate that he had repeated it many, many times, so as to convince his neighbors in the other cells, who were to be shown the photograph, that he had indeed been inducted into the service of the Shabak and, consequently, represented a target for their violent revenge. However, his Palestinian neighbors in the next cell, for the benefit of whose ears and eyes this spectacle had been staged, had abused and tortured 'Ubeid not, as the Shabak had threatened, because he was a collaborator, but because they themselves had been forced into collaboration and had been ordered to become the torturers of 'Ubeid: "Abu A. told me: Now I'll show you something that if the young men see, they'll kill you. Abu A. covered the bed with blankets and then showed me the picture that Benny took of me. Now you have to prove to us that you're not a collaborator.... Two of them held my arms and legs and a third lit a cigarette and started burning my hands" (figure 8.2).[8]

The photograph of 'Abed A-Nasser 'Ubeid in which he's shown with surgical tape on his chest inscribed with the word "collaborator" was supposed to incriminate him due to the truth that it seemingly conveyed. In fact, given the circumstances in which the Shabak used it, the photograph was totally superfluous. What was apparently not superfluous in the interrogators' view was performing the ritual of photographing and enacting the threat that the act of photography posed to a person held in custody in circumstances of horror and terror. The photograph was superfluous because those to whom it was presented — imprisoned collaborators at the disposal of the Shabak — did not acquire it by accident. As stated, they were accomplices, albeit forced ones, in its production and in creating its effects. They were ordered to cause 'Ubeid to prove, under torture, that in contrast to what was graphically shown in the photograph, he was not a collaborator with the Shabak, but rather a member of Hamas. Like him, they too, had been tortured as a way of forcing them to become collaborators. Unlike him, however, they had broken down and become collaborators. For this reason, perhaps, symbolically, when 'Ubeid displayed his cigarette-burned forearms to the camera, he did not reach away from himself, but rather drew his

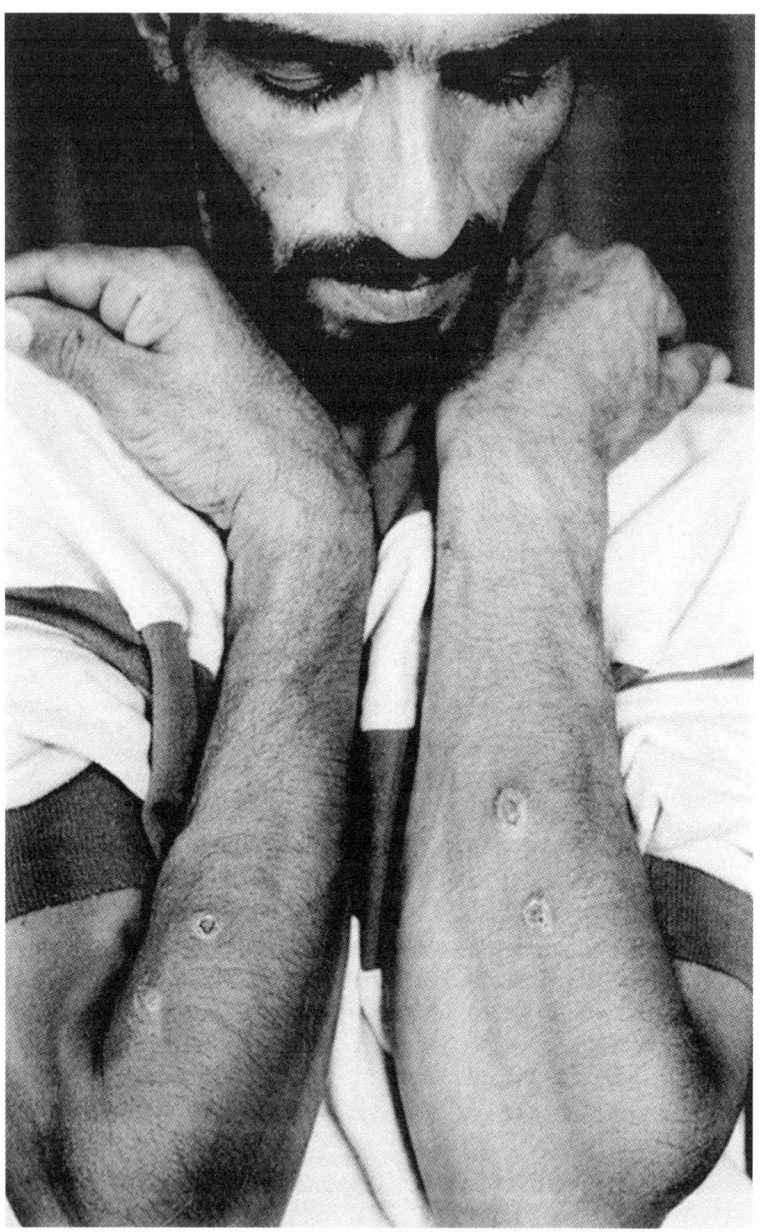

Figure 8.2. 'Abed A-Nasser 'Ubeid, September 17, 1993 (B'Tselem).

arms toward himself, folded them in an intimate gesture of closeness and embrace, signifying a containment of sorts on the part of one who is angry at the act, but cannot place himself totally in an external judgmental position. 'Ubeid is seen in the photograph bowing his head toward his arms, looking down at them as if seeking to guide the viewer's gaze toward the burns, looking at them, beaten and ashamed, posing and hiding simultaneously, perhaps because the only visual evidence that he can display publicly for the torture he experienced is evidence of the act perpetrated by his brothers, those who (like him) were tortured and coerced until (unlike him) they obeyed the order to torture him. This photograph, then, should be displayed as a photograph of double torture.

A careful reconstruction of the complex circumstances of the photograph I have just shown and the inclusion of photographs that are not viewable at present in the visual field allow us to extend the field of vision that the Israeli ruling apparatus seeks to instrumentalize completely. This extension thus allows the spectator to avoid the trap of reducing the meaning of the photograph to the last event in a chain documented by it in isolation: a display of the burn marks left by the cigarettes that Palestinian collaborators stubbed out on the forearms of 'Ubeid.

In the early 1990s, at the height of Israel's use of torture under the aegis of the law, the human-rights information center B'Tselem, produced a series of photographs as part of the struggle against torture in Israel. At press conferences and various other conferences, the organization publicly performed several common kinds of torture from which it produced these photographs, which it then proceeded to disseminate as part of its various reports on torture (see figures 8.3–8.5). Despite the fact that these photographs were simulations produced by people working to stop torture in Israel, they bear testimony to the use of torture. The fact that these photographs, presenting the kinds of positions commonly used in interrogation, were displayed publicly while no attempts were made by any state institutions, including the Shabak, to challenge their accuracy or deny them makes it possible to assign them the status of an agreed testimony to torture. Not only was it the case that no parties in the Shabak ever denied what they depicted, but the Shabak actually

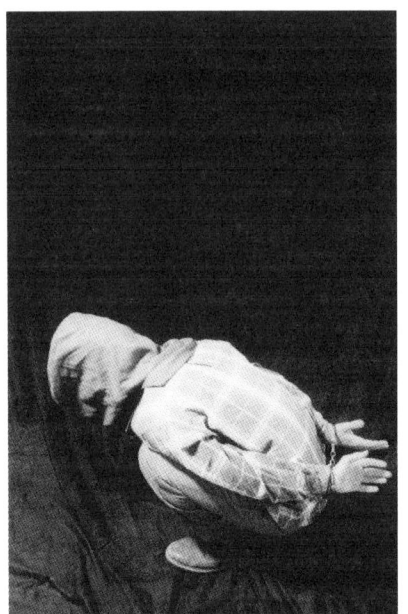

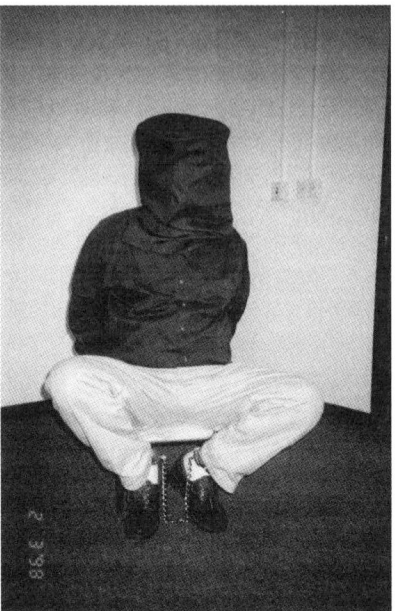

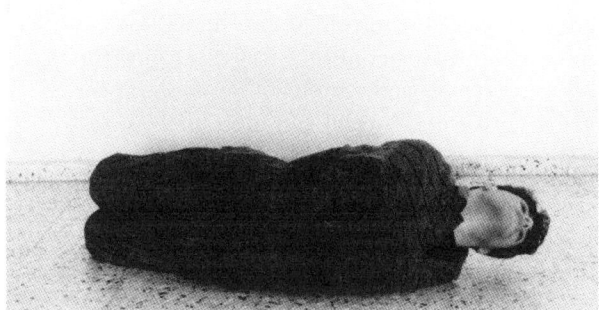

Figures 8.3–8.5. Torture poses used by Shabak (B'Tselem).

sought the authorization of the legal system to continue using the techniques represented in them.

These photographs, too, whose explicit content paradoxically came to be agreed on universally, do not speak for themselves and are not sufficient in and of themselves. Some of the positions shown seem fairly innocent at first glance. The photographs lack the dimensions of duration, intensity, and the infliction of violence that transform a crouching position or sitting on a chair with one's arms handcuffed, folded behind one's back, into torture. When it emerges that the size of the chair is adapted to the body of a preschool child or that the back leaning on the wall has been banged against it repeatedly thirty times every few minutes, one grasps that the photographs in question were produced in sterile laboratory conditions, intentionally avoiding the application of direct violence to the body.

Although these photographs are devoid of violence, reading them in combination with the testimonies providing the precise instructions for the reconstruction of the positions they depict allows a reillumination of the photographs that *are* accessible to the public eye, most of which were taken outside the detention facilities, but that nevertheless show some of the methods of torture used on a daily and continuing basis within such facilities. They demonstrate that handcuffed hands and bound feet, hooded eyes, and limbs that are forcefully stretched against their normal direction, are more than a means of humiliation and oppression. They also constitute torture, carried out openly, in the broad daylight of the occupation, and not just in its unseen shadows (figure 8.6).

The ruling apparatus is everywhere, pervasive and scattered throughout the entire penal colony, intentionally blurring distinctions between its various branches, legislative, juridical, and executive. The penal colony is based on a system of physical, linguistic, and human measures — obstructive trenches and concrete blocks, permits, magnetic ID cards and other identifying documents, bureaucratic forms, metal detectors, manned roadblocks, permanent roadblocks, obstructive earth mounds, jeeps, billy clubs, tanks, and rifles. This apparatus intercepts the spatial movement of Palestinians to the point of stopping it completely when it takes their lives. Being noncitizens, Palestinians' encounter with the regime always involves

429

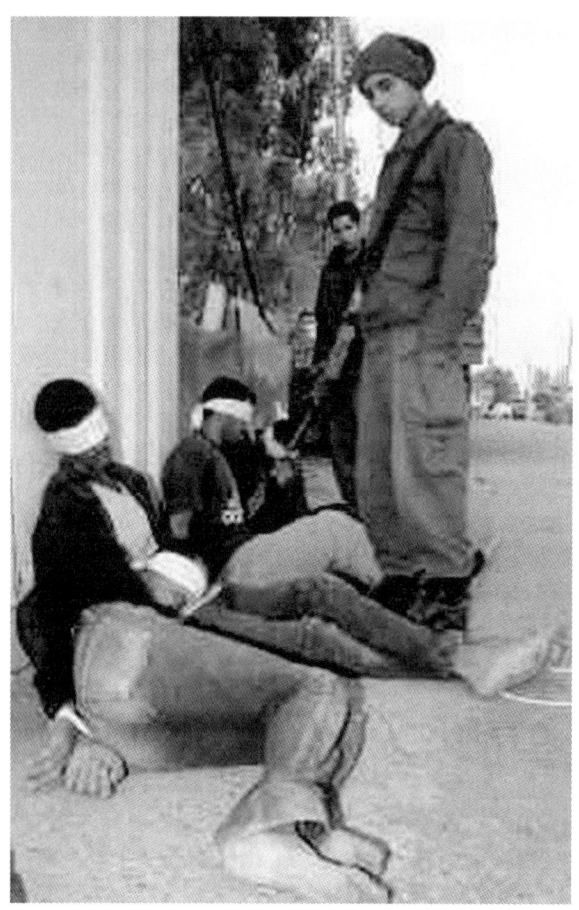

Figure 8.6. Raffah crossing, October 2004 (Assafir).

the use of violence by the ruling apparatus, whether withheld, suspended, or open, abrupt, and direct.[9] From the permits they are required to obtain, through their detainment at checkpoints, through mass arrests, to targeted assassinations, the law in the territories runs wild and hunts down the Palestinian, marks him, and operates on him prior to the collection of any suspicious evidence.

According to the Addameer association, which works to uphold the rights of Palestinian prisoners in the Occupied Territories (*addameer* is Arabic for "conscience"), six hundred and fifty thousand Palestinians, mainly men, have been incarcerated for varying periods since the beginning of the occupation.[10] This amounts to about 40 percent of the adult male population of the territories. The data concerning women is much less exhaustive. It indicates that there are currently about one hundred incarcerated women, including one woman who has given birth in prison and has now been imprisoned along with her infant for almost two years. The enormous number of men however, six hundred and fifty thousand, includes only those actually sent to prisons and therefore fails to reflect the true statistics on the hundreds of thousands of people whose hands have been handcuffed and whose eyes have been blindfolded with strips of flannel cloth (used to clean rifle barrels in the army), detained from five to twelve hours and "hung out to dry" in the street or at some military facility until their totally arbitrary release. Neither does it reflect the entire population whose homes sporadically turn into prison cells under military orders.

To grasp the continuum between the prisons designated as such and the way in which the Palestinians' living space is organized and administered, one merely needs to note the similarity between the procedures used in both types of space, which together make up the penal colony, procedures through which the denial of freedom of movement and action is inscribed on the Palestinian's body. The incarceration of six hundred and fifty thousand Palestinians does not mean that these people have experienced due process. Many were and still are imprisoned in a manner very similar to the one in which closure is imposed on the territories, in which imprisonment does not imply guilt, trial, conviction, a ruling, or a sentence. The initial encounter with the law, which is actually the initial encounter with naked violence, centers on a lack of knowledge, on the part of the Palestinian, as to why the law is seeking him out and demanding that he stop moving. The Palestinian, who is well versed in this encounter, expects it at any moment and is probably preoccupied with speculations and conjectures as to when this encounter will occur. But the knowledge that the encounter is pending, as certain as it may be, does nothing at all to dispel the basic absence of knowledge at its very core.

Traces of this uncertainty are manifested in a series of photographs taken by Musa Al Shaer in April 2002 in Bethlehem, when Israel was conducting mass arrests there (figures 8.7–8.8). The photograph, taken from the point of view of the armed Israeli soldier pointing his rifle at the crowd, presents hundreds of Palestinian men crowded together. In forming this tight body, they are expected to obey a series of orders that have been issued arbitrarily, as if they were prison inmates being summoned to morning roll call: "Come out," "Go over there," "Stop," "All together," "Closer," "Form a line," "Turn left," "No shouting," "No moving," "Raise your hands," "Wait." These specific orders are a local manifestation of the real order hidden behind them — the order to suspend private life, with everything that this implies: work, family, friends, leisure, health care.

Needless to say, the injury to be caused them from this point on, including the very act of suspending their lives, is not subject to negotiation and is most certainly not grounds for demanding compensation of any kind. The suspending order is indefinite in duration, aside from the generalized specification "for as long as necessary." As the photo shows, the body of these hundreds of men is turned, orchestrated, in a single direction, doubtless in response to an order they have been given. But they have no idea where they are headed. The looks of a few dozen of these men, turned to the left, toward the soldier whose gun is cocked and aimed — or possibly toward the photographer whose picture we are studying — seek some sliver of an answer. Since the outbreak of the second intifada, numerous mass arrests have been carried out by Israeli forces. They are conducted under degrading conditions and in total contradiction with the international standards intended to ensure the minimal rights of detainees, such as access to legal counsel, notice to one's family, and due process.

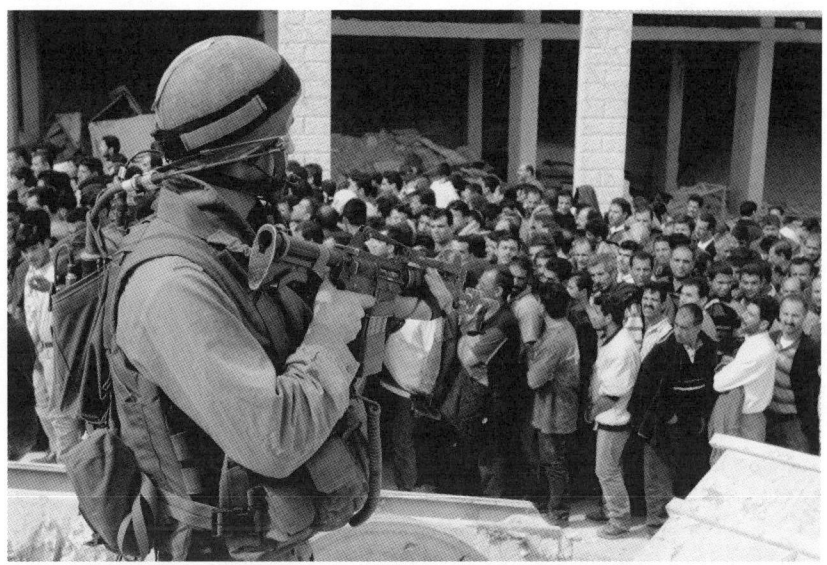

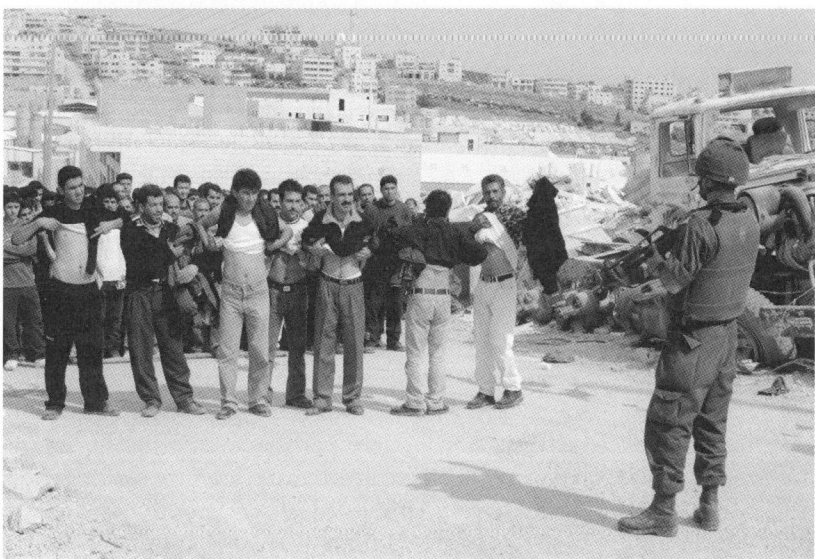

Figures 8.7 and 8.8. Musa Al Shaer, arrest campaign, refugee camp, Daheisha, March 11, 2002. (Please see Color Plates.)

The detainees in the picture have not even been served with Military Summons No. 1500. The state justifies this summons and the detaining of Palestinians incommunicado on the grounds that it is "necessary for handling the large number of detainments."[11] In addition, the military justifies the "detainment of wanted persons" by claiming that "these detainments are carried out following intensive collection of intelligence material, in a limited, localized manner, making the utmost effort to avoid injury or damage to the civilian population and to the wanted persons."[12]

Such detainments indeed occur along the tense fault line between the mass and individuation. After the Palestinians have been assembled in a single body whose contours can be supervised so as to ensure that no part of it evades the order, a more focused treatment of each individual is possible (figure 8.8). Seven at a time, the men are ordered to separate from the crowd, to approach the soldier, and to lift up their shirts. The gun remains cocked and aimed, the soldier's gaze pierces the men's body, looks them over one by one, negotiates with them regarding clothing items, after which the group of seven is ordered to move on to the next station. All this takes place in the public space, as it were, in a space that common usage would call "open," although it is in fact a sealed outdoor space, which, despite its relative closure, is nevertheless accessible to the gaze of the camera, from which the ongoing events seek no cover.

The ritual of stripping the Palestinian man takes place as a public spectacle before the eyes of his brothers. The soldier and the Palestinians who participate in this ritual are well versed in its details. This is not the first time the soldier has forbidden the Palestinian to do anything besides appear before him peeled of parts of his clothing, and this isn't the first time that the Palestinian has been required to follow orders precisely, with a loaded gun aimed at him. This photograph, taken without interference, perhaps even officially authorized, faces us with the repeated ritual enacted by the sovereign in order to inscribe its orders on the Palestinian's body. The act of inscription is carried out in conditions of a sweeping suspension of all the ties and contacts within which individual Palestinian lives are woven, turning the individual body into a raw and easily accessible base on which to inscribe the order.

434

The open space, the events' accessibility from the point of view of the camera, and the dissemination of these photographs with no ensuing scandal whatsoever, distances this type of photograph from the label "photograph of torture." Only when a similar situation, such as that of a Palestinian stripped down to his underpants and hooded with a sack, takes place in a space that common usage describes as closed, for instance in what looks like the receiving space of a detention facility, where the camera can, at best, capture a distant image without permission, does the application of physical and mental violence on the Palestinian reappear as a forbidden act, exposed by the camera (figures 8.9 and 8.10).

The ritual of mass arrest may, in the end, come "to nothing." The Palestinian may be released to go his way, bearing with him the seal of the order on his body. In many cases, though, it is just the beginning of an extended incarceration that starts out in the open, when the Palestinian is required to bare his body so that the soldier can scan him like a piece of information, as shown in the photographs, and then progresses into the darkness, out of bounds of the camera, where there are accordingly no accessible photographs (figures 8.11 and 8.12).

Over the years, photographs of the first part of the detention, carried out in the light of day, have accumulated by the hundreds. Easily deducible from them are the procedures employed for reminding the Palestinian of the citizenship he lacks and rendering him a detainee or a prisoner. His arms are raised under orders, the fingers of both hands, laced together, are placed on the back of the neck, an open ID card either hangs from these fingers or is tucked into the strip of flannel cloth so it can be speedily perused, the folded arms frame the face so that it echoes the photo on the ID card, his few belongings are bundled into a plastic bag, and in some cases, his upper body is already bared, covered only by an undershirt. He, along with many others, is channeled toward an impromptu pathway constructed out of a roll of barbed wire stretched between a cement mixer and a wooden crate, while in the background, an armored truck waits to transport him and all the other detainees to the next station.

Inside the truck, he and the others are crowded together standing,

435

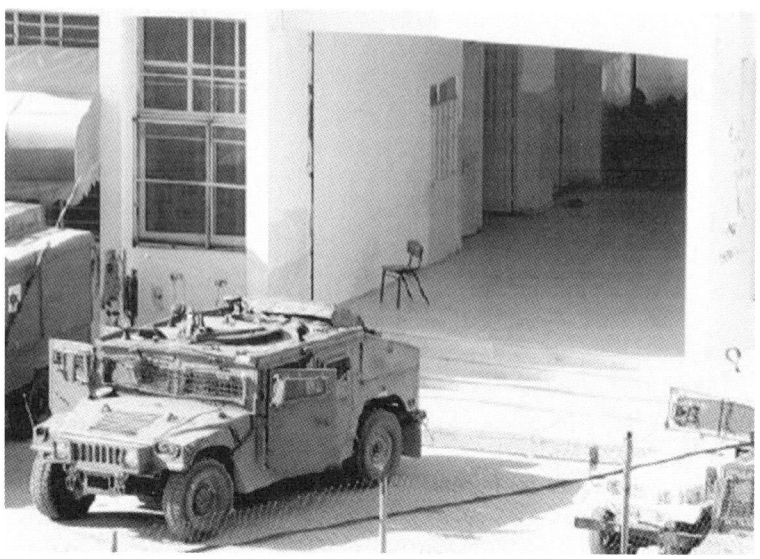

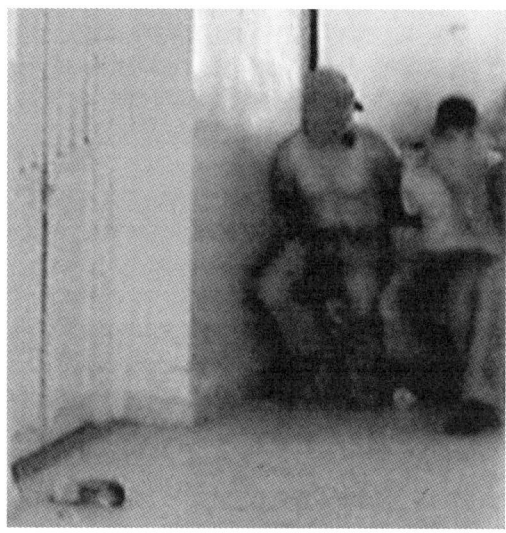

Figures 8.9 and 8.10. Refugee camp El-Ein near Nablus,
photo by a volunteer in the International Solidarity
Movement (ISP), August 19, 2004.

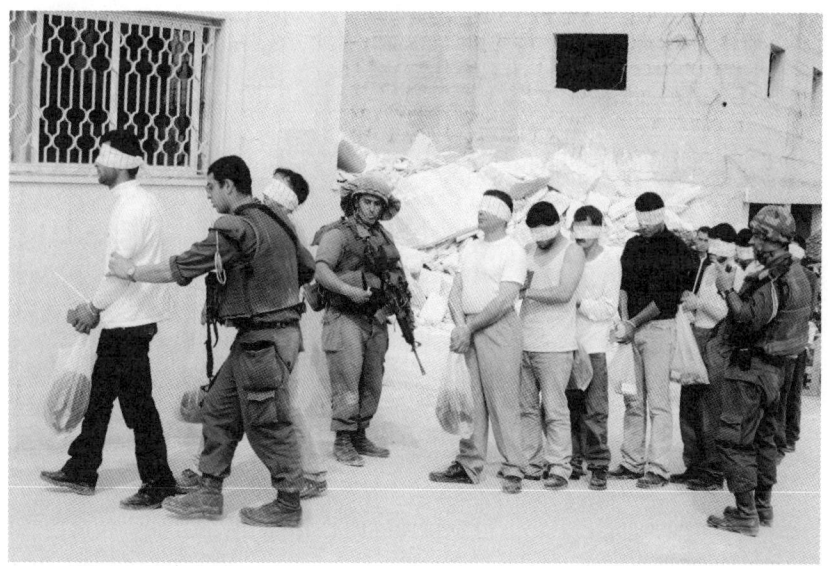

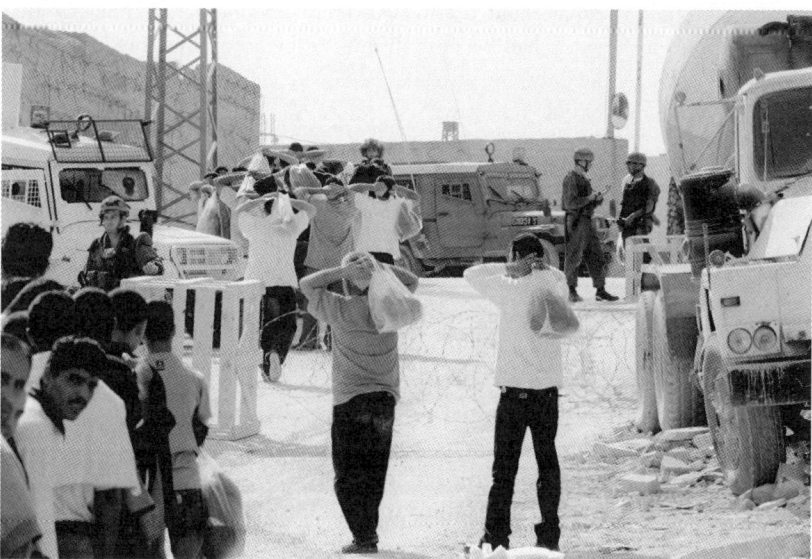

Figures 8.11 and 8.12. Musa Al Shaer, arrest campaign, refugee camp, Daheisha, March 11, 2002.

pushed against each other, "in order to get in as many as possible," as I was told by one of the activists, a conscientious objector of the group Breaking the Silence, who sent me the photograph (figure 8.13).[13] A number of armed soldiers supervise the traffic, signaling "no shenanigans" to the men in transit. The soldier at the head of the line is gripping two Palestinian detainees, one in each hand, straightening them into line with the queue.

> We were transferred to Ofer in an armored truck. At Ofer we were about 200 people ... our hands were tied and our heads were hooded ... we were left that way till one A.M., when a soldier came to pick up our ID cards and frisk us; they took everyone's cell phone. Then they took a few people and gave them tents, which they told them to set up — there were four tents for 200, about 50 in each tent. From two-thirty to three A.M. we finished setting up the tents and asked for bedding and they refused. They brought us wooden planks from the kind of poor material that coffins are made of. On the first night, we had no blankets — they brought them at about ten-thirty P.M. on Wednesday evening. By that time five people had become ill due to the cold; they took them to a doctor but he didn't do anything. We were given food for the first time on Wednesday at eight P.M.[14]

For at least eighteen days, Awni Said and two hundred other Palestinians were detained without being allowed to make contact of any kind with the world outside the prison. Later, when they were transferred to court, they were again handcuffed and blindfolded. According to the testimonies of numerous Palestinians, blindfolding usually takes place before they enter and leave the detention facilities. The use of blindfolds in transit to and from the detention facilities is commonly justified as a security measure to prevent Palestinians from seeing what they shouldn't. The testimonies of soldiers who have organized over the past year in Breaking the Silence confirm unofficial assumptions that blindfolding is actually used as a form of abuse — or even torture — referred to by the soldiers themselves as "dehydrating": "In the territories there are 'wanted persons' and 'dehydrated persons.' The latter are people who have committed minor offenses, such as passing through a street during

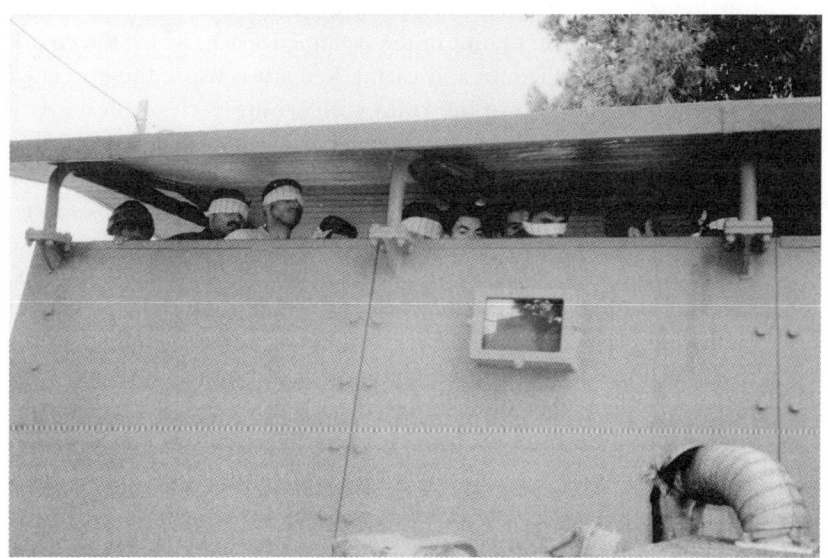

Figure 8.13. Breaking the Silence, Ramallah, 2002.

curfew or being in the wrong place at the wrong time" (figures 8.14 and 8.15).[15]

This description is chillingly precise in the way it reveals the spatial logic of the penal colony. The soldiers are spread throughout the territories and rule the Palestinians actually or potentially, personally or with instruments, be these light or harsh, declared or hidden, doing so at every point in the occupied space, which they mark and parcel into subzones and earmarked sites, while the governed are required to observe the rules concerning each of these. At a checkpoint, you stand in line. During curfew, you're incarcerated at home; you don't walk the streets after nightfall; you don't drive a car from village to village; you don't arrive at a checkpoint with a large bag — and so on and so forth. The soldiers are on their guard to make sure that the orders are obeyed. That is why they are holding guns, sheets of paper with printed orders and injunctions, strips of flannel cloth, and plastic handcuffs. Every soldier who serves in the territories is equipped with a three-meter strip of flannel cloth and with plastic handcuffs that allow him to mark out for and on the Palestinian his deviation from his place in space. Like prison wardens who guard their inmates, ascertaining that they do not escape from their cells, the soldiers monitor what is going on in the governed lives in the penal colony. Whether the blindfold serves them for security purposes or in an attempt to cause the Palestinian cognitive interference concerning the space around him, whether it serves exclusively as a form of abuse meant to terrorize, humiliate, or embarrass, the flannel strip covering the eyes aids the soldiers in doing their jobs.

Managing a penal colony for such a long period requires the regular employment of three procedures forming the core of the detainment facility throughout the whole of the space in question: marking, punishment, and suspension of the gaze (figure 8.16). Blindfolding marks every individual as indistinguishable within the series of men being handled. There are no exceptions. Everyone on the assembly line is granted the same treatment. Behind the prefab concrete cubicles of the Chawara checkpoint, they sit for hours, "hung out to dry" — two blindfolded, handcuffed Palestinians. This photograph shows a heterogeneous group of men, women, and children. The act of marking these particular two men is designed to

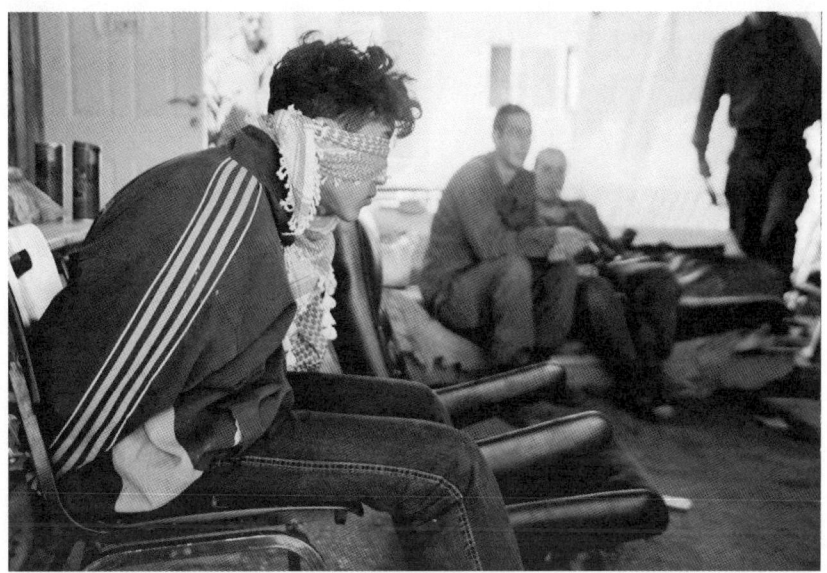

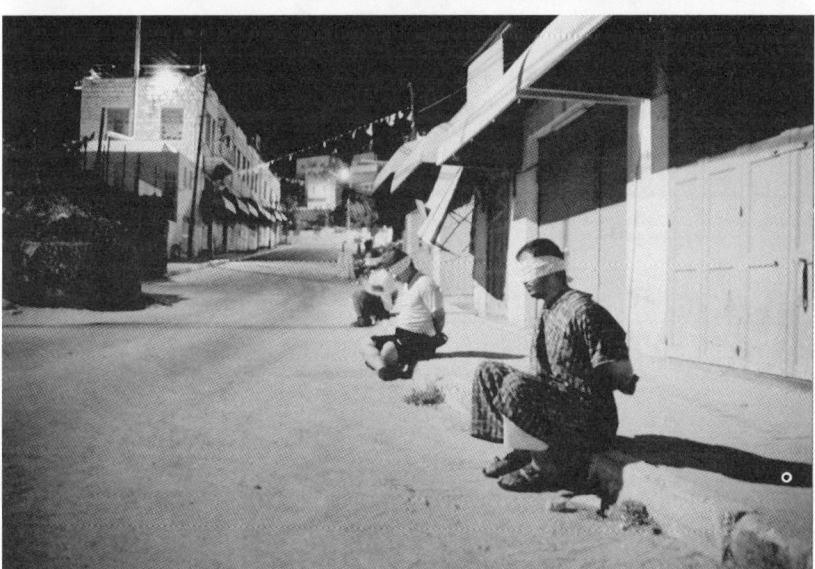

Figures 8.14 and 8.15. Breaking the Silence, Hebron, 2003.

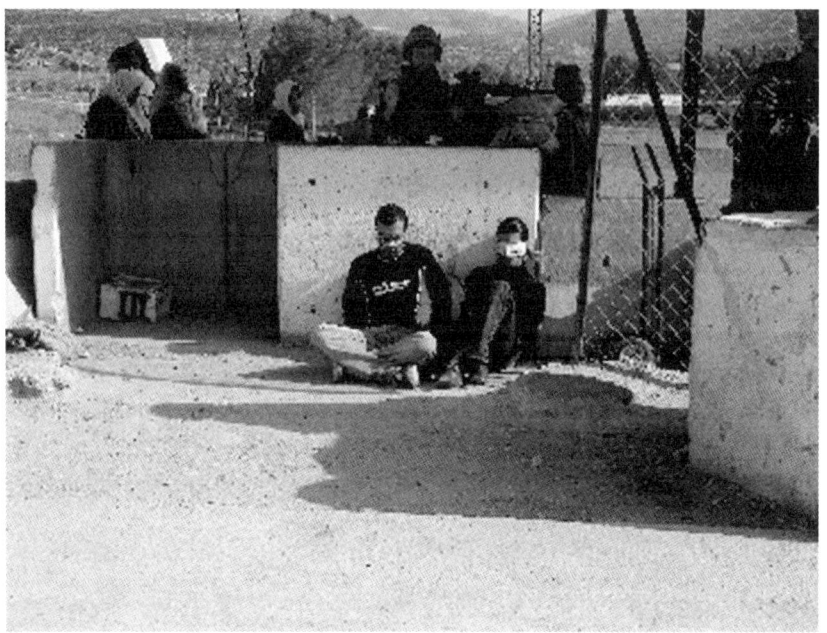

Figure 8.16. Chawara checkpoint, November 23, 2003 (B'Tselem).

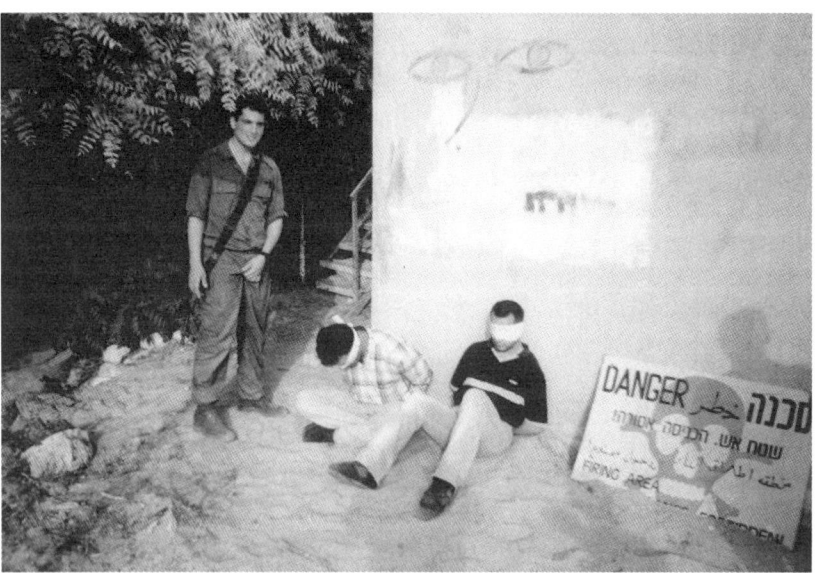

Figure 8.17. Breaking the Silence, Hebron, 2003.

distinguish the "resisters" who have refused to follow the soldiers' order to clean up the checkpoint.

In this case, then, the blindfold clearly serves as a form of immediate, on-the-spot punishment. No one passing through the checkpoint can miss the punished "resisters" or the lesson the army is trying to teach through them. For the Palestinian, the procedure of random arrest has become a routine; for the Israeli soldier, as described to me by one of the founders of Breaking the Silence, "It's the landscape you grow up in."

Blindfolded, transformed into a kind of still life, the Palestinian indeed can become part of the landscape from the soldier's point of view. The soldier uses a strip of flannel rifle cleaner to erase the presence of the Palestinian facing him. In other words, denying the Palestinian a gaze allows the soldier not to see the Palestinian by canceling out the possibility that he himself might become the object of the Palestinian's gaze (figure 8.17). Forcefully brought to mind, in this context, is Freud's confession that in circumstances much friendlier and more caring than the ones before us, he felt compelled to erase his patient's gaze, whose continual presence, over the long hours of work, could become insufferable.

The soldier neutralizes the gaze of the Palestinian, suspends it, and turns him into a mark within the soldier's space. It is a mark that the soldier can appropriate and use as a vehicle of self-expression. In this photograph, the soldier has positioned himself in front of the camera, seeking an appropriate pose through which he can demonstrate to the camera his indifference toward the tortured Palestinians on the ground, who are struggling with the pain that the handcuffs and their enforced posture are sending through their arms, legs, and bodies, while the sensations of their eyes have long been lost due to the overly tight flannel blindfold. The sudden appearance of another Palestinian without a blindfold would suffice to remind the soldier how fragile is this gaze of his that acts momentarily as if it were within his power to rule another's life space, to be its master. He has his picture taken beside the blindfolded men, thus attempting to preserve this moment and lengthen it as much as possible.

The Palestinians with whom he is now taking his picture have been punished for resisting the initial punishment imposed on them

443

— that of curfew. They have "breached curfew." The Palestinians sitting on the curbstone a few meters away from each other in figure 8.15 — supposedly to prevent them from talking to each other — have also "breached curfew." These photographs clearly exemplify the penal colony and the way in which the desire to rule the Palestinians is manifested. The Palestinian must obey rules and regulations that he usually has no way of knowing before becoming an object of their application. In most cases, these rules themselves already amount to a punishment. They restrict the Palestinian's movement and deny him his freedom. If he transgresses them, that is, if he rejects the punishment imposed on him, he will of course be punished — punished for failing to serve his term of punishment.

This is the penal colony. This is its logic. Hundreds of thousands of Palestinians are shut up, day in, day out, within their homes, which, under orders, become the prison cells of the penal colony. Decades of ongoing management of this space through its violent labeling as a space not owned by its owners has laid the groundwork for its transformation into this penal colony. In the penal colony, every movement is a mitigated punishment, and every superfluous movement is grounds for harshening punishment. Imprisoned and isolated under extremely difficult conditions, denied freedom of movement and action, dependent on the goodwill of their wardens — this is how the inhabitants of the penal colony are forced to pass their lives.

The continuous control of their movements and actions has prepared them to become inhabitants of the colony. They need not commit any offense in order to be sentenced to life imprisonment in this colony. They always already are within it, deserving of the punishment that it inscribes on their bodies, a punishment that is unique in that its duration is unspecified. It is the suspension of all punishments; it is suspension itself *as* punishment. The punishment imposed on them, suspending their encounter with the legal system in which punishments are supposed to be specified and limited, requires no prior notice, no legal counsel, no procedures of trial or appeal.

Curfew, siege, and closure are the main mechanisms employed continuously by the authorities for purposes of restricting move-

ment in the territories for varying periods. Curfew prohibits residents from exiting their homes, at times for weeks, just as zones of
siege prevent them from leaving the village or town or the area
on which it is imposed, and closure prohibits their entrance into
Israel.[16] The Emergency Defense Regulations (Regulation 124 of
1945) and the Command Concerning Security Instructions (Item 89
of 1970) authorize the military commander to impose curfew exclusively at his discretion, without specifying a maximum duration.
Curfew is a common mode of military operation and is used "following demonstrations and violent events, in searching for wanted
persons and for purposes of arrest, locating arms or explosives, and
preventing clashes during the demolition of the homes of suspects of
security offenses." Although the High Court of Justice ruled in the
early 1990s that curfew should not be employed as a means of punishment and limited its use to cases in which "clear security reasons"
exist, this ruling is regularly transgressed, and curfew continues to
serve the army on a routine basis.

Curfew acts as a substitute for staged trials. It allows the army to
convey messages to the subjects by inscribing these messages on
their bodies. During the first intifada, as well as during the second,
the number of annual days of curfew in many communities reached a
third or even half of a year.[17] The inhabitants imprisoned in their
homes are physically prevented from appealing this decision during
the time it is imposed and, moreover, there exists no orderly procedure for appealing it at other times.

The Pale of Security

The Jewish civilians living in the terrritory where the penal colony
was installed, are not authorized to use flannel strips to avoid seeing
the gaze of the Palestinians confronting them in their lives and
deeds. As civilians, they are limited in their authorization to use
force. However, from time to time, at certain sites, they nevertheless
let loose against Palestinians, forcefully organizing their living space
and, as part of it, the space covered by the gaze. Most of the time,
though, the ruling system administers the penal colony through its
soldiers in order to allow the Jewish civilians within it to manage
their lives unseen. What is possible on the operational maps of the

war rooms is possible on the ground too. Suffice it to move the colored pins from place to place: "We issued orders"; "We built bypass roads"; "We have allowed passage"; "We've fit cars with armor"; "We've separated routes"; "We've dug tunnels"; "We have imposed closure"; "We have eased the closure"; "We have opened up alternative traffic routes." It's not that the Jews don't see the Palestinians. It's not that the Palestinians don't see the Jews. They most certainly do. It's not that the Jews don't want the Palestinians to see them. On the contrary. Let them see well and fear. What Jewish soldiers and civilians in the penal colony alike are seeking to prevent is the possibility that the other might steal their gaze, forcing them to see what it is that he sees; that he will see that the Jew sees him or, worse, that he will be seen to the Jew as one who sees the Jew. As long as the Palestinians' gaze can be suspended, as long as the civilian living among them can be spared from seeing the Palestinians seeing him, no common object will materialize in the penal colony to juxtapose the gazes of the Jew and the Palestinian.

The discourse about land prevents perception of this demon's dance in action. Only scrutiny of the inscrutable, complicated maps of the areas of Palestine enables an understanding of the dual desire that is characteristic of the Jewish settlement of the territories: on the one hand, the desire to enter into pockets that are situated between large Arab communities, extending the surface on which Jews and Palestinians can see one another; on the other hand, the desire to control the field of vision while setting up obstacles that preclude the possibility of the Jew seeing the Palestinian seeing him. As I will try to demonstrate through photographs taken by Efrat Shvili, building serves the Jews as a means of blocking, in advance, any possibility of a public space of gaze and action.

From the early 1990s until the end of the decade, Efrat Shvili took two series of photographs, both of which focused on homes. The first was taken in new cities (or in some cases, new neighborhoods) constructed inside the Green Line. The second was taken on the other side of the Green Line, within the Jewish settlements there. The two series seem quite similar (figures 8.18 and 8.19). Although I'll work back and forth between the two series, I'll begin with the second — and with my difficulty in writing about it — my

446

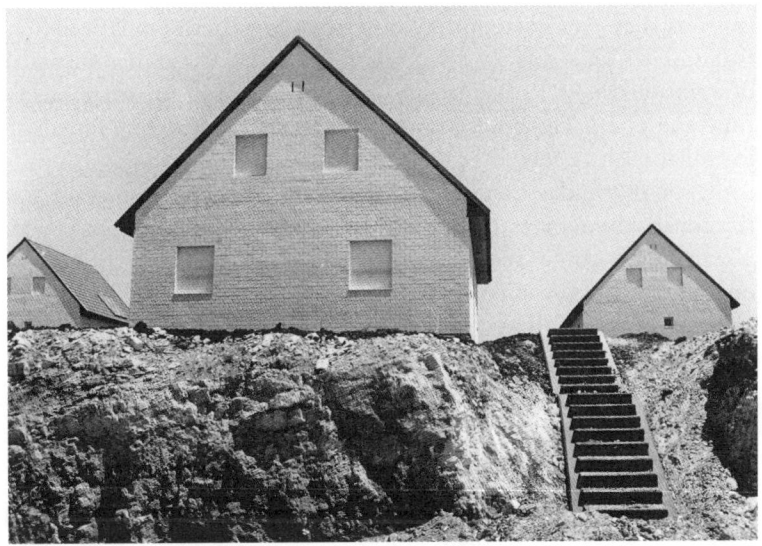

Figure 8.18. Efrat Shvili, Talmon, 1993.

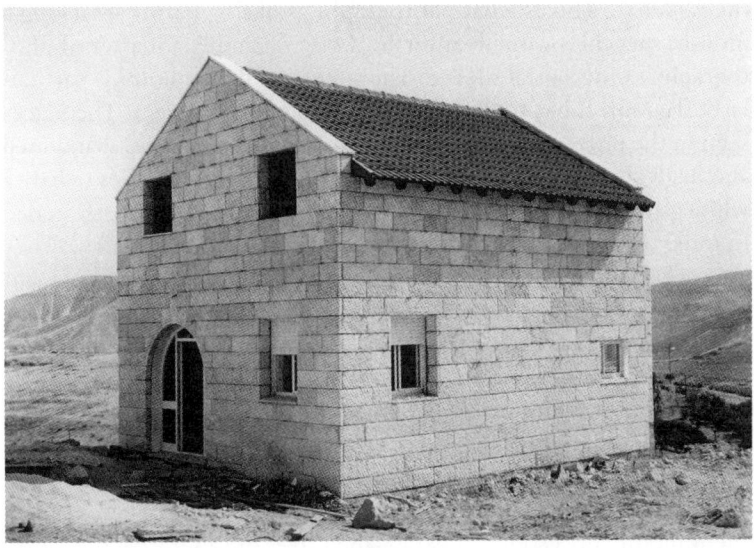

Figure 8.19. Efrat Shvili, Mitzpe Jericho, 1993.

sense is that every attempt to describe the series comes across as fraudulent. This was the case when I tried to depart from initial descriptions, basic facts allowing an anchoring of the photographs in time and place. The descriptions were trapped in existing linguistic formulae such as "newly built" or "building boom." Seemingly innocent, such formulae describe the state of the real-estate market and the construction industry, perhaps also saying something about style. Nevertheless, their ready availability, along with the difficulty I encountered in escaping them — the fact that they were employed almost automatically — made them suspect. One after another, I deleted entire paragraphs that sought to describe what I saw. Despite attempts to confine these descriptions to the visual plane, they failed dismally. Even the leanest language sounded tainted. Even when I ascribed what could be seen in the photos to those responsible for creating it — the Jewish settlers, Israel's succession of governments, military personnel, and right-wing voters — the descriptions sounded false. They functioned like a layer of insulation meant to seal off the photos and to silence them even more.

As I watched the photos, looked at them long and hard, I heard their silence. This is what photography is like by nature — lacking a mouth, speechless, dumb at birth. It wasn't simply a matter of photography's ontological silence. The silence of these photos is particularly flagrant. It has to do with the photographed object. The places seen in the photos are barren, devoid of human presence, abandoned and neglected. An aura hovers over them; their stone bodies radiate a white glare; the sun's rays accentuate their outlines. They are shrouded in milky light that screens them and makes them inaccessible. They are packaged like a picture on a wall. "But isn't a photo always meant to be like a picture on a wall?" I said to myself. Yes . . . but.

Even when a photo turns into a silent picture on a wall, the traces of teeming life in the framework of which it was taken are usually not entirely erased. Photos are always dangling between two modes — between what's depicted on the photographic paper and the traces of the photographic act, between the two-dimensional image and the chaos of reality out of which it was forged, between being a silent picture on a wall and being (the traces of) a scrap of the world teeming with life.

But these photos of Shvili's appear to obey a different logic that eludes this wandering between two modes, a logic that resolves the contrasts so that the traces of the photographic act are erased before the image fixed on the photographic paper. They are reduced to a picture on a wall that lacks any sign of life. The photographed object seems to be disconnected from any spatial or temporal context.[18] This impression is reinforced in those photos in which the buildings look like architectural models. The buildings appear to float, with no connection to anything but themselves. They look like a computer simulation, which from an ontological aspect is the polar opposite of photography. A computer simulation exists as an image devoid of any encounter with concrete reality, whereas a photo is sampled from reality and unwittingly bears its traces. "But no," I said to myself again, "these are photos and not computer simulations. These are actual buildings, and not models, actual settlements and not simply open spaces."

A photo's context is never given and must always be woven out of the intertextual fabric, by means of which it is possible to fill in what cannot be read directly from the photo: Israel of the 1990s, the continued occupation of the Palestinian territories, a surge of construction on both sides of the Green Line, satellite towns and Jewish settlements, suburban homes and lawns beside buildings that faintly echo the forms of "the ideal city." In conversation with Shvili, she said that she is trying to show in her photos that construction in the Jewish settlements is motivated by the need to grab more land, rather than by the desire to create life, that the buildings are outlandish, and everything looks more like an ideal rather than like reality.[19]

Construction in the Jewish settlements, as can be seen from these photos, brings together the archetypal idea of the home, simplicity, precision, and purposefulness, with the fantasy of the ideal home, stylistic and symbolic superfluity.[20] Both the idea and the ideal combine in the framework of a distinctive procedure, which does not refer to one or two random buildings, but to a multitude of buildings designed by different architects, in which the same procedure has been applied. In the phrase "construction in the Jewish settlements," the occupation is separated from the settlements, marking the Palestinians as inhabitants of bounded territory that is

449

far away, isolated from lives of the Jewish settlers — "theirs," "there," "not here," "not ours." The description "construction in the Jewish settlements" supports the delusion that the settlements are a separate entity, a clearly delineated territory in the heart of the Occupied Territories outside of and around which the occupation swirls, as if these were two homogenous, continuous, and separate spaces, one a branch of the state of Israel into which it can accordingly fold and the other totally distinct and foreign to the state. Clients, developers, and architects' concerted recourse to idealistic forms and ideas to implement this separation is part of an attempt to bypass the prosaic, to avoid the concrete, and to eliminate anything that might disturb, disrupt, spoil, or, worst of all, inflict shock.

An ideal city built in one of the most conflict-ridden places on Earth: This is a camouflage that establishes itself in its place of residence while denying that it does so, sinks stakes into the ground, straddles the land, and in time, by the simple fact of being there, becomes part of the landscape — taken for granted in the landscape. "Construction in the Jewish settlements" erases the Palestinian gaze over the landscape and the fact that, for the Palestinian, this construction eviscerates the landscape into which it has been transplanted, establishing itself as the object of the gaze, an object that can no longer be erased.

Even when the gaze on "construction in the Jewish settlements" seeks to be critical, to reconstruct the Palestinian gaze in regard to it, it is forced to constitute this construction as its object and thus to recognize its existence, form, content, and validity. The phrase "construction in the Jewish settlements" is so deceptive that it threatens to snare not only Shvili's photos in its trap, but the discourse of anyone who might attempt to write about them, including, of course, those who might propose to replace the positivist description of what can be seen in them — a type of "ideal" construction that claims to be insularly detached from the landscape while occupying it — with more of a critical description — "euphemistic construction," that is, construction designed to substitute the agreeable and inoffensive for something that is unpleasant — the forced occupation of Palestinian land. Euphemistic construction is an effort to euphemize the entire field of vision in the Occupied Territories.

The prevalent description of Shvili's photos as "construction in the Jewish settlements," has in fact become part of the surge of euphemistic construction itself; it has been wholly assimilated by the euphemistic procedure. It is not only the settlers who are interested in perpetuating this delusion; it is widespread throughout public and political discourse and feeds into the cartography that offers various maps toward the end of the Israeli-Palestinian conflict, maps that attempt the spatial acrobatics of delimiting the settlements within the Occupied Territories and either shrinking them or annexing them to the state of Israel. Even the language of those supporting the "evacuation of settlements" and viewing them as "obstacles to peace" legitimizes the euphemistic worldview. As a result, discussion of the occupation can proceed as a Jewish-Israeli matter, while solutions to the controversy about possible concessions are consequently required to remain within the framework of these ethnic boundaries.

The territorial focus, the ethnic segregation, and the imagining of an existence outside of the occupation or the settlements support the state's evasion of its responsibility toward the population of its ruled subjects. Accepting the territorial category — "settlements" — and describing the construction that occurs within this framework combine to obscure the organized crime that has detached the territory from its surroundings. It requires the expropriation of land to evict the formerly indigenous Palestinian residents, requiring their deportation and transformation into refugees, shattering their sense of security, mounting roadblocks to restrict their travel, building bypass roads that reflect the ethnic discrimination, uprooting orchards and trees, destroying their livelihood in myriad other ways, inflicting hunger, wounding them in body and spirit, and in general exposing them to the arbitrary ravages and tyranny of the occupation.[21] When one gazes at the photos, they remain silent and give away nothing. The question regarding what language is best suited to describe them leaves them completely indifferent.

The photo's indifference is the secret of its strength. It doesn't give away what's described in it, leaving perplexed anyone seeking to understand what's described in it. Sometimes the description succeeds in making contact with what's described. At other times, it fails to satisfy. As stated above, photos are dumb and speechless;

they will not let down their guard and be caught in momentary weakness. To formulate what is seen, to get it to speak out, is the task of the spectator — be it the photographer or anybody else. "I needed *hundreds* of pictures in order to understand this attraction to the landscape, to the innovation, to the integration between the construction and the landscape," Shvili has said — not one or two photos, but hundreds. It is a strained gaze, rolling from house to house, lingering on one or another and then passing on. It is accompanied by observation of the photographic results, a transition between focused and floating observation, an obstinate search for an insight that will arise, augurlike, from the depths of the photo's black and white dance, attaching itself to the photo so as to appear to be its reflection.

Taking "hundreds of pictures" — or, for that matter, looking at them — in order to see something or to arrive at a certain insight displaces (the gaze of) the photo, as it does observation of the photo, from being anchored in the visible. The repetition that characterizes Shvili's photos, her dedication to photographing dozens of buildings systematically in the same way, distances the gaze from the specific nature of what appears before it. The search of the gaze — during the photographic act and during observation — takes place on a different level. It isn't looking for new information to be gleaned from the next photo. The repetitive gaze and the profusion of photos are intended not to amplify the syntagmatic chain of details, but to forge an intimate, unconscious encounter with something that is inherent in them, which can be produced only out of the profusion and the repetition and the connection between them. Perhaps it is some paradigmatic pattern that the reiteration of the gaze can capture and impress on the observer's consciousness. Perhaps it's like the process that takes place in certain cognitive apprehension tests, where once the gaze has recognized a particular shape, it can no longer *not* see it, and the shape becomes an inseparable part of both the image, as well as of the gaze on the image.

Walter Benjamin calls what the mechanical gaze of the photo exposes to the eyes of the spectator "the optical unconscious."[22] The gaze I'm talking about is slightly different. Benjamin has described a procedure that refers to the gaze on a single photo, whereas I'm talking about the different experience of what might be called a "floating gaze"[23] that roams past a series of images. To judge from the examples that Benjamin gives, what he's referring to is indeed new information that the photo provides, whereas I'm talking about something that doesn't belong to the photo's informative or symbolic order and cannot be predicated on it. The repetitive gaze is looking for a different space of relations that will allow a different connection between itself and its object.[24] It is a floating, but resolute gaze, systematic, but superficial, knowledgeable, but naïve, intermittent, but obstinate. It rejects the meaning of photography.

Instead, it clings to photography in order not to participate in the euphemization of the field of vision, the machinery of camouflage that disguises injustice. The customary, canonical formulation, employed by Benjamin at the end of "The Work of Art in the Age of Mechanical Reproduction," distinguishes between the aestheticization and the politicization of images.[25] Here, however, I am concerned with the euphemism lurking in wait for any photo of horror, which is dependent not only on the image, but on the chain of observation and interpretation that develops from it. This gaze's discomfort with the image is supposed to enable it to penetrate the photo's insularity and reach beyond it to the photographic event. As described above, Shvili's photos tend to reduce the two modes of photography into one — they lack any traces of the life from which they've been sampled — and therefore make it difficult to pass from the photo to the photographic act or situation. In their indifference, they waylay the spectator and lure her into the trap of euphemism. But euphemism is not an essential characteristic of photography. It threatens to attach itself only when photography turns horror into its object. Even then, photography itself remains indifferent to euphemism. If euphemism does attach itself to anything, it is to the spectator who consumes it. Resistance to euphemism can take different forms. One of them is repeated observation, not only of dozens of photos that belong to a single series, as in Shvili's case, but repeated observation of the same photos dozens of times.[26]

Efrat Shvili exhibits her photos under a single, all-inclusive title that unites them into a series — *Untitled* — plus the year of the photo. Deletion of titles from the photos and their assimilation under a title that negates their title — that negates any title whatsoever, in fact — serves as a mirror that obliquely shifts the observer's gaze to the next photo in the series, another photo devoid of a title. In this way, the spectator is invited to do some horizontal viewing, to perform a movement from one photo to the next. In the absence of any indicative title, a spectator who would like to disregard the fact that this construction is taking place in the Palestinian Occupied Territories and to regard these buildings as if they were rooted in "Jerusalem's new neighborhoods" can do so more readily. But as regards any such spectator, even a specific title bearing the stamp of a specific place would not have sufficed to get her to call the settlements of Gilo or Ma'ale Ha-Edomim "the Palestinian Occupied Territories." The anonymity of the buildings, some built in the Palestinian Occupied Territories and others within the state of Israel's borders, offers itself to the spectator as a thought. The photos, as I've said, function as a mirror. They send the spectator on to additional images in the series, but they also turn the spectator's gaze directly back on herself.

Although these photos have also been exhibited in recent years in various venues in Europe and the United States, it's hard for me to think of them as not being addressed primarily to a local spectator first and foremost, to an Israeli Jew. The houses she sees, whether built inside or outside the Green Line, are the houses of Israeli Jews. In the course of the occupation, before, during, and after the Oslo peace process, Israeli Jews have been building their homes in the Occupied Territories. It's not just "them," the Jewish "settlers," but the entire state of Israel that has thus been branded by the occupation. The photos avoid presenting themselves as an indictment or as a manifesto, and Shvili, so it appears, is interested in preventing the observer from regarding them as a concrete store of information.[27] Even if, to the nonlocal spectator, they might echo the familiar appearance of photos of buildings from the history of photography,[28] they provide enough signs to enable the reconstruction of the context in which they were made from what can be seen in them. One such sign is the trace of time. Following the "Untitled" attached to each photo comes the year — not that of the photographed object, but of the photo itself.

I will linger here on two photos, both taken in 1997 (figures 8.20

and 8.21). Both are unusual in the context of Shvili's photos of build-ings as a whole. But even if their appearance allows them to be lost sight of within the series, they are caught within a lethal duality that extricates them from the anonymity of the series, enabling them to become an index to it.

In October of 1996, several months before these photos were taken, Nahum Korman, an Israeli citizen residing in the settlement of Hadar Beitar and responsible for its security, set out from there to the neighboring village of Hussan in pursuit of several Palestinian boys whom he suspected of having thrown stones at some settlers' vehicles a few hours earlier. Korman caught one of the boys, Hilmi Shusha, and beat him to death. The pathologist's report determined that "the injury to the left side of the neck that led to the death of the deceased was caused by a direct blow (kick), and so, too, the injury to the scalp (in the top and rear) was also caused by a direct blow (pistol-whipping)."[29] The defendant was kept under house arrest for a few months and released on the conclusion of the crimi-nal proceedings without serving any additional time.[30] The testi-monies of the only two witnesses to the murder, the two other Palestinian boys, was insufficient to convict the citizen. The court undersigned the abandoned life of Hilmi Shusha.

These two photos look like ordinary components of Shvili's series: two houses, located in neighborhoods just a few hundred yards apart. Only one of them was taken in a "Jewish settlement," however. The other was taken in "the Occupied Territories," that is, in the Palestinian sphere of life. The first house belongs to an Israeli citizen, the second to a Palestinian subject. The two photos were taken in the wake of Hilmi Shusha's murder.

Any trace of events is missing from Shvili's entire series of photographed buildings. This isn't only because these are photos of buildings, rather than snapshots of events, but also because the buildings are largely lifeless — either abandoned or not yet inhabited. They themselves are not places of life.[31] They play a semiotic role in the conquest of the space, its demarcation, its Judaization, and the redrawing of its borders. As defined above, the emptiness that char-acterizes the objects of these photos creates the impression that the two modes of photography are reduced to one. But this is only an

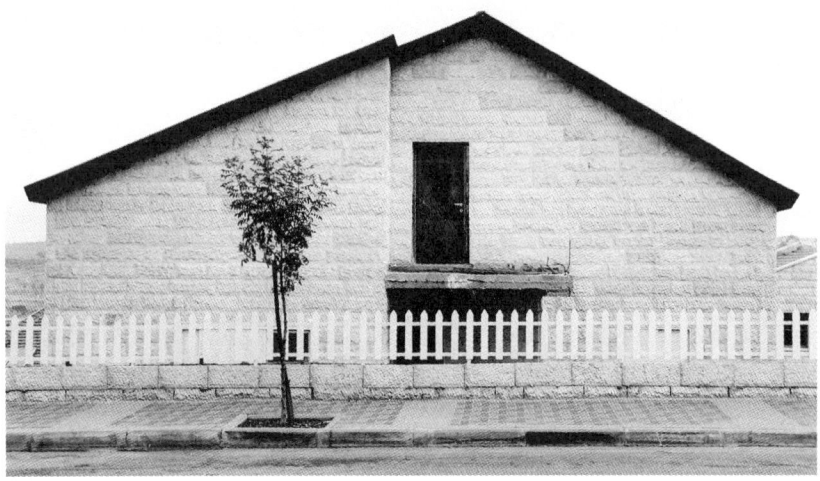

Figure 8.20. Efrat Shvili, Hadar Beitar, 1997.

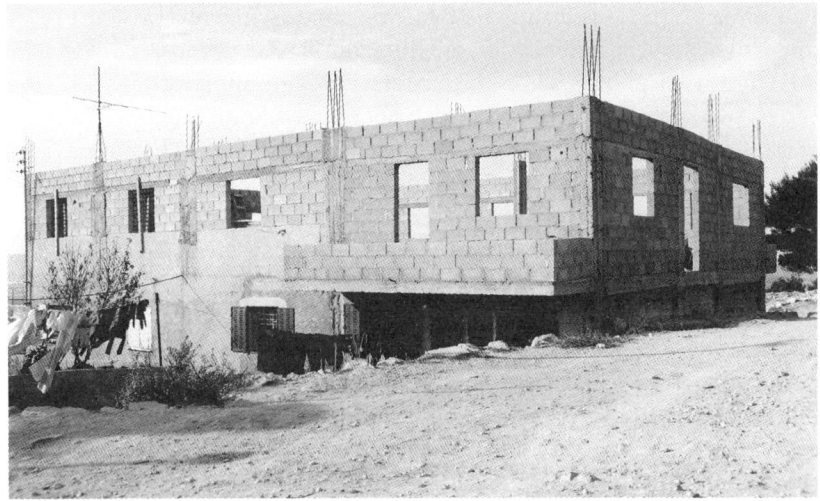

Figure 8.21. Efrat Shvili, Hussan village, 1997.

apparent reduction, because the parallel existence of both is essential to photography.[32] Shvili's camera could not have recorded an object that doesn't exist (teeming life). But her obstinate presence in these ghost towns, the encounter between them and her gaze resting on them — these are the traces of life sampled by her camera. Shvili's calm and tranquil photos, which repeat the same objective format again and again, testify to the discomfort of the gaze that has constituted them. It is a gaze that cannot be reconciled to the horror of what it looks at, so it trains itself to see even where there is nothing to be seen.

In each of the two photos, a residential home appears. One is simple and functional: exposed building blocks lie atop one another in layers, creating the shape of a residential box. The box lacks a roof; it is defenseless. Only the steel rods of the foundations rear upward in a way that might ostensibly deter any would-be invaders. But the upright steel rods are only temporarily symbolic. They'll be there only until the construction phase has been concluded, after which they'll be swallowed up inside the building, fufilling their prosaic function as its support. The house isn't bordered by a fence. It is open to all. Not just anyone is allowed to fence his home, draw a border beyond which entrance is prohibited. Lacking sovereign power, being noncitizens, Palestinians lack the authority to draw a border and decide who may or may not enter their homes.

The house in the first photo is more tawdry. Its lines give it the appearance of a fairy-tale house — a cube with a slanting, tiled roof. There is a symbolic fence out in front. It is not meant for defense, but to mark the point beyond which lies the private domain of the family that resides therein. Defense isn't something that the occupants of this house apparently require. They are the masters here, and their mastery requires nothing more than a flimsy fence, more decoration than anything else. They are protected by the fence of Israeli sovereignty, which has invaded the Occupied Territories and by force of arms entrenches the Jewish settlers' destructive presence in the heart of the Palestinian space.

On the morning of October 29, 1996, the boy Hilmi Shusha set out from the house in the second photo, Nahum Korman from the house in the first. Their particular encounter, the encounter that cannot be seen in the photos, was accidental. It might not have happened — after all, it's not every day that the occupation exacts its price in children. On the other hand, however, it was almost inevitable, structured into the logic of the occupation.

In the penal colony, it is not just the sovereign's proxy who can set up and operate a kangaroo court.[33] The settler does so too, sometimes in full view of the sovereign's low-ranking proxy, sometimes, as in Korman's case, unseen. As in a kangaroo court set up by a soldier, the occupier is the party who determines the procedures, the practices of hearing testimony, the order of the witnesses, the rulings, and the sentences. The occupied can only hope that his life won't be taken in the process.

Placed side by side, each of the two photos respectively appears to demonstrate one of photography's two modes. The photo of Nahum Korman's house looks like a picture on a wall. In it, we see an ideal model of a house, with all the required attributes: façade, window, tiled roof, fence, and a tree. The leveled earth on which the house stands testifies to the identity of the owners. The house testifies to a desire to disregard the surface of the terrain and to establish an ideal model of a house on it at any cost. The perfect structure appears lifeless, deserted, and derelict. As regards the house in the second photo, which belongs to the Shusha family, only one end of it rests on the earth, most of it being suspended on columns along the slope of the hill. Its construction testifies to a willingness to take pleasure in the site's topographical conditions. In fact, it appears to be still in the process of construction: The workers have perhaps stepped out — it is lunchtime, and they have gathered in a small spot of shade to satisfy their hunger.

However, the signs can also be read the other way around. The residents of the Korman family home might perhaps be sitting at table in the privacy of their abode, the sounds of commotion and laughter rising. But the price of this joie de vivre is the sequestration of the house from the outside. The sole window in the structure's façade appears dark, its shutters battened; the interior has been locked away from the outside in order to maintain the routine of life. As regards the second house, its apparent exuberance, to which I pointed earlier, might simply be testimony to an interruption of

458

construction, to a ban on any further work imposed as part of the IDF's overall policy of preventing any expansion of Palestinian housing. The unfinished building might stand like this for months or years, awaiting the necessary authorizations or better days to reach completion. The many openings gouged out in it, which haven't yet been sealed with windows, allow the gaze to move about freely, to look through it. Behind the unfinished building's appearance of levity lies a life constricted by prohibitions and restrictions. Behind the apparently perfect structure's ponderousness lies a life that arbitrarily determines the rules and imposes them on others.

Following this description, what seems to be called for is to say that in one house resides a family of Jewish citizens, in the other a family of Palestinian subjects. But this description too, even though there is some truth to it, is problematic and again confronts us with the traps laid by language when we try to describe the occupation, including its traces in photography. Formally, the Palestinian is a subject, the Israeli a citizen. The Palestinian is the exception, the Israeli, the rule. And yet, when the Israeli is a settler, he, too, is an exception. He is a citizen of the state of Israel who lives in territories that are ruled by the state, but to which it abstains from applying its laws, with the exception of cases concerning him. In other words, the state avoids applying its laws to the Palestinian subjects over whom it rules and therefore avoids applying them to the Occupied Territories as a whole. The settlers enjoy the privileged status of exceptional citizens. They benefit from the civil rights granted to all citizens of the state of Israel and, in addition, they are also granted special privileges and benefits in many areas, intended to recompense them for the security risk involved in living in what are defined as high-risk zones.[34]

While no similarity exists or can exist between the living conditions of the Palestinians and those of the settlers, I wish to emphasize the structural analogy between them, both being exceptions, and to illuminate its meanings. The Palestinian's incarceration in the penal colony is insufficient, for the settler doesn't actually live outside of the territory of the colony. To turn his living space into a sterile zone, he must enclose himself behind opaque walls, fences, borders, and barricades. To maintain his life uninterrupted in the fortresses he has erected, he must allow the ruling power to pene-

459

trate ever larger areas of his life: provisions, security, health, education, mobility, and so forth. Of course, the ruling power doesn't exert violence against him, as it does in dealing with the Palestinians who live in the penal colony, but the violence does overflow.

In practical terms, the settlers request that this power *not* stop expanding. The desire for more and more of this power stems from the fact that the laws designed to protect them, the special laws of those who are the exceptions, are insufficient without the daily presence of the ruling apparatuses. This is precisely the status of the exception. If citizenship is measured by its capacity to limit force and to serve as a protective shield against power, then the exception does not command such a capacity. The Palestinian lacks it, for his status as an exception is forced on him and does not include components of consent or negotiable conditions. The settler, conversely, even if he has come to the territories encouraged by the state, has chosen his exceptional status and enjoys the benefits this involves. The privileges (money, means, protection) with which the regime pampers the exception prevent him from recognizing the price that these privileges exact from the exception at whose expense he benefits. In addition, though, they also prevent him from recognizing the temporariness of the privileges granted him and thus of his own status. The "disengagement" under which settlers were evacuated from the Gaza Strip exposed the exceptional citizen's inability to realize his citizenship and to circumscribe the ruling power. Unlike the Palestinian, who stands totally exposed before the power of the regime, the settler is not totally a subject, but neither is he totally a citizen.

The gaze continues on its path, moving from photo to photo, from one residential home to the next: dark windows, few and far between, an accumulation of residential structures, gouging boundaries in the land. The houses serve as protective walls, borderlines, and ramparts (figures 8.22–8.23). In many of the photos, the houses are either arranged in rows standing on top of the hill, overlooking their surroundings, or planted inside excavated trenches, like fortified outposts. To the obstinate gaze, it becomes evident that the logic joining these buildings together is the logic of security, which pushes aside the logic of citizenship. After looking at dozens of pictures hundreds of times, a public space — a civilian space, where the

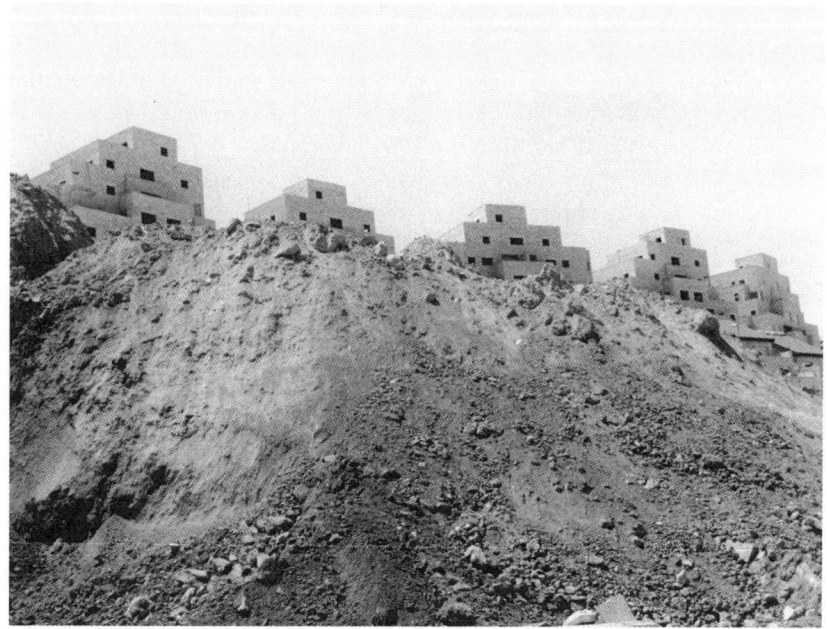

Figure 8.22. Efrat Shvili, Pisgat Ze'ev, Jerusalem, 1993.

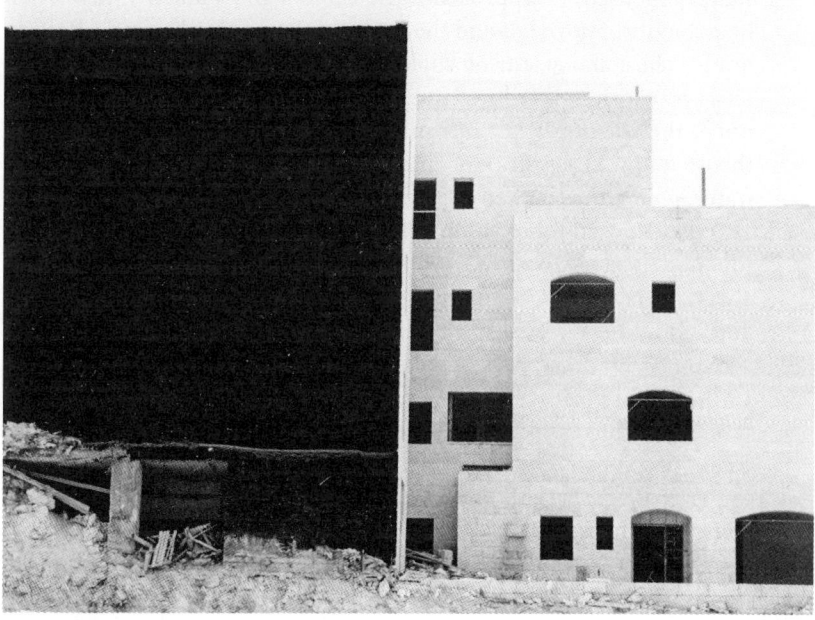

Figure 8.23. Efrat Shvili, Malha, Jerusalem, 1995.

citizens, if they were rightful citizens, could gather and discuss the *res publica* without the presence of the governmental power — is prominently missing from the Jewish colonies.

The ruling power is everywhere, there in order to protect the would-be assemblers, but first and foremost to ensure that all those who assemble are wanted, that all of them are Jews. In the absence of stable borders, the presence of this power demarcates the contours of the borders of the penal colony: the pale of security.

Chic Point: *Irony and the Field of Vision in the Penal Colony*

The video *Chic Point* by Sharif Waked proposes a peep into the field of vision created by the checkpoint. From the point of view of the Palestinian, whether an Israeli citizen or a noncitizen, the field of vision where the Palestinian is becoming an object of scrutiny is not limited to the checkpoints in the occupied areas of Palestine. Suffice it for someone who looks like an Arab to walk down the street in order for his body to become the object of an invasive gaze, at times hesitant and unfelt, at times direct and blunt.

The video begins with a view of a young, stylish man walking toward the spectator (figures 8.24–8.25). Elegantly dressed, his eye sharply focused, he approaches the camera and suddenly, just when he is about to move beyond the limits of the screen, he stops. Puffing out his chest and gesturing slightly with his hand, he shows the spectator his clothes: a tailored suit, its jacket shorter than usual. All at once, the spectator is confronted with the model's exposed belly, thrust at him in a gesture of charming defiance. The man briefly hesitates, giving the spectator time to examine not only his clothes, but also the exposed bit of flesh, before turning right and left like a fashion model on a catwalk. Afforded recourse to the model's profile, the spectator is allowed to improve her view, while the man moves right and left and even winks at the spectator before vanishing from the screen. As he disappears, a second young man appears, also dressed stylishly and perfectly barbered, made up and shaved. He resolutely takes the same course. He is followed by another model, and another, each one exposing his chest, ribs, stomach muscles, solar plexus, and upper or lower back. Sometimes the model appears already exposed, sometimes he slowly bares himself in front of the camera.

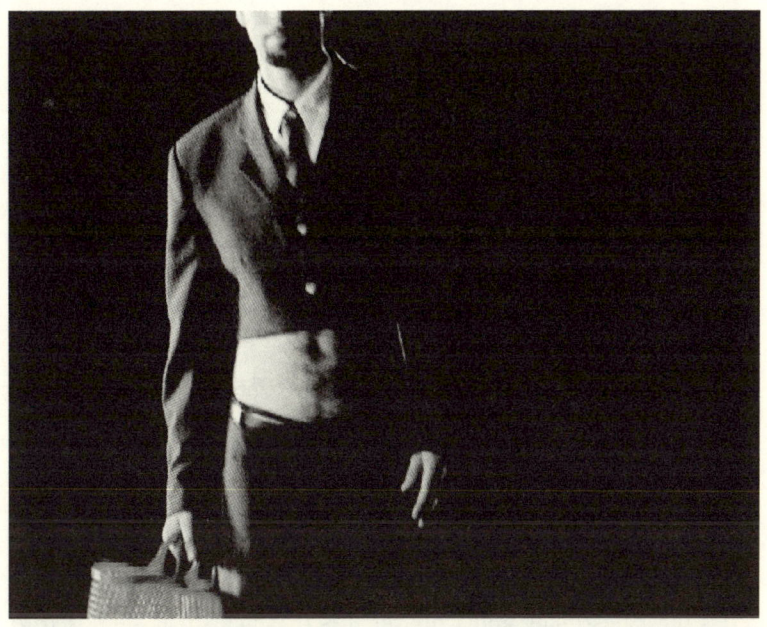

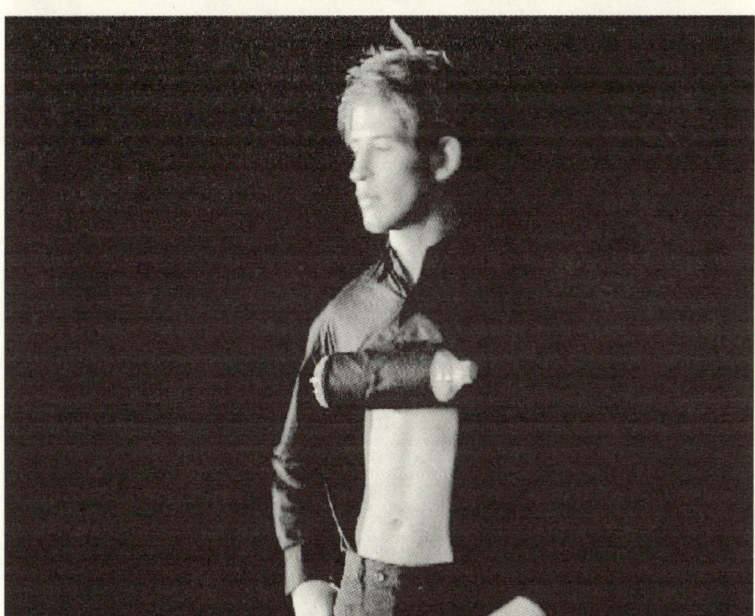

Figures 8.24 and 8.25. Sharif Waked, *Chic Point: Fashion for Israeli Checkpoints*, video, 7 minutes, 2003.

Following the practices of the fashion world, the spectator's glimpse at the models' bodies is managed by way of the apparel they are wearing. The clothes are relatively conventional — jackets, shirts, T-shirts, and undershirts — but in each of them, an out-of-the-ordinary peep hole has been excised, exposing the midsection (from chest to waist), permitting scrutiny of the gap between skin and cloth. If not on seeing the first model in the parade, then by the second or at most the third, the spectator understands that she is not watching a routine fashion show. The accumulation of altered pieces of clothing emphasizes that we are dealing here with fashion designed to make removal an integral part of style.

The video's subtitle, *Fashion for Israeli Checkpoints*, directs the understanding to the ironic reference being invoked here. The Israelis guard the checkpoints, while the people being checked are Palestinian; what is fashionable for Israeli checkpoints are the Palestinians being checked — in Nablus, in Bir Naballah, in Ramallah, in Tulkarm, yes, but also in Jaffa, Tel-Aviv, Nazareth, the Sharon coastal plain, at the center of the country. Sometimes the checkpoint precedes the Palestinian, and whoever it is that mans it is supposed to identify him in the crowd pressing toward the entrance. Sometimes the checkpoint is produced ad hoc, there, where the Palestinian is.

At the side of a main road in the heart of the Sharon plain, under a billboard covered with Hebrew ads, in view of thousands of cars, the three Palestinians in Pavel Wolberg's photo are stopped and ordered to raise their shirts. Since Israel is still in a declared state of emergency and has been since its creation, there are always "alerts," "warnings," and "manhunts" to justify these orders (figure 8.26).

Waked's fashion show, which — at first glance — seems like any routine catwalk production, actually positions the spectator in a way that slowly reveals itself as a rehearsal of the gaze at the checkpoint. The model parading in front of her is a Palestinian. The look she gives him erects a checkpoint ad hoc. In this video, the models' steps along the catwalk undergo an ironic transformation into an echo of the meeting between the Palestinian's free motion and the obstruction of a surveillance point. The viewer, as she watches, takes the place of the camera that serves as a checkpoint in this video. From this vantage point, the spectator can best stare at the body that

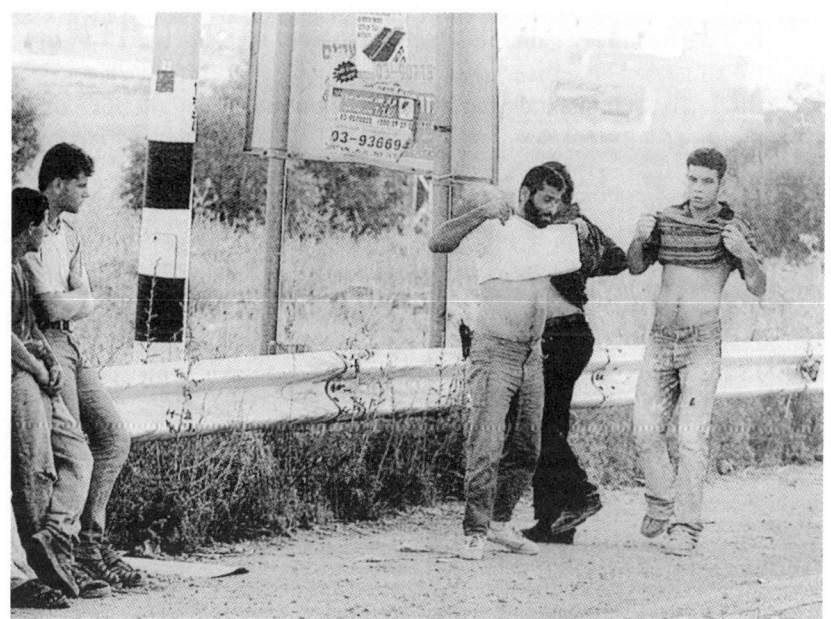

Figure 8.26. Pavel Wolberg, seam line, *Ha'aretz*, July 30, 2002.

appears before her. The checkpoint marks the Palestinian body; Waked's fashion line shifts the marking from the body to the apparel and to the playful possibilities inherent in the relations between the clothes and those who wear and remove them. In Waked's work, the body wearing these fashion articles is not turned into the site of a truth that the clothing merely conceals. Rather, the body plays a part in a performative game in which the model stylizes himself in relation to a set of signs imposed on him from the outside. He wears those signs on his body like prize jewels, intensifying them or turning them upside down.

The first model walks at a measured, deliberate pace directly toward the spectator as though about to bump into her. It is difficult to imagine him not enjoying the spectator's discomfort at the prospect. While he stops and turns, he genially winks at the spectator, as if sharing a secret, yet the spectator knows that she is not really the addressee of the wink, but at most its object. The model is in alliance with the model who follows him, who is similarly marked with a patch consisting of a hole. It is the second model whom he turns to welcome. Whereas at the checkpoint the people being checked pass one after another under the classificatory scrutiny of the soldier on watch, awaiting his verdict, the people being checked in Waked's video welcome each other, each giving the one after him the signal to appear. Thus, sharing a destiny that has become a secret and translated into an ironic gaze, they negate the spectator's function as the one who is supposed to confirm their appearance, leaving her behind.

The next model down the runway is as resolute as his predecessor, his outfit complete and intact. After approaching the spectator, he turns around. Only then does the gaping hole in the back of his suit come into view. The model takes another two or three steps and then turns unexpectedly in an attitude of defiance: *Hey*, he appears to be saying to the spectator, *you wanted to see some more, I'll show you more!* He jerks open the zipper that crisscrosses his garment. *There's nothing to see, but come on anyway — this time I'll show you that there's nothing to see. Take a good look. Maybe you're missing something. Try from this angle.*

The next model, or perhaps the one after the next, does not strut or wiggle his hips at all, but walks directly toward the spectator, as if to say: *Here is my body, like an open book before your eyes. But look at your own gaze, at the data it's collecting, at the hundreds of thousands of bodies it's torturing, stripping them of their clothes, trespassing on their territory as though it has the power to uncover their truth. Take a very good look. You've got an opportunity to see your own gaze spread out before you like an open book.* And so on and so forth, one model after another, an entire show. Toward the end, there appears a model with his arm thrust inside an opening in his garment, directly above his midsection. He advances toward the spectator, his hand dangling and touching his body. He appears to have something in his grip, something that he will brandish forthwith. But he may simply be toying intimately with himself, a provocation by its very intimacy, defiant in its control over what the other would like to penetrate with her gaze in order to bring what is hidden inside out into the light.

At any given moment, the Israeli Jew can demand that the Palestinian's body be exposed. If he's a soldier or a security guard, he can give the order directly, himself. If he's a civilian, he can enlist the assistance of one of the tens of thousands of soldiers and security guards who cover the entire area of the state of Israel. In the penal colony, at any given moment a small kangaroo court can be created, a mobile kit for passing judgment and sealing fates. The tools at the soldier's disposal are almost infinite; the authority he wields is almost absolute.[35] Although the instrument he uses to make his decision precludes contact, sometimes the gaze retreats before it. As has already been said, if asked what he's looking for, he would say it's a belt of explosives. But if we examine his gaze in an effort to understand how it works, we find that the Palestinian's body, wherever it might be, serves as a pretext for drawing a border from which it may be observed. The Palestinian's body is the carrier of a truth that he either denies or conceals. The truth is in his body, but he frustrates its appearance. As we've noted, the sovereign's junior proxy is there to prove that the person in front of him is not really who he claims to be. He is looking for the truth, the truth of identity and identity as truth, and therefore he must gaze directly at the Palestinian's body, removing all the disguises that the Palestinian has draped over it.

It is not enough that he knows the Palestinian's true identity; he wants the Palestinian to know it as well. As the "military element" informed me, "at the checkpoints, we nevertheless succeed in capturing dozens of people whom we need for intelligence purposes. They don't always know that that's what they are." This underlies the ritual of the sovereign gaze, which decides that the person before it is not who he is pretending to be. When his gaze tires, he does not require the Palestinian body to know the truth, for it lies open before him, even when absent. He can seal shut the checkpoint and bar anyone from passing or he can dismantle the checkpoint and let everyone pass through until each and all are caught at the next checkpoint. It is obvious that they all have stolen, borrowed, or forged identities. They are all suspect a priori of not being who they claim to be.

The sovereign's proxy manufactures meaning out of his encounter with the Palestinian at the checkpoint. The spectacle of the Palestinian's body displays this meaning. Waked strips this meaning of its content, confounding Israeli bodies with Palestinian bodies and Palestinian citizens of Israel with Palestinians from the Occupied Territories. His men are handsome, determined, robust, threatening, provocative, soft, unshaven, and tired. Their names, which mark their origins, do not correspond to their onscreen appearances. The "Israeli" cannot be distinguished from the "Palestinian" or the "Arab" from the "Jew," and vice versa. To become an expert at turning political entities into bodies under investigation, you have to hunker down behind protective armor, plated glass, a wire-screened counter, cocked weapon, or instruction manual. The tactics employed by the guard at the checkpoints — humiliation, abuse, disruption of movement, callowness — have justification and purpose because they assist his gaze in discovering the truth. While knowing that the truth may not reveal itself, he assumes that he may hasten its disclosure by bringing the subjects to the point of exhaustion. That is the reason for the attrition and humiliation. *Yes, there's no choice*, he'll say and go on working in utter seriousness and out of a sense of responsibility.[36] Every day he and other links in the chain of command further divide the territory and plant more contrivances in order to surprise the Palestinian and expose his schemes. These various peculiar contrivances — "enclosure checkpoint," "surprise checkpoint," "manned checkpoint" or "mobile checkpoint"—make the Palestinian's movement unpredictable. On Monday, he may be permitted to pass through a checkpoint that no longer stands on Tuesday, and the permit he holds is invalid at the checkpoint that suddenly rises on another road. On the other hand, he may draw back from the checkpoint after hours of waiting and begin trudging home, only to hear a commotion arise. He turns, only to find the checkpoint gone.

The Hebrew word *machsom*, which means both "barrier" or "obstacle" and "checkpoint," isn't uttered at all in the video, even though it regularly serves both Hebrew and Arabic speakers. "In Arabic, there is no word for checkpoint."[37] The use of the term "checkpoint," which has come to stand for inspection stations at border crossings around the world, disguises the violent context of the Hebrew term: the stoppage of movement and the obstruction of passage. In Waked's video, the checkpoint has turned into a "chic point." The examination has become chic—rational, elegant, sophisticated, and charming—and the point has become a peephole into the body that the Palestinian is required to provide.

At the end of his video Waked has compiled a sequence of press photos similar to some of the photos that I have analyzed in this chapter. When one looks at these photos, it is evident that the Palestinian has become an obstacle to the Israeli gaze, which is constantly looking for the "checkpoint," eyeing that strip of flesh between the chest and waist. The checkpoint, for the army, restricts the infiltration of Palestinians who seek to carry out terror attacks in Israel. The army assumes that the Palestinian is likely to strike by surprise, so it is always best to surprise him first. This is why the army breaks into homes, destroys infrastructures, deploys troops on rooftops, plants observation posts, raids businesses and public institutions, wakes people in the dead of night, breaks down doors, undresses men, and ransacks drawers, why the army tortures, humiliates, shoots, insults, and kills. Throughout the West Bank and the Gaza Strip, this is what the army does. The checkpoints are part of the same logic, because they help the army accomplish such tasks.

In a paradoxical fashion, the checkpoints moderate the army's ferocity and brutality elsewhere. The daily body count does not rise out of the checkpoints. One might surmise that the checkpoints serve less as an obstacle to the Palestinians than as a muzzle for the voracious governmental monster (indeed, the original meaning of the Hebrew word *machsom* was just that — a muzzle for an animal), which prevents it from rampaging, biting, and devouring anyone who passes near it. The muzzled violence that occurs each day at the checkpoints serves, so it seems, to suspend and delay the massive eruption of direct violence of the kind that is perpetrated daily in the nonnegotiable living space of the penal colony, the space that has been left between the various checkpoints. The massive deployment of withheld violence restrains the Israeli army and avoids the outburst of direct, full-scale military violence. It enables the ruling apparatus to continue governing millions of Palestinians without naturalizing them — citizenship would entail ideological state apparatuses, recognition, and participation in the ruling power — *but without war as well.* Such a war, were it to break out under the present conditions, in the absence of a cohesive Palestinian military force, would entail some form of ethnic cleansing: be it the transfer, expulsion, or annihilation of the Palestinians.[38] Their territories are already occupied, and there is no sovereign enemy to be destroyed.

CHAPTER NINE

The Woman Collaborator Does Not Exist

Administration of the Palestinian's private space by the Israeli ruling apparatus doesn't stop at the front door. The Palestinian home is a cell in the penal colony, and various operative factors can lead to a realization of the army's potential control over it and over its contours: searches for wanted persons, demolition commands, proximity to the homes of people whom the army has decided to punish with a home demolition, or the army's need for a local headquarters, an outpost, or a vantage point.[1]

Evening. Hard knocking at the door. Banging. Soldiers taking family members out of the house. If they refuse, they'll be hurt. Of course they obey. They stand huddled at the entrance of their home (figure 9.1). The women's hands are full. Two of them are holding babies; a younger girl is pressing her palms together in a seemingly pleading gesture, as if she were saying "Not this, just not this." The children are less disciplined; they stand outside the line that has been drawn for the family. If there's a shootout, their position will endanger them. At the moment, they're mesmerized by the sight of the gun in the hands of the soldier who is covering the soldier with his gun pointed into the home. It's a cliffhanger. The spectator wants to cover her ears, too, to shut out the sound of a soldier firing into the home. Make him go away already, now, with his gun. That will happen in a few moments. In this house, too, he will find nothing. He has many more homes in which to sow fear. A photographer has been accompanying the unit since morning. He says that by the end of the day he had counted thirty homes that he entered along with the army. This time, the visit was brief. The family was returned to its home the same evening.

> Most of the time we were in homes. No, there are no pictures of the Palestinians inside the homes, because in most homes they're locked into one room, the entire family is in a room downstairs in the basement. "Being in a home" has two meanings — for a short time, four or five days or [for a longer time] a week or two. And then you leave the family imprisoned there, and there are times when you turn the home into an outpost and then you throw the family out. It's just in houses that you turn into headquarters that you throw out the family.[2]

The precise statistics on the scope of these operations doesn't affect the principle common to them: The Palestinian and his property are permeable to the exertion of direct force. The Palestinian does not need to commit any offense for the power to realize this permeability and hurt him. His living area is imprinted with the presence of the Israeli ruling apparatuses, and reducing the level of friction with this power does not depend on him. The permeability of his body and home exposes his private life and makes them vulnerable in a way that circumscribes his capacity to limit the power, to prevent it from taking control of his life, his soul, and his deeds.

"In the room was a man named Q., who said, 'I know a lot about you and I can send you to jail. It's important for me to know about your activity in the village.'" He also said: "There is no one who can approve your departure except me, and your whole future is in my hands. You want my help now, and in return, I want your help."[3] The things the Shabak interrogator told "H. A." in an attempt to recruit him as a collaborator indicate the manner in which the Palestinians' dependence on the security forces is thus created as a mirror image, albeit not a symmetrical or an even one, of the way in which the security forces are dependent on the Palestinians for their operation. The actions and services the Palestinians provide encompass many areas, such as information collection, translation, the identification of detainees, population management, the procurement of lands, acting as "human shields," policing and interrogation activities, collaborating in threats, and exerting psychological and physical force.

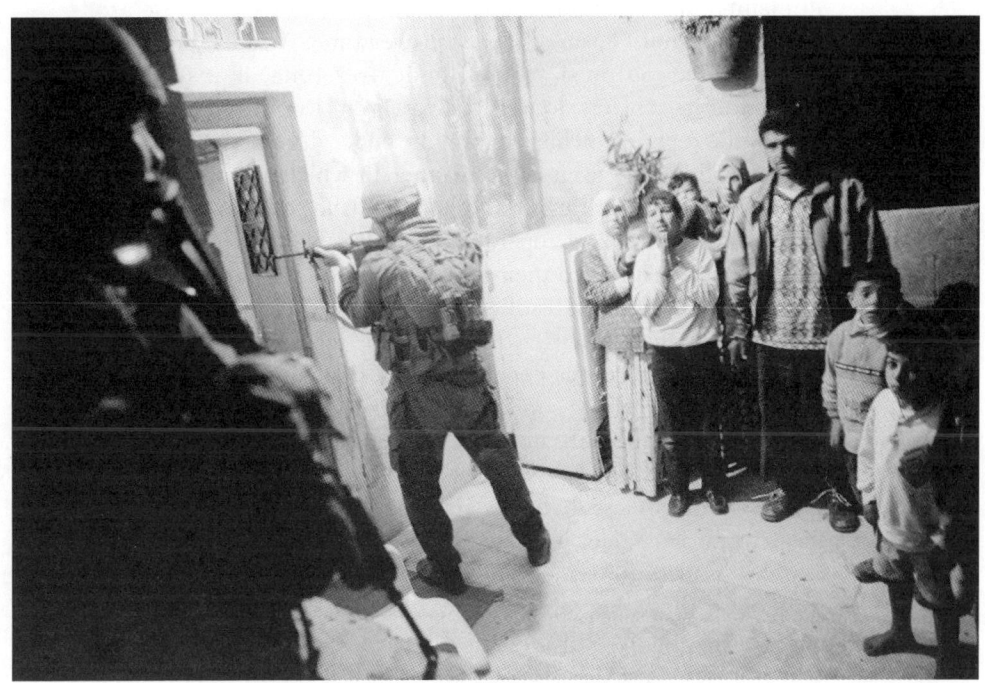

Figure 9.1. Pavel Wolberg, Tufach, 2002.

These services, which are often termed "collaboration," are pro-cured by the security services through various means and levels of coercion.

Through the specific products it is capable of creating — informa-tion, lands, and blood — collaboration assists the ruling apparatuses in maintaining the regime in the territories. However, these prod-ucts alone cannot ensure this result over time. A ruling power can-not operate, and most certainly not over time, if at least some portion of its subjects do not take part in it. Even if their participa-tion in the regime is achieved forcibly, under duress, through threats and extortion, and even if the manner in which they participate is impaired, those Palestinians known as collaborators in point of fact take part in the ruling apparatus. The impaired character of their participation testifies to their inferior position in the ruling appara-tus, but it also, equally, testifies to the impaired character of the rul-ing power in the territories.

The ruling apparatus depends on the population that it seeks to rule, but its rule is not conducted as an orderly power. Its relations with the population are based on extortion, fear, duress, violence, uncertainty, and instability. These are the characteristics of the rul-ing apparatus no less than they are descriptions of the way in which Palestinians live under it.

The security forces commonly call the Palestinians whom they include in the ruling apparatus *mashtapim*, a pluralization of the acronym *mashtap* denoting the two-word idiom *meshatef peula*, which means "collaborator" in Hebrew. It is a term that enhances the scorn and repulsion toward them. The epithet is part of the mechanism through which they are controlled — the means by which they are turned into part of the ruling apparatus, the means of their integration as part of the logic of this action and their simultaneous distancing from the regime, purifying the system of any trace of them.

This duality is unfailingly manifested in the stories of collabora-tors who were dismissed from their roles after a short period, not always as a direct result of the services that they did or did not suc-ceed in providing. Thus, despite the massive mixing of Palestinians into the ruling apparatus, the latter succeeds in maintaining its image as separate from the local population and in representing those who take part in it as evidence of the impaired character of the Palestinians, who are no more than *mashtapim*, that is, traitors to their own people. This is how the use of the term to describe some of the workings of the ruling apparatus serves to create a dichotomous world in which the individual can ostensibly either be or refrain from being a collaborator. This dichotomy activates a lethal demon's dance that includes all — both Jews and Palestinians.

What is more important, however, is that the mechanism for recruiting collaborators threatens to trap the Palestinian in the category "collaborator" even when he has refused to collaborate, thus exposing him to simultaneous threats from both the Shabak — including the threats mediated by Palestinian collaborators — and Palestinians seeking to resist the Shabak by reinstating the boundary lines between collaborators and noncollaborators. In the course of interrogations and as part of the means of exerting pressure on candidates for recruitment, the Shabak, too, attempts to instate the boundary lines that it usually undoes between collaborator and noncollaborator. In addition, it recruits collaborators in order to injure those who refuse to collaborate. Accordingly, the instability of the boundary line between the two increasingly spins and spirals.[4] The instability occurs not only between collaborator and noncollaborator but, as I will show shortly, is also reproduced between those attempting to injure collaborators, for the methods of the ruling apparatus include posing as Palestinians — or using real Palestinians — who are in pursuit of collaborators.

"'S.' told me I had to honor my commitment. I said I was absolutely unwilling to collaborate and that I had signed the document only because I had been tortured.... I am afraid that he might send collaborators who will beat me or burn my house, and then the people in the village will say it was done because I was a collaborator."[5]

The report on collaborators produced by B'Tselem in 1994 deals with the first intifada. It was an important report, because it is almost the only source for learning about collaborators and the methods of their recruitment by the Shabak.[6] Brief allusions to collaborators in the press or in the existing literature are usually made as if they were part of the normal world order: "M. N. was the son of a family of Palestinian collaborators."[7] Collaborators fear for their lives and speak sparingly, while the activity of the men of the Shabak is shrouded in a thunderous silence. Confronting this phenomenon, as the authors of the report indicate, is an extremely difficult task. A close reading of the report reveals that the difficulties facing those who seek to handle this topic extend far beyond the mere issue of their ability to collect reliable information and facts. The difficulties, as I will try to show, stem from the way in which the field of vision within which the "collaborator" appears to others' gaze and speech is already contaminated by collaboration. To allow a grasp of this, I will offer a rereading of the testimonies provided by the report. My aim is not to propose a more precise description of the figure of the collaborator, but rather to reconstruct the arena of speech, gaze, and action within which the collaborator's image is depicted.

Collaboration Does Not Exist

The report opens with the statement that it will deal with six kinds of collaborators. It actually lists only five: "the intelligence agent" (*'amil al-mukhabarat* in Arabic), "collaborators in prisons and detention facilities" (*al-'asfor*), "the land dealers" (*al-samsar*), "the intermediary" (*al-wasit*), and "government appointees and associates" (*mukhtars* and others). Instead of a sixth, it offers the following vague description of a value system: "morality, family honor, and collaboration." This heading itself already indicates that this type of collaboration poses a problem.

The linguistic difficulty that the authors encountered in characterizing the sixth kind of collaboration in the same way as they characterized the other five is merely the tip of an iceberg of difficulties raised by the question of women as collaborators. Collaboration involving women is intertwined with the discussion of matters of silence and silencing that deviate from the public toward the private and intimate sphere in which physical contact leaves the body with a stain that only silence can remove. Halting language is one facet of the silence. The lack of women's testimonies is its other facet. The absence of women's testimonies in the report emerges as highly significant in the context of the multiplicity and variety of the testimonies of men who have collaborated, men who were targeted by the Shabak for recruitment as collaborators, but refused, and men who acted on behalf of Palestinian factions or on behalf of the Shabak to injure both male and female collaborators. The report documents "five incidents of the killing of women in the intifada." The vague language that also characterizes their treatment of these cases itself participates in turning the attacks against women from a political to a moral issue, thus removing from the picture the role played by Israeli men in the violent relations between Palestinian men and women, of which killing is merely the visible manifestation.

This treatment renders injury to these women prior to their murder irrelevant, representing it instead as an offense to be considered relative to the punishment to which the women were sentenced. In its treatment of the other types of collaborators that it lists, the report discusses their torture and murder as a distinct topic meriting a separate chapter. With regard to the women, the authors are extremely careful with language and avoid any characterizations of the type of collaboration at issue. They also avoid claiming that the women in question were murdered due to suspicions of collaboration, thus leaving them in a twilight zone controlled by questions of morality and family honor that signify the point of separation between Jewish-Israeli society as an advanced community and Palestinian-Arab society as a conservative one that injures women due to their sexual activities.

If the report had avoided using the term "collaborators" for the other Palestinians whose deeds it describes, its decision to do so with regard to women could have been seen as an effort on the part of the authors to challenge the taken-for-granted use of the category and to propose a new and different grid for understanding and analyzing the phenomenon. However, as stated above, in its discussion of the first five categories, the report uses the term "collaborator" to denote the Palestinians it describes. In many instances, by comparing evidence, the report takes pains to clear the Palestinian men or women who were suspected of collaboration. It turns out that "many Palestinians were killed for baseless suspicions, due to errors in identification" or other errors.[8] The authors understand that they are dealing with highly explosive materials and seek, therefore, throughout the report, to qualify their claims in an attempt to find eminently reliable sources for a formulation of the phenomenon at issue: "This report does not offer an independent definition of the term 'collaborator.' It tries, rather, to focus on the definitions of the Palestinian organizations and address them, for those definitions, and not external criteria, determine against whom violent action is taken."[9] Because the category of "collaborator" is harmful and degrading, the authors are careful not to determine which people are collaborators. They accordingly choose to rely on the judgments made by Palestinians on this matter. And yet, in point of fact, they adopt the perspective of the ruling apparatus regarding this topic, a perspective based on the assumed possibility of both separating and stabilizing the separation between Palestinians and Israelis with regard to the workings of the ruling apparatus in the territories.

The authors are saying, in effect, "We are neutral and merely observe the ways in which collaborators are caught by the Palestinians." In practice, though, they create an artificial split within the field of vision, as if "collaborators" were managed by the Palestinians alone. The attempt to discuss only the collaborators whom the Palestinians killed as punishment for their collaboration, as if their murder were some final evidence of their deeds or identity, is doomed to fall into precisely the same trap.[10] No less problematic is the report's attribution of its central categories to "Palestinian organizations," as if these formed a single fabric and agreed among themselves on the categories. This is in direct contradiction to the testimonies — quoted in the report — of central figures in these organizations, most of whom describe unsynchronized, quarrelsome activities, born of uncertainty, of multiple, varied, and clashing interests, of disinformation, of the activities of impostors and counterimpostors, and so on. In addition, the testimonies indicate a high level of heterogeneity regarding actions, categories, and motives among all of those operating in the arena of collaboration.

In short, it is a tainted arena revealing, perhaps in the most unbearable terms, the perversity of the ruling apparatus in the territories in its accounts for its actions in the causal, linear, rational terms of security considerations — "searching for wanted people," "stopping ticking bombs," or seeking "sensitive security information" — while acting through the opposite procedures of expansion, contact, contamination, obscuration, and destabilization, all guided by a single principle: reaching everywhere, interfering in everything, staining and touching all.

> For a few months afterward there was an upsurge in the phenomenon of "repentance" among collaborators.... PLO activists claimed that at the beginning of the Intifada collaborators were given the opportunity to repent without endangering themselves, but that Israel prevented this.[11]

> At the beginning of the Intifada they said not to kill.... I did a lot to prevent murders. The authorities do not want the Palestinians to stop the murders.[12]

> At the beginning of the Intifada, we still didn't know about the under-cover units, and they also eliminated people while placing the responsibility on us.[13]

> In most cases we get the right person, but there have also been mistakes when we have executed people who were not guilty. Sometimes there are internal liquidations for other reasons, [such as] when people disguise themselves as wanted men and murder people as if they were suspected collaborators.[14]

These are difficult testimonies, revealing a crazed picture — that of a branding/staining machine propelled by an uncontrollable desire to foil every attempt on the part of Palestinian society to shore up areas that are inaccessible to the ruling system. The authors apparently find it difficult to believe the testimonies that they themselves present. They accordingly weave them into a well-ordered worldview in which, on the one hand, there are the Shabak and the collaborators and, on the other, there are Palestinians who seek to harm the collaborators and who also harm innocent victims killed by mistake. Close attention to these testimonies, in which the insanity is reflected from the reality they describe, will clarify that the entire report is an attempt to restore a degree of logic and sanity to the picture it draws of the occupation. In doing so, in an effort to restabilize a worldview centered on crime and punishment, it employs the Palestinians as a tribunal, meanwhile positioning the report as a moral standard for critiquing the operation of this "judicial" system.

Since I first received this report, I have repeatedly gone back and read parts of it. Not one of my readings was the same as its predecessor. Following the authors, I first read the testimonies within the framing narrative in which they were embedded. I was shocked by the killing of collaborators and by the attitudes of Palestinian society toward these people. However, every such reading ended in a sense of uneasiness. The testimonies I read tugged in the opposite direction, toward the possibility of another story, one that is hard to believe and that, probably for this reason, is hard to tell. It was only when I understood the role of photography in the practices employed by the Shabak, through an analysis of the case of 'Abed A-Nasser 'Ubeid (see Chapter Eight), that I thought I had a possible lead on a slightly different account of this tale. Through his testimony, I grasped that the Shabak collaborates in the killing of suspects of collaboration and, moreover, that the killing of suspects of collaboration is part of the Shabak's mode of operation vis-à-vis collaborators.

The role of photography also reappeared in the description of women's recruitment as collaborators: "He said that he was going to undress, that I should undress, and that we would get on the table to be photographed so my family would know I was having fun."[15] In their case too, the actual photographs remained outside the accessible field of vision, and the role played by the act of photography could only be reconstructed. However, in the case of the women, not only the photographs were absent, but also their first-person testimonies.[16] My understanding that the women are both present in and at the same time absent from the report became the beginning of my understanding that the woman collaborator *does not exist* — and, in its wake, the understanding that *collaboration itself* does not exist.

The Woman Collaborator Does Not Exist

The stories of the women left me very uneasy. One by one, the report analyzes five cases of the murder of women from the one hundred killed in a similar context during the first intifada, claiming that these women had not been collaborators. According to the report, the women in question therefore had in fact been murdered in vain. This formulation, implying as it does that some murders are not in vain, however, is contaminated and is therefore worth scrutiny.

"The study [in this report] reveals that most of the women killed by Palestinians during the Intifada did not have any contacts with the security forces."[17] And yet, in the first testimony included in the report after this statement, A. Q. testifies that he was involved in the killing of Warda Al-Safriyah: "She had already been interrogated twice in the past by the Fatah, and she confessed to having been involved in *isqat* [exerting pressure, usually through sexual means], but she denied that she had relationships with the enemy. She ran a sewing factory with twenty-five women employees, almost all of whom she had involved in *isqat.* . . . Al-Safriyah's house is in the Barbah neighborhood, most of whose residents are armed collaborators."[18] The details reported by A. Q. regarding Al-Safriyah distance her story from the title of the chapter in which it is depicted: "Morality, Family Honor, and Collaboration." The claim that Al-Safriyah had had no contacts with the enemy while carrying out *isqat* at the rate of a cottage industry (twenty-five women), leaves "the enemy" innocent, untainted and unstained, while ignoring its mode of operation through a network of subcontractors who may sometimes refrain for years from creating direct contacts between "the enemy" and "the woman collaborator." The branding/staining is also performed geographically, as a result of the woman's residence among "collaborators," such that even if she were to deny her involvement in sexual *isqat*, she could not have protected herself completely from the machine.

Understanding the ways in which the branding/staining machine works to create instability as regards the identity of collaborators requires an understanding of the mechanisms that it puts in motion to stabilize their identities. The Shabak employs violent practices to induct people who will collaborate with it, and many of these practices can be learned about from the report. Most of these share the use of the tool of identity in order to exert pressure. The Shabak threatens the candidate for induction with disclosure of his "true" identity. This is a terrifying game, for what is at stake is life itself, and in a reality where Palestinians are constantly brushing against Shabak agents, there are myriad potential signs that could be decisive — incriminating signs of collaboration. The "true" identity of the candidate for induction as a collaborator may well therefore cost him his life.

His "true" identity, turned into a weapon against him, is never "his," but rather an identity that others seek to attribute to him as they "extract" it from him. This identity, seemingly the kernel of truth at the core of his being, is composed of signs that only others have the power to stabilize and determine as disclosing his "true" identity. As stated, despite the broad range of signs that are potentially capable of conviction, all of them testify to the fact that the suspected collaborator has been in contact with the Shabak. But one of the Shabak's most common practices is manufacturing such signs, regardless of whether the attempted induction was successful or not. Every attempt on the part of the Shabak to induct a candidate manufactures a sign of the contact that it has conducted with the Palestinian.

Evening. Dark. Tufach Village. A flashlight beams toward a Palestinian (figure 9.2). A Shabak agent signals him to approach the wall. The beam is powerful enough to create a huge shadow that his face casts against the wall — a terrifyingly enlarged, incriminating, convicting portrait. His expression is fearful. The Shabak agent mumbles to the photographer "No photographs." And yet, the photographer is there. He's not alone. Everyone there sees a Palestinian talking to a Shabak agent. Whoever was there or in the vicinity also saw how he was released and sent on his way at the end of the encounter. He was caused no harm. Maybe he got something in return. Maybe he passed something on. Maybe he didn't. His body has been branded. Stained. The machine can go on working. His contaminated body will create its effects. It will stream added uncertainty into the system.

From here on, the Palestinian is trapped in the snare of impossible proof — he must prove that he is not a collaborator.[19] However, as illustrated by the case of 'Ubeid, once the candidate has refused to collaborate, the Shabak is interested in incriminating him as a collaborator, thus intensifying the pressure exerted on him to accede to collaboration. However, those Palestinians in whose view the Shabak acts to incriminate him are already part of the collaborating network.

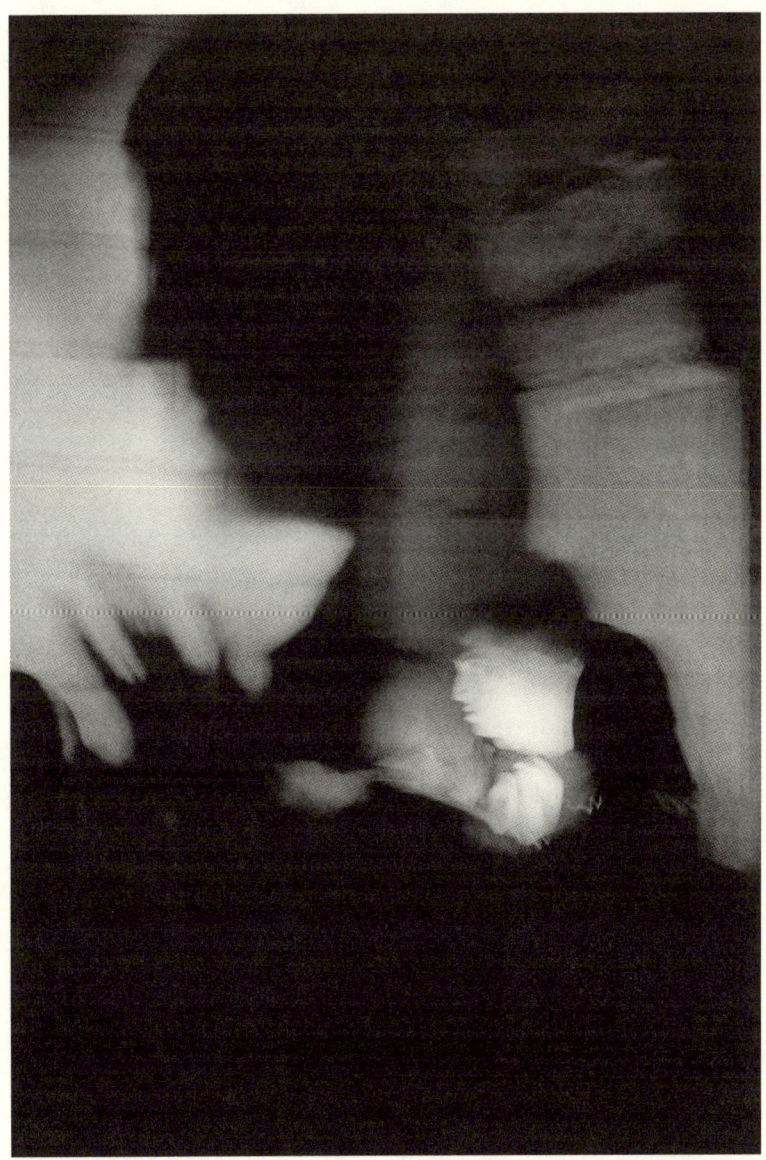

Figure 9.2. Pavel Wolberg, Tufach, 2002.

Consequently, their action on him, intended to disclose his real identity, is merely part of the attempt to manufacture and fit him with an identity at the behest of or under direct orders from the Shabak. In the process, the Palestinian can mislead his inductors and disguise his refusal to collaborate as collaboration. The Shabak takes this into account and acts accordingly. It ensures that the information it collects through its Palestinian sources is backed up by additional sources, most of the time Palestinian too. Thus, the other potential implications of being misled by Palestinians become part of what feeds into and spirals the questions of identity in the violent arena of collaboration.

Whether or not the Palestinian collaborates while seeming to, he is making his own contribution to the threatening instability that allows the Shabak to trap everyone in its web. Thus, the very use of the unproblematized category "collaborator" to signify the "true" identity of given Palestinians, even when it occurs for purposes of their "exoneration," serves as part of the arena of collaboration and is subject to the rules set by the Shabak. The classification of various collaborators into different types of identities such as "the intelligence agent (*'amil al-mukhabarat*)," "collaborators in prisons and detention facilities (*al-'asfor*)," "the land dealers (*al-samsar*)" or "the intermediary (*al-wasit*)," traps them into a lethal identity, as if it had the power to convey something substantial about them and about the society they belong to that treats "its" collaborators this way. The unproblematized use of the category of "collaborator" leaves the activity of the Shabak limited to the induction and operation of collaborators and fails to allow a view of the lethal arena created by the Shabak through which it continues to rule.

A candidate for induction into the Shabak is trapped. On the one side are the Shabak agents, pressuring him with threats that if he should refuse them, they will spread information and photographs that incriminate him as a collaborator. On the other side are the Palestinians who have already caved in under such pressures and have begun to collaborate, threatening the life of the candidate for induction and demanding that he prove the impossible — that he is not a collaborator.[20] Through the system of collaboration, the Palestinian is abandoned and exposed to harm, whether or not he has, in fact, collaborated.

And the Palestinian woman, even if she is a collaborator, is easier to get rid of on the pretense that she is a slut. Consequently, in the final analysis, she cannot be part of this game. The section of the second chapter of the report, which presents the various ways of inducting collaborators under the title *isqat*, describes the procedure: "Literally, the word means 'knocking down,' in the sense of tripping someone up or causing his moral deterioration. In this context, it refers to extortion or exerting pressure, usually through sexual means, in order to recruit collaborators."[21]

However, when the report turns to a description of the phenomenon of *isqat*, the authors' language departs from the style they use in describing other phenomena in other sections of the report. They present the phenomenon of *isqat* as it is described by "Palestinian organizations": "On many occasions, in leaflets and in other published material, the Palestinian organizations have warned against *isqat*.... According to the Palestinian organizations, *isqat* is carried out in a variety of ways."[22] The authors of the report, exposed as they are to hair-raising data and evidence regarding the murder of more than one hundred women and the injury of hundreds more over a six-year period during the first intifada (from its outbreak until compilation of the report), understand that what is at issue is a phenomenon that exists, is reported on, and discussed in Palestinian society, that this is no pack of unfounded rumors or disjointed episodes that it will be up to them to connect and to characterize as a phenomenon. Nevertheless, they find it difficult to believe in the phenomenon of sexual *isqat*. Ending the subsection that deals with it, they say:

> As part of the research involved in producing this report, B'Tselem made considerable efforts to find evidence supporting or refuting the claim that *isqat* exists. Despite these efforts, we found no clear proof that systematic and widespread use of *isqat* is made to recruit collaborators. Nevertheless, we thought it proper to address these claims because of their place in the Palestinian national consciousness and because of their wide implications for interrogations, confessions, and executions of suspected collaborators.[23]

They have no difficulty in believing that these women were murdered and injured as punishment for collaboration. Their difficulty is in believing that the Israeli ruling apparatus actually employs practices of sexual violence against Palestinian women.[24]

In the sixth subsection, the authors, compelled to describe the induction of women collaborators, in fact describe the practices of their assassination, for which they rely on the testimonies of Palestinian men who are members of "Palestinian organizations." In attempting to describe the modes of operation of these "Palestinian organizations," the authors return to descriptive language, readopting the voice of omniscient narrators:

> During the Intifada, the local cells, which are identified with the various organizations, have taken the place of the *hamulah* as the source of power and authority in the family issues as well, and the concept of "family honor" has acquired national significance. If traditionally only the father's family was held responsible for the woman's behavior, during the Intifada, the street leadership itself began to take on this "authority." The leadership began to lay down rules of behavior for women in circulars telling them to ensure modest behavior and traditional dress, including head covering. Women who did not behave as expected became vulnerable to attack by Palestinian activists. These attacks included pouring acid on their bodies, throwing stones at them, threats, and even rape.[25]

Those actions of the Palestinians that are related to the oppression and injury of women raise no doubts here and are seen as fully consistent with conventional ways of representing Palestinian society. The context provided by this familiar, safe description neutralizes the involvement of Israeli men, Shabak agents, in contact with Palestinian women and in their sexualized injury, meanwhile allowing the authors of the report to formulate a critical, unbiased position on the "Palestinian organizations": "The findings of the investigation point to widespread phenomena of killings, torture, and brutal punishment inflicted on suspected collaborators by Palestinian organizations and their activists. These phenomena are an extremely grave breach of human rights, and cannot be justified in any situation whatsoever."[26] However, even as the omniscient narrator relates how the Palestinian street has replaced the patriarchal family since the outbreak of the intifada, thus allowing the reader to understand that the women in question were killed and raped due to loose sexual conduct, the authors of the report, who are well aware that this description is lacking, not to say totally mistaken, simultaneously reveal that "women and girls who were attacked by their families or by others for reasons connected with family honor are not included in this report, unless any person or organization announced that the grounds for the attack were of a 'nationalist' nature, that is to say, suspicion of collaboration."[27]

The authors of the report recognize, then, that the women who have been injured were not hurt in the context of what is termed "family honor," but rather as a result of the fact that they were viewed as collaborators by their executioners. However, as stated, the research conducted prior to the compilation of the report led its authors to the conclusion that "most of the women killed by Palestinians during the Intifada did not have any contacts with the security forces" and also to the decision that the accusations against them were "based only on rumors and unverified information."[28] The convoluted language used by the report creates the illusion that had the information been "verified," the kangaroo courts to which these women were subjected would have turned, as if by magic, into due process.

But the matter is even more complicated than this. I reread the testimonies of the "Palestinian organizations" in an effort to understand just how information is obtained about these women. "Generally, the authorities recruit women through photographing them naked or engaged in some immoral activity. They threaten that if they do not collaborate, they will show the pictures to their family and publish them in the newspapers. Women who have already been recruited as collaborators tempt other women to have sex with men, and so it continues."[29]

The procedure is familiar. It's not just in the context of framing women that photography serves the security forces. I have already dealt with this practice in the context of 'Abed A-Nasser 'Ubeid. The photograph of the Palestinian in the hands of the security forces, deployed through their various agents — both Israelis and Palestinians — frames the Palestinian as a target. When the photographed figure is a Palestinian woman, the photograph traps her in a merry-go-round of horrors.

As stated, the research found that "most of the women killed by Palestinians during the Intifada did not have any contacts with the security forces."[30] This conclusion is meant to undermine the judgment of those who executed these women, those who determined that they were collaborators. It is reached on the assumption that it is possible to make a definite distinction, one established as true, between women collaborators and women who are not collaborators. However, the women pose a problem, for if the research had verified that they were truly collaborators, the authors of the report would have had to state what they consistently avoid stating — thus joining the tradition of prolonged silence — that is, that the activities of the security forces in the territories involves, among other things, sexual violence. But proving that these women did not collaborate with the security forces in fact allows the statement, in the voice of an omniscient narrator — notably, in contrast to the voices of the Palestinians who claim the existence of sexualized violence — that the security forces do not employ sexual violence as a means of inducting women collaborators. Thus, the story of these Palestinian women is reduced to a tale of their murder by Palestinians on the grounds of "family honor" or "immoral conduct." However, when one's reading of the statement made by the report — that "most of the women killed by Palestinians during the Intifada did not have any contacts with the security forces" — is not oriented toward achieving conclusive certainty as to whether or not these women were truly collaborators, then its meaning is totally transformed. The statement itself is most probably true, but under the conditions created by the Shabak, one might ask whether this isn't in fact the cause of the women's death, rather than proof that their death was unjustified. Isn't it precisely because they refused to collaborate that their pictures were spread around in order to defame and frame them?

A document quoted in the report and disseminated by the Popular Front for the Liberation of Palestine describes the methods employed by the Shabak. Many of them involve photography: "A collaborator rapes a young woman while another collaborator photographs the act. The collaborators or the GSS threaten to shame the girl publicly if she does not cooperate with them," or "Collaborators follow a pair of lovers and photograph them at the climax of their sexual activity, even if she is innocent [not involved in *isqat*]. They [then] threaten to display the photographs if they [the lovers] do not cooperate."[31]

An exhaustive comparison of these methods, one by one, as they are described in the testimonies, in the quoted document, and in the literature on the topic, shows the scope of the photography attributed to the security forces and their proxies to be enormous.[32] Yussef al-Arjani, commander of a cell of Fateh Eagles in the Rafah area, relates in his testimony that the ongoing hunt for photographs of women in sexual situations or in the nude permeates very different areas of life: "There are clothing stores in which the *isqat* process takes place. The cameras were hidden in the women's fitting rooms, and the women were photographed in the nude. Yes, there are beauty salons where women were photographed in immoral positions, and the same is so in video supply stores that sell pornographic films that tempt people into immoral crimes."[33]

The sexual *isqat* is also employed, to a minimal degree, with men, but it is mainly focused on women.[34] The production of the photographs is carried out by Israeli men and by Palestinian men who — whether the latter are collaborators or not — apparently collaborate to create the cottage industry of erotic photographs of women. These photos change hands, but stay in the hands of men as incriminating evidence against the women in question. The evidence incriminates them as collaborators or noncollaborators, depending on who is the viewer. Either way, those looking at the photographs can continue exchanging them among themselves while keeping their circulation well hidden from public eyes and while explaining the silence that shrouds the sexual *isqat* with the claim that "the women don't complain for understandable reasons."

In any case, the photographs are silent. Even if they had been exposed, they could not have stabilized the upheaval they caused and determined whether or not the photographed woman was a collaborator. These photographs, which are meant to betray the people photographed, in fact betray another area of collaboration between Israelis and Palestinians, a twilight zone in which Israeli and Palestinian men can exchange nude photos of women to explosive effect. When the explosion kills or injures the victim, they can divide up the loot between them — one side will declare her a collaborator, while the other will declare her a noncollaborator.

When a woman's figure has been framed by the camera of a Shabak agent, the civil contract of photography seems like a legend about the state of nature. And citizenship seems like a legend about democratic society. Photography, it seems, has turned into a tool of concentrated violence, and the photos have turned into sentences that determine the fates of people, not just that of the contract. The Shabak agent, his superiors and subordinates, the force that has transformed photography into a weapon, into a guided missile, seem to hold it completely in their hands, subject to the goals that they have sought to impose on it. Nevertheless, photography "was there," not fully compliant to the rules that the Shabak agents wish to impose on it. The contract that accompanies photography always reminds the spectators that photography cannot be totally controlled, that it exists in relations of plurality, even in the darkest of circumstances, relations that no one can totally manage and whose development is unpredictable.

The fact that photography has become similar to the violent situations in which it is operated clarifies the urge to invent, restore, or maintain a civil contract of photography as a collection of escape routes from situations in which a stranglehold is tightening around the photographed people. This is the backyard of the democratic regimes in which photography is thus operated, and often, perhaps paradoxically, it is in the power of photography to trace the first line of flight when the water rises and the wave swells. Through it, it is possible to see the corrosion, even if very slight, at the edges of the sovereignty supposedly possessed by those holding the means of photography or operating them through others.

When the photographs remain inaccessible to the civil gaze, these possibilities are reduced. Even then, however, the inaccessibility of the photographs to the gaze is never final. And in any case, the photographs are only a small part of the picture. Merely knowing that these photographs exist allows a reconstruction of the act of photography, of the situation in which it was operated. In the cases with which I have dealt in the last two chapters, in the absence of photographed testimonies, it was the verbal testimonies that allowed the reconstruction of the act of photography that allowed an undermining of the construct of collaborator and the claim in the spirit of the absent photographs: The woman collaborator does not exist.

A Comment on the Photographs

The decision to print some of the photographs included in this book was a difficult one that I reversed several times during my work on the manuscript. The question facing me again and again was whether or not to reprint photographs that show the photographed persons in situations so harsh as to entail humiliation or to cause injury to them. This question cannot be answered through the adoption of any single inclusive principle or generalization. It is imperative to scrutinize each individual case separately. The conditions in which the photograph was produced need to be reconstructed as exhaustively as possible, as do the circumstances of its dissemination and the specific conditions enabling its role as an emergency claim, a demand for ceasing the horror to which it testifies. On these grounds, one should then make a careful attempt to assess the damage that the photograph might cause the person portrayed in it (damage that will compound the injury already caused to her or to him in the degrading situation itself and through previous dissemination of the photograph) and to gauge this possible damage against the photograph's potential contribution toward realizing the address of the photographed subject or of those who speak on their behalf. No less important is trying to assess the photograph's perception within the cultural milieu of the photographed subject. Also to be taken into account is the possibly weakened line of argument within this discussion, when it substitutes a verbal description for the photograph itself.

As regards the rape of the women of Nanking, I decided to include the photographs in the book. The key factor affecting my decision was the scope of the horror of the rapes perpetrated there, the taboo against photographing rape, which I note in the fifth chapter, and the length of time that had passed since the rape took place. (Most of the women who were victims of this act of rape, as well as those who knew them, are no longer alive.)

To the best of my knowledge, the photographs of the women slaves, Drana and Delia, are the only visual evidence for assaults on women slaves. The way in which the two women conduct themselves in the photographic situation is difficult to describe in words, and here, too, the photographed subjects are women who have long been dead. I therefore decided to print these photographs as well. In contrast, my decision regarding the photograph of Imad Qwasma was of a different kind. Qwasma was detained in 2004 by soldiers of the Israel Defense Force, stripped, and left waiting for a long time in his undershorts. I decided to leave Qwasma's lower body (a thin strip one-tenth the size of the photo) out of the reprinted frame. In my view, this is a case in which substituting a verbal description for the photo segment does not detract substantially from the information transmitted through the photograph, while printing the entire photograph might constitute a continuation of Qwasma's humiliation by the soldiers.

Finally, in spite of great efforts to identify and locate all the photographers to request their permission for publication, there are still several photographs whose importance has justified publication in spite of my failure to locate the names of the photographers. Unfortunately, naming the people photographed has been even more problematic, and most of them appear unnamed.

Color Plates

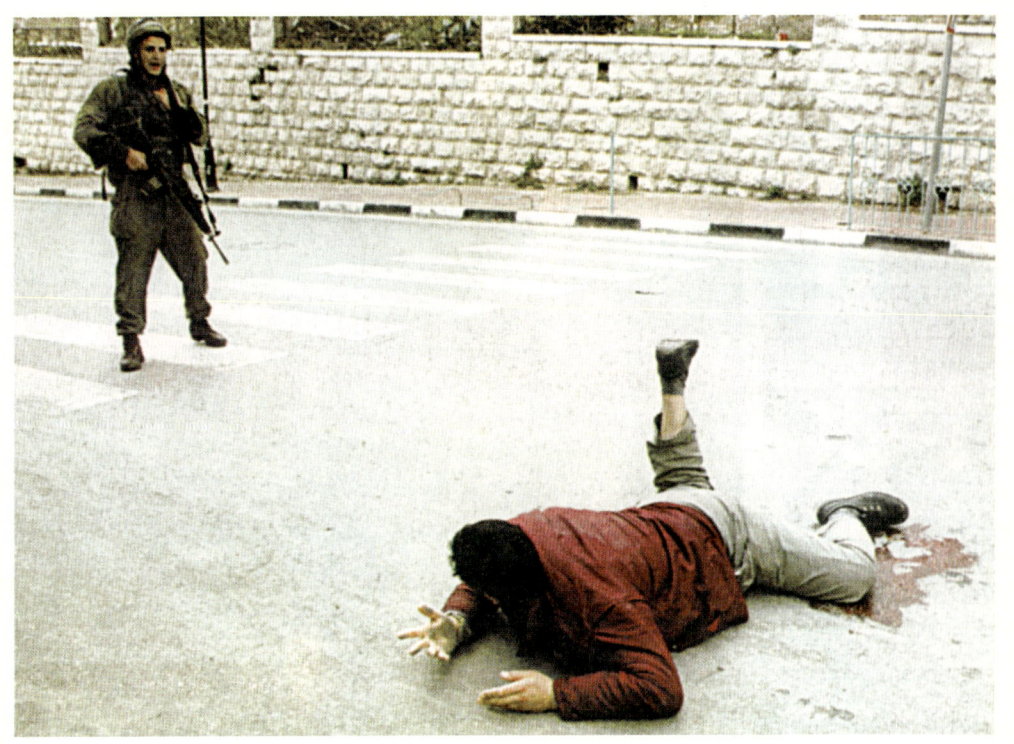

Figure 1.2. Alex Levac, Hebron, 2000.

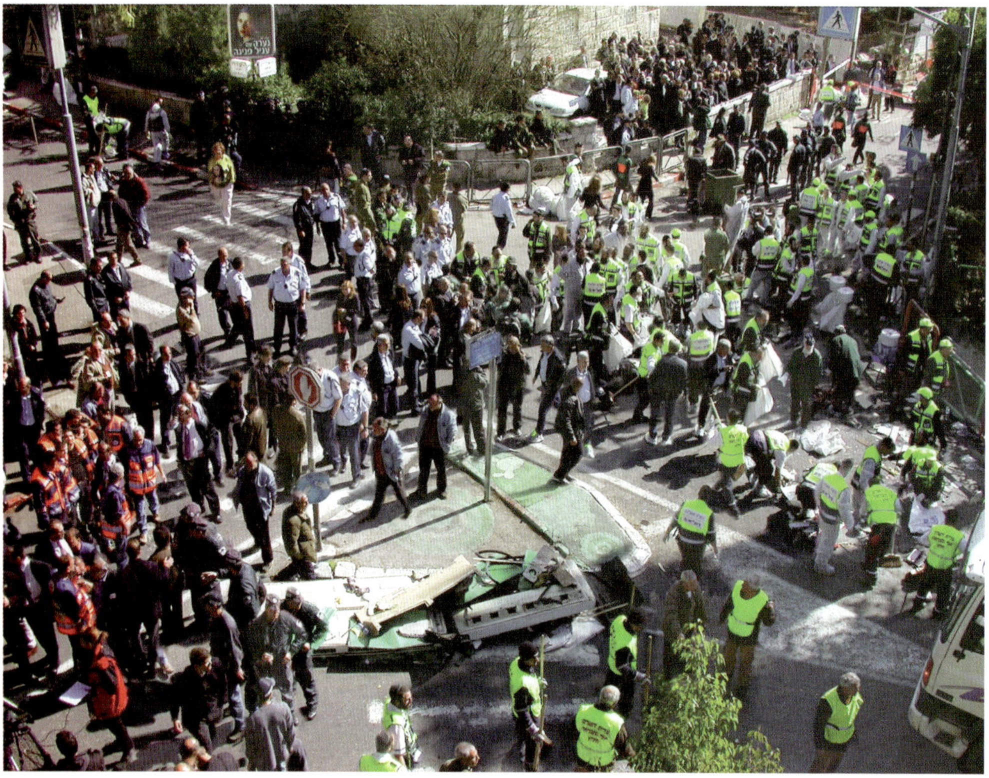

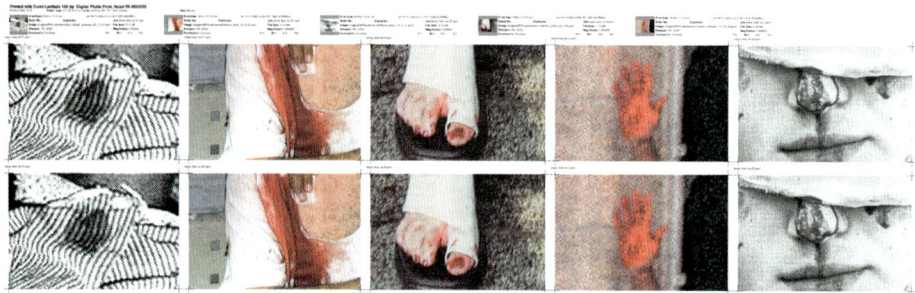

Figure 6.1. Boaz Aharonovitch, *Time Capsule No. 1 (3 minutes): Girl with a Pearl Earring*, digital image, 160 x 120 cm, 2004.

Figure 6.8. Michal Heiman, *Blood Test #4 (Series A)*, color print, 52 x 101 cm, 2002.

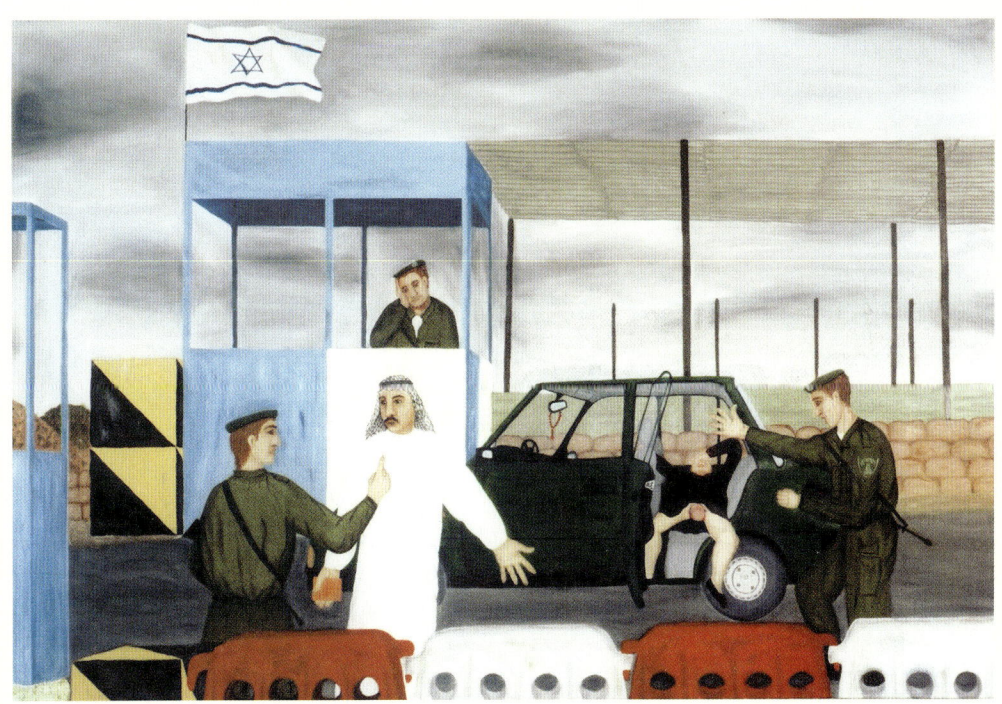

Figure 6.12. Faten Nastas, *Birth and Death at the Checkpoint*, 1996.

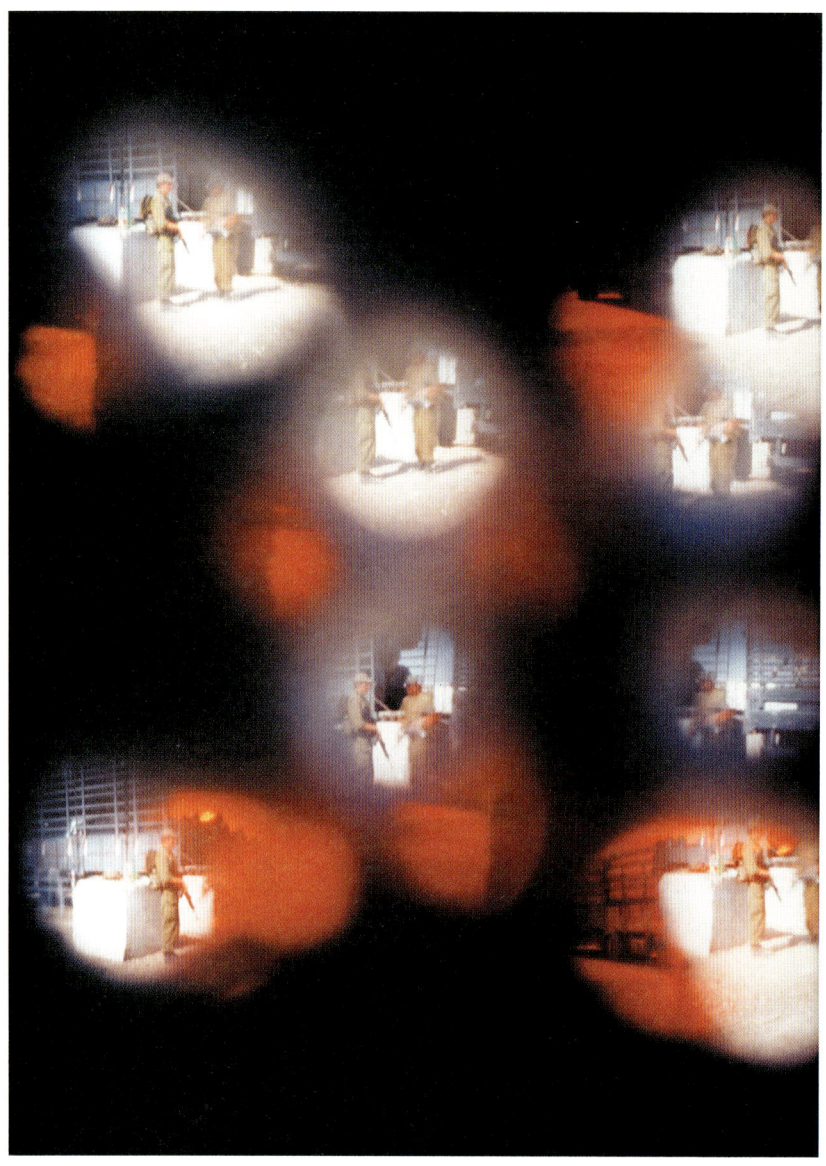

Figure 6.17. Aïm Deüelle Lüski, *Back-to-Back*, Bitounia, photo taken with Pita camera, color negative, 4 x 5 inches, 2003.

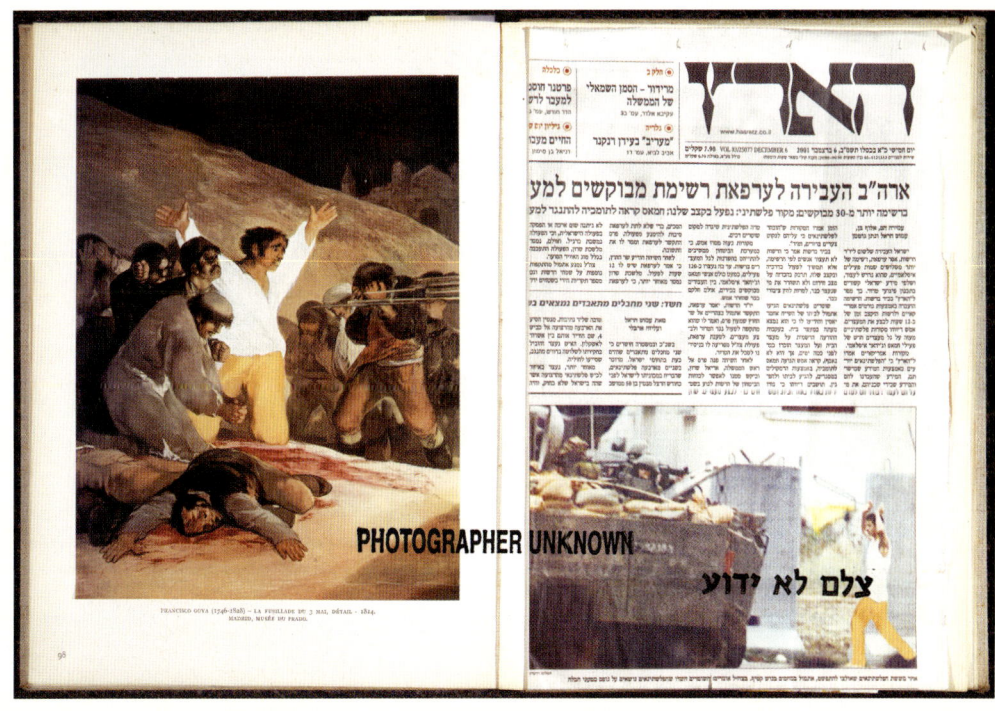

Figure 6.26. Michal Heiman, *May 3, 1814 – December 6, 2001 (Francisco Goya – 1814, Photographer Unknown – 2011)*, color print, 120 x 176 cm, 2002.

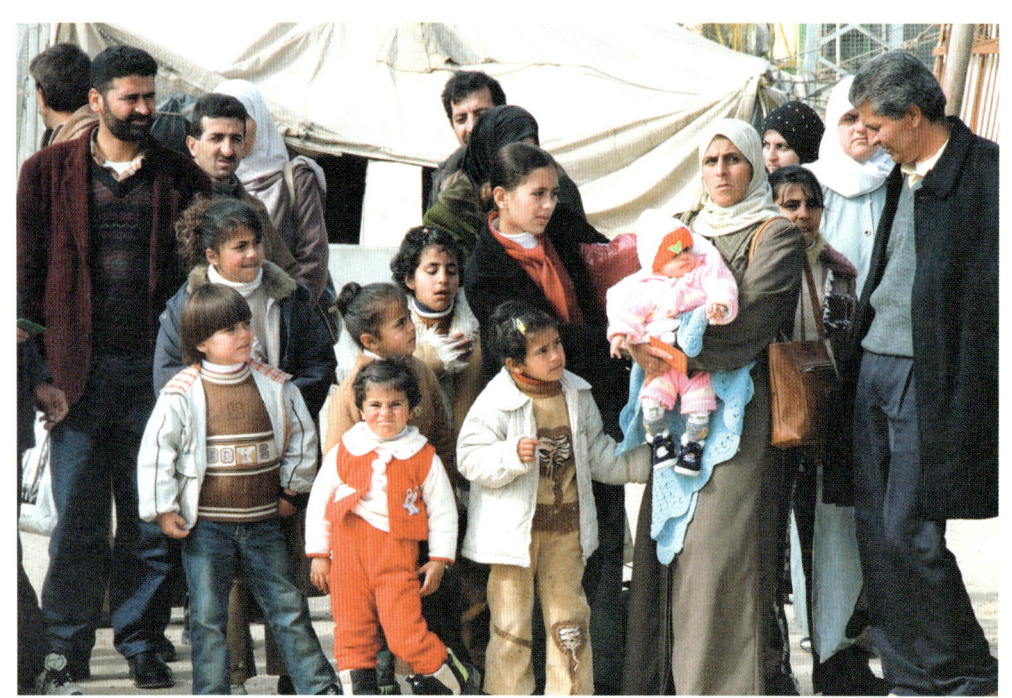

Figure 6.28. Miki Kratsman, Beit Ibba checkpoint, 2004.

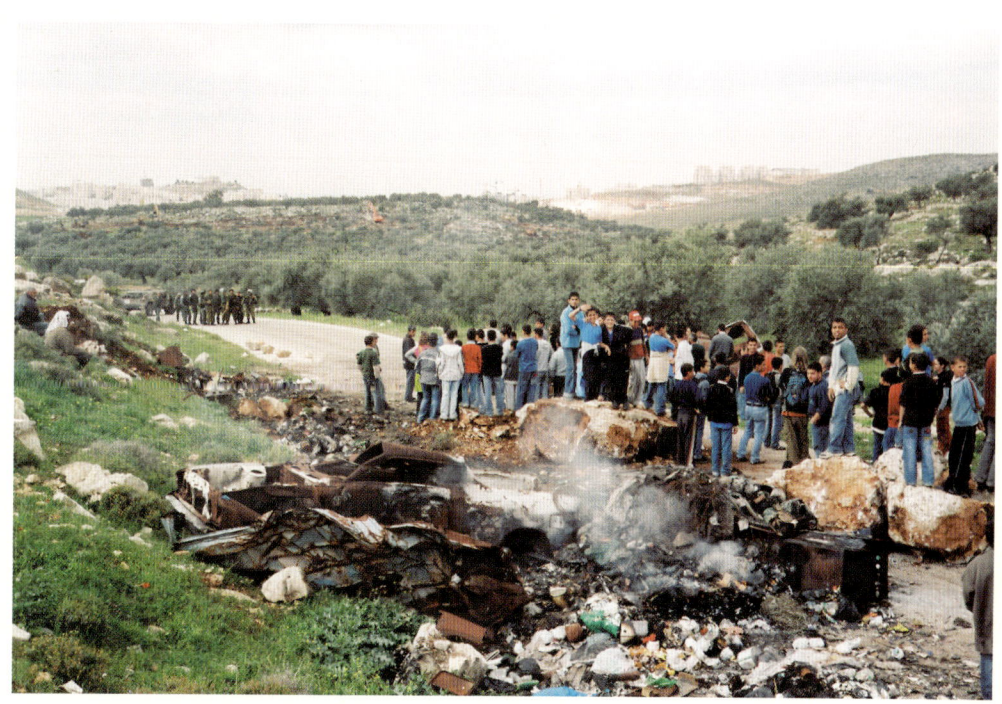

Figure 6.36. Oded Yedaya, diversion demonstration, Harbata, 2004.

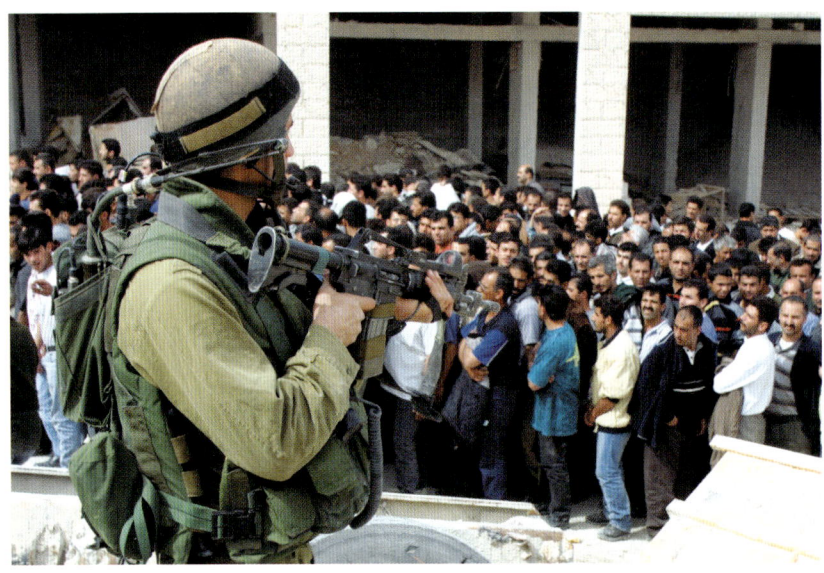

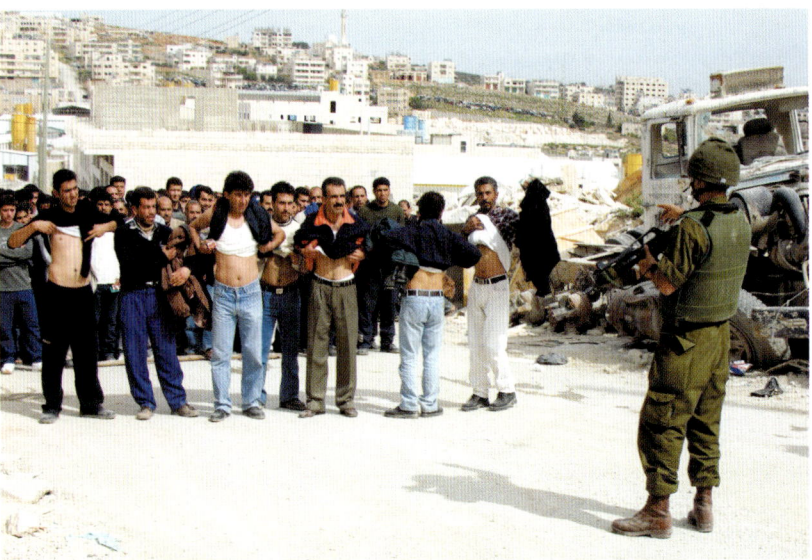

Figures 8.7–8.8. Musa Al Shaer, arrest campaign, refugee camp, Daheisha, March 11, 2002.

Notes

497

INTRODUCTION

1. Citizenship, like power, is not and should not be considered as property. Nevertheless, under the Israeli regime, citizenship resembles property more than all its other descriptions within political theory. Citizenship is something Israeli Jews own and distribute, which Israeli Palestinians might lose as a result of their conduct. Citizenship, as I'll show in the following chapter, is not merely a status, but a form of participation in a political space that in some aspects resemble Hannah Arendt's conception of power. In *On Violence*, Arendt criticizes the way power is conceived as property: "Power corresponds to the human ability not just to act, but to act in concert. Power is never the property of an individual." Hannah Arendt, *On Violence* (New York: Harvest Books, 1970), p. 143.

2. The Palestinians governed by the state of Israel are noncitizens, but because their situation as noncitizens long ago lost its temporary status and became their permanent status in the state of Israel, I prefer to transform the description of their status into a noun: noncitizen *of* the State of Israel.

3. Several months after publication of the Hebrew version of this book, a collection dealing with nongovernmental politics was published by Michel Feher: *Nongovernmental Politics*, Michel Feher (ed.), with Gaëlle Krikorian and Yates McKee (New York: Zone Books, 2007). According to Feher, "To be involved in politics without aspiring to govern, be governed by the best leaders, or abolish institutions of government: such are the constraints that delineate the condition common to all practitioners of nongovernmental politics" (p. 12). Feher analyzes activism, the distinctive form of this type of politics, as regards its sources of legitimacy. The civil contract of photography offers a similar description of the sphere of political

497

relations as a space in which such relations are not mediated by a sovereign regime. In the case of the contract, however, the protagonists conducting these relations are not necessarily declared activists operating within protest movements or nongovernmental organizations. This book makes a sustained effort to rehabilitate and reactivate the space and practice of political and nongovernmental relations as essential components of citizenship, whether or not in connection with an institutionalized organization.

4. On the trial and the branded hand see Alvin F. Oickle, *Jonathan Walker: the Man with the Branded Hand* (Everett, MA: Lorelli Slater, 1998).

5. See Feher, "The Governed in Politics," p. 13.

6. Jean-Jacques Rousseau, *The Social Contract, Or Principles of Political Right*, trans. G. D. H. Cole, http://www.constitution.org/jjr/socon_01.htm#005.

7. Ariella Azoulay, *Once Upon a Time: Photography after Walter Benjamin* [in Hebrew] (Ramat-Gan: Bar Ilan University Press, 2006).

CHAPTER ONE: CITIZENS OF DISASTER

1. This classification into three types is a synthesis based on the numerous definitions found in various dictionaries, both in Hebrew and English, including Even Shushan, Ben Yehuda, http://www.ravmilim.co.il, the online glossary of Google, and *Webster's*.

2. On political participation see Carole Pateman, *Participation and Democratic Theory* (Cambridge: Cambridge University Press, 1970).

3. This lack also applies to most definitions of the "citizen" in historical and philosophical discourses.

4. From the UN report "Clarifying and Expanding the Rights of Non-Citizens," 2004, available on-line at http://www.justiceinitiative.org/activities/ec/ec_noncitizens (last accessed June 13, 2007).

5. Citizenship as membership in a distinct collective of people was the way in which citizenship was originally understood in Athens, the Roman Republic, the Roman Empire, some Italian city-states, and all of the colonial empires. My discussion, however, focuses only on citizenship in the modern era, after the French Revolution.

6. Unlike the noncitizen, the citizen participates, at least potentially, in government. He or she will have fulfilled the conditions of citizenship, however, only by exercising it, only by viewing citizenship not as a permanent status, but as an ongoing negotiation. It is precisely at this point that the citizen can share common ground with the noncitizen under civilian frameworks that are not nationalistic.

This exercising of citizenship takes place in photography (see the next chapter), for example, when the noncitizen becomes a citizen long before his or her civil situation in the state is formally regulated.

7. An anonymous reviewer of an early draft of this text wrote: "Even from a purely conceptual viewpoint, the use of the term citizenship . . . in order to describe stateless people beside others is problematic." Taking for granted the characterization of the Palestinians as stateless people means ignoring the fact that they have been governed for a long time by the sovereign authority in the framework of which I am a citizen.

8. As Michel Feher notes with regard to the realm of nongovernmental politics: "it shows that politics extends beyond the realm of representation . . . taking nongovernmental politics seriously not only expands the realm of what counts as politics, but also emphasizes the open-endedness of the political process." Michel Feher, "The Governed in Politics," in *Nongovernmental Politics*, Michel Feher (ed.), with Gaëlle Krikorian and Yates McKee (New York: Zone Books, 2007), p. 26.

9. When does the temporary become permanent? The answer could be calculated by reference to a certain number of years of residence or parameters as employment, family, social connections, and so on. I will not formulate such parameters here, since in the Palestinian case, which I have before my eyes as I write these lines, there is no doubt that their governance by the state of Israel over several decades cannot be discussed under the category of temporariness.

10. Pateman, *Participation and Democratic Theory*, p. 173.

11. Feher, "The Governed in Politics," p. 17.

12. Adi Ophir, "The Sovereign, the Humanitarian, and the Terrorist," in Feher, *Nongovernmental Politics*, p. 161.

13. The discussion below will not address cases of disaster-stricken areas in which the entire population of a country is exposed to disaster and there are hardly any citizens left unharmed who can negotiate with the sovereign power over the position of the victims and the administration of the disaster. I limit my discussion to cases in which disaster and citizenship intersect and differentiate each other in a given territory.

14. When I first presented my discussion of both cases together, I was criticized on the grounds that, even from a purely conceptual viewpoint, the use of the term "citizenship" to describe stateless people living alongside others is problematic. From my point of view, taking for granted the characterization of the Palestinians as stateless people means ignoring the fact that they have been governed for a long time by a sovereign authority in the framework of which I am a citizen.

15. Milton Viorst, *The Great Documents of Western Civilization* (Philadelphia: Chilton Books, 1965), pp. 185–88.

16. On the normative mechanism at the foundation of modernism, as well as the gap within this mechanism that appears as the unfulfilled ideal — the actual realization of which is a possible engine of progress — see Jürgen Habermas, *Legitimation Crisis* (Boston: Beacon Press, 1975). The principle of universalization is what enabled the spread of political participation from the bourgeoisie to the other classes. The potential for diffusion was realized in a violent manner immediately after the Revolution ended, when France went to war against most of her neighbors with the pretension of spreading the word of the declaration.

17. On unnecessary suffering, see Adi Ophir, *The Order of Evils* (New York: Zone Books, 2005).

18. Étienne Balibar, "'Rights of Man' and 'Rights of Citizen': The Modern Dialectic of Equality and Freedom," in *Masses, Classes, Ideas: Studies on Politics and Philosophy before and after Marx*, trans. James Swenson (New York: Routledge, 1994), p. 50. Balibar bases his understanding of freedom as an equal right to freedom, what he has designated as "equaliberty," on an identification of the man with the citizen: "Underneath the equation of man and citizen, or rather *within* it, as the very reason of its universality — as its *presupposition* — lies the proposition of equaliberty" (p. 47).

19. On the different versions, see Lucien Jaume, *Les déclarations des droits de l'homme: 1789* (Paris: Flammarion, 1989).

20. *A Chronicle of the French Revolution* (New York: Vintage Books, 1990). On the limitation of women's participation in the political sphere following the French Revolution see Joan Wallach Scott, *Only Paradoxes to Offer: French Feminists and the Rights of Man* (Cambridge, MA: Harvard University Press, 1996) or Dorinda Outram, *The Body and the French Revolution* (New Haven: Yale University Press, 1989).

21. Olympe de Gouges, *Déclaration des droits de la femme et de la citoyenne* (Paris: Mille et une nuit, 2003), p. 13–19. Olympe de Gouges was executed on the guillotine in 1793 on account of her political work, which in addition to writing included various actions with the aim of enabling her to become a *homme d'État*. On de Gouges, see Scott, *Only Paradoxes to Offer*, Emanuèle Gaulier, "Femme, réveille-toi," in de Gouges, *Déclaration des droits de la femme*; Sophie Mousset, *Olympe de Gouges et les droits de la femme* (Paris: Félin, 2003); Benoîte Groult, "Olympe de Gouges: La première féministe moderne," in *Olympe de Gouges: Oeuvres* (Paris: Mercure de France, 1986); and Carla Hesse, *The Other Enlightenment: How French Women Became Modern* (Princeton, NJ: Princeton University Press, 2001).

22. In her text, de Gouges doesn't offer an ideological critique of universalism,

but shows in a performative fashion that universalism is always tainted with particularism. Over two hundred years later, in her essay on universalism, Judith Butler has made universalism politically relevant in a similar manner when she speaks of the conventional norms of the universal and points to the way in which "the reiterative speech act thus offers the possibility — though not the necessity — of depriving the past of the established discourse of its exclusive control over defining the parameters of the universal within politics." Judith Butler, "Restaging the Universal: Hegemony and the Limits of Formalism," in Judith Butler, Ernesto Laclau, and Slavoj Žižek (eds.), *Contingency, Hegemony, Universality: Contemporary Dialogues on the Left* (New York: Verso, 2000), p. 41.

23. *Ibid.*, pp. 39–41.

24. On the historical importance of "man" over "citizen," see Lucien Jaume, "Citizen and State under the French Revolution," in Quentin Skinner and Bo Stråth (eds.), *States and Citizens* (Cambridge: Cambridge University Press, 2003).

25. See Pierre Lascoumes, "Géographie de l'*intolérable:* A la recherché d'une internationale des gouvernés," *Vacarme*, no. 29 (Autumn 2004), where he sketches the history of Foucault's political interventions and revisits the texts written in connection with them.

26. Michel Foucault, *Dits et écrits, vol. III* (Paris: Gallimard, 1994), p. 361.

27. This wording appeared as the subtitle of Lascoumes' article in the table of contents of the special issue of *Vacarme* devoted to Foucault. *Ibid.*, p. 2.

28. Hannah Arendt, "The Decline of the Nation-State and the End of the Rights of Man," in *Imperialism* (San Diego: Harvest Books, 1968).

29. On citizens' religion, see Ariella Azoulay and Adi Ophir, *Bad Days: Between Disaster and Utopia* [in Hebrew] (Tel Aviv: Resling, 2002).

30. Hannah Arendt describes this as a conflict between the state and the nation — one in which the nation has won. This conflict, she asserts, emerged already in the Declaration of the Rights of Man and the Citizen, which combined the demand for national sovereignty with the protection of rights. The state then became an instrument in the nation's hands, rather than a protector of the individual.

31. There are states that have been established with such language at their foundation, such as the State of Israel — "It is the natural right of the Jewish people" (from Israel's Declaration of Independence) — and there are states that are exemplars of such a constitution, despite not having been thus founded, "like any other people," as Israel's Declaration of Independence goes on to say.

32. These organizations sprang up immediately following World War II, but have massively proliferated since the 1960s. See William Korey, *NGOs and the Universal*

Declaration of Human Rights: A Curious Grapevine (New York: St. Martin's Press, 1998).

33. See Michel Foucault, "Qu'est-ce que la critique?" *Bulletin de la société française de philosophie* 84, no. 2 (1990), pp. 35–63.

34. Feher, "The Governed in Politics," p. 14.

35. Parallel to the urgent relief that organizations provide to disaster-stricken areas, most democratic countries also have various organizations that assist in routine operations within their own territory. At times, these latter groups may attempt to project a dimension of urgency onto the cases with which they deal. However, in most of these situations, the logic of their operation is to provide ongoing services in ordinary times. Examples of this kind of organization are locally based human-rights and civil-rights movements.

36. This affiliation of the two is not an attempt to strike an equality between these two populations, but only to point to the connection between being exposed to disaster and citizenship.

37. In the past few years, these organizations have begun treating male victims of sexual assault as well. Most male victims were victimized before growing into citizens — that is, they shared the reality of sexual victimization of both boys and girls — but on reaching maturity they exited the at-risk group. I focus on women, rather than on children — both boys or girls — specifically because, as adults, they constitute a population of citizens whose citizenship fails to protect them.

38. Even today, more than three decades after appearing on the scene, these organizations are operated only by volunteers, and only a small part of their budgets is funded by government.

39. This manifests itself in creating awareness of the issue and in training, but also in campaigning for legal change.

40. The French text reads: "cette liberté assure la légitimité des pères envers les enfants."

41. De Gouges, *Déclaration des droits de la femme et de la citoyenne*, pp. 13–19.

42. *Ibid.*

43. In 1976, Letty Cottin Pogrebin published in her regular column in the *Ladies' Home Journal* an article on sexual harassment that drew a "storm of responses." She described in detail the daily experience of sexual harassment. The article begins as follows: "A restaurant owner grabs a waitress' rear whenever she passes the cash register. A police officer makes advances to the woman cop with whom he shares a patrol car. A politician bombards his female staff with regular remarks about their breasts," and so on. Letty Cottin Pogrebin, "Sex Harassment," in Adele

M. Stan (ed.), *Debating Sexual Correctness* (New York: Delta, 1995), p. 3. In the movie *Im redet Ha-chashecha* (At nightfall), which I directed in 2005, I interviewed five women about the experience of abandonment on a sexual basis. One of the things that continuously emerged from the interviewees' responses was the difficulty women have in calling sexual relations that have been forced on them by a familiar partner a rape and the way in which their discourse is torn between their recognition of the relations as having been forced and their cultural inclination to protect the partner and show understanding of his actions. This film is part of an experimental cinematic project, Why Don't You Say It? curated by Michal Heiman.

44. In *The Sexual Contract* (Stanford, CA: Stanford University Press, 1988), Carole Pateman shows the sexual contract as being the other side of the social contract. Pateman contends that the marriage contract has been overlooked by the social contract, thus pointing to the way in which the social contract, which espouses the values of equality, is in effect based on a prior contract that subjugates the woman to the man (pp. 1–19).

45. On raped women and unwanted pregnancy in the eighteenth century see Tracy Rizzo, "Between Dishonor and Death," *Women's History Review* 13, no. 1 (2004).

46. See Giorgio Agamben, *Homo Sacer: Sovereign Power and Bare Life*, trans. Daniel Heller-Roazen (Stanford, CA: Stanford University Press, 1998).

47. *Ibid*, pp. 65, 83. Agamben does not fully account for the replacement of one pair of opposites (political life and natural life) by another pair of opposites (natural life and exposed, or sacred life), which is in fact nothing but the division of one of the elements (*zoē*) of the first pair of opposites, which has disappeared: "Once the *zoē*, is politicized by declarations of rights, the distinctions and thresholds that make it possible to isolate a sacred life must be newly defined." *Ibid.*, p. 131.

48. *Ibid.*, pp. 82, 83. In *State of Exception*, a sequel to *Homo Sacer*, Agamben presents the state of the exception as the paradigm of governmentality. See Giorgio Agamben, *State of Exception,* trans. Kevin Attell (Chicago: University of Chicago Press, 2005).

49. The rights in question are "freedom, property, security and resistance to oppression."

50. For a systematic presentation of Agamben's essay, see Adi Ophir, "Life between Abandonment and Sacredness: An Introduction to *Homo Sacer*," in Shai Lavi (ed.), *Technologies of Justice: Law, Science, and Society* (Tel Aviv: Ramot, 2003). In her last book, *Imagine There Is No Woman*, Joan Copjec points out that Agamben does not deal at all with the question regarding what life has become the foundation

of the political order. This blindness is related to the blindness which I am pointing to here. Joan Copjec, *Imagine There's No Woman: Ethics and Sublimation* (Cambridge, MA: MIT Press, 2002).

51. Agamben, *Homo Sacer*, p. 128.

52. *Ibid.*, p. 28.

53. From another perspective, but in a move similar to my own here, Carole Pateman and Juliet Flower MacCannell perform a critical analysis of the concept of fraternity, which has become a cornerstone of modern citizenship, but is just another incarnation of the patriarchy from which women are excluded and in the framework of which they are abandoned. See Pateman, *The Sexual Contract* and Juliet Flower MacCannell, *The Regime of the Brother* (London: Routledge, 1991).

54. De Gouges, *Déclaration des droits de la femme et de la citoyenne*, pp. 13–19. On the illegitimate child, see de Gouges' real and fictive correspondence with her own father, who refuses to recognize her as his own child, "Mémoire de Madame de Valmont," in *Œuvres* (Paris: Mercure de France, 1986).

55. "Many women in the [Saint-Simonian] movement were abandoned to raise illegitimate children on their own." Scott, *Only Paradoxes to Offer*, p. 73.

56. See Pateman, *The Sexual Contract*.

57. Susan Buck-Morss, "Hegel and Haiti," *Critical Inquiry* 26 (Summer 2006). The inclusion of the marriage contract in de Gouges' declaration was part of her demand to recognize women's right to divorce. This right was supposed to transform marriage from a relation of master and slave into a voluntary contractual engagement that the two parties have right to terminate. See Olympe de Gouges "Black Slavery, or The Happy Shipwreck," in *Translating Slavery: Gender and Race in French Women's Writing, 1783–1823*, eds. Doris Y. Kadish and Françoise Massardier-Kenny (Kent, OH: Kent State University Press, 1994), and, on the presence and engagement of blacks in the French Revolution, Emmanuel Genvrin, *Études suivi de l'esclavage des negres* (Saint Denis: Théatre Vollard, 1988).

58. See Frances Ferguson's discussion of the synonymous link between consent and nonconsent in Hebrew and Saxons law in "Rape and the Rise of the Novel," *Representations*, no. 20 (1987), and Orit Kamir, *Feminism, Rights, and the Law* (Tel Aviv: Universita Meshuderet, Ministry of Defense, Israel, 2002) [in Hebrew].

59. The marriage contract, in which the legal status of women was in effect defined, is a primary manifestation of this and demonstrates the crucial difference in the status of the two sides to the contract. In *The Second Sex*, trans. H. M. Parshley (New York: Vintage Books, 1989), Simone de Beauvoir dispels any illusions regarding the institution of marriage throughout history.

60. In her discussion of Jeanne Deroin and later responses to the constitution of men's rights in relation to the family a few decades after the 1789 declaration, Scott writes: "formal political rights could not be extended to women, because universality among men was secured by making women (under the sign of property and family) a right of man." Scott, *Only Paradoxes to Offer*, p. 69. What Scott describes in relation to the later constitution can also be shown, as I tried to do here, regarding the declaration of 1789.

61. See MacCannell, *The Regime of the Brother*, Lynn Hunt, *The Invention of Pornography* (New York: Zone Books, 1993), and Catherine MacKinnon, *Toward a Feminist Theory of the State* (Cambridge, MA: Harvard University Press, 1989).

62. I will discuss the visible dimension of rape in Chapter Five. On the change in regard to the rape of a woman by her husband see Nizza Berkowitz, "Globalization of Human Rights and of Women's Rights," *Theoriya Ve-Bikoret*, no. 23 (2003) and Kamir, *Feminism, Rights, and the Law*.

63. In France, universal suffrage was established by law in 1848.

64. See MacCannell, *The Regime of the Brother*.

65. On the participation of women in different social, political, and cultural domains see Scott, *Only Paradoxes to Offer* and Hesse, *The Other Enlightenment*.

66. Over the years women have gradually won the right to vote – in France this finally happened in 1945.

67. In parallel to women, criminals and the insane were also made exceptions to the rule.

68. On the history of female nudity, see Lynda Nead, *Female Nude* (New York: Routledge, 1992).

69. In Arendt's words: "we were not born equal, we became equal." Arendt, "The Decline of the Nation-State," p. 181.

70. Agamben, *Homo Sacer*, p. 128.

71. *Ibid.*, p. 128.

72. *Ibid.*, pp. 128–29.

73. Introduction to the Declaration of Women's Human and Civil Rights.

74. In Finland, this happened in 1906; in Norway, 1913; in Germany, 1919; in England, 1928; in France, 1944; and in Switzerland 1971.

75. For more on the way in which the Declaration of the Rights of Man and the Citizen linked and segregated the two, see Agamben, *Homo Sacer*, pp. 131–33.

76. *Ibid.*, pp. 130–31.

77. In 1942, three years before French women were given the vote, abortion was defined as a crime that carried the death penalty.

78. For instance, contraceptives began to be legalized only in the late seventies.

79. Agamben, *Homo Sacer*, pp 168–69.

80. On the challenge to the sovereign as demonstrated by the case of humanitarian organizations, see Ophir, "Life between Abandonment and Sacredness." On women imposing new objects on the hegemonic discourse, see Linda Alcoff and Laura Gray-Rosendale, "Survivor Discourse: Transgression or Recuperation?" in Sidonie Smith and Julia Watson (eds.), *Getting a Life: Everyday Uses of Autobiography* (Minneapolis: University of Minnesota Press, 1996).

81. Copjec, *Imagine There's No Woman*, p. 47.

82. This term is used by rape centers all over the world, as well as by theoretical discourse.

83. On the (in)visible conditions of rape, see Ariella Azoulay, *Once Upon a Time: Photography following Walter Benjamin* [in Hebrew] (Ramat-Gan: Bar Ilan University Press, 2006).

84. See Catherine A. MacKinnon, *Sex Equality: Rape Law* (New York: Foundation Press, 2001) and Kamir, *Feminism, Rights, and the Law*.

85. The situation in the territories is explicitly defined as such in the Ziegler report, Jean Ziegler, *United Nations Special Rapporteur on the Right to Food, Addendum, Mission to the Palestinian Occupied Territories*, available online as a PDF file at http://www.unhchr.ch/pdf/chr60/10add2AV.pdf (last accessed January 22, 2007).

86. I have analyzed the twofold aspect of this situation in the exhibition catalogue *Everything Could Be Seen* (Tel Aviv: Um el Fachem Art Gallery, 2004).

87. On the refugees, see Arendt, "The Decline of the Nation-State." Noncitizens are distinguished from refugees in that they belong de facto to the state — for example, the Palestinians to the state of Israel — even though the latter, in effect, governs them while refusing to acknowledge them as its citizens.

88. For more on the apparatus of rule in the territories, see *ibid.*

89. See my article on famine as an event that never happened, "Hunger in Palestine: The Event That Never Was," in *Territories: Islands, Camps, and Other States of Utopia*, exhibition catalogue (Berlin: KW-Institute for Contemporary Art, 2003).

90. Entire populations of citizens may be exposed to disasters, especially of the environmental kind — in Chernobyl, Dimona, by the Ural Sea, or on the Pacific islands. Their ability, or that of individuals among them, to escape from the verge of catastrophe is a result of their ability to fulfill and realize their capacities as citizens. There are occasions in which a disaster occurs even before the populations have had time to negotiate, in which case their citizenship and the capacities that constitute it are of no service.

91. On the topography of extreme violence, see Étienne Balibar, "Outlines of a Topography of Cruelty: Citizenship and Civility in the Era of Global Violence," *Constellations* 8, no. 1 (March 2001).

92. On the Israeli checkpoint system in Palestine, see B'Tselem, The Israeli Information Center for Human Rights in the Occupied Territories, "Ground to a Halt: Denial of Palestinians' Freedom of Movement in the West Bank" (2007), http://www.btselem.org/english/publications/summaries/20070807_ground_to _a_halt.asp (last accessed November 13, 2007).

93. After several requests to the Israeli army spokesman to access the checkpoint procedures were rejected, I was permitted to conduct a telephone interview with a major in the Israeli Defense Forces spokesman's office and was instructed to call him a "military source." The citations below are all from that same conversation, held on February 5, 2004.

94. On the relation between these two authorities in the actions of the army and police, see Walter Benjamin, *Selected Writings Volume 1, 1913–1926*, eds. Marcus Bullock and Michael W. Jennings (Cambridge, MA: Belknap Press of Harvard University Press, 1996) and my own essay on this text by Benjamin, Ariella Azoulay, "The Loss of Critique and the Critique of Violence," *Cardozo Law Review* 26, no. 3 (2005).

95. Judith Butler, "Indefinite Detention," in *Precarious Life: The Powers of Mourning and Violence* (New York: Verso, 2004), p. 56.

96. *Ibid.*, pp. 56, 55.

97. Based on the testimony of a soldier regarding his own actions, as told at an evening for draft resisters held in the Tsavta Auditorium, Tel Aviv, in the spring of 2004.

98. The nature of this sovereign power, however, is not to be taken for granted. Traditional definitions of sovereignty do not sufficiently explain the relationship between this power and the "petty sovereigns": neither the sovereign as "the form of power that ensures the representational standing of the political institutions" nor the power appointed to preserve and defend the territory (which are the two definitions that Butler rejects by claiming they do not characterize the new form of sovereignty, p. 53), or even the sovereign as the exception to the rule (Schmitt).

99. In the rare cases in which the chain of command is exposed, the sovereign does stand behind its representatives and may even send a note of apology for their actions to the press.

100. Beside him stand representatives of humanitarian organizations, such as Machsom (checkpoint) Watch, Physicians for Human Rights, and so on, who assist

the noncitizen. But their presence does not change the structure of relations described.

101. Balibar, "Outlines of a Topography of Cruelty."

102. This is certainly true if the concept of citizenship is based on a principle of universality.

103. In reality, citizenship is never a fully actualized status but always a set of procedures of becoming-citizen.

104. See Giorgio Agamben, *The Coming Community*, trans. Michael Hardt (Minneapolis: University of Minnesota Press, 1993).

105. The population of noncitizens also includes those who by entering into various forms of exchange relations are forced to divest themselves of citizenship. On this, see, for example the population of women who earn less than the minimum wage as described in Barbara Ehrenreich, *Nickel and Dimed: On (Not) Getting By in America* (New York: Henry Holt, 2002).

106. Arendt, "The Decline of the Nation-State," pp. 170–77.

107. Just as the "system" has no agency, so, too, the possibilities of rebelling against the system don't converge on an active agency. The concept of "insurrection," Balibar claims, has taken the place of the concept of "resistance" in modern political discourse. Balibar, "Outlines of a Topography of Cruelty." Insurrection is characterized by the proliferation and compartmentalization of points of friction within the "system," and this type of reaction constitutes an integral part of it.

108. I use the term rigorously here, as "a contagious or infectious epidemic disease that is virulent and devastating." Whether one wishes to renounce the concept of citizenship or to recuperate it, the noncitizen is becoming increasingly visible as infecting and devastating the world system.

109. The formal naturalization of outcast populations in countries occurred in parallel with the displacement of the political game to spheres of action organized around market principles that remained blocked to many citizens is part of the same global process of reorganizing the world's populations, a process with which I will not deal here.

110. Conceit regarding the concept of "global" citizenship has today become a hallmark of various corporations and educational institutions. The former take pride in their contributions to the global community and the way in which they manufacture "global citizens," and the latter offer to teach "global skills," from teacher training programs to university programs.

111. Giorgio Agamben, "We Refugees," trans. Michael Rocke (2004) http://

www.egs.edu/faculty/agamben/agamben-we-refugees.html (last accessed June 13, 2007).

112. Both in his writings and in his parliamentary work, Azmi Bishara has developed this idea, which has emerged as an object of discussion in political discourse as "the state of all its citizens." On the separation of the nation from the state, see the opening and concluding chapters of Ariella Azoulay and Adi Ophir, *Bad Days: Between Disaster and Utopia* [in Hebrew] (Tel Aviv: Resling, 2002)

113. Azmi Bishara, in his writings and parliamentary work at the Israeli Knesset, articulated this idea of a "State of All its Citizens." See my conversations with him in the film *I Also Dwell among Your Own People: Conversations with Azmi Bishara* (DVD, Alma Productions, Tel Aviv, 2005).

114. A state can maintain the citizenship of people who have left its territory, but under no circumstances is the state entitled to deny citizenship to the people who live and work within it.

115. The concept of online citizenship compels us therefore to define new categories of the political and remove, first and foremost, old concepts such as sovereignty or representation, which prevent us from seeing the possibility of such citizenship. Citizenship no longer requires a transcendent dimension and consists of a flexible package of rights, constantly subject to negotiation and alteration.

Chapter Two: The Civil Contract of Photography

1. It does not matter for the purpose of this discussion whether the decision is over the exception (Carl Schmitt, *Political Theology: Four Chapters on the Concept of Sovereignty* [Cambridge, MA: MIT Press, 1985]), or over the distinction between friend and enemy, or over the borders of the space where the sovereign's laws apply.

2. Giorgio Agamben, *Homo Sacer: Sovereign Power and Bare Life*, trans. Daniel Heller-Roazen (Stanford, CA: Stanford University Press, 1998), p. 90.

3. *Ibid.*, pp. 106–107.

4. *Ibid.*, p. 109.

5. *Ibid.*

6. Giorgio Agamben, *The Coming Community*, trans. Michael Hardt (Minneapolis: University of Minnesota Press, 1993), p. 1.

7. "In current usage," Arendt adds, "when we speak of a 'powerful man' or a 'powerful personality,' we already use the word 'power' metaphorically; what we refer to without metaphor is strength." Hannah Arendt, *On Violence* (New York, Harvest Books, 1970), p. 44.

8. See the comprehensive, but still not exhaustive survey compiled in the essays and interviews in Michel Feher (ed.), with Gaëlle Krikorian and Yates McKee, *Nongovernmental Politics* (New York: Zone Books, 2007).

9. In 1989, for instance, the one hundred and fiftieth anniversary of the invention of photography was celebrated in various places throughout the world.

10. Walter Benjamin, *Selected Writings, Volume 2, 1927–1934*, eds. Michael W. Jennings, Gary Smith, and Howard Eiland (Cambridge, MA: Belknap Press of Harvard University Press, 1999), p. 507.

11. Quoted in Geoffrey Batchen, *Burning with Desire* (Cambridge, MA: MIT Press, 1999), p. 62.

12. Pinson, for instance, wrote that the discovery of a 1837 portrait ascribed to Daguerre and pronounced the first photographic portrait resulted in an exclusively internal, French debate, one of the only debates about the invention of the daguerreotype, which had long before been marginalized by the discussion of photography as a technology of print on paper. Stephen Pinson, "Revers de fortune," in *Le daguerreotype français: Un objet photographique* (Paris: Musée d'Orsay, 2003).

13. André Gunthert, "La boite noire de Daguerre," in *Le daguerreotype francais: Un objet photographique* (Paris: Musée d'Orsay, 2003), p. 35.

14. *Ibid.*, p. 39.

15. Drawing on the study by Nathalie Boulouch, Gunthert links this accessibility to the invention of the autochrome by the Lumière brothers and to the uses to which it was put. Nathalie Boulouch, "Peindre avec le soleil? Les enjeux du problème de la photographie des couleurs," *Études Photographiques*, no. 10 (2002).

16. The names are listed in Alan Trachtenberg, *Reading American Photographs: Images as History* (New York: Hill and Wang, 1989), p. 3.

17. In *Techniques of the Observer*, Jonathan Crary shows that during the years from 1810 to 1840 — that is, before the invention of photography — a new observer figure was institutionalized, along with the conditions for a new visual experience that involved a break from the model manifested by the *camera obscura*, and "new modes of circulation, communication, production, consumption and rationalization all demanded and shaped a new observer-consumer." Jonathan Crary, *Techniques of the Observer* (Cambridge, MA: MIT Press, 1992), p. 14. Many of the characteristics that Crary attributes to the viewer at the beginning of the century are also typical of spectators of photography, but do not adequately describe them.

18. Roland, Barthes, *Camera Lucida: Reflections on Photography*, trans. Richard Howard (New York: Vintage, 2000), p. 76, translation modified·

19. In *Camera Lucida* and in his lectures, Barthes attempted to grasp the essence

of photography in its specificity as a medium. This formulation, which has since become classic, fails to exhaust the essence of photography, as Barthes wished, but undoubtedly offers a precise description of the social attitude toward photography. Barthes' expression, which he arrived at one hundred and fifty years after the invention of photography, succinctly captures the particular characteristic of the photographic medium as it is grasped by the users of photography since its invention. Without adding the civil contract of philosophy to our understanding of the medium, however, it is impossible to understand the institutionalization of photography as a medium of truth that attests to that to what "was there."

20. On the distinction between the *vita contemplative* and *vita activa*, along with the history of this distinction, see Hannah Arendt, *The Human Condition* (1958; Chicago: University of Chicago Press, 1998).

21. This description is quoted in Geoffrey Batchen, *Burning with Desire* (Cambridge, MA: MIT Press, 1999), p. 130. Most likely, the faithful description of what was visible in the daguerreotype is based on a reproduction that continues to be distributed as "the first daguerreotype." I am grateful to André Gunthert of the SFP in Paris for showing me the first actual daguerreotype and informing me of its condition and the fact of its omission from the Daguerre exhibition in 2003.

22. In the exhibition catalogue, the image appears as an expression of Daguerre's preference for "the readable aspect of the image." Quentinc Bajac and Dominique Planchon-de Font-Réalux, *Le daguerréotype français: Un objet photographique* (Paris: Musée d'Orsay, 2004), p. 58.

23. Crary, *Techniques of the Observer*, p. 112.

24. *Ibid,* p. 13.

25. For some crucial moments in the history of the ownership of photographs, see John David Viera, "Images as Property," in Larry Gross, John Katz, Jay Ruby (eds.), *Image Ethics: The Moral Rights of Subjects in Photographs, Film, and Television* (New York: Oxford University Press, 1988). An interesting case in point is the free access to use photographer David Rubinger's image of Israeli paratroopers in front of the Wailing Wall in the 1967 War.

26. Celebrities don't automatically turn into the owners of the photographs taken of them in the public space, but they can demand economic rights for the use of their images.

27. One of the first cases to challenge the photographed's lack of ownership of his own image, as something self-evident — although there was no demand for ownership — involved a photograph of Miss Abigail Roberson on packages of flour. See Viera, "Images as Property," pp. 140–41.

28. The artist Michal Heiman has systematically demonstrated this in her project "Unknown Photographer."

29. It is important to note that in the nineteenth century, people collected *cartes de visite* with the photographs of the famous, and Bisson was only following the common commercial practice of the period.

30. Giselle Freund is the source of this story, although she does not point to the fact that the photographed subject is not part of the legal dispute. See Gisèle Freund, *Photographie et société* (Paris: Seuil, 1996), pp. 80–81.

31. Lange is quoted in Marie Monique Robin, *Les 100 photos du siècle* (Paris: Editions du Chêne, 2000).

32. Geoffrey Dunn, "Photographic License," San Luis Obispo (CA) *New Times*, http://www.newtimes-slo.com/archives/cov_stories_2002/cov_01172 002.html, last accessed January 31, 2007.

33. This is mainly true of celebrities who have turned their images into an economic resource, and therefore their use by others detracts from the economic capital they themselves might derive from them. An "ordinary" person, however, as in the case of Florence Owens Thompson (in Dorothea Lange's photograph), will be given nothing, even though their photograph has made others a fortune.

34. Numerous catalogues published in the last few decades manifest these assumptions. See Carol Squiers, *The Body at Risk: Photography, Illness and Healing* (New York: International Center of Photography, 2005); Deborah Willis, *Reflections in Black* (New York: W. W. Norton, 2000); Roy Guttman and David Rieff (eds.), *Crimes of War* (London: W. W. Norton, 1999); and Thomas Y. Levin, Ursula Frohne, and Peter Weibel (eds.), *Ctrl (Space): Rhetorics of Surveillance from Bentham to Big Brother* (Cambridge, MA: MIT Press, 2002).

35. One example is the cameras distributed in the Occupied Territories during the first intifada. See the interview with Haim Brayshit in Ariella Azoulay, *How Does It Look to You?* (Tel Aviv: Babel, 2000).

36. The stalking of celebrities by paparazzi and the political photo opportunity are two examples.

37. Thomas Hobbes, *Leviathan*, ed. C. B. MacPherson (London: Penguin, 1987), p. 193.

38. *Ibid.*, pp. 227, 228.

39. See Arendt, *The Human Condition* and Carole Pateman, *The Sexual Contract* (Stanford, CA: Stanford University Press, 1988) for readings of the social contract. Both detail various stories that the civil contract sought to replace.

40. See Pateman, *The Sexual Contract*.

41. Jean Sagne, "All Kinds of Portraits: The Photographer's Studio," in Michel Frizot (ed.), *A New History of Photography* (Cologne: Könemann, 1998), p. 106.

42. In 1827, when Niépce presented the invention of the haliograph to the Royal Society, it was poorly received. In the wake of this failure, most of Daguerre's efforts, after joining forces with Niépce to develop the invention, were devoted to preparing the ground for its widespread acceptance. This, indeed, came to pass once the Chamber of Deputies authorized the purchase of the invention, and photography quickly spread throughout the Western world.

43. In a lecture during the exhibition Act of State: 1967–2007 at Minsha Art Gallery, Tel Aviv, July 2007, the journalist Joseph Algazy described the prohibition on taking photos during this time in Gaza. Military Proclamation No. 101 prohibits "photographing or any other manner of representation or of communicating expressions." Quoted in Jaja Shehadeh and Jonathan Kuttab, *The West Bank and the Rule of Law: A Study* (New York: The International Commission of Jurists and Law in the Service of Man), p. 126.

44. Thus, for instance, the American military government's prohibition of photography at Hiroshima and Nagasaki was demarcated in space and limited in time and could not have continued without being violated by local photographers. It certainly could not have become a constitutional law.

45. See Georges Didi-Huberman, *Images malgré tout* (Paris: Minuit, 2003).

46. The description of the violence of the photographic act is frequent in recent writings on photography. Barthes describes its ontology in *Camera Lucida*: "In terms of the image-repertoire, the Photograph (the one I *intend*) represents that very subtle moment when, to tell the truth, I am neither subject not object but a subject who feels he is becoming an object: I then experience a micro-version of death (of parenthesis): I am becoming a specter," (pp. 13–14).

47. By "public appearances," I refer to the simple distinction between photography at the heart of the family and those that can be seen to be a matter of "public interest." This distinction, of course, needs to be problematized, and it is easy to show this in the migration of family photographs into the press coverage of disasters.

48. For more on this, see Allan Sekula, "The Body and the Archive," in Richard Bolton (ed.), *The Contest of Meaning* (Cambridge, MA: MIT Press, 1989); Carol Squiers (ed.), *Overexposed: Essays on Contemporary Photography* (New York: New Press, 1999); and Sandra S. Phillips, Mark Haworth-Booth, and Carol Squiers (eds.), *Police Pictures: The Photograph as Evidence* (San Francisco: Chronicle Books, 1997).

49. On the state's use of photography, see John Tagg, "Evidence, Truth and

Order: Photographic Records and the Growth of the State," in Liz Wells (ed.), *The Photography Reader* (London: Routledge, 2003).

50. This inequality does receive mention in various places, but without leading to an in-depth discussion. For instance, in the album issued on the occasion of the millennial year 2000, in the case of inequality regarding the photograph of Florence Owens Thompson, emphasis on the fact that she considered taking those who published it to court (although she didn't, of course, as she lacked the financial ability) is presented as an amusing anecdote. See Robin, *Les 100 photos du siècle*.

51. On the distinction between citizenship and becoming a citizen, see Ariella Azoulay and Adi Ophir, *Bad Days: Between Disaster and Utopia* [in Hebrew] (Tel Aviv: Resling, 2002).

52. Israeli readers need not be reminded how quickly the bodies of Jewish casualties are covered after terror attacks.

53. This is the legislative proposal of 1839 as presented by the French interior minister to the Chamber of Deputies on June 15, 1839.

54. By contrast, such inventions as the washing machine or vacuum cleaner have no doubt changed the life of the individual, but the benefit they bring is personal and private.

55. On the formation of the observer in the end of the eighteenth century and the beginning of the nineteenth, see Crary, *Techniques of the Observer*.

56. The same process occurred among the black population in the United States, who, although deprived of citizenship, participated in the nascent practice of photography from the beginning, transforming it into a weapon in the abolitionist struggle. See Deborah Willis, *Reflections in Black* (New York: W. W. Norton, 2000).

57. Needless to say, their photographs, as well as those produced by African Americans, were not treated like those produced by white men, and their existence has only come to light in recent years. The research on women's use of photography (and daguerreotype) in the first years of photography is still only beginning, but one may already affirm their participation in the nascent practice of photography.

58. "Any Person today can lay claim to being filmed." Walter Benjamin, *Selected Writings, Volume 3, 1935–1938*, eds. Howard Eiland and Michael Jennings (Cambridge, MA: Belknap Press of Harvard University, 2002), p. 115.

59. Susan Sontag, *On Photography* (New York: Picador, 1977), p. 22.

60. On the legal protection of the right to privacy, see Viera, "Images as Property."

61. These remarks appear in Robin, *Les 100 photos du siècle*.

62. The proliferation of local photographers during the first intifada is an instructive case in point.

63. On deterritorialization and reterritorialization see Gilles Deleuze and Félix Guattari, *A Thousand Plateaus: Capitalism and Schizophrenia*, trans. Brian Massumi (Minneapolis: University of Minnesota Press, 1987).

64. See Dorothea Lange, "The Assignment I'll Never Forget," in Liz Heron and Val Williams (eds.), *Illuminations: Women's Writings on Photography from the 1850s to the Present* (London: I. B.Tauris, 1996).

65. Susan Sontag, *On Photography* (New York: Picador, 1977), p. 3.

66. *Ibid.*, p. 107.

67. See Arendt, *The Human Condition.*

68. For more on the flawed citizenship of citizens living beside noncitizens, see Azoulay and Ophir, *Bad Days.*

69. See Michel Foucault, *The Birth of the Clinic: An Archaeology of Medical Perception* (New York: Random House, 1975).

70. See, for example, Georges Didi-Huberman's book on the photography department in Charcot's clinic, *Invention de l'hystérie: Charcot et l'iconographie photographique de la Salpêtrière* (Paris: Macula, 1995) and Denis Bernard and André Gunthert's book on Albert Lande, who was one of the photographers who worked there, *L'instant revé: Albert Londe* (Nîmes: Jacqueline Chambon, 1993).

71. Because citizenship is never fully achieved, practices of civilianization are needed in order to become a citizen, thus preserving the gap between the citizen and power.

72. On the contribution of the Englishman Henry Fox Talbot, see Frizot (ed.), *A New History of Photography.*

73. The specific prohibitions that various states apply to the publication of photos, usually on an ad hoc basis in order to serve political interests, doesn't take the place of the missing discussion.

74. The contention that every technology poses the same challenge from the user's point of view is false. Thus, for example, the vacuum cleaner invites the purchaser to use it in a certain way, and in most cases the user will indeed do it correctly. However, the use of the vacuum cleaner doesn't take place in the framework of social, political, and civil practices that bind individuals together, shape their citizenship and horizon of action, represent their actions, and structure their identities.

CHAPTER THREE: THE SPECTATOR IS CALLED TO TAKE PART

1. A photo, like a product of work, can be destroyed, and in extreme cases, it can even be systematically annihilated. The treatment by the Nazis of the large quantities of photos they produced is one well-known case. This is an extreme

example in the framework of which the total prohibition on photography was constantly transgressed, as in the case of SS officer Max Täubner, judged in the secret tribunal of the SS. His verdict stated: "The accused took a number of photographs of the executions and allowed SS-Sturmmann Fritsch to take further photographs, although he knew that the photographing of such incidents was not permitted. These were for the most part pictures which showed the most deplorable excesses, many are shameless and utterly revolting." Ernst Klee, Willi Dressen, and Volker Riess (eds.), *"The Good Old Days": The Holocaust as Seen by Its Perpetrators and Bystanders*, trans. Deborah Burnstone (New York: Free Press, 1991), p. 199; Georges Didi-Huberman, *Images malgré tout* (Paris: Minuit, 2003).

2. Although I could not include the photograph by Yariv Katz in this book, it can be seen can be seen at (the photographer's name is misspelled there — Yarif Katz) http://commondreams.org/headlines02/0224-04.htm (last accessed on March 20, 2008).

3. I rely here on Gilles Deleuze's discussion of sense in *The Logic of Sense*, trans. Mark Lester with Charles Stivale, ed. Constantin V. Boundas (New York: Columbia University Press, 1990). The sense of an *énoncé* — a photo, in this case — can never be found in the photo itself, but is always caught in an infinite regression of *énoncés* where a new one is required to express the sense of the previous one.

4. Deleuze describes this node as a singular point. *The Logic of Sense*, pp. 28–35.

5. See Lyotard's fourth conversation in Jean-François Lyotard and Jean-Loup Thébaud, *Just Gaming*, trans. Wlad Godzich (Minneapolis: University of Minnesota Press, 1985), pp. 64, 71.

6. *Ibid.*, p. 69.

7. I'm not dealing here with the Kantian and Levinasian influences on Lyotard or with his critical stance toward both, which he addresses in *The Differend: Phrases in Dispute*, trans. Georges Van Den Abbeele (Minneapolis: University of Minnesota Press, 1988), as well as in *Just Gaming*.

8. Lyotard and Thébaud, *Just Gaming*, p. 72.

9. Hannah, Arendt, *The Human Condition* (1958; Chicago: University of Chicago Press, 1998, pp. 179–80).

10. I refer here only to still photographs rather than television images, which create a new type of here and now. On the new status of television images see Thomas Keenan, "Publicity and Indifference: Media, Surveillance, 'Humanitarian Intervention,'" in Thomas Y. Levin, Ursula Frohne, and Peter Weibel (eds.), *Ctrl [Space]: Rhetorics of Surveillance from Bentham to Big Brother* (Cambridge, MA: MIT Press, 2002).

11. In reference to time, see Benjamin's "On the Concept of History," *Selected Writings, Volume 4, 1938–1940* (Cambridge, MA: Belknap Press of Harvard University Press, 2003), where he writes of the past as the time of moral duty, and Hans Jonas, "The Imperative of Responsibility," in which Jonas writes about the future as the time of moral duty. Hans Jonas, *The Imperative of Responsibility: In Search of an Ethics in the Technological Age* (Chicago: University of Chicago Press, 1984). In regard to space, see Luc Boltanski, *La souffrance à distance: Morale humanitaire, médias et politique* (Paris: A. M. Metaillie, 1993).

12. According to Hans Jonas, the anthropocentric dimension characterized ethics until modernism: "The ethical meaning belonged to the direct treatment of man by man, including his treatment of himself: all traditional ethics is anthropocentric." Jonas, *The Imperative of Responsibility*, p. 4.

13. *Ibid.*, pp. 5–6.

14. On this expression from Martin Heidegger's "The Age of the World Picture," in *The Question concerning Technology and Other Essays*, trans. William Lovitt (New York: Harper & Row, 1977), p. 134, see Ariella Azoulay, *Death's Showcase: The Power of Image in Contemporary Democracy*, trans. Ruvik Danieli (Cambridge, MA: MIT Press, 2001).

15. Heidegger, "The Age of the World Picture," pp. 129–30. Insertions within brackets are Heidegger's.

16. An analysis of photography's omnipresence in connection with a discussion of merchandise and the transformation of the entire world into merchandise could well be rewarding, although it would miss the crucial difference between the two. Merchandise is part of the world of labor and production, a significant part of which is established through contracts, agreements, and strictly defined employer-worker relations. Photography is fundamentally different.

17. While Heidegger described the modern era as the age of "conquering the world as picture" and Guy Debord described this era as "the society of spectacle" in (*The Society of Spectacle* [New York: Zone Books, 1995]), these two discussions, which speak of the omnipresence of the image in the modern era, do not explicitly address photography and the particular ramifications of the conquest of the world by means of it, although they both undoubtedly relate to the photographed image.

18. Even Israeli law, which once avoided the use of photography in actual court hearings, introduced it into the evidentiary hearing. See Tal Golan, "Learning to See: The Beginning of Visual Technologies in Medicine and Law," in *Law, Society and Culture*, Buchman Faculty of Law Series (Tel Aviv: Tel Aviv University, 2003).

19. The ban on photography is still exceptional in the Western world. Hiroshima and Nagasaki are famous examples where, during the first years of the American occupation, films were confiscated

20. Since the middle of the 1990s, following the terrorist attacks in Israel, and since 9/11 in the United States, newspapers occasionally report of photographers or citizens who have been asked to stop taking photos in different public areas. The fact that prior to these attacks terrorists gathered photographic information in open public space has led to attempts by a few police agencies to limit photographic activity, but as of yet, no law has been legislated.

21. In this respect, it is similar to power as described by Foucault. Michel Foucault, *The History of Sexuality, Volume 1: An Introduction*, trans. Robert Hurley (New York: Vintage, 1980).

22. On photography as omnipresent, and used by "everyone," see Pierre Bourdieu, with Luc Boltanski, Robert Castel, Jean-Claude Chamboredon, and Dominique Schnapper, *Photography: A Middle-brow Art*, trans. Shaun Whiteside (Stanford, CA: Stanford University Press, 1990).

23. See Stefano Boeri, "Eclectic Atlases," *Documenta X Documents*, no. 3 (Stuttgart: Cantz, 1996). A distinct example is the controversy among various institutions over the number of participants in demonstrations seen from aerial photos, spawning various methods to interpret the visible. See Farouk El Baz, "Crowd Space — Bodies Count," *Wired*, June 2003.

24. This is true of the critical ones as well which attempt to depict the invention as the product of a period, rather than of a unique inventor.

25. Jonathan Crary has described the various instruments that were used to produce images on the eve of photography's emergence as the hegemonic means to mechanically obtain images. See Jonathan Crary, *Techniques of the Observer* (Cambridge, MA: MIT Press, 1992). Aïm Deüelle Lüski's "cameras" testify to some of the options repressed by the emergence of photography as we know it today. On his instruments see Chapter Six.

26. Despite the decision to confer the invention on the entire world, a patent was taken out in England on the invention of the daguerreotype, and for several years it was not accessible to everyone. See Elizabeth Eastlike, "Photography," in Alan Trachtenberg (ed.), *Classic Essays on Photography* (New Haven, CT: Leete's Island Books, 1980).

27. Dominique François Arago, "Report," in Trachtenberg (ed.), *Classic Essays on Photography*, p. 19.

28. *Ibid.*

29. Walter Benjamin briefly discusses this in "Little History of Photography," in *Selected Writings, Volume 2, 1927–1934*, eds. Michael W. Jennings, Gary Smith, and Howard Eiland (Cambridge, MA: Belknap Press of Harvard University Press, 1999).

30. Charles Baudelaire, who was dominant among those who opposed photography, wrote regarding the Salon of 1859 that a vengeful god had responded to wishes to reproduce nature with exactitude and nominated Daguerre as its messiah. From that moment on, he wrote, the whole society rushed like Narcissus to contemplate its trivial image on a metal plate. Charles Baudelaire, "Salon de 1859," in *Baudelaire: Oeuvres Completes*, vol. 2 (Paris: NRF Bibliothèque de la Pléiade, 1976), pp. 617–18.

31. For a discussion of the denial of the logic of photography, see my discussion of Aïm Deüelle Lüski's cameras in Chapter Six.

32. Arago, "Report," p. 24.

33. The invention is usually attributed to Daguerre, thus forgetting the contribution of those who contributed to its invention. To purchase the invention, the state paid both Daguerre and Nicéphore Niépce's son, Isidore.

34. The state paid for the invention, but did not take possession of it, thus renouncing both the monopoly it might have had by virtue of its purchase and the possibility of having the government play an explicit role in the processes of institutionalizing the invention. Although the state relinquished its rights to the invention, one must not underestimate its role in regard to photography and its functions. The purchase of the invention and the concurrent renunciation of any rights obtaining to this purchase entailed that both a national (French) and a universal stamp were at once imprinted on the invention. Thus, France sought to retain the spiritual monopoly, but also hoped to turn photography itself into a symbol of democratization. From its very beginning, photography had been presented as a gift given to the nation, a blessing bestowed on it, and a right granted it; to this day it has been conceived as an instrument with positive attributes of assistance and support.

35. On this choice see Michel Frizot (ed.), *A New History of Photography* (Cologne: Könemann, 1998) and Geoffrey Batchen, *Burning with Desire* (Cambridge, MA: MIT Press, 1999).

36. I base my argument here on many conversations I have had with journalistic photographers, some of whom are published in *Death's Showcase*, as well as on an ongoing analysis of press photos.

37. Jacques Lacan, *The Four Fundamental Concepts of Psychoanalysis*, ed. Jacques-Alain Miller, trans. Alan Sheridan (New York: Norton, 1978), p. 253.

38. For more on this subject, see my discussion of Roni Kempler, who happened to document Rabin's assassination, in *Death's Showcase*, pp. 171–75.

39. On the disrupted process of secularization with regard to art and sovereign rule, see *ibid.*, pp. 266–86.

40. Since the 1980s, museums have started to work consistently with photography as photography. Previously, photographs in museum spaces were frequently used as a reference, remainder, or sometimes even a type of relic of artistic events. By the 1980s, however, the photographic image began to receive a different treatment, along with the opening of new museum wings devoted to photography that officially established photography's representation in museum contexts.

41. On the political economy of the museum, see Ariella Azoulay, *Training for Art* [in Hebrew] (Tel Aviv: The Porter Institute for Poetics and Semiotics, Tel Aviv University, Hakibbutz Hameuchad, 1999).

42. The English version, *Mythologies*, trans. Annette Lavers (New York: Hill and Wang, 1972), contains only essays selected from the original by the translator. The "Shock-Photos" essay is included in Roland Barthes, *The Eiffel Tower and Other Mythologies*, trans. Richard Howard (New York: Hill and Wang, 1977), pp. 71–73.

43. *Ibid.*, p. 71

44. *Ibid.*

45. *Ibid.*

46. I rely here on Deleuze's concept of a pure event. A pure event does not happen in space and time, but is an a priori form of all the possible realizations within a given set of relations, like the infinitive form of a verb. See Deleuze, *The Logic of Sense*. See also my reading of the collapse of the Twin Towers in terms of a pure event in "A Moment of Quiet, Please, the Disaster Would Like to Say Something," *(a): the journal of culture and the unconscious* 2, no. 1 (2002).

47. Crary's use of the term "observer" does not pertain to photography. See *Techniques of the Observer*.

48. *Merriam-Webster's Collegiate Dictionary*, 11th ed., s.v. "spectator."

49. Throughout this work on the civil contract, I am trying to show that photography is embedded in a complex system of power relations that undermine any attempt to demonstrate a unidirectional flow of power from the camera to the photographed subjects.

50. Out of over seven hundred plates in which Muybridge deals with the dissection of motion, two-thirds are devoted to the human body. Most of the subjects are in the nude and in positions that arouse no less wonder than the image of the woman spanking the boy: a woman undressing another woman, a woman crawling

on all fours, and so on. On the gender bias of his photographs — men are photographed in displays of power and strength as weightlifters and other athletes, whereas women are shown in absurd and humiliating postures — see Janine A. Mileaf, "Poses for the Camera: Eadweard Muybridge's Studies of the Human Figure," *American Art: The Journal of the Smithsonian's American Art Museum* 16, no. 3 (2002). Mileaf analyzes Muybridge's photographs and his own pronouncements regarding his models: "If the men provided a standard of achievement, then the women served as a standard of the mundane" (p. 7). See also Rebecca Solnit, *River of Shadows: Eadweard Muybridge and the Technological Wild West* (New York: Viking, 2003).

51. On sexuality under the Victorian regime, see Michel Foucault, *The History of Sexuality, Volume 1: An Introduction*, trans. Robert Hurley (New York: Vintage, 1980).

52. Benjamin, "Little History of Photography," in *Selected Writings, Volume 2*, p. 510.

53. Giselle Freund describes the dramatic decrease in photographic costs with the invention of calling cards by Andre-Adolphe-Eugene Disderi, who replaced metal with glass plates and thus slashed the cost from 100 to 20 francs. In addition he divided the negative into twelve pictures, so the photographed subject could get several copies of his image. Gisèle Freund, *Photographie et société* (Paris: Seuil, 1996), pp. 56–57.

54. On the beginning of identity picture see Allan Sekula, "The Body and the Archive," in Richard Bolton (ed.), *The Contest of Meaning* (Cambridge, MA: MIT Press, 1989). On the abuse of identity picture in political violence see Jean-Luc Nancy, *Being Singular Plural*, trans. Robert O. Richardson and Anne E. O'Byrne (Stanford, CA: Stanford University Press, 2000).

55. Brian Wallis notes that the population of Columbia at the time included five thousand whites who owned a total of one hundred thousand slaves. Brian Wallis "Black Bodies, White Science: Louis Aggasiz's Daguerreotypes," in Coco Fusco and Brian Wallis (eds.) *Only Skin Deep: Changing Visions of the American Self* (New York: Harry Abrams, 2003), p. 170.

56. Elinor Reichlin, "Survivors of a Painful Epoch: Six Rare Pre-Civil War Daguerreotypes of Southern Slaves," undated, Archive, Peabody Museum, Harvard University. The photographs were discovered by Reichlin in the storerooms of the Peabody Museum in 1975.

57. For an analysis of the pictures, see Wallis, "Black Bodies, White Science"; Sandra S. Phillips, Mark Haworth-Booth, and Carol. Squiers (eds.), *Police Pictures:*

The Photograph as Evidence (San Francisco: Chronicle Books, 1997); Melissa Banta, *A Curious and Ingenious Art: Reflexions on Daguerreotypes at Harvard* (Iowa City: University of Iowa Press, 2000); and Manning Marable and Leith Mullings, *Freedom: A Photographic History of the African American Struggle* (London: Phaidon, 2002).

58. Wallis quotes from a letter written by Agassiz to his mother detailing his repulsion and shock at his first meeting with a black person, but there is no mention of his encounter with the slaves on the plantation. Wallis, "Black Bodies, White Science," p. 167.

59. As Carrie Mae Weems wrote in the text she superimposed on the photograph of Drana and Delia in her work *From Here I Saw What Happened and I Cried* (1995–96), "YOU BECAME A SCIENTIFIC PROFILE." For the series, see www.moma. org/collection/browse_results.php?object_id= 45579 (last accessed March 23, 2007).

60. The museum prohibits viewings of the daguerreotypes themselves, even for purposes of research, and anything written about them is based exclusively on reproductions.

61. Wallis, "Black Bodies, White Science," p. 178. On the participation of blacks in the nascent practice of photography, and more specifically on the use of photography in the production of abolitionist pamphlets by the African American abolitionist and daguerreotypist James Presley Ball, see Deborah Willis, *Reflections in Black* (New York: W. W. Norton, 2000).

62. Wallis, "Black Bodies, White Science," p. 170.

63. On the use of sexual violence in the exclusion of black women from citizenship, see Louise Michele Newman, *White Women's Rights: The Racial Origins of Feminism in the United States* (New York: Oxford University Press, 1999).

64. On the vulnerability of women slaves and the helplessness of their husbands in the face of their sexual violation, see Deborah Gray White, *Aren't I a Woman?: Female Slaves in the Plantation South* (New York: W. W. Norton, 1985); Linda Brent, *Incidents in the Life of a Slave Girl*, ed. Lydia Maria Child (San Diego: Harcourt Brace Jovanovich, 1973); and Patricia, C. McKissack, *A Picture of Freedom: The Diary of Clotee, a Slave Girl* (New York: Scholastic Inc., 1997).

65. On this matter, see also the brief discussion by Judith Butler, following Orlando Patterson's research, in *Antigone's Claim: Kinship between Life and Death* (New York: Columbia University Press, 2002), pp. 73–74.

66. On the violation of men's and fathers' capacity to protect their wives and children see White, *Aren't I a Woman?*, and Willie Lee Rose, *Slavery and Freedom*, ed. William Freehling (Oxford: Oxford University Press, 1982).

67. Their posture resembles the way other weak populations were photo-graphed scientifically in the nineteenth century. See Sekula, "The Body and the Archive"; Carol Squiers, *Overexposed: Essays on Contemporary Photography* (New York: The New Press, 1999); James C. Faris, *Navajo and Photography: A Critical History of the Representation of an American People* (Salt Lake City: University of Utah Press, 2003); and Georges Didi-Huberman, *Invention de l'hystérie: Charcot et l'iconographie photographique de la Salpêtrière* (Paris: Macula, 1995).

68. Reichlin also claims that her eyes are tearful. However, the seeming tears are most probably a very common effect of daguerreotype portraits made in this period, when extended exposure resulted in a misting over of the eyes of the pho-tographed people.

69. Shortly after writing about these images, I came on a paper published by African Americans in New York at the end of the 1840s and edited by Frederick Douglass. A passage from a text published there describes the opportunities that were opened up for the black population through their use of the daguerreotype: "It is one of the best answers to the charge of natural inferiority we have lately met with." Willis, *Reflections in Black*, p. 6. The photographed slaves, who couldn't have read this passage, seem to have recognized this possibility in the setup of the studio and the photographic ceremony, as witnessed by their posture in front of the camera.

70. White, *Aren't I a Woman?* p. 32.

71. In this context, it is worth mentioning the photograph of the scourged back taken thirteen years later, which is also a rare instance of visual traces of the white man's cruelty toward the body of his slaves.

CHAPTER FOUR: EMERGENCY CLAIMS

1. On the fantasy of the new age see my discussion of 9/11 in Ariella Azoulay, "A Moment of Quiet, Please, the Disaster Would Like to Say Something," *(a): the journal of culture and the unconscious* 2, no. 1 (2002).

2. Professionals involved in covering the war — news editors, journalists, pho-tographers, politicians, and even editorial-page writers — all have used variations of these terms. See Andrew Hoskins, *Televising War: From Vietnam to Iraq* (London: Continuum, 2004).

3. Susan Sontag, *Regarding the Pain of Others* (New York: Picador, 2003), p. 66.

4. *Ibid.*, p. 67. See also the various articles on the torture photographs of Iraqi prisoners collected in *Abu Ghraib: The Politics of Torture*, The Terra Nova Series (Berkeley, CA: North Atlantic Books, 2004).

5. Near the end of *Regarding the Pain of Others*, written twenty-six years after her *On Photography*, Susan Sontag sums up the power of photography from a remote, abstract viewpoint that looks not at the photographs themselves, but at the ideal of what photography is: "Even if they are only tokens, and cannot possibly encompass most of the reality to which they refer, they still perform a vital function. The imagery says: This is what human beings are capable of doing—may volunteer to do, enthusiastically, self-righteously. Don't forget." (p. 115).

6. One may recall the images distributed in which, in the center, a target icon could be seen, whether in the form of a crosshairs or square brackets.

7. It suffices to mention some prominent examples: the photograph of the charred corpse of an Iraqi soldier taken by Kenneth Jarecke of the Contact Press Images Agency on February 28, 1991; the photograph of the "cemetery" of vehicles on the so-called "Highway of Death" from Kuwait to Basra in Iraq taken by Cassandra Garner; Web sites of American soldiers showing their war albums, such as "Tim's Desert Storm Photo Album," by Tim Cobble, which exhibited side-by-side photographs of him and his comrades, photographs from the "Highway of Death," photographs showing Iraqi soldiers being taken prisoner, and more.

8. Besides the generalized "end of the image" discourse, which turns the writer's eyes away from the visible, essays are constantly being written that stubbornly observe the visible out of a commitment to the civil contract of photography. For example, the work of Wendy Kozol on Kosovo, "Domesticating NATO's War in Kosovo: (In)Visible Bodies and the Dilemma of Photojournalism," *Meridians: Feminism, Transnationalism, Race* 4, no. 2 (2004), pp. 1–38, and articles by Susan Jeffords, Lauren Rabinovitz, and others on the media in the First Gulf War in the volume they edited, *Seeing through the Media: The Persian Gulf War* (New Brunswick, NJ: Rutgers University Press, 1994).

9. Available online at http://digitaljournalist.org/issue0212/pt_index. html, last accessed March 27, 2007.

10. Publication of Jarecke's photograph of the Iraqi soldier's charred corpse, for example, was suspended by *Life* magazine and made available only three days later, not spread over the magazine's front pages. In his book on the visual coverage of the Gulf War, Andrew Hoskins unfolds the photograph's story from the time of its suspension until its publication. Hoskins, *Televising War*, p. 20.

11. Available online at http://www.geocities.com/Pentagon/3153 (last accessed October 2, 2007).

12. Jean Baudrillard writes: "In this manner, everyone is amnestied by the ultra-rapid succession of phony events and phony discourses." Jean Baudrillard, *The*

Gulf War Did Not Take Place (Bloomington: Indiana University Press, 1991). Sontag proposes the painter Goya as the author of a new age in response to the suffering of others: "The account of war's cruelties is fashioned as an assault on the sensibility of the viewer." Sontag, *Regarding the Pain of Others*, p. 45.

13. The exhibition featured works by the following artists: Raeda Adon, Ariella Azoulay, Iman Abu-Hmid, Boaz Arad, Daniel Bauer, Aïm Deüelle Lüski, Michal Heiman, Sandi Hilal, Sharif Waked, Alex Levac, Avi Mograbi, Manal Mahamid, Faten Fawzy Nastas, Allesandro Petti, Miki Kratsman, David Reeb, and Dina Shenhav.

14. Walter Benjamin, *Selected Writings, Volume 3, 1935–1938*, eds. Howard Eiland and Michael W. Jennings (Cambridge, MA: Belknap Press of Harvard University Press, 2002), p. 108.

15. See Jean-François Lyotard, *The Differend: Phrases in Dispute*, trans. Georges Van Den Abbeele (Minneapolis: University of Minnesota Press, 1988).

16. *Metsudat David*, commentary on Isaiah 28:19. I am grateful to Rachel Gordin for her assistance in finding the sources.

17. Power has the authority and the means to turn statements of horror into, or depict them as, emergency claims, but it is not always able to do so. One example might be the attempt by the Israeli government to dissuade its citizens from traveling to Sinai on the pretext of emergency, while the citizens dispute the meaning which the government seeks to attach to the statement.

18. "The Twilight Zone," a column by Gideon Levy and Miki Kratsman that appears weekly in *Ha'aretz*, is one of the sole enclaves in which photographer and journalist (in a rare instance of cooperation in the press) attempt to engineer a meeting between what's visible and what's written in order to facilitate the addressing of the Palestinian who can be seen in the photograph. Here I do not treat Amira Hass's important work regarding statements of horror, insofar as those she deals with exist only on the textual level and are generally indifferent to the visual level I'm dealing with here.

19. I've discussed this matter in a forthcoming book coauthored with Adi Ophir, *This Regime Which Is Not One* (Tel Aviv: Resling, 2008).

20. Foreign workers constitute another group within the population over which the state of Israel has ruled for a long time without formalizing their political status. The foreign workers themselves are not wanted in Israel. What is wanted is what they have in their possession — labor, sex, ability in certain fields — but what they have in their possession doesn't suffice to free them from their transience.

21. *Ha'aretz*, January 19, 2004, p. A2.

22. I do not share the reluctance of many sympathizers of the Palestinian

struggle to represent Palestinians' suffering and their cause. This reluctance implies a fantasy of an authentic voice belonging to the "other" and constrains access to the position of the addresser of statements of horror and atrocities. But in times of emergency anyone should — and should be allowed to — cry for help. The purists who care for the Palestinians' authentic voice divest the photographs of their plight of their emergency claim and contribute to the perpetuation of the distinction between occupiers and occupied. In so doing, they make it difficult to see an important dimension of the Palestinian struggle — the fact that it is a struggle of noncitizens against the state that has long abandoned them. The demand for the victims' authentic voice is contrary to the logic of the statement in general and to the duty to transmit emergency claims of atrocities in particular.

CHAPTER FIVE: HAS ANYONE EVER SEEN A PHOTOGRAPH OF A RAPE?

1. Recent decades, which paradoxically enough may be termed the "golden age" of images of horror, have been characterized by a dizzying rise in the production and distribution of picture albums whose declared purpose is to gather visual testimonies of horrors that have struck humanity in the modern era. Such albums may include documentation of the daily distress of circumscribed populations whose names only few know how to pronounce or of spectacular events, such as 9/11 or the tsunami disaster. Photos of events that haven't been gathered together as a book or album in hardcover or softcover can be found at many sites on the Internet.

2. In the Israeli context that is the focus of this book, I have heard here and there some information about Palestinian women raped by Israeli soldiers and civilians in 1948, but I was never able to find images from these events or information about them. Susan Slymovics's paper on the rape of Qula is illuminating in its reconstruction of the events and of the apparatuses which made them, leaking out of the main narrative of 1948. "The Rape of Qula, A Destroyed Palestinian Village," in Lila Abu-Lughod and Ahmad Sa'adi (eds.), *Touching a Painful Past: The Nakba as a Site of Palestinian Collective Memory* (New York: Columbia University Press, 2007).

3. I'm relying here on Michel Foucault's notion of an object of discourse. In his theory of discourse developed in *The Birth of the Clinic*, Foucault notes of the medical gaze: "New objects were to present themselves...in the sense that, and at the same time as, the knowing subject reorganizes himself, changes himself, and begins to function in a new way. It was not, therefore, the conception...that changed first and later the way in which it was recognized; nor was it the signatelic system that was changed first and then the theory; but together, and at a deeper level." "At this

level," he continues, one must "read the deep structures of visibility in which field and gaze are bound together by *codes of knowledge*." Michel Foucault, *The Birth of the Clinic: An Archaeology of Medical Perception*, trans. A. M. Sheridan Smith (New York: Vintage Books, 1975), p. 90.

4. Maria Bevacqua reconstructs the history of rape in the feminist struggle and points to the 1970s as the time when it became an explicit, agreed-on object of contention in *Rape on the Public Agenda: Feminism and the Politics of Sexual Assault* (Boston: Northeastern University Press, 2000).

5. For an analysis of rape from a legal perspective, see Catherine A. MacKinnon, *Sex Equality: Rape Law* (New York: Foundation Press, 2001); Susan Estrich, *Real Rape: How the Legal System Victimizes Women Who Say No* (Cambridge, MA: Harvard University Press, 1987), and Orit Kamir, *Feminism, Rights, and the Law* (Tel Aviv: Universita Meshuderet, Ministry of Defense, Israel, 2002).

6. On the analysis of rape victims' presence on talk shows, see Linda Alcoff and Laura Gray-Rosendale, "Survivor Discourse: Transgression or Recuperation?" in Sidonie Smith and Julia Watson (eds.), *Getting a Life: Everyday Uses of Autobiography* (Minneapolis: University of Minnesota Press, 1996).

7. To comprehend how often the term "rape" appears in the titles of books from different fields such as cinema, criminology, law, and psychology, it suffices to glance at the bibliography of this book, which is undoubtedly only partial, and to compare it with the meager bibliography compiled by Joan Mathews in the early 1970s, "Rape Bibliography," in New York Radical Feminists, *Rape: The First Sourcebook for Women by New York Radical Feminists*, eds. Noreen Connell and Cassandra Wilson (New York: New American Library, 1974).

8. Paul Tabori, *The Social History of Rape* (London: New English Library, 1971), p. 13.

9. New York Radical Feminists, *Rape*, p. xv.

10. Bevacqua has pointed to the antirape declaration of the radical feminist movement of New York in 1971 and the conference conducted by the movement on this subject in April of that year as the two key events that heralded the dawn of the antirape movement in the United States. See *Rape on the Public Agenda*, pp. 18–21.

11. These goals are presented in both New York Radical Feminists, *Rape* and in Bevacqua, *Rape on the Public Agenda*.

12. The writing on rape in recent years describes rape as an event of prominent visibility in the public sphere. "The 1971 speak-out and conference," Maria Bevacqua writes, for example, "both reflected the newly raised awareness of rape as a women's issue and made that issue publicly visible." Bevacqua, *Rape on the Public*

Agenda, p. 56. Sharon Marcus writes that "one common conjunction of rape and language refers to the many images of rape which our culture churns out." Sharon Marcus, "Fighting Bodies, Fighting Words: A Theory and Politics of Rape Prevention," in Judith Butler and Joan W. Scott (eds.), *Feminists Theorize the Political* (New York: Routledge, 1992), p. 389.

13. In their essay "Survivors' Discourse: Transgression or Recuperation," Linda Alcoff and Laura Gray-Rosendale analyze the discourse on rape in terms borrowed from Michel Foucault. They write about the importance of talking about rape and point to its presence in discourse — on television, in books and newspapers, and so on. Despite the nature of their discussion, they don't linger over the fact that rape has remained an invisible object. Reference to the visual dimension of rape occurs only once, when the two deal with the question that has stood at the center of a public debate: whether it's right to expose a rape victim or whether a woman should reveal herself to be a rape victim. At the beginning of the essay, the authors identify themselves as women who have survived rape. They write: "And the visual image of the survivor, although it can be used to objectify, has the potential to explode stereotypes about who survivors are as well as counter an invisibility that in the long run serves only to hide the true nature of patriarchy, a patriarchy that condones, if not promotes, sexual violence." Alcoff and Gray-Rosendale, "Survivor Discourse." According to Alcoff and Gray, exposing women who have survived rape to the gaze is supposed to render rape visible. But an injured person who has survived a traffic accident is not the accident, and when you see a woman who has been raped, you don't see rape. Exposing a rape victim to the gaze doesn't show rape, but merely creates the illusion that rape has become an object of the gaze.

14. What has become to be known in Israel as "the Shomrat gang rape" was an ongoing rape of a fourteen-year-old girl from Kibbutz Shomrat by several sixteen-year-old and seventeen-year-old years old boys. The affair, the ruling of the district court, and the lenient punishment to which it sentenced the boys led to an important change in Israeli rape law.

15. Keith Burgess-Jackson, *Rape: A Philosophical Investigation* (Aldershot, UK: Dartmouth, 1996), p. 36.

16. Burgess-Jackson describes which social contract is breached according to each of these conceptions.

17. See especially the brief history of the law regarding rape presented in Chapter Three of the *Rape: A Philosophical Investigation*.

18. Georges Vigarello, *A History of Rape* (Cambridge: Polity, 2001). Likewise, Tabori's *Social History of Rape*, which doesn't problematize its subject at all and

describes rape as formulated on the back cover of his book: "The history of rape is as ancient as life on planet earth."

19. Vigarello, *A History of Rape*, p. 88.

20. *Ibid.*

21. New York Radical Feminists, *Rape*, p. 3.

22. See the story about the rape of the painter Artemisia Gentilecci, which led to her father's suing the rapist in court for having damaged his property and not having wed her, as he'd promised. This story, as well as the protocol of the rape trial, appears in her biographies and in the exhaustive catalogue of an exhibition of her works. See Mary, D. Garrard, *Artemisia Gentileschi: The Image of the Female Hero in Italian Baroque Art* (Princeton, NJ: Princeton University Press, 1989).

23. In the nineteenth century, there were known instances of public figures who took an interest in isolated rape cases and openly condemned them and demanded justice for the victims. In these cases, it was damage to public morals that stirred people to action, not a damage to property claimed by a husband or father demanding restitution.

24. An exceptional case in this context is that of the Marquis de Sade, who brutally raped and beat Rose Keller, whom he'd hired to work in his home. When the story came to light, de Sade's family paid the victim an unusually large sum of money relative to her economic situation in return for her silence. The affair was nevertheless exposed by public figures who sought public condemnation of it. The full story appears in Vigarello, *A History of Rape*, pp. 69–72.

25. Vigarello, who quotes Gaubard in reference to medieval times, notes that this statement is true of the eighteenth century as well. Vigarello, *A History of Rape*, p. 18.

26. I am not dealing here with the historical origins of this sanctity, but only with the fact that from the French Revolution onward, with the emergence of the modern citizen, women were left imprisoned in this conceptual world, whereas the citizen status of men was structured in secular terms and conceived as a political entity.

27. Jean Paul Sartre, *Being and Nothingness* (London: Methuen, 1957), p. 349.

28. See Naomi Wolf, *The Beauty Myth* (New York: Harper Perennial, 2002).

29. See especially the chapters "Personal Testimonies" and "The Red Ribbons" in New York Radical Feminists, *Rape*, in which women talk about their experiences.

30. According to the report on sexual violence in Israel, which was released in 2002 by the Central Association for Victims of Sexual Assault in Israel, only 17 percent of all rape incidents were instigated by a stranger.

31. This discussion is of no relevance, of course, to rape in its traditional sense, wherein the rapist is a stranger.

32. Robin Warshaw, *I Never Called It Rape: The* Ms. *Report on Recognizing, Fighting, and Surviving Date and Acquaintance Rape*, with an afterword by Mary P. Koss (New York: HarperPerennial, 1994), p. 253.

33. When Susan Estrich wrote *Real Rape* in 1987, she was attempting to contend with all those cases in which sexual relations are forced on a woman against her will and without her consent, cases that "are not dealt with as crimes by the criminal justice system, nor even considered rape by the women themselves." Estrich, *Real Rape*, p. 8.

34. From the film *At Nightfall*, directed by Ariella Azoulay (2005).

35. New York Radical Feminists, *Rape*, p. 45.

36. I will deal more fully below with the relation between these arenas, in which women are abandoned and sanctified, and those in which women are raped.

37. The abandonment of women on the basis of their sex has made them, exactly in what concerns their sex, abandoned. A woman's womb, from which all men and women have emerged, has turned into a place of control and a place of abandonment. The birth of gynecology as a science of men and the removal of the management of birth from women, who historically had handled it, occurred simultaneously. See Hilary Maraland and Anne Marie Rafferty (eds.), *Midwives, Society and Childbirth: Debates and Controversies in the Modern Period*, Studies in the Social History of Medicine (New York: Routledge, 1997).

38. See Geoffrey Robertson, *Crimes against Humanity: The Struggle for Global Justice* (London: Penguin, 1999), Vigarello, *A History of Rape*, Catherine A. MacKinnon, *Sex Equality*, and Kamir, *Feminism, Rights, and the Law*. On the reliability accorded in the 1970s to women who'd been raped after the term "rape trauma syndrome" entered the medical debate, see José Bruner, "Trauma and Justice: Moral, Legal, and Political Trajectories of Trauma Discourse from Wilhelmine Germany to Post-Apartheid South Africa," in Austin Sarat, Nadav Davidovitch, and Mical Alberstein (eds.), *Trauma and Memory: Subjective and Collective Experiences: Legal, Medical, and Cultural Perspectives* (Stanford, CA: Stanford University Press, 2008) and Ann W. Burgess and Lynda L. Holmstrom, "Rape Trauma Syndrome," *American Journal of Psychiatry* 131 (1974).

39. See Linda Nead's critical discussion of the sanctified boundary between high art and pornography, which made nudity acceptable in art, *Female Nude* (New York: Routledge, 1992). See also Catherine A. MacKinnon's discussion of pornographic images in *Toward a Feminist Theory of the State* (Cambridge, MA: Harvard

University Press, 1989), Frances Ferguson's *Pornography, the Theory: What Utilitarianism Did to Action* (Chicago: University of Chicago Press, 2004), which analyzes the rise of pornography at the end of the eighteenth century, and the activist practice of the Guerrilla Girls in revealing the data on the frequency of female nudity inside the museum.

40. On the constitution of woman as a visual fetish, see Wolf, *The Beauty Myth*.

41. See Orly Lubin, *Women Reading Women* (Haifa: Haifa University Press, Zmora-Modan, 2003) and Mieke Bal, *Double Exposures* (New York: Routledge, 1996).

42. See for example MacKinnon, *Sex Equality*.

43. See, for example, the battle against pornography being waged by MacKinnon, Andrea Dworkin, Robin Morgan, and others; see also the anthology edited by Laura Lederer, *Take Back the Night: Women on Pornography* (New York: Morrow, 1980).

44. In her discussion of the Iranian director Abbas Kiarostami's film *The Wind Will Carry Us*, Joan Copjec analyzes private space as a space ascribed to the subject that is independent of the spaces recognized as public or private. This private space must remain "inviolable," she writes in *The Descent into Shame* (unpublished manuscript). She attempts to sketch a private space that upsets the distinction between private and public and is independent of it. I, too, am trying to sketch such a space, but to point to its constitution as a result of the violence that seeks to disrupt it.

45. The collection of these data was not dependent on the formulation of a single definition of rape, and to this day it remains difficult to find any such that will satisfy all the various agents responsible for dealing with it.

46. In "Black Slavery," written in 1782, Zamor, a black slave, kills a white guard because the guard ordered him to hit his beloved Mirza, a black woman slave, who didn't respond to his advances. When Mirza tells Zamor that she will ask for the Master's pardon, he answers her: "what could you say to him?" In this rhetorical question, de Gouges captured simultaneously the discursive silence on both gender and race. Olympe de Gouges, "Black Slavery, or The Happy Shipwreck," In Doris Y. Kadish and Françoise Massardier-Kenny (eds.), *Translating Slavery: Gender and Race in French Women's Writing, 1783–1823* (Kent, OH: Kent State University Press, 1994), p. 110.

47. History records countless such cases in which, as Frances Ferguson puts it, the woman's lack of consent at the time of the rape is supplanted by agreement to a wedding ceremony. "Rape and the Rise of the Novel," *Representations*, no. 20 (1987).

48. These are categories used for the definition of sexual assault widely prevalent among rape-victim treatment centers.

49. According to the Association of Rape Crisis Center in Israel.

50. The abandonment of women in their own countries is only one side of the problem, in addition to the rape of women in wartime as a customary weapon of war. I am not dealing with these types of rape cases here, however, nor with rape in traditional societies where complaining about rape could be more dangerous to the woman than the rape itself.

51. Foucault, *The Birth of the Clinic*, pp. 107–25. Foucault explicitly discusses the gaze and speech in regard to new objects that are intervened with, but doesn't explicitly thematize this level of intervention. On these three levels in Foucault, see Adi Ophir, *The Order of Evils* (New York: Zone Books, 2005), pp. 61–79.

52. I'm focusing on photographic images, and not with cinematic representations of rape, where the situation is slightly different. On rape in the cinema see Juliet Flower MacCannell, "Between The Two Fears," *Cardozo Law Review* 24, no. 6 (August 2003); Sarah Projansky, *Watching Rape: Film and Television in Postfeminist Culture* (New York: New York University Press, 2001); Molly Haskell, *From Reverence to Rape: The Treatment of Women in the Movies* (Chicago: University of Chicago Press, 1973); Lynne Farrow, "The Independent Woman and the Cinema of Rape," in New York Radical Feminists, *Rape*; and Orit Kamir, *Framed: Women in Law and Film* (Durham, NC: Duke University Press, 2005).

53. Several dozen sites on the Internet facilitate perusal of the hundreds of slogans and catch phrases coined over the course of the past thirty-five years. Some of them offer their services to graffiti artists and sign painters, while others purvey ready-made pins and banners. See www.kersplebedeb.com (last accessed April 6, 2007).

54. The ad appeared on page 5 of *The Daily Free Press* on January 31, 2005, and the endorsement at the bottom assigns the rights to the rape treatment center of Santa Monica Hospital.

55. This is also true of books that deal with rape.

56. See John Berger, *Ways of Seeing* (Harmondsworth, UK: Penguin, 1990); Griselda Pollock, *Vision and Difference: Femininity, Feminism and the Histories of Art* (London: Routledge, 1988); Bal, *Double Exposures*; Nead, *Female Nude*; and Linda Nochlin, *Women, Art and Power: And Other Essays* (New York: HarperCollins, 1988).

57. Walter Kälin, Lars Müller, and Judith Wyttenbach (eds.), *The Face of Human Rights* (Baden: Lars Müller Publishers, 2004), p. 605. Throughout this comprehensive book, rape isn't mentioned as a category at all. It is missing from the table of

contents, which lists the various rights with which the book deals: the right to think and to believe, the right to education, the right to work, the right to food and health, the right to habitation and privacy, and so on. Rape is also missing from the index, which lists various categories in regard to women: discrimination, domestic violence, murder for the sake of family honor, and trade in women.

58. In 1949, in the framework of the Fourth Geneva Convention, rape, as a way of fighting the enemy, was made illegal. However, it wasn't included in the definition of grave breaches, which has made it difficult to enforce the provision. Thus, for example, the rape of millions of German women by Stalin's soldiers was never brought to court, and the rapes committed by Nazi war criminals weren't mentioned in their indictments. Only much later, in the late 1980s, did the rape of women by Nazi criminals appear as a topic in its own right. On the rape of German women, see Robertson, *Crimes against Humanity* and Irit Rogoff, "From Ruins to Debris: The Feminization of Fascism in German History Museums," in Daniel J. Sherman and Irit Rogoff (eds.), *Museum Culture: Histories, Discourses, Spectacles* (Minneapolis: University of Minnesota Press, 1994). On rape in colonial contexts, see Juliet Flower MacCannell, *The Hysteric's Guide to the Future Female Body* (Minneapolis: University of Minnesota Press, 2000), as well as J. M. Coetzee's *Disgrace* (New York: Viking, 1999) and the essays on it in *scrutiny2* 7, no. 1 (2002) by Hannan Hever, "Facing *Disgrace*: Coetzee and the Israeli intellectual," Louise Bethlehem, "Pliant/Complaint; Grace/Disgrace; Plaint/Complaint," and Ariella Azoulay, "An Alien Woman / A Permitted Woman: On J. M. Coetzee's *Disgrace*." It was only in the 1990s, after the establishment of the rape camps in Bosnia, that rape was defined as a crime against humanity. But even then, explicitly identified and defined at last, it still wasn't presented as a crime against women.

59. In 1937, the Japanese army invaded Nanking, killing some three hundred thousand Chinese in a week, including tens of thousands of women who were brutally raped before they were murdered. On the rape in Nanking, see Iris Chang, *The Rape of Nanking: The Forgotten Holocaust of World War II* (New York: Penguin, 1997).

60. On rape in Sudan, see the report issued on July 19, 2004, by Amnesty International, entitled "Darfur: Rape as a Weapon of War: Sexual Violence and its Consequences," available on-line at http://web.amnesty.org/library/Index/ENGA FR540882004?open&of=ENG-SDN (last accessed November 29, 2007).

61. On the rape camps in Bosnia, see Beverly Allen, *Rape WarFare: The Hidden Genocide in Bosnia-Herzegovina and Croatia* (Minneapolis: University of Minnesota Press, 1996).

62. The accessibility of data banks, including visual resources, in the Internet age makes it possible at least to chart the inventory in any field. A more significant exception to the rule is constituted by pornography sites, to which I will also refer below.

63. Camille Paglia, a prominent opponent of rape's presentation as violence, writes: "For the course of a decade feminists instructed their students to say 'Rape is a crime of violence, not of sex.' This Shirley Temple folly in candy wrapping has exposed young women to disaster. Having been misled by feminism, they didn't expect rape from the nice boys from good homes who sat next to them in class." "Rape and the Modern Sex War," in Adele M. Stan (ed.), *Debating Sexual Correctness* (New York: Delta, 1995), p. 23. The argument between two philosophers, Christina Somers and Marilyn Friedman, whether Rhett Butler raped Scarlet O'Hara succinctly represents the general argument. It is summarized in Burgess-Jackson, *Rape*.

64. Since I am dealing here with the issue of consent, I am constrained to simplify the complex debate that presents different variations on the theme: "against her will," "by means of force," and so on. Books and essays have been written on these essential variations, including those by MacKinnon, Estrich, Burgess-Jackson, and Kamir already cited.

65. I also received explanations of this kind from several agents with whom I was in contact in my search for rape photographs. Those providing the explanations, both men and women, also hedged their bets and said it didn't mean that rape photographs don't exist.

66. One group of images to which access is restricted to the expert gaze consists of photographs of the rape victim's genitalia, which are taken by the police as part of the procedure of investigating complaints of rape. These images, too, join what might be termed the hard core of rape images. The gaze on them is restricted, delineated, compartmentalized, and managed.

67. According to Iris Chang, these are just some of the photographs of rape victims taken by the Japanese rapists. She provides no explanation as to what may have become of the other photographs. It is unclear whether they were kept in public archives, destroyed, or fell into private hands. *The Rape of Nanking*, pp. 9–13.

68. Garcia was raped and immediately afterward killed one of her assailants. She was charged with second-degree manslaughter, and her defender wasn't allowed to present evidence relating to the rape on account of which she performed her action. From a legal perspective, this wasn't a rape trial (hence the quotation marks), but specifically for that reason, the trial drew intense attention from the antirape movement, which demonstrated overwhelming sympathy for Garcia and

attempted to change the categories of reference toward her and to establish a new gender agenda through her. See Bevacqua, *Rape on the Public Agenda*, pp. 127–28.

69. The emphasis is on the present, because the display of bodies from the past, of both exalted figures and simple people, has never stood at the center of such a public debate.

70. My initial search for images of rape led me to dozens of sex sites on the Internet in which rape is one of the routine categories.

71. The case of former Israeli beauty queen and Miss World, Linor Aberjil, who was raped on the eve of her coronation by someone who volunteered to drive her to the ceremony, shows the difficulty of the rape victim in dealing not with the act of confession itself, which is generally seen as a heroic action and garners support, but with the identification between her and the rapist. Since the evening when she confessed during a live television broadcast to having been raped, Aberjil has avoided mentioning the rape in her interviews. The media's abstention from asking her about it suggests that Aberjil conditions her consent to being interviewed on not being asked about the rape and that the media have accepted her terms. I'm grateful to Merav Michaely for her assistance in reconstructing the depiction of the case in the media.

72. Quoted in Vigarello, *A History of Rape*, p. 209.

73. Alcoff and Gray-Rosendale, "Survivor Discourse," p. 27.

74. In "Rape and the Rise of the Novel," Frances Ferguson sketches the outline of a rape scenario in the framework of which the woman is assigned a role that manufactures her as a vulnerable and penetrable inner space, pp. 90–94.

75. The problematic contention that seeks to protect and in effect sanctify women's speech is also voiced by Susan Brownmiller in *Men, Women, and Rape* (New York: Ballantine, 1975) and Susan Estrich in *Real Rape*. Ferguson disagrees with them in "Rape and the Rise of the Novel."

76. Sylvia Plath, *The Journals of Sylvia Plath*, eds. Ted Hughes and Frances McCullough (New York: Ballantine, 1991), pp. 5–6.

77. *Ibid.*, p. 5.

78. I have deliberately broken off the quotation from Plath at a point where it is unclear whether she was ultimately raped or not. The situation that Plath describes is something that I would like to negotiate in public, to propose seeing the image that arises from it as part of the iconography of rape and not to reject it only because continued perusal of the diary would enable the reader to say, "Oh well, she wasn't raped, he only kissed her." Plath continues: "And suddenly his mouth was on mine, hard, vehement, his tongue darting between my lips, his arms like iron around me.

"Ilo, Ilo!," I don't know whether I screamed or whispered, struggling to break free, my hands striking wildly, futilely against his great strength. At last he let me go, and stood back." Plath, *Journals*, p. 6.

79. I am referring here both to the practice of instrumental uses of photographs, especially in nationalist contexts, and to theory, of which Sontag is a distinct representative, that considers the viewing of photographs to be mainly in the service of gestures of remembrance.

80. Contemporary studies in the history of art point to a recurring model in the presentation of women who've been raped — reconciliation with the rapist and the rape, culminating in marriage and offspring. See Diane Wolfthal, *Images of Rape: The "Heroic" Tradition and Its Alternatives* (Cambridge: Cambridge University Press, 1999). See also a study that defends masterpieces anew from being stained with the imprint of rape, Roger Kimball, *The Rape of the Masters: How Political Correctness Sabotages Art* (San Francisco, CA: Encounter Books, 2004), as well as the exhaustive catalogue of works by Artemisia Gentileschi in Mary D. Garrard, *Artemisia Gentileschi: The Image of the Female Hero in Italian Baroque Art* (Princeton, NJ: Princeton University Press, 1989).

81. Such images include those by Ana Mendieta documenting herself staged as a rape victim, those by Lorna Simpson, the texts affixed to which pit the rape victim's personal testimony against the police and judicial discourse that would turn her body into evidence, into an exhibit, a photograph by Yehudit Levin in which she's seen lying on the ground with a helicopter hovering over her, and the image of the bloodied feminine sex by Yocheved Weinfeld.

82. The installation was shown in the framework of the exhibition titled The Doll's House, curated by Sarit Shapira.

83. These are lyrics from a song by Sharon Ben Ezer and Pollyanna Frank for my film *On the Threshold* (2001).

84. The text unfolds the context of the assault. It concerns a mute young woman who was brutally raped one day by an unknown man. The attack restored her capacity for speech all at once, and with it as well the childhood memory of the moment she had fallen silent. That moment, too, had been defined by a rape. She was raped by her father.

85. Such images do exist in cinema, but as I've already mentioned, I'm not dealing here with the specific problematic of rape in cinema.

86. This body of work includes studies by Mieke Bal, John Berger, Griselda Pollock, Irit Rogoff, Joan Copjec, Juliet Flower MacCannell, Wendy Kozol, Mary Ann Duane, Amelia Jones, Orly Lubin, Linda Nead, Molly Nesbit, Diane Wolfthal, and Laura Mulvey.

87. Later in the same interview, Varda describes the difficulties in overcoming the pervasive conventions of exhibiting the female body and her way of dealing with them: "I was interested in showing a nude woman alone, without any other purpose than her own in feeling herself alone and naked." Agnès Varda, filmed interview.

88. See Carole Pateman, *The Sexual Contract* (Stanford, CA: Stanford University Press, 1988).

89. In order to fight rape, Marcus asserts, this movement needs to be augmented also by the struggle to change the status of woman's sexuality from an "inner space" to a fluctuating sexuality in constant motion. Marcus, "Fighting Bodies, Fighting Words," pp. 398–400.

90. Even the use of force during rape cannot always be seen in still photographs. However, rape may occur without the need to exercise violence. The very expectation of seeing traces of violence in rape images is a regression regarding the common understanding and has been recognized by the law in many countries.

91. This is a familiar statement. Ofer Glazer, who was charged with making obscene advances toward two women, was recently recorded saying exactly this to one of the complainants at his trial. See the report by Zvi Harel, *Ha'aretz*, May 23, 2005.

92. On the difficulty in identifying an event as rape and in getting others to acknowledge it, see Estrich's *Real Rape*, especially the first chapter, "Is This Rape?" Estrich attempts to reconstruct the difficulties in turning rape into something that the legal system can discuss as rape, or as the subtitle of the book puts it: "How the Legal System Victimizes Women Who Say No."

93. I am grateful to Orit Kamir for illuminating me on this point regarding the uncertainty generated by legislation, allowing me to forge a link between this uncertainty in the legal and visual fields.

94. A comprehensive discussion of these issues would take me too far from the topic of the present chapter. However, I can demonstrate this through the example of the work of Laura Mulvey. In her key essay on visual pleasure, she formulates the position of the cinematic spectator as a masculine position from which women can be constituted only as fetish. This theoretical tool proposed by her, which was brilliant at the time, became over the years, in her hands and in those of her followers, an approach that perpetuates the same power relations that it seeks to describe critically. In the films that she made in parallel to her theoretical work, Mulvey formulated a different kind of cinema that avoids the traps she described and that in doing so topples the traditional structure of the spectator's function, constructs a new spectator's position, and outlines new ways of structuring the cinematic narrative.

95. Joan Copjec, *The Descent into Shame*, unpublished manuscript.

96. Sharon Marcus, in an essay on rape that outlines a strategy for fighting and preventing it, points to the way in which rape structures woman's sexuality as an invaded interiority as the first thing that needs to be fought. "Fighting Bodies, Fighting Words: A Theory and Politics of Rape Prevention," in Judith Butler and Joan W. Scott (eds.), *Feminists Theorize the Political* (New York: Routledge, 1992).

97. Various factors involved in treating rape attest that it is one of the less-reported crimes, contributing to the difficulty of processing statistical data in regard to it. In an evening discussion on rape conducted at Mishkenot Shaananim in the winter of 2004, Ruth Wind, one of the founders of the Rape Crisis Center in Tel Aviv, tried to explain the astonishing finding she presented, according to which there has been no decrease in the number of rape incidents, despite the intense activities of rape treatment centers. The more that the awareness of rape grows, she contended, the more incidents are reported, and it is impossible to know whether the overall number of rape incidents has risen or dropped, since the data regarding the past was collected in times and conditions in which women didn't report rape.

98. In Chapter 1, I tried to show that the treatment of rape and women's abandonment is conducted along the lines of humanitarian assistance, rather than by dint of the sovereign's responsibility for its own citizens.

99. These photographs can currently be found on several Internet sites. Their publication is mentioned in Susan J. Brison, "Torture or 'Good Old American Pornography'?" *Chronicle of Higher Education*, June 4, 2004.

100. In that article, Brison mentions the photographs and describes their repudiation as forged. She also wonders at the significance of the scandal accompanying the publication of photographs of Iraqi prisoners in the context of the pornography industry: "Why should the sexual molestation and humiliation of Iraqi prisoners (and their photographing) arouse an international outcry when such things are done to women around the world (and are photographed) in a multi-billion-dollar pornographic industry that is considered entertainment?" See http://ics.leeds.ac.uk/papers/vp01.cfm?outfit=ks&requesttimeout=500&folder= 42&paper=141 (last accessed November 29, 2007).

101. In an unpublished essay on the photographs from Abu Ghraib, Wendy Kozol mentions the women's photographs, but doesn't elaborate on them. Kozol, "Abu Ghraib and the Dilemma of Spectatorship," unpublished essay.

102. Susan Sontag, "Regarding the Torture of Others," *New York Times*, May 23, 2004, available on-line at http://southerncrossreview.org/35/sontag.htm (last accessed November 29, 2007).

103. *Ibid.*

104. My discussion focuses only on the photographs from Abu Ghraib in which sexual injury is shown. Kozol has attempted to oppose the hegemonic spectator's position proposed to the viewer of these photographs in "Abu Ghraib and the Dilemma of Spectatorship."

105. Luke Harding, "Focus Shifts to Jail Abuse of Women," *Guardian Unlimited*, March 24, 2005.

106. I cannot say for sure whether this is all that is shown at these sites, or whether they also purvey porn that doesn't directly involve crude violence, nor do I know anything about the presence or frequency of rape images in pornographic books and magazines.

107. On viewing pornography on Internet sites and on the type of connection with those who log into them, see Zabet Patterson, "Going On-Line: Consuming Pornography in the Digital Era," in Linda Williams (ed.), *Porn Studies* (Durham, NC: Duke University Press, 2004).

108. I surfed only the public domain, which is accessible without payment, and looked only at stills, avoiding video material.

109. As mentioned above, in this essay I am not referring at all to the issue of rape in cinema.

110. The book edited by Linda Williams entitled *Porn Studies* is a landmark in this field, and many of the essays in it were written by students from her seminars, who are today the heralds of this new field.

111. In *Porn Studies*, there is not one essay dealing with the topic of rape, and it is mentioned only twice in two brief passages.

112. Linda Williams, *Hard Core: Power, Pleasure, and the "Frenzy of the Visible"* (Berkeley: University of California Press, 1989), p. 50.

113. In her introduction to *Porn Studies*, Linda Williams presents these data, including also the figures regarding cinema production: Hollywood makes 400 films each year, whereas the porn industry makes 10,000 (pp. 1–2).

114. See Ilana Hammerman, *In Foreign Parts: Trafficking in Women in Israel* [in Hebrew] (Tel Aviv: 'Am 'oved, 2004)

115. In *Pornography, the Theory*, Frances Ferguson attempts to deal seriously with the assertion by Justice Potter Stuart, who explained how he knew something was obscene: "When I see it, I know it for what it is." Ferguson makes use of this statement, which drew fierce criticism from Katherine MacKinnon, to attack the expectation that "the law should not try to regulate anything that generates less than universal agreement" (p. 8).

116. The question that looms over Gorris's film, as it does over any film that chooses to show its spectators a rape scene, is not how to represent rape, but how to behave within the cinematic medium, which requires staging another rape on the set in order to deal with rape.

117. In the summer of 2001, the Center for Assistance to Victims of Sexual Assault in Tel Aviv published on the cover of one of its publications the photograph of a woman holding a camera to her eyes. The figure is photographed at a neutral and featureless site and so remains an *énoncé* of the possibility of woman's taking photographs and returning her gaze, rather than an *énoncé* of the production and distribution of rape photographs.

118. This is not the first time that an artist or scholar will have identified clear traces of rape and sexual injury in images from the past. It is part of the struggle against rape that has been going on since the 1970s and points to the glorification of rape in art. See, among others, Wolfthal, *Images of Rape*, Lynn Farrow's essay "The Independent Woman and the Cinema of Rape," in which she analyzes rape to the strains of Mozart's music in *A Clockwork Orange*, and Kamir, *Framed*.

CHAPTER SIX: PHOTOGRAPHING THE VERGE OF CATASTROPHE

1. Most cases of destruction in the Occupied Territories — house demolitions, eradications, the digging of trenches, the placing of obstacles, the blocking of wells, and the operation of what Amira Hess has called "weapons of light construction," which have utterly transformed the Palestinian living space — are not the result of any outburst of direct violence in response to resistance, but the deliberate application of instruments meant to damage buildings, objects, and the space itself without directly harming human beings. Amira Hess, "Colonialism under the Guise of a Peace Process" [in Hebrew], *Theoria ve-Bikoret* 24 (2004).

2. Another distinctive example that Heiman addresses is the use of the icon of mother and child, whose artistic standing exchanges its Christian particularity with universal compassion. Michal Heiman, "Attacks on Linking," paper presented at the Art and War conference, Goethe-Platform, Tel Aviv, 2004. On the use of this icon in the war in Yugoslavia see Wendy Kozol, "Domesticating NATO's War in Kosovo: (In)Visible Bodies and the Dilemma of Photojournalism," *Meridians: Feminism, Transnationalism, Race* 4, no. 2 (2004).

3. On the various descriptions of the postmodernist condition, see Jean-François Lyotard, *The Postmodern Condition: A Report on Knowledge*, trans. Geoff Bennington and Brian Massumi (Minneapolis: University of Minnesota Press, 1984), David Harvey, *The Condition of Postmodernity* (Oxford: Blackwell, 1989), and Jean

Baudrillard *Simulacra and Simulation*, trans. Sheila Faria Glaser (Ann Arbor: University of Michigan Press, 1994), Mark Seltzer, *Serial Killers* (New York: Routledge, 1998), and others.

4. On this topic see Mark Seltzer, "Wound Culture: Trauma in the Pathological Public Sphere," *October*, no. 80 (Spring 1997).

5. On the appearance of needs as an object of political intervention, see Hannah Arendt's discussion of the French Revolution in *On Revolution* (Harmondsworth, UK: Penguin, 1990), pp. 59–114.

6. On photographs of the wounded and sick in hospitals, see Adam Baruch, *Seder Yom* [in Hebrew] (Jerusalem: Keter, 2000).

7. Michal Heiman, "Holding," in *Everything Could Be Seen*, exhibition catalogue (Tel Aviv: Um el Fachem Art Gallery, 2004).

8. Heiman in conversation with me, November 28, 2005.

9. Ruthie Sinai, "They're Expected to Contain the Horrors of the Intifada and Keep Silent," *Ha'aretz*, November 11, 2005, p. B4. The title is derived from the figures relating to a rise in sexual assaults that was oddly accompanied by a drop in the number of applications to assistance centers.

10. On this in connection with the first intifada and the occupation in general, see my film *A Sign from Heaven* and the work of Professor Simcha Landau, who was interviewed for the film.

11. On the illustrative photograph and its role in determining the limits of discourse and demarcating the objects that can be seen in its framework, see in Chapter Four my discussion of the figure of the blindfolded Palestinian.

12. *Photo Rape* is part of a larger series *Attacks on Linking, 2001–2004*. Heiman titled this series after Wilfred Bion's article from 1959 that focuses on issues of destruction and attacks on linking in thinking and communication.

13. See the regular column by Gideon Levy and Miki Kratsman in *Ha'aretz*. This is one of the few media sites that regularly covers Palestinian victims, but it is nevertheless a weekly magazine, produced days after the event has elapsed.

14. See Adam Baruch's analyses of the assimilation of the military reporter into the figure of the military spokesperson in *Seder Yom* and in *Betom Lev* [in Hebrew] (Jerusalem: Keter, 2001) and Daniel Dor's analyses of the media coverage of the intifada in *Newspapers Under the Influence* (Tel Aviv: Babel, 2001).

15. Roland Barthes, *Camera Lucida: Reflections on Photography*, trans. Richard Howard (New York: Hill and Wang, 1981), p. 3.

16. In the *Tests* (1 and 2) she created, following the TAT (Thematic Apperception Test), Michal Heiman employed the model of projection as a practice of

looking at photographs. See *Michal Heiman Test No. 1* (Kassel: Documenta X, 1996) and *Michal Heiman Test (M.H.T.) No 2: My Mother-in-Law, Test for Women* (Quimper: Le Quartier, 1998). In the manual that accompanied these tests, I have discussed photography's double role in the discourse on the museum and in psychoanalytic discourse. Ariella Azoulay, "Michal Heiman Test — Manual," in *Michal Heiman Test No. 2: My Mother-in-Law — a Test for Women Only* (Quimper: Le Quartier, 1998).

17. Barthes, *Camera Lucida*, p. 8.

18. *Ibid.*, p. 4.

19. *Ibid.*

20. *Ibid.*, p. 6.

21. All quotations from Miki Kratsman are from a series of unpublished conversations we held between 2000 and 2006.

22. Tens of thousands of workers used to pass from Gaza through the Erez crossing every year, from the beginning of the occupation in 1967 until the beginning of the first intifada. On the changes in the number of Palestinian workers in Israel, see B'Tselem, "Builders of Zion: Human Rights Violations of Palestinians from the Occupied Territories Working in Israel and the Settlements," available online at http://www.btselem.org/English/Publications/Index.asp ?YF=1999& image.x=10&image.y=7 (last accessed November 30, 2007).

23. Israel has used checkpoints since 1967, but it was only after the Oslo Accords that they covered the whole territory and became the main control apparatus. On the connection between Oslo Accords and the system of checkpoints see Hess, "Colonialism under the Guise of a Peace Process."

24. Painting from photographs is another way to make the photograph speak, as exemplified by the work of David Reeb. See Ariella Azoulay, "Let's Have Another War," in *Let's Have Another War (David Reeb)*, exhibition catalogue (Tel Aviv: Mpublishers, 1996).

25. Faten Fawzy Nastas, "It Was Already Too Late," in *Everything Could Be Seen*, exhibition catalogue (Tel Aviv: Um el Fahem Art Gallery, 2004), p. 19.

26. Throughout his book on the checkpoints, Azmi Bishara calls all those who participate in the constriction of the Palestinians' movements "masters of the land." *Checkpoint* (Arles: Actes Sud, 2004).

27. Both quotations are from interviews I conducted for the purpose of making the film *The Food Chain* (2003).

28. See Aïm Deüelle Lüski, "Fragments of Horizontal Thinking," *Plastika*, no. 3 (1999).

29. On photography's entry into the American judicial discourse, see Tal

Golan, "Learning to See: The Beginning of Visual Technologies in Medicine and Law," in *Law, Society and Culture*, The Buchman Faculty of Law Series (Tel Aviv: Tel Aviv University, 2003).

30. I am relying on remarks made by Richard Cook, UNRWA general manager, East Jerusalem, as spoken in the film *The Food Chain*.

31. Interview from *The Food Chain*.

32. On the infinite regression of meaning, which can only ever be stated on the occasion of the next *énoncé*, see Gilles Deleuze, *The Logic of Sense*, trans. Mark Lester with Charles Stivale, ed. Constantin V. Boundas (New York: Columbia University Press, 1990).

33. Even then, as I have shown in Chapter Two, a photograph cannot belong to anyone.

34. He did not measure the lighting or focus the lens, either, but thanks to automatic cameras, conventional photographers also do not have to perform such operations.

35. The discussion of the instrument is restricted to the professional's dimension of "achieving the objective" and therefore if it takes place, it is generally among "professionals."

36. On the "photographer unknown" see Adam Baruch, "Michal Heiman's Installation: *At the Edge of the Museum*, the Poet Rachel and Artist Aviva Uri," in John Stathatos (ed.), *Persistence of Memory*, exhibition catalogue, The Third Israeli Photography Biennale (Ein Harod: Mishkan Le'Omanut, 1991).

37. See, for example, the exhibition of Yakov Agor's work, which Heiman curated at the Camera Obscura Gallery in the early 1990s, which was one of the first to express concern for the history of Israeli photography.

38. On the attempt to erase this gap, see Baudrillard, *Simulacre et simulations*.

39. In the chapter on history in my book on Benjamin, *Once Upon a Time: Photography following Walter Benjamin* [in Hebrew] (Ramat-Gan: Bar Ilan University Press, 2006), I have attempted to reconstruct these relations on the basis of his understanding of the camera's modus operandi.

40. In the last chapter of *The Human Condition*, Arendt analyzes the loss of the shared sense since Descartes: "This is the spirit's game with itself, which occurs when the spirit becomes sealed off from reality and 'feels' only itself." Hannah Arendt, *The Human Condition* (1958; Chicago: University of Chicago Press, 1998), p. 284.

41. The interview is taken from the film *Angel of History*. See also Heiman's exhibition *Photo Rape*, in which she handles photographs in different ways, empha-

sizing that the therapeutic language which she employs is directed toward both the photographed women and the photograph.

42. Only with the onset of the French Revolution did the common practice of stripping and beating women in public as punishment for adultery, in a sort of field court-martial, finally come to an end.

43. Heiman's work on the press photograph in the context of the newspaper page already had begun in the 1980s. See Adam Baruch, "Art-Chronicle: The Option for Creative and Informed Israeli Photography," in *The Second Israeli Photography Biennale* (Jerusalem: The Domino Press, 1988).

44. Kratsman, in an unpublished conversation with me.

45. From a conversation with Kratsman held in May 2003 (unpublished).

46. Heiman in conversation with me, September 25, 2003.

47. In this context, two additional projects should be mentioned, both by women artists — Sigalit Landau and Alice Klingman — who have systematically collected newspapers printed since the beginning of the second intifada. Both Landau and Klingman extend the domain of the gaze at images of horror into a tactile, energetic, and physical experience. Landau used them as papier-mâché to create poisoned "fruits" for at her exhibition The Country at the Alon Segev Gallery. See Sigalit Landau, *The Country* (Jerusalem: Spartizan / D. K. Graubart Ltd., 2003). Klingman wrapped balloons in them.

48. Heiman in conversation with me, November 28, 2005.

49. For more on this, see the beginning of Chapter Four. In this article "Mobilizing Shame," Thomas Keenan analyzes the dissolution of the paradigm of the concealment of information together with the paradigm of mobilizing shame. Thomas Keenan, "Mobilizing Shame," *South Atlantic Quarterly* 103, no. 2/3 (Spring/Summer, 2004), pp. 435–49.

50. Miki Kratsman in the movie *Angel of History* (2001).

51. After the beginning of the second intifada, the army declared the Occupied Territories to be closed military zones. The few Israeli photographers who insist on working in the Occupied Territories have to sign a document that waives any responsibility by the army for their security.

52. Most of the images published in *Hadashot* during the first intifada were primarily taken over the course of roaming through the Occupied Territories, the camera capturing moments of violent physical confrontation that are not necessarily defined as "events." Today, it is almost impossible for such photographs to be captured by Israeli cameras working for the Israeli press.

53. Additional details about the difficulties which the Israeli government places

in the way of Palestinian photographers can be read in the various reports of the Committee to Protect Journalists, www.cpj.org (last accessed on April 24, 2007).

54. In Hebrew, "to rape" is used also to mean "to force someone to do something."

55. See, for example, the way in which the question of showing the photographs of suicide bombings or of dead and wounded soldiers was smoothed over in the media.

56. From the standpoint of assistance agencies, media interests, and so on, it's impossible to erase the gaps between the situation of people devoid of citizen status who have been struck by disaster and citizens whose civilian protection is suspended for a limited time by disaster. Just the same, during times of sudden disaster, citizens are cast into a situation without civilian protection that gives them common ground with individuals devoid of citizen status.

57. In *The Body At Risk*, Carol Squiers retraces various photographic projects during the twentieth century sharing this objective. Carol Squiers, *The Body at Risk: Photography, Illness and Healing* (New York: International Center of Photography, 2005).

58. On famous instances in which the photographer with his camera stood aside and didn't warn the photographed of the danger threatening him, see Vincent Lavoie, *L'instant-monument* (Montreal: Dazibao, 2001).

59. In conversations I had with several press photographers, their commitment to universal values was reiterated and formulated differently by each. See the conversations with Miki Kratsman, Alex Levac, Shlomo Arad, Khaled Zigary, and others in Ariella Azoulay, *How Does It Look to You?* (Tel Aviv: Babel, 2000). A few of them were integrated in Ariella Azoulay, *The Power of Image in Contemporary Democracy*, trans. Ruvik Danieli (Cambridge, MA: MIT Press, 2001).

60. In my movie *Chaira's Smile*, I interviewed a conscientious objector who had been in charge of a soldier who prevented a woman in labor from reaching the hospital. In reply to my questions concerning the nature of the inspection, he answered: "Every woman with a bit of a belly could be pregnant." The body of the Palestinian, male or female, deceptively disguises its truth, which the soldier knows before he has even seen the body.

61. For more on the Palestinian body at the checkpoint, see the discussion of Sharif Waked's work in Chapter Eight.

62. From a conversation with "Y," representing the IDF spokesman, Central Command, on February 5, 2004.

63. In *Cappuccino in Ramallah*, Suad Amiri describes the frenzy that gripped the

soldiers checking her on her return from London after she told them that she had gone to dance. They were willing to accept any actual reason — just not that one. Suad Amiri, *Cappuccino in Ramallah* (Tel Aviv: Babel Publishers, 2003).

64. From the exhibition catalogue *Everything Could Be Seen.*

65. Oded Yedaya in regard to two demonstrations held on July 8 and September 2, 2004, from Yedaya's diary.

66. For more on the encounter between them, see Chapter 1, "Citizens of Disaster."

67. This is the modus operandi of the activists at the checkpoints in operations such as Mahsom Watch. In the past two years, the army has begun commissioning humanitarian units of its own or enlisting ex-soldiers in order to instill humanitarian logic into its activities, thus rendering superfluous any intervention by Israeli citizens who would do so by means other than the army. In the same conversation with "Y" of the IDF Spokesman's Office, I was given the following reply to my question, "What qualifies the soldiers at a checkpoint to decide whether a woman is pregnant or a patient really ill": "They aren't experts on pregnancy; they aren't doctors and not even medics. It's a harsh reality. It's hard for them to know. To deal with this, at the Kalandia checkpoint, we've added older people, volunteers, family men who come to provide that humane aspect — people who are parents and of sound judgment."

68. See the chapter "The Silver Platter" on photographs of Palestinian funerals and deaths in Ariella Azoulay and Adi Ophir, *Bad Days: Between Disaster and Utopia* [in Hebrew] (Tel Aviv: Resling, 2002).

69. From a text in preparation by Oded Yedaya, to be issued in conjunction with new photographs from the anarchists' demonstrations he has participated in regularly over the past several years.

Chapter Seven: The Gaze

1. Walter Benjamin formulated this exquisitely when he claimed that the cult value "does not give way without resistance. It falls back to a last entrenchment: the human countenance." Walter Benjamin, "The Work of Art in the Age of Its Technological Reproducibility," second version, in *Selected Writings, Volume 3, 1935–1938*, eds. Howard Eiland and Michael W. Jennings (Cambridge, MA: Belknap Press of Harvard University Press, 2002), p. 108.

2. Michal Heiman in an interview I conducted with her. Ariella Azoulay, *How Does It Look to You?* [in Hebrew] (Tel Aviv: Babel, 2000), p. 230.

3. Walter Benjamin, "Little History of Photography," in *Selected Writings,*

Volume 2, 1927–1934, eds. Michael W. Jennings, Howard Eiland, and Gary Smith (Cambridge, MA: Belknap Press of Harvard University Press, 1999), p. 510.

4. Jacques Lacan, *The Four Fundamental Concepts of Psychoanalysis*, ed. Jacques-Alain Miller, trans. Alan Sheridan (New York: Norton, 1978), p. 84. On the gaze in Lacan and Sartre, see Joan Copjec, *Imagine There's No Woman: Ethics and Sublimation* (Cambridge, MA: MIT Press, 2002).

5. Miki Kratsman and Eldad Rafaeli, "What Do You Have to Do There?" *Plastika*, no. 2 (1998), p. 71.

6. I'm referring to a gap different from the one characteristic of old reflex cameras, which produced a large, but foreseeable gap between the result and what was seen through the viewer, where the photographer knows the type of adjustment she should be making. (Another variation of this gap exists today, too, in digital photography.)

7. Kratsman talking with me, October 17, 2003.

8. This is what Benjamin called the "optical unconscious." Walter Benjamin, "The Work of Art in the Age of Its Technological Reproducibility," in *Selected Writings, Volume 4, 1938–1940*, eds. Howard Eiland and Michael W. Jennings (Cambridge, MA: Belknap Press of Harvard University Press, 2003), p. 266.

9. The photograph was printed in the *Hadashot* daily, which was the first newspaper that made a point of attaching a name to every Palestinian whose story was published. The fact that this photograph was printed without the name of the dead man (February 23, 1988) seems to indicate that the project undertaken by the paper did not go without saying and was beset by circumstantial or intentional difficulties.

10. According to Heiman, among the pages of the magazine offering instructions for amateur photographers on displaying their work, in between photographs of flower arrangements and fashion photography by the most prominent photographers, the magazine regularly displayed pictures of suicides or hangings, cleared for publication because the time that had elapsed since their archiving had made publication legal. All these photographs were presented without photographers' names — as "photographer unknown," in the wording of Heiman's stamp "with no consideration for the photographed people and their families."

11. The addressee's proxy, who can be the photographed person himself, may need the photograph for journalistic use, for sexual purposes, for family purposes, for illegal use, for political use, and so forth.

12. In a paraphrase on the Lacanian "subject supposed to know." See *The Four Fundamental Concepts of Psychoanalysis*, pp. 230–43.

13. Kratsman in a conversation with me, May 2003.

14. See Joan Copjec, *Imagine There's No Woman: Ethics and Sublimation* (Cambridge, MA: MIT Press, 2002), p. 220.

15. Kratsman in a conversation with me, May 2003.

16. From time to time, photographers organize protests against attempts to breach the contract and to prevent them from taking pictures. For instance, forty-one thousand members of the German journalists union decided to boycott Bob Dylan when he prohibited taking pictures of him. (See the item by Reuters in *Ha'aretz,* October 19, 2003.)

17. From a conversation I conducted with Kratsman, October 16, 2003.

18. During the same conversation, Kratsman continued: "When the funeral was over there was army outside and they [the Palestinians] were afraid to leave and didn't let us leave the cemetery, either. Time passed, and they started leaving one by one, and when they saw that the army wasn't doing anything to them, they all left. When I left, some officer who was there came up to me and hugged me. That really pissed me off, because he hugged me beside the Palestinians. He wanted the Palestinians to think we were friends or something. I pushed him away."

19. *Ibid.*

20. He first began working there as a photojournalist for the daily *Hadashot* and later for the daily *Ha'aretz* and the weekly *Ha'ir.*

21. In a special supplement on the second year anniversary of the outbreak of the first intifada (December 7, 1989), the editors of the *Hadashot* weekend magazine amassed a collection of sayings expressing this situation: "We won't let stone throwers dictate our political agenda" (Itzhak Shamir, December 1987); "The situation is calming down. We'll soon be back to usual" (Dan Shomron, December 1987); "I believe we're in a slow process of restoring the peace" (Itzhak Rabin, January 1988); "No matter what they do, they'll have to calm down in the end. We'll station more troops here; it'll take time, but we'll overcome it" (Shmuel Goren, January 1988).

22. Among the photojournalists working at *Hadashot* at the time and pushing for this change were Alex Levac, Miki Kratsman, Moshe Shai, Yaron Kaminski, and Daniel Cohen.

23. I'm indirectly referring here to Lyotard's concept of the *différend* and to the fact that the Palestinian is positioned in a permanent *différend* relative to the logic of the judiciary in Israel, which disallows the voicing of his claim on grounds of "security," "state secrecy," and so forth. Jean-François Lyotard, *The Differend: Phrases in Dispute,* trans. Georges Van Den Abbeele (Minneapolis: University of Minnesota Press, 1988).

24. In the period between the first intifada and the second one, the army's attitude toward photography underwent a transformation. Photography continued to be viewed by commanders and soldiers as an enemy, but as one that could not be vanquished and that therefore should be collaborated with and used.

25. In English and French usage the act of photography retains the violent action of "taking" the picture from another.

26. Bernard Edelman, *Le droit saisi par la photographie: Éléments pour une théorie marxiste du droit* (Paris: Maspero, 1973). Images of comic-strip heroes or other commercial figures feature in litigation and discussions of ownership that usually focus on the question of profits. One of the first cases in the history of photography in which the ownership of a photograph was contested in court occurred as part of a lawsuit filed by Napoleon Sarony, the portrait photographer who photographed Oscar Wilde, against the printmakers Burrow-Giles, who had distributed 85,000 unauthorized copies of the portrait. In 1883, the court ruled in favor of Sarony. Needless to say, the photographed man was not a party in this lawsuit. The parties were the photographer and the distributing agency. On copyrights, the law, and images see Jane M. Gaines, *Contested Culture: The Image, the Voice, and the Law* (Chapel Hill: University of North Carolina Press, 1991).

27. Gaines, *Contested Culture*, p. 92.

28. There is no difference whatsoever between the legal presumption of determining the status of the technology and Barthes' philosophical presumption of determining the unique status of photography. Both treat photography as a medium for which specific essences can be determined, regardless of the social context in which it is operated.

29. See the discussion of the photograph by Wendy Kozol and Wendy Hesford in Wendy S. Hesford and Wendy Kozol (eds.), *Just Advocacy? Women's Human Rights, Transnational Feminisms, and the Politics of Representation* (New Brunswick, NJ: Rutgers University Press, 2005). They present it as a part of the construction of the United States as a "culture of security" through the individuation and control of visual images of the other.

30. "'This is the face that so captivated not only *National Geographic* readers but also anyone who saw her image around the world,' said Boyd Matson, host of the National Geographic television show *Explorer*, who was with the group that met with Gula." David Braun, "How They Found National Geographic's 'Afghan Girl,'" available online at http://news.nationalgeographic. com/news/2002/ 03/0311_ 020312_sharbat.html.

31. The magazine attributes the initiative to channel donations toward building

a school to Gula herself. In the various articles reporting on the barter, it was emphasized that Gula chose not to put the money to her own individual use, but rather to invest it for the benefit of the community. In this way, the magazine could retain Gula's exoticism, this time in a new form — she is a party in the barter, but remains pure within its framework, allowing the magazine not to expose itself as acting out of economic interests and to seem, rather, as a philanthropic institution.

32. Many donations were collected following the second photograph, totaling about half a million dollars. The largest donation from an individual donor was $18,000.

33. See the beginning of the discussion in the Chapter Six.

34. The test was activated at Documenta X. A few years later Heiman created a second test box that was activated at Quimper and the Herzelya Museum of Art. See Michal Heiman, *Michal Heiman Test No. 1* (Kassel: Documenta X, 1996) and *Michal Heiman Test (M.H.T.) No 2: My Mother-in-Law, Test for Women* (Quimper: Le Quartier, 1998).

35. On Heiman's tests see Dominique Abensour, *D'Israël*, exhibition catalogue (Quimper: Le Quartier, 1999), Meir Agassi, "M.H.T.: Looking as a Test of the Test of Looking: Michal Heiman and the Examination of the Subject Life of the Image," in *Michal Heiman Test (M.H.T.)*, Supplement (Kassel: Documenta X, 1997), and Ariella Azoulay, "Michal Heiman Test-Manual," in *Michal Heiman Test No. 2: My Mother-in-Law — a Test for Women Only* (Quimper: Le Quartier, 1998).

CHAPTER EIGHT: THE PUBLIC EDGE OF PHOTOGRAPHY

1. This isn't the first time the paper has published a photograph of this type. See my discussion of Michal Heiman's work based on a similar photograph in Chapter Six and the editorial in the journal *Plastika* 4, in which I discuss avoiding printing the photograph. Ariella Azoulay, "Editorial," *Plastika*, no. 4 (2002).

2. See Amos Harel and Arnon Regular, "After a Two-Month Siege — Arrest of the Head of Hamas in Hebron Who Sent the Suicide Bombers to the Double Attack in Beersheba," *Ha'aretz*, October 14, 2004, p. A2.

3. For more on this regime, see Ariella Azoulay and Adi Ophir, *This Regime Which Is Not One* (Tel Aviv: Resling, 2008).

4. The few photographs from prisons archived in the Government Press Office's (GPO), repeating the same scene — a few prisoners in a group portrait in their room — testify to the conditions of possibility of taking photos in prison.

5. His testimony is excerpted from B'Tselem, *The "New Procedure" in GSS Interrogation: The Case of 'Abd A-Nasser 'Ubeid,* Case Study No. 3, November 1993, p. 11.

6. Another testimony is, for example, that of Amin Ibrahim Galaban: "The interrogations continued in this form for 86 days. They tried to press me by showing me pictures of my brother Yasser who was also detained in Ashkelon prison, weeping from the torture, and they would show him to me weeping from the torture, and they would show him to me when they were beating him, and they threatened me that they would bring in my whole family." "Back to the Torture Routine — The Torture and Abuse of Palestinian Prisoners during Detainment and Interrogation," September 2001 – April 2003, www.stoptorture.org.il (last accessed May 2, 2007).

7. Bassem Eid, former B'Tselem researcher, described this as follows in a conversation: "The [interrogators] didn't distribute the picture in the village. They gave it to the collaborators' cell known as the "birds' cell," whose assistance the Shabak employed very frequently. The collaborator who's in prison is called a 'bird,' and at every detention center where the Shabak interrogates Palestinian detainees, these birds extricate confessions from people and transmit them to the Shabak, and the Shabak uses them as eye witnesses." The conversation took place on October 16, 2005.

8. B'Tselem, The "New Procedure" in GSS Interrogation, p. 13.

9. This distinction between withheld or suspended and direct and eruptive violence is developed further in Azoulay and Ophir, This Regime Which Is Not One.

10. It is clear from the testimonies of the dissenting Israeli reserve soldiers' group Breaking the Silence that the commands of mass arrest pertain to men: "Arrest every man aged 18 to 45 who is outside" was the order repeated to me by one of the group founders with whom I spoke.

11. This was the state's response to a petition to the High Court of Justice by three Palestinians who were held at the Ofer detention center, along with seven human-rights groups who joined the petition. The response is quoted on the Amnesty Israel Web site: www.amnesty.org.il.

12. The response of the military spokesperson is quoted in B'Tselem, Take No Prisoners: The Fatal Shooting of Palestinians by Israeli Security Forces during "Arrest Operations," Information Sheet, May 2005, view: summary.

13. Based on a conversation with Yehuda Shaul of Breaking the Silence, October, 13, 2005.

14. Awni Said, of the al-Amari refugee camp, Ramallah, describing the events following his detainment on March 12, 2002, as quoted in an Amnesty International report. Amnesty International Report, "Israel: Briefing for the Committee against Torture, May 2002," available online at http://www.amnesty.org/en/library/info/MDE15/075/2002 (last accessed March 19, 2008).

15. From soldiers' testimonies (in Hebrew) on the Breaking the Silence Web site, www.shovrimshtika.org (last accessed May 2, 2007).

16. On these three mechanisms, see B'Tselem, "Civilians under Siege: Restrictions on Freedom of Movement as Collective Punishment," available online at http://www.btselem.org/English/Publications/Index.asp?YF=2001& image.x= 9&image.y=13 (last accessed March 19, 2008).

17. See B'Tselem, *Comprehensive Report*, January 1992.

18. Or, alternatively, it appears anchored in a mythical context. On Shvili's photos as helping to preserve past Hebraic architecture, see Sarit Shapira, *Mar'it Ayin*, exhibition catalogue [in Hebrew] (Jerusalem: Israel Museum Press, 2000).

19. The conversation was published in the catalogue of the From Israel exhibition. Dominique Abensour, *D'Israël*, exhibition catalogue (Quimper: Le Quartier, 1999).

20. One example of the idealistic dimension of construction is the protective concrete wall around the settlement of Gilo, on which a realistic depiction of the landscape it conceals has been painted. After all, a house that is connected to the land must enjoy the view of the landscape. The landscape undergoes a process of condensation and is painted on the fortification that isolates the Jewish settlement from its surroundings. As an example of the ideal dimension, I would mention the way in which this construction obliterates the uneven surface of the land, leveling it to allow for the "growth" of an ideal complex that is not dependent on local or contingent characteristics, but that preserves forms, compositions, and hallmarks of ideal conceptions.

21. On the settlements, see Idit Zertal and Akiva Eldar, *Lords of the Land* [in Hebrew] (Or Yehuda: Kinneret, 2004).

22. Walter Benjamin, "The Work of Art in the Age of Its Technological Reproducibility," in *Selected Writings, Volume 4, 1938–1940*, eds. Howard Eiland and Michael W. Jennings (Cambridge, MA: Belknap Press of Harvard University Press, 2003), p. 266. Benjamin doesn't distinguish here between the mechanical gaze of photography and that of cinema in his discussion of the unconscious of photography.

23. I speak of a "floating gaze" in an analogy with the concept of "floating attention," which Freud discusses in *The Interpretation of Dreams* as a way of following what is important in a dream to its source, rather than being distracted by particulars.

24. This space can be defined, following Julia Kristeva, as the semiotic of photography, or as the space of semiotic traces impressed on the photo. Kristeva distin-

guishes between the symbolic and the semiotic: The symbolic is a network of signi-fiers that organizes enunciations into language, sense, and logic, whereas the semi-otic is the prelinguistic layer, including everything concerned with the more corporeal dimension of language, with melody and rhythm, and with nonsensical enunciations such as murmurs and whispers. Julia Kristeva, *The Kristeva Reader*, ed. Toril Moi (Oxford: Basil Blackwell, 1986).

25. Benjamin, "The Work of Art in the Age of Its Technological Reproducibil-ity," in *Selected Writings, Volume 4*, p. 269.

26. David Reeb's painting exemplifies this procedure in the way he paints the same photographs again and again. On his works in this context, see Ariella Azoulay, "Let's Have Another War," in *Let's Have Another War (David Reeb)*, exhibition cata-logue (Tel Aviv: MPublishers, 1996).

27. It is difficult not to see Efrat Shvili's works as being fed by the publications of various organizations involved in collecting information about what is happening in the Occupied Territories (B'Tselem, the Center for Alternative Information, Between the Lines, and so on), and feeding them in turn. Each of them is trying to create a specific and different framework for handling the information that they col-lect, including visual information. Shvili's works, as I attempt to show here, not only try to do the same, but also try to render an account of the gaze on the horror and to fashion unique patterns of observation for photos.

28. Her photos appear to be in the tradition of photographed buildings such as those of Walker Evans and Dan Graham. See Jean François Chevrier, "Dual Read-ing," in *Walker Evans and Dan Graham*, exhibition catalogue (Rotterdam: Witte de With, 1992). However, limiting the discussion of Shvili's photos to a selection of "photos of buildings" seems partial and insufficient.

29. Cited in the decision by Justice Yehudit Tsur to keep the defendant in cus-tody until the conclusion of legal proceedings.

30. In 1997, Aïm Deüelle Lüski and I coedited a book in memory of Hilmi Shusha in which these two photos of Shvili's appeared. Aïm Deüelle Lüski and Ariella Azoulay, *Hilmi Shusha — The Silver Platter* (Tel Aviv: published indepen-dently, 1997).

31. For years, the Peace Now movement has been monitoring the empty houses in the Jewish settlements.

32. Again, this is based on Kristeva's discussion of the symbolic and the semi-otic, which are the two necessary dimensions of linguistic action. The one cannot exist without the other, even if certain linguistic forms obscure the traces of one of them.

33. "Administrative detention," "precise targeting," "elimination," "roughing," or "extracting information from a ticking bomb" — these are all concrete and linguistic examples of the principle of the field court-martial. A field court-martial is an instrument that can turn any victim into a hangman and any hangman into a victim. A field court-martial of the kind that has developed under the regime of Israel occupation reverses the situation in a twofold way. The occupier — that is, the hangman — behaves like an intended victim. The judge, who is the occupier himself, cannot see himself as anything but a victim, and he therefore depicts the Palestinian subject as the intended hangman. Thus both the occupier and the occupied exist in the range between the hangman and the victim, both of them occupying the same positions. The field court-martial enables the Israeli to deny that the Palestinian, even when he casts his eye toward the hangman's position, is merely the product of a brutal and ongoing occupation.

34. These include benefits in all areas, from housing through education, from employment through culture.

35. The main tool at the soldier's disposal, as the selfsame "military element" reiterated to me again and again, is his reasonable fair-mindedness. He receives the following training: "They undergo all sorts of preparations relating to operational activity. A young soldier who has finished his basic training and his fighter's training — it's always fighters at the checkpoints, not just plain soldiers — such a soldier goes through several hours relating to his activity at the checkpoint, commanders' briefings, mandatory briefings regarding activity at the checkpoint, all sorts of standing orders. A soldier working at the checkpoint has to have been briefed by a commander." "The soldiers we've got aren't Ph.Ds," says one IDF colonel, "but they're the best we have. Suddenly they're being required to demonstrate a proficiency in the field of permits. You have to know where the expiration date appears on the permit and whether the permit is authentic or forged. Regretfully, a huge number of false documents are in circulation. In this case, a policeman arrives and teaches the men what a forged document looks like and how to tell them apart. These are fields of knowledge that, as a result of the conflict, we have had to teach the soldiers to deal with, not the basic fields studied in basic or noncom training. But we have internalized it so that they will act in an appropriate fashion on duty at the checkpoints, and [we have] educational corps classes relating to human dignity. Ultimately, however, with all these procedures, there is no substitute for the on-site training of the commanders in the field" (conversation with the author on February 5, 2004).

36. On the futility of the checkpoints policy and the malice inherent in it, see Gideon Levy, "The Great Prison Warden," *Ha'aretz,* January 18, 2004.

37. Azmi Bishara in the film *I Also Dwell Among Your Own People: Conversations with Azmi Bishara*, directed by Ariella Azoulay.

38. On the "final solutions" of the exceptions see Hannah Arendt, "The Decline of the Nation-State and the End of the Rights of Man," in *Imperialism* (San Diego: Harvest Books, 1968).

Chapter Nine: The Woman Collaborator Does not Exist

1. According to the testimonies of the soldiers who established Breaking the Silence, it is evident that in some cases, entry into homes lacks any logical operational grounds whatsoever and can be carried out as a drill for soldiers, or just to let off steam, or to overcome boredom and distraction. Such descriptions were repeated in the guided tours that group members gave at the photography exhibition Soldiers Talk about Hebron at the Gallery of the Geo Photo College (June 2004).

2. This is a description I heard from Yehuda Shaul, one of the members of Breaking the Silence, regarding his prolonged term of duty in the territories, in an unpublished conversation with me.

3. From the testimony of H. A., a resident of the village of Dura, Mount Hebron, given on September 1, 1992. B'Tselem, *Collaborators in the Occupied Territories: Human Rights Abuses and Violations, Bi-Annual Report 1990/1991: Violations of Human Rights in the Occupied Territories*, p. 18.

4. About half of the B'Tselem report on collaborators is dedicated to the way in which Palestinian organizations handle this problem. While the authors also attribute indirect responsibility for the injury of collaborators to the Israeli ruling apparatus, they research the phenomenon as if it were possible, under the conditions created by the ruling apparatus, to stabilize the boundary between collaborator and noncollaborator or between a denouncer of collaborators who acts on behalf of the Palestinians and a denouncer of collaborators who acts on behalf of the Shabak.

5. From the testimony of Mohammad F., *ibid*, p. 22.

6. Hillel Cohen's book, *The Army of Shadows*, addresses the history of the enlistment of collaborators by the Zionist movement but does not deal with the past few decades. Hillel Cohen, *The Army of Shadows* (Jerusalem: Ivrit Publisher, 2005). Amos Harel and Avi Issacharoff, in *The Seventh War*, briefly mention instances of collaboration or suspected collaboration in passing, but do not deal specifically with this subject or with its problematic character. Amos Harel and Avi Issacharoff, *The Seventh War* (Tel Aviv: Miskal Yedioth Ahronoth Books and Chemed Books, 2004).

7. Harel and Issacharoff, *The Seventh War*, p. 128.

8. B'Tselem, *Collaborators in the Occupied Territories*, p. 8.

9. *Ibid.*

10. Hillel Cohen, too, formulates the boundary lines of his research on collaborators based on those that were drawn by Palestinians. Following a lecture at Zochrot, January 8, 2006, he proposed the killing of collaborators by Palestinians as proof of the fact that they were perceived in Palestinian society as collaborators. Fatmeh Kassem, who responded to his claims, disagreed with his formulation and suggested the need for reexamining the alleged murders of Palestinians by Palestinians.

11. Testimony of Feisal al-Husseini, B'Tselem, *Collaborators in the Occupied Territories*, p. 112.

12. *Ibid.*

13. Testimony of Hussein 'Awwad, *ibid.*, p. 8.

14. Testimony of Abu Qayid, *ibid.*, p. 8.

15. Fatma Salama, quoted in Teresa Thornhill, *Making Woman Talk: The Interrogation of Women Detainees* (London: Lawyers for Palestinian Human Rights, 1992), p. 32.

16. Several women's testimonies can be read in Thornhill, *Making Woman Talk*, however.

17. B'Tselem, *Collaborators in the Occupied Territories*, p. 61.

18. *Ibid*, p. 63.

19. This snare is a terrifying one: "I was presented as a collaborator," says Muneir Manasreh, the governor of Jenin. Quoted in Harel and Issacharoff, *The Seventh War*, p. 95. It can also cause symbolic assassination, as in the case of Jibril Rajoub. *Ibid.*, pp. 242–45.

20. See the discussion by Jean-François Lyotard on the impossibility of proving innocence, *The Differend: Phrases in Dispute*, trans. Georges Van Den Abbeele (Minneapolis: University of Minnesota Press, 1988), p. 9.

21. B'Tselem, *Collaborators in the Occupied Territories*, p. 22.

22. *Ibid.*

23. *Ibid.*, p. 24.

24. The possibility of sexual violence against Palestinian women by Israelis, both soldiers and civilians, remains totally unspoken, but there is no reason to believe it doesn't exist. The information available today on violence against women inside Israel and on violence against women under military regimes elsewhere makes it impossible to assume that things here are any different. And yet, only occasionally does some rumor materialize here or there proceeding to disappear swiftly.

In this context, see Susan Slymovics, "The Rape of Qula, A Destroyed Palestinian Village," in Lila Abu-Lughod and Ahmad Sa'adi (eds.), *Touching a Painful Past: The Nakba as a Site of Palestinian Collective Memory* (New York: Columbia University Press, 2007).

25. *Ibid.*, p. 61.

26. *Ibid.*, p. 69.

27. *Ibid.*, p. 61.

28. *Ibid.*

29. From the testimony of Hussein 'Awwad, known as "al 'Aqra '," commander of the Fateh Eagles in the Khan Yunis area, in *Ibid.*, p. 62.

30. *Ibid.*, p. 61.

31. *Ibid.*, pp. 23–24.

32. The B'Tselem report cites two books on the subject: *al-Dahiyyah Taataraf* (The victim confesses), a book describing the deeds of Mazen Fahwami, and another book on the same affair that was apparently disseminated in over ten thousand copies. *Ibid.*, p. 23.

33. *Ibid.*, pp. 22–23.

34. This emerges from the B'Tselem report, but was also stressed to me repeatedly by Bassem Eid, who is one of the researchers who prepared the report and who is currently director of the BADIL information center. "I heard it more from women, not from men. A woman who went out with her boyfriend and then either the boyfriend or someone else photographed her with the boyfriend, and then the Shabak came and said look what a pretty picture of you. Either you agree to work with us, or we'll print a hundred copies of it and spread it around the village." Conversation conducted in November 2005.

Bibliography

Abensour, Dominique, *D'Israël*, exhibition catalogue (Quimper: Le Quartier, 1999).

Abu Ghraib: The Politics of Torture, The Terra Nova Series (Berkeley, CA: North Atlantic Books, 2004).

Abu-Lughod, Lila, and Ahmad Sa'adi (eds.), *Touching a Painful Past: The Nakba as a Site of Palestinian Collective Memory* (New York: Columbia University Press, 2007).

Agassi, Meir, "M.H.T.: Looking as a Test of the Test of Looking: Michal Heiman and the Examination of the Subject Life of the Image," in *Michal Heiman Test (M.H.T.)*, Supplement (Kassel: Documenta X, 1997).

Agamben, Giorgio, *The Coming Community*, trans. Michael Hardt (Minneapolis: University of Minnesota Press, 1993).

———, *Homo Sacer: Sovereign Power and Bare Life*, trans. Daniel Heller-Roazen (Stanford, CA: Stanford University Press, 1998).

———, "Non au tatouage bio-politique." *Le Monde*, November 1, 2004.

———, *State of Exception*, trans. Kevin Attell (Chicago: University of Chicago Press, 2005).

———, "We Refugees," trans. Michael Rocke, 2004, available online at http://www.egs.edu/faculty/agamben/agamben-we-refugees.html.

Alcoff, Linda, and Laura Gray-Rosendale, "Survivor Discourse: Transgression or Recuperation?" in Sidonie Smith and Julia Watson (eds.), *Getting a Life: Everyday Uses of Autobiography* (Minneapolis: University of Minnesota Press, 1996).

Allen, Beverly, *Rape WarFare: The Hidden Genocide in Bosnia-Herzegovina and Croatia* (Minneapolis: University of Minnesota Press, 1996).

Allyn, David, *Make Love, Not War: The Sexual Revolution, An Unfettered History* (New York: Routledge, 2001).

Amiri, Suad, *Cappuccino in Ramallah* (Tel Aviv: Babel Publishers, 2003).

Arago, Dominique François, "Report," in Alan Trachtenberg (ed.), *Classic Essays on Photography* (New Haven, CT: Leete's Island Books, 1980).

Arendt, Hannah, "The Decline of the Nation-State and the End of the Rights of Man," in *Imperialism* (San Diego: Harvest Books, 1968).

——, *The Human Condition* (1958; Chicago: University of Chicago Press, 1998).

——, *On Revolution* (Harmondsworth, UK: Penguin, 1990).

——, *On Violence* (New York, Harvest Books, 1970).

Azoulay, Ariella, "An Alien Woman / A Permitted Woman: On J. M.Coetzee's *Disgrace*," *scrutiny2* 7, no. 1 (2002).

——, *Death's Showcase: The Power of Image in Contemporary Democracy*, trans. Ruvik Danieli (Cambridge, MA: MIT Press, 2001).

——, "Editorial," *Plastika*, no 4 (2002).

—— (ed.), *Everything Could Be Seen*, exhibition catalogue (Tel Aviv: Um el Fachem Art Gallery, 2004).

——, "Female Trauma," in Austin Sarat, Nadav Davidovitch, and Mical Alberstein (eds.), *Trauma and Memory: Subjective and Collective Experiences: Legal, Medical, and Cultural Perspectives* (Stanford, CA: Stanford University Press, 2008).

——, *The Food Chain* (film, 2003).

——, *How Does It Look to You?* (Tel Aviv: Babel, 2000).

——, "Hunger in Palestine: The Event That Never Was," in *Territories: Islands, Camps and Other States of Utopia*, exhibition catalogue (Berlin, KW-Institute for contemporary art, 2003). Also available in Anselm Franke (ed.), *Territories: Islands, Camps and Other States of Utopia* (Berlin: KW-Institute for Contemporary Art, 2005).

——, *I Also Dwell among Your Own People: Conversations with Azmi Bishara*, film, DVD, Alma Productions, Tel Aviv, 2005.

——, "Let's Have Another War," in *Let's Have Another War (David Reeb)*, exhibition catalogue (Tel Aviv: Mpublishers, 1996).

——, "The Loss of Critique and the Critique of Violence," *Cardozo Law Review* 26, no. 3 (2005).

——, "Michal Heiman Test – Manual," in *Michal Heiman Test No. 2: My Mother-in-Law – a Test for Women Only* (Quimper: Le Quartier, 1998).

——, "A Moment of Quiet, Please, the Disaster Would Like to Say Something," *(a): the journal of culture and the unconscious* 2, no. 1 (2002).

– – – –, *Once Upon a Time: Photography following Walter Benjamin* [in Hebrew] (Ramat-Gan: Bar Ilan University Press, 2006).

——, *Training for Art* [in Hebrew] (Tel Aviv: The Porter Institute for Poetics and Semiotics, Tel Aviv University, Hakibbutz Hameuchad, 1999).

Azoulay, Ariella, and Adi Ophir, *Bad Days: Between Disaster and Utopia* [in Hebrew] (Tel Aviv: Resling, 2002).

——, *This Regime Which Is Not One* (Tel Aviv: Resling, 2008).

Baber, H. E., "How Bad is Rape?" *Hypatia* 2, no, 2 (1987).

Bachar, Karen, and Mary P. Koss, "From Prevalence to Prevention: Closing the Gap between What We Know about Rape and What We Do," in Claire M. Renzetti., Jeffrey L. Edleson, and Raquel Kennedy Bergen (eds.), *Sourcebook on Violence against Women* (Thousand Oaks, CA: Sage, 2001).

Bajac, Quentin, and Dominique Planchon-de Font-Réalux, *Le daguerréotype français: Un objet photographique* (Paris: Musée d'Orsay, 2004).

Bal, Mieke, *Double Exposures* (New York: Routledge, 1996).

Balibar, Étienne, "Outlines of a Topography of Cruelty: Citizenship and Civility in the Era of Global Violence," *Constellations* 8, no. 1 (March 2001).

——, *Politics and the Other Scene*, trans. Christine Jones, James Swenson, and Chris Turner (London: Verso, 2002).

——, "'Rights of Man' and 'Rights of Citizen': The Modern Dialectic of Equality and Freedom," In *Masses, Classes, Ideas. Studies on Politics and Philosophy before and after Marx*, trans. James Swenson (New York: Routledge, 1994).

Banta, Melissa, *A Curious and Ingenious Art: Reflexions on Daguerreotypes at Harvard* (Iowa City: University of Iowa Press, 2000).

Barthes, Roland, *Camera Lucida: Reflections on Photography*, trans. Richard Howard (New York: Vintage, 2000).

——, *Mythologies*, trans. Annette Lavers (New York: Hill and Wang, 1972).

——, "Shock Photos," in *The Eiffel Tower and Other Mythologies*, trans. Richard Howard (New York: Hill and Wang, 1977).

Baruch, Adam, "Art-Chronicle: The Option for Creative and Informed Israeli Photography," in *The Second Israeli Photography Biennale* (Jerusalem: The Domino Press, 1988).

——, *Betom Lev* [in Hebrew] (Jerusalem: Keter, 2001).

——, "Michal Heiman's Installation: *At the Edge of the Museum*, the Poet Rachel and Artist Aviva Uri," in John Stathatos (ed.), *Persistence of Memory*, exhibition catalogue, The Third Israeli Photography Biennale (Ein Harod: Mishkan Le'Omanut, 1991).

——, *Seder Yom* [in Hebrew] (Jerusalem: Keter, 2000).

Batchen, Geoffrey, *Burning with Desire* (Cambridge, MA: MIT Press, 1999).

Baudelaire, Charles, "Salon de 1859," in *Baudelaire: Œuvres Complètes*, vol. 2 (Paris: NRF Bibliothèque de la Pléiade, 1976).

Baudrillard, Jean, *The Gulf War Did Not Take Place* (Bloomington: Indiana University Press, 1991).

——, *Simulacra and Simulation*, trans. Sheila Faria Glaser (Ann Arbor: University of Michigan Press, 1994).

Beauvoir, Simone de, *The Second Sex*, trans. H. M. Parshley (Vintage Books, 1989).

Benjamin, Walter, *Selected Writings Volume 1, 1913–1926*, eds. Marcus Bullock and Michael W. Jennings (Cambridge, MA: Belknap Press of Harvard University Press, 1996).

——, *Selected Writings, Volume 2, 1927–1934*, eds. Michael W. Jennings, Gazy Smith and Howard Eiland (Cambridge, MA: Belknap Press of Harvard University Press, 1999).

——, *Selected Writings, Volume 3, 1935–1938*, eds. Howard Eiland and Michael Jennings (Cambridge, MA: Belknap Press of Harvard University Press, 2002).

——, *Selected Writings, Volume 4, 1938–1940*, eds. Howard Eiland and Michael W. Jennings (Cambridge, MA: Belknap Press of Harvard University Press, 2003).

Berger, John, *Ways of Seeing* (Harmondsworth, UK: Penguin, 1990).

Bergoffen, Debra, B., "How Rape Became a Crime Against Humanity: History of an Error," in Alan D. Schrift (ed.), *Modernity and the Problem of Evil* (Bloomington: Indiana University Press, 2005).

Berkowitz, Nizza, "Globalization of Human Rights and of Women's Rights," *Theoriya Ve-Bikoret*, no. 23 (2003).

Bernard, Denis, and André Gunthert, *L'instant revé: Albert Londe* (Nîmes: Jaqueline Chambon, 1993).

Bethlehem, Louise, "Pliant/Complaint; Grace/Disgrace; Plaint/Complaint," *scrutiny2* 7, no. 1 (2002).

Bevacqua, Maria, *Rape on the Public Agenda: Feminism and the Politics of Sexual Assault* (Boston: Northeastern University Press, 2000).

Bishara, Azmi, *Checkpoint* (Arles: Actes Sud, 2004).

Boeri, Stefano, "Eclectic Atlases," *Documenta X Documents*, no. 3 (Stuttgart: Cantz, 1996).

Boltanski, Luc, *La souffrance à distance: Morale humanitaire, médias et politique* (Paris: A. M. Metaillie, 1993).

Boulouch, Nathalie, "Peindre avec le soleil?: Les enjeux du problème de la photographie des couleurs," *Études Photographiques*, no. 10 (2002).

Bourdieu, Pierre, with Luc Boltanski, Robert Castel, Jean-Claude Chamboredon, and Dominique Schnapper, *Photography: A Middle-brow Art*, trans. Shaun White-side (Stanford, CA: Stanford University Press, 1990).

Braun, David, "How They Found National Geographic's 'Afghan Girl,'" available online at http://news.nationalgeographic.com/news/2002/03/0311_ 020312_ sharbat.html.

Brent, Linda, *Incidents in the Life of a Slave Girl*, ed. Lydia Maria Child (San Diego: Harcourt Brace Jovanovich, 1973).

Brison, Susan, "Torture or 'Good Old American Pornography'?" *Chronicle of Higher Education*, June 4, 2004, available online at http://ics.leeds.ac.uk/papers/vp01. cfm?outfit=ks&requesttimeout=500&folder=42&paper=141.

Brownmiller, Susan, *Men, Women, and Rape* (New York: Ballantine, 1975).

Bruner, José, "Trauma and Justice: Moral, Legal, and Political Trajectories of Trauma Discourse from Wilhelmine Germany to Post-Apartheid South Africa," in Austin Sarat, Nadav Davidovitch, and Mical Alberstein (eds.), *Trauma and Memory: Subjective and Collective Experiences: Legal, Medical, and Cultural Perspectives* (Stanford, CA: Stanford University Press, 2008).

Buchwald, Emilie, Pamela Fletcher, and Martha Roth (eds.), *Transforming a Rape Culture* (Minneapolis: Milkweed Editions, 1993).

Buck-Morss, Susan, "Hegel and Haiti," *Critical Inquiry* 26 (Summer 2000).

Burgess, Ann W., and Lynda L. Holmstrom, "Rape Trauma Syndrome," *American Journal of Psychiatry* 131 (1974).

Burgess-Jackson, Keith, *A Most Detestable Crime: New Philosophical Essays on Rape* (New York: Oxford University Press, 1999).

——, *Rape: A Philosophical Investigation* (Aldershot, UK: Dartmouth, 1996).

Butler, Judith, *Antigone's Claim: Kinship between Life and Death* (New York: Columbia University Press, 2002).

——, "Indefinite Detention," in *Precarious Life: The Powers of Mourning and Violence* (New York: Verso, 2004).

——, "Restaging the Universal: Hegemony and the Limits of Formalism," in Judith Butler, Ernesto Laclau, and Slavoj Žižek (eds.), *Contingency, Hegemony, Universality: Contemporary Dialogues on the Left* (New York: Verso, 2000).

Chang, Iris, *The Rape of Nanking: The Forgotten Holocaust of World War II* (New York: Penguin, 1997).

Chevrier, Jean François, "Dual Reading," in *Walker Evans and Dan Graham*, exhibition catalogue (Rotterdam: Witte de With, 1992).

Coetzee, J. M., *Disgrace* (New York: Viking, 1999).

Cohen, Hillel, *The Army of Shadows* (Jerusalem: Ivrit Publisher, 2005).

563

Copjec, Joan, *The Descent into Shame*, unpublished manuscript.

——, *Imagine There's No Woman: Ethics and Sublimation* (Cambridge, MA: MIT Press, 2002).

Crary, Jonathan, *Techniques of the Observer* (Cambridge, MA: MIT Press, 1992).

Debord, Guy, *The Society of Spectacle* (New York: Zone Books, 1995).

Deleuze, Gilles. *The Logic of Sense*, trans. Mark Lester with Charles Stivale, ed. Constantin V. Boundas (New York: Columbia University Press, 1990).

Deleuze, Gilles, and Félix Guattari, *A Thousand Plateaus: Capitalism and Schizophrenia*, trans. Brian Massumi (Minneapolis: University of Minnesota Press, 1987).

Didi-Huberman, Georges, *Images malgré tout* (Paris: Minuit, 2003).

——, *Invention de l'hystérie: Charcot et l'iconographie photographique de la Salpêtrière* (Paris: Macula, 1995).

Dor, Daniel, *Newspapers Under the Influence* (Tel Aviv: Babel, 2001).

Deüelle Lüski, Aïm, "Fragments of Horizontal Thinking," *Plastika*, no. 3 (1999).

Deüelle Lüski, Aïm, and Ariella Azoulay, *Hilmi Shusha — The Silver Platter* (Tel Aviv: published independently, 1997).

Eastlike, Elizabeth, "Photography," in Alan Trachtenberg (ed.), *Classic Essays on Photography* (New Haven, CT: Leete's Island Books, 1980).

Edelman, Bernard, *Le droit saisi par la photographie: Éléments pour une théorie marxiste du droit* (Paris: Maspero, 1973).

Ehrenreich, Barbara, *Nickel and Dimed: On (Not) Getting By in America* (New York: Henry Holt, 2002).

Ehrenreich, Barbara, and Arlie Russel Hochschild (eds.), *Global Woman: Nannies, Maids, and Sex Workers in the New Economy* (New York: Metropolitan/Owl Books, 2004).

El Baz, Farouk, "Crowd Space — Bodies Count," *Wired* (June 2003).

Erlich, Susan, *Representing Rape: Language and Sexual Consent* (New York: Routledge, 2001).

Estrich, Susan, *Real Rape: How the Legal System Victimizes Women Who Say No* (Cambridge, MA: Harvard University Press, 1987).

Faris, James, C., *Navajo and Photography: A Critical History of the Representation of an American People* (Salt Lake City: University of Utah Press, 2003).

Farrow, Lynne, "The Independent Woman and the Cinema of Rape," in New York Radical Feminists, *Rape: The First Sourcebook for Women by New York Radical Feminists*, eds. Noreen Connell and Cassandra Wilson (New York: New American Library, 1974).

Feher Michel, "The Governed in Politics," in *Nongovernmental Politics*, Michel Feher (ed.), with Gaëlle Krikorian and Yates McKee (New York: Zone Books, 2007).

Felder, Deborah, G., *A Century of Women: The Most Influential Events in 20th Century Women's History* (Secaucus, NJ: Carol Publishing Group, 1999).

Ferguson, Frances, *Pornography, the Theory: What Utilitarianism Did to Action* (Chicago: University of Chicago Press, 2004).

———,"Rape and the Rise of the Novel," *Representations*, no. 20 (1987).

Ferrato, Donna, *Living with the Enemy* (New York: Aperture, 1991).

Foucault, Michel, *The Archaeology of Knowledge*, trans. A. M. Sheridan Smith (1969; New York: Pantheon, 1972).

———, *Dits et écrits, vol. III* (Paris: Gallimard, 1994).

———, *The History of Sexuality, Volume 1: An Introduction*, trans. Robert Hurley (New York: Vintage, 1980).

———, *The Birth of the Clinic: An Archaeology of Medical Perception* (New York: Random House, 1975).

Freund, Gisèle, *Photographie et société* (Paris: Seuil, 1996).

Frizot, Michel (ed.), *A New History of Photography* (Cologne: Könemann, 1998).

Gaines, Jane, M., *Contested Culture: The Image, the Voice, and the Law* (Chapel Hill: University of North Carolina Press, 1991).

Garrard, Mary, D., *Artemisia Gentileschi: The Image of the Female Hero in Italian Baroque Art* (Princeton, NJ: Princeton University Press, 1989).

Gaulier, Emanuèle, "Femme, réveille-toi," in Olympe de Gouges, *Déclaration des droits de la femme et de la citoyenne* (Paris: Mille et une nuit, 2003).

Genvrin, Emmanuel, *Études suivi de l'esclavage des negres* (Saint Denis: Théatre Vollard, 1988).

Golan, Tal, "Learning to See: The Beginning of Visual Technologies in Medicine and Law," in *Law, Society and Culture*, The Buchman Faculty of Law Series (Tel Aviv: Tel Aviv University, 2003).

Gouges, Olympe de, "Black Slavery, or The Happy Shipwreck," in. Doris Y. Kadish and Françoise Massardier-Kenny (eds.), *Translating Slavery: Gender and Race in French Women's Writing, 1783–1823* (Kent, OH: Kent State University Press, 1994).

———, *Déclaration des droits de la femme et de la citoyenne* (Paris: Mille et une nuit, 2003).

———, "Mémoire de Madame de Valmont," in *Œuvres* (Paris: Mercure de France, 1986).

Groult, Benoîte, "Olympe de Gouges: La première féministe moderne," in *Olympe de Gouges: Oeuvres* (Paris: Mercure de France, 1986).

Guerilla Girls, *The Guerilla Girls' Bedside Companion to the History of Western Art* (London: Penguin, 1998).

Gunthert, André, "La boite noire de Daguerre," *Le daguerréotype français: Un objet photographique* (Paris: Musée d'Orsay, 2003).

——, "Daguerre ou la promptitude: Archéologie de la rédaction du temps de pose," *Études Photographiques*, no. 5 (1998).

——, "L'image numérique s'en va-t'en guerre: Les photographies d'Abou Ghraib," *Études photographiques*, no. 15 (November 2004).

Guttman, Roy, and David Rieff (eds.), *Crimes of War* (London: Norton, 1999).

Habermas, Jürgen, *Legitimation Crisis* (Boston: Beacon Press, 1975).

Hammerman, Ilana, *In Foreign Parts: Trafficking in Women in Israel* [in Hebrew] (Tel Aviv: 'Am 'oved, 2004).

Harding, Luke, "Focus Shifts to Jail Abuse of Women," *Guardian Unlimited*, March 24, 2005.

Harel, Amos and Avi Issacharoff, *The Seventh War* (Tel Aviv: Miskal Yedioth Ahronoth Books and Chemed Books, 2004).

Harel, Amos, and Arnon Regular, "After a Two-Month Siege — Arrest of the Head of Hamas in Hebron Who Sent the Suicide Bombers to the Double Attack in Beersheba," *Ha'aretz*, October 14, 2004, p. A2.

Harvey, David, *The Condition of Postmodernity* (Oxford: Blackwell, 1989).

Haskell, Molly, *From Reverence to Rape: The Treatment of Women in the Movies* (Chicago: University of Chicago Press, 1973).

Heidegger, Martin, "The Age of the World Picture," in *The Question concerning Technology and Other Essays*, trans. William Lovitt (New York: Harper & Row, 1977).

Heiferman, Marvin, and Carole Kismaric, *Talking Pictures: People Speak about the Photographs that Speak to Them* (San Francisco: Chronicle Books, 1994).

Heiman, Michal, "Attacks on Linking," paper presented at the Art and War conference, Goethe-Platform, Tel Aviv, 2004.

——, "Holding," in Ariella Azoulay (ed.), *Everything Could Be Seen*, exhibition catalogue (Tel Aviv: Um el Fachem Art Gallery, 2004).

——, *Michal Heiman Test No. 1* (Kassel: Documenta X, 1996).

——, *Michal Heiman Test (M.H.T.) No 2: My Mother-in-Law, Test for Women* (Quimper: Le Quartier, 1998).

Hersh, Seymour, M., *Chain of Command: The Road from 9/11 to Abu Ghraib* (New York: Harper Collins, 2004).

Hesford, Wendy S., and Wendy Kozol (eds.), *Haunting Violations: Feminist Criticism and the Crisis of the Real* (Urbana: University of Illinois Press, 2001).

——— (eds.), *Just Advocacy? Women's Human Rights, Transnational Feminisms, and the Politics of Representation* (New Brunswick, NJ: Rutgers University Press, 2005).

Hess, Amira, "Colonialism under the Guise of a Peace Process" [in Hebrew], *Theoria ve-Bikoret* 24 (2004).

Hesse, Carla, *The Other Enlightenment: How French Women Became Modern* (Princeton, NJ: Princeton University Press, 2001).

Hever, Hannan, "Facing *Disgrace*: Coetzee and the Israeli intellectual," *scrutiny2* 7, no. 1 (2002).

Hobbes, Thomas, *Leviathan,* ed. C. B. MacPherson (London: Penguin, 1987).

Hoskins, Andrew, *Televising War: From Vietnam to Iraq* (London: Continuum, 2004).

Hunt, Lynn, *The Invention of Pornography* (New York: Zone Books, 1993).

Jaume, Lucien, "Citizen and State under the French Revolution," in Quentin Skinner and Bo Stråth (eds.), *States and Citizens* (Cambridge: Cambridge University Press, 2003).

———, *Les déclarations des droits de l'homme: 1789* (Paris: Flammarion, 1989).

Jeffords, Susan, and Lauren Rabinovitz (eds.), *Seeing through the Media: The Persian Gulf War* (New Brunswick, NJ: Rutgers University Press, 1994).

Jonas, Hans, *The Imperative of Responsibility: In Search of an Ethics in the Technological Age* (Chicago: University of Chicago Press, 1984).

Johnson, Brooks, *Photography Speaks* (New York: Aperture, 1995).

Kälin, Walter, Lars Müller, and Judith Wyttenbach (eds.), *The Face of Human Rights* (Baden: Lars Müller Publishers, 2004).

Kamir, Orit, *Framed: Women in Law and Film* (Durham, NC: Duke University Press, 2005).

———, *Feminism, Rights, and the Law* (Tel Aviv: Universita Meshuderet, Ministry of Defense, Israel, 2002).

Kant, Immanuel, "A Renewed Attempt to Answer the Question: 'Is the Human Race Continually Improving?'" in Hans Reiss (ed.), *Political Writings*, trans. H. B. Nisbet (Cambridge: Cambridge University Press, 1991).

Keenan, Thomas, *Fables of Responsibility: Aberrations and Predicaments in Ethics and Politics* (Stanford, CA: Stanford University Press, 1997).

———, Mobilizing Shame," *South Atlantic Quarterly*, 103, no. 2/3 (Spring/Summer, 2004), pp. 435–49.

———, "Publicity and Indifference: Media, Surveillance, 'Humanitarian Intervention,'" in Thomas. Y. Levin, Ursula Frohne, and Peter Weibel (eds.), *Ctrl [Space]: Rhetorics of Surveillance from Bentham to Big Brother* (Cambridge, MA: MIT Press, 2002).

Kimball, Roger, *The Rape of the Masters: How Political Correctness Sabotages Art* (San Francisco, CA: Encounter Books, 2004).

Klee, Ernst, Willi Dressen, and Volker Riess (eds.), *"The Good Old Days": The Holocaust as Seen by Its Perpetrators and Bystanders*, trans. Deborah Burnstone (New York: Free Press, 1991).

Korey, William, *NGOs and the Universal Declaration of Human Rights: A Curious Grapevine* (New York: St. Martin's Press, 1998).

Kozol, Wendy, "Abu Ghraib and the Dilemma of Spectatorship," unpublished essay.

——, "Domesticating NATO's War in Kosovo: (In)Visible Bodies and the Dilemma of Photojournalism," *Meridians: Feminism, Transnationalism, Race* 4, no. 2 (2004), pp. 1–38.

Kratsman, Miki, and Eldad Rafaeli, "What Do You Have to Do There?" *Plastika*, no. 2 (1998), p. 71.

Kristeva, Julia, *The Kristeva Reader*, ed. Toril Moi (Oxford: Basil Blackwell, 1986).

Lacan, Jacques, *The Four Fundamental Concepts of Psychoanalysis*, ed. Jacques-Alain Miller, trans. Alan Sheridan (New York: Norton, 1978).

Landau, Sigalit, *The Country* (Jerusalem: Spartizan / D. K. Graubart LTD, 2003).

Lange, Dorothea, "The Assignment I'll Never Forget," in Liz Heron and Val Williams (eds.), *Illuminations: Women's Writings on Photography from the 1850s to the Present* (London: I. B. Tauris, 1996).

Lascoumes, Pierre, "Géographie de l'*intolérable:* A la recherché d'une internationale des gouvernés," *Vacarme*, no. 29 (Autumn 2004).

Lavoie, Vincent, *L'instant-monument* (Montreal: Dazibao, 2001).

Lederer, Laura (ed.), *Take Back the Night: Women on Pornography* (New York: Morrow, 1980).

Levin, Thomas Y., Ursula Frohne, and Peter Weibel (eds.), *Ctrl (Space): Rhetorics of Surveillance from Bentham to Big Brother* (Cambridge, MA: MIT Press, 2002).

Levy, Gideon, "The Great Prison Warden," *Ha'aretz,* January 18, 2004.

Lubin, Orly, *Women Reading Women* [in Hebrew] (Haifa: Haifa University Press, Zmora-Modan, 2003).

Lyotard, Jean-François, *The Differend: Phrases in Dispute*, trans. Georges Van Den Abbeele (Minneapolis: University of Minnesota Press, 1988).

——, *The Postmodern Condition: A Report on Knowledge*, trans. Geoff Bennington and Brian Massumi (Minneapolis: University of Minnesota Press, 1984).

Lyotard, Jean-François, and Jean Loup Thébaud, *Just Gaming*, trans. Wlad Godzich (Minneapolis: University of Minnesota Press, 1985).

MacCannell, Juliet Flower, "Between The Two Fears," *Cardozo Law Review* 24, no. 6 (August 2003).

——, *The Hysteric's Guide to the Future Female Body* (Minneapolis: University of Minnesota Press, 2000).

——, *The Regime of the Brother* (London: Routledge, 1991).

Maraland, Hilary, and Anne Marie Rafferty (eds.), *Midwives, Society and Childbirth: Debates and Controversies in the Modern Period*, Studies in the Social History of Medicine (New York: Routledge, 1997).

McNutt, Kristen, "Sexualized Violence Against Iraqi Women by US Occupying Forces," paper presented to The United Nations Commission on Human Rights, Geneva, March 2005, available online at http://psychoanalystsoppose-war.org/resources_files/SVIW–1.doc.

MacKinnon, Catherine, A., *Sex Equality: Rape Law* (New York: Foundation Press, 2001).

——, *Toward a Feminist Theory of the State* (Cambridge, MA: Harvard University Press, 1989).

Marable, Manning, and Leith Mullings, *Freedom: A Photographic History of the African American Struggle* (London: Phaidon, 2002).

Marcus, Sharon, "Fighting Bodies, Fighting Words: A Theory and Politics of Rape Prevention," in Judith Butler and Joan W. Scott (eds.), *Feminists Theorize the Political* (New York: Routledge, 1992).

Mathews, Joan, *"Rape Bibliography,"* in New York Radical Feminists, *Rape: The First Sourcebook for Women by New York Radical Feminists*, eds. Noreen Connell and Cassandra Wilson (New York: New American Library, 1974).

McKissack, Patricia, C., *A Picture of Freedom: The Diary of Clotee, a Slave Girl* (New York: Scholastic Inc., 1997).

Mileaf, Janine, A. "Poses for the Camera: Eadweard Muybridge's Studies of the Human Figure," *American Art: The Journal of the Smithsonian's American Art Museum* 16, no. 3 (2002).

Mousset, Sophie, *Olympe de Gouges et les droits de la femme* (Paris: Félin, 2003).

Nancy, Jean Luc, *Being Singular Plural*, trans. Robert O. Richardson and Anne E. O'Byrne (Stanford, CA: Stanford University Press, 2000).

Nastas, Faten Fawzy, "It Was Already Too Late," in Ariella Azoulay (ed.), *Everything Could Be Seen*, exhibition catalogue (Tel Aviv: Um el Fahem Art Gallery, 2004).

Nead, Lynda, *Female Nude* (New York: Routledge, 1992).

Newhall, Beaumont, *The History of Photography: From 1839 to the Present* (New York: Museum of Modern Art, 1982).

Newman, Louise Michele, *White Women's Rights: The Racial Origins of Feminism in the United States* (New York: Oxford University Press, 1999).

New York Radical Feminists, *Rape: The First Sourcebook for Women by New York Radical Feminists*, eds. Noreen Connell and Cassandra Wilson (New York: New American Library, 1974).

Nochlin, Linda, *Femmes: Art et pouvoir* (Paris: Editions Jacqueline Chambon, 1993).

Oickle, Alvin F., *Jonathan Walker: the Man with the Branded Hand* (Everett, MA: Lorelli Slater, 1998).

Ophir, Adi, "Life between Abandonment and Sacredness: An Introduction to *Homo Sacer*," in Shai Lavi (ed.), *Technologies of Justice: Law, Science, and Society* (Tel Aviv: Ramot, 2003).

——, "Moral Technologies: The Administration of Disaster and the Abandonment of Life," *Theoria ve-Bikoret* 22 (2003).

——, *The Order of Evils* (New York: Zone Books, 2005).

——, "The Sovereign, the Humanitarian, and the Terrorist," in Michel Feher (ed.), with Gaëlle Krikorian and Yates McKee, *Nongovernmental Politics* (New York: Zone Books, 2007).

Outram, Dorinda, *The Body and the French Revolution* (New Haven: Yale University Press, 1989).

Paglia, Camille, "Rape and the Modern Sex War," in Adele M. Stan (ed.), *Debating Sexual Correctness* (New York: Delta, 1995).

Pateman, Carole, *Participation and Democratic Theory* (Cambridge: Cambridge University Press, 1970).

——, *The Sexual Contract* (Stanford, CA: Stanford University Press, 1988).

Patterson, Zabet, "Going On-Line: Consuming Pornography in the Digital Era," in Linda Williams (ed.), *Porn Studies* (Durham, NC: Duke University Press, 2004).

Phillips, Sandra S., Mark Haworth-Booth, and Carol Squiers (eds.), *Police Pictures: The Photograph as Evidence* (San Francisco: Chronicle Books, 1997).

Pinson, Stephen, "Revers de fortune," in *Le daguerréotype français: Un objet photographique* (Paris: Musée d'Orsay, 2003).

Planchon-de Font-Réaulx, Dominique, "Splendeurs et mystères de la chamber noire: Le daguerreotype sous l'oeil des critiques," in *Le daguerréotype français: Un objet photographique* (Paris: Musée d'Orsay, 2003).

Plath, Sylvia, *The Journals of Sylvia Plath*, eds. Ted Hughes and Frances McCullough (New York: Ballantine, 1991).

Pogrebin, Letty Cottin, "Sex Harassment," in Adele M. Stan (ed.), *Debating Sexual Correctness* (New York: Delta, 1995).

Pollock, Griselda, *Vision and Difference: Femininity, Feminism and the Histories of Art* (London: Routledge, 1988).

Projansky, Sarah, *Watching Rape: Film and Television in Postfeminist Culture* (New York: New York University Press, 2001).

Reichlin, Elinor, "Faces of Slavery," *American Heritage* 29 (June 1977).

——, "Survivors of a Painful Epoch: Six Rare Pre-Civil War Daguerreotypes of Southern Slaves," undated, Archive, Peabody Museum, Harvard. First version of Reichlin, "Faces of Slavery."

Riot Sarcey, Michèle, "Citizenship and the Equality of the Sexes: The French Model Question," in Quentin Skinner and Bo Stråth (eds.), *States and Citizens* (Cambridge: Cambridge University Press, 2003).

Rizzo, Tracy, "Between Dishonor and Death," *Women's History Review* 13, no. 1 (2004).

Robertson, Geoffrey, *Crimes against Humanity: The Struggle for Global Justice* (London: Penguin, 1999).

Robin, Marie Monique, *Les 100 photos du siècle* (Paris: Editions du Chêne, 2000).

Rogoff, Irit, "From Ruins to Debris: The Feminization of Fascism in German History Museums," in Daniel J. Sherman and Irit Rogoff (eds.), *Museum Culture: Histories, Discourses, Spectacles* (Minneapolis: University of Minnesota Press, 1994).

Rose, Willie Lee, *Slavery and Freedom*, ed. William Freehling (Oxford: Oxford University Press, 1982).

Rosenblum, Naomi, *A History of Women Photographers* (New York: Abbeville Press, 1994).

Sagne, Jean, "All Kinds of Portraits: The Photographer's Studio," in Michel Frizot (ed.), *A New History of Photography* (Cologne: Könemann, 1998).

Sandler, Martin W., *Against the Odds: Women Pioneers in the First Hundred Years of Photography* (New York: Rizzoli, 2002).

Sartre, Jean Paul, *Being and Nothingness* (London: Methuen, 1957).

Schama, Simon, *Citizens: A Chronicle of the French Revolution* (New York: Vintage Books, 1990).

Schmitt, Carl, *Political Theology: Four Chapters on the Concept of Sovereignty* (Cambridge, MA: MIT Press, 1985).

Scott, Joan Wallach, *Only Paradoxes to Offer: French Feminists and the Rights of Man* (Cambridge, MA: Harvard University Press, 1996).

Sekula, Allan, "The Body and the Archive," in Richard Bolton (ed.), *The Contest of Meaning* (Cambridge, MA: MIT Press, 1989).

Seltzer, Mark, *Serial Killers* (New York: Routledge, 1998).

——, "Wound Culture: Trauma in the Pathological Public Sphere," *October*, no. 80 (Spring 1997).

Shapira, Sarit, *Not to Be Looked At*, exhibition catalogue (Jerusalem: The Israel Museum Press, 2000).

Shehadeh, Raja, and Jonathan Kuttab, *The West Bank and The Rule of Law: A Study* (New York: The International Commissiom of Jurists and Law in Service of Man, 1982).

Slymovics, Susan, "The Rape of Qula, A Destroyed Palestinian Village," in Lila Abu-Lughod and Ahmad Sa'adi (eds.), *Touching a Painful Past: The Nakba as a Site of Palestinian Collective Memory* (New York: Columbia University Press, 2007).

Solnit, Rebecca, *River of Shadows: Eadweard Muybridge and the Technological Wild West* (New York: Viking, 2003).

Sontag, Susan, *On Photography* (New York: Picador, 1977).

——, *Regarding the Pain of Others* (New York: Picador, 2003).

——, "Regarding the Torture of Others," *New York Times*, May 23, 2004.

Squiers, Carol, *The Body at Risk: Photography, Illness and Healing* (New York: International Center of Photography, 2005).

—— (ed.), *Overexposed: Essays on Contemporary Photography* (New York: The New Press, 1999).

Tabori, Paul, *The Social History of Rape* (London: New English Library, 1971).

Tagg, John, "Evidence, Truth and Order: Photographic Records and the Growth of the State," in Liz Wells (ed.), *The Photography Reader* (London: Routledge, 2003).

Thomas, Hugh, *The Slave Trade* (New York: Simon and Schuster, 1997).

Thornhill, Teresa, *Making Woman Talk: The Interrogation of Women Detainees* (London: Lawyers for Palestinian Human Rights, 1992).

Trachtenberg, Alan, *Reading American Photographs: Images as History* (New York: Hill and Wang, 1989).

Truth, Sojourner, *Narrative of Sojourner Truth* (New York: Penguin, 1998).

Varda, Agnès, filmed interview.

Viera, John David, "Images as Property," in Larry Gross, John Katz, Jay Ruby (eds.), *Image Ethics: The Moral Rights of Subjects in Photographs, Film, and Television* (New York: Oxford University Press, 1988).

Vigarello, Georges, *A History of Rape* (Cambridge: Polity, 2001).

——, *L'histoire du viol* (Paris: Seuil, 1998).

Viorst, Milton, *The Great Documents of Western Civilization* (Philadelphia: Chilton Books, 1965).

Wallis, Brian, "Black Bodies, White Science: Louis Agassiz's Daguerreotypes," in Coco Fusco and Brian Wallis (eds.), *Only Skin Deep: Changing Visions of the American Self* (New York: Harry Abrams, 2003).

Warshaw, Robin, *I Never Called It Rape: The Ms. Report on Recognizing, Fighting, and Surviving Date and Acquaintance Rape*, with an afterword by Mary P. Koss (New York: HarperPerennial, 1994).

White, Deborah Gray, *Aren't I a Woman?: Female Slaves in the Plantation South* (New York: W. W. Norton, 1985).

Williams, Linda, *Hard Core: Power, Pleasure, and the "Frenzy of the Visible"* (Berkeley: University of California Press, 1989).

Willis, Deborah, *Reflections in Black* (New York: W. W. Norton, 2000).

Wolf, Naomi, *The Beauty Myth* (New York: Harper Perennial, 2002).

Wolfthal, Diane, *Images of Rape: The "Heroic" Tradition and Its Alternatives* (Cambridge: Cambridge University Press, 1999).

Zertal, Idit, and Akiva Eldar, *Lords of the Land* [in Hebrew] (Or Yehuda: Kinneret, 2004).

Reports

Amnesty International, "Darfur: Rape as a Weapon of War: Sexual Violence and its Consequences," available online at http://web.amnesty.org/library/Index/ENGAFR540882004?open&of=ENG-SDN.

——, "Israel: Briefing for the Committee against Torture, May 2002," available online at http://web.amnesty.org/library/index/ENGMDE150752002.

B'Tselem, The Israeli Information Center for Human Rights in the Occupied Territories, *Bi-Annual Report 1990/1991: Violations of Human Rights in the Occupied Territories.*

——, "Builders of Zion: Human Rights Violations of Palestinians from the Occupied Territories Working in Israel and the Settlements," available online at http://www.btselem.org/English/Publications/Index.asp?YF=1999&image.x=10&image.y=7.

— — — —, "Civilians under siege: restrictions on freedom of movement as collective punishment," 2001, available online at http://www.btselem.org/English/Publications/Index.asp?YF=2001&image.x=9&image.y=13.

——, *Collaborators in the Occupied Territories: Human Rights Abuses and Violations*, January 1994.

——, *Comprehensive Report*, January 1992.

——, "Ground to a Halt: Denial of Palestinians' Freedom of Movement in the

West Bank," 2007, available online at http://www.btselem.org/english/publications/summaries/20070807_ground_to_a_halt.asp.

——, *The "New Procedure" in GSS Interrogation: The Case of 'Abd A-Nasser 'Ubeid,* Case Study No. 3, November 1993, p. 11.

——, *Take No Prisoners: The Fatal Shooting of Palestinians by Israeli Security Forces during "Arrest Operations,"* Information Sheet, May 2005. View: summary.

The Public Committee against Torture in Israel, "Back to the Torture Routine — The Torture and Abuse of Palestinian Prisoners during Detainment and Interrogation September 2001 – April 2003, available online at www.stoptorture.org.il.

Sexual Violence in Israel, 2003–2004 (Jerusalem: The Association of Rape Crisis Centers in Israel, Jerusalem, 2004).

Ziegler, Jean, *United Nations Special Rapporteur on the Right to Food, Addendum, Mission to the Palestinian Occupied Territories* (2003), available online as a PDF file at http://www.unhchr.ch/pdf/chr60/10add2AV.pdf.

Web Sites

http://www.justiceinitiative.org/activities/ec/ec_noncitizens.
http://www.amnesty.org.il.
http://www.btselem.org/English/.
http://www.shovrimshtika.org/index_he.asp.
http://www.stoptorture.org.il.

Index

Zone Books series design by Bruce Mau
Typesetting by Archetype
Image placement & production by Julie Fry
Printed and bound by Maple Press